GO!
with Microsoft® Office

Excel 2003
Volume 1

John Preston, Sally Preston,
Robert L. Ferrett

Shelley Gaskin, Series Editor

PEARSON
Prentice Hall

Upper Saddle River, New Jersey

Library of Congress Cataloging-in-Publication Data

Preston, John M.
  Go! with Microsoft Office Excel 2003 / John Preston, Sally Preston, Robert L. Ferrett.
    p. cm.—(Go! with Microsoft Office 2003)
Includes index.
  ISBN 0-13-143420-9 (spiral edition : alk. paper)—ISBN 0-13-145119-7 (perfect bound
edition : alk. paper)
  1. Microsoft Excel (Computer file) 2. Business—Computer programs. 3. Electronic
spreadsheets. I. Preston, Sally. II. Ferrett, Robert. III. Title. IV. Series.
HF5548.4.M523P727 2004
005.54—dc22

2003026106

Vice President and Publisher: Natalie E. Anderson
Executive Acquisitions Editor: Jodi McPherson
Marketing Manager: Emily Williams Knight
Marketing Assistant: Nicole Beaudry
Associate Director IT Product Development: Melonie Salvati
Senior Project Manager, Editorial: Mike Ruel
Project Manager, Supplements: Melissa Edwards
Senior Media Project Manager: Cathi Profitko
Editorial Assistants: Jasmine Slowik, Jodi Bolognese, Alana Meyers
Senior Managing Editor, Production: Gail Steier de Acevedo
Senior Project Manager, Production: Tim Tate
Manufacturing Buyer: Tim Tate
Design Manager: Maria Lange
Art Director: Pat Smythe
Cover Designer: Brian Salisbury
Interior Designer: Quorum Creative Services
Full Service Composition: Black Dot Group
Printer/Binder: Von Hoffmann Corporation
Cover Printer: Phoenix Color Corporation

Credits and acknowledgments borrowed from other sources and reproduced,
with permission, in this textbook are as follows or on the appropriate page
within the text.

Microsoft, Windows, PowerPoint, Outlook, FrontPage, Visual Basic, MSN, The
Microsoft Network, and/or other Microsoft products referenced herein are
either trademarks or registered trademarks of Microsoft Corporation in the
U.S.A. and other countries. Screen shots and icons reprinted with permission
from the Microsoft Corporation. This book is not sponsored or endorsed by or
affiliated with Microsoft Corporation.

Microsoft and the Microsoft Office Specialist logo are trademarks or registered
trademarks of Microsoft Corporation in the United States and/or other countries. Pearson Education is independent from Microsoft Corporation and not
affiliated with Microsoft in any manner. This text may be used in assisting
students to prepare for a Microsoft Office Specialist Exam. Neither Microsoft,
its designated review company, nor Pearson Education warrants that use of
this text will ensure passing the relevant exam.

10 9 8 7 6 5 4 3 2 1
ISBN 0-13-145119-7

What does this logo mean?

It means this courseware has been approved by the Microsoft® Office Specialist Program to be among the finest available for learning **Microsoft® Office Word 2003, Microsoft® Office Excel 2003, Microsoft® Office PowerPoint® 2003, and Microsoft® Office Access 2003**. It also means that upon completion of this courseware, you may be prepared to take an exam for Microsoft Office Specialist qualification.

What is a Microsoft Office Specialist?

A Microsoft Office Specialist is an individual who has passed exams for certifying his or her skills in one or more of the Microsoft Office desktop applications such as Microsoft Word, Microsoft Excel, Microsoft PowerPoint, Microsoft Outlook, Microsoft Access, or Microsoft Project. The Microsoft Office Specialist Program typically offers certification exams at the "Specialist" and "Expert" skill levels.* The Microsoft Office Specialist Program is the only program approved by Microsoft for testing proficiency in Microsoft Office desktop applications and Microsoft Project. This testing program can be a valuable asset in any job search or career advancement.

More Information:

To learn more about becoming a Microsoft Office Specialist, visit **www.microsoft.com/officespecialist**

To learn about other Microsoft Office Specialist approved courseware from Pearson Education, visit **www.prenhall.com/phit**

GO!
Series for Microsoft® Office System 2003

Series Editor: **Shelley Gaskin**

Office
Getting Started
Brief
Intermediate
Advanced

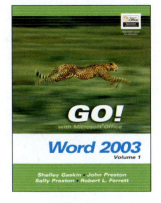

Word
Brief
Volume 1
Volume 2
Comprehensive

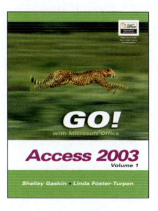

Access
Brief
Volume 1
Volume 2
Comprehensive

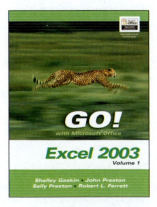

Excel
Brief
Volume 1
Volume 2
Comprehensive

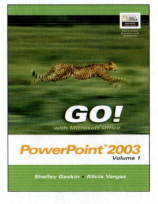

PowerPoint
Brief
Volume 1
Volume 2
Comprehensive

GO! Series Reviewers

We would like to thank the following "Super Reviewers" for both their subject matter expertise and attention to detail from the instructors' perspective. Your time, effort, hard work, and diligence has helped us create the best books in the world. Prentice Hall and your author partners thank you:

Rocky Belcher	Sinclair CC
Judy Cameron	Spokane CC
Gail Cope	Sinclair CC
Larry Farrer	Guilford Tech CC
Janet Enck	Columbus State CC
Susan Fry	Boise State
Lewis Hall	Riverside CC
Jeff Howard	Finger Lakes CC
Jason Hu	Pasadena City College
Michele Hulett	Southwest Missouri State U.
Donna Madsen	Kirkwood CC
Cheryl Reindl-Johnson	Sinclair CC
Jan Spaar	Spokane CC
Mary Ann Zlotow	College of DuPage

We would also like to thank our valuable student reviewers who bring us vital input from those who will someday study from our books:

Nicholas J. Bene	Southwest Missouri State U.
Anup Jonathan	Southwest Missouri State U.
Kimber Miller	Pasadena City College
Kelly Moline	Southwest Missouri State U.
Adam Morris	Southwest Missouri State U.
Robert Murphy	Southwest Missouri State U.
Drucilla Owenby	Southwest Missouri State U.
Vince Withee	Southwest Missouri State U.

Finally, we have been lucky to have so many of you respond to review our chapter manuscripts. You have given us tremendous feedback and helped make a fantastic series. We could not have done it without you.

Abraham, Reni	Houston CC
Agatston, Ann	Agatston Consulting
Alejandro, Manuel	Southwest Texas Junior College
Ali, Farha	Lander University
Anik, Mazhar	Tiffin University
Armstrong, Gary	Shippensburg University
Bagui, Sikha	Univ. West Florida
Belton, Linda	Springfield Tech. Com College
Bennett, Judith	Sam Houston State University
Bishop, Frances	DeVry Institute- Alpharetta (ATL)
Branigan, Dave	DeVry University
Bray, Patricia	Allegany College of Maryland
Buehler, Lesley	Ohlone College
Buell, C	Central Oregon CC
Byars, Pat	Brookhaven College
Cacace, Rich	Pensacola Jr. College
Cadenhead, Charles	Brookhaven College
Calhoun, Ric	Gordon College
Carriker, Sandra	North Shore CC

Challa, Chandrashekar	Virginia State University
Chamlou, Afsaneh	NOVA Alexandria
Chapman, Pam	Wabaunsee CC
Christensen, Dan	Iowa Western CC
Conroy-Link, Janet	Holy Family College
Cosgrove, Janet	Northwestern CT Community Technical College
Cox, Rollie	Madison Area Technical College
Crawford, Hiram	Olive Harvey College
Danno, John	DeVry University/ Keller Graduate School
Davis, Phillip Md.	Del Mar College
Doroshow, Mike	Eastfield College
Douglas, Gretchen	SUNY Cortland
Driskel, Loretta	Niagara CC
Duckwiler, Carol	Wabaunsee CC
Duncan, Mimi	University of Missouri-St. Louis
Duvall, Annette	Albuquerque Technical Vocational Institute

Reviewers continues

Ecklund, Paula	Duke University	Menking, Rick	Hardin-Simmons University
Edmondson, Jeremy	Mount Pisgah School	Meredith, Mary	U. of Louisiana at Lafayette
Erickson, John	University of South Dakota	Mermelstein, Lisa	Baruch College
Falkenstein, Todd	Indiana University East	Metos, Linda	Salt Lake CC
Fite, Beverly	Amarillo College	Meurer, Daniel	University of Cincinnati
Foltz, Brian	East Carolina University	Monk, Ellen	University of Delaware
Friedrichsen, Lisa	Johnson County CC	Morris, Nancy	Hudson Valley CC
Fustos, Janos	Metro State	Nadas, Erika	Wright College
Gallup, Jeanette	Blinn College	Nadelman, Cindi	New England College
Gentry, Barb	Parkland College	Ncube, Cathy	University of West Florida
Gerace, Karin	St. Angela Merici School	Nicholls, Doreen	Mohawk Valley CC
Gerace, Tom	Tulane University	Orr, Claudia	New Mexico State University
Ghajar, Homa	Oklahoma State University	Otieno, Derek	DeVry University
Gifford, Steve	Northwest Iowa CC	Otton, Diana Hill	Chesapeake College
Gregoryk, Kerry	Virginia Commonwealth State University	Oxendale, Lucia	West Virginia Institute of Technology
Griggs, Debra	Bellevue CC	Paiano, Frank	Southwestern College
Grimm, Carol	Palm Beach CC	Proietti, Kathleen	Northern Essex CC
Helms, Liz	Columbus State CC	Pusins, Delores	HCCC
Hernandez, Leticia	TCI College of Technology	Reeves, Karen	High Point University
Hogan, Pat	Cape Fear CC	Rhue, Shelly	DeVry University
Horvath, Carrie	Albertus Magnus College	Richards, Karen	Maplewoods CC
Howard, Chris	DeVry University	Ross, Dianne	Univ. of Louisiana in Lafayette
Huckabay, Jamie	Austin CC	Rousseau, Mary	Broward CC
Hunt, Laura	Tulsa CC	Sams, Todd	University of Cincinnati
Jacob, Sherry	Jefferson CC	Sandoval, Everett	Reedley College
Jacobs, Duane	Salt Lake CC	Sardone, Nancy	Seton Hall University
Johnson, Kathy	Wright College	Scafide, Jean	Mississippi Gulf Coast CC
Jones, Stacey	Benedict College	Scheeren, Judy	Westmoreland County CC
Kasai, Susumu	Salt Lake CC	Schneider, Sol	Sam Houston State University
Keen, Debby	Univ. of Kentucky	Scroggins, Michael	Southwest Missouri State University
Kirk, Colleen	Mercy College		
Kliston, Linda	Broward CC	Sever, Suzanne	Northwest Arkansas CC
Kramer, Ed	Northern Virginia CC	Sheridan, Rick	California State University-Chico
Laird, Jeff	Northeast State CC	Sinha, Atin	Albany State University
Lange, David	Grand Valley State	Smith, T. Michael	Austin CC
LaPointe, Deb	Albuquerque TVI	Smith, Tammy	Tompkins Cortland CC
Lenhart, Sheryl	Terra CC	Stefanelli, Greg	Carroll CC
Letavec, Chris	University of Cincinnati	Steiner, Ester	New Mexico State University
Lightner, Renee	Broward CC	Sterling, Janet	Houston CC
Lindberg, Martha	Minnesota State University	Stroup, Tracey	Pasadena City College
Linge, Richard	Arizona Western College	Sullivan, Angela	Joliet Junior College
Loizeaux, Barbara	Westchester CC	Szurek, Joseph	University of Pittsburgh at Greensburg
Lopez, Don	Clovis- State Center CC District		
Low, Willy Hui	Joliet Junior College	Taylor, Michael	Seattle Central CC
Lowe, Rita	Harold Washington College	Thangiah, Sam	Slippery Rock University
Lucas, Vickie	Broward CC	Thompson-Sellers, Ingrid	Georgia Perimeter College
Lynam, Linda	Central Missouri State University	Tomasi, Erik	Baruch College
		Toreson, Karen	Shoreline CC
Machuca, Wayne	College of the Sequoias	Turgeon, Cheryl	Asnuntuck CC
Madison, Dana	Clarion University	Turpen, Linda	Albuquerque TVI
Maguire, Trish	Eastern New Mexico University	Upshaw, Susan	Del Mar College
Malkan, Rajiv	Montgomery College	Vargas, Tony	El Paso CC
Manning, David	Northern Kentucky University	Vicars, Mitzi	Hampton University
Marghitu, Daniela	Auburn University	Vitrano, Mary Ellen	Palm Beach CC
Marks, Suzanne	Bellevue CC	Wahila, Lori	Tompkins Cortland CC
Marquez, Juanita	El Centro College	Wavle, Sharon	Tompkins Cortland CC
Marucco, Toni	Lincoln Land CC	White, Bruce	Quinnipiac University
Mason, Lynn	Lubbock Christian University	Willer, Ann	Solano CC
Matutis, Audrone	Houston CC	Williams, Mark	Lane CC
McCannon, Melinda (Mindy)	Gordon College	Wimberly, Leanne	International Academy of Design and Technology
McClure, Darlean	College of Sequoias		
McCue, Stacy	Harrisburg Area CC	Worthington, Paula	NOVA Woodbridge
McEntire-Orbach, Teresa	Middlesex County College	Yauney, Annette	Herkimer CCC
McManus, Illyana	Grossmont College	Zavala, Ben	Webster Tech

Dedications

We dedicate this book to our granddaughters, who bring us
great joy and happiness: Clara and Siena & Alexis and Grace.

—John Preston, Sally Preston, and Robert L. Ferrett

This book is dedicated to my students,
who inspire me every day, and to my husband, Fred Gaskin.

—Shelley Gaskin

About the Authors/Acknowledgments

About John Preston, Sally Preston, and Robert L. Ferrett

John Preston is an Associate Professor at Eastern Michigan University in the College of Technology, where he teaches microcomputer application courses at the undergraduate and graduate levels. He has been teaching, writing, and designing computer training courses since the advent of PCs and has authored and co-authored over 60 books on Microsoft Word, Excel, Access, and PowerPoint. He is a series editor for the *Learn 97*, *Learn 2000*, and *Learn XP* books. Two books on Microsoft Access that he co-authored with Robert Ferrett have been translated into Greek and Chinese. He has received grants from the Detroit Edison Institute and the Department of Energy to develop Web sites for energy education and alternative fuels. He has also developed one of the first Internet-based microcomputer applications courses at an accredited university. He has a BS from the University of Michigan in Physics, Mathematics, and Education and an MS from Eastern Michigan University in Physics Education. His doctoral studies were in Instructional Technology at Wayne State University.

Sally Preston is president of Preston & Associates, which provides software consulting and training. She teaches computing in a variety of settings, which provides her with ample opportunity to observe how people learn, what works best, and what challenges are present when learning a new software program. This diverse experience provides a complementary set of skills and knowledge that blends into her writing. Prior to writing for the *GO! series*, Sally was a co-author on the *Learn* series since its inception and has authored books for the *Essentials* and *Microsoft Office User Specialist (MOUS) Essentials* series. Sally has an MBA from Eastern Michigan University. When away from her computer, she is often found planting flowers in her garden.

Robert L. Ferrett recently retired as the director of the Center for Instructional Computing at Eastern Michigan University, where he provided computer training and support to faculty. He has authored or co-authored more than 60 books on Access, PowerPoint, Excel, Publisher, WordPerfect, and Word and was the editor of the *1994 ACM SIGUCCS*

Conference Proceedings. He has been designing, developing, and delivering computer workshops for nearly two decades. Before writing for the *GO! series*, Bob was a series editor for the *Learn 97, Learn 2000,* and *Learn XP* books. He has a BA in Psychology, an MS in Geography, and an MS in Interdisciplinary Technology from Eastern Michigan University. His doctoral studies were in Instructional Technology at Wayne State University. For fun, Bob teaches a four-week Computers and Genealogy class and has written genealogy and local history books.

Acknowledgments from John Preston, Sally Preston, and Robert L. Ferrett

We would like to acknowledge the efforts of a fine team of editing professionals, with whom we have had the pleasure of working. Jodi McPherson, Jodi Bolognese, Mike Ruel, and Shelley Gaskin did a great job managing and coordinating this effort. We would also like to acknowledge the contributions of Tim Tate, Production Project Manager, and Emily Knight, Marketing Manager, as well as the many reviewers who gave invaluable criticism and suggestions.

About Shelley Gaskin

Shelley Gaskin, Series Editor, is a professor of business and computer technology at Pasadena City College in Pasadena, California. She holds a master's degree in business education from Northern Illinois University and a doctorate in adult and community education from Ball State University. Dr. Gaskin has 15 years of experience in the computer industry with several Fortune 500 companies and has developed and written training materials for custom systems applications in both the public and private sector. She is also the author of books on Microsoft Outlook and word processing.

Acknowledgments from Shelley Gaskin

Many talented individuals worked to produce this book, and I thank them for their continuous support. My Executive Acquisitions Editor, Jodi McPherson, gave me much latitude to experiment with new things. Editorial Project Manager Mike Ruel worked with me through each stage of writing and production. Emily Knight and the Prentice Hall Marketing team worked with me throughout this process to make sure both instructors and students are informed about the benefits of using this series. Also, very big thanks and appreciation goes to Prentice Halls' top-notch Production and Design team: Associate Director Product Development Melonie Salvati, Manager of Production Gail Steier de Acevedo, Senior Production Project Manager and Manufacturing Buyer Tim Tate, Design Manager Maria Lange, Art Director Pat Smythe, Interior Designer Quorum Creative Services, and Cover Designer Brian Salisbury.

Thanks to all!
Shelley Gaskin, Series Editor

Why I Wrote This Series

Dear Professor,

If you are like me, you are frantically busy trying to implement new course delivery methods (e.g., online) while also maintaining your regular campus schedule of classes and academic responsibilities. I developed this series for colleagues like you, who are long on commitment and expertise but short on time and assistance.

The primary goal of the **GO! Series**, aside from the obvious one of teaching **Microsoft® Office 2003** concepts and skills, is ease of implementation using any delivery method—traditional, self-paced, or online.

There are no lengthy passages of text; instead, bits of expository text are woven into the steps at the teachable moment. This is the point at which the student has a context within which he or she can understand the concept. A scenario-like approach is used in a manner that makes sense, but it does not attempt to have the student "pretend" to be someone else.

A key feature of this series is the use of Microsoft procedural syntax. That is, steps begin with where the action is to take place, followed by the action itself. This prevents the student from doing the right thing in the wrong place!

The *GO! Series* is written with all of your everyday classroom realities in mind. For example, in each project, the student is instructed to insert his or her name in a footer and to save the document with his or her name. Thus, unidentified printouts do not show up at the printer nor do unidentified documents get stored on the hard drives.

Finally, an overriding consideration is that the student is not always working in a classroom with a teacher. Students frequently work at home or in a lab staffed only with instructional aides. Thus, the instruction must be error-free, clearly written, and logically arranged.

My students enjoy learning the Microsoft Office software. The goal of the instruction in the *GO! Series* is to provide students with the skills to solve business problems using the computer as a tool, for both themselves and the organizations for which they might be employed.

Thank you for using the **GO! Series for Microsoft® Office System 2003** for your students.

Regards,

Shelley Gaskin, Series Editor

Preface

Philosophy

Our overall philosophy is ease of implementation for the instructor, whether instruction is via lecture, lab, online, or partially self-paced. Right from the start, the *GO! Series* was created with constant input from professors just like you. You've told us what works, how you teach, and what we can do to make your classroom time problem free, creative, and smooth running—to allow you to concentrate on not what you are teaching from but who you are teaching to—your students. We feel that we have succeeded with the *GO! Series*. Our aim is to make this instruction high quality in both content and presentation, and the classroom management aids complete—an instructor could begin teaching the course with only 15 minutes advance notice. An instructor could leave the classroom or computer lab; students would know exactly how to proceed in the text, know exactly what to produce to demonstrate mastery of the objectives, and feel that they had achieved success in their learning. Indeed, this philosophy is essential for real-world use in today's diverse educational environment.

How did we do it?

- All steps utilize **Microsoft Procedural Syntax**. The *GO! Series* puts students where they need to be, before instructing them what to do. For example, instead of instructing students to "Save the file," we go a few steps further and phrase the instruction as "On the **Menu** bar, click **File**, then select **Save As**."

- A unique teaching system (packaged together in one easy to use **Instructor's Edition** binder set) that enables you to teach anywhere you have to—online, lab, lecture, self-paced, and so forth. The supplements are designed to save you time:

    - *Expert Demonstration Document*—A new project that mirrors the learning objectives of the in-chapter project, with a full demonstration script for you to give a lecture overview quickly and clearly.

    - *Chapter Assignment Sheets*—A sheet listing all the assignments for the chapter. An instructor can quickly insert his or her name, course information, due dates, and points.

    - *Custom Assignment Tags*—These cutout tags include a brief list of common errors that students could make on each project, with check boxes so instructors don't have to keep writing the same error description over and over! These tags serve a dual purpose: The student can do a final check to make sure all the listed items are correct, and the instructor can check off the items that need to be corrected.

- **Highlighted Overlays**—These are printed and transparent overlays that the instructor lays over the student's assignment paper to see at a glance if the student changed what he or she needed to. Coupled with the Custom Assignment Tags, this creates a "grading and scoring system" that is easy for the instructor to implement.

- **Point Counted Chapter Production Test**—Working hand-in-hand with the Expert Demonstration Document, this is a final test for the student to demonstrate mastery of the objectives.

Goals of the GO! Series

The goals of the *GO! Series* are as follows:

- Make it *easy for the instructor to implement* in any instructional setting through high-quality content and instructional aids and provide the student with a valuable, interesting, important, satisfying, and clearly defined learning experience.

- Enable true diverse delivery for today's diverse audience. The *GO! Series* employs various instructional techniques that address the needs of all types of students in all types of delivery modes.

- Provide *turn-key implementation* in the following instructional settings:

  - Traditional computer classroom—Students experience a mix of lecture and lab.

  - Online instruction—Students complete instruction at a remote location and submit assignments to the instructor electronically—questions answered by instructor through electronic queries.

  - Partially self-paced, individualized instruction—Students meet with an instructor for part of the class, and complete part of the class in a lab setting.

  - Completely self-paced, individualized instruction—Students complete all instruction in an instructor-staffed lab setting.

  - Independent self-paced, individualized instruction—Students complete all instruction in a campus lab staffed with instructional aides.

- Teach—*to maximize the moment*. The *GO! Series* is based on the Teachable Moment Theory. There are no long passages of text; instead, concepts are woven into the steps at the teachable moment. Students always know what they need to do and where to do it.

Pedagogical Approach

The *GO! Series* uses an instructional system approach that incorporates three elements:

- *Steps are written in **Microsoft Procedural Syntax**, which prevents the student from doing the right thing but in the wrong place. This makes it easy for the instructor to teach instead of untangle. It tells the student where to go first, then what to do. For example—"On the File Menu, click Properties."

- *Instructional strategies* including five new, unique ancillary pieces to support the instructor experience. The foundation of the instructional strategies is performance based instruction that is constructed in a manner that makes it *easy for the instructor* to demonstrate the content with the GO Series Expert Demonstration Document, guide the practice by using our many end-of-chapter projects with varying guidance levels, and assess the level of mastery with tools such as our Point Counted Production Test and Custom Assignment Tags.

- *A physical design* that makes it *easy for the instructor* to answer the question, "What do they have to do?" and makes it easy for the student to answer the question, "What do I have to do?" Most importantly, you told us what was needed in the design. We held several focus groups throughout the country where we showed ***you*** our design drafts and let you tell us what you thought of them. We revised our design based on your input to be functional and support the classroom experience. For example, you told us that a common problem is students not realizing where a project ends. So, we added an "END. You have completed the Project" at the close of every project.

Microsoft Procedural Syntax

Do you ever do something right but in the wrong place?

That's why we've written the *GO! Series* step text using Microsoft procedural syntax. That is, the student is informed where the action should take place before describing the action to take. For example, "On the menu bar, click File," versus "Click File on the menu bar." This prevents the student from doing the right thing in the wrong place. This means that step text usually begins with a preposition—a locator—rather than a verb. Other texts often misunderstand the theory of performance-based instruction and frequently attempt to begin steps with a verb. In fact, the objectives should begin with a verb, not the steps.

The use of Microsoft procedural syntax is one of the key reasons that the *GO! Series* eases the burden for the instructor. The instructor spends less time untangling students' unnecessary actions and more time assisting students with real questions. No longer will students become frustrated and say "But I did what it said!" only to discover that, indeed, they *did* do "what it said" but in the wrong place!

Chapter Organization—Color-Coded Projects

All of the chapters in every *GO! Series* book are organized around interesting projects. Within each chapter, all of the instructional activities will cluster around these projects without any long passages of text for the student to read. Thus, every instructional activity contributes to the completion of the project to which it is associated. Students learn skills to solve real business problems; they don't waste time learning every feature the software has. The end-of-chapter material consists of additional projects with varying levels of difficulty.

The chapters are based on the following basic hierarchy:

Project Name

Objective Name (begins with a verb)

Activity Name (begins with a gerund)

Numbered Steps (begins with a preposition or a verb using Microsoft Procedural Syntax.)

Project Name → **Project 1A Exploring Outlook 2003**

Objective Name → **Objective 1**
Start Outlook and Identify Outlook Window Elements

Activity Name → **Activity 1.1 Starting Outlook**

Numbered Steps → **1** On the Windows taskbar, click the Start button, determine from your instructor or lab coordinator where the Microsoft Office Outlook 2003 program is located on your system, and then click Microsoft Office Outlook 2003.

A project will have a number of objectives associated with it, and the objectives, in turn, will have one or more activities associated with them. Each activity will have a series of numbered steps. To further enhance understanding, each project, and its objectives and numbered steps, is color coded for fast, easy recognition.

In-Chapter Boxes and Elements

Within every chapter there are helpful boxes and in-line notes that aid the students in their mastery of the performance objectives. Plus, each box has a specific title—"Does Your Notes Button Look Different?" or "To Open the New Appointment Window." Our GO! Series Focus Groups told us to add box titles that indicate the information being covered in the box, and we listened!

Alert!

Does Your Notes Button Look Different?

The size of the monitor and screen resolution set on your computer controls the number of larger module buttons that appear at the bottom of the Navigation pane.

Alert! boxes do just that—they alert students to a common pitfall or spot where trouble may be encountered.

Another Way

To Open the New Appointment Window

You can create a new appointment window using one of the following techniques:

- On the menu bar, click File, point to New, and click Appointment.
- On the Calendar Standard toolbar, click the New Appointment button.

Another Way boxes explain simply "another way" of going about a task or shortcuts for saving time.

Note — Server Connection Dialog Box

If a message displays indicating that a connection to the server could not be established, click OK. Even without a mail server connection, you can still use the personal information management features of Outlook.

Notes highlight additional information pertaining to a task.

More Knowledge — Creating New Folders

A module does not have to be active in order to create new folders within it. From the Create New Folder text box, you can change the type of items that the new folder will contain and then select any location in which to place the new folder. Additionally, it is easy to move a folder created in one location to a different location.

More Knowledge is a more detailed look at a topic or task.

Organization of the GO! Series

The *GO! Series for Microsoft® Office System 2003* includes several different combinations of texts to best suit your needs.

- **Word, Excel, Access, and PowerPoint 2003** are available in the following editions:

  - **Brief:** Chapters 1–3 (1–4 for Word 2003)

  - **Volume 1:** Chapters 1–6
    ~ Microsoft Office Specialist Certification

  - **Volume 2:** Chapters 7–12 (7–8 for PowerPoint 2003)

  - **Comprehensive:** Chapters 1–12 (1–8 for PowerPoint 2003)
    ~ Microsoft Office Expert Certification for Word and Excel 2003.

- Additionally, the *GO! Series* is available in four combined **Office 2003** texts:

  - **Microsoft® Office 2003 Getting Started** contains the Windows XP Introduction and first chapter from each application (Word, Excel, Access, and PowerPoint).

  - **Microsoft® Office 2003 Brief** contains Chapters 1–3 of Excel, Access, and PowerPoint, and Chapters 1–4 of Word. Four additional supplementary "Getting Started" books are included (Internet Explorer, Computer Concepts, Windows XP, and Outlook 2003).

  - **Microsoft® Office 2003 Intermediate** contains Chapters 4–8 of Excel, Access, and PowerPoint, and Chapters 5–8 of Word.

  - **Microsoft® Office 2003 Advanced** version picks up where the Intermediate leaves off, covering advanced topics for the individual applications. This version contains Chapters 9–12 of Word, Excel, and Access.

Microsoft Office Specialist Certification

The *GO! Series* has been approved by Microsoft for use in preparing for the Microsoft Office Specialist exams. The Microsoft Office Specialist program is globally recognized as the standard for demonstrating desktop skills with the Microsoft Office System of business productivity applications (Microsoft Word, Microsoft Excel, Microsoft Access, Microsoft PowerPoint, and Microsoft Outlook). With Microsoft Office Specialist certification, thousands of people have demonstrated increased productivity and have proved their ability to utilize the advanced functionality of these Microsoft applications.

Instructor and Student Resources

Instructor's Resource Center and Instructor's Edition

The *GO! Series* was designed for you—instructors who are long on commitment and short on time. *We asked you how you use our books and supplements and how we can make it easier for you and save you valuable time.* We listened to what you told us and created this Instructor's Resource Center for you—different from anything you have ever had access to from other texts and publishers.

What is the Instructor's Edition?

1) Instructor's Edition

New from Prentice Hall, exclusively for the *GO! Series*, the Instructor's Edition contains the entire book, wrapped with vital margin notes—things like objectives, a list of the files needed for the chapter, teaching tips, Microsoft Office Specialist objectives covered, and MORE! Below is a sample of the many helpful elements in the Instructor's Edition.

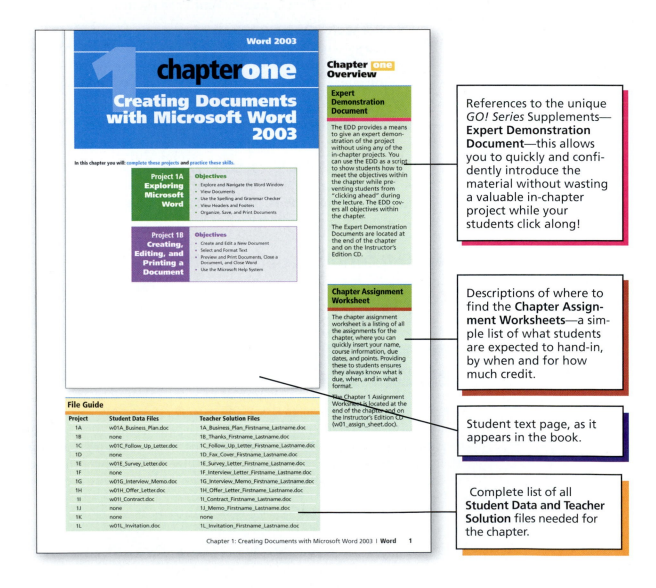

References to the unique *GO! Series* Supplements—**Expert Demonstration Document**—this allows you to quickly and confidently introduce the material without wasting a valuable in-chapter project while your students click along!

Descriptions of where to find the **Chapter Assignment Worksheets**—a simple list of what students are expected to hand-in, by when and for how much credit.

Student text page, as it appears in the book.

Complete list of all **Student Data and Teacher Solution** files needed for the chapter.

Reference to Prentice Hall's Companion Website for the *GO! Series*: **www.prenhall.com/go**

Companion Website

CW

www.prenhall.com/go

The Companion Website is an online training tool that includes personalization features for registered instructors. Data files are available here for download as well as access to additional quizzing exercises.

Each chapter also tells you where to find another unique *GO! Series* Supplement—the **Custom Assignment Tags**—use these in combination with the highlighted overlays to save you time! Simply check off what the students missed or if they completed all the tasks correctly.

Custom Assignment Tags

Custom Assignment Tags, which are meant to be cut out and attached to assignments, serve a dual purpose: the student can do a final check to make sure all the listed items are correct, and the instructor can quickly check off the items that need to be corrected and simply return the assignment.

The Chapter 1 Custom Assignment Tags are located at the end of the chapter and on the Instructor's Edition CD (w01_assign_tags.doc).

The Perfect Party

The Perfect Party store, owned by two partners, provides a wide variety of party accessories including invitations, favors, banners and flags, balloons, piñatas, etc. Party-planning services include both custom parties with pre-filled custom "goodie bags" and "parties in a box" that include everything needed to throw a theme party. Big sellers in this category are the Football and Luau themes. The owners are planning to open a second store and expand their party-planning services to include catering.

© Getty Images, Inc.

Getting Started with Microsoft Office Word 2003

Word processing is the most common program found on personal computers and one that almost everyone has a reason to use. When you learn word processing you are also learning skills and techniques that you need to work efficiently on a personal computer. Use Microsoft Word to do basic word processing tasks such as writing a memo, a report, or a letter. You can also use Word to do complex word processing tasks, including sophisticated tables, embedded graphics, and links to other documents and the Internet. Word is a program that you can learn gradually, adding more advanced skills one at a time.

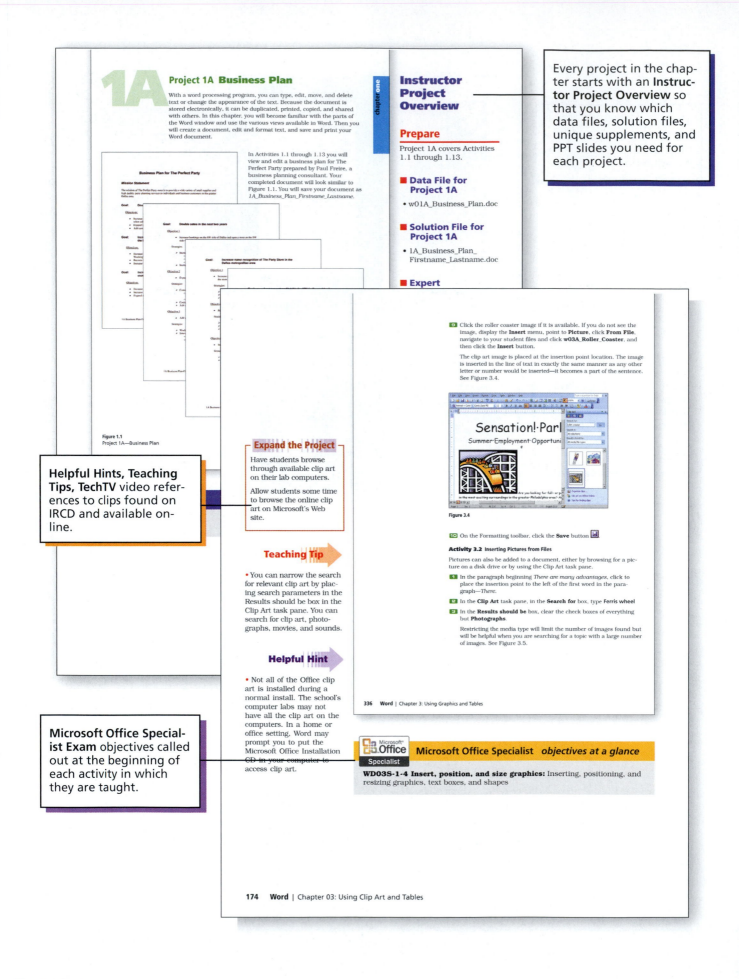

Every project in the chapter starts with an **Instructor Project Overview** so that you know which data files, solution files, unique supplements, and PPT slides you need for each project.

Helpful Hints, Teaching Tips, TechTV video references to clips found on IRCD and available on-line.

Microsoft Office Specialist Exam objectives called out at the beginning of each activity in which they are taught.

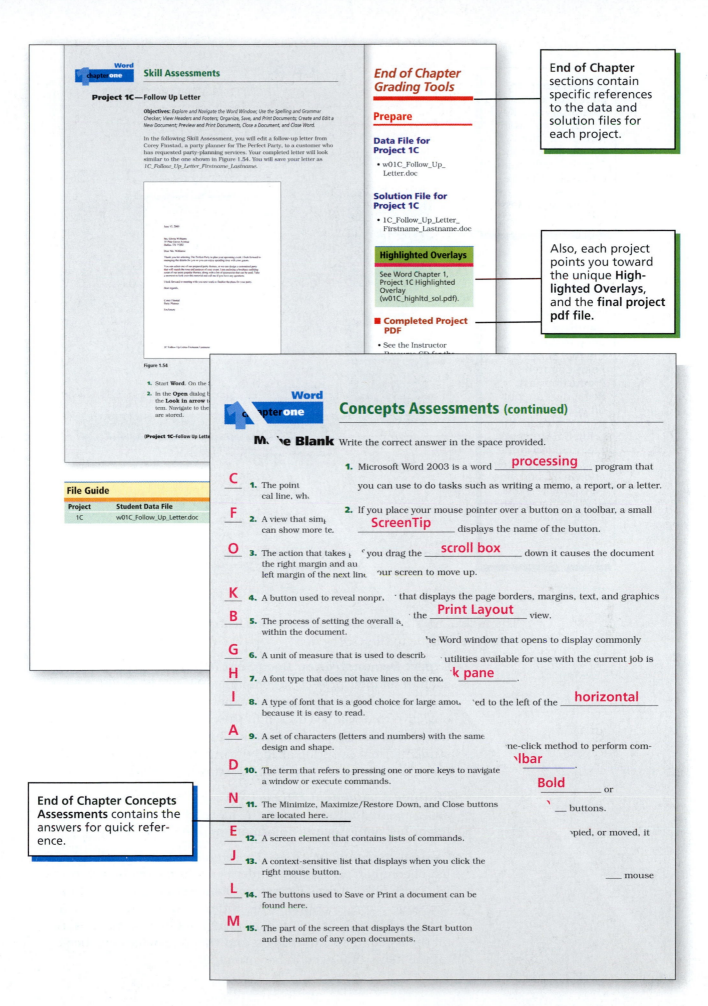

End of Chapter sections contain specific references to the data and solution files for each project.

Also, each project points you toward the unique **Highlighted Overlays**, and the **final project pdf file**.

End of Chapter Concepts Assessments contains the answers for quick reference.

Word
chapter one

Skill Assessments

Project 1C—Follow Up Letter

Objectives: *Explore and Navigate the Word Window; Use the Spelling and Grammar Checker; View Headers and Footers; Organize, Save, and Print Documents; Create and Edit a New Document; Preview and Print Documents, Close a Document, and Close Word.*

In the following Skill Assessment, you will edit a follow-up letter from Corey Finstad, a party planner for The Perfect Party, to a customer who has requested party-planning services. Your completed letter will look similar to the one shown in Figure 1.54. You will save your letter as *1C_Follow_Up_Letter_Firstname_Lastname*.

Figure 1.54

1. Start **Word**. On the S...
2. In the **Open** dialog b... the **Look in arrow** t... tem. Navigate to the... are stored.

(Project 1C–Follow Up Letter...

File Guide

Project	Student Data File
1C	w01C_Follow_Up_Letter.doc

End of Chapter Grading Tools

Prepare

Data File for Project 1C

• w01C_Follow_Up_Letter.doc

Solution File for Project 1C

• 1C_Follow_Up_Letter_Firstname_Lastname.doc

Highlighted Overlays

See Word Chapter 1, Project 1C Highlighted Overlay (w01C_highltd_sol.pdf).

■ **Completed Project PDF**

• See the Instructor Resource CD for the...

Word
chapter one

Concepts Assessments (continued)

Fill the Blank Write the correct answer in the space provided.

C 1. The point... cal line, wh...

F 2. A view that simp... can show more te...

O 3. The action that takes... you drag the... the right margin and au... left margin of the next line... our screen to move up.

K 4. A button used to reveal nonpr... that displays the page borders, margins, text, and graphics

B 5. The process of setting the overall a... the... within the document.

G 6. A unit of measure that is used to describ... utilities available for use with the current job is

H 7. A font type that does not have lines on the end...

I 8. A type of font that is a good choice for large amou... because it is easy to read.

A 9. A set of characters (letters and numbers) with the same design and shape.

D 10. The term that refers to pressing one or more keys to navigate a window or execute commands.

N 11. The Minimize, Maximize/Restore Down, and Close buttons are located here.

E 12. A screen element that contains lists of commands.

J 13. A context-sensitive list that displays when you click the right mouse button.

L 14. The buttons used to Save or Print a document can be found here.

M 15. The part of the screen that displays the Start button and the name of any open documents.

1. Microsoft Word 2003 is a word **processing** program that you can use to do tasks such as writing a memo, a report, or a letter.

2. If you place your mouse pointer over a button on a toolbar, a small **ScreenTip** displays the name of the button.

3. The action that takes... you drag the **scroll box** down it causes the document... our screen to move up.

...the **Print Layout** view.

...he Word window that opens to display commonly

k pane

horizontal

...ne-click method to perform com-

lbar

Bold or

_ buttons.

...pied, or moved, it

_ mouse

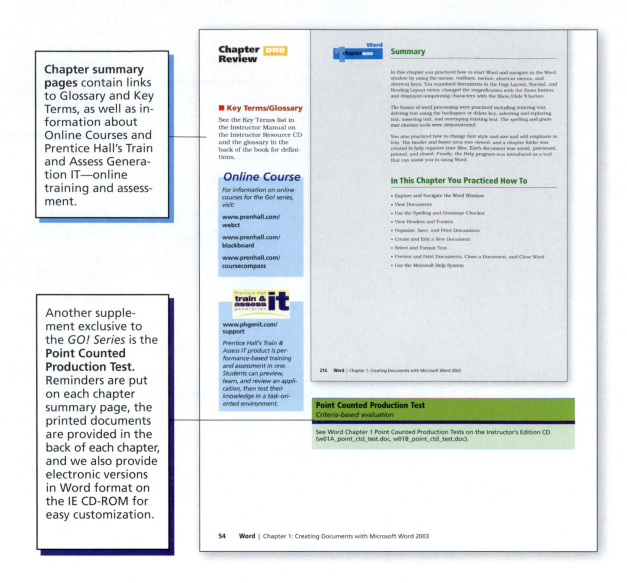

Chapter summary pages contain links to Glossary and Key Terms, as well as information about Online Courses and Prentice Hall's Train and Assess Generation IT—online training and assessment.

Another supplement exclusive to the *GO! Series* is the **Point Counted Production Test.** Reminders are put on each chapter summary page, the printed documents are provided in the back of each chapter, and we also provide electronic versions in Word format on the IE CD-ROM for easy customization.

The Instructor's Edition also contains printed copies of these supplement materials *unique* to the *GO! Series*:

- *Expert Demonstration Document (EDD)*—A mirror image of each in-chapter project, accompanied by a brief script. The instructor can use it to give an expert demonstration of each objective that will be covered in the chapter, without having to use one of the chapter's projects. This EDD also prevents students from "working ahead during the presentation," as they do not have access to this document/project.

- *Chapter Assignment Sheets*—With a sheet listing all the assignments for the chapter, the instructor can quickly insert his or her name, course information, due dates, and points.

- *Custom Assignment Tags*—These cutout tags include a brief list of common errors that students could make on each project, with check boxes so instructors don't have to keep writing the same error description over and over! These tags serve a dual purpose: The student can do a final check to make sure all the listed items are correct, and the instructor can check off the items that need to be corrected.

- **Highlighted Overlays**—These are printed and transparent overlays that the instructor lays over the student's assignment paper to see at a glance if the student changed what he or she needed to. Coupled with the Custom Assignment Tags, this creates a "grading and scoring system" that is easy for the instructor to implement.

- **Point Counted Chapter Production Test**—Working hand-in-hand with the EDD, this is a final test for the student to demonstrate mastery of the objectives.

2) Enhanced Instructor's Resource CD-ROM

The Instructor's Resource CD-ROM is an interactive library of assets and links. The Instructor's Resource CD-ROM writes custom "index" pages that can be used as the foundation of a class presentation or online lecture. By navigating through the CD-ROM, you can collect the materials that are most relevant to your interests, edit them to create powerful class lectures, copy them to your own computer's hard drive, and/or upload them to an online course management system.

The new and improved Prentice Hall Instructor's Resource CD-ROM includes tools you expect from a Prentice Hall text:

- The Instructor's Manual in Word and PDF formats—includes solutions to all questions and exercises from the book and Companion Website

- Multiple, customizable PowerPoint slide presentations for each chapter

- Data and Solution Files

- Complete Test Bank

- Image library of all figures from the text

- TestGen Software with QuizMaster

  - TestGen is a test generator that lets you view and easily edit test bank questions, transfer them to tests, and print in a variety of formats suitable to your teaching situation. The program also offers many options for organizing and displaying test banks and tests. A built-in random number and text generator makes it ideal for creating multiple versions of tests that involve calculations and provides more possible test items than test bank questions. Powerful search and sort functions let you easily locate questions and arrange them in the order you prefer.

  - QuizMaster allows students to take tests created with TestGen on a local area network. The QuizMaster utility built into TestGen lets instructors view student records and print a variety of reports. Building tests is easy with TestGen, and exams can be easily uploaded into WebCT, Blackboard, and CourseCompass.

3) Instructor's Edition CD-ROM

The Instructor's Edition CD-ROM contains PDF versions of the Instructor's Edition as well as Word versions of the *GO! Series* unique supplements for easy instructor customization.

Training and Assessment— www2.phgenit.com/support

 Prentice Hall offers performance-based training and assessment in one product— Train&Assess IT. The training component offers computer-based training that a student can use to preview, learn, and review Microsoft Office application skills. Web or CD-ROM delivered, Train IT offers interactive, multimedia, computer-based training to augment classroom learning. Built-in prescriptive testing suggests a study path based not only on student test results but also on the specific textbook chosen for the course.

The assessment component offers computer-based testing that shares the same user interface as Train IT and is used to evaluate a student's knowledge about specific topics in Word, Excel, Access, PowerPoint, Outlook, the Internet, and Computing Concepts. It does this in a task-oriented environment to demonstrate proficiency as well as comprehension of the topics by the students. More extensive than the testing in Train IT, Assess IT offers more administrative features for the instructor and additional questions for the student.

Assess IT also allows professors to test students out of a course, place students in appropriate courses, and evaluate skill sets.

Companion Website @ www.prenhall.com/go

This text is accompanied by a Companion Website at www.prenhall.com/go. Features of this new site include an interactive study guide, downloadable supplements, online end-of-chapter materials, additional practice projects, Web resource links, and technology updates and bonus chapters on the latest trends and hottest topics in information technology. All links to Web exercises will be constantly updated to ensure accuracy for students.

CourseCompass— www.coursecompass.com

 CourseCompass is a dynamic, interactive online course-management tool powered exclusively for Pearson Education by Blackboard. This exciting product allows you to teach market-leading Pearson Education content in an easy-to-use, customizable format.

Blackboard— www.prenhall.com/blackboard

 Prentice Hall's abundant online content, combined with Blackboard's popular tools and interface, result in robust Web-based courses that are easy to implement, manage, and use—taking your courses to new heights in student interaction and learning.

WebCT—www.prenhall.com/webct

Course-management tools within WebCT include page tracking, progress tracking, class and student management, gradebook, communication, calendar, reporting tools, and more. Gold Level Customer Support, available exclusively to adopters of Prentice Hall courses, is provided free-of-charge on adoption and provides you with priority assistance, training discounts, and dedicated technical support.

TechTV—www.techtv.com

TechTV is the San Francisco-based cable network that showcases the smart, edgy, and unexpected side of technology. By telling stories through the prism of technology, TechTV provides programming that celebrates its viewers' passion, creativity, and lifestyle.

TechTV's programming falls into three categories:

1. **Help and Information**, with shows like *The Screen Savers*, TechTV's daily live variety show featuring everything from guest interviews and celebrities to product advice and demos; *Tech Live*, featuring the latest news on the industry's most important people, companies, products, and issues; and *Call for Help*, a live help and how-to show providing computing tips and live viewer questions.

2. **Cool Docs**, with shows like *The Tech Of...*, a series that goes behind the scenes of modern life and shows you the technology that makes things tick; *Performance*, an investigation into how technology and science are molding the perfect athlete; and *Future Fighting Machines*, a fascinating look at the technology and tactics of warfare.

3. **Outrageous Fun**, with shows like *X-Play*, exploring the latest and greatest in videogaming; and *Unscrewed* with Martin Sargent, a new late-night series showcasing the darker, funnier world of technology.

For more information, log onto www.techtv.com or contact your local cable or satellite provider to get TechTV in your area.

Visual Walk-Through

Project-based Instruction

Students do not practice features of the application; they create real projects that they will need in the real world. Projects are color coded for easy reference.

Projects are named to reflect skills the student will be practicing, not vague project names.

Word 2003

1 chapterone

Creating Documents with Microsoft Word 2003

In this chapter you will: complete these projects and practice these skills.

Project 1A
Exploring Microsoft Word

Objectives
- Explore and Navigate the Word Window
- View Documents
- Use the Spelling and Grammar Checker
- View Headers and Footers
- Organize, Save, and Print Documents

Project 1B
Creating, Editing, and Printing a Document

Objectives
- Create and Edit a New Document
- Select and Format Text
- Preview and Print Documents, Close a Document, and Close Word
- Use the Microsoft Help System

Learning Objectives

Objectives are clustered around projects. They help students to learn how to solve problems, not just learn software features.

The Greater Atlanta Job Fair

The Greater Atlanta Job Fair is a nonprofit organization that holds targeted job fairs in and around the greater Atlanta area several times each year. The fairs are widely marketed to companies nationwide and locally. The organization also presents an annual Atlanta Job Fair that draws over 2,000 employers in more than 70 industries and generally registers more than 5,000 candidates.

©Getty Images, Inc.

Each chapter opens with a story that sets the stage for the projects the student will create, not force them to pretend to be someone or make up a scenario themselves.

Getting Started with Outlook 2003

Do you sometimes find it a challenge to manage and complete all the tasks related to your job, family, and class work? Microsoft Office Outlook 2003 can help. Outlook 2003 is a personal information management program (also known as a PIM) that does two things: (1) it helps you get organized, and (2) it helps you communicate with others efficiently. Successful people know that good organizational and communication skills are important. Outlook 2003 electronically stores and organizes appointments and due dates; names, addresses, and phone numbers; to do lists; and notes. Another major use of Outlook 2003 is its e-mail and fax capabilities, along with features with which you can manage group work such as the tasks assigned to a group of coworkers. In this introduction to Microsoft Office Outlook 2003, you will explore the modules available in Outlook and enter data into each module.

Each chapter has an introductory paragraph that briefs students on what is important.

Visual Summary

Shows students up front what their projects will look like when they are done.

Objective

The skills they will learn are clearly stated at the beginning of each project and color coded to match projects listed on the chapter opener page.

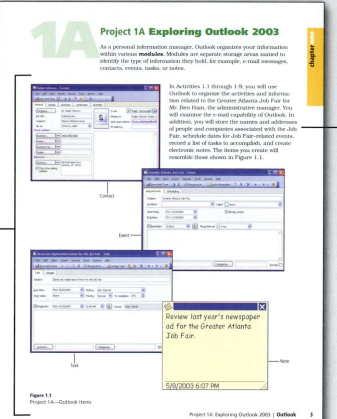

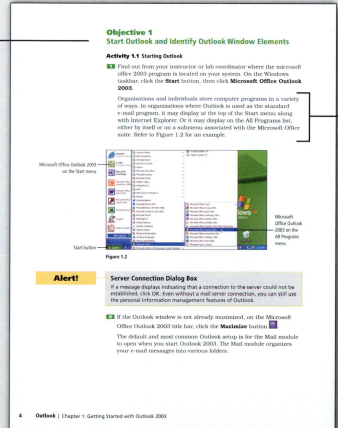

Project Summary

Stated clearly and quickly in one paragraph with the Visual Summary formatted as a caption so your students won't skip it.

Teachable Moment

Expository text is woven into the steps—at the moment students need to know it—not chunked together in a block of text that will go unread.

Steps

Color coded to the current project, easy to read, and not too many to confuse the student or too few to be meaningless.

Sequential Page Numbering

No more confusing letters and abbreviations.

Microsoft Procedural Syntax

All steps are written in Microsoft Procedural Syntax in order to put the student in the right place at the right time.

End of Project Icon

All projects in the *GO! Series* have clearly identifiable end points, useful in self-paced or on-line environments.

Objective 5
Organize, Save, and Print Documents

In the same way that you use file folders to organize your paper documents, Windows uses a hierarchy of electronic folders to keep your electronic files organized. Check with your instructor or lab coordinator to see where you will be storing your documents (for example, on your own disk or on a network drive) and whether there is any suggested file folder arrangement. Throughout this textbook, you will be instructed to save your files using the file name followed by your first and last name. Check with your instructor to see if there is some other file naming arrangement for your course.

Activity 1.12 Creating Folders for Document Storage and Saving a Document

When you save a document file, the Windows operating system stores your document permanently on a storage medium—either a disk that you have inserted into the computer, the hard drive of your computer, or a network drive connected to your computer system. Changes that you make to existing documents, such as changing text or typing in new text, are not permanently saved until you perform a Save operation.

1 On the menu bar, click **File**, and then click **Save As**.

The Save As dialog box displays.

2 In the **Save As** dialog box, at the right edge of the **Save in** box, click the **Save in arrow** to view a list of the drives available to you as shown in Figure 1.30. The list of drives and folders will differ from the one shown.

Figure 1.30

Activity 1.13 Printing a Document From the Toolbar

In Activity 1.13, you will print your document from the toolbar.

1 On the Standard toolbar, click the **Print** button.

One copy of your document prints on the default printer. A total of four pages will print, and your name and file name will print in the footer area of each page.

2 On your printed copy, notice that the formatting marks designating spaces, paragraphs, and tabs, do not print.

3 From the **File** menu, click **Exit**, saving any changes if prompted to do so.

Both the document and the Word program close.

> **Another Way**
>
> **Printing a Document**
>
> *There are two ways to print a document:*
>
> • On the Standard or Print Preview toolbar, click the Print button, which will print a single copy of the entire document on the default printer.
>
> • From the File menu, click Print to display the Print dialog box, from which you can select a variety of different options, such as printing multiple copies, printing on a different printer, and printing some but not all pages.

End You have completed Project 1A

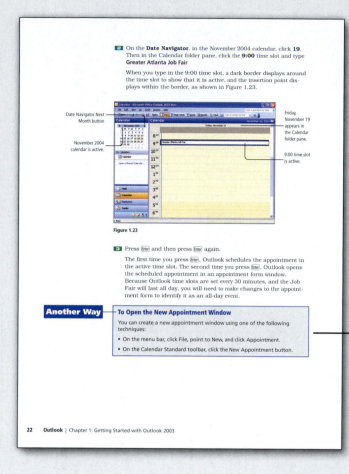

Alert box

Draws students' attention to make sure they aren't getting too far off course.

Another Way box

Shows students other ways of doing tasks.

More Knowledge box

Expands on a topic by going deeper into the material.

Note box

Points out important items to remember.

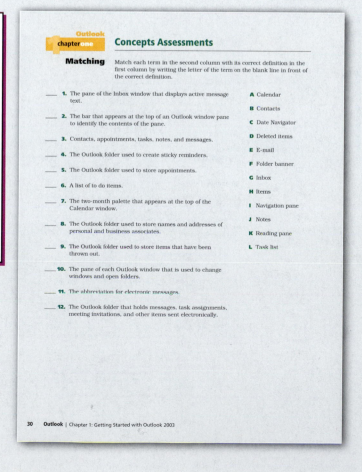

End-of-Chapter Material

Take your pick... Skills Assessment, Performance Assessment, or Mastery Assessment. Real-world projects with high, medium, or low guidance levels.

Objectives List

Each project in the GO! Series end-of-chapter section starts with a list of the objectives covered, in order to easily find the exercises you need to hone your skills.

Performance Assessments

Project 1D — Creating Folders for College Fairs

Objectives: *Start Outlook and Create Outlook Folders.*

The fairs for Mercer College and Georgia Tech have been set for April 2005. As a result, you need to create folders to hold vendor information for the fairs. When you have created the contact folders for these two fairs, your Contacts list will appear as in Figure 1.35.

Figure 1.35

1. Start Outlook, open the **Contacts** module, open the main **Contacts** folder, and on the menu bar, click **File**, point to **Folder**, and click **New Folder** to open the **Create New Folder** dialog box.

2. In the **Name** text box, type **Mercer College Fair 2005** ensure that **Contact Items** appears in the **Folder contains** text box, and click **OK**.

3. Repeat the procedures in Steps 1 and 2 to create another contacts folder named **Georgia Tech Fair 2005**

End You have completed Project 1D

End of Each Project Clearly Marked

Groups of steps that the student performs; the guided practice in order to master the learning objective.

On the Internet

In this section, students are directed to go out to the Internet for independent study.

On the Internet

Locating Friends on the Web

The World Wide Web not only stores information about companies, Web sites for bidding on items, and so forth, but it also contains telephone book information as well as e-mail addresses for many people—especially those who are students at universities! Search the Web for the colleges that three of your friends attend. After you locate the sites, search each university's e-mail directory for one of your friends. Then record these friends and their university e-mail addresses in your contacts list. Print a copy of each contact form as you create it.

GO! with Help

Training on Outlook

Microsoft Online has set up a series of training lessons at its online Web site. You can access Microsoft.com and review these training sessions directly from the Help menu in Outlook. In this project, you will work your way through the links on the Microsoft Web site to see what training topics they currently offer for Outlook. Log onto the required networks, connect to the Internet, and then follow these steps to complete the exercise.

1. If necessary, start Outlook. On the menu bar, click **Help** and then click **Office on Microsoft.com**.

   The Microsoft Office Online Web page opens in the default browser window.

2. On the left side of the Microsoft Office Online Web page, click the **Training** link.

   The Training Home Web page opens.

3. On the Training Home page, under Browse Training Courses, click **Outlook**.

   The Outlook Courses Web page opens.

4. On the Outlook Courses Web page list, click **Address your e-mail: Get it on the To line fast**.

   The Overview Web page displays information about the training session, identifies the goals of the session, and displays links for continuing the session. Navigation buttons appear in a grey bar toward the top of the Overview page for playing, pausing, and stopping the session. Yellow arrows appear above the navigation bar to advance to the next session page.

5. In the upper right side of the Overview page, on the gray navigation bar, click **Play**.

GO! with Help

A special section where students practice using the HELP feature of the Office application.

Contents in Brief

Table of Contents

Excel 2003

chapterone

Getting Started with Excel 2003

In this chapter, you will: complete these projects and practice these skills.

Project 1A
Navigating a Workbook

Objectives
- Start Excel and Navigate a Workbook
- Create Headers and Footers
- Preview and Print a Workbook
- Save and Close a Workbook and Exit Excel

Project 1B
Creating a New Workbook

Objectives
- Create a New Workbook
- Enter and Edit Data in a Worksheet
- Create Formulas
- Use Zoom and the Spelling Checker Tool
- Print a Worksheet Using the Print Dialog Box
- Use Excel Help

The City of Desert Park

Desert Park, Arizona, is a thriving city with a population of just under 1 million in an ideal location serving major markets in the western United States and Mexico. Desert Park's temperate year-round climate attracts both visitors and businesses, and it is one of the most popular vacation destinations in the world. The city expects and has plenty of space for long-term growth, and most of the undeveloped land already has a modern infrastructure and assured water supply in place.

© Getty Images, Inc.

Working with Spreadsheets

Using Microsoft Office Excel 2003, you can create and analyze data organized into columns and rows. After the data is in place, you can perform calculations, analyze the data to make logical decisions, and create a visual representation of the data in the form of charts. In addition to its spreadsheet capability, Excel can manage your data, sort your data, and search for specific pieces of information within your data.

In this chapter you will learn to create and use an Excel workbook. You will learn the basics of spreadsheet design, how to create a footer, how to enter and edit data in a worksheet, how to navigate within a workbook, and how to save, preview, and print your work. You will create formulas to add and multiply numbers. You will use AutoComplete, Excel's spelling checker tool, and access Excel's Help feature.

Project 1A Gas Usage

In Activities 1.1 through 1.12, you will **edit** (update and make changes to) an existing Excel workbook for Dennis Johnson, Police Chief of Desert Park. The Desert Park Police Department has three 12-passenger vans—one at each of the three police stations in the city. Chief Johnson has asked all station captains to track the amount of gasoline and mileage for the vans by recording the number of miles traveled each time gasoline is purchased. The four worksheets of your completed workbook will look similar to Figure 1.1. You will save your workbook as *1A_Gas_Usage_Firstname_Lastname*.

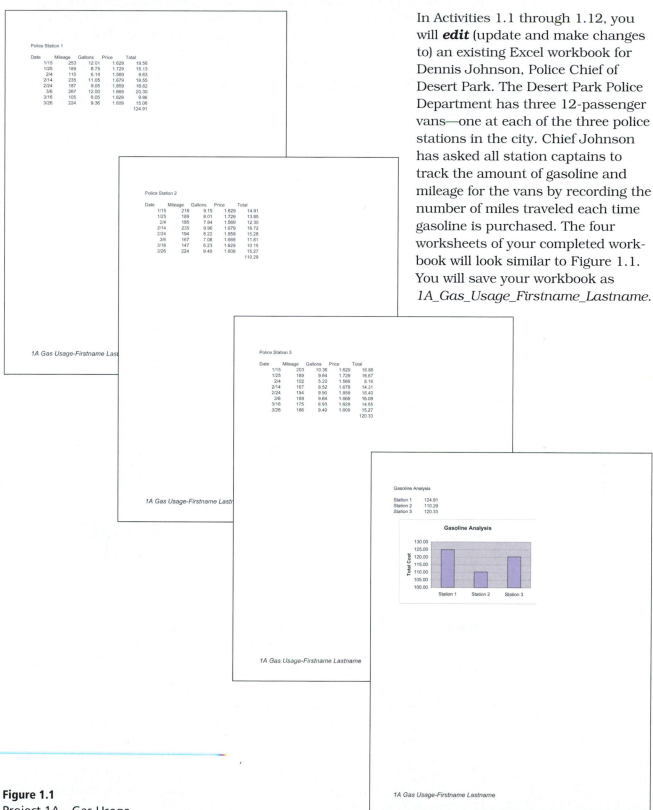

Figure 1.1
Project 1A—Gas Usage

Project 1A: Gas Usage | **Excel**   3

Objective 1
Start Excel and Navigate a Workbook

When you start the Excel program, a new blank *workbook* displays. Within a workbook are one or more pages called *worksheets*. A worksheet is formatted as a pattern of uniformly spaced horizontal and vertical lines. This grid pattern of the worksheet forms vertical columns and horizontal rows. The intersection of a column and a row forms a small rectangular box referred to as a *cell*.

Activity 1.1 Starting Excel and Identifying the Parts of the Window

You start Excel in the same manner as you start other Microsoft Office System 2003 programs.

1 On the Windows taskbar, click the **Start** button [start].

The Start menu displays. Organizations and individuals store computer programs in a variety of ways. The Excel program might be installed under "All Programs" or "Microsoft Office" or some other arrangement. See Figure 1.2 for an example.

All Programs

Start button

Figure 1.2

Microsoft Excel Office 2003

2 Point to **All Programs**, determine where the Excel program is located, point to **Microsoft Office Excel 2003**, and then click once to start the program.

Excel opens, and a blank workbook displays. The default Excel working environment consists of a menu bar, toolbars across the top of the window, and a main window divided into two sections—the *task pane* on the right and the worksheet on the left. The task pane is a window within a Microsoft Office application that displays commonly used commands. Its location and small size give you easy access to these commands while still working on your workbook. See Figure 1.3.

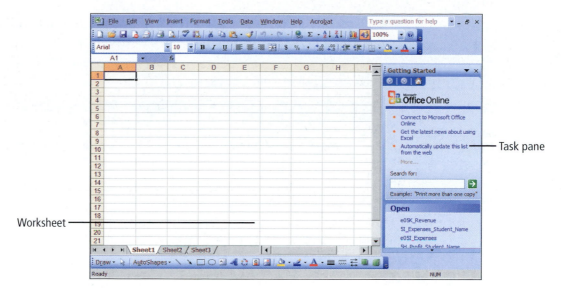

Worksheet

Figure 1.3

3 In the upper right corner of the task pane, click the **Close** button ⊠ to close the task pane.

The task pane closes. When not in use, you can close the task pane in this manner to allow the maximum amount of screen space for your worksheet. See Figure 1.4.

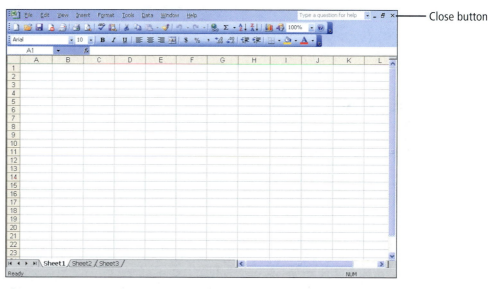

Close button

Figure 1.4

4 Take a moment to study Figure 1.5a-b and the table in Figure 1.6 to become familiar with the parts of the Excel window.

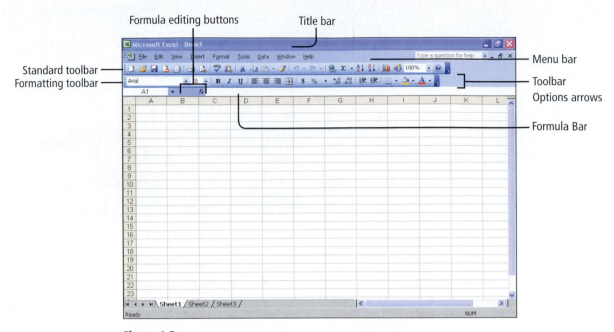

Figure 1.5a

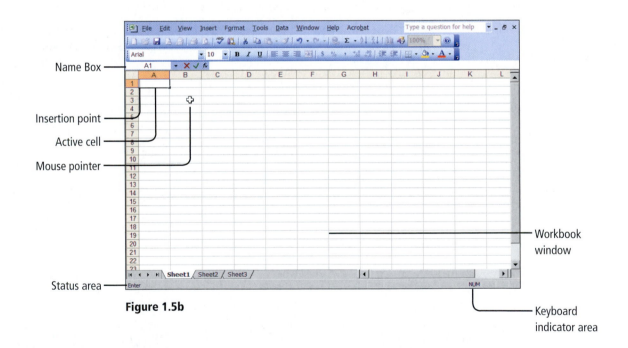

Figure 1.5b

Parts of the Excel Window

Excel Window Element	Description
Title bar	Displays the program icon, the program name, and the workbook name. The Minimize, Maximize or Restore, and Close buttons are at the extreme right edge of the title bar.
Menu bar	Contains the menus of commands. Display a menu by clicking on its name in the menu bar or by pressing Alt and pressing the underlined letter in the menu name.
Standard toolbar	Contains buttons for some of the most common commands in Excel, for example, Print and Save. It may occupy an entire row or share a row with the Formatting toolbar.
Formatting toolbar	Contains buttons for some of the most common formatting commands in Excel. It may occupy an entire row or share a row with the Standard toolbar.
Toolbar Options arrow	Displays additional buttons on the Formatting and Standard toolbars and also permits moving the toolbar to a separate or shared row.
Name Box	Identifies the selected cell, chart item, or drawing object. Also used to type a name for a cell or range of cells.
Formula editing buttons	Display when you are entering or editing data in a cell and assist in editing. The X button cancels the entry; the check mark button functions in the same manner as pressing Enter—it locks in your information; and the *fx* button displays the Insert Function dialog box to assist you in building a formula.
Formula Bar	Displays the value or formula contained in the active cell. Also permits entry or editing of values or formulas in cells or charts.
Insertion point	A blinking vertical bar that indicates where typed text or numbers will be inserted.
Active cell	The cell in which the next keystroke or command will take place. A black border surrounds the cell when it is active.
Mouse pointer	A graphic screen image controlled by your movement of the mouse.
Workbook window	The area of the Excel window containing the worksheets and the rows, columns, and cells of the active worksheet. The area of the workbook window ruled with horizontal and vertical lines makes up the worksheet's cells.
Status area	Displays information about the active cell.
Keyboard indicator area	Displays the current status of various keyboard functions such as the on or off status of NumLock.

Figure 1.6

Activity 1.2 **Using the Menu Bar, ScreenTips, and the Toolbars**

1 On the menu bar, click **File**.

The File menu displays in either the full format, as shown in Figure 1.7, or in a short format, as shown in Figure 1.8. Excel's commands are organized in *menus*—lists of commands within a category. A short menu will display fully after a few seconds, or you can click the double arrows at the bottom to display the full menu. The File menu, when displayed in full, lists the last four to nine workbooks used on your computer. Whether your full menu displays immediately or is delayed by a few seconds depends on the options that are set for this software. Likewise, the number of previous workbook names displayed depends on how the software was set up. These default settings can be changed in the Options dialog box (displayed from the Tools menu) on systems where it is permissible to do so.

Full format —

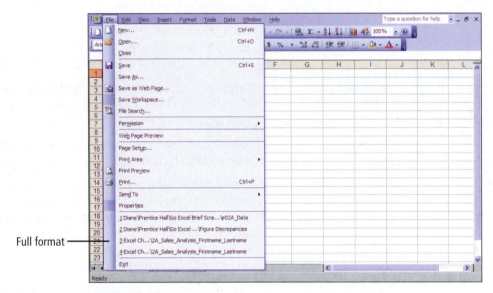

Figure 1.7

Short format —

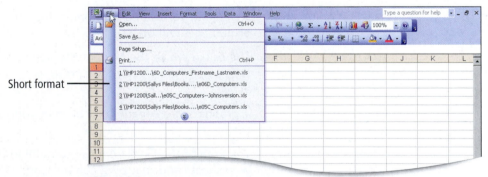

Figure 1.8

Note — Displaying Full Menus

Many Excel users prefer the automatic full menu display. To set a system to always display full menus, display the Tools menu, click Customize, and then click the Options tab. Under Personalized Menus and Toolbars, select the Always show full menus check box. Click the Reset menu and toolbar usage data button, click Yes, and then click Close.

2 If the full menu is not displayed, pause your mouse pointer over the **Expand arrows** to expand the **File** menu. See Figure 1.9.

On the left side of some command names is an image of the button that represents this command on a toolbar. This is a reminder that you can use the toolbar button to start the command with only one click. Likewise, to the right of some commands is a reminder that you can use a keyboard shortcut (holding down a combination of keys) to start the command.

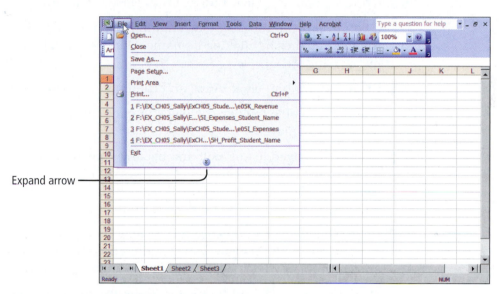

Expand arrow

Figure 1.9

3 Look at the full **File** menu on your screen.

Following or to the right of some menu commands, you will see various symbols, characters, or formatting, which are standard across all Microsoft products. The table in Figure 1.10 lists these characteristics and describes what will happen when you select the command.

Microsoft Menu Characteristics

Characteristic	Description	Example
... (ellipsis)	Indicates that a dialog box requesting more information will display.	Print...
▶ (triangle)	Indicates that a submenu—another menu of choices—will display.	Send to ▶
No symbol	Indicates that the command will perform immediately.	Exit
✓ (check mark)	Indicates that a command is turned on or active.	✓ Standard
Gray option name	Indicates that the command is currently unavailable (grayed out).	Properties

Figure 1.10

4 On the menu bar, click **File** again to close the menu.

If you decide not to select a command from a displayed menu, close the menu either by clicking its name, clicking outside the menu, or by pressing Esc.

5 On the menu bar, click **View**, and then point to **Toolbars**.

A list of available toolbars displays. A check mark indicates that the toolbar is displayed.

6 On the displayed list of toolbars, be sure that **Standard** and **Formatting** are both checked. Clear any other checked toolbar on the list by clicking its check mark to clear it, and then, if the list is still displayed, click outside the menu to close it.

7 Below the menu bar, be sure two rows of toolbars display, as shown in Figure 1.11. If, instead, your toolbars are sharing one row, as shown in Figure 1.12, at the end of the toolbar click the **Toolbar Options** button ▐, and then click **Show Buttons on Two Rows**.

The toolbars will display on two rows, as shown in Figure 1.11. Alternatively, from the Tools menu, click Customize, click the Options tab, and then select the Show Standard and Formatting toolbars on two rows check box.

Toolbars on two rows —

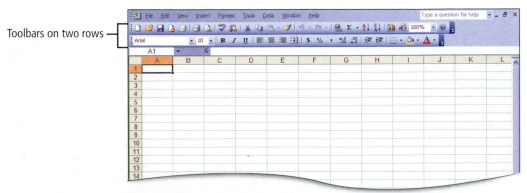

Figure 1.11

Toolbars on one row ——

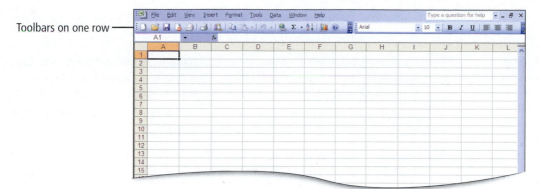

Figure 1.12

8 On the Standard toolbar, locate and pause your mouse pointer over the **New** button .

When you position the mouse pointer over a button, Excel displays the button's name in a **ScreenTip**. The ScreenTip *New* displays, indicating that clicking this button will activate the command to create a new workbook. See Figure 1.13.

New button ——
ScreenTip ——

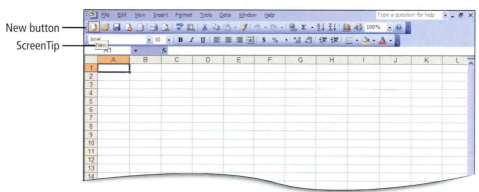

Figure 1.13

9 Pause your pointer over several buttons on both the Standard and Formatting toolbars to become familiar with the commands available to you. A toolbar button is a one-click method to activate frequently used commands that are also available from the menus. The ScreenTip describes the command that will be activated when you click the toolbar button.

Activity 1.3 Opening an Existing Workbook

1 From the menu bar, display the **File** menu, and then click **Open**. Alternatively, click the Open button on the Standard toolbar.

The Open dialog box displays.

2 At the right side of the **Look in** box, click the **Look in arrow**, and then navigate to the student files that accompany this textbook.

3 Click to select the file **e01A_Gas_Usage**, and then, in the lower right corner of the dialog box, click **Open**.

The workbook e01A_Gas_Usage displays. Alternatively, you can double-click a file name to open it. The workbook includes data already captured from gas slips, including the number of gallons purchased and the total amounts printed on the actual slips. Excel calculates the total of all slips by using a formula.

4 Take a moment to study Figures 1.14a and 1.14b and the table in Figure 1.15 to become familiar with the Excel workbook window.

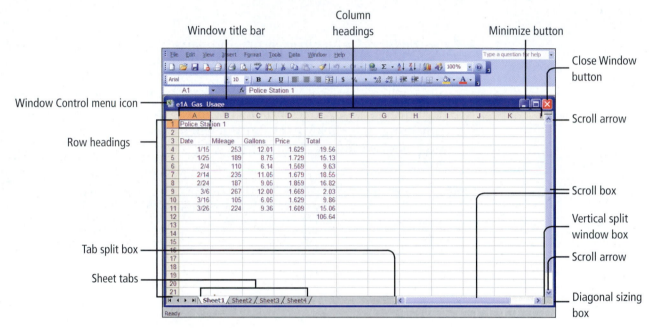

Figure 1.14a

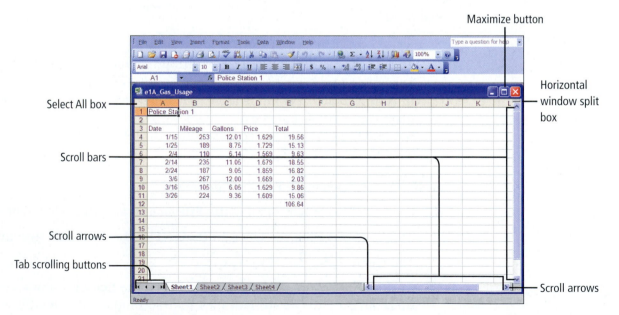

Figure 1.14b

Excel Workbook Elements

Workbook Element	Description
Close Window button	Closes the workbook.
Column headings	Indicate the column letter.
Diagonal sizing box	Indicates that the window can be resized; dragging this box changes the window size.
Horizontal window split box	Splits the worksheet into two vertical views of the same worksheet.
Maximize button	Displays the active window in its full size in the Excel workspace.
Minimize button	Collapses the active window to a button on the taskbar.
Row headings	Indicates the row number.
Scroll arrows	Scroll one column or row at a time.
Scroll bars	Scroll the Excel window up and down or left and right.
Scroll boxes	Used with the mouse to drag the position of a window up and down or left and right.
Select All box	Selects all cells in a worksheet.
Sheet tabs	Changes the active worksheet in a workbook.
Tab scrolling buttons	Display sheet tabs that are not in view; used when there are more sheet tabs than will display in the space provided.
Tab split box	Adjusts the space available for sheet tabs.
Vertical split window box	Splits the worksheet into two horizontal views of the same worksheet.
Window Control menu icon	Also known as the control program box. Allows keyboard access to move, resize, minimize, maximize, and close the worksheet window.
Window title bar	Displays the application name along with the name of the current workbook.

Figure 1.15

Activity 1.4 Selecting Columns, Rows, Cells, Ranges, and Worksheets

Recall that a **cell** is the rectangular box formed by the intersection of a column and a row. **Selecting** refers to highlighting, by clicking or dragging with your mouse, one or more cells so that the selected range of cells can be edited, formatted, copied, or moved. Excel treats the selected range of cells as a single unit; thus, you can make the same change, or combination of changes, to more than one cell at a time.

1 In the upper left corner of the displayed worksheet, position your mouse pointer over the letter **A** until the pointer ⬇ displays, as shown in Figure 1.16, and then click once.

Column A is selected (highlighted). A **column** is a vertical group of cells in a worksheet. Beginning with the first letter of the alphabet, A, a unique letter identifies each column—this is called the **column heading**. After using the entire alphabet from A to Z, Excel begins naming the columns AA, AB, AC, and so on.

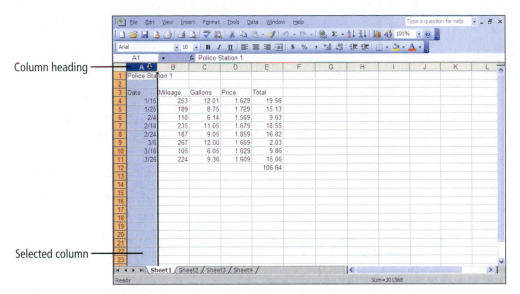

Figure 1.16

2 At the left edge of the workbook, position your mouse pointer over the number **3** until the pointer ➡ displays, as shown in Figure 1.17, and then click once.

Row 3 is selected. A **row** is a horizontal group of cells in a worksheet. Beginning with number 1, a unique number identifies each row—this is the **row heading**, located at the left side of the worksheet.

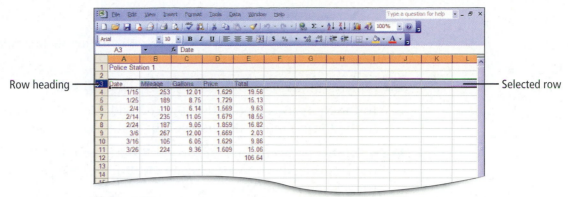

Row heading ——

—— Selected row

Figure 1.17

3 In the displayed worksheet, click the word **Date**. See Figure 1.18.

A black border surrounds the cell, indicating that it is the *active cell*. The active cell in a worksheet is the cell ready to receive data or be affected by the next Excel command. A cell is identified by the intersecting column letter and row number, which forms the *cell address*. A cell address is also referred to as a *cell reference*.

4 At the left end of the Formula Bar, look at the **Name Box**.

The cell address of the active cell, A3, displays.

5 Look at the Formula Bar.

The value of the cell—the word *Date*—displays. See Figure 1.18.

Intersecting row   Value displayed in
and column   Formula Bar

Cell reference (cell address)
displayed in Name box ——

Intersecting row and column ——

Active cell ——

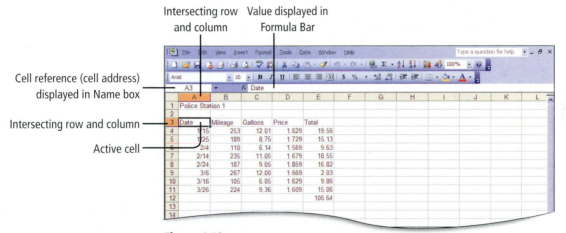

Figure 1.18

6 On the keyboard, press ↓ three times.

Cell A6 becomes the active cell. Pressing an arrow key relocates the active cell.

7 With your mouse, point to and then click cell **B4**.

In the Name Box, notice that the cell address, *B4*, is indicated, and in the Formula Bar, the value of the cell, *253*, is indicated.

8 With the mouse pointer ⊕ over cell **B4**, hold down the left mouse button, drag down to select cells **B5**, **B6**, and **B7**, and then release the left mouse button.

The four cells, B4 through B7, are selected. This **range** (group) of cells is referred to as *B4:B7*. When you see a colon (:) between two cell references, the range includes all the cells between the two cell addresses—in this instance, all the cells from B4 through B7. Use this technique to select a range of cells adjacent (next) to one another in a worksheet. See Figure 1.19.

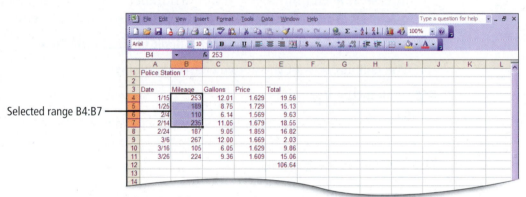

Selected range B4:B7 ——

Figure 1.19

9 Point to and then click cell **B4** to make it the active cell.

10 Press and hold down Ctrl, click cell **B7**, and then click cell **C6**.

Cells B4, B7, and C6 are all selected. See Figure 1.20.

Use this technique to select cells that are nonadjacent (not next to one another). A range of cells can be adjacent or nonadjacent. A range of cells that is nonadjacent is separated with commas instead of a colon. In this instance, the range is referred to as *B4, B7, C6*.

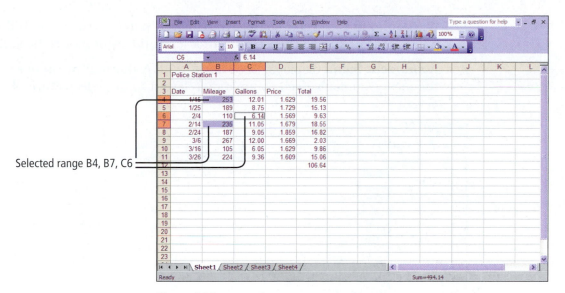

Figure 1.20

Selected range B4, B7, C6

11 Select **column C**.

Notice that when you select an entire column, the address of the first cell in the column displays in the Name Box. See Figure 1.21.

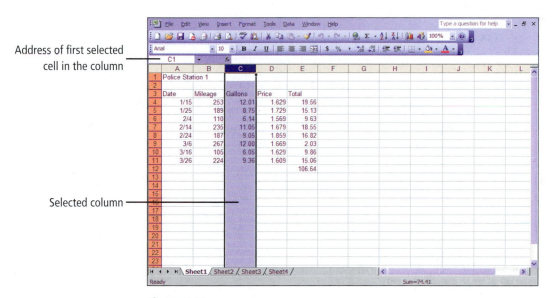

Address of first selected cell in the column

Selected column

Figure 1.21

12 With **column C** selected, pause your mouse pointer anywhere in the highlighted area, and then ***right-click*** (click the right mouse button).

A ***shortcut menu*** displays. See Figure 1.22. A shortcut menu offers the most commonly used commands relevant to the selected area.

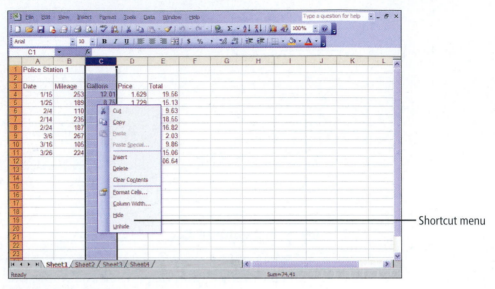

Figure 1.22

13 Move the pointer anywhere outside **column C** and away from the shortcut menu, and then click the left mouse button.

You have canceled the selection of—***deselected***—column C. The column is no longer highlighted, and the shortcut menu is closed.

14 At the left edge of the worksheet, move your mouse pointer over the **row 4** heading, and click to select the row.

When you select an entire row, the address of the first cell in the row displays in the Name Box. See Figure 1.23.

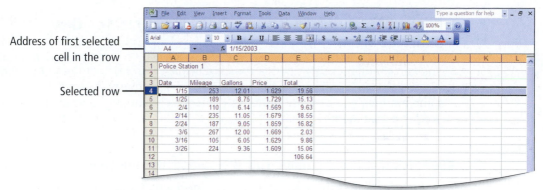

Address of first selected cell in the row ────

Selected row ────

Figure 1.23

15 With **row 4** selected, move the mouse pointer anywhere over the highlighted area, and right-click.

A shortcut menu displays the most commonly used row commands, as shown in Figure 1.24.

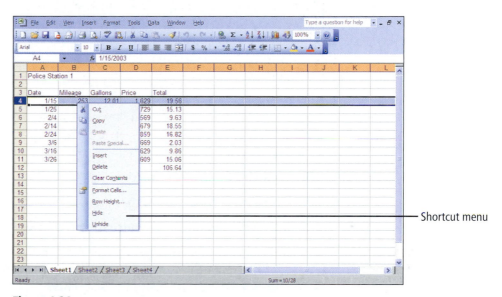

──── **Shortcut menu**

Figure 1.24

More Knowledge — Right-clicking to See the Shortcut Menu

You can simultaneously select a row and display the shortcut menu by pointing to the row heading and then clicking the right mouse button. In the same manner, you can simultaneously select a column and display its associated shortcut menu.

16 Click anywhere outside **row 4** to cancel the selection.

17 At the upper left corner of your worksheet, locate the **Select All** button—the small gray box above row heading 1 and to the left of column heading A—as shown in Figure 1.25.

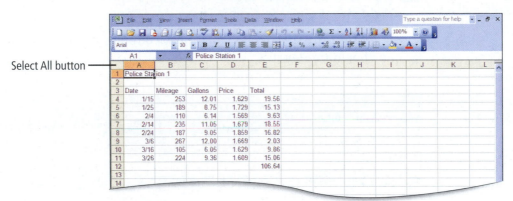

Select All button

Figure 1.25

18 Click the **Select All** button.

All the cells in the worksheet are selected.

19 Move your pointer anywhere in the worksheet and click once.

The selection is canceled.

Activity 1.5 Navigating Using the Scroll Bars

An Excel worksheet contains 256 columns and 65,536 rows. Of course, you cannot see that many rows and columns on your computer's screen all at the same time, so Excel provides scroll bars for you to display and view different parts of your worksheet. A scroll bar has a scroll box and two scroll arrows. **Scroll** is the action of moving the workbook window either vertically (up and down) or horizontally (side to side) to bring different areas of the worksheet into view on your screen. See Figure 1.26.

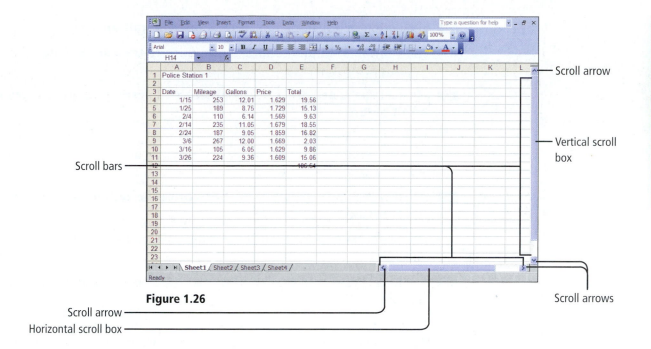

Scroll arrow

Vertical scroll box

Scroll bars

Figure 1.26

Scroll arrow

Horizontal scroll box

Scroll arrows

1 In the horizontal scroll bar, point to and then click the **right scroll arrow**.

The workbook window moves one column to the right so that column A moves out of view, as shown in Figure 1.27. The number of times you click the arrows on the horizontal scroll bar determines the number of columns by which the window shifts—either to the left or to the right.

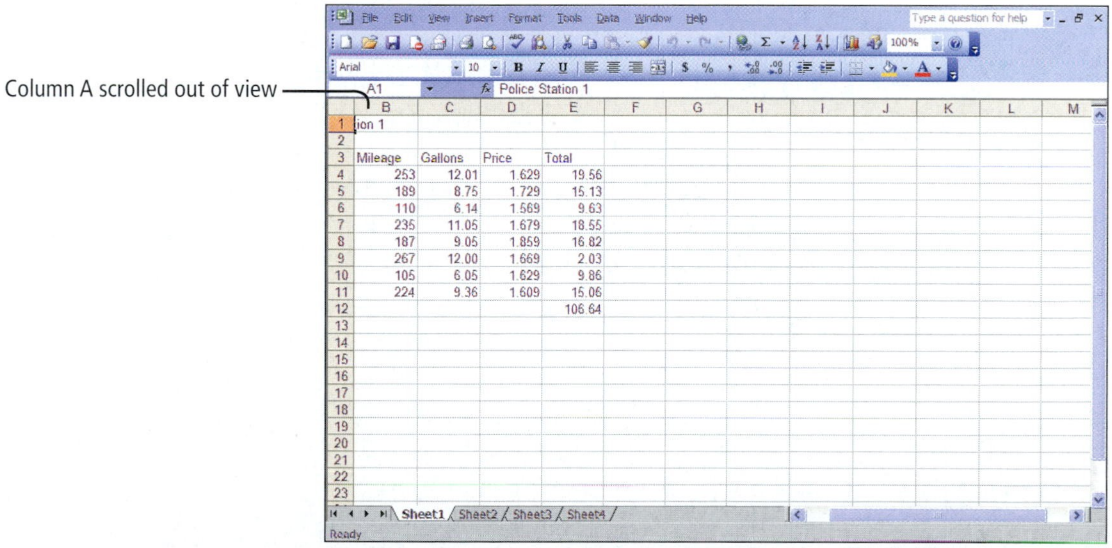

Column A scrolled out of view

Figure 1.27

2 In the horizontal scroll bar, click the **left scroll arrow**.

The workbook window shifts one column to the left, moving column A back into view.

3 Click in the space between the **horizontal scroll box** and the **right scroll arrow**.

An entire group of columns, equivalent to the number visible on your screen, scrolls to the left and out of view; in fact, the data has moved out of view.

4 Click in the space between the **horizontal scroll box** and the **left scroll arrow**.

The first group of columns, beginning with column A, moves back into view.

5 In the vertical scroll bar, point to and then click the **down scroll arrow**.

Row 1 is no longer in view. The number of times you click the arrows on the vertical scroll bar determines the number of rows shifted either up or down.

6 In the vertical scroll bar, point to and then click the **up scroll arrow**.

Row 1 comes back into view.

Activity 1.6 Navigating Using the Name Box

1 To the left of the Formula Bar, point to the **Name Box** to display the **I-beam** pointer ⬚, as shown in Figure 1.28, and then click once.

Name Box with I-beam pointer displayed

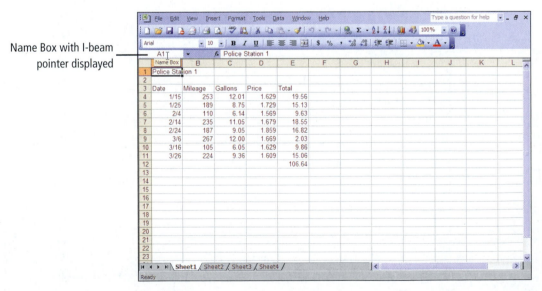

Figure 1.28

The cell reference that was displayed is highlighted in blue and aligned at the left. In Microsoft products, when text is highlighted in blue within a box, it is an indication that when you begin to type, the existing text will be deleted and replaced with your new keystrokes.

2 Using the keyboard, type **b6** and then press Enter.

Cell B6 becomes the active cell. Typing a cell address in the Name Box is another way to select a cell and cause it to become the active cell. Notice that you do not have to use the capital letter B—typing in either uppercase or lowercase will result in *B6* displaying in the Name Box.

3 Selecting a cell to make it the active cell can also be accomplished using the keys on the keyboard. Take a moment to study the table shown in Figure 1.29 to become familiar with these keyboard commands.

Keyboard Commands

To Move the Location of the Active Cell:	Press:
Left, right, up, or down one cell	←, →, ↑, or ↓
Down one cell	Enter
Up one cell	Shift + Enter
Up one full screen	Page Up
Down one full screen	PageDown
Left one full screen	Alt + Page Up
Right one full screen	Alt + PageDown
To column A of the current row	Home
To the last cell in the last column of the **active area** (the rectangle formed by all the rows and columns in a worksheet that contain or contained entries.)	Ctrl + End
To cell A1	Ctrl + Home
Right one cell	Tab
Left one cell	Shift + Tab

Figure 1.29

Activity 1.7 Navigating Among the Worksheets in a Workbook

The default setting for the number of worksheets in a workbook is three. You can add worksheets or delete worksheets. Each worksheet has a total of 16,777,216 cells (256 columns × 65,536 rows). Sometimes a project may require that you enter data into more than one worksheet.

When you have more than one worksheet in a workbook, you can *navigate* (move) among worksheets by clicking the *sheet tab*. Sheet tabs identify each worksheet in a workbook. Sheet tabs are located along the lower border of the worksheet window. When you have more worksheets in the workbook than can be displayed in the sheet tab area, use the four tab scrolling buttons to move sheet tabs into and out of view. See Figure 1.30.

Notice that the background color for the Sheet1 tab displays in the same color as the background color for the worksheet and also displays as bold characters. See Figure 1.30. This indicates that *Sheet1* is the active worksheet within the current workbook.

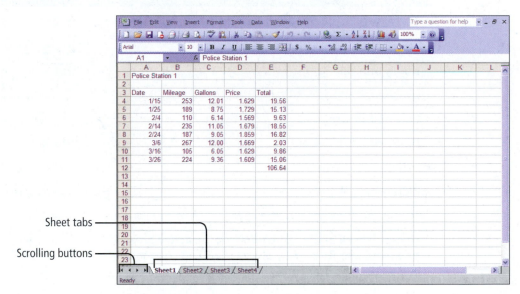

Figure 1.30

1 Point to and then click the **Sheet2 tab**.

The second worksheet in the workbook displays and becomes the active worksheet. Notice that cell A1 displays the text *Police Station 2* because the second worksheet of this workbook contains data for the 12-passenger van at Police Station 2.

2 Click the **Sheet1 tab**.

The first worksheet in the workbook becomes the active worksheet, and cell A1 displays *Police Station 1*.

Activity 1.8 Viewing a Chart

Excel can produce a graphical representation of your data. Data presented as a graph is easier to understand than rows and columns of numbers. Within Excel, a visual representation of your data using graphics is called a *chart*.

1 In the row of sheet tabs, click the **Sheet4 tab**.

A worksheet containing a chart displays. See Figure 1.31. The chart represents the total gasoline expenses for the 12-passenger vans at each of the three police stations—graphically displaying the differences. The chart uses data gathered from the other three worksheets to generate the graphical representation. If you change the numbers in any of the worksheets, Excel automatically redraws the chart to reflect those changes.

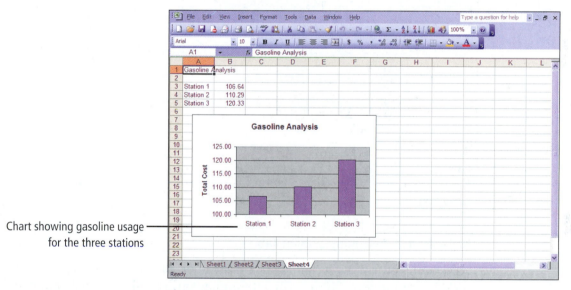

Chart showing gasoline usage for the three stations

Figure 1.31

2 Notice the height of the bar for Station 1. Then, click the **Sheet1 tab**, and click to select cell **E9**.

3 Notice the column total of 106.64 in cell **E12**. In cell **E9**, replace the current value of *2.03* by typing **20.30** and then press (Enter).

When you type a value into a cell that already contains a value, the new value replaces the old. It is not necessary to delete the original contents of the cell first. With a new value in cell E9, pressing (Enter) caused Excel to recalculate the column total and display the new total, 124.91, in cell E12.

4 Click the **Sheet4 tab**.

The size of the bar representing Station 1 in the chart has changed to reflect the new total from the Station 1 worksheet as shown in Figure 1.32. This is an example of Excel's powerful ability to perform calculations and then update the visual representations of the data.

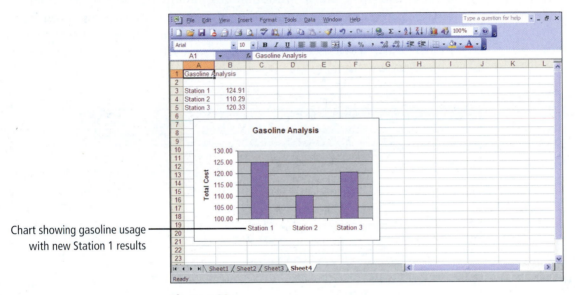

Chart showing gasoline usage with new Station 1 results

Figure 1.32

Activity 1.9 Renaming a Sheet Tab

Excel names the first worksheet in a workbook Sheet1 and each additional worksheet in order—Sheet2, Sheet3, and so on. Usually you will want to assign names to your worksheets that are more meaningful to you. Use either of two methods to rename a worksheet within a workbook:

• Right-click the sheet tab to display the shortcut menu, and then click the Rename command.

• Double-click the sheet tab, and then type a new name directly on the tab.

In this activity, you will rename the worksheets so that they are more descriptive.

1 Point to the **Sheet4 tab** and right-click. On the displayed shortcut menu, click **Rename**.

The Sheet tab name is selected.

2 Type **Chart** and then press Enter.

3 *Double-click* (click the left mouse button twice in rapid succession, keeping the mouse still between the clicks) the **Sheet1 tab** to select its name, and then type **Station 1**

4 Using either method, rename **Sheet2** to **Station 2** and **Sheet3** to **Station 3**

Objective 2
Create Headers and Footers

Headers and *footers* are text, page numbers, graphics, and formatting that print at the top (header) or bottom (footer) of every page.

Throughout this textbook, you will type the project name and your name on each of your worksheets by placing them in a footer. This will make it easier for you to identify your printed documents in a shared printer environment such as a lab or classroom.

Activity 1.10 Creating Headers and Footers

1 Point to the **Station 1 tab** and right-click. On the displayed shortcut menu, click **Select All Sheets**.

When a group of worksheets is selected, the word *Group* displays in the title bar to the right of the file name, as shown in Figure 1.33. By selecting all sheets, you will cause the Header and Footer information that you create to print on each worksheet in this workbook—not only on the active sheet.

Alert!

What Is "Read-Only"?

In addition to [Group], your title may display [Read-Only]. Workbook files provided by the textbook publisher frequently have this designation. It means that you cannot make permanent changes to the workbook. To make permanent changes, you will have to save the workbook with a new name, which you will be instructed to do.

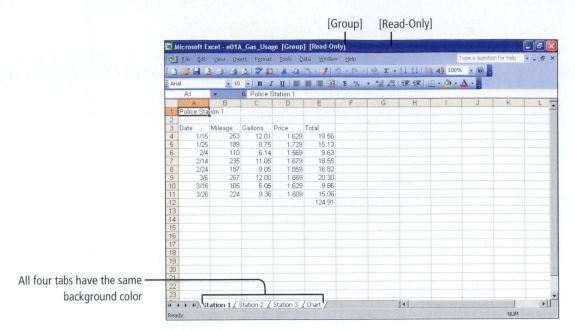

[Group]   [Read-Only]

All four tabs have the same background color

Figure 1.33

2 On the menu bar, click **View**, and then click **Header and Footer**.

The Page Setup dialog box displays, as shown in Figure 1.34.

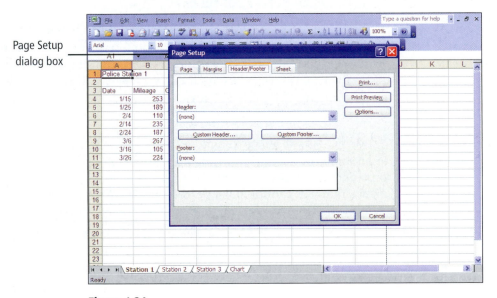

Page Setup dialog box

Figure 1.34

3 In the top portion of the **Page Setup** dialog box, click the **Header/Footer tab** once if necessary.

4 In the center of the dialog box, click the **Custom Footer** button.

The Footer dialog box displays, as shown in Figure 1.35. A flashing vertical line displays at the left edge of the *Left section* box. This is the ***insertion point***, the point at which anything you type will be inserted. The insertion point in this box is left-aligned—text you enter will begin at the left.

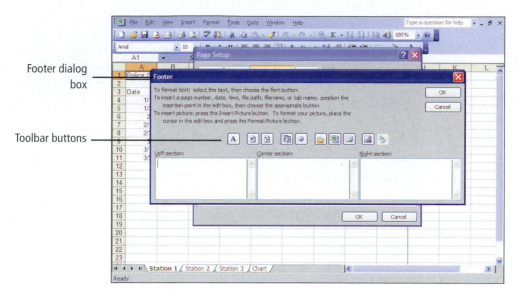

Footer dialog box

Toolbar buttons

Figure 1.35

5 In the center of the **Footer** dialog box, locate the toolbar buttons shown in Figure 1.35, and then click the **Font** button. These toolbar buttons do not display ScreenTips.

The Font dialog box displays, as shown in Figure 1.36.

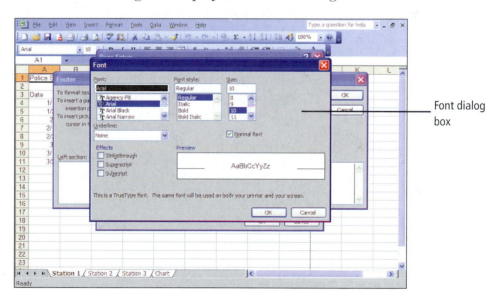

Font dialog box

Figure 1.36

6 Under **Font**, click the **scroll bar arrows** as necessary, and then click **Arial**. Under **Font style**, scroll as necessary, and then click **Italic**. Under **Size**, scroll as necessary, and then click **14**. Then, in the lower right corner, click the **OK** button.

7 Using your own first and last name, type **1A Gas Usage-Firstname Lastname** and notice that as you type, Excel wraps the text to the next line in the box. When you print your workbook, the footer will print on one line.

Compare your screen with Figure 1.37.

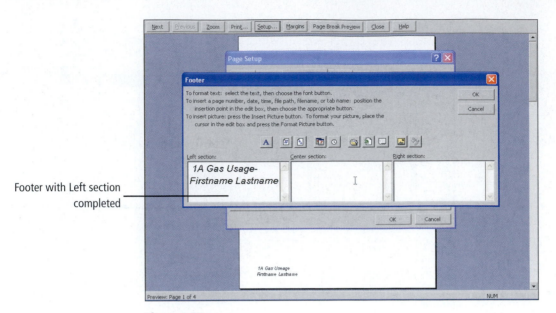

Footer with Left section completed ————

Figure 1.37

8 In the upper right of the **Footer** dialog box, click **OK**, and then at the lower right of the **Page Setup** dialog box, click **OK** to return to the workbook.

Headers and footers that you create do not display in the worksheet window; they display only on the page preview screen and on the printed page. The vertical dotted line between columns indicates that as currently arranged, only the columns to the left of the dotted line will print on the first page, as shown in Figure 1.38. The exact position of the dotted line will depend on the default printer settings. Yours may fall elsewhere.

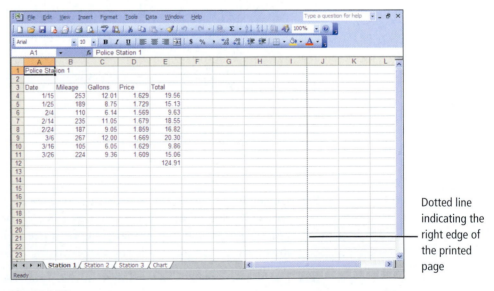

Dotted line indicating the right edge of the printed page

Figure 1.38

9 Right-click the **Station 1 tab**, and then click **Ungroup Sheets** to ungroup the sheets.

The word *Group* no longer displays in the worksheet title bar, indicating that the worksheet grouping has been removed.

More Knowledge — Removing the [Group] Indicator on the Title Bar

If sheets in a workbook are grouped, clicking any sheet tab other than that of the active sheet ungroups the sheets and removes the [Group] indicator from the title bar.

Objective 3
Preview and Print a Workbook

Before you print your worksheet or an entire workbook, you will want to check the formatting, placement, and layout. Excel's Print Preview feature lets you do this before printing your worksheets on paper.

From your instructor or lab coordinator, determine the default printer for the computer at which you are working, and check to see whether it is available for you to use.

Activity 1.11 Previewing and Printing a Workbook

1 Point to the **Station 1 tab** and right-click. On the displayed shortcut menu, click **Select All Sheets**.

The title bar shows [Group] indicating that multiple worksheets in the workbook are selected.

2 On the Standard toolbar, click the **Print Preview** button .

Your worksheet displays as an image of a piece of paper so that you can see how your worksheet will be placed on the page, including the footer. See Figure 1.39. Because more than one worksheet is being previewed, in the lower left of the preview window *Page 1 of 4* displays.

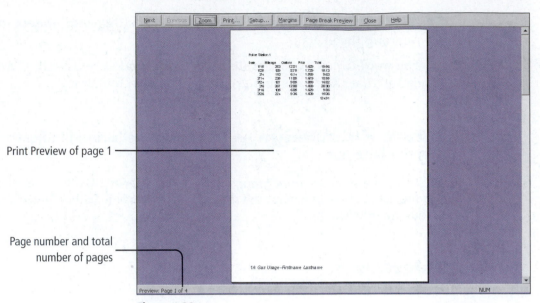

Print Preview of page 1

Page number and total number of pages

Figure 1.39

3 On the Print Preview toolbar, click the **Next** button to view page 2. Then, click the **Next** button two more times to view pages 3 and 4.

As you scroll forward and backward using the Next and Previous buttons, the words in the lower left of the Preview window change to indicate the page you are currently viewing—*Page 3 of 4* and so forth.

4 On the Print Preview toolbar, click the **Close** button to exit Print Preview.

5 On the Standard toolbar, click the **Print** button 🖨.

One copy of each worksheet in the workbook prints—a total of four sheets.

6 Right-click the **Station 1 tab**, and then click **Ungroup Sheets**.

The [Group] indication in the title bar is removed and the worksheets are no longer grouped together.

Objective 4
Save and Close a Workbook and Exit Excel

In the same way you use file folders to organize your paper documents, Windows uses a hierarchy of electronic folders to store and organize your electronic files (workbooks). In the following activities you will save the workbook with a name and in a location that will be easy for you to find.

Activity 1.12 Creating a New Folder and Saving a Workbook with a New Name

Creating a new folder in which to save your work will make finding the workbooks you create easier. Before saving, you will need to determine where you will be storing your workbooks, for example, on your own disk or on a network drive.

1 On the menu bar, click **File** to display the File menu, and then click **Save As**.

The Save As dialog box displays, as shown in Figure 1.40.

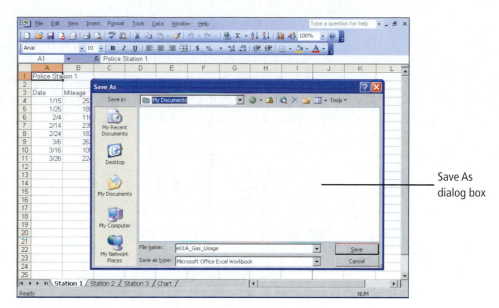

Save As
dialog box

Figure 1.40

2 Click the **Save in arrow** to view a list of the drives available to you, and then navigate to the drive on which you will be storing your folders and documents; for example, 3½ Floppy (A:).

3 In the upper right of the dialog box, click the **Create New Folder** button.

The New Folder dialog box displays.

4 In the displayed **New Folder** dialog box, in the **Name** box, type **Excel Chapter 1** as shown in Figure 1.41 and then click **OK**.

Windows creates the *Excel Chapter 1* folder and makes it the active folder in the Save As dialog box.

New Folder dialog box with folder name typed

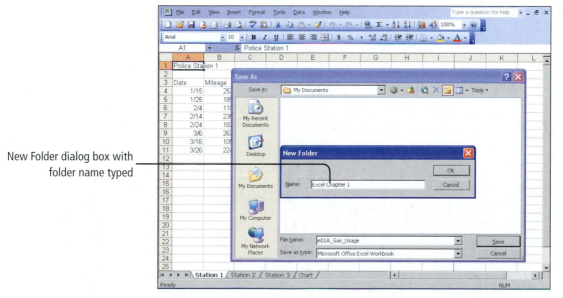

Figure 1.41

5 In the **File name** box, delete any existing text by selecting it and pressing the `Delete` key, and type **1A_Gas_Usage_Firstname_Lastname** replacing *Firstname* with your first name and *Lastname* with your last name, being sure to include the underscore (`Shift` + `-`) instead of spaces between words.

Windows recognizes file names that use spaces between words. However, many electronic file transfer programs do not. In this text, you will use underscores instead of spaces between words for your file names. In that manner, you can be assured that if you need to transfer files on the Web, for example, using Blackboard or WebCT for online courses, your files will move easily on the Internet.

6 In the lower right corner of the **Save As** dialog box, click **Save**.

The file is saved in the new folder with the new name. The workbook redisplays, and the new name displays in the title bar.

7 On the menu bar, click **File**, and then click **Close**.

Your workbook closes. The Excel program remains open, even when no workbooks are open.

8 At the extreme right of the title bar, click the **Close** button ☒ to close Excel.

Note — Renaming Folders

You can rename folders by right-clicking a folder and selecting Rename from the shortcut menu. The folder name will display in an edit mode and you can type to rename the folder. You can also click once on the folder name, and then click a second time to invoke the edit mode, and then type a new folder name.

End **You have completed Project 1A** ────────────────────

Project 1B Salary Analysis

In this project, you will create a new workbook and enter data into it. Then you will create formulas to perform mathematical calculations and use the spelling checker to check for misspelled words in your spreadsheet.

In Activities 1.13 through 1.29, you will create a new workbook for Police Chief Johnson that contains an employee list showing the name, shift, date of hire, and current weekly salary of the police officers assigned to each police station. You will enter the data for Police Station 1. The resulting workbook will look similar to Figure 1.42. You will save your workbook as *1B_Salary_Analysis_Firstname_Lastname*.

Police Station 1 Weekly Salaries

Emp	Shift	Hired on	Salary	Annual
J Bryon	Day	5/13/1996	460	23920
T Cassidy	Day	6/11/1998	685	35620
L Shasta	Night	7/30/1998	550	28600
G Adams	Day	3/15/1999	526	27352
S Front	Day	4/17/2001	767	39884
M Pong	Night	5/17/2002	389	20228
Total			3377	175604

1B Salary Analysis-Firstname Lastname

Figure 1.42
Project 1B—Salary Analysis

Objective 5
Create a New Workbook

When you save a file, the Windows operating system stores your work-book permanently on a storage medium—either a disk that you have inserted into the computer, the hard drive of your computer, or a net-work drive to which your computer system is connected. Changes that you make to existing workbooks, such as changing data or typing in new data, are not permanently saved until you perform a Save operation.

Save your workbooks frequently to avoid losing the data you have created in a new workbook or the changes you have made to an existing work-book. In rare instances, problems arise with your computer system or your electrical power source.

Activity 1.13 Creating a New Workbook

In the following activity, you will begin a new workbook and then save it in your Excel Chapter 1 folder.

1 If the Excel program is open, close it now.

2 **Start** the Excel program. If the **Getting Started** task pane is open, click its **Close** button ☒. Notice that *Book1* displays in both the title bar and the taskbar. See Figure 1.43.

Excel displays the file name of a workbook in both the blue title bar at the top of the screen and on a button in the taskbar at the bottom of the screen—including new, unsaved workbooks. The unsaved workbook displays as *Book1* or *Book2*, depending on the number of times you have started a new workbook during your current Excel session.

Figure 1.43

Alert! ── **The complete file name is not visible in the taskbar?**

The size of taskbar buttons varies, depending on your computer setup. To view the full file name in the taskbar, pause the mouse pointer over the button to display a ScreenTip containing the complete workbook name.

3 Display the **File** menu, and then click **Close**. Click **No** if you are prompted to save any changes to the workbook.

When all Excel workbooks are closed, most of the toolbar buttons display in gray, indicating that they are unavailable, and the workbook area displays in a darker shade. See Figure 1.44. Your screen will look like this when the Excel program is running but no workbooks are open.

Unavailable (grayed) toolbar buttons

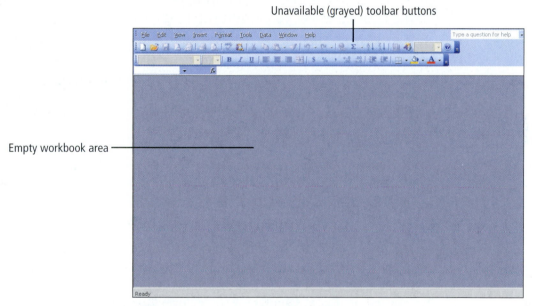

Empty workbook area

Figure 1.44

4 On the Standard toolbar, click the **New** button.

Recall that a toolbar button is a one-click method of performing a command. Alternatively, you could display the File menu and then click New, but this would require more than one click.

A new blank workbook displays, the toolbar buttons are reactivated, and *Book2* displays in the title bar and in the taskbar. Each time you open a new workbook during an Excel session, the number will increase by one. There is no limit to the number of blank workbooks. Each time you exit and then restart Excel, the numbering of blank workbooks begins again with the number 1.

You can begin a new workbook in any of the following ways:

- Start Excel. The program opens with a new workbook displayed.

- From the File menu, click New.

- On the keyboard, press [Ctrl] + [N].

- From the Getting Started task pane, click *Create a new workbook.*

- From the New Workbook task pane, click *Blank workbook.*

Activity 1.14 Saving and Naming a New Workbook

When Excel displays *Book* followed by a number, for example, *Book1*, *Book2*, and so forth, it indicates that this workbook has never been saved. To save the workbook, perform a Save As to specify a file name and the location where you want to store the workbook.

Your computer's memory stores changes you make to your workbook until you perform another Save operation. Get in the habit of saving changes you have made to an existing workbook by clicking the Save button on the Standard toolbar. The Save button saves any changes you have made to the file—without changing the file name or storage location.

1 On the Standard toolbar, click the **Save** button [image].

Because this workbook has never been saved with a name, the Save As dialog box displays. Alternatively, you can display the File menu and then click Save As.

2 In the **Save As** dialog box, click the **Save in arrow** to view a list of the drives available to you.

3 Navigate to the drive and folder in which you are storing your projects for this chapter; for example, 3½ Floppy (A:). Recall that you created an **Excel Chapter 1** folder previously for this purpose.

4 In the **File name** box, delete any existing text and type **1B_Salary_Analysis_Firstname_Lastname** as shown in Figure 1.45.

Recall that in this textbook, you will use underscores instead of spaces in your file names. This will make it easier to send files over the Internet if you need to do so.

Save As dialog box

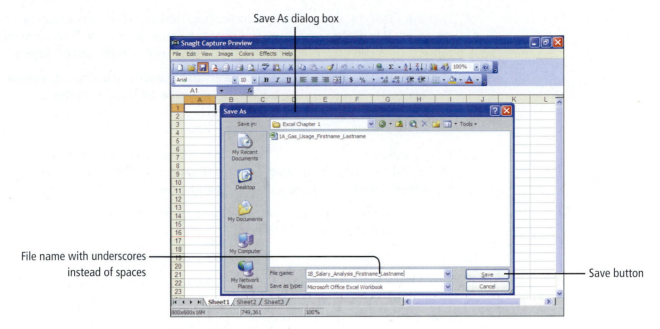

File name with underscores
instead of spaces

Save button

Figure 1.45

5 In the lower right corner of the **Save As** dialog box, click **Save**, or press Enter. The new workbook name displays in the title bar and on the taskbar.

Objective 6
Enter and Edit Data in a Worksheet

Every cell in a worksheet contains **_formatting_** information—information about how data typed into the cell will look. Formatting is easily changed, and as you progress in your study of Excel, you will practice applying various formats that will make your worksheets visually appealing.

Anything typed into a cell is referred to as **_cell content_**. Cell content can be one of only two things: a **_constant value_** or a **_formula_**. A constant value, also referred to simply as a **_value_**, can be numbers, text, dates, or times of day that you type into a cell. A formula, on the other hand, is an equation that you type into a cell. A formula acts as an instruction for Excel to perform mathematical calculations (such as adding and subtracting) on values in other cells.

In the next group of activities, you will enter various types of constant values. After you enter values into a cell, they can be edited (changed) or cleared from the cell.

Activity 1.15 Entering Text

Words (text) typed in a worksheet usually provide information about numbers in other worksheet cells. For example, *Police Station 1* gives the reader an indication that the data in this worksheet relates to information about Police Station 1. To enter text into a cell, activate the cell and type. Before entering text in this activity, you will create the footer with your name.

1 Point to the **Sheet1 tab** and right-click. On the displayed shortcut menu, click **Select All Sheets**.

[Group] displays in the title bar, indicating that the three worksheets are grouped. Recall that grouping the sheets in this manner will place your footer on all the sheets in the workbook—not only on the active sheet.

2 Display the **View** menu, click **Header and Footer**, click the **Custom Footer** button, and under **Left section**, type **1B Salary Analysis-Firstname Lastname** using your own first and last name. Do not change the font or font size—use the default font and font size.

3 In the upper right corner of the **Footer** dialog box, click **OK**. In the lower right corner of the **Page Setup** dialog box, click **OK**. Right-click the **Sheet2 tab**, and then click **Ungroup Sheets**.

The sheets are no longer grouped together, and [Group] no longer displays in the worksheet title bar.

4 On the Standard toolbar, click the **Save** button .

Recall that adding the footer causes the dotted line to display, indicating where the page would end if printed on the default printer. This may vary among printers.

5 Click the **Sheet1 tab** so that Sheet 1 is the active sheet. In cell **A1** type **Police Station 1 Weekly Salaries** and then press Enter.

After you type data into a cell, you must lock in the entry to store it in the cell. One way to do this is to press the Enter key, which makes another cell active and locks in the entry. You can use other keyboard movements, such as Tab, or one of the arrow keys on your keyboard to make another cell active and lock in the entry.

6 Look at the text you typed in cell **A1**.

Notice that the text is aligned at the left edge of the cell. Left alignment is the default for text entries and is an example of the formatting information stored in a cell. Cell A2 is the active cell, as indicated by the black border surrounding it.

7 Look at the **row 2 heading** and **column A heading**, as shown in Figure 1.46.

The shading indicates that the active cell is at the intersection of column A and row 2. In addition, the Name Box displays the cell reference, *A2*.

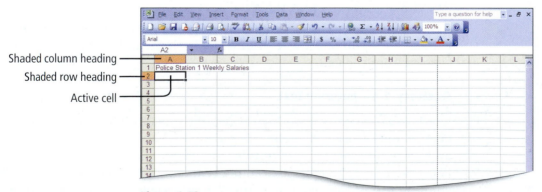

Figure 1.46

8 Press and hold down Ctrl and then press Home to make cell **A1** the active cell.

Recall that this keyboard shortcut is a quick way to move to cell A1 and make it the active cell.

9 Press Enter two times to move to cell **A3**. Type **Emp** and if you make a typing error press Bksp. Notice that as you type, a vertical line called the *insertion point* blinks, indicating where your keystrokes will be inserted. Press Enter.

10 Click cell **A1** to make it the active cell, look at the Formula Bar, and notice that the words *Police Station 1 Weekly Salaries* display.

11 Click cell **B1** and look at the Formula Bar.

No text displays in the Formula Bar. Although the display of the value in cell A1 overlaps into cell B1, the value itself is contained within cell A1. When a value is too wide for its cell, Excel will display the value in the adjacent cell—if the adjacent cell is empty. If the adjacent cell is *not* empty, Excel displays only as much of the value as there is space to do so.

12 Click cell **A4**, and then type the remaining text into **column A** as shown in Figure 1.47. Press Enter after you type the text for each cell to lock in the entry and move down to the next cell. While typing in a cell, press Bksp to correct any errors.

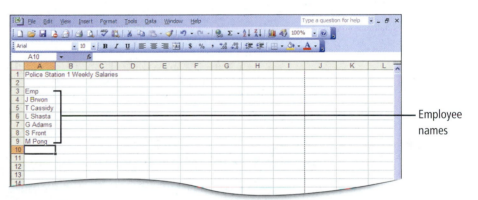

Employee names

Figure 1.47

13 Click cell **B3** to make it the active cell, type **Shift** and then press Tab to move to cell **C3**.

More Knowledge — More Ways to Use the Enter Key

Pressing the ⟨Tab⟩ key makes the cell to the right the active cell. Pressing the ⟨Enter⟩ key makes the cell in the next row the active cell. If you prefer to have the ⟨Enter⟩ key make the cell to the right the active cell, select a group of horizontal cells, and then begin typing in the first cell. Then press ⟨Enter⟩—the cell to the right will become the active cell. This is useful if you are entering data from the numeric keypad, where ⟨Enter⟩ is the only key available on the keypad to lock in the entry.

14 In cell **C3** type **Date** and then press ⟨Tab⟩.

15 In cell **D3** type **Salary** and then press ⟨Enter⟩.

B4 becomes the active cell. Because you used ⟨Tab⟩ to move the active cell to column C and then to column D, pressing ⟨Enter⟩ causes the active cell to return to the column in which you first pressed ⟨Tab⟩.

16 Compare your screen with Figure 1.48.

Column headings

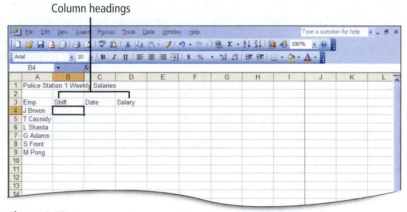

Figure 1.48

Activity 1.16 Using AutoComplete to Enter Data

Excel assists you in typing. If the first few characters you type in a cell match an existing entry in the column, Excel fills in the remaining characters for you. This feature, called ***AutoComplete***, speeds your typing. It is useful because, in a spreadsheet, you frequently type the same information over and over. AutoComplete assists only with alphabetic values; it does not assist with numeric values.

1 To check that the AutoComplete feature is available on your system, display the **Tools** menu, click **Options,** and then in the displayed **Options** dialog box, click the **Edit tab**. Under **Settings**, determine whether *Enable AutoComplete for cell values* is selected (checked) as shown in Figure 1.49. If a check mark appears, click **OK** to close the dialog box. If no check mark appears, click to select the option, and then click **OK**.

Options dialog box ——————

Edit tab ——————

Enable AutoComplete for cell values check box ——————

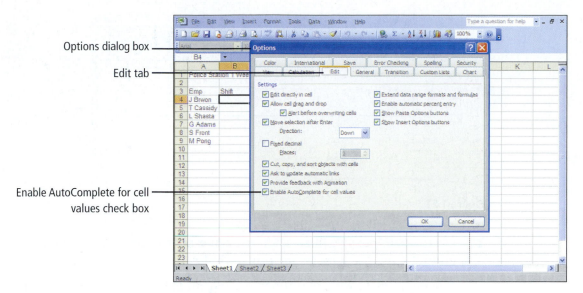

Figure 1.49

2 Be sure that cell **B4** is the active cell. Type **Day** and then press Enter.

3 In cell **B5**, type **D**

Excel completes the word *Day* because the first character matches an existing text entry in column B. See Figure 1.50.

AutoComplete fills in the *ay* of *Day* ——————

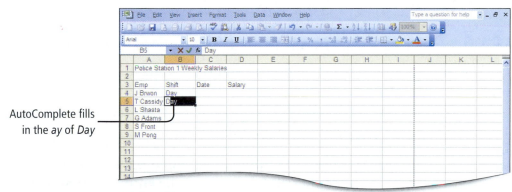

Figure 1.50

4 Press Enter to accept the entry.

Day is automatically entered in the cell, saving you from typing the entire word. The completed entry will match the pattern of upper-case and lowercase letters of the existing entry. If you do not want to accept an AutoComplete suggestion, press Bksp to delete the characters, or continue typing to replace the characters with your own typing.

5 Enter the remaining data in **column B** as shown in Figure 1.51, using **AutoComplete** when it is useful to complete the cell entry.

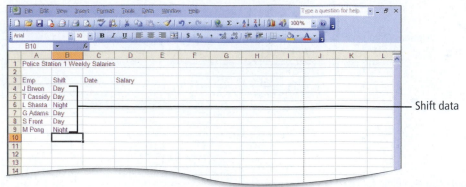

Figure 1.51

6 On the Standard toolbar, click the **Save** button 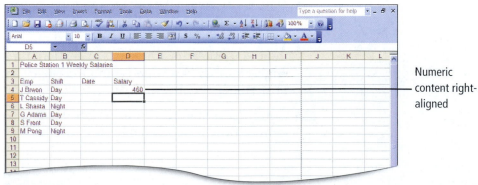 to save the changes you have made to your worksheet.

> The changes to your workbook are saved. Recall the importance of saving your work periodically.

Activity 1.17 Entering Numbers

When typing numbers, you can use either the number keys across the top of your keyboard or the number keys and Enter key on the numeric keypad. Try to develop some proficiency in touch control of the numeric keypad. On a desktop computer, the Num Lock light indicates that the numeric keypad is active. If necessary, press the Num Lock key to activate the numeric keypad.

1 In **column D**, under *Salary*, click cell **D4**, type **500** and then press Esc (located in the upper left corner of your keyboard).

> Your typing is canceled, and D4 remains the active cell. If you change your mind about an entry while typing in a cell, press Esc or click the Cancel button on the Formula Bar.

2 With **D4** as the active cell, type **460** and then press Enter.

> The weekly salary of 460 is locked into cell D4, as shown in Figure 1.52. Notice that after you lock in the entry, the numbers align at the right edge of the cell. This is called *right alignment*. When you type a value consisting of numbers in a cell, the default alignment is right. Right alignment of numbers is another example of formatting information that is stored in a cell.

Figure 1.52

3 Click cell **D5**, type **685** and then press Enter. Continue entering the weekly salary amounts for **column D,** as shown in Figure 1.53.

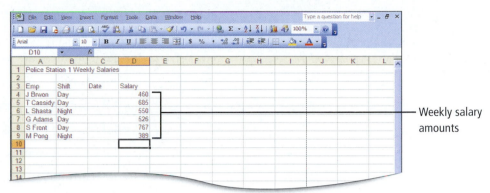

Weekly salary amounts

Figure 1.53

4 These numbers will affect your final worksheet, so take a moment to check that you have typed accurately. To correct a cell, click it and type the data again. There is no need to delete the old value—typing a new value replaces any existing cell values.

5 On the Standard toolbar, click the **Save** button.

Activity 1.18 Typing Dates into a Worksheet

Date values are a type of content frequently typed into a worksheet. Date values entered in any of the following formats will be recognized by Excel as a date:

- m/d/yy   For example, 7/4/05

- d-mmm   For example, 4-Jul

- d-mmm-yy   For example, 4-Jul-05

- mmm-yy   For example, Jul-05

On your keyboard, - (the hyphen key) and / (the forward slash key) function identically in any of these formats and can be used interchangeably. You may abbreviate the month name to three characters or spell it out. You may enter the year as two digits, four digits, or even leave it off. When left off, the current year is assumed but does not display in the cell.

A two-digit year value of 30 through 99 is interpreted by the Windows operating system as the four-digit years of 1930 through 1999. All other two-digit year values are assumed to be in the 21st century. Get in the habit of typing year values as four digits, even though only two digits may display in the cell. In that manner, you can be sure that Excel interprets the year value as you intended. See the table in Figure 1.54 for examples.

How Excel Interprets Dates

Date Typed As:	Completed by Excel As:
7/4/05	7/4/2005
7-4-96	7/4/1996
7/4	4-Jul (current year assumed)
7-4	4-Jul (current year assumed)
July 4	4-Jul (current year assumed)
Jul 4	4-Jul (current year assumed)
Jul/4	4-Jul (current year assumed)
Jul-4	4-Jul (current year assumed)
July 4, 1996	4-Jul-96
July 2005	Jul-05
July 1996	Jul-96

Figure 1.54

1 In **column C**, under *Date*, click cell **C4** to make it the active cell, type **5/13/2004** and then press Enter.

The date right-aligns in the cell and displays as 5/13/2004, using the m/d/yyyy format.

Alert!

The date does not display as 5/13/2004?

The Windows setting in the Control Panel under Regional and Language Options determines the default format for dates. If your result is different, it is likely that the formatting of the default date was adjusted on the computer at which you are working.

2 Click cell **C4** again to make it the active cell, press and hold down Ctrl, and then press ; (the semicolon key) on your keyboard. Press Enter to lock in the entry.

Excel enters the current date, obtained from your computer's internal calendar, into the selected cell using the m/d/yyyy formatting that was previously created in that cell. This is a convenient keyboard shortcut for entering the current date.

3 Click cell **C4** again, type **5/13/96** and press Enter. Then, enter the remaining dates as shown in Figure 1.55.

Because the year was between 30 and 99, Excel assumed a 20th century date and changed *96* to *1996* to complete the four-digit year.

4 On the Standard toolbar, click the **Save** button.

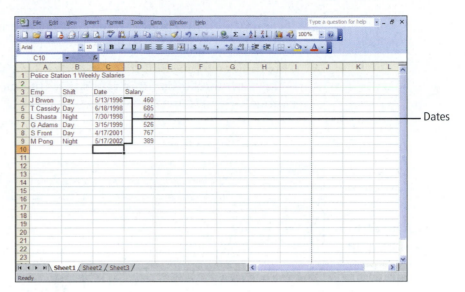

Dates

Figure 1.55

Activity 1.19 Editing Data in Cells

Before you lock in a cell entry by pressing [Enter] or by making another cell the active cell, you can correct typing errors in one of three ways:

- Press [Bksp] to delete characters to the left of the insertion point, one character at a time.

- Press [Esc] to cancel the entire entry.

- On the Formula Bar, click the Cancel button to cancel the entire entry.

Corrections can also be made after locking in the entry by either making the cell active and typing in new data, in which case the existing data will be replaced by your new keystrokes, or by activating Edit mode and editing a portion of the data in the cell. Once you activate Edit mode, you can perform editing directly in the cell or in the Formula Bar.

1 At the lower left corner of your screen, in the Status area, locate the word *Ready*.

Ready indicates that the active cell is ready to accept new data.

2 Point to cell **C4** and double-click to select the cell and simultaneously activate Edit mode. Alternatively, you can select the cell and then press [F2] to activate Edit mode.

The blinking vertical insertion point displays somewhere within the cell. The cell is active and ready to be edited (modified).

> **Note — Performing a Double-Click**
>
> Double-clicking may take some practice, but remember that it is not the speed of the two clicks that is important. What is important is that the mouse remain still between the two clicks. Mouse devices with an extra button on the side that functions as a double-click are available.

3 Look at the Status area and notice that *Ready* has been replaced with *Edit*.

This indicates that Edit mode is active. Now you can use the ← and → keys on the keyboard to reposition the insertion point and make changes. See Figure 1.56.

Content visible in Formula Bar

Formula editing buttons

Insertion point indicates editing can be performed

Edit mode indicator

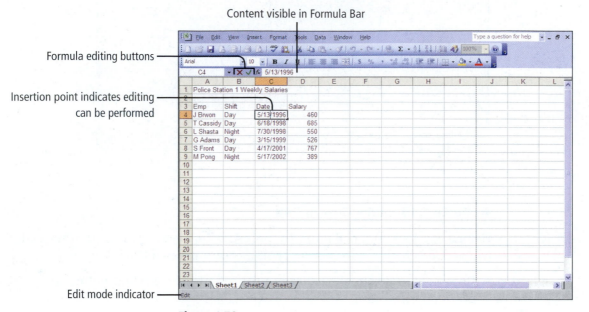

Figure 1.56

4 On the Formula Bar, locate the formula editing buttons. Refer to Figure 1.56.

The Cancel and Enter buttons are visible only when you are entering or editing data in a cell.

5 On the Formula Bar, click the **Cancel** button ![X] to exit Edit mode.

The cell remains active, but the insertion point no longer displays.

6 To activate Edit mode using the keyboard, click cell **C5** to make it the active cell, and then press F2. Move your mouse pointer away from the cell so you can see the insertion point.

Edit mode is activated, and the insertion point displays at the right edge of the cell. *Ready* is replaced with *Edit* in the Status area.

7 Using either ← or your mouse pointer, position the insertion point to the left of the number *8* in *18*. Press Delete to delete the number *8*.

The cell displays *6/1/998*. Recall that Bksp removes text to the left of the insertion point one character at a time, and Delete removes text to the right of the insertion point one character at a time.

8 Press Enter to lock in the entry.

9 Click cell **C5** again to make it the active cell. Pause the mouse pointer in the Formula Bar until the I-beam pointer ⌶ displays. Click to position the pointer ⌶ before the *1* in *6/1* as shown in Figure 1.57.

Sometimes it is easier to perform your editing in the Formula Bar, where you have a better view of the cell contents.

Insertion point in Formula Bar indicates
that editing can be performed

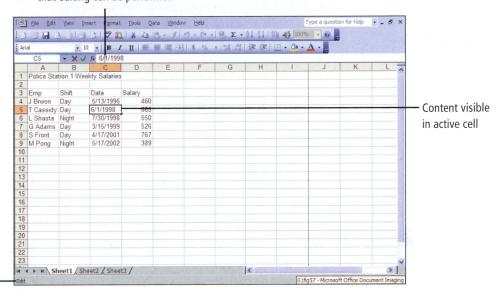

Content visible in active cell

Edit mode indicator

Figure 1.57

10 Type **1** and then click the **Enter** button ✓ on the Formula Bar.

The date changes to *6/11/1998* and C5 remains the active cell. Recall that clicking the Enter button on the Formula Bar locks in the entry while keeping the current cell active.

More Knowledge — Insert and Overtype Mode

The default for editing data in a worksheet is insert mode. Characters you type are inserted, and the existing characters move to the right to make space for your new typing. You can activate overtype mode, in which your typing replaces any existing characters, by pressing Insert when you are in *Edit* mode. In overtype mode, the letters *OVR* display in the status area, and the insertion point displays as a blinking block. Pressing Insert again turns off overtype mode, removes *OVR*, and reactivates insert mode.

Activity 1.20 Using Undo and Redo

You can reverse an action or a series of actions while entering data into an Excel worksheet by using the Undo command. You can Undo up to your past 16 keyboard actions. If you Undo something by mistake, the Redo command will reverse a previous Undo. Undo an action in any of the following ways:

- On the Standard toolbar, click the Undo button.

- Display the Edit menu, and then click Undo.

- From the keyboard, hold down the Ctrl key and press Z.

- On the Standard toolbar, click the Undo arrow and choose one or more actions to undo.

1 Click cell **A3** to make it the active cell, type **Name** and then press Enter.

The column heading *Emp* is replaced by your new entry, *Name*. Recall that typing a new value into a cell will delete the old value.

2 On the menu bar, click **Edit** to display the Edit menu.

The Undo command line describes the action that the Undo command will replace if you decide to do so. To the left is a reminder that a toolbar button can carry out this command, and to the right is a reminder that a keyboard shortcut can also carry out the command.

3 On the **Edit** menu, click **Undo Typing 'Name' in A3**.

The cell entry *Name* is deleted, and *Emp* displays again in cell A3.

4 Click cell **C3**, type **Hired on** and then press Enter.

Date is replaced with *Hired on*.

5 On the Standard toolbar, click the **Undo** button. Alternatively, you can press Ctrl + Z on the keyboard to reverse the last action.

Date is restored and *Hired on* is deleted—your action was undone. Recall that a toolbar button is a one-click method of performing a command that would otherwise take several clicks to perform from the menu.

6 On the Standard toolbar, click the **Redo** button.

Hired on replaces *Date*.

7 Rename the **Sheet1 tab** to **Station 1** and then press Enter.

8 On the Standard toolbar, click the **Save** button to save the changes you have made to your workbook.

Activity 1.21 Clearing a Cell

You can clear (delete) the contents of a selected cell in one of two ways:

- From the Edit menu, point to the Clear command, and then click Contents.

- Press the Delete key.

Recall that if you type anything into a cell, it is considered to have content—either a value or a formula. Recall also that every cell has some formatting instructions attached to it that determine how the content will display. As you progress in your study of Excel, you will learn to format cells with different looks, such as color or bold text, and to attach comments to a cell. Clearing the contents of a cell deletes the value or formula typed there, but it does *not* clear formatting and comments.

1 Click cell **A4** to make it the active cell. Display the **Edit** menu, point to **Clear**, and then on the displayed submenu, click **Contents**.

2 Click cell **A5,** display the **Edit** menu, and then point to **Clear**.

The displayed submenu indicates *Del* (the Del key) as the keyboard shortcut for the Clear Contents command.

3 Click any empty cell in the worksheet window to close the menu without activating a command.

4 Select cell **A5** again, press Del to clear the contents of the cell.

5 From the keyboard, hold down the Ctrl key and press Z twice to undo the last two actions, which will restore the contents of cells **A5** and then **A4**.

6 On the Standard toolbar, click the **Save** button 🖫 to save your changes.

Objective 7
Create Formulas

Excel performs calculations on numbers. That is why people use Excel. You can arrange data in a format of columns and rows in other application programs—in a word processing program, for example—and even perform simple calculations. Only a spreadsheet program such as Excel, however, can perform complex calculations on numbers.

Recall that the content of a cell is either a constant value or a formula. Formulas contain instructions for Excel to perform mathematical calculations on values in other cells and then to place the result of the calculations in the cell containing the formula. You can create your own formulas, or you can use one of Excel's prebuilt formulas called a *function*.

When you change values contained in any of the cells referred to by the formula, Excel recalculates and displays the new result immediately. This is one of the most powerful and valuable features of Excel.

Activity 1.22 Typing a Formula in a Cell

In this activity, you will sum the weekly salaries to calculate the total weekly payroll.

1 Click cell **A10** to make it the active cell, type **Total** and then press Enter.

2 Click cell **D10** to make it the active cell, and press ⊟.

The equal sign (=) displays in the cell with the insertion point blinking, ready to accept more data. All formulas begin with the = sign, which is the signal that directs Excel to begin a calculation. The Formula Bar shows the = sign, and the Formula Bar Cancel and Enter buttons are displayed.

3 At the insertion point, type **d4**

Cell D4 is surrounded by a blue border with small corner boxes, as shown in Figure 1.58. This indicates that the cell is part of an active formula. The color used in the box matches the color of the cell reference in the formula.

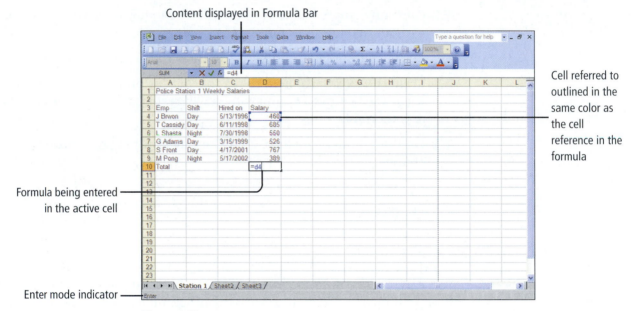

Figure 1.58

4 At the insertion point, press the ⊞ key ((Shift) + ⊟) and then type **d5**

A border of another color surrounds cell D5, and the color matches the color of the cell address in the active formula. Recall that when typing cell references, it is not necessary to use uppercase letters.

5 At the insertion point, type **+d6+d7+d8+d9** and then press (Enter).

The result of the calculation—*3377*—displays in the cell.

6 Click cell **D10** again to make it the active cell, and look at the Formula Bar, as shown in Figure 1.59.

You created a formula that added the values in cells D4 through D9, and the result of adding the values in those cells displays in cell D10. Although cell D10 displays the result of the formula, the formula itself is displayed in the Formula Bar. This is referred to as the ***underlying formula***. Always view the Formula Bar to be sure of the exact content of a cell—a displayed number might actually be a formula.

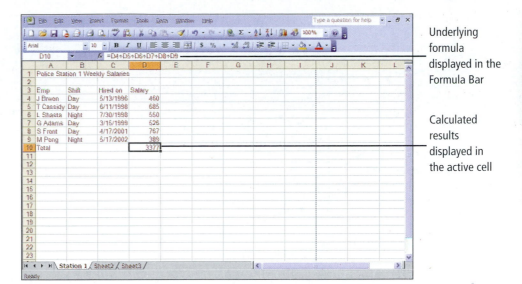

Underlying formula displayed in the Formula Bar

Calculated results displayed in the active cell

Figure 1.59

7 On the Standard toolbar, click the **Save** button ![save] to save the changes you have made to your workbook.

Activity 1.23 Using Point and Click to Enter Cell References in a Formula

In this activity, you will calculate the annual salary for each officer by multiplying the weekly salary by the number of pay periods in a year. So far, you have entered cell references into a formula by typing them. Another method is to point to the cell you want to refer to and click. The selected cell address is placed in the formula without any typing.

1 Click cell **E3** to make it the active cell, type **Annual** and then press Enter .

2 In cell **E4**, type **=** to signal the beginning of a formula.

3 With your mouse, point to cell **D4** and click once.

The reference to the cell, D4, is added to the active formula. A moving border surrounds the cell referred to, and the border color and the color of the cell reference in the formula are color coded to match. See Figure 1.60.

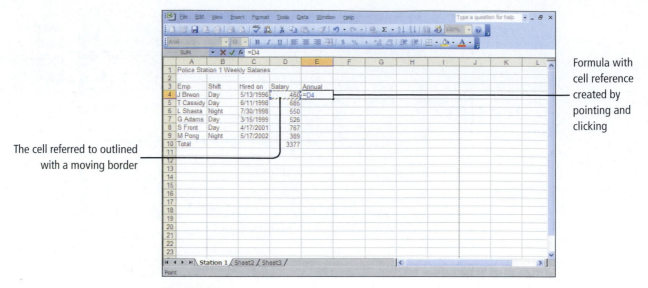

The cell referred to outlined with a moving border

Formula with cell reference created by pointing and clicking

Figure 1.60

4 On your keyboard, locate the [*] key ([Shift] + [8]), type ***52** and press [Enter].

The calculated annual salary, *23920*, displays in cell E4. The * symbol, called an ***asterisk***, functions in Excel as an ***operator***. Operators are symbols that represent mathematical operations. The mathematical operation of multiplication is represented by the asterisk. Thus, you multiplied the weekly salary (the value in cell D4) by the constant value 52 (the number of weeks in a year) to calculate the annual salary—and placed the result in cell E4.

5 Take a moment to study the symbols you will use to perform mathematical operations in Excel, as shown in the table in Figure 1.61.

Mathematical Symbols Used in Excel

Operator Symbol	Operation
[+]	Addition
[−]	Subtraction
[*]	Multiplication
[/]	Division
[^]	Exponentiation

Figure 1.61

For reading ease, you may include spaces before and after the operators in a formula. Also, when you use more than one operator in a formula, Excel follows a mathematical rule called the ***order of operations***. As you progress in your study of Excel and develop your own formulas, you will practice applying this rule, which has three basic parts:

- Expressions within parentheses are processed first.

- Exponentiation is performed before multiplication and division, which are performed before addition and subtraction.

- Consecutive operators with the same level of precedence are calculated from left to right.

6 In cell **E5**, type **=** to begin a formula.

7 With your mouse, point to cell **D5** and click once.

8 Type ***52** and then press Enter.

The annual salary, *35620*, displays.

9 In cell **E6**, type **=d6*52** and press Enter.

When constructing a formula, you can either type cell references or use the point-and-click method to insert the cell reference. The annual salary, *28600*, displays in cell E6.

10 In cells **E7**, **E8**, and **E9**, use either the point-and-click method or the typing method to construct a formula to multiply each officer's weekly salary by 52. Then compare your screen with Figure 1.62.

11 On the Standard toolbar, click the **Save** button 💾 to save the changes you have made to your worksheet.

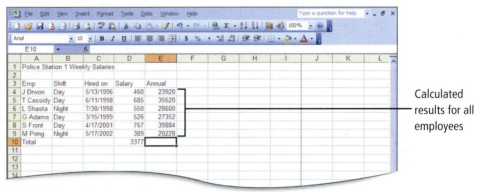

Calculated results for all employees

Figure 1.62

Activity 1.24 Summing a Column of Numbers with AutoSum

Excel has some prebuilt formulas, which are called ***functions***. One function, ***AutoSum***, is frequently used to add columns of numbers. Because it is used so frequently, a toolbar button was created for the AutoSum function. Other functions that are not so frequently used are available through the Insert Function dialog box.

1 Be sure **E10** is the active cell. On the Standard toolbar, click the **AutoSum** button Σ.

As shown in Figure 1.63, cells E4:E9 are surrounded by a moving border, and =SUM(E4:E9) displays in cell E10. The = sign signals the beginning of a formula, SUM indicates the type of calculation that will take place (addition), and (E4:E9) indicates the range of cells on which the sum operation will be performed. A ScreenTip provides additional information about the action.

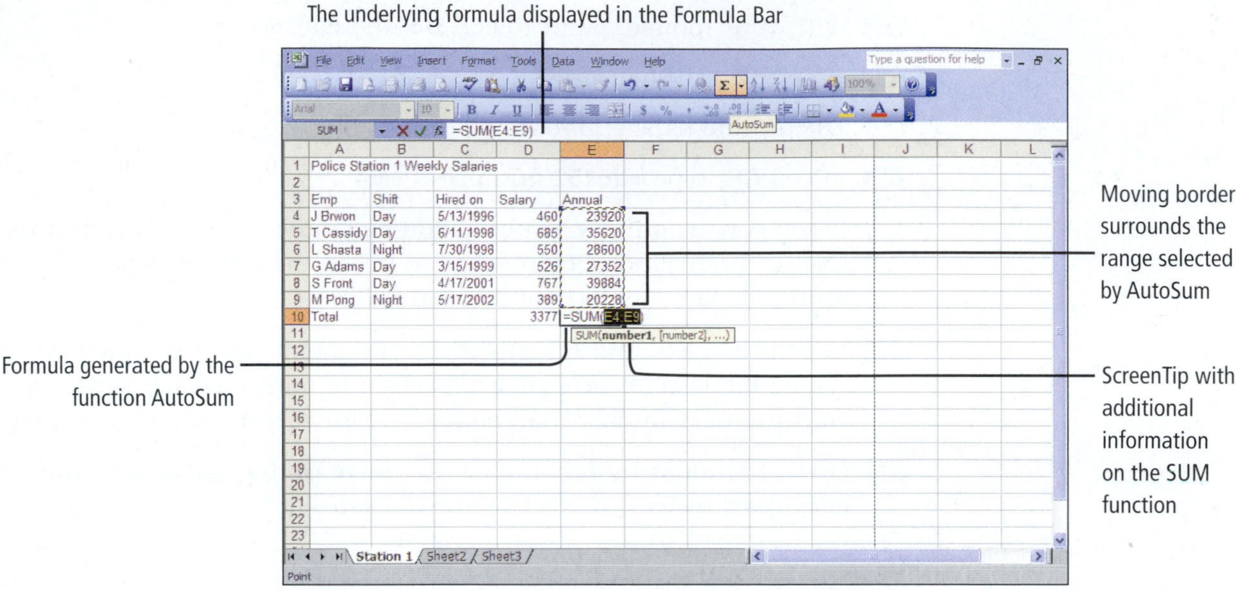

The underlying formula displayed in the Formula Bar

Moving border surrounds the range selected by AutoSum

Formula generated by the function AutoSum

ScreenTip with additional information on the SUM function

Figure 1.63

2 Look at the Formula Bar, and notice that the formula also displays there. Then, look again at the cells surrounded by a moving border.

When the AutoSum function is activated, Excel first looks above the active cell for a range of cells to sum. If no range is above the active cell, Excel will look to the left for a range of cells to sum. Regardless, Excel will propose a range of cells to sum, and if the proposed range is not what you had in mind, simply drag to select a different group of cells.

3 Press Enter. The total annual payroll amount of *175604* displays in cell E10.

4 On the Standard toolbar, click the **Save** button to save the changes you have made to your workbook.

Objective 8
Use Zoom and the Spelling Checker Tool

The Zoom command magnifies or shrinks the columns and rows of a worksheet to increase or decrease the number of cells displayed in the workbook window. Excel's default setting for the magnification size of a worksheet window is 100%, but you can increase the magnification to as much as 400% or decrease it to as little as 10%.

Excel's spelling checker tool checks for misspelled words in your workbook. A word that is not in Excel's dictionary is considered to be misspelled. For example, proper names of cities and people may be correctly spelled, but because Excel's dictionary does not include many of them, they will be flagged as misspelled words. Fortunately, you can add words to the dictionary or have Excel ignore words that are correctly spelled but that are not in Excel's dictionary.

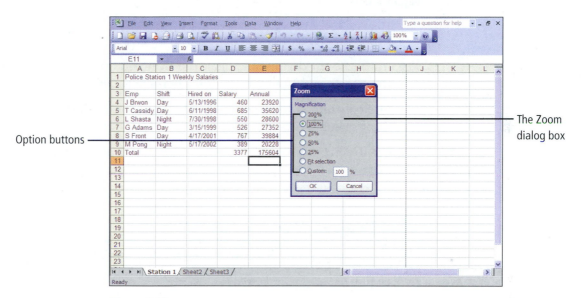

Option buttons

The Zoom dialog box

Figure 1.64

Activity 1.25 Zooming a Worksheet

1 Display the **View** menu, and then click **Zoom**.

The Zoom dialog box displays a list of Magnification options, as shown in Figure 1.64. The round buttons to the left of each option are referred to as *option buttons*.

2 In the **Zoom** dialog box, click the **75%** option button, and then click **OK**.

As shown in Figure 1.65, the sizes of the columns and rows are reduced, and more cells are visible in the worksheet window.

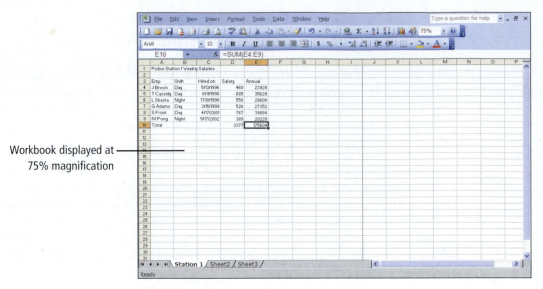

Workbook displayed at 75% magnification

Figure 1.65

3 From the **View** menu, click **Zoom**.

4 In the **Zoom** dialog box, click the **Custom** option button, type **150** in the box to right of *Custom,* and then click **OK**.

The columns and rows are much larger, and fewer cells are visible in the worksheet window.

5 On the Standard toolbar, click the **Zoom button arrow**, as shown in Figure 1.66.

The Zoom button arrow

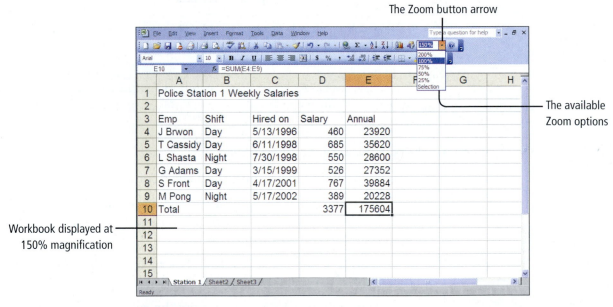

The available Zoom options

Workbook displayed at 150% magnification

Figure 1.66

6 In the displayed list, click **100%**.

The worksheet window returns to its default magnification size of 100%.

Activity 1.26 Checking for Spelling Errors in a Worksheet

1 Hold down Ctrl and press Home to make **A1** the active cell.

2 On the Standard toolbar, click the **Spelling** button 📋.

The Spelling dialog box displays, as shown in Figure 1.67.

The Spelling dialog box

Word indicated as Not in Dictionary

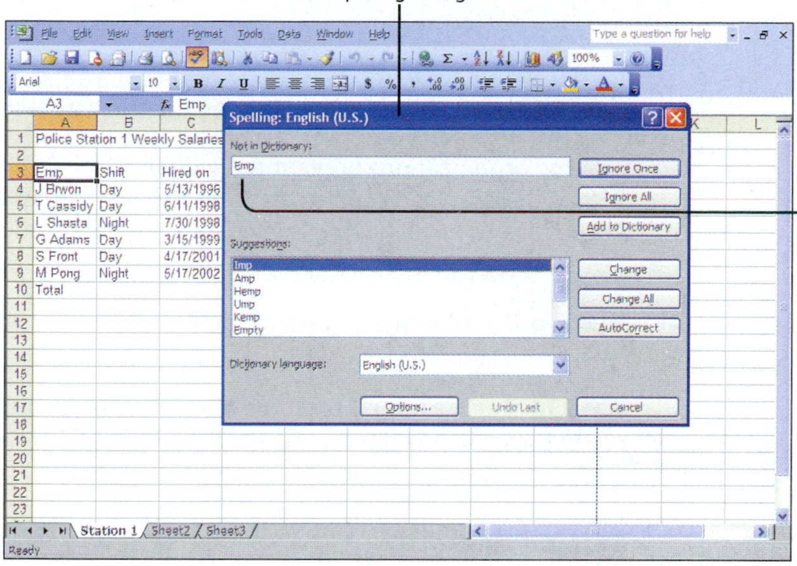

Figure 1.67

Alert!

Does Your Screen Differ?

Your first and last name, which are in the footer, may not be recognized by Excel. If your name displays under Not in Dictionary, click the Ignore Once button until Emp displays as shown in Figure 1.67. If the active cell was not A1, an informational dialog box displays, asking you whether you want to continue checking at the beginning of the sheet. Clicking Yes continues the spelling check from cell A1. Clicking No will end the spelling check command.

---

3 Under **Not in Dictionary**, notice the word *Emp*.

The spelling checker tool does not recognize the abbreviation you used for *Employee*. Under *Suggestions*, Excel provides a list of suggested spellings.

4 Under **Suggestions**, use the scroll bar to scroll through Excel's list of suggested spellings. Because *Emp* is an abbreviation that is useful in this worksheet but does not appear on the **Suggestions** list, click **Ignore All**.

Ignore All instructs Excel to ignore this particular spelling anywhere it is encountered in this worksheet. Excel stops at the next unrecognized word, *Brwon*.

5 Under **Suggestions**, click **Bryon** and then click the **Change** button.

Brwon, which was a typing error, is changed to Bryon. The spelling checker did not find *Brwon* in its dictionary. Although a number of proper names, such as *Brown* and *Bryon* are in the dictionary, many are not. Click Ignore All for those that are not contained in Excel's dictionary. You may want to add proper names that you expect to use often, such as your own last name, to the dictionary if you are permitted to do so.

Note — Can't Add Names to the Dictionary?

Some organizations prevent individuals from adding names to the dictionary to avoid overloading the server or disk drive where the software is located and also to avoid having misspellings inadvertently added to the dictionary.

6 On the displayed message, *The spelling check is complete for the entire sheet*, click **OK**.

7 On the Standard toolbar, click the **Save** button 🖫 to save the changes you have made to your workbook.

Objective 9
Print a Worksheet Using the Print Dialog Box

Clicking the Print button on the Standard toolbar prints one complete copy of the active worksheet or all the selected sheets. To choose more options, such as printing additional copies or selecting a different printer, display the Print dialog box.

Activity 1.27 Previewing the Worksheet

1 With the Station 1 worksheet of your workbook **1B_Salary_Analysis** on your screen, display the **File** menu, and then click **Print Preview**.

The active worksheet displays as an image of a piece of paper so that you can see how the worksheet will be placed on the page.

2 On the Print Preview toolbar, click **Zoom**.

The worksheet zooms to 100%—you can read the contents of the page.

3 Click the **Zoom** button again to return to the full-page preview.

4 On the Print Preview toolbar, locate the **Print** button, and notice that the button name includes an ellipsis (...).

Recall that the ellipsis indicates that a dialog box will follow.

5 Click the **Print** button.

6 As shown in Figure 1.68, in the displayed **Print** dialog box, under **Print range** verify that the **All** option button is selected. Under **Print what** verify that **Active sheet(s)** is selected, under **Copies** verify that the Number of copies is **1**, and then click **OK**.

Print dialog box

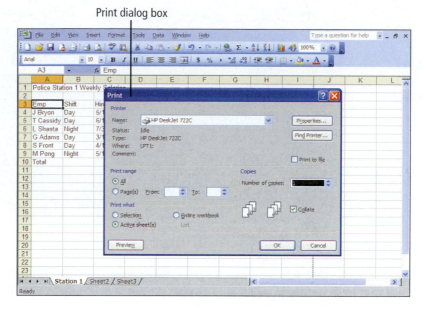

Figure 1.68

Activity 1.28 Closing a Workbook from the File Menu

When you have completed your work, save and close your workbook. Develop the habit of saving your workbook before closing it. If you forget to save it, however, Excel will display a reminder.

1 With your **1B_Salary_Analysis** worksheet still displayed, display the **File** menu, and then click **Close**, saving any changes if prompted to do so.

The workbook closes, leaving the workbook window empty and shaded in gray. Alternatively, close a workbook by clicking its

Close button.

Objective 10
Use Excel Help

Excel's Help feature provides information about all of Excel's features and displays step-by-step instructions for performing many tasks.

Activity 1.29 Using the Type a question for help Box

1 At the right side of the menu bar, locate the box containing the words *Type a question for help*. See Figure 1.69.

The Type a question for help box

Figure 1.69

2 Click in the **Type a question for help** box. At the insertion point, type **How do I create a new workbook?** and then press Enter.

The Search Results task pane displays a list of Help topics with hyperlinks (blue text) listed. Clicking on these hyperlinks will link you to additional information about the topic. See Figure 1.70.

The Search Results task pane

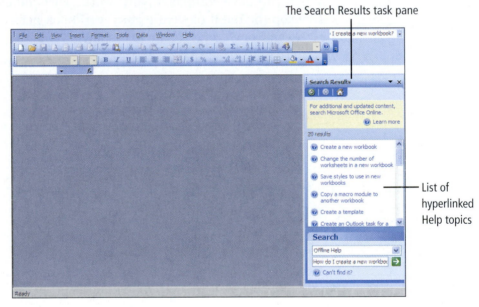

List of hyperlinked Help topics

Figure 1.70

3 On the list of Help topics, click **Create a new workbook**.

4 Click the blue hyperlink **Create a new, blank workbook**.

The topic expands to display additional information.

5 In the upper right corner, click **Show All** to expand the information.

6 Locate and then click the word **task pane** that is displayed in blue.

A definition of the term *task pane* displays in green.

7 Click the word **task pane** again to collapse (hide) the definition.

8 Read the information about creating a new workbook.

9 In the Excel Help window, on the toolbar, click the **Print** button 🖨. See Figure 1.71.

The expanded Microsoft
Excel Help window

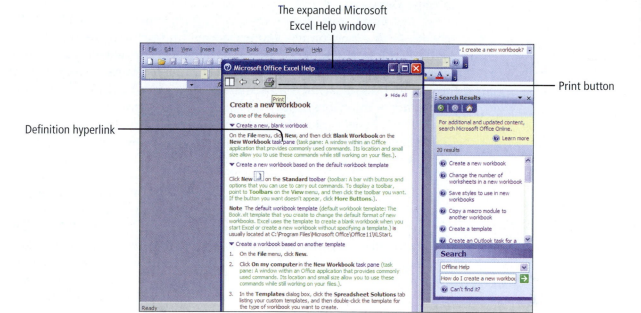

Print button

Definition hyperlink

Figure 1.71

10 In the **Print** dialog box, click **Print**.

The Help topic you have displayed is printed. Keep this document for your reference.

11 On the Microsoft Excel Help title bar, click the **Close** button ❌, and then on the task pane, click the **Close** button ❌.

12 On the right side of the title bar, click the **Close** button ❌.

End **You have completed Project 1B** ──────────────

Summary

Microsoft Excel 2003 is a spreadsheet application that can display and analyze data both numerically and graphically. Excel formulas are both powerful and easy to create.

In this chapter, you opened an existing workbook, added a footer, saved the file with a new name, and previewed and printed the file. The basics of using menus, toolbars and ScreenTips were reviewed. You practiced selecting cells, columns, rows and cell ranges. You navigated within a worksheet using the scroll bars and the name box, and among multiple worksheets in a workbook. You learned how to name a sheet tab so you can clearly label and identify information contained on each worksheet. You also examined an existing chart and saw how changing data also changes the chart.

In Project 6B a new workbook was created. You practiced entering and editing data in a worksheet. You edited text in the formula bar and in a cell, and used the Undo and Redo commands. The power of Excel lies in its ability to perform calculations on numbers. The basic techniques for creating formulas were introduced and then you created simple formulas by typing, by using the point-and-click method, and by using the AutoSum function. You changed the magnification of a worksheet with the Zoom button and used the Spelling Checker tool to ensure that the information was free of spelling mistakes. Finally, you asked a question of the Excel Help feature to explore this tool which is available to assist you as you work with the program.

In This Chapter You Practiced How To

- Start Excel and Navigate a Workbook
- Create Headers and Footers
- Preview and Print a Workbook
- Save and Close a Workbook and Exit Excel
- Create a New Workbook
- Enter and Edit Data in a Worksheet
- Create Formulas
- Use Zoom and the Spelling Checker Tool
- Print a Worksheet Using the Print Dialog Box
- Use Excel Help

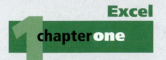
Concepts Assessments

Matching   Match each term in the second column with its correct definition in the first column by writing the letter of the term on the blank line in front of the correct definition.

_____ **1.** Located at the lower left of the Excel window, the identifier of individual worksheets within a workbook.

_____ **2.** The basic Excel document, consisting of one or more worksheets.

_____ **3.** The action of moving the workbook window horizontally or vertically to view areas of the worksheet.

_____ **4.** A symbol that represents a mathematical operation.

_____ **5.** A graphical representation of the values in a worksheet.

_____ **6.** A reference to a group of cells, for example, *A1:C18*.

_____ **7.** Data—numbers, text, dates, or times of day—that you type in a cell.

_____ **8.** The intersection of a column and a row.

_____ **9.** Text or graphics that print at the top or bottom of a worksheet.

_____ **10.** The cell bordered in black and ready to receive data or to be modified.

_____ **11.** Highlighting by clicking or dragging with your mouse.

_____ **12.** A window within a Microsoft Office application that displays commonly used commands.

_____ **13.** An instruction in Excel used to perform mathematical operations.

_____ **14.** An Excel feature that assists with your typing by automatically completing data entered in a cell based on similar values in the column.

_____ **15.** The column letter and row number that identify a specific cell.

A Active cell

B AutoComplete

C Cell

D Cell address

E Chart

F Constant value

G Formula

H Headers and footers

I Operator

J Range

K Scrolling

L Selecting

M Sheet tabs

N Task pane

O Workbook

Fill in the Blank Write the correct answers in the space provided.

1. The two most frequently used toolbars are the _____ and the _____ toolbars.

2. To reduce the magnification and thus view more columns and rows on one screen, use the _____ feature.

3. When viewing a menu, an _____ following a command name indicates that a dialog box will display.

4. If a workbook has never been saved, clicking the Save button causes the _____ dialog box to open.

5. To group worksheets for the purpose of applying a header or footer, from the sheet tab shortcut menu click _____.

6. Nonadjacent cells can be selected by holding down the _____ key while clicking the desired cells.

7. The address of the active cell is always displayed in the _____.

8. Switch to another worksheet in the workbook by clicking on the _____.

9. Editing can be performed either in the cell or in the _____.

10. To select all the cells in the worksheet, click the _____ button.

Project 1C — Computer Passwords

Objectives: *Start Excel and Navigate a Workbook, Create Headers and Footers, Preview and Print a Workbook, Save and Close a Workbook and Exit Excel, Enter and Edit Data in a Worksheet, and Use Zoom and the Spelling Checker Tool.*

In the following Skill Assessment, you will complete a workbook for the Desert Park Police Department listing the assigned computer system passwords for the officers. Your completed workbook will look similar to Figure 1.72. You will save the workbook as *1C_Computer_Passwords_Firstname_Lastname*.

Police Department Computer Passwords

Officer	Password
Jones, M	4t23s2
Gray, T	5a62t4
Silva, M	32du72
Som, K	9a247z
Britto, P	8gh446
Rivard, C	652u6x

1C Computer Passwords-Firstname Lastname

Figure 1.72

1. Start Excel. Display the **File** menu, and then click **Open**.

2. Navigate to the student files that accompany this textbook, and then open the workbook *e01C_Computer_Passwords*.

3. Display the **View** menu, click **Header and Footer**, click the **Custom Footer** button, and in the **Left section**, type **1C Computer Passwords-Firstname Lastname** using your own first and last name. Use the default font and font size.

(Project 1C–Computer Passwords continues on the next page)

(Project 1C–Computer Passwords continued)

4. In the upper right corner of the **Footer** dialog box, click **OK**. In the lower right corner of the **Page Setup** dialog box, click **OK**. Recall that the dotted line indicates the number of columns that will print on the page as the page is currently set up.

5. From the **File** menu, click **Save As**, and then navigate to the location where you are storing your projects for this chapter. In the **File name** box, type **1C_Computer_Passwords_Firstname_Lastname** and then click the **Save** button.

6. In cell **A4**, type **Jones, M** and then press Enter to lock in the entry.

7. Display the **View** menu, and then click **Zoom**. In the **Zoom** dialog box, click the **200%** option button, and then click **OK**. This gives you an enlarged view, which is helpful when you are entering complex statistical data such as passwords.

8. Beginning in cell **A5**, add the following names to column A. Recall that pressing Enter after each entry relocates the active cell to the next row.

   Gray, T
   Silva, M
   Som, K
   Britto, P
   Rivard, C

9. In cell **B4**, type **4t23s2** and then press Enter.

10. Beginning in cell **B5**, add the remaining passwords to column B:

    5a62t4
    32du72
    9a347z
    8gh446
    652u6x

11. Point to cell **B7** and double-click to select the cell and simultaneously activate Edit mode. Using the arrow keys on the keyboard, place the insertion point before the *3*. Press Delete, type **2** and then press Enter to display the corrected password, *9a247z*.

12. On the Standard toolbar, click in the **Zoom** box so that *200%* is highlighted, type **100** and then press Enter. This is another method for changing the Zoom setting.

13. On the Standard toolbar, click the **Save** button to save your changes, and then click the **Print Preview** button.

14. On the Print Preview toolbar, click the **Print** button. In the displayed **Print** dialog box, click **OK** to print one complete copy of your worksheet on the default printer. From the **File** menu, click **Close** to close the workbook. Display the **File** menu again, and click **Exit** to close Excel.

End You have completed Project 1C ──────────────

Project 1D — Crossing Guards

Objectives: *Start Excel and Navigate a Workbook, Create Headers and Footers, Preview and Print a Workbook, Save and Close a Workbook and Exit Excel, Enter and Edit Data in a Worksheet, Create Formulas, and Use Zoom and the Spelling Checker Tool.*

In the following Skill Assessment, you will complete a Crossing Guard report for the month of January for the Desert Park Police Department, whose officers volunteer as school crossing guards. Your completed workbook will look similar to the one shown in Figures 1.73a and 1.73b. You will save the workbook as *1D_Crossing_Guards_Firstname_Lastname*.

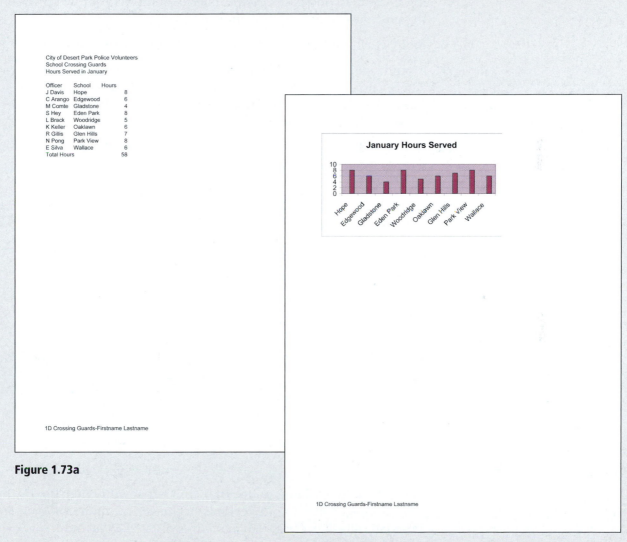

Figure 1.73a

Figure 1.73b

1. Start Excel. On the Standard toolbar, click **Open**.

2. Navigate to the student files that accompany this textbook, and then open the workbook **e01D_Crossing_Guards**.

(Project 1D–Crossing Guards continues on the next page)

(Project 1D–Crossing Guards continued)

3. Right-click the **Sheet1 tab**, and on the displayed shortcut menu, click **Select All Sheets**.

4. Display the **View** menu, click **Header and Footer**, click the **Custom Footer** button, and in the **Left section**, type **1D Crossing Guards-Firstname Lastname** using your own first and last name. Use the default font and font size.

5. In the upper right corner of the **Footer** dialog box, click **OK**. In the lower right corner of the **Page Setup** dialog box, click **OK**. Recall that the dotted line indicates the number of columns that will print on the page as the page is currently set up.

6. Right-click the **Sheet1 tab**, and click **Ungroup Sheets**.

7. From the **File** menu, click **Save As**, and then navigate to the location where you are storing your projects for this chapter. In the **File name** box, type **1D_Crossing_Guards_Firstname_Lastname** and then click the **Save** button.

8. In cells **A6** through **A14**, type the following list of volunteer crossing guards:

   J Davis
   C Arango
   M Comte
   S Hey
   L Brack
   K Keller
   R Gillis
   N Pong
   E Silva

9. In cells **B6** through **B11**, enter the following list of school names:

   Hope
   Park View
   Gladstone
   Eden Park
   Woodbridge
   Oaklawn

10. In cell **B12**, type **G** and notice that as soon as you enter the *G*, the AutoComplete feature of Excel fills in the school name *Gladstone*. Type **len Hills** to enter the school name of *Glen Hills* and to overwrite the AutoComplete entry. Press Enter.

11. In cells **B13** and **B14**, type the remaining two school names, **Edgewood** and **Wallace** overwriting the AutoComplete entries as you type.

12. Click cell **B10** to make it the active cell. Pause the mouse pointer in the Formula Bar until the **I-beam** pointer displays. Click to position

(Project 1D–Crossing Guards continues on the next page)

(Project 1D–Crossing Guards continued)

the pointer before the *b* in *Woodbridge*, press Delete to remove the *b* and correct the school name to *Woodridge*. Click the **Enter** button on the Formula toolbar to lock in the change.

13. In cells **C6** through **C14**, enter the following list of hours that each volunteer worked. Because these are numeric values, as you lock them in by pressing Enter, they are right-aligned in each cell.

    8
    6
    4
    6
    5
    6
    7
    8
    6

14. In cell **A15**, type **Total Hours** and then press the Tab key twice to make **C15** the active cell.

15. With **C15** as the active cell, move to the Standard toolbar and click the **AutoSum** button. AutoSum borders the cells above and proposes a formula. Press Enter to accept the formula. The total in C15 is *56*.

16. Click cell **C15** again. Compare what is displayed in the cell, *56*, with what is displayed in the Formula Bar, *=SUM(C6:C14)*. Recall that this is called the underlying formula. The formula indicates that the contents of the cells in the range C6:C14 are summed.

17. Right-click the **Sheet1 tab**, click **Rename**, type **Hours** and then press Enter. Rename Sheet2 as **Chart** and then be sure that the Chart sheet is displayed.

18. View the graphical chart of the schools and number of hours worked. Notice the height of the Eden Park entry—6 hours. Click the **Hours tab** to return to the previous worksheet.

19. Change the number of hours for Officer *Hey* to **8** and press Enter. The calculated result in C15 changes to *58*. Click the **Chart tab** and notice the new height of the Eden Park entry. When you changed the number of hours worked on the Hours worksheet, the entry in the chart was also updated by Excel. Return to the Hours worksheet by clicking the **Hours sheet tab**.

20. On the Hours worksheet, click cell **B13**. Type **P** and notice that the existing value is deleted and that AutoComplete assists with your typing. With *Park View* in the cell, press Enter to accept it. Recall that when you type a new value in a cell, the existing value is deleted and replaced by your typing.

(Project 1D–Crossing Guards continues on the next page)

(Project 1D–Crossing Guards continued)

21. Change the school name for Officer *Davis* to **Edgewood** overriding AutoComplete, and then press ⏎. On the Standard toolbar, click **Undo** to restore the original value of *Hope*. Change the school name for Officer *Arango* to **Edgewood** and press ⏎.

22. Click in the **Name Box**, type **a1** and then press ⏎ to make **A1** the active cell. Recall that you can navigate to a cell address by typing it in the Name Box and that you may type the column reference as either lower- or uppercase.

23. On the Standard toolbar, click the **Spelling** button. If necessary, click the Ignore All button as necessary to ignore the spelling of your name. The first word interpreted by Excel to be misspelled is *Crosing*. Under **Suggestions**, be sure that *Crossing* is selected, and then click the **Change** button. Correct the spelling for *January* and *School*.

24. Click **Ignore All** for the proper names that Excel does not have in its dictionary. Click **OK** when the spelling complete message displays.

25. From the **File** menu, click **Save** to save the changes you have made to your workbook since the last Save operation. Then, display the **File** menu again and click **Print Preview** to view the worksheet page as it will print on paper. Close Print Preview, click the **Chart** worksheet, and then click the **Print Preview** button.

26. On the Print Preview toolbar, click the **Print** button. On the displayed **Print** dialog box, under **Print what**, click the **Entire workbook** option button, and then click **OK** to print one copy of the workbook. Two sheets will print. From the **File** menu, click **Close**, and then exit Excel.

 End **You have completed Project 1D** ─────────────────

Project 1E — AV Equipment

Objectives: *Start Excel and Navigate a Workbook, Create Headers and Footers, Preview and Print a Workbook, Save and Close a Workbook and Exit Excel, Create a New Workbook, Enter and Edit Data in a Worksheet, and Create Formulas.*

In the following Skill Assessment, you will create a new workbook to generate an inventory report for the audiovisual equipment at the Desert Park Public Library. Your completed workbook will look similar to the one shown in Figure 1.74. You will save the workbook as *1E_AV_Equipment_Firstname_Lastname*.

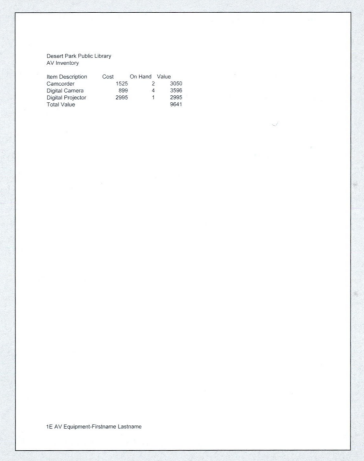

Desert Park Public Library
AV Inventory

Item Description	Cost	On Hand	Value
Camcorder	1525	2	3050
Digital Camera	899	4	3596
Digital Projector	2995	1	2995
Total Value			9641

1E AV Equipment-Firstname Lastname

Figure 1.74

1. Start the Excel program. *Book1* displays in both the title bar and the taskbar, indicating a new, unnamed workbook.

2. Display the **View** menu, click **Header and Footer**, click the **Custom Footer** button, and in the **Left section**, type **1E AV Equipment-Firstname Lastname** using your own first and last name. Use the default font and font size.

(Project 1E–AV Equipment continues on the next page)

(Project 1E–AV Equipment continued)

3. In the upper right corner of the **Footer** dialog box, click **OK**. In the lower right corner of the **Page Setup** dialog box, click **OK**. Recall that the dotted line indicates the number of columns that will print on the page as the page is currently set up.

4. If necessary, close the Getting Started task pane by clicking its small black **Close** button. From the **File** menu, click **Save As**, and then navigate to the location where you are storing your projects for this chapter. In the **File name** box, delete the existing text, type **1E_AV_Equipment_Firstname_Lastname** and then click **Save**.

5. In cell **A1**, type **Desert Park Public Library** and press Enter. Because cells B1 and C1 are empty, the content of cell A1 can display into the adjacent cells. Recall, however, that the text is contained entirely within cell A1. In cell A2, type **AV Inventory** and press Enter.

6. Right-click the **Sheet1 tab**, click **Rename**, type **AV Equipment** and notice that the tab expands to accommodate the name. Press Enter.

7. Move to cell **A4**, type **Item Description** and then press Tab twice. In cell **C4**, type **Cost** and then press Tab once. In cell **D4**, type **On Hand** and in cell **E4**, type **Value** and press Enter. Recall that when you use Tab, the cell entry is locked in and the cell to the right becomes the active cell. When Enter is pressed, the active cell becomes the cell below the first cell in which Tab was pressed. A5 is the active cell.

8. Beginning in the active cell, **A5**, enter the following descriptions in cells **A5:A7**:

Camcorder
Digital Camera
Digital Projector

9. Beginning in cell **C5**, enter the following costs in the Cost column:

1525
899
2995

10. Beginning in cell **D5**, enter the following On Hand quantities.

2
4
1

11. Click in cell **E5** and type = to begin a formula. Click cell **C5** to insert it in the formula, type * (the operator for multiplication), and then click cell **D5**. This will multiply the camcorder cost in cell C5 by the number on hand in cell D5. Press Enter to display the result of *3050*.

(Project 1E–AV Equipment continues on the next page)

(Project 1E–AV Equipment continued)

12. Click cell **E5** again, and compare what is displayed in the cell (3050) with what is displayed in the Formula Bar (=C5*D5). Recall that this is called the underlying formula and that to determine the exact content of a cell, check the Formula Bar.

13. In cells **E6** and **E7**, use the point-and-click method to construct similar formulas to multiply the cost of the item by the number on hand. Compare your results with Figure 1.74. Click **Save** to save your changes.

14. In cell **A8**, type **Total Value** and then click cell **E8**. Using the point-and-click method to add the column, type = to begin a formula, click cell **E5**, press +, click cell **E6**, press +, and click cell **E7** and press Enter. The result, *9641*, displays in cell E8.

15. On the Standard toolbar, click **Save** to save the changes to your workbook.

16. On the Standard toolbar, click the **Print Preview** button to view the worksheet page. On the Print Preview toolbar, click the **Print** button. In the displayed dialog box, click **OK** to print one copy of your worksheet. Close the workbook, saving any changes if prompted, and then exit Excel.

End **You have completed Project 1E**

Project 1F—Phone Charges

Objectives: *Start Excel and Navigate a Workbook, Create Headers and Footers, Preview and Print a Workbook, Save and Close a Workbook and Exit Excel, Enter and Edit Data in a Worksheet, Create Formulas, Use Zoom and the Spelling Checker Tool, and Use Excel Help.*

In the following Performance Assessment, you will complete a list of phone charges for Desert Park's City Manager, Madison Romero. Your completed workbook will look similar to the one shown in Figure 1.75. You will save the workbook as *1F_Phone_Charges_Firstname_Lastname.*

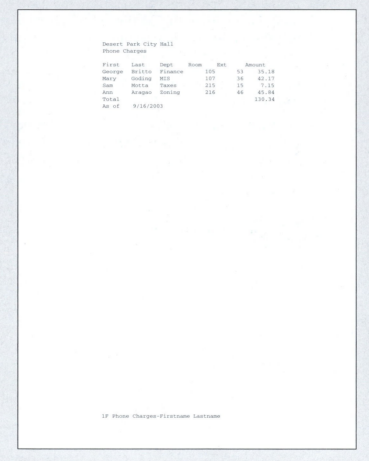

Figure 1.75

(**Project 1F**–Phone Charges continues on the next page)

(Project 1F–Phone Charges continued)

1. Start Excel, navigate to the location where the student files for this textbook are stored, and then open workbook **e01F_Phone_Charges**. Display the **View** menu, click **Header and Footer**, click the **Custom Footer** button, and in the **Left section**, type **1F Phone Charges-Firstname Lastname** using your own first and last name. Use the default font and font size. In the upper right corner of the **Footer** dialog box, click **OK**. In the lower right corner of the **Page Setup** dialog box, click **OK**.

2. From the **File** menu, click **Save As**, and then navigate to the location in which you are storing your projects for this chapter. In the **File name** box, type **1F_Phone_Charges_Firstname_Lastname** and then click **Save**.

3. Beginning in cell **A4**, type the following, using the ⌜Tab⌝ key to move across each row:

First	Last	Dept	Room	Ext	Amount
George	Britto	Finance	105	53	35.18
Mary	Goding	MIS	107	36	16.05
Sam	Motta	Taxes	215	15	7.15
Ann	Aragao	Zoning	216	46	45.84

4. In cell **A9**, type **Total** and then press ⌜Enter⌝. In cell **F9**, using the point-and-click method to create a formula to add up the total phone charges, type **=** to start the formula, click cell **F5**, press ⌜+⌝, and then continue in the same manner for the remaining cells. Alternatively, click the **AutoSum** button. The total charges add up to *104.22*.

5. In cell **A10**, type **As of** and then press ⌜Tab⌝. In cell **B10**, hold down ⌜Ctrl⌝ and then press ⌜;⌝ to insert today's date.

6. Change the amount for the MIS department to 42.17 and press ⌜Enter⌝ to recalculate the total—130.34.

7. Press ⌜Ctrl⌝ + ⌜Home⌝ to move to cell **A1**, and then on the Standard toolbar, click the **Spelling** button. For proper names, including your own, click Ignore All as necessary. Correct the word *Charges* and then click **Ignore All** for the proper names.

8. Save your changes, and then preview and print the worksheet. Close the file and exit Excel.

End **You have completed Project 1F**

Project 1G — Building Permits

Objectives: *Start Excel and Navigate a Workbook, Create Headers and Footers, Preview and Print a Workbook, Save and Close a Workbook and Exit Excel, Enter and Edit Data in a Worksheet, Create Formulas, and Use Zoom and the Spelling Checker Tool.*

In the following Performance Assessment, you will complete a workbook for the Desert Park Deputy Mayor, Andrew Gore, that summarizes the number of building permits issued for the second quarter. Your completed workbook will look similar to Figure 1.76. You will save the workbook as *1G_Building_Permits_Firstname_Lastname*.

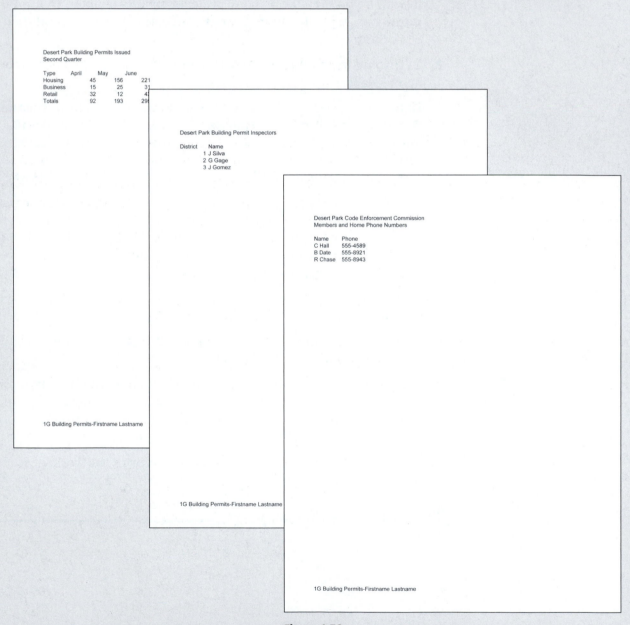

Figure 1.76

(Project 1G–Building Permits continues on the next page)

(Project 1G–Building Permits continued)

1. Start Excel, navigate to your student files, and then open the workbook **e01G_Building_Permits**. Right-click the **Sheet1 tab** and click **Select All Sheets**.

2. From the **View** menu, click **Header and Footer**, click the **Custom Footer** button, and in the **Left section**, type **1G Building Permits-Firstname Lastname** using your own first and last name. Use the default font and font size. In the upper right corner of the **Footer** dialog box, click **OK**. In the lower right corner of the **Page Setup** dialog box, click **OK**. Right-click the **Sheet1 tab**, and click **Ungroup Sheets**.

3. From the **File** menu, click **Save As**, and then navigate to the location where you are storing your projects for this chapter. In the **File name** box, type **1G_Building_Permits_Firstname_Lastname** and then click **Save**.

4. In **Sheet1**, be sure that cell **A1** is the active cell. Click in the **Formula Bar** so that you can edit the text. Click to the left of the *P* in *Permits*, insert the word **Building** followed by a space, and then press [Enter].

5. Double-click cell **A2** to display the insertion point within the cell. Alternatively, select the cell and press [F2]. Edit the text by changing the word *First* to **Second** and then press [Enter].

6. In cells **A4:D7**, enter the following data. Use [Tab] to move across the row and [Enter] to move down to a new row:

Type	April	May	June
Housing	45	156	221
Business	15	25	31
Retail	32	12	43

7. In cell **A8**, type **Totals** and then, using either the **AutoSum function** button or the point-and-click method, create formulas to sum each month's permits. Your results should be 92, 193, and 295. Rename Sheet1 **2nd Quarter**

8. Select **Sheet2**. Rename the sheet **Inspectors** and then enter the following data in cells **A3:B6**:

District	Name
1	J Silva
2	G Gage
3	J Gomez

(Project 1G–Building Permits continues on the next page)

(Project 1G–Building Permits continued)

9. Select **Sheet3**, rename the sheet **Commission Members** and then in cells **A4:B7**, enter the following data:

Name	Phone
C Hall	555-4589
B Date	555-8921
R Chase	555-8943

10. For each worksheet, make **A1** the active cell and then check the spelling. (Hint: Each worksheet contains one spelling error.) Save your changes. Right-click the **2nd Quarter Sheet** tab, and then click **Select All Sheets** so that all three sheets display in Print Preview.

11. Use Print Preview to review the overall look of your workbook. Display the **Print** dialog box. Because the sheets are still grouped, all are active and will print; thus you need not select the Entire workbook option. Print, close the file, saving any changes, and close Excel.

End You have completed Project 1G ———————————————

Project 1H—Public Service

Objectives: *Create Headers and Footers, Preview and Print a Workbook, Save and Close a Workbook and Exit Excel, Create a New Workbook, Enter and Edit Data in a Worksheet, Create Formulas, Use Zoom and the Spelling Checker Tool, Print a Worksheet Using the Print Dialog Box, and Use Excel Help.*

In the following Performance Assessment, you will create a new workbook for the Desert Park Deputy Mayor, Andrew Gore, that reports the number of students that attended a public service presentation at their school. Your completed workbook will look similar to the one shown in Figure 1.77. You will save the workbook as *1H_Public_Service_Firstname_Lastname*.

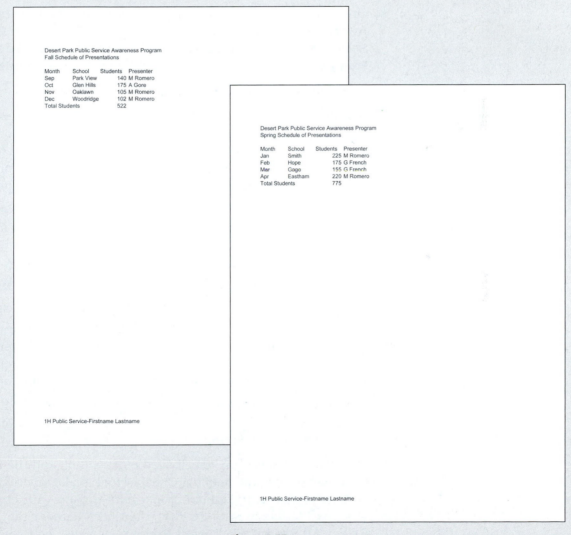

Figure 1.77

(Project 1H–Public Service continues on the next page)

(Project 1H–Public Service continued)

1. Start Excel. On the new blank workbook, right-click the **Sheet1 tab** and click **Select All Sheets**. From the **View** menu, click **Header and Footer**, click the **Custom Footer** button, and in the **Left section**, type **1H Public Service-Firstname Lastname**. Use the default font and font size. In the upper right corner of the **Footer** dialog box, click **OK**. In the lower right corner of the **Page Setup** dialog box, click **OK**. Right-click the **Sheet1 tab**, and click **Ungroup Sheets**.

2. From the **File** menu, click **Save As**, navigate to the location where you are storing your projects for this chapter, and in the **File name** box, type **1H_Public_Service_Firstname_Lastname** and then click **Save**. If necessary, close the task pane.

3. On Sheet1, select cell **A1** and type **Desert Park Public Service Awareness Program** and in cell **A2**, type **Fall Schedule of Presentations** Select **Sheet2**. In cell **A1**, type **Desert Park Public Service Awareness Program** and in cell **A2**, type **Spring Schedule of Presentations**

4. Select **Sheet1**. In cells **A4:D8**, enter the following data:

Month	School	Students	Presenter
Sep	Park View	140	M Romero
Oct	Glen Hills	175	A Gore
Nov	Oaklawn	105	M Romero
Dec	Woodridge	102	M Romero

5. In cell **A9**, type **Total Students** and then, in cell **C9**, use any method (typing, point-and-click, or AutoSum) to construct a formula to sum the total number of students. The total should be 522. Rename the Sheet1 tab to **Fall**

6. Select Sheet2 and enter the following data in cells **A4:D8**:

Month	School	Students	Presenter
Jan	Smith	225	M Romero
Feb	Hope	175	G French
Mar	Gage	155	G French
Apr	Eastham	220	M Romero

7. In cell **A9**, type **Total Students** and then, in cell **C9**, construct a formula to add the total number of students. The total should be *775*. Rename Sheet2 as **Spring**

8. On each worksheet, make cell **A1** the active cell, and then check the spelling by using the Spelling Checker tool; make any necessary corrections. If necessary, ignore proper names. Save your changes. To view both sheets in Print Preview, right-click a **sheet tab**, and click **Select All Sheets**. Click **Print Preview** to review both sheets, and then close Print Preview. From the **File** menu, click **Print**, and in the **Print** dialog box, under **Print what**, click the **Entire workbook** option button. Two sheets will print. Close the workbook, and exit Excel.

End **You have completed Project 1H**

Project 1I — Police Cars

Objectives: *Start Excel and Navigate a Workbook, Create Headers and Footers, Preview and Print a Workbook, Enter and Edit Data in a Worksheet, Create Formulas, and Use Zoom and the Spelling Checker Tool.*

In the following Mastery Assessment, you will create a workbook for the Desert Park Police Department with an inventory of the police cars, including license tag number, date placed in service, and total number of miles driven. Your completed workbook will look similar to the one shown in Figure 1.78. You will save the workbook as *1I_Police_Cars_Firstname_Lastname.*

Figure 1.78

1. Start Excel. In a new workbook, create a custom footer, and in the **Left section**, type **1I Police Cars-Firstname Lastname**

2. Save the file in your storage location for this chapter as **1I_Police_Cars_Firstname_Lastname**

(**Project 1I**–Police Cars continues on the next page)

(Project 1I–Police Cars continued)

3. On **Sheet1**, in cell **A1**, type **Desert Park Police Department** and, in cell **A2**, type **Police Car Inventory**

4. In cells **A4:C7**, enter the following data:

Tag	Date	Mileage
423-MFG	5-Mar-97	152576
342-QZY	8-May-99	120945
525-KYW	7-Jun-01	65098

5. Type **Total** in column A in the cell below the last car's data. In the appropriate cell, construct a formula to sum the total miles driven. The result should be 338619.

6. Rename the **Sheet1 tab Police Cars**

7. In cell **D4**, type **Expense** and then, using the following rules, create a formula in cells **D5**, **D6**, and **D7** to compute the expenses for each car:

Rule 1: Cars placed in service before the year 2000 have an expense value of 50 cents per mile.

Rule 2: Cars placed in service after January of 2000 have an expense value of 30 cents per mile.

8. Change the mileage for **525-KYW** to **165098** and press Enter to recalculate. Create a formula to sum the total expenses. The result should be 186289.9.

9. Click cell **A1**, and then check the spelling. Save your changes. Use Print Preview to review the overall look of your worksheet. Print the worksheet, close the workbook, and exit Excel.

End You have completed Project 1I ———————————————

Project 1J — Cell Phones

Objectives: *Start Excel and Navigate a Workbook, Create Headers and Footers, Preview and Print a Workbook, Enter and Edit Data in a Worksheet, Create Formulas, and Use Zoom and the Spelling Checker Tool.*

The Desert Park Police Department uses cell phones to communicate with the officers. Chief Dennis Johnson wants an analysis of the cell phones that shows the number of minutes per phone used last month and the total cost of each phone. Your completed workbook will look similar to the one shown in Figure 1.79. You will save the workbook as *1J_Cell_Phones_Firstname_Lastname.*

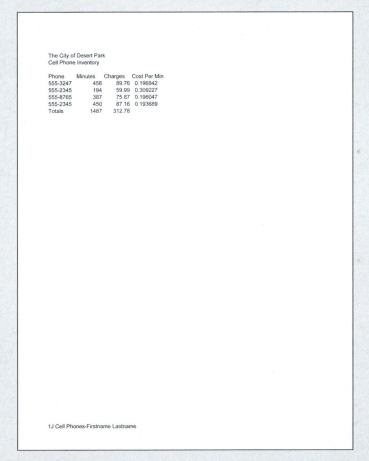

The City of Desert Park
Cell Phone Inventory

Phone	Minutes	Charges	Cost Per Min
555-3247	456	89.76	0.196842
555-2345	194	59.99	0.309227
555-8765	387	75.87	0.196047
555-2345	450	87.16	0.193689
Totals	1487	312.78	

1J Cell Phones-Firstname Lastname

Figure 1.79

1. Start Excel, navigate to your student files, and then open the workbook **e01J_Cell_Phones**. Create a custom footer, and in the **Left section** type 1J_Cell_Phones_Firstname_Lastname

2. Save the file in your storage location for this chapter as **1J Cell Phones-Firstname Lastname**

(Project 1J–Cell Phones continues on the next page)

(Project 1J–Cell Phones continued)

3. Beginning in cell **A4**, enter the following data:

Phone	Minutes	Charges
555-3247	456	89.76
555-2345	194	59.99
555-8765	387	75.87
555-3356	450	87.16

4. In cell **A9**, enter **Totals** and construct a formula to sum the total Minutes used and the total Charges. Your results should be 1487 and 312.78.

5. In cell **D4**, enter **Cost Per Min** and then, in cell **D5**, type = to begin a formula. Click cell **C5** and then type , which is the operator for division. (This key is next to the Right Shift on most keyboards.) Click cell **B5**, and press Enter. Your result, 0.196842, indicates the *per minute charge* for this phone (charges divided by minutes). Construct similar formulas for the remaining phones, and then compare your results with Figure 1.79.

6. Rename the **Sheet1 tab Cell Phones**

7. Check for and correct spelling errors. (Hint: There are at least three spelling errors.) Save your changes. Use Print Preview to review the overall look of your worksheet. Print the worksheet, close the workbook, and exit Excel.

End **You have completed Project 1J** ──────────────

Project 1K — Permit List

Objectives: *Start Excel and Navigate a Workbook, Create Headers and Footers, Preview and Print a Workbook, Save and Close a Workbook and Exit Excel, Create a New Workbook, Enter and Edit Data in a Worksheet, and Create Formulas.*

The Director of Arts and Parks, Roy Hamilton, wants to compile a list of all community organizations that have requested a summer picnic permit. Additionally, he would like to know the approximate number of people who will be attending each organization's picnic. This will help the department plan for park maintenance and trash collection. Three parks have picnic shelters: North Park, South Park, and Mariposa Park.

Create a workbook that has three worksheets, one for each of the three parks. For each park, create the name of at least three community organizations, the dates of their picnics, and the approximate number of people who will attend each. You might visit your community's Web site to get ideas of various community organizations. Total the number of picnic attendees for each park. Create a footer that includes your name as you have in the past, and save the file as **1K_Permit_List_Firstname_Lastname**.

 End **You have completed Project 1K** ──────────────────────────

Project 1L — Museum Visits

Objectives: *Start Excel and Navigate a Workbook, Create Headers and Footers, Preview and Print a Workbook, Enter and Edit Data in a Worksheet, and Create Formulas.*

Gloria French, Public Information Officer for Desert Park, wants to report the number of students who have visited the city's museum over the past year. Create a workbook with one worksheet that lists the names of at least six schools. For each school, list the number of students that visited the museum for both the fall semester and the spring semester. Include totals by school and by semester. For school names, use school names from your local area. Create a footer that includes your name as you have in the past, and save the file as **1L_Museum_Visits_Firstname_Lastname**.

 End **You have completed Project 1L** ──────────────────────────

On the Internet

Learning More About Excel 2003

Additional information about using Microsoft Office 2003 Excel is available on the official Microsoft Web site. Take a look at the Top 10 Questions about Excel found at the following URL: **www.microsoft.com/office/excel/using/**

Many additional pages at this site have tips, help, downloads, and more. Plan to visit this site on a regular basis.

GO! with Help

Becoming Familiar with Excel Help

The easiest way to become successful with Microsoft Excel is to get in the habit of using the Help feature. In this exercise, you will access tips from Microsoft Help.

1. If necessary, start Excel to open a new workbook.

2. At the right edge of the menu bar, click in the **Type a question for help** box, type **How do I get Help?** and then press Enter.

   The Search Results task pane displays a list of results.

3. Click **About getting help while you work**.

   A Microsoft Excel Help window displays with a detailed list of various ways to access Help for Excel.

4. Using the **Print** button at the top of the Help window, print the contents of the Help window. Recall that your printed document will not contain any document identifier containing your name.

5. Close the Help window, and close the task pane.

2 chaptertwo

Editing Workbooks, Formulas, and Cells

In this chapter, you will: complete these projects and practice these skills.

Project 2A **Creating a Quarterly Sales Analysis**	**Objectives** • Enter Constant Values with AutoFill and the Fill Handle • Insert, Delete, and Adjust Rows and Columns • Align Cell Contents Horizontally • Copy and Move Cell Contents
Project 2B **Calculating Annual Sales**	**Objectives** • Format Numbers Using the Toolbar • Edit Formulas • Copy Formulas • Conduct a What-if Analysis • Display and Print Underlying Formulas • Change Page Orientation

The Perfect Party

The Perfect Party store, owned by two partners, provides a wide variety of party accessories including invitations, favors, banners and flags, balloons, piñatas, etc. Party-planning services include both custom parties with pre-filled custom "goodie bags" and "parties in a box" that include everything needed to throw a theme party. Big sellers in this category are the Football and Luau themes. The owners are planning to open a second store and expand their party-planning services to include catering.

© Getty Images, Inc.

Editing Workbooks, Formulas, and Cells

In this chapter you will expand your knowledge of Excel by copying formulas and conducting a what-if analysis. You will enhance the appearance of workbooks by centering headings and adjusting the size of rows and columns and discover how easy it is to create a series of numbers without typing.

While working with the formulas in this chapter, you will discover how Excel can easily replicate formulas without having to retype them. You will also move and copy the contents of cells within a worksheet, within worksheets in the same workbook, and between worksheets from one workbook to another workbook.

Project 2A **Sales Analysis**

In this project, you will use a quick method to enter constant values in a spreadsheet. You will also insert, delete, and adjust columns and rows and copy and move cell contents.

In Activities 2.1 through 2.13, you will create a workbook for Angie Nguyen and Gabriela Quinones, owners of The Perfect Party, that shows the sales totals for each quarter for the previous fiscal year. You will import data for last year from another workbook. The resulting workbook will look similar to Figure 2.1. You will save your workbook as *2A_Sales_Analysis_Firstname_Lastname.*

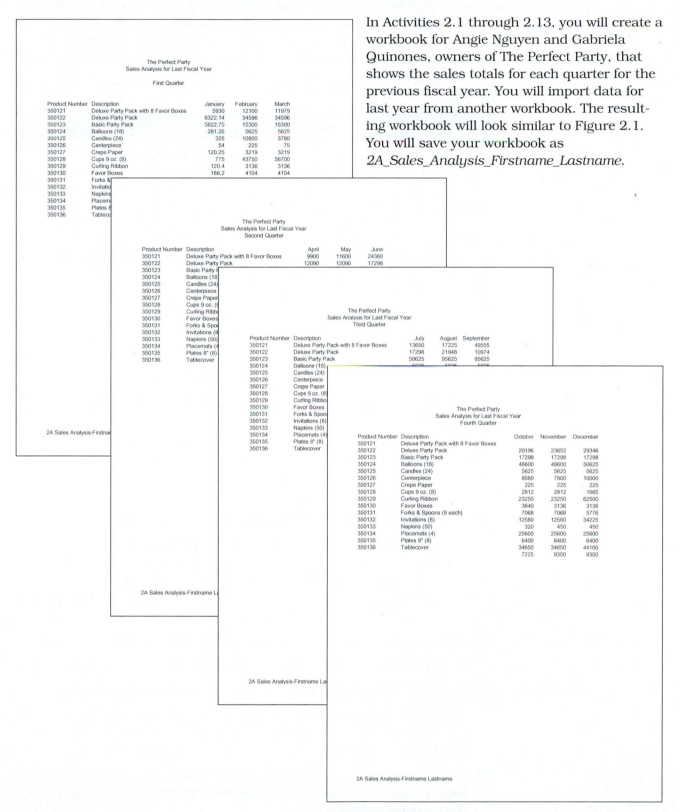

Figure 2.1—Sales Analysis

Objective 1
Enter Constant Values with AutoFill and the Fill Handle

Excel provides shortcuts for entering and editing data within cells. For example, AutoComplete, which you practiced in Chapter 1, assists you in typing duplicate entries in the same column. Shortcuts are designed to reduce typing. Excel has a shortcut called **AutoFill** that generates a series of constant values such as the months of the year in order or the days of the week in order. The table in Figure 2.2 lists some of the series that Excel can generate.

AutoFill Series

Start with:	AutoFill generates this series:
Jan	Feb, Mar, Apr…
January	February, March, April…
Mon	Tue, Wed, Thu…
Monday	Tuesday, Wednesday, Thursday…
Qtr 1	Qtr 2, Qtr 3, Qtr 4…
Quarter 1	Quarter 2, Quarter 3, Quarter 4…
Oct-99	Nov-99, Dec-99, Jan-00…
15-Jan	16-Jan, 17-Jan, 18-Jan…
1st Period	2nd Period, 3rd Period, 4th Period…
Product 1	Product 2, Product 3, Product 4…
Text 1	Text 2, Text 3, Text 4…
10:00 AM	11:00 AM, 12:00 PM, 1:00 PM…

Figure 2.2

Activity 2.1 Inserting Titles and Headings

In a new worksheet, the first information you enter is usually a title and perhaps one or more subtitles that describe the purpose of the worksheet. Additionally, each column of data normally has a column heading describing the type of information in the column. Likewise, each row may have a description in the left column that describes the data in the row.

1 Start Excel and, if necessary, close ☒ the **Getting Started** task pane.

Excel displays a new workbook named *Book1*.

2 Right-click the **Sheet1 tab**, and then click **Select All Sheets**.

In the blue title bar, *[Group]* displays, indicating that the three sheets are grouped. When worksheets are grouped, information such as a header or footer is placed on all the sheets in the workbook.

3 From the **View** menu, click **Header and Footer**. In the displayed **Page Setup** dialog box, click the **Header/Footer tab**, and then click the **Custom Footer** button.

4 In the displayed **Footer** dialog box, under **Left section**, type **2A Sales Analysis-Firstname Lastname** using your own first and last name, and then in the upper right corner, click **OK** to close the **Footer** dialog box. Click **OK** again to close the **Page Setup** dialog box.

A dotted vertical line may display on the worksheet, indicating the right edge of the page as currently formatted. Recall that headers and footers do not display in the worksheet on your screen. They display only in the Print Preview and on the printed worksheets. Because you grouped the sheets, your footer will print on all the sheets in the workbook.

5 Right-click the **Sheet1 tab**, and then click **Ungroup Sheets**.

[Group] no longer displays in the blue title bar.

6 In cell **A1**, type **The Perfect Party** as the title of the worksheet, and then press Enter.

7 In cell **A2**, type **Sales Analysis for Last Fiscal Year** as the first subtitle, and then press Enter two times.

8 Be sure cell **A4** is the active cell, type **Product Number** as the column heading for this column of data, and then press Enter. Compare your screen with Figure 2.3.

Worksheet heading and subheading ——
Column heading ——

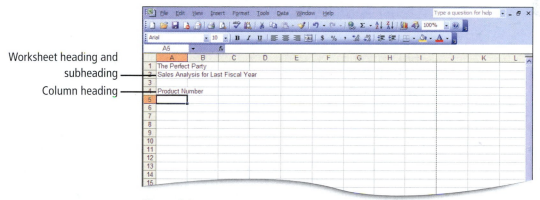

Figure 2.3

9 Display the **File** menu, and then click **Save As**.

10 In the displayed **Save As** dialog box, click the **Save in arrow**. Navigate to the drive and folder where you are storing your projects for this chapter, creating a new folder for Chapter 2 if you want to do so.

11 In the **File name** box, delete **Book 1**, type **2A_Sales_Analysis_Firstname_Lastname** and then in the lower right corner, click **Save** or press Enter.

The workbook name displays in both the title bar and the taskbar. Recall that when saving files, using the underscore character instead of spaces will facilitate sending your files over the Internet.

Activity 2.2 Creating a Series Using AutoFill

A *series* is a group of things that come one after another in succession. For example, January, February, March, April, and so on, is a series. The days of the week form a series. Quarter 1, Quarter 2, Quarter 3, and Quarter 4 form a series. The numbers 1, 2, 3, 4, 5 and 10, 15, 20, 25 are series. Excel's *AutoFill* feature completes a series so that you do not have to type every value. AutoFill is the ability to extend a series of values into adjacent cells, based on the value of other cells.

1 With your workbook **2A_Sales_Analysis** displayed, click cell **B4**.

Although text displays in cell B4, the text *Product Number* is contained within cell A4. Recall that if a cell is not wide enough to accommodate a text value, its display will spill over to the next cell, provided the cell is empty. If you look at the Formula Bar, you can see that cell B4 does not contain a value.

2 In cell **B4** type **January** and then press Tab to make cell **C4** the active cell.

January will form the heading for its column, which will contain January sales amounts. *Product Number* no longer overlaps into cell B4. Now that cell B4 contains a value, the value in cell A4 is **truncated**—cut off. Although not completely visible, the underlying value of cell A4 remains unchanged.

3 In cell **C4**, type **February** and then press Tab.

February will form the column heading for this column, which will contain February sales amounts. One by one you could enter the months from March through December, but AutoFill will complete the series for you without additional typing.

4 Click cell **C4** to make it the active cell, and then notice the small black square in the lower right corner of the cell, as shown in Figure 2.4.

This is the *fill handle*. You can drag the fill handle to adjacent cells to fill them with values based on the first cell in the series.

Fill handle —

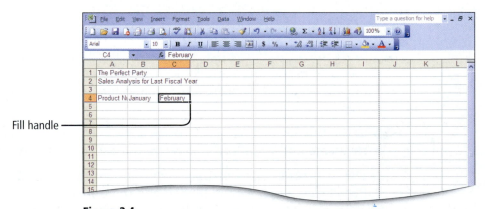

Figure 2.4

5 Point to the **fill handle** until your mouse pointer changes from a white cross ⊕ to a black cross ✛, hold down the left mouse button, drag to the right through cell **M4**, and as you do so, notice that a ScreenTip displays for each month, as shown in Figure 2.5. Release the left mouse button.

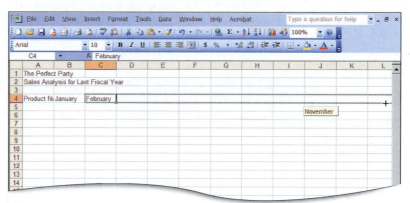

Figure 2.5

6 After you release the mouse button, the months March through December are filled in. On your screen, locate and then point to the *Auto Fill Options button* 🖭 to display its ScreenTip, as shown in Figure 2.6.

The Auto Fill Options button is a type of *smart tag*. When Excel recognizes certain types of data, Excel labels the data with a smart tag. Some smart tags, for example, the Auto Fill Options button, provide a menu of options related to the current task. Because the options are related to the current task, the tag or button is referred to as being *context-sensitive*.

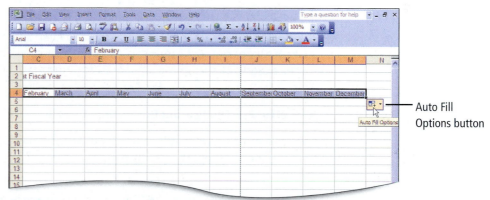

Auto Fill Options button

Figure 2.6

7 Point to and then click the **Auto Fill Options button arrow** to display a menu, as shown in Figure 2.7.

The menu offers options about how to fill the selected cells. On the displayed menu, *Fill Series* is selected, indicating the action that was taken. From the displayed menu, you could also select other actions. For example, if you clicked Copy Cells, February would fill each of the selected cells because February was the selected cell when you began to drag the mouse. As you progress in your study of Excel, you will encounter additional smart tags.

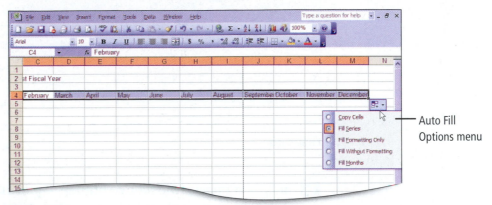

Figure 2.7

8 Click any empty cell to close the **Auto Fill Options** menu without changing the selection.

The smart tag will remain visible until you perform another screen action.

9 On the Standard toolbar, click the **Save** button.

More Knowledge — Smart Tags

Smart tags were first introduced in Microsoft Office XP. In Microsoft Office System 2003, smart tags have been made even smarter. Using various types of software, organizations can develop their own custom smart tags, and smart tags can automatically search for information on the Web.

Activity 2.3 Duplicating Data Using AutoFill

AutoFill not only extends a series of values, but it also duplicates data into adjacent cells. This is another way that Excel helps to reduce your typing.

1 Click cell **A5**, type **350121** and then press Enter.

Product Number 350121 displays in cell A5.

2 Click cell **A5** again, position your pointer over the **fill handle** in the lower right corner of the cell to display the pointer ⊞, and then drag downward through cell **A10**.

The value 350121 is duplicated in all the cells, and the Auto Fill Options button displays.

3 Point to and then click the **Auto Fill Options button arrow** to display the menu, as shown in Figure 2.8.$I~AutoFill;duplicating data with>

The default option *Copy Cells* is selected. Because Excel did not interpret the single value of 350121 to be part of a series, it copied (duplicated) the value in the selected cells.

Auto Fill Options menu ————

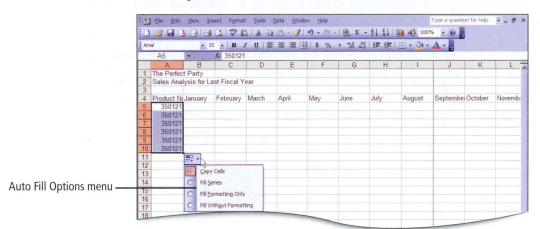

Figure 2.8

4 From the displayed menu, click **Fill Series**.

A series of numbers, 350121–350126, replaces the duplicate numbers. You can use AutoFill to create a series or to duplicate data in adjacent cells. Compare your screen with Figure 2.9.

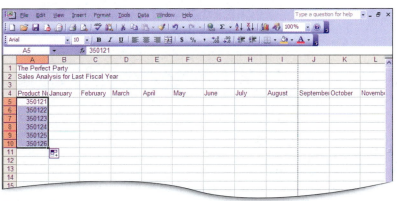

Figure 2.9

5 Click in any empty cell to cancel the selection. On the Standard toolbar, click the **Save** button ⊞ to save the changes you have made to your worksheet.

Recall that the Auto Fill Options button will remain visible until you perform another screen action. This is characteristic of the various smart tags in Excel.

Objective 2
Insert, Delete, and Adjust Rows and Columns

Within the spreadsheet grid you can control the size of cells in various ways. For example, you can change the width of columns and the height of rows to accommodate your data. You can also insert new columns and rows and delete existing columns and rows—even after data has been typed into them. You also have the ability to merge several cells into one cell.

Activity 2.4 Adjusting Column Width and Row Height

The size of cells is controlled by either adjusting the width of a column or by increasing the height of a row. The cell size you need is determined by the amount of data you type into the cell and by the *font* and *font size* of the data. A font is a set of characters with the same design and shape. Font size is measured in *points*, with one point equal to ½ of an inch, and abbreviated as *pt*.

1 Click **A4** to make it the active cell.

2 In the **column heading area**, position the pointer over the vertical line between **column A** and **column B** until the white cross ⊕ changes to a double-headed arrow ↔, and then hold down the left mouse button. See Figure 2.10.

A ScreenTip displays information about the width of the column. The default width of a column is 64 pixels, or 8.43 characters, which is the average number of digits that will fit in a cell using the default font. The default font in Excel is Arial, and the default font size is 10 pt.

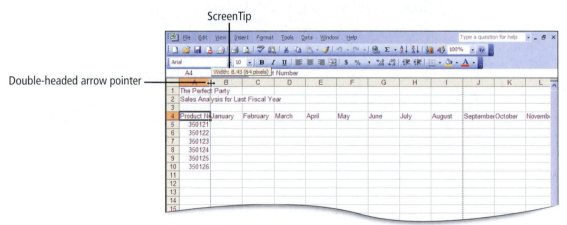

Figure 2.10

3 Drag to the right until the number of pixels indicated in the ScreenTip reaches **200 pixels**, as shown in Figure 2.11, and then release the mouse button. If you are not satisfied with your result, click the **Undo** button ↩ and begin again.

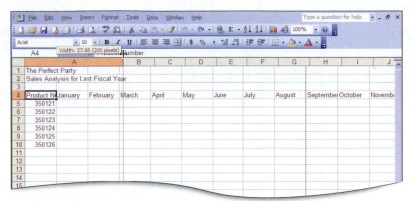

Figure 2.11

4 Using the technique you just practiced, decrease the width of **column A** to **40 pixels**.

A pattern, #####, displays in cells A5:A10. When a column is too narrow to display the entire numeric value in a cell, the cell displays as a series of number signs (also called pound signs), as shown in Figure 2.12.

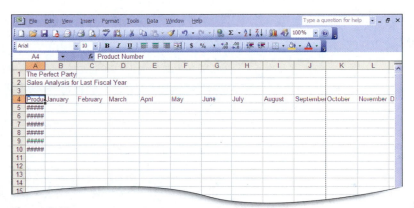

Figure 2.12

5 Click cell **A5**, and then look at the value in the Formula Bar.

Although the cell displays #####, the underlying value is unchanged; it is still 350121.

6 Click cell **A4**, display the **Format** menu, point to **Column**, and then click **AutoFit Selection**.

This command adjusts the width of a column to accommodate the value in the selected cell, cell A4 in this instance.

7 Click cell **A2**, and notice that the text in cell **A2** still overlaps into **columns B** and **C**. See Figure 2.13.

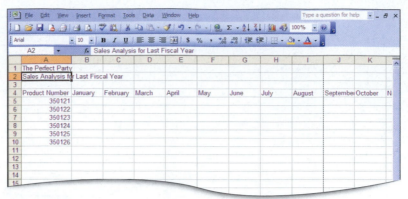

Figure 2.13

8 In the **column heading area**, position your pointer over the **column B** heading until the pointer changes to a black down arrow 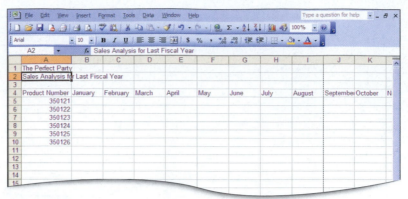, hold down the left mouse button, and then drag to the right through **column M**.

Columns B though M are selected, as shown in Figure 2.14.

Columns B through M selected

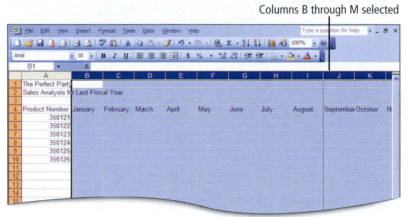

Figure 2.14

9 With the columns still selected, in the **column heading area**, position the pointer over the vertical line between **column B** and **column C** to display the double-headed arrow pointer, and then drag to the right until **75 pixels** displays in the ScreenTip. Release the mouse. If you are not satisfied with your result, click Undo and begin again. Alternatively, from the Format menu, point to Column, click Width, and type **75**

All the selected columns are increased in width to 75 pixels.

10 Click anywhere to cancel the selection. In the **row heading area**, position the pointer over the horizontal line between **row 3** and **row 4** until the double-headed arrow pointer displays, as shown in Figure 2.15.

Double-headed arrow pointer —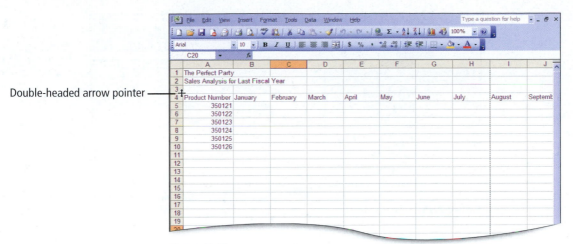

Figure 2.15

11 Hold down the left mouse button, and then watch the ScreenTip while dragging downward until the height is **27 pixels**. If you are not satisfied with your result, click **Undo** and begin again.

The height of the row is increased. The height of rows is measured in points. Recall that one point equals ½ of an inch. The default height of a row is 12.75 points.

More Knowledge — Adjusting Cell Height

Excel adjusts the height of a row to accommodate the largest font used in that particular row. Thus, you need not be concerned that your characters are too tall for the row.

Activity 2.5 Inserting and Deleting Rows and Columns

You can insert columns or rows in the following ways:

• From the Insert menu, click Rows or click Columns.

• In the column heading or the row heading, right-click to simultaneously select the column or row and display a shortcut menu. From the displayed shortcut menu, click Insert.

You can delete columns or rows in the following ways:

• Select the column or row, and then from the Edit menu, click Delete.

• In the column heading or the row heading, right-click to simultaneously select the column or row and display a shortcut menu. From the displayed shortcut menu, click Delete.

1 Right-click the **column B** heading to simultaneously select the column and display the shortcut menu, as shown in Figure 2.16.

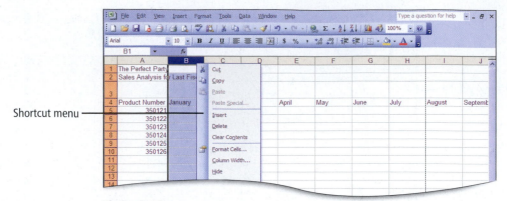

Shortcut menu ——

Figure 2.16

2 From the displayed shortcut menu, click **Insert**.

A new column B is inserted to the left of the selected column, and the existing columns are shifted to the right. Additionally, the Insert Options button displays.

3 Point to the **Insert Options** button to display its ScreenTip and its arrow, and then click the arrow to display the menu, as shown in Figure 2.17.

From this menu, you can format the new column like the column to the left or the column to the right, or you can leave it unformatted. The default is *Format Same As Left*.

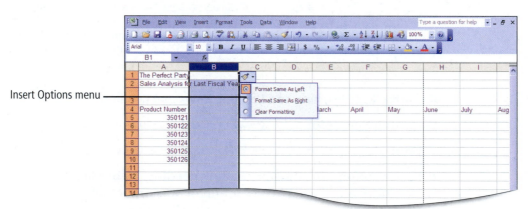

Insert Options menu ——

Figure 2.17

More Knowledge — Inserting and Deleting Cells

You can also insert or delete individual cells in a worksheet using a similar technique. Right-click the cell position where you want to add a cell, and from the shortcut menu click Insert. In the Insert dialog box click the option button for the direction you wish to shift the existing cells—down or to the right. All the cells in the column are shifted down one, or the cells in the row are shifted to the right one cell. Similarly, when you delete a cell, the delete dialog box will display so you can choose to shift the remaining cells up or to the left.

4 Click anywhere outside the selected column to cancel the selection and accept the default value.

The new column is formatted in the same width as column A to the left. The Insert Options button remains visible until you perform another screen action.

5 Click cell **B4**, type **Description** and then press Enter.

6 Right-click the **row 4 heading** to simultaneously select the row and display the shortcut menu, and then from the displayed menu, click **Insert**.

A new row 4 is inserted, formatted in the same height as the row above it. The Insert Options button displays. New rows are inserted above the selected row.

7 Select cell **A3**, type **First Quarter** and then press Enter.

Businesses frequently track their yearly financial information by dividing a year into four equal parts called **quarters**. Thus, *First Quarter* refers to the period from January through March, *Second Quarter* refers to April through June, *Third Quarter* refers to July through September, and *Fourth Quarter* refers to October through December.

8 Right-click the **column F heading**, and then from the displayed shortcut menu, click **Delete**.

Column F is deleted from the worksheet, and the columns to the right shift one letter to the left. Thus, the former column G becomes column F.

9 In the **column heading area**, hold down the left mouse button and drag to select **columns F through M**. Pause your pointer anywhere over the selected area, right-click, and from the shortcut menu, click **Delete**. Click anywhere to cancel the selection.

The selected range of columns is deleted. Both columns and rows can be deleted in this manner—individually or as a range (group).

10 Hold down Ctrl and press Home to make cell **A1** the active cell and bring the left side of the worksheet into view. On the Standard toolbar, click the **Save** button 💾 to save the changes you have made to your workbook. Compare your screen with Figure 2.18.

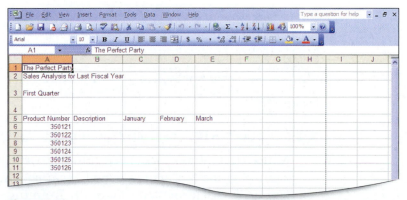

Figure 2.18

Objective 3
Align Cell Contents Horizontally

Within cells, data can be aligned at the left edge of the cell—*left-aligned*—or at the right edge of the cell—*right-aligned*. Within a cell, data can also be centered, or data can be centered across a group of cells using a feature called *Merge and Center*.

Activity 2.6 Aligning Cell Contents

By default, Excel aligns numeric values at the right edge of a cell and aligns text values at the left edge of the cell. These default settings can be changed as needed.

1 Look at the data in cells **A3:A11**, and notice that text values, for example, *First Quarter*, are aligned at the left edge of the cell and that the numeric product numbers are aligned at the right edge of the cell.

2 Click cell **A6**, and then on the Formatting toolbar, click the **Center** button.

Product Number *350121* is aligned in the center of the cell.

3 With **A6** still the active cell, on the Formatting toolbar click the **Align Left** button.

Product Number *350121* is aligned at the left of the cell. Because this numeric value is used for reference and not in a mathematical calculation, it can be aligned at the left. Numeric values that are not used for calculations, such as phone numbers, postal codes, and taxpayer identification numbers, are commonly left-aligned so that it is obvious that they are not numbers to be used in calculations.

4 Select the range **A7:A11**, and then click **Align Left**.

The entire group of cells is left-aligned. Compare your screen with Figure 2.19.

Align Left button

Center button

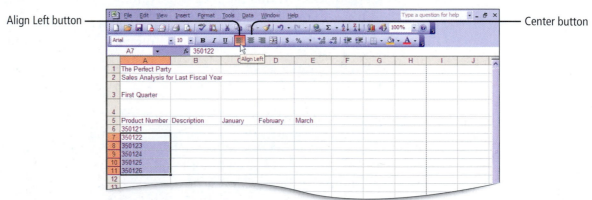

Figure 2.19

5 Select cell **A12**, type **350127** and press Enter.

Notice that although this is a number, Excel did not apply the default right-alignment. This happened because when three or more adjacent cells are formatted differently from the default, Excel applies the same formatting to the next three adjacent cells.

6 Select cell **A16**, which is more than three cells away from the previous entry, type **350128** and press Enter. Notice the alignment.

Because this cell was more than three cells down from the last active cell containing the left-align format, Excel used its default alignment for numeric values, which is right-align.

7 Select **column A**, on the Formatting toolbar click **Align Left** ▤, and then click outside the selected area to cancel the selection.

All the cells in column A are formatted with left alignment. You can format entire rows and columns in this manner. Now that left alignment has been applied to all the cells in the column, any new numeric entries in column A will be left-aligned.

8 Right-click cell **A16**, and on the shortcut menu, click **Clear Contents** to remove *350128*.

9 Select the range **C5:E5**. On the Formatting toolbar click **Align Right** ▤, and then click outside the selected area to cancel the selection. Click **Save** 🖫.

The column headings for January through March are right-aligned. When entered, the data in these columns will be numeric values that are right-aligned. Visually, it is useful if the heading for a numeric column lines up with the data it describes.

Activity 2.7 Using Merge and Center

In addition to widening columns and making rows taller, you can control the size of cells in another way. Several cells can be merged into one large cell. When you merge cells, the result is a single cell that comprises all the original cells.

Because the title information in a worksheet is so frequently centered across the columns of the worksheet, Excel provides a command that combines the merging of cells with center alignment. This command is *Merge and Center*.

1 Select the range **A1:E1**, and then, on the Formatting toolbar, click the **Merge and Center** button 🔳. Click outside the selected area to cancel the selection.

Cells A1:E1 are merged into one cell, and the heading, *The Perfect Party*, is centered across the columns in the newly formed cell. Cells B1:E1 cease to exist because they are contained with cell A1.

2 Select the range **A2:E2**, and then, on the Formatting toolbar, click the **Merge and Center** button 🔳.

Cells A2:E2 are merged into one cell, and the data is centered in the cell.

3 Click the **Merge and Center** button 🔳 again.

The text value returns to cell A2, and the merged cells are changed back to their individual cells. In this manner, you can reverse the Merge and Center command.

4 With cells **A2:E2** still selected, click the **Merge and Center** button 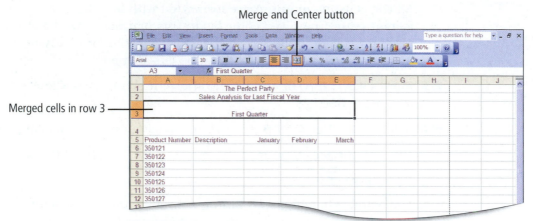 again to merge and center the data.

5 Using the technique you have just practiced, in **row 3**, merge and center the subtitle *First Quarter* across the range **A3:E3**. Compare your results with Figure 2.20.

6 On the Standard toolbar, click the **Save** button.

Merge and Center button

Merged cells in row 3 ——

Figure 2.20

Objective 4
Copy and Move Cell Contents

Data from individual cells and groups of cells can be copied to other cells in the same worksheet, to other sheets in the same workbook, or to sheets in another workbook. Likewise, data can be moved (*cut*) from one place to another. The action of placing cell contents that have been copied or moved from one location to another location is called *paste*.

Data from other sources can also be copied into a worksheet. For example, if your instructor uses a course management program such as BlackBoard or WebCT, data from the program can be copied into an Excel worksheet. In the following activities, you will use various methods to copy and move cell contents.

Activity 2.8 Copying Cell Contents

The *Office Clipboard* is a temporary storage area maintained by your Windows operating system. When you perform the Copy command or the Cut command, the data you select is placed on the Clipboard. From this Clipboard storage area, the data is available for pasting into other cells, worksheets, workbooks, and even other Office programs.

1 From the **Edit** menu, click **Office Clipboard**.

2 The **Clipboard** task pane displays.

3 Check to see whether the top of the Clipboard indicates *Clipboard empty*, and if it does not, at the top of the task pane click the **Clear All** button.

4 Click cell **A1**, the merged and centered cell, and then on the Standard toolbar, click the **Copy** button ⧉.

A moving border surrounds the merged cell, and the contents of cell A1, including its formatting, are copied to the Clipboard, as shown in Figure 2.21. A moving border indicates cells that have been copied, and the border will remain until you perform another screen action.

Moving border ⟶ 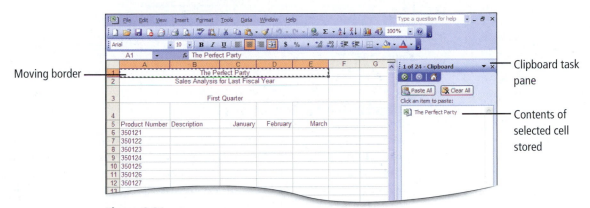 ⟵ Clipboard task pane

⟵ Contents of selected cell stored

Figure 2.21

5 In the lower left of the grid area, click the **Sheet2 tab**, and be sure that cell **A1** is the active cell.

6 On the Standard toolbar, click the **Paste** button ⧉▾.

The Clipboard entry is pasted into cell A1, with the identical formatting, and the Paste Options button displays, as shown in Figure 2.22.

Paste Options button ⟶ 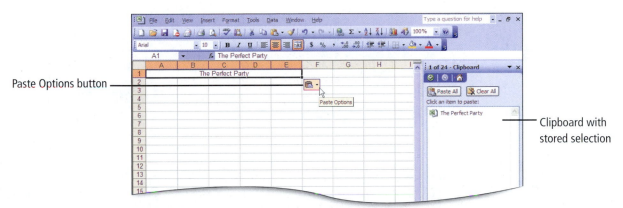 ⟵ Clipboard with stored selection

Figure 2.22

7 Point to the **Paste Options** button, and then click its **arrow** to display a menu of options.

The Paste Options menu displays, as shown in Figure 2.23. Notice that *Keep Source Formatting* is the default. You can see that the original formatting, merge and center, was retained.

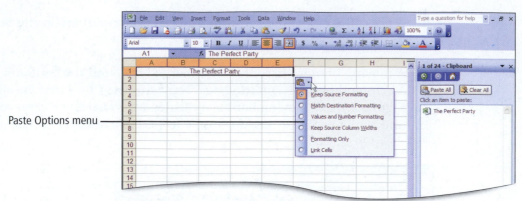

Paste Options menu ——

Figure 2.23

Note — Paste Options

When pasting items you can also choose the Paste Special command from the Edit menu or from the shortcut menu. This gives you even greater control over what is pasted. Using the Paste Special command you can choose the values, formulas, formats or other specific characteristics of the cell that has been cut or copied.

8 Click outside the menu to close it without changing the selection. Navigate back to **Sheet1**, select the range **A2:A3**, and then hold down `Ctrl` and press `C`.

`Ctrl` + `C` is the keyboard shortcut for the Copy command. The contents of the two cells are copied to the top of the Clipboard, as shown in Figure 2.24, and the first copied item on the Clipboard moves down. A moving border surrounds the copied cells.

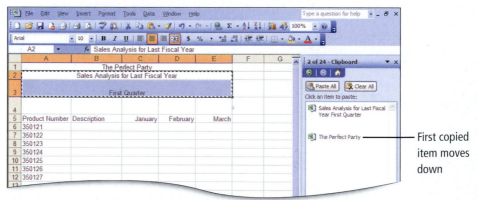

First copied item moves down

Figure 2.24

9 Navigate to **Sheet2**, select cell **A2**, and then press `Ctrl` + `V`.

The content of the copied cells is copied to the same cells in Sheet2. Notice that you did not have to select both cells A2 and A3. You need only select the top left cell of the paste range before performing the paste. Excel will select the correct cells for the remaining data.

10 In the upper left corner of your keyboard, press Esc to remove the **Paste Options** button.

Because you want to retain the source formatting, it is not necessary to display the Paste Options menu.

11 Using one of the copy techniques you have just practiced, navigate to **Sheet1**, select the range **A5:E5**, and then copy it. Navigate to **Sheet2**, and then paste to cell **A5**.

Notice that the widths of the columns on Sheet2 are not the same as those you have formatted on Sheet1.

12 Click the **Paste Options button arrow**, and then click **Keep Source Column Widths**.

The columns are adjusted to the same widths as those on Sheet1. This is a good example of the usefulness of smart tags in Excel.

13 On **Sheet2**, select **C5:E5**, and then press Delete. Select cell **C5**, type **April** and press Enter.

14 Click cell **C5**, and then drag the **fill handle** to the right to fill in *May* and *June* in cells **D5** and **E5**.

15 Select cell **A3**, click to place the insertion point in the Formula Bar, and then edit the heading as necessary to read **Second Quarter** Press Enter, and then compare your screen with Figure 2.25.

Second Quarter inserted ⎯⎯⎯

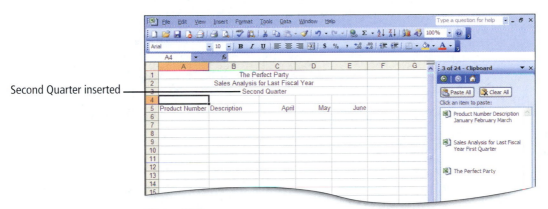

Figure 2.25

16 **Save** 💾 the changes you have made to your workbook.

Note — Copying and Pasting a Single Item

When copying and then pasting one item at a time, as you have done in the previous steps, it is not necessary to display the Clipboard task pane. The Paste command always takes its data from the top of the Clipboard, and as new items are stored on the Clipboard, they occupy the top position. It was useful to display the Clipboard here, however, so that you could have a visual indication of how the Clipboard works.

Activity 2.9 Copying Multiple Selections Using Collect and Paste

When copying and then pasting a single item, you can do so without displaying the Clipboard task pane. As you saw in the previous activity, each time you perform the Copy command, the selected cells move to the top of the Clipboard list, and each time you perform the Paste command, the item at the top of the list is pasted to the desired location.

Displaying the Clipboard is essential, however, if you want to collect a group of items and then paste them where you want them. The Clipboard can hold up to 24 items, and as you have seen, the Clipboard task pane displays a short representation of each item.

You can display the Clipboard task pane in one of three ways:

- If a different task pane is displayed, click the Other Task Panes arrow, and then click Clipboard.

- From the Edit menu, click Office Clipboard.

- Select the first cell or cells that you want to copy, hold down Ctrl, and then quickly press C two times.

1 Navigate to **Sheet3**, click cell **A1**, and then at the top of the **Clipboard** task pane, click the **Paste All** button 📋 Paste All.

The three copied entries are all pasted into Sheet3, beginning in cell A1. The empty row above the monthly column headings was not copied, so it is not included. Compare your screen with Figure 2.26.

Paste All button

Entries pasted from Clipboard —

Figure 2.26

2 In the **row heading area**, right-click to simultaneously select **row 4** and display a shortcut menu. From the displayed menu, click **Insert**.

A blank row is inserted above the selected rows, and the rows are renumbered accordingly.

3 Select **columns A** and **B**, and then drag to increase the width to **102 pixels**. Use the same technique to widen **columns C** through **E** to **75 pixels**.

4 Delete *January*, *February*, and *March*, and then use **AutoFill** to change the months to *July*, *August*, and *September*.

5 Edit cell **A3** to read **Third Quarter** and then compare your results with Figure 2.27.

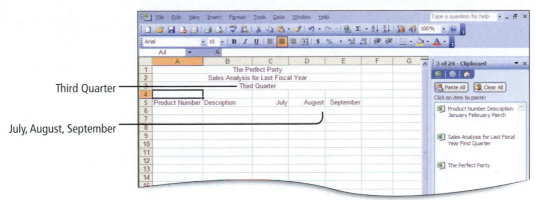

Third Quarter

July, August, September

Figure 2.27

6 On the **Clipboard**, click the **Clear All** button ![Clear All], and **Close** ![X] the **Clipboard** task pane. **Save** ![save icon] your workbook.

The collection of copied items is removed from the Clipboard.

Activity 2.10 Copying an Entire Worksheet to a New Worksheet

You can copy an entire worksheet to another worksheet in the same workbook.

1 Be sure that **Sheet3** is displayed. From the **Edit** menu, click **Move or Copy Sheet**.

The Move or Copy dialog box displays.

2 In the **Move or Copy** dialog box, under **Before sheet**, click **(move to end)**, and then select the **Create a copy** check box. Click **OK**.

A fourth worksheet named *Sheet3 (2)* displays, as shown in Figure 2.28. It contains a duplicate of all the data and formatting from Sheet3, from which it was copied.

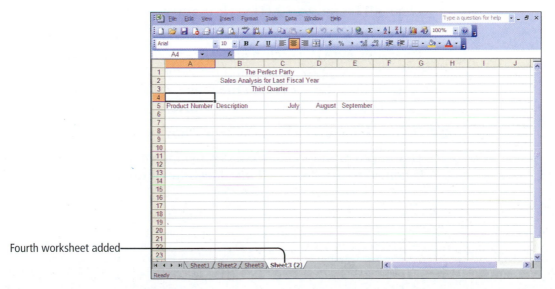

Fourth worksheet added

Figure 2.28

3 Right-click the **Sheet1 tab**, click **Rename**, type **First Qtr** and then rename the remaining sheets as **Second Qtr** and **Third Qtr** and **Fourth Qtr**

4 Display the **Fourth Qtr** sheet. Use **AutoFill** to change the months to *October*, *November*, and *December*.

5 Edit cell **A3** to read **Fourth Quarter** and compare your screen with Figure 2.29. Click **Save** to save the changes you have made to your workbook.

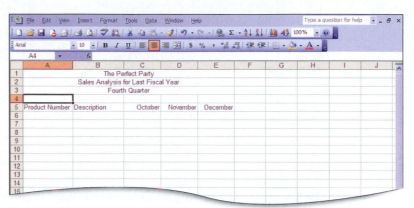

Figure 2.29

Activity 2.11 Pasting Data from Another Workbook

You can paste data from one workbook into another workbook.

1 From the **File** menu, click **Open**, click the **Look in arrow**, and then navigate to the student files that accompany this textbook. Click to select the file **e02A_Data**, and then click **Open**.

The workbook e02A_Data displays. This workbook contains a year of sales data for The Perfect Party.

2 From the **Edit** menu, click **Office Clipboard**. If necessary, click the **Clear All** button [Clear All] to clear any items from the Clipboard. Click cell **A2**, hold down Shift, and then click cell **B17**.

The range A2:B17 is selected. You can select a range of consecutive cells by clicking the first cell in the range, holding down Shift, and then clicking the last cell in the range. Alternatively, you can drag from the first to the last cell in the range.

3 On the Standard toolbar, click the **Copy** button.

The selected range is surrounded by a moving border, and the range is copied to the Clipboard, as shown in Figure 2.30.

Range copied to Clipboard

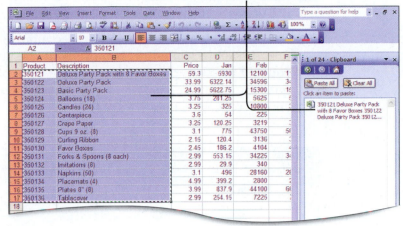

Figure 2.30

4 Click cell **D2**, hold down ⇧Shift, and then click cell **F17** to select the range. Click the **Copy** button 📋.

The dollar amounts for the first quarter, January through March, are copied to the Clipboard. Compare your screen with Figure 2.31.

Range copied to Clipboard

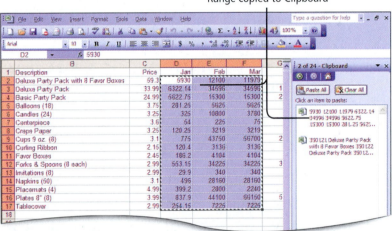

Figure 2.31

5 On the menu bar, click **Window**, and then at the bottom of the menu, click the **2A_Sales_Analysis** workbook containing your name. Alternatively, click the name of your workbook on the taskbar.

6 Display the **First Qtr** worksheet. Click cell **A6** to set the active cell, and then on the task pane, click the second entry, which begins *350121 Deluxe Party Pack*.

The product numbers and descriptions are copied from the Clipboard to the active worksheet beginning at the active cell. Data in cells A2:A12 was overwritten by the paste operation. It was not necessary to clear the cells first.

7 Click cell **C6** to set the active cell, and then on the task pane, click the entry beginning *5930*.

The sales amounts for the first three months of the year are copied into the active worksheet beginning at the active cell. This process of copying multiple pieces of data to the Clipboard and then pasting the data into another location is called ***collect and paste***. Compare your screen with Figure 2.32.

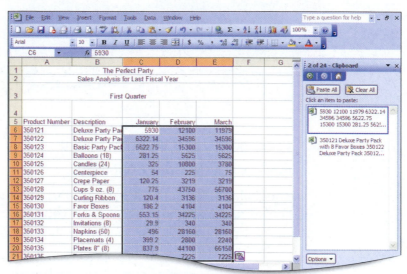

Figure 2.32

8 From the **Window** menu, click **e02A_Data** to return to the worksheet with the sales amounts. Scroll as necessary to view **columns G** through **I**. To select the second quarter dollar amounts, click cell **G2**, hold down Shift, and then click cell **I17**.

9 Right-click in the selected area, and then from the shortcut menu, click **Copy**.

The second quarter's data is copied and moves to the top of the Clipboard.

10 On the taskbar, click your workbook **2A_Sales_Analysis**.

Recall that the taskbar can also be used to switch between open workbooks.

11 Display the **Second Qtr** worksheet. Click **A6** to set the active cell, and then on the Clipboard, click the entry beginning with *350121 Deluxe Party Pack*.

The product numbers and descriptions are copied from the Clipboard and pasted to the active worksheet beginning at the active cell in the second quarter's sheet. Items collected on the Clipboard can be pasted as many times as needed.

12 Click **C6** to set the active cell, and then on the Clipboard click the entry beginning with *9900*.

The sales amounts for the second three-month quarter of the year are copied into the active worksheet beginning at the active cell.

13 Navigate to the **e02A_Data** workbook, select the range **J2:L17**, and copy the range to the Clipboard. Then, display your **2A_Sales_Analysis** workbook and click the sheet tab for the **Third Qtr**.

14 Click cell **A6**, and then from the Clipboard, paste the last item, which begins *350121 Deluxe Party Pack*. Then click cell **C6**, and from the Clipboard, paste the first item, which begins *13650*.

The sales amounts for the third quarter are pasted into the Third Qtr worksheet. Compare your screen with Figure 2.33.

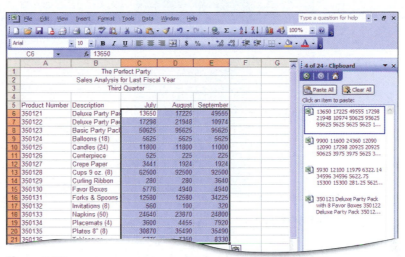

Figure 2.33

15 From the **e02A_Data** workbook, copy the range **M2:O17** to the Clipboard. Then display the **Fourth Qtr** worksheet of your **2A_Sales_Analysis** workbook. In cell **A6**, paste the last item on the Clipboard—the product numbers and descriptions. In cell **C6**, paste the first item on the Clipboard, which begins *20196*.

The sales amounts for the fourth quarter are pasted into the Fourth Qtr worksheet. Compare your screen with Figure 2.34.

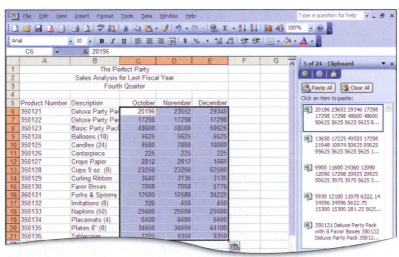

Figure 2.34

16 Right-click on the **First Qtr tab**, and then click **Select All Sheets**.

[Group] displays in the title bar.

17 Select **column B**, display the **Format** menu, point to **Column**, and then click **AutoFit Selection**.

Column B is widened to accommodate the longest entry in the column. Because you selected all sheets, this action is applied to all four sheets in the workbook. Compare your screen with Figure 2.35.

Column B widened ——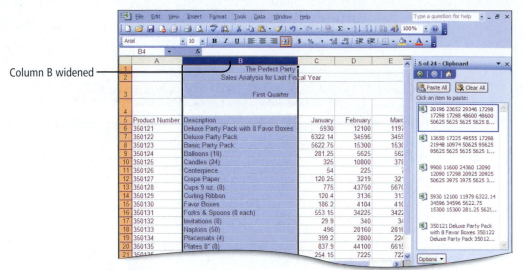

Figure 2.35

18 Display the **Second Qtr**, **Third Qtr**, and **Fourth Qtr** worksheets to verify that **column B** was widened on each.

By displaying other worksheets, the sheets are automatically ungrouped, and the word *[Group]* is removed from the title bar.

19 With your **2A_Sales_Analysis** workbook displayed, on the Standard toolbar, click the **Save** button [icon].

20 On the taskbar, click the **e02A_Data** button to display the workbook. From the **File** menu, click **Close**. If prompted to save the changes, click **No**.

21 On the **Clipboard** task pane, click the **Close** button [X].

Activity 2.12 Moving Cell Contents Using the Cut Command

1 Be sure that your **2A_Sales_Analysis** workbook is open, and then display the **First Qtr** worksheet. If necessary, close the task pane.

2 Click cell **E21**, and then on the Standard toolbar, click the **Cut** button [icon].

A moving border surrounds the cell that has been cut, and a copy of the contents of the cell is moved to the Clipboard. Because you are not going to collect or paste multiple items, it is not necessary to view the Clipboard. As you have seen, the most recent Clipboard item goes to the top of the Clipboard list.

3 Pause your mouse pointer over cell **F21**, right-click, and then from the displayed shortcut menu, click **Paste**.

The content of cell E21 is moved from the Clipboard to cell F21. The

Cut command removes text from one location and lets you paste it to another location. The Paste operation automatically uses the first Clipboard item. Thus, unless you need to choose some other pasted item, it is not necessary to display the Clipboard.

4 Select the range **E6:E20**. Pause the pointer over the selection, and right-click. From the displayed shortcut menu, click **Cut**.

A moving border surrounds the selection, and a copy of the cell content is moved to the top of the Clipboard list. Compare your screen with Figure 2.36.

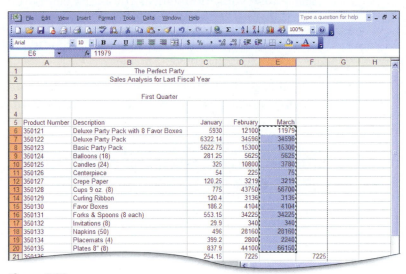

Figure 2.36

5 Select cell **F6**, hold down [Ctrl], and press [V].

[Ctrl] + [V] is the keyboard shortcut for the Paste command. The range of cells cut from E6:E21 is moved from the Clipboard and pasted into a similar range beginning in cell F6. When pasting a range of cells, it is necessary only to select the starting cell.

6 On the Standard toolbar, click **Undo** two times to restore the contents of cells **E6:E21**, and then press [Esc] to clear the moving border surrounding cell **E21**. Compare your screen with Figure 2.37.

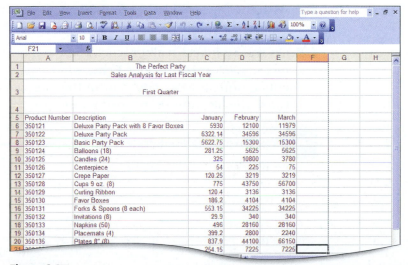

Figure 2.37

7 Click **Save** 🖫.

Activity 2.13 Moving Cell Contents Using Drag-and-Drop

The Cut command is one way to move the contents of one or more cells from one location to another. In this activity, you will use the mouse to move the contents of a cell.

1 With your **2A_Sales_Analysis** workbook open and the **First Qtr** worksheet displayed, select the range **E17:E21**.

2 Pause your mouse over the black cell border until the **move** pointer 🔀 displays, and then drag to the right until the ScreenTip displays **G17:G21**, as shown in Figure 2.38, and then release the mouse to complete the move.

Using this technique, cell contents can be moved from one location to another. This is referred to as *drag-and-drop*.

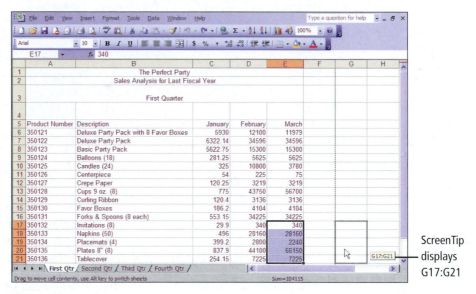

Figure 2.38

3 With the range **G17:G21** still selected, use the same technique to drag and then drop the range back to its original location, **E17:E21**.

4 On the Standard toolbar, click the **Save** button 🖫. From the **File** menu, click **Print**. Under **Print what**, click the **Entire workbook** option button. Click **OK** to print the four worksheets in the workbook. Close the file, and then close Excel.

End **You have completed Project 2A** ────────────

2B Project 2B Annual Sales

In this project, you will edit numbers from the Formatting toolbar and copy and edit formulas. You will also conduct a what-if analysis—a business technique in which you determine what will happen if you change values in one or more cells.

In Activities 2.14 through 2.25, you will edit a workbook for Angie Nguyen and Gabriela Quinones, owners of The Perfect Party, that shows the sales totals and product percentages for the previous fiscal year. The resulting workbook will look similar to Figure 2.39. You will save your workbook as *2B_Annual_Sales_ Firstname_Lastname*.

Figure 2.39

Objective 5
Format Numbers Using the Toolbar

Financial data is formatted with thousand comma separators, decimals, and dollar signs ($). By default, numbers in Excel are right-aligned in the cell and have no formats applied. To apply formats, you must either type them or use Excel features to apply them.

Dollar amounts such as sales figures are usually shown with two decimal places and commas inserted to separate values into thousands, millions, and so forth. Additionally, the first row of dollar amounts and the total row of dollar amounts usually display the dollar sign.

Activity 2.14 Formatting Cells with the Currency Style Button

The Currency Style button on the Formatting toolbar applies several cell formatting attributes in a single mouse click, including the dollar sign ($), thousand commas, separator and two decimal places to the selected cell. This is the style used for **currency** (monetary values) displayed in dollars and cents.

1 **Start** Excel. Display the **File** menu, and then click **Open**. Navigate to the student files that accompany this textbook, and then open the workbook **e02B_Annual_Sales**.

2 From the **File** menu, click **Save As**. In the displayed **Save As** dialog box, use the **Look in arrow** to navigate to the location where you are storing your projects for this chapter. In the **File name** box, type **2B_Annual_Sales_Firstname_Lastname** and press Enter.

3 Right-click the **First Qtr sheet tab**, and then click **Select All Sheets**.

4 Display the **View** menu, click **Header and Footer**, click the **Custom Footer** button, and under **Left section**, type **2B Annual Sales-Firstname Lastname** using your own first and last name.

5 Click **OK** to close the **Footer** dialog box, and then click **OK** again to close the **Page Setup** dialog box.

A dotted vertical line displays, indicating how many columns will print on the page as the page is currently set up. Do not be concerned if it appears that the columns will not fit on a single page—you will have an opportunity to adjust this before you complete the project.

6 Click the **Second Qtr sheet tab**, and then click the **First Qtr sheet** tab again.

Notice that *[Group]* no longer displays in the title bar. Displaying another worksheet automatically ungroups the sheets.

7 With the **First Qtr** worksheet displayed, select the range **C6:F6**, and then on the Formatting toolbar, click the **Currency Style** button $\boxed{\$}$.

As shown in Figure 2.40, some cells display ########, indicating that the cell is not wide enough to accommodate the newly formatted numeric data.

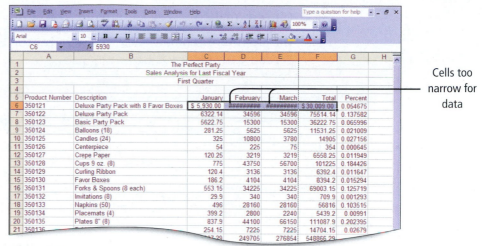

Cells too
narrow for
data

Figure 2.40

8 Select the range **C22:F22**, and then on the Formatting toolbar, click the **Currency Style** button [$].

The overall total, *$548,866.29*, is properly formatted, but the column width is not large enough to accommodate the monthly totals—they display as ##########.

9 From the **column heading area**, drag to select **columns C**, **D**, **E**, and **F**.

Recall that when multiple columns are selected, any changes you make are applied to all the selected columns.

10 In the **column heading area**, move the pointer over the vertical line that separates **columns C** and **D** until the double-headed arrow pointer displays, as shown in Figure 2.41, and then double-click.

This is the mouse shortcut to AutoFit selected columns to accommodate their longest entry. Alternatively, from the Format menu, point to Column and then click AutoFit selection. Each column now accommodates the totals with the currency format applied.

Double-headed arrow pointer

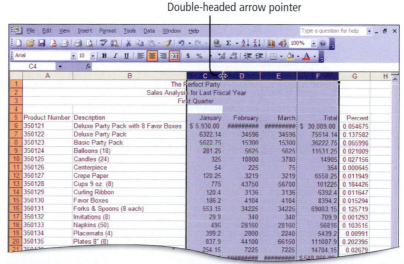

Figure 2.41

11 Click outside the selected area to cancel the selection, and then, on the Standard toolbar, click the **Save** button ⊟. Compare your screen with Figure 2.42.

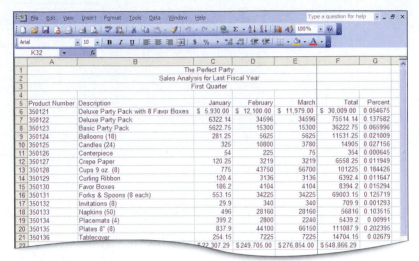

Figure 2.42

Activity 2.15 Formatting Cells with the Percent Style Button

A percentage is a part of a whole expressed in hundredths. For example, .75 is the same as 75% percent of one dollar. The Percent Style button on the Formatting toolbar formats the selected cell as a percentage rounded to the nearest hundredth.

1 Click cell **G6**, and notice the number *0.054675*.

This number is the result of dividing the value in F6 (total quarterly sales for Product Number 350121) by the total in cell F22 (total quarterly sales for all products combined). Applying the Percent Style to 0.054675 will result in 5%—0.0545675 rounded up to the nearest hundredth and expressed as a percentage.

2 With cell **G6** selected, on the Formatting toolbar, click the **Percent Style** button ⟨%⟩.

The result, 5%, indicates that 5 percent of the total sales for the first quarter of the fiscal year resulted from selling the *Deluxe Party Pack with 8 Favor Boxes* product.

3 Select the range **G7:G21**, click the **Percent Style** button ⟨%⟩ to format the remaining cells, and then click outside the selected area to cancel the selection. Compare your screen with Figure 2.43.

4 **Save** ⊟ your workbook.

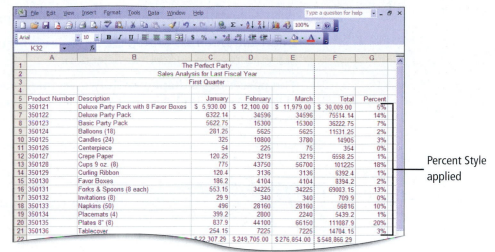

Figure 2.43

Activity 2.16 Increasing and Decreasing Decimal Places

Rounding percentages to the nearest hundredth may not offer a percentage precise enough to analyze important financial information such as sales data. For example, on your displayed worksheet, some product percentages indicate 0%. To make data more precise, Excel can add additional decimal places.

1 With your **2B_Sales_Analysis** workbook open and the **First Qtr** worksheet displayed, locate the percentages for the products in **row 11** and **row 17**.

Obviously, there were sales of these two products, but the sales were less than 1%; thus, the percentage, as currently expressed, indicates 0%.

2 Select the range **G6:G21**, and then on the Formatting toolbar, click the **Increase Decimal** button three times.

The percentages display with three decimal places, as shown in Figure 2.44. The cells that displayed 0% now contain a more meaningful value. The Increase Decimal command increases the display by one decimal position each time it is clicked.

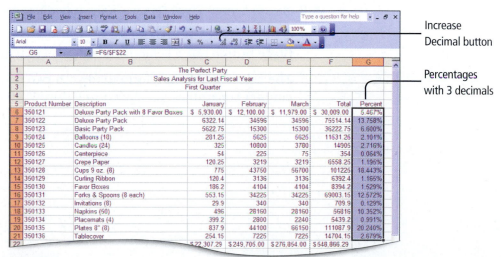

Figure 2.44

3 With cells **G6:G21** selected, on the Formatting toolbar click the **Decrease Decimal** button 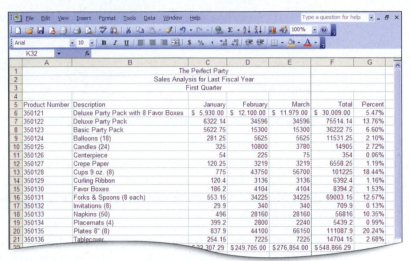 once, and then click outside the selected area to cancel the selection.

The percentages display with two decimal places. The Decrease Decimal command decreases one decimal position each time it is clicked.

4 Compare your screen with Figure 2.45. Click **Save** .

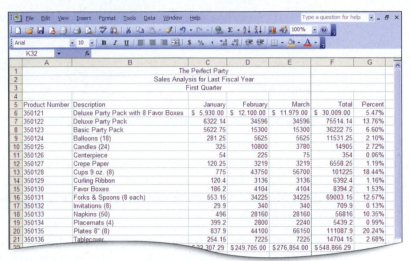

Figure 2.45

Activity 2.17 Formatting Cells with the Comma Style Button

When preparing spreadsheets with financial information, the first row of dollar amounts and the total rows of dollar amounts are formatted in the Currency Style; that is, with thousand comma separators, dollar signs, and two decimal places.

All other dollar amounts in the worksheet are usually formatted only with thousand comma separators and two decimal places. This format, referred to as **Comma Style**, is easily applied with the Comma Style button on the Formatting toolbar.

1 Be sure your **First Qtr** worksheet is displayed. Select the range **C7:F21**, and then on the Formatting toolbar, click the **Comma Style** button . Click outside the selected area to cancel the selection.

The selected cells are formatted with two decimals and thousand comma separators, as shown in Figure 2.46.

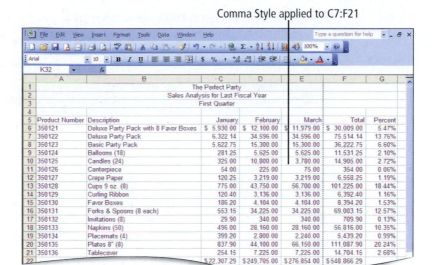

Comma Style applied to C7:F21

Figure 2.46

2 On the Standard toolbar, click the **Save** button 🖫.

Objective 6
Edit Formulas

Recall that data in a cell can be only one of two things—either a formula, which is an instruction for a mathematical calculation, or a constant value. Constant values fall into three main categories:

- Numeric values (numbers)

- Text values (text or a combination of text and numbers such as a street address)

- Date and time values

Activity 2.18 Selecting Ranges Using the AutoSum Function

Recall that AutoSum is one of many *functions*—formulas that Excel has already built for you. AutoSum is frequently used, and thus has its own button on the Standard toolbar. When you initiate the AutoSum command, Excel first looks *above* the cell to propose a group of numbers to add. In this activity, you will discover that there is additional versatility in the AutoSum function.

1 Be sure that your **2B_Annual_Sales** workbook is open. Then, click the **Second Qtr sheet tab**.

2 In cell **F5** type **Total** and in cell **G5** type **Percent**

3 Click cell **A1** and notice that this is a merged cell encompassing the range **A1:E1**.

Now that you have added two additional columns, it will be necessary to adjust the centering of the title and the two subtitles.

4 Select the range **A1:G1** as shown in Figure 2.47.

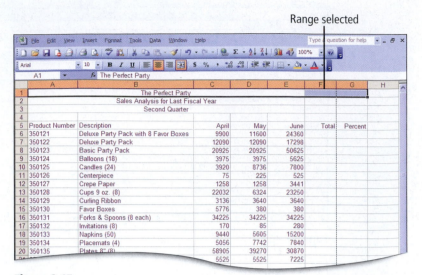

Range selected

Figure 2.47

5 On the Formatting toolbar, click the **Merge and Center** button 🔲 once.

Recall that if a cell has been merged and centered, clicking the Merge and Center button again reverses the action, as shown in Figure 2.48.

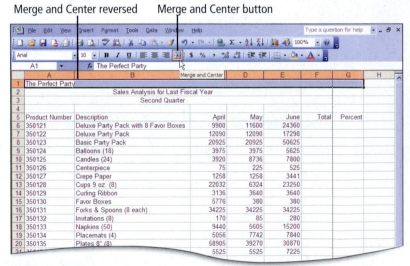

Merge and Center reversed   Merge and Center button

Figure 2.48

6 With the range still selected, click **Merge and Center** 🔲 again.

Cells A1:G1 are merged into one cell, and the text is centered in the cell.

7 Use the technique you just practiced to merge and center the subtitle *Sales Analysis for Last Fiscal Year* across the range **A2:G2**, and then repeat the process for the subtitle *Second Quarter* across the range **A3:G3**. Compare your screen with Figure 2.49.

Title and subtitles centered

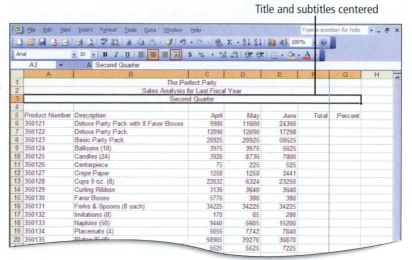

Figure 2.49

8 Click **C22** to make it the active cell, and then on the Standard toolbar, click the **AutoSum** button [Σ ▾].

A moving border surrounds the April sales numbers, as shown in Figure 2.50.

Formula in Formula Bar   AutoSum button

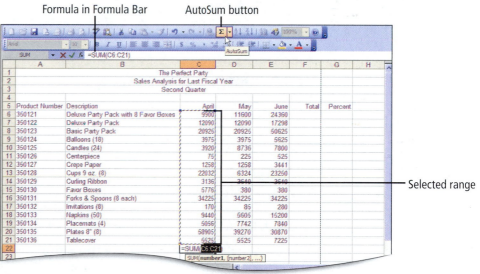

Selected range

Figure 2.50

9 Look at the Formula Bar.

The word *SUM*, the function name, indicates that Excel will add (sum) the values contained in the cells referenced in the range *(C6:C21)*. See Figure 2.50.

10 Press [Enter] to accept the formula created by AutoSum.

The sum *196408* displays in cell C22.

11 Click cell **C13**, type **483** and then press Enter.

483 displays in cell C13, and Excel recalculates the sum in cell C22 as *174859*. Recall that this is Excel's great strength. After formulas are in place, Excel recalculates the formula each time a value changes in any of the cells referenced in the formula.

12 Select the range **D6:D21**—the May sales amounts.

13 On the Standard toolbar, click the **AutoSum** button Σ▾.

The result, *161605*, displays in cell D22. This is another way that you can use AutoSum. Using this method, Excel places the formula in the first empty cell following the selected range.

14 Click cell **D22** and look at the Formula Bar.

The underlying formula, inserted by AutoSum, displays, as shown in Figure 2.51.

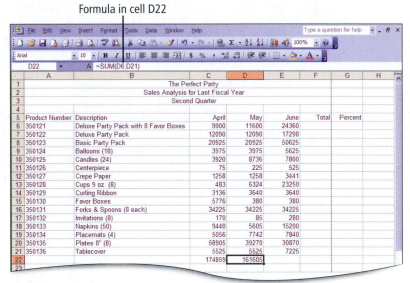

Figure 2.51

15 Click **E11**, and then press Delete to clear the value from the cell.

16 Click cell **E22**, and then on the Standard toolbar, click **AutoSum** Σ▾.

As shown in Figure 2.52, Excel selects only the range E12:E21 because E11 does not contain a value.

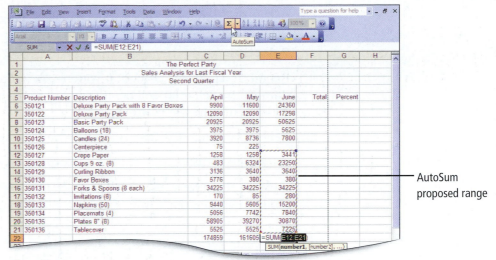

AutoSum
proposed range

Figure 2.52

17 With the moving border still displayed, drag to select the range **E6:E21**.

Excel changes the selection and displays the new range of referenced cells in the formula. Because AutoSum will not automatically include an empty cell in a range, use this method to select a range containing an empty cell. In this manner, you can still take advantage of the ease with which AutoSum creates a formula.

18 Press Enter to insert the formula and calculate the total. In cell **E11**, type **75** and press Enter again to recalculate the formula.

The result, *232134*, displays. Compare your screen with Figure 2.53.

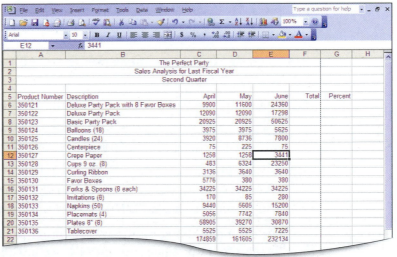

Figure 2.53

19 Select the range **C22:E22** and apply the **Currency Style** [$]. Then, display the **Format** menu, point to **Column**, and click **AutoFit Selection**.

Recall that AutoFit Selection widens the column to accommodate the data in the selected cell or, if the entire column is selected, for the widest entry in the column.

20 Select the range **C6:E6** and apply the **Currency Style** [$]. Select the range **C7:E21** and apply the **Comma Style** [,]. On the Standard toolbar, click **Save**. Click outside the selection to deselect it, and compare your screen with Figure 2.54.

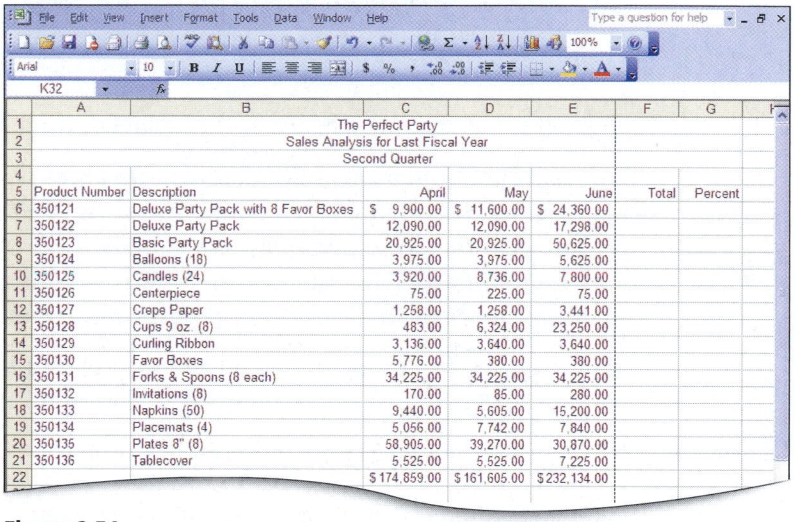

	A	B	C	D	E	F	G
1	The Perfect Party						
2	Sales Analysis for Last Fiscal Year						
3	Second Quarter						
4							
5	Product Number	Description	April	May	June	Total	Percent
6	350121	Deluxe Party Pack with 8 Favor Boxes	$ 9,900.00	$ 11,600.00	$ 24,360.00		
7	350122	Deluxe Party Pack	12,090.00	12,090.00	17,298.00		
8	350123	Basic Party Pack	20,925.00	20,925.00	50,625.00		
9	350124	Balloons (18)	3,975.00	3,975.00	5,625.00		
10	350125	Candles (24)	3,920.00	8,736.00	7,800.00		
11	350126	Centerpiece	75.00	225.00	75.00		
12	350127	Crepe Paper	1,258.00	1,258.00	3,441.00		
13	350128	Cups 9 oz. (8)	483.00	6,324.00	23,250.00		
14	350129	Curling Ribbon	3,136.00	3,640.00	3,640.00		
15	350130	Favor Boxes	5,776.00	380.00	380.00		
16	350131	Forks & Spoons (8 each)	34,225.00	34,225.00	34,225.00		
17	350132	Invitations (8)	170.00	85.00	280.00		
18	350133	Napkins (50)	9,440.00	5,605.00	15,200.00		
19	350134	Placemats (4)	5,056.00	7,742.00	7,840.00		
20	350135	Plates 8" (8)	58,905.00	39,270.00	30,870.00		
21	350136	Tablecover	5,525.00	5,525.00	7,225.00		
22			$ 174,859.00	$ 161,605.00	$ 232,134.00		

Figure 2.54

21 Click the **Third Qtr sheet tab**. In cell **F5** type **Total** and in cell **G5** type **Percent**

22 Select the range **A1:G1** and click the **Merge and Center** button two times to merge the cells and recenter the title. Repeat the process for the range **A2:G2** and for **A3:G3**.

23 In row 22, use **AutoSum** [Σ] to total the columns for each of the three months in the quarter. Select the range **C6:E6**, hold down Ctrl and select the range **C22:E22**, and then apply the **Currency Style** [$]. To make the columns wide enough to accommodate their newly formatted data, select **columns C**, **D**, and **E**, and use either the double-click method between two of the column headings, or display the Format menu to apply AutoFit Selection to the selected columns.

24 Select the range **C7:E21** and apply the **Comma Style** [,]. Click anywhere to deselect the range, and compare your screen with Figure 2.55.

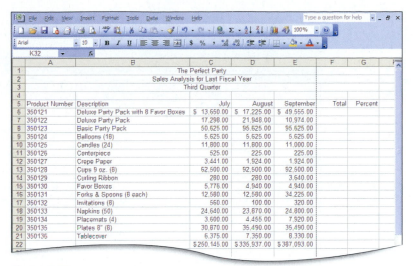

Figure 2.55

25 Select the **Fourth Qtr sheet tab**. In cell **F5** type **Total** and in cell **G5** type **Percent** and then repeat Steps 22–24. Compare your result with Figure 2.56.

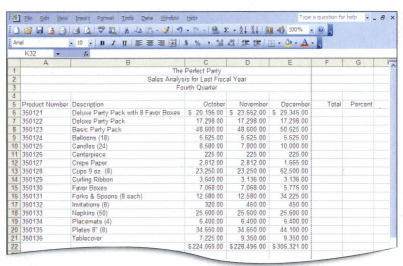

Figure 2.56

26 On the Standard toolbar, click **Save** to save your workbook.

Activity 2.19 Editing Within the Formula Bar

1 In your **2B_Annual_Sales** workbook, display the **Second Qtr** worksheet.

2 Click cell **F6**, click the **AutoSum** button , and compare your screen with Figure 2.57.

Recall that AutoSum first looks above the selected cell, and then, if no values are present, looks to the left for a proposed range of values to sum.

AutoSum proposed range

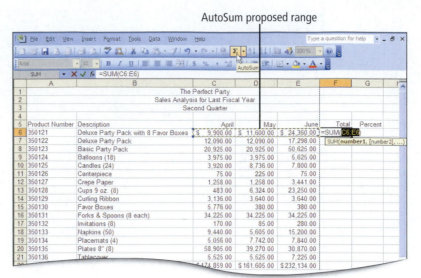

Figure 2.57

3 Press Enter.

The total, *$45,860.00*, displays in cell F6 and is formatted in the Currency Style. Recall that if adjacent cells have formatting applied, the next three cells to the right will have the same formatting applied.

4 Select cell **F6**. On the Formula Bar, position the **I-beam** pointer ⌶ between *C* and *6*, and then double-click to select the cell reference **C6**. Point to cell **D6**, as shown in Figure 2.58.

C6 selected in Formula Bar   Point to cell D6

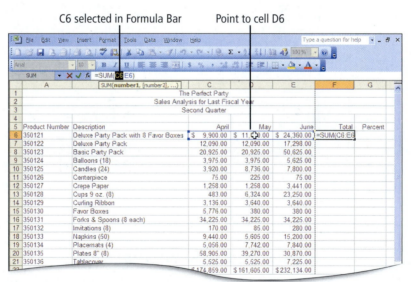

Figure 2.58

5 Click once to border cells **D6:E6** in blue, and then press Enter to accept this change to the formula. In cell **F6**, locate the small green triangle in the upper left corner, as shown in Figure 2.59.

The green triangle is the ***Trace Error*** smart tag, which indicates a potential error in a formula.

Green triangle in cell

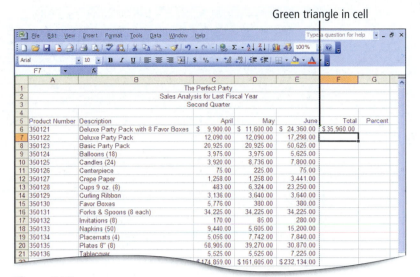

Figure 2.59

6 Select cell **F6** and then point to the displayed **Trace Error** button, as shown in Figure 2.60.

The ScreenTip indicates *The formula in this cell refers to a range that has additional numbers adjacent to it.* This is Excel's method for alerting you that, logically, it would appear that you want to total all three cells.

Trace Error button

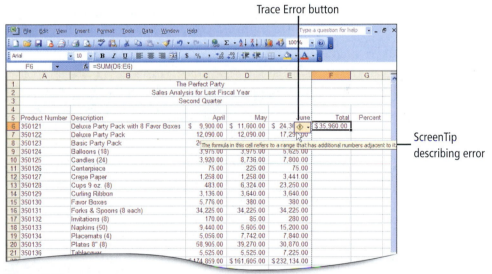

ScreenTip describing error

Figure 2.60

7 On the displayed button, click the **arrow** to display the list of options, as shown in Figure 2.61.

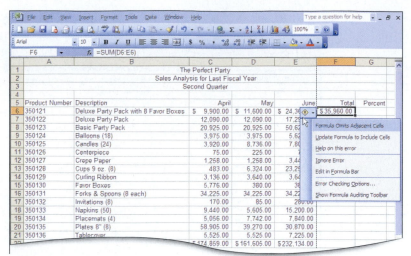

Figure 2.61

8 From the displayed menu, click **Ignore Error**, and click **Save** 💾.

The Trace Error option button and the green triangle are both removed. In this manner, you can override Excel's suggested formula.

Activity 2.20 Editing Within a Cell Using Edit Mode

1 Double-click cell **F6**.

Double-clicking a cell that contains a formula causes the result of the calculation to be replaced with the underlying formula in the cell. The Formula Bar also displays the formula for editing, as shown in Figure 2.62.

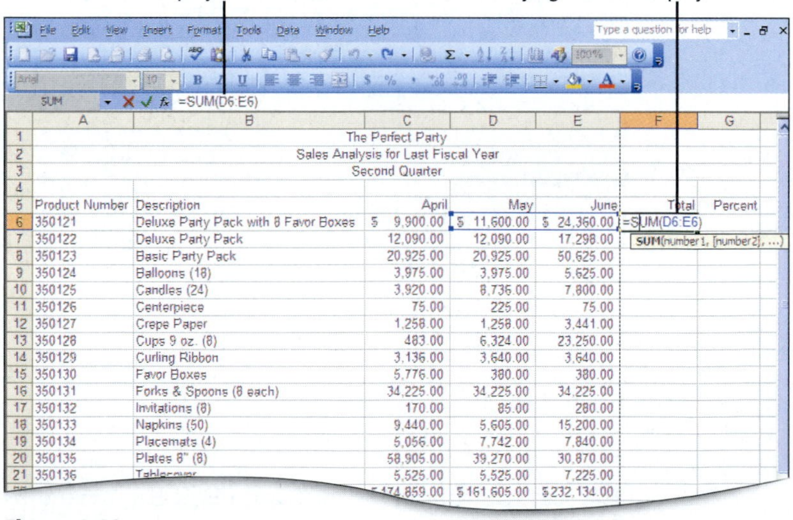

Formula displayed in Formula Bar   Underlying formula displayed in cell

Figure 2.62

2 Move your mouse pointer away from the cell so that you have a clear view. Then, click to position the insertion point within the cell to the left of *D6*, as shown in Figure 2.63.

Position insertion point here

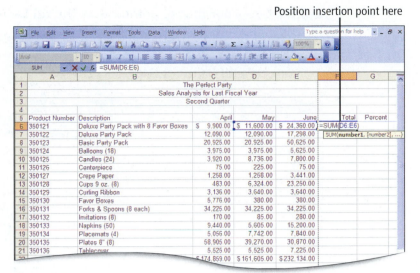

Figure 2.63

3 Press [Delete], and then type **c** so that the formula indicates *=SUM(c6:E6)*.

The cell range C6:E6 is surrounded in blue, indicating the new range in the formula. Recall that although cell references are converted to uppercase letters, it is not necessary to type uppercase letters. You can edit a formula either in the Formula Bar or directly in the cell as you have done here.

4 Press [Enter] to display the three-month total *$45,860.00* in the cell, and on the Standard toolbar, click the **Save** button [icon].

Objective 7
Copy Formulas

Excel provides a quick method to create formulas without typing them and without clicking a toolbar button. This method is known as ***copying formulas***. For example, you have a quarterly total of $45,860.00 for the product *Deluxe Party Pack with 8 Favor Boxes*. Obviously, you would like to calculate similar totals for each of the remaining products in rows 7 through 22.

When a formula is copied from one cell to another, Excel adjusts the cell references to fit the new location of the formula. This is known as a ***relative cell reference***.

Activity 2.21 Copying a Formula with Relative Cell References Using the Fill Handle

1 With your **2B_Annual_Sales** workbook open and the **Second Qtr** worksheet displayed, click cell **F6**.

You can see that in cells F7:F22, you need a formula similar to the one in F6, but one that properly refers to the cells in row 7, row 8, and so forth.

2 Position your mouse pointer over the **fill handle** in the lower right corner of cell **F6** until the pointer ⊞ displays. Then, drag downward through cell **F22** and release the left mouse button. Compare your screen with Figure 2.64.

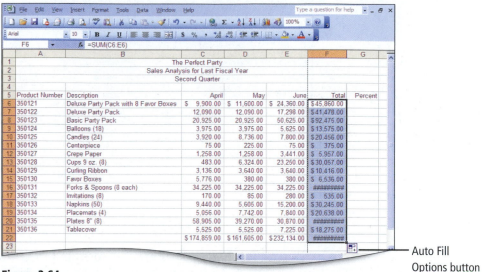

Auto Fill Options button

Figure 2.64

Totals display in the selected cells, formatted with Currency Style because the formula you copied was formatted in Currency Style. Also, several values are now too wide for the column and display ######. The Auto Fill Options button displays.

3 **Point** to the **Auto Fill Options** button, click the **arrow**, and from the displayed menu, click **Fill Without Formatting**.

All formatting is removed from the selected cells so that you can apply the formatting of your choice.

4 Select the range **F7:F21** and apply the **Comma Style** ⊡. Click cell **F22** and apply the **Currency Style** ⊡. If any cells still display #####, select column F, display the Format menu, point to Column, and then click AutoFit Selection.

5 Click cell **F7**, look at the Formula Bar, and notice the formula *=SUM(C7:E7)*. Click cell **F8**, look at the Formula Bar, and notice the formula *=SUM(C8:E8)*.

In each row, Excel copied the formula but adjusted the cell references *relative to* the row number. This is called a relative cell reference. The calculation is the same, but it is performed on the cells in that particular row. This is a quick method to insert numerous formulas into large spreadsheets.

6 Click the **Third Qtr sheet tab**.

7 Click cell **F6**. On the Standard toolbar, click **AutoSum** ⊡, and then move up to the Formula Bar and click the **Enter** button ☑.

Recall that clicking the Enter button on the Formula Bar retains the cell in which you are working as the active cell.

8 Position your pointer over the **fill handle** of cell **F6**, display the pointer ⊞, and then drag downward through cell **F22** to copy the formula to the remaining rows.

9 Point to the **Auto Fill Options** button, click the **arrow**, and from the displayed menu, click **Fill Without Formatting**.

10 Select the range **F7:F21** and apply the **Comma Style** 🔘. Click cell **F22** and apply the **Currency Style** 💲. If any cells display ######, select column F, display the Format menu, point to Column, and then click AutoFit Selection.

11 Click the **Fourth Qtr sheet tab**, repeat Steps 7–10, and then click **Save** 💾.

You can see how fast it is to insert formulas using the copy method and how helpful Excel is because it adjusts the cell references for you as you copy the formula.

More Knowledge — Copy Formulas with the Copy and Paste Command

You can also copy formulas with relative cell references using the Copy and Paste commands. Click the cell containing the first formula, and then click the Copy button. Select the range to which you want to copy formulas, and then click the Paste button. The formula will be copied and the relative cell references adjusted accordingly. Recall that the Copy and Paste commands can also be initiated from the Edit menu or with the keyboard shortcuts Ctrl + C and Ctrl + V, respectively.

Activity 2.22 Copying Formulas Containing Absolute Cell References

You have seen that a relative cell reference refers to cells by their position in relation to the cell that contains the formula. **Absolute references**, on the other hand, refer to cells by their fixed position in the worksheet, for example, the cell at the intersection of column F and row 22.

A relative cell reference automatically adjusts when a formula is copied. An absolute cell reference does *not* adjust; rather, it remains the same when the formula is copied—and there are times when you will want to do this. To make a cell reference absolute, dollar signs are inserted into the cell reference. The use of dollar signs to denote an absolute reference is not related in any way to whether or not the values you are working with are currency values. It is simply the symbol used by Excel to denote an absolute cell reference.

1 In your **2B_Annual_Sales** workbook, click the **Second Qtr sheet tab**.

2 In cell **G6** type = to begin a formula, click cell **F6** to insert its reference into the formula, type / (on your keyboard, next to the right Shift key) to insert the division operator, click cell **F22**, and then on the Formula Bar click the **Enter** button ✓.

The formula created, *=F6/F22*, indicates that the value in cell F6 will be divided by the value in cell F22. Why? Because the owners of The Perfect Party want to know the percentage by which each product contributes to total sales. Arithmetically, the percentage is computed by dividing the sales for the specific product by the total sales, and that is accomplished with this formula.

3 Be sure cell **G6** is selected. Position your pointer over the **fill handle**, and then drag down to cell **G21**.

As shown in Figure 2.65, each cell displays an error message; each cell displays a Trace Error triangle in the upper left corner, and the Auto Fill Options button displays.

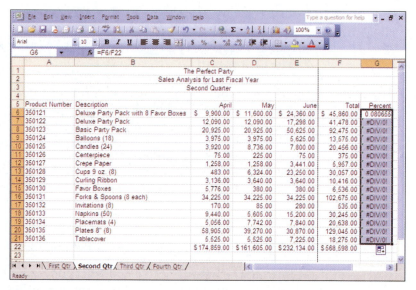

Figure 2.65

4 Click cell **G7**, and then point to the **Trace Error** button.

As shown in Figure 2.66, the ScreenTip displays *The formula or function used is dividing by zero or empty cells.*

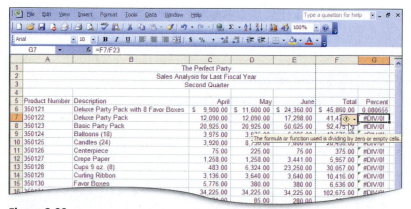

Figure 2.66

5 Look at the Formula Bar to examine the formula.

Indeed, the cell reference following the divisor operator (/) is F23, and F23 is an empty cell.

6 Click cell **G8**, and in the Formula Bar, notice the cell reference following the divisor operator is **F24**, also an empty cell.

Because the cell references are relative, Excel attempts to build the formula by increasing the row number for each equation. In this particular calculation, however, the divisor must always be the value in cell F22—the total sales.

7 Click cell **G6**. In the Formula Bar, edit the formula so that it indicates **=F6/$F$22** as shown in Figure 2.67, and then click the **Enter** button ✓ on the Formula Bar to finish editing the formula.

Enter button on Formula Bar ——

Edit formula with dollar signs ——

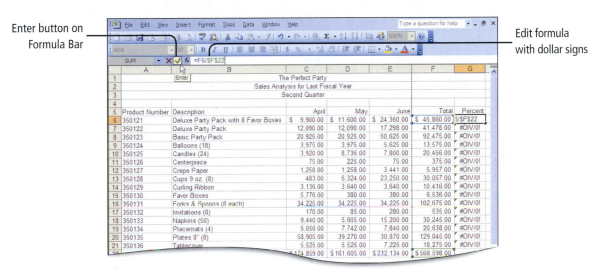

Figure 2.67

8 Using the **fill handle** in cell **G6**, copy the formula down through cell **G21**, and then compare your screen with Figure 2.68.

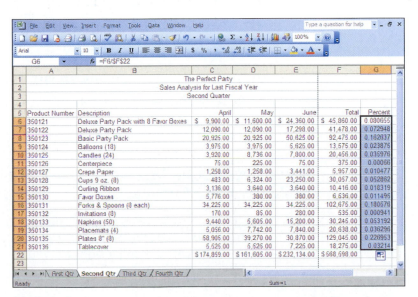

Figure 2.68

9 Click in several of the copied cells, and observe the formula in the Formula Bar. You can see that for each formula, the cell reference for the product's total sales changed relative to its row, but the value used as the divisor—total sales—the value in cell F22, remained absolute. Thus, using either relative or absolute cell references, it is easy to duplicate formulas without typing them.

10 Select the range **G6:G21**, apply the **Percent Style** ![%], and then click **Increase Decimal** ![.00] two times. Compare your screen with Figure 2.69.

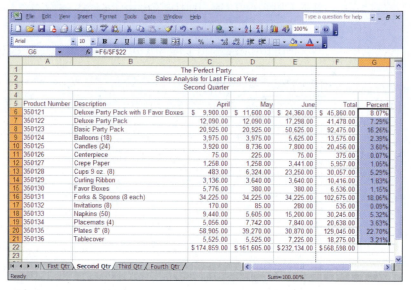

Figure 2.69

11 Click the sheet tab for **Third Qtr**.

12 Click cell **G6**, construct the formula **=F6/$F$22** and then click the **Enter** button ![✓] on the Formula Bar. Copy the formula to cells **G7:G21**. Apply the **Percent Style** ![%] to the range **G6:G21**, and then click **Increase Decimal** ![.00] two times on the selected range.

13 Repeat Step 12 above on the **Fourth Qtr** worksheet.

14 On the Standard toolbar, click **Save** ![💾] to save the changes to your workbook.

More Knowledge — Make a Cell Reference Absolute While Creating a Formula

To make a cell reference absolute while creating a formula, click to select the cell to which you want to refer, press F4, and then continue creating the formula. Excel will insert the dollar signs for you.

Objective 8
Conduct a What-if Analysis

A ***what-if analysis*** is a business management technique in which you ask *what* happens *if* something else happens. For example, the owners of The Perfect Party plan to increase their marketing efforts in the third quarter of next year for the major events that people celebrate during those months—specifically, Independence Day parties in July and the increasingly popular wedding month of September. They estimate that the increased marketing will result in a 20% increase in third quarter sales.

Activity 2.23 Conducting a What-if Analysis

1 Display the **Third Qtr** worksheet. In cell **A24**, type **Projected Third Quarter Revenue With a 20% Increase in Sales**

2 In cell **D24**, type the formula **=F22*1.20** and then compare your screen with Figure 2.70.

Cell F22 is the total sales for the third quarter just finished, the asterisk (*) represents the multiplication operator, and *1.20* represents the current total sales plus 20%.

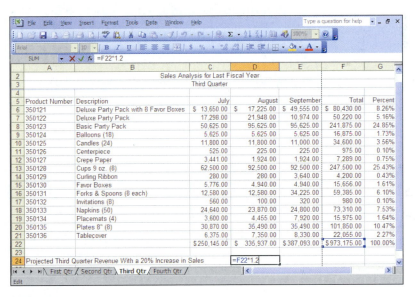

Figure 2.70

3 Press ⌷Enter⌷ to view the result.

If next year's sales for the third quarter are increased by 20% over the last year, the total sales for the quarter will be $1,167,810.

4 On the Standard toolbar, click the **Save** button ⌷🖫⌷ to save the changes you have made to your workbook.

Objective 9
Display and Print Underlying Formulas

When you have a formula in a cell, the cell displays the results of the formula. Recall that this value is called the *displayed value*. To see the actual formula—the *underlying formula*—you must activate the cell and look at the Formula Bar.

There are two ways to display all the underlying formulas in your worksheet:

- From the Tools menu, click Options, display the View tab, and select the Formulas check box.

- Press Ctrl + ` to display the formulas, and then activate the same keyboard shortcut to toggle back to the displayed values. The ` is called the *grave accent* and is located below the Esc key on most keyboards.

Activity 2.24 Displaying and Printing Underlying Formulas

1 Be sure that your **2B_Annual_Sales** workbook is open, and then click the **First Qtr sheet tab**.

2 Hold down Ctrl and press ` (below Esc). If the Formula Auditing tool bar displays, click the **close** button ☒ on the toolbar.

3 If necessary, use the horizontal scroll bar to view the formulas in **columns F** and **G**, as shown in Figure 2.71.

It is frequently useful to view the formulas in all the cells, especially if you are trying to locate an error in your worksheet.

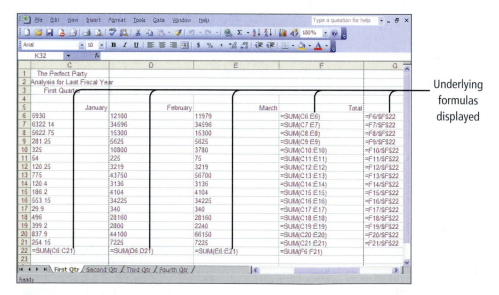

Figure 2.71

4 Hold down Ctrl and press ˋ again.

The normal view of your worksheet redisplays.

5 Click **Save** 🖫.

Objective 10
Change Page Orientation

Thus far you have printed your worksheets in *Portrait orientation*. In this orientation, the paper is taller than it is wide. Excel can also print in *Landscape orientation*, in which the paper is wider than it is tall. Landscape orientation is frequently used in Excel because worksheets tend to have numerous columns.

Activity 2.25 Changing Page Orientation

1 With your **2B_Annual_Sales** workbook open, if necessary, display the **First Qtr** worksheet.

2 Press Ctrl + Home to move to the top left corner of the worksheet. A vertical dotted line may display. If it does not, click **Print Preview** 🔍, and then close **Print Preview**.

This line indicates where the first page would end and the second page would begin if you printed your worksheet. It is likely that columns F and G would fall onto another page if printed in the current setup.

3 Right-click the **First Qtr sheet tab**, and click **Select All Sheets**.

[Group] displays in the title bar. For the purpose of changing the orientation, select all the sheets in the workbook so that you have to make the change only once.

4 From the **File** menu, click **Page Setup**.

The Page Setup dialog box displays.

5 In the displayed **Page Setup** dialog box, if necessary, click the **Page tab**. Under **Orientation**, click the **Landscape** option button. See Figure 2.72.

Page tab   Landscape option button

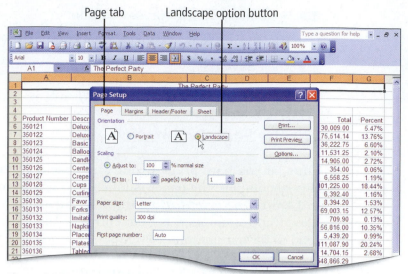

Figure 2.72

6 In the upper right corner of the **Page Setup** dialog box, click the **Print Preview** button and compare your screen with Figure 2.73.

Notice the landscape orientation. In the lower left corner, notice that there are 4 sheets. This is the result of grouping the sheets.

Landscape orientation

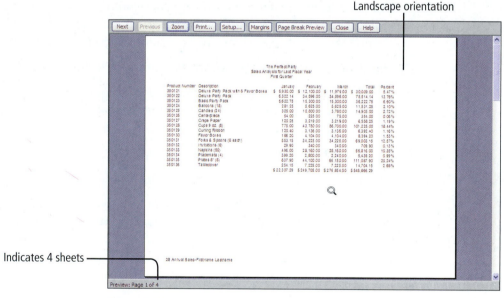

Indicates 4 sheets

Figure 2.73

7 Press PageDown as many times as necessary to view each of the four worksheets in the workbook. Then, on the Print Preview toolbar, click the **Print** button.

Because you selected all sheets, all four sheets will print, and thus it is not necessary to select the Entire Workbook option button.

8 **Save** 🖫 your workbook. Close the file and close Excel.

End **You have completed Project 2B**

Summary

With Excel, it is easy to create complex, multipage workbooks to analyze financial information such as quarterly sales. You can create formulas and copy them easily within a single spreadsheet and among spreadsheets in the same workbook. Numeric data can be formatted in a way that is meaningful to the reader. Flexibility in the layout of a spreadsheet is accomplished by controlling the size of columns, rows, and cells. Finally, Excel helps with your typing by completing a series, such as the days of the week or the months of the year.

In This Chapter You Practiced How To

- Enter Constant Values with AutoFill and the Fill Handle
- Insert, Delete, and Adjust Rows and Columns
- Align Cell Contents Horizontally
- Copy and Move Cell Contents
- Format Numbers Using the Toolbar
- Edit Formulas
- Copy Formulas
- Conduct a What-if Analysis
- Display and Print Underlying Formulas
- Change Page Orientation

Concepts Assessments

Matching   Match each term in the second column with its correct definition in the first column. Write the letter of the term on the blank line to the left of the correct definition.

_____ **1.** A cell reference with a fixed position in the worksheet that does not automatically change based on its location.

_____ **2.** The process of copying multiple pieces of data to the Office Clipboard and then pasting the data into another location.

_____ **3.** A small black box in the lower right corner of a selected cell that can be used to complete a series with AutoFill.

_____ **4.** A temporary storage area maintained by your Windows operating system where data is stored for the Cut and Paste commands.

_____ **5.** The ability to extend a series of values into adjacent cells based on the value of other cells.

_____ **6.** During the formula copying process, the automatic adjustment of cell references to fit the new location of the formula.

_____ **7.** The style of data formatted with thousand comma separators and two decimal places, but with no dollar sign.

_____ **8.** A button or other screen indication that displays when Excel recognizes certain types of data and that offers a list of commands related to the data.

_____ **9.** A page orientation in which the paper is wider than it is tall.

_____ **10.** A group of things that come one after another in succession.

_____ **11.** A set of characters with the same size and shape.

_____ **12.** A business management technique in which one asks _what_ happens _if_ something else happens.

_____ **13.** Monetary values.

_____ **14.** A small green triangle in the upper left corner of a cell that indicates a potential error in a formula.

_____ **15.** The term used to refer to data that is aligned at the left edge of a cell.

A Absolute cell reference

B AutoFill

C Collect and paste

D Comma style

E Currency

F Fill handle

G Font

H Landscape orientation

I Left-aligned

J Office Clipboard

K Relative cell reference

L Series

M Smart tag

N Trace Error

O What-if analysis

Concepts Assessments (continued)

Fill in the Blank Write the correct answers in the space provided.

1. In the formula =B6/$C$52, the absolute cell reference is

_____.

2. AutoSum is a _____, predefined by Excel, which

generates a formula.

3. Font size is measured in _____, one being equal to

$\frac{1}{72}$ of an inch.

4. A pattern of number signs (#######) displays in a cell when the data

is too _____ for the existing size of the column.

5. Using the keyboard, you can copy a selected range of cells to the

Clipboard by pressing _____.

6. Right-clicking on a column heading letter or row heading number

will display a _____.

7. In the series JAN, APR. . . the next month in the series is

_____.

8. Data aligned at the right edge of a cell is said to be

_____.

9. The _____ Style button is used to format the numbers

in a cell to display commas, two decimal places, and a dollar sign.

10. The ☐ key is called the _____ accent.

Project 2C—Bonuses

Objectives: *Enter Constant Values with Autofill and the Fill Handle; Insert, Delete, and Adjust Rows and Columns; Align Cell Contents Horizontally; and Format Numbers Using the Toolbar.*

In the following Skill Assessment, you will edit a workbook for the owners of The Perfect Party that tracks monthly sales and the bonuses paid on monthly sales to sales associates. Bonuses are paid at the end of each year. Your completed workbook will look similar to the one shown in Figure 2.74. You will save the workbook as *2C_Bonuses_Firstname_Lastname.*

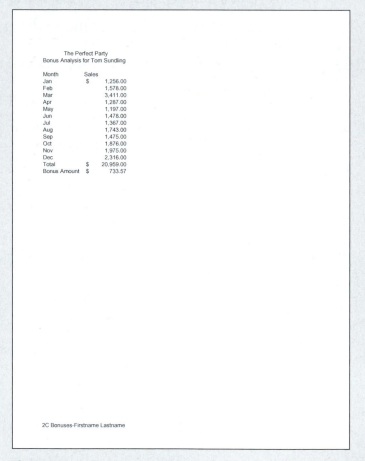

The Perfect Party
Bonus Analysis for Tom Sundling

Month	Sales	
Jan	$	1,256.00
Feb		1,578.00
Mar		3,411.00
Apr		1,287.00
May		1,197.00
Jun		1,478.00
Jul		1,367.00
Aug		1,743.00
Sep		1,475.00
Oct		1,876.00
Nov		1,975.00
Dec		2,316.00
Total	$	20,959.00
Bonus Amount	$	733.57

2C Bonuses-Firstname Lastname

Figure 2.74

1. Start Excel. On the **File** menu, click **Open**. In the **Open** dialog box, navigate to the student files that accompany this textbook, and open the file **e02C_Bonuses**. Display the **View** menu, click **Header and Footer**, and then click the **Custom Footer** button. In the **Left section** type **2C Bonuses-Firstname Lastname** and then click OK to close the dialog boxes.

(Project 2C–Bonuses continues on the next page)

(Project 2C–Bonuses continued)

2. From the **File** menu, click **Save As**. In the **Save As** dialog box, navigate to the location where you are storing your projects for this chapter. In the **File name** box, type **2C_Bonuses_Firstname_Lastname** and then click **Save** or press ⏎Enter.

3. Click cell **A5**, type **Jan** and press ⏎Enter. Select cell **A5** again, point to the **fill handle**, and then drag downward through cell **A16** to create a series containing the months from Jan through Dec. In cell **A17**, type **Total** and in cell **A18**, type **Bonus Amount**

4. Click cell **A18**, display the **Format** menu, point to **Column**, and then click **AutoFit Selection**. Rename Sheet1 as **Bonus**

5. Select **column B**, point to the vertical line between **columns B** and **C** to display the double-headed arrow pointer, and then drag to the right until the width of the column is **105 pixels**. Select the range **A1:B1** and then click the **Merge and Center** button.

6. Click cell **B17**, on the Standard toolbar click **AutoSum**, and then press ⏎Enter to accept the formula and display the total, *20959*.

7. Click cell **B5**, hold down Ctrl and click cell B17, and then apply **Currency Style**. Select the range **B6:B16** and apply **Comma Style**.

8. The total sales generated by Mr. Sundling for the year is $20,959. Sales associates are paid a bonus of 3.5% of total annual sales. Click cell **B18** and enter the formula **=B17*.035** to multiply the total in cell B17 by the bonus rate of 3.5%. The bonus will be $733.57. Cell B18 displays Currency Style formatting because the referenced cell used Currency Style.

9. On the Standard toolbar, click **Save** to save the changes you have made to your workbook. Then, on the Standard toolbar, click the **Print Preview** button to view your worksheet. On the Print Preview toolbar, click the **Print** button.

10. Close your file, and close Excel.

 You have completed Project 2C ————————————

Project 2D — Expense Report

Objectives: *Enter Constant Values with AutoFill and the Fill Handle; Insert, Delete, and Adjust Rows and Columns; Align Cell Contents Horizontally; Format Numbers Using the Toolbar; Edit Formulas; Copy Formulas; and Change Page Orientation.*

In the following Skill Assessment, you will edit a workbook that details business travel expenses for the owners of The Perfect Party. Your completed workbook will look similar to the one shown in Figure 2.75. You will save the workbook as *2D_Expense_Report_Firstname_Lastname.*

The Perfect Party
Weekly Expense Report

Traveler	Gabriela Quinones
Report Date	5/21/2005
Destination	Boston
Purpose of Trip	Meet with new vendor

	Monday 5/19/2005	Tuesday 5/20/2005	Wednesday 5/21/2005	Thursday 5/22/2005	Friday 5/23/2005	Saturday 5/24/2005	Sunday 5/25/2005	Total
Airfare			$ 369.00					$ 369.00
Hotel					289.72			289.72
Breakfast				12.95	15.56			28.51
Lunch				17.50				17.50
Dinner			37.85	42.95				80.80
Bus								-
Train								-
Taxi			20.00	10.00	20.00			50.00
Gratuity								-
Auto Rental								-
Gasoline								-
Parking					60.00			60.00
Telephone & Fax								-
Tolls								-
Other								-
Total	$ -	$ -	$ 426.85	$ 83.40	$ 385.28	$ -	$ -	$ 895.53

2D Expense Report-Firstname Lastname

Figure 2.75

1. Start Excel. On the **File** menu, click **Open**. In the **Open** dialog box, navigate to the student files that accompany this textbook, and then open the file **e02D_Expense_Report**. Display the **View** menu, click **Header and Footer**, and then click the **Custom Footer** button. In the **Left section**, type **2D Expense Report-Firstname Lastname** and then click **OK** to close the dialog boxes.

2. From the **File** menu, click **Save As**. In the **Save As** dialog box, navigate to the location where you are storing your projects for this chapter. In the **File name** box, type **2D_Expense_Report_Firstname_Lastname** and then click **Save** or press ⏎ Enter.

(**Project 2D**–Expense Report continues on the next page)

(Project 2D–Expense Report continued)

3. Click cell **B8**, type **Monday** and press Enter. Select cell **B8** again, and then using the fill handle, drag to the right to create a series containing the days of the week from Monday through Sunday. Click cell **I8**, type **Total** and then rename Sheet1 as **Expense Report**

4. Select the range **A1:I1**, and then on the Formatting toolbar, click **Merge and Center**. Merge and center the range **A2:I2**.

5. Right-click the **row 8 heading**, and on the displayed shortcut menu, click **Insert** to insert a blank row. Select **row 9**, and on the Formatting toolbar, click the **Align Right** button.

6. Select **columns B** through **I**. Position the mouse pointer between any two of the selected column headings until the double-headed pointer displays, and then drag right until the ScreenTip indicates **80 pixels**. This will increase the width of all the selected columns to 80 pixels.

7. Right-click the **row 10 heading**, and then on the displayed shortcut menu, click **Insert**. Point to the displayed **Insert Options** button, click the **arrow** to display the menu, and then click **Format Same As Above**. In your newly created **row 10**, you will enter dates, and they will be right-aligned, the same as the row above.

8. Position your pointer in the column heading area between **columns A** and **B** until the double-headed arrow displays, and then double-click. The width of column A adjusts to accommodate its longest entry.

9. Select the range **B11:I11**, and then on the Formatting toolbar, click the **Currency Style** button. Select the range **B27:I27** and click the **Currency Style** button. Values in this row will be formatted with the Currency Style. Select the range **B12:I26**, and on the Formatting toolbar, click the **Comma Style** button.

10. Click cell **B27**, on the Standard toolbar click the **AutoSum** button, and then select the range **B11:B25** to select the cell references for the formula. Press Enter. Recall that to include empty cells in an AutoSum formula, you must manually select the cells. In cell B27, only the dollar sign and a small line display because there are no values in the range to sum.

11. Click cell **B27**, and then drag the fill handle to the right through cell **I27** to copy the formula. For the days that have expenses reported, totals display. For the days that have no expenses reported, only the dollar sign and a small line display. Recall that because the cell references are relative, Excel adjusts the cell references relative to their location in the worksheet.

(Project 2D–Expense Report continues on the next page)

(Project 2D–Expense Report continued)

12. Click cell **I11**, click the **AutoSum** button, and then select the range **B11:H11** to select the cell references to be included in the formula. This technique will include the empty cells of B11 and C11 in the formula. Press Enter. The total Airfare for the week, $369.00, displays in cell I11.

13. Select cell **I11**, and then from the **Edit** menu, click **Copy**. Select the range **I12:I25** and then, from the **Edit** menu, click **Paste**. The formula in I11 is copied to the selected range of cells, and the relative cell references are changed to fit the receiving cells. Because the copied formula was formatted with Currency Style, the resulting formulas also retain the Currency Style. With the range **I12:I25** still selected, click the **Comma Style** button.

14. Press Ctrl + Home to return to cell **A1**. On the Standard toolbar, click the **Spelling** button, and correct any spelling errors. (Hint: You should discover three misspelled words. Click Ignore All to Ignore proper names.) On the Standard toolbar, click **Save** to save your work.

15. In cells **B4:B7** enter the following values regarding this two-day trip Gabriela Quinones made to Boston:

Traveler	**Gabriela Quinones**
Report Date	**5/21/2005**
Destination	**Boston**
Purpose of Trip	**Meet with new vendor**

16. In cell **B10**, type **5/19/2005** and press Enter. Select cell **B10** again, and then using the fill handle, drag to the right through cell **H10** to extend the dates in the series.

In **row 27**, the totals display the Trace Error smart tags (green triangles) that indicate a potential formula error. These appear because not all the cells contain values; in this instance, that is acceptable because Gabriela did not travel on all days, and she did not incur every type of expense allowable on any of the days. Thus, the worksheet will contain blank cells.

17. Click anywhere to cancel the selection in row 10. In cell **I27**, verify that Gabriela spent a total of $895.53 on this trip.

18. On the Standard toolbar, click the **Save** button. If you see the vertical dotted line on your screen, this indicates that, as currently set up, the entire worksheet will not print on one page. From the **File** menu, click **Page Setup**. On the **Page tab**, click the **Landscape** option button, and then click **OK**. The vertical dotted line moves to the right, indicating that all the columns will now print on one page.

(Project 2D–Expense Report continues on the next page)

(Project 2D–Expense Report continued)

19. On the Standard toolbar, click the **Print Preview** button, visually check your worksheet, and then, on the Print Preview toolbar, click **Print**.

20. Close the file, saving any changes, and then close Excel.

 You have completed Project 2D

Project 2E — Profit Loss

Objectives: *Insert, Delete, and Adjust Rows and Columns; Align Cell Contents Horizontally; Format Numbers Using the Toolbar; Edit Formulas; and Copy Formulas.*

In the following Skill Assessment, you will edit a workbook that contains a Profit & Loss Statement for The Perfect Party for the month of June. Your completed workbook will look similar to the one shown in Figure 2.76. You will save the workbook as *2E_Profit_Loss_Firstname_Lastname.*

The Perfect Party
Profit & Loss Statement for June

Ordinary Income/Expense		% of Total Income
Income		
Bridal Shower theme	61,164.45	38.94%
Luau theme	63,816.03	40.63%
All Others	32,075.16	20.42%
Total Income	**$ 157,055.64**	
Cost of Goods Sold		
Raw Materials	65,330.63	
Packaging Materials	12,089.36	
Shipping Boxes	1,516.00	
Total COGS	**$ 78,935.99**	
Gross Profit	**$ 78,119.65**	
Expenses		
Automobile	967.66	
Bad debt	33.99	
Bank Service Charges	47.50	
Freight & Delivery	1,239.60	
Insurance	4,050.00	
Interest Expense	651.77	
Job Expenses	12,925.07	
Payroll Expenses	23,880.19	
Professional Fees	250.00	
Rent	2,400.00	
Repairs	220.00	
Tools and Machinery	1,160.00	
Utilities	439.64	
Total Expenses	**$ 48,265.42**	
Net Ordinary Income	**$ 29,854.23**	
Other Income/Expense		
Other Income	593.42	
Rebates Received	975.92	
Interest Income	237.50	
Total Other Income	**$ 1,806.84**	
Net Income	**$ 31,661.07**	

2E Profit Loss-Firstname Lastname

Figure 2.76

(Project 2E–Profit Loss continues on the next page)

(Project 2E–Profit Loss continued)

1. Start Excel. On the **File** menu, click **Open**. In the **Open** dialog box, navigate to the student files that accompany this textbook, and then open the file **e02E_Profit_Loss**. Display the **View** menu, click **Header and Footer**, and then click the **Custom Footer** button. In the **Left section**, type **2E Profit Loss-Firstname Lastname** and then click **OK** to close the dialog boxes.

2. From the **File** menu, click **Save As**. In the **Save As** dialog box, navigate to the location where you are storing your projects for this chapter. In the **File name** box, type **2E_Profit_Loss_Firstname_ Lastname** and then click **Save** or press Enter.

3. Click cell **A2**. Move your pointer to the Formula Bar, click to position the insertion point following the word *Statement*, edit as necessary to add **for June** and then press Enter. Rename Sheet1 to **P&L for June**

4. Select the range **A1:C1**, and then, on the Formatting toolbar, click the **Merge and Center** button. Select the range **A2:C2** and click **Merge and Center**. Select **column B**, and then, on the Formatting toolbar, click the **Comma Style** button.

5. In cell B9 you will add the three items that make up Total Income. Click cell **B9**, on the Standard toolbar, click the **AutoSum** button, and then press Enter to display a Total Income of *157,055.64*.

6. In cell B15 you will add the three items that make up the Cost of Goods Sold. Click **B15**, click **AutoSum**, and then press Enter to display Total COGS (Cost Of Goods Sold) of *78,935.99*.

7. The accounting formula for calculating Gross Profit is *TOTAL INCOME MINUS COST OF GOODS SOLD*.

   Click cell **B17** and type **=** to begin a formula. Click cell **B9** to enter the cell reference using the point-and-click method, type **–** (the subtraction operator), click cell **B15** to insert the cell reference, and then press Enter. The Gross Profit is *78,119.65*.

8. In cell **B33**, use **AutoSum** to add the items that make up Total Expenses. The Total Expenses are *48,265.42*.

9. The accounting formula for calculating Net Ordinary Income is *GROSS PROFIT MINUS TOTAL EXPENSES*.

   In cell **B35**, construct a formula that calculates the value in cell B17 (Gross Profit) minus the value in cell B33 (Total Expenses). The Net Ordinary Income should be 29,854.23. If necessary, edit your formula to get the correct result.

10. In cell **B41**, use **AutoSum** to add the three items that make up Total Other Income. Your result should be *1,806.84*.

(Project 2E–Profit Loss continues on the next page)

(Project 2E–Profit Loss continued)

11. The accounting formula for calculating Net Income is *NET ORDINARY INCOME PLUS TOTAL OTHER INCOME.*

In cell **B43**, construct a formula to calculate Net Income. Your result should be 31,661.07. Click **Save**.

12. In **column B**, apply the **Currency Style** to all the cells that are gray. (Hint: Hold down Ctrl to select all the nonadjacent cells.) Widen the column by selecting the column and then applying the **AutoFit Selection** command from the **Format** menu.

13. The Luau and Bridal Shower themes are big sellers in June, and Angie and Gabriela want to compute the percentage of their Total Income that comes from these two party packages. In cell **C6**, type **=b6/b9** and press Enter. Apply the **Percent Style** to the result, and click **Increase Decimal** two times. Almost 39% of income in June was derived from the Bridal Shower theme packages.

14. Click cell **C6** again. In the Formula Bar, position the I-beam pointer over *B9*, and double-click. The entire Formula Bar from *B9* on will be selected. Press F4. Recall that this is a keyboard shortcut for making a cell an absolute reference by inserting dollar signs. On the Formula Bar, click the **Enter** button, and then use the fill handle to copy this formula to cells **C7** and **C8**. Cell C7 will contain 40.63%. Cell C8 will contain 20.42%.

15. Press Ctrl + Home to move to cell **A1**. On the Standard toolbar, click the **Spelling** button, and correct any spelling errors in the worksheet. (Hint: There are two spelling errors.) Click **Save**.

16. On the Standard toolbar, click the **Print Preview** button, visually check your worksheet, and then on the Print Preview toolbar, click **Print**.

17. Close the file, saving any changes, and then close Excel.

End **You have completed Project 2E** ———————————————

Project 2F — Product Inventory

Objectives: *Align Cell Contents Horizontally; Copy and Move Cell Contents; Format Numbers Using the Toolbar; and Copy Formulas.*

At the end of each month, the owners of The Perfect Party count the number of products on hand to determine what to order for next month. In the following Performance Assessment, you will create a new workbook to display the results of this physical inventory. Your completed workbook will look similar to the one shown in Figure 2.77. You will save the workbook as *2F_Product_Inventory_Firstname_Lastname*.

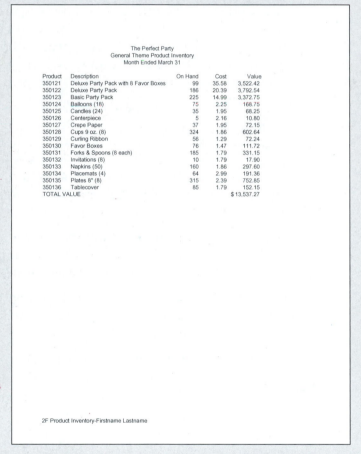

The Perfect Party
General Theme Product Inventory
Month Ended March 31

Product	Description	On Hand	Cost	Value
350121	Deluxe Party Pack with 8 Favor Boxes	99	35.58	3,522.42
350122	Deluxe Party Pack	186	20.39	3,792.54
350123	Basic Party Pack	225	14.99	3,372.75
350124	Balloons (18)	75	2.25	168.75
350125	Candles (24)	35	1.95	68.25
350126	Centerpiece	5	2.16	10.80
350127	Crepe Paper	37	1.95	72.15
350128	Cups 9 oz. (8)	324	1.86	602.64
350129	Curling Ribbon	56	1.29	72.24
350130	Favor Boxes	76	1.47	111.72
350131	Forks & Spoons (8 each)	185	1.79	331.15
350132	Invitations (8)	10	1.79	17.90
350133	Napkins (50)	160	1.86	297.60
350134	Placemats (4)	64	2.99	191.36
350135	Plates 8" (8)	315	2.39	752.85
350136	Tablecover	85	1.79	152.15
TOTAL VALUE				$ 13,537.27

2F Product Inventory-Firstname Lastname

Figure 2.77

1. Start Excel and display a new, blank workbook. Display the **View** menu, click **Header and Footer**, and then click the **Custom Footer** button. In the **Left section**, type **2F Product Inventory-Firstname Lastname** and then click **OK** to close the dialog boxes.

2. From the **File** menu, click **Save As**. In the **Save As** dialog box, navigate to the location where you are storing your projects for this chapter. In the **File name** box, type **2F_Product_Inventory_Firstname_ Lastname** and then click **Save** or press Enter.

(Project 2F–Product Inventory continues on the next page)

(Project 2F–Product Inventory continued)

3. Rename Sheet1 to **March Inventory** and then, in cells **A1** through **A3**, enter the following titles:

The Perfect Party
General Theme Product Inventory
Month Ended March 31

4. On the **File** menu, click **Open**. Navigate to the student files that accompany this textbook, click to select the file **e02F_Data**, and then click **Open**.

5. Click cell **A1**, hold down Shift, and then click cell **B17**. On the Standard toolbar, click the **Copy** button to copy the product numbers and descriptions to the Office Clipboard.

6. On the taskbar, click the button to return to your **2F_Product_ Inventory** workbook. Click cell **A5**, and then on the Standard toolbar, click the **Paste** button. Excel pastes the range of cells, beginning with the selected destination cell.

7. Change the width of **column B** to fit all the entries in column B. Merge and Center each of the three titles in **A1** through **A3** across **columns A:E**.

8. In cell **C5**, type **On Hand** in cell **D5**, type **Cost** and in cell **E5**, type **Value**

9. From the taskbar, return to the **e02F_Data** workbook. From the **Edit** menu, click **Office Clipboard**. If the Clipboard is not empty, at the top of the **Clipboard** task pane, click the **Clear All** button.

10. Select the range **C2:C17**, pause the pointer over the selection, right-click to display the shortcut menu, and then click **Copy**. The selection is copied to the Office Clipboard.

11. Select the range **D2:D17**, and copy the range to the Office Clipboard. From the **File** menu, click **Close**. The **e02F_Data** workbook closes, your 2F_Product_Inventory workbook displays, and the **Office Clipboard** task pane remains open.

12. Click cell **C6**. Point to the first item on the Clipboard, which begins *99 186*, and click to paste the selection into column C. Click cell **D6**, point to the **Clipboard**, and paste the second selection, which begins *35.38 20.39*. Close the task pane.

13. Using the Align Right command, align the column titles in **C5:E5**.

14. In cell **E6**, construct a formula to multiply the number On Hand (C6) by the Cost per item (D6). Then, using the fill handle, copy the formula in cell **E6** through cell **E21**.

15. In cell **E22**, using **AutoSum**, create a formula to add the total value of all products, and then apply the **Currency Style** to cell **E22**. Widen the column if necessary. The total value is $13,537.27. Select the range **E6:E21**, and apply the comma style.

(Project 2F–Product Inventory continues on the next page)

(Project 2F–Product Inventory continued)

> **16.** In cell **A22**, type **TOTAL VALUE** and then save your workbook. Click the **Print Preview** button to view the worksheet page. Print your worksheet. Close the workbook and close Excel.

 You have completed Project 2F ——————————————

Project 2G—Profit Analysis

Objectives: *Enter Constant Values with AutoFill and the Fill Handle; Insert, Delete, and Adjust Rows and Columns; Align Cell Contents Horizontally; Copy and Move Cell Contents; Format Numbers Using the Toolbar; Edit Formulas; Copy Formulas; and Display and Print Underlying Formulas.*

At the end of each quarter, the owners of The Perfect Party analyze profit by product. In the following Performance Assessment, you will complete a workbook that calculates the total profit for the quarter for each of the products in one theme. Your completed workbook will look similar to the one shown in Figure 2.78. You will save the workbook as *2G_Profit_Analysis_Firstname_Lastname.*

The Perfect Party
Profit Analysis for First Quarter

Product	Qty Sold	Cost	Selling Price	Profit Per Unit
350121	1,724	35.58	59.30	23.72
350122	1,764	20.39	33.99	13.60
350123	2,602	14.99	24.99	10.00
350124	878	2.25	3.75	1.50
350125	1,139	1.95	3.25	1.30
350126	190	2.16	3.60	1.44
350127	609	1.95	3.25	1.30
350128	2,623	1.86	3.10	1.24
350129	639	1.29	2.15	0.86
350130	825	1.47	2.45	0.98
350131	1,986	1.79	2.99	1.20
350132	249	1.79	2.99	1.20
350133	1,759	1.86	3.10	1.24
350134	900	2.99	4.99	2.00
350135	2,453	2.39	3.99	1.60
350136	1,028	1.79	2.99	1.20
	21,368			

2G Profit Analysis-Firstname Lastname

Figure 2.78

(Project 2G–Profit Analysis continues on the next page)

(Project 2G–Profit Analysis to Contacts continued)

1. Start Excel. On the **File** menu, click **Open**. In the **Open** dialog box, navigate to the student files that accompany this textbook, and open the file **e02G_Profit_Analysis**. Display the **View** menu, click **Header and Footer**, and then click the **Custom Footer** button. In the **Left section**, type **2G Profit Analysis-Firstname Lastname** and then click **OK** to close the dialog boxes.

2. From the **File** menu, click **Save As**. In the **Save As** dialog box, navigate to the location where you are storing your projects for this chapter. In the **File name** box, type **2G_Profit_Analysis_Firstname_ Lastname** and then click **Save** or press Enter.

3. Click cell **B4**, and then in the Formula Bar, edit as necessary to include the word **Sold** after *Qty*. Rename Sheet1 as **Profit Analysis** and then **Merge and Center** the title and subtitle in **row 1** and **row 2** across **columns A:E**.

4. In **row 4**, right-align the titles in **columns B4:E4**, and then set the width of **columns B:E** to **90 pixels**.

5. Click cell **A2**, press F2 to activate Edit mode. Edit as necessary so that the subtitle is **Profit Analysis for First Quarter** Edit cell **E4** to indicate **Profit Per Unit** and edit cell **D4** to indicate **Selling Price** Adjust the column width of columns D and E if necessary.

6. The accounting formula for calculating Profit Per Unit is SELLING PRICE MINUS COST.

   In cell **E5**, enter a formula to calculate the profit per unit of **Product 350121**. The result should be *23.72*.

7. Using the fill handle, copy the formula in cell **E5** down through cell **E20**. Select the range **C5:E20**, and apply the **Comma Style**.

8. In cell **B21**, using **AutoSum**, create a formula to sum the total number of items sold. Your result should be *21368*.

9. Select the range **B5:B21**, apply the **Comma Style**, and then click **Decrease Decimal** two times. Because these are products and not monetary values, it is not necessary to display two decimal places.

10. Press Ctrl + ` to display the underlying formulas. On the Standard toolbar, click the **Print Preview** button. Notice that there are two pages. Displaying formulas usually makes the workbook wider. Click the **Print** button. Two pages will print. Close Print Preview, and then press Ctrl + ` to return to the normal view of your workbook.

11. Save your workbook, and then click the **Print Preview** button to view the worksheet page. Print your worksheet, close the file, and close Excel.

End You have completed Project 2G

Project 2H — Sales Tax

Objectives: *Insert, Delete, and Adjust Rows and Columns; Align Cell Contents Horizontally; Format Numbers Using the Toolbar; Edit Formulas; Copy Formulas; Conduct a What-if Analysis; and Display and Print Underlying Formulas.*

In the following Performance Assessment, you will complete a workbook that calculates the total sales tax due for each of the products in one theme. Your completed workbook will look similar to the one shown in Figure 2.79. You will save the workbook as *2H_Sales_Tax_Firstname_Lastname.*

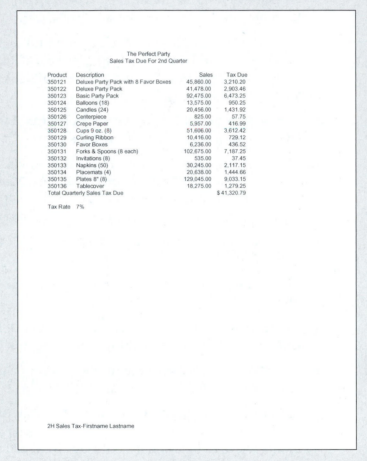

The Perfect Party
Sales Tax Due For 2nd Quarter

Product	Description	Sales	Tax Due
350121	Deluxe Party Pack with 8 Favor Boxes	45,860.00	3,210.20
350122	Deluxe Party Pack	41,478.00	2,903.46
350123	Basic Party Pack	92,475.00	6,473.25
350124	Balloons (18)	13,575.00	950.25
350125	Candles (24)	20,456.00	1,431.92
350126	Centerpiece	825.00	57.75
350127	Crepe Paper	5,957.00	416.99
350128	Cups 9 oz. (8)	51,606.00	3,612.42
350129	Curling Ribbon	10,416.00	729.12
350130	Favor Boxes	6,236.00	436.52
350131	Forks & Spoons (8 each)	102,675.00	7,187.25
350132	Invitations (8)	535.00	37.45
350133	Napkins (50)	30,245.00	2,117.15
350134	Placemats (4)	20,638.00	1,444.66
350135	Plates 8" (8)	129,045.00	9,033.15
350136	Tablecover	18,275.00	1,279.25
Total Quarterly Sales Tax Due			$ 41,320.79

Tax Rate 7%

2H Sales Tax-Firstname Lastname

Figure 2.79

1. Start Excel. On the **File** menu, click **Open**. In the **Open** dialog box, navigate to the student files that accompany this textbook, and open the file **e02H_Sales_Tax**. Display the **View** menu, click **Header and Footer**, and then click the **Custom Footer** button. In the **Left section**, type **2H Sales Tax-Firstname Lastname** and then click **OK** to close the dialog boxes.

2. From the **File** menu, click **Save As**. In the **Save As** dialog box, navigate to the location where you are storing your projects for this chapter. In the **File name** box, type **2H_Sales_Tax_Firstname_Lastname** and then click **Save** or press Enter.

(Project 2H–Sales Tax continues on the next page)

(Project 2H–Sales Tax continued)

3. Select **rows 1**, **2**, and **3**. From the **Insert** menu, click **Rows**. Excel inserts as many new rows as you selected—three. In cell **A1**, type **The Perfect Party** and in cell **A2**, type **Sales Tax Due for 2nd Quarter** Click cell **A21**, and type **Total Quarterly Sales Tax Due** Rename Sheet1 as **2nd Quarter**

4. Select **column B**, display the **Format** menu, point to **Column**, and then click **AutoFit Selection**. **Merge and Center** the titles in **row 1** and **row 2** across columns **A:D**.

5. In cell **B22**, type **.07** as the sales tax rate. Select **B22**, click the **Align Left** button, and apply the **Percent Style**. Insert a blank row above **row 22**, moving the Tax Rate down to **row 23**. Select the range **C5:C20**, and apply the **Comma Style**.

6. For each item, the sales tax due will be calculated by multiplying the Sales amount in column C by the tax rate in cell B23. Thus, the formula will require a relative cell reference for sales and an absolute cell reference for the tax rate, which is fixed in cell B23. In cell **D5**, construct the formula to multiply cell **C5** by cell **B23**. Edit as necessary to make cell **B23** an absolute cell reference. The sales tax amount for the first product should be *3,210.20*.

7. Copy the formula down through cell **D20**. With the range **D5:D20** selected, click **AutoSum**, and then widen the column as necessary. To cell **D21**, apply the **Currency Style**. The total sales tax due is $41,341.79.

8. Double-click cell **C14**, and edit as necessary to change the value to **6236.00** The new calculated tax for Favor Boxes is *436.52*.

9. To find out what would happen if the sales tax rate changed from 7% to 8%, click cell **B23**, and in the Formula Bar, edit as necessary to change the number to 8%, and then press Enter. The tax rate displays as 8% and the new tax due amount is *$47,223.76*.

10. Change the tax rate back to 7%. Your result is $41,320.79.

11. Press Ctrl + ` to view the underlying formulas, and then use the same keyboard shortcut to return to normal view. Save your workbook, and then click the **Print Preview** button to view the worksheet page. Print the worksheet, and then close the file and close Excel.

End **You have completed Project 2H**

Project 2I — Open Invoices

Objectives: *Enter Constant Values with AutoFill and the Fill Handle; Insert, Delete, and Adjust Rows and Columns; Align Cell Contents Horizontally; Format Numbers Using the Toolbar; and Copy Formulas.*

Most customers of The Perfect Party pay when their orders are received. A few larger customers have open accounts, and it is necessary to track how much they owe. In the following Mastery Assessment, you will complete a workbook that lists all open invoices. Your completed workbook will look similar to the one shown in Figure 2.80. You will save the workbook as *2I_Open_Invoices_Firstname_Lastname*.

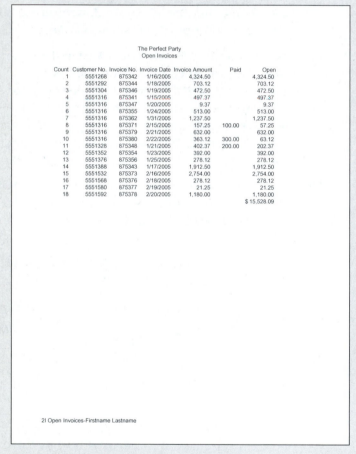

Count	Customer No.	Invoice No.	Invoice Date	Invoice Amount	Paid	Open
			The Perfect Party			
			Open Invoices			
1	5551268	875342	1/16/2005	4,324.50		4,324.50
2	5551292	875344	1/18/2005	703.12		703.12
3	5551304	875346	1/19/2005	472.50		472.50
4	5551316	875341	1/15/2005	497.37		497.37
5	5551316	875347	1/20/2005	9.37		9.37
6	5551316	875355	1/24/2005	513.00		513.00
7	5551316	875362	1/31/2005	1,237.50		1,237.50
8	5551316	875371	2/15/2005	157.25	100.00	57.25
9	5551316	875379	2/21/2005	632.00		632.00
10	5551316	875380	2/22/2005	363.12	300.00	63.12
11	5551328	875348	1/21/2005	402.37	200.00	202.37
12	5551352	875354	1/23/2005	392.00		392.00
13	5551376	875356	1/25/2005	278.12		278.12
14	5551388	875343	1/17/2005	1,912.50		1,912.50
15	5551532	875373	2/16/2005	2,754.00		2,754.00
16	5551568	875376	2/18/2005	278.12		278.12
17	5551580	875377	2/19/2005	21.25		21.25
18	5551592	875378	2/20/2005	1,180.00		1,180.00
						$ 15,528.09

2I Open Invoices-Firstname Lastname

Figure 2.80

1. Start Excel. On the **File** menu, click **Open**. In the **Open** dialog box, navigate to the student files that accompany this textbook, and open the file **e02I_Open_Invoices**. Display the **View** menu, click **Header and Footer**, and then click the **Custom Footer** button. In the **Left section**, type 2I Open Invoices-Firstname Lastname and then click **OK** to close the dialog boxes.

(Project 2I–Open Invoices continues on the next page)

(Project 2I–Open Invoices continued)

2. From the **File** menu, click **Save As**. In the **Save As** dialog box, navigate to the location where you are storing your projects for this chapter. In the **File name** box, type **2I_Open_Invoices_Firstname_Lastname** and then click **Save** or press Enter.

3. Rename Sheet1 as **Open Invoices** Select **rows 1** through **4**, display the **Insert** menu, and then click **Rows** to insert four empty rows above row 1. In cell **A1**, type **The Perfect Party** and in cell **A2**, type **Open Invoices** In cells **A4** through **D4**, type the following column headings:

   Customer No.
   Invoice No.
   Invoice Date
   Invoice Amount

4. Merge and center the title and subtitle in **row 1** and **row 2** across **columns A:F**. Select **Columns A:D** and then, using either the **Format** menu or the double-click method, AutoFit to set the width to display the longest entry in each column. In cell **E4**, type **Paid** and then, in cell **F4**, type **Open** Select the range **A4:F4** and right-align.

5. Select the range **D5:F25** and apply **Comma Style**. Enter the following paid amounts, being careful to locate the correct invoice number. The invoice numbers are not in numerical order.

Invoice No.	Amount Paid
875348	**200.00**
875349	**87.50**
875370	**9.37**
875371	**100.00**
875375	**722.00**
875380	**300.00**

6. The accounting formula to calculate the Open amount is INVOICE AMOUNT MINUS PAID.

   In cell **F5**, create a formula to calculate the amount Open, also referred to as the open balance. For some customers, the invoice amount has been paid in full; thus, some customers will have no open balance.

7. Using the fill handle, copy the formula in cell **F5** down through cell **F25**. With the range **F5:F25** still selected, click **AutoSum** to calculate the total in the empty cell following the range. Widen the column as necessary, and apply **Currency Style** to cell **F26**. The total Open amount is $15,528.09.

8. Hold down Ctrl and then select each row that shows no open amount. (Hint: There are three rows with no open amount.) With the three rows selected, display the **Edit** menu, and then click **Delete**. Click anywhere to cancel the selection.

(Project 2I–Open Invoices continues on the next page)

(Project 2I–Open Invoices continued)

9. Select **column A**, and then insert a new column to the left of **column A**. Adjust the two titles in **rows 1–2** to **Merge and Center**, starting with the new column A. Type **Count** in cell **A4**, and then type **1** in cell **A5**. Using AutoFill, select cell **A5**, and drag the fill handle down through cell **A22**. On the **Auto Fill Options** button, click the **arrow** to display the menu, and then click **Fill Series**. This will assign a sequential number to each invoice entry by creating a series in **A5:A21**. See Figure 2.80. This is an easy way to determine the number of invoices that are open.

10. Save your workbook, view it in Print Preview, and then print it. Close the file, and then close Excel.

 You have completed Project 2I

Project 2J—Product Order

Objectives: *Enter Constant Values with AutoFill and the Fill Handle; Insert, Delete, and Adjust Rows and Columns; Align Cell Contents Horizontally; Copy and Move Cell Contents; Format Numbers Using the Toolbar; Copy Formulas; and Conduct a What-if Analysis.*

In the following Mastery Assessment, you will edit a workbook that lists all products in the general theme category, the current inventory levels, and average monthly sales by quantity. You will calculate a quantity to order for each product. Your completed workbook will look similar to the one shown in Figure 2.81. You will save the workbook as *2J_Product_Order_Firstname_Lastname*.

1. Start Excel. On the **File** menu, click **Open**. In the **Open** dialog box, navigate to the student files that accompany this textbook, and open the file **e02J_Product_Order**.

2. Right-click the **Sheet1 tab**, and then click **Select All Sheets**. Display the **View** menu, click **Header and Footer**, and then click the **Custom Footer** button. In the **Left section**, type **2J Product Order-Firstname Lastname** and then click **OK** to close the dialog boxes. Right-click the **Sheet 1 tab**, and click **Ungroup Sheets**.

3. From the **File** menu, click **Save As**. In the **Save As** dialog box, navigate to the location where you are storing your projects for this chapter. In the **File name** box, type **2J_Product_Order_Firstname_Lastname** and then click **Save** or press Enter.

4. Select **rows 1–3**, display the **Insert** menu, and then click **Rows** to insert three new blank rows. In cell **A1**, type **The Perfect Party** and in cell **A2**, type **Product Order Report** Rename Sheet1 to **Order** and then **Merge and Center** the titles in **rows 1 and 2** across **columns A:E**.

(Project 2J–Product Order continues on the next page)

(Project 2J–Product Order continued)

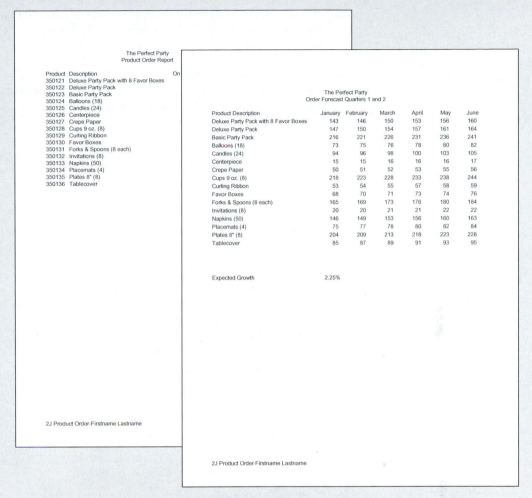

The Perfect Party
Product Order Report

Product	Description	On
350121	Deluxe Party Pack with 8 Favor Boxes	
350122	Deluxe Party Pack	
350123	Basic Party Pack	
350124	Balloons (18)	
350125	Candles (24)	
350126	Centerpiece	
350127	Crepe Paper	
350128	Cups 9 oz. (8)	
350129	Curling Ribbon	
350130	Favor Boxes	
350131	Forks & Spoons (8 each)	
350132	Invitations (8)	
350133	Napkins (50)	
350134	Placemats (4)	
350135	Plates 8" (8)	
350136	Tablecover	

2J Product Order-Firstname Lastname

The Perfect Party
Order Forecast Quarters 1 and 2

Product Description	January	February	March	April	May	June
Deluxe Party Pack with 8 Favor Boxes	143	146	150	153	156	160
Deluxe Party Pack	147	150	154	157	161	164
Basic Party Pack	216	221	226	231	236	241
Balloons (18)	73	75	76	78	80	82
Candles (24)	94	96	98	100	103	105
Centerpiece	15	15	16	16	16	17
Crepe Paper	50	51	52	53	55	56
Cups 9 oz. (8)	218	223	228	233	238	244
Curling Ribbon	53	54	55	57	58	59
Favor Boxes	68	70	71	73	74	76
Forks & Spoons (8 each)	165	169	173	176	180	184
Invitations (8)	20	20	21	21	22	22
Napkins (50)	146	149	153	156	160	163
Placemats (4)	75	77	78	80	82	84
Plates 8" (8)	204	209	213	218	223	228
Tablecover	85	87	89	91	93	95

Expected Growth	2.25%

2J Product Order-Firstname Lastname

Figure 2.81

5. Select **columns A:B** and AutoFit the width to display the longest entry in each column. Select **columns C:E**, adjust the width to **60 pixels** wide, and then click the **Align Right** button so that all cells in these columns will be right-aligned.

6. Column D contains the average quantity sold of each product number, each month. The owners like to maintain a two-month average supply of products. In cell **E5**, create a formula to calculate the quantity that should be ordered to maintain a two-month supply, taking into account the number currently on hand. (Hint: Average multiplied by 2 months minus On Hand.) Recall that the **Average column** contains the average monthly sales quantities. The Order quantity for the first product should be *214*.

7. Using the fill handle, copy the formula in cell **E5** down through the remaining rows. Select the range **C5:E20**, apply **Comma Style**, and then click **Decrease Decimal** two times. Click anywhere to cancel the selection, and then, on the Standard toolbar, click **Save**.

(Project 2J–Product Order continues on the next page)

(Project 2J–Product Order continued)

8. Select **Sheet2**, and then rename the sheet as **Forecast** Display the **Order** sheet, copy the title in cell **A1**, and paste it to cell **A1** on the **Forecast** sheet.

9. In cell **A2** of the **Forecast** sheet, type **Order Forecast Quarters 1 and 2** In cell **A4** of the **Forecast** sheet, type **Product Description** Display the **Order** sheet, copy the range **B5:B20**, and then return to the **Forecast** sheet.

10. On the **Forecast** sheet, click cell **A5**, and then click the **Paste** button. Adjust **column A** on the **Forecast** sheet so that it is wide enough to accommodate the longest product description.

11. On the **Forecast** sheet, change the height of **rows 5 through 20** to **20** pixels. This taller row size will make it easier to view the entries in each row.

12. Beginning in cell **B4** on the Forecast sheet, create a series of month names for the first and second quarters, beginning with January and ending with June, and then apply right alignment to the month names.

13. Display the **Order** sheet. Copy the range **D5:D20**, display the **Forecast** sheet, and paste the range beginning in cell **B5** under *January*.

14. **Merge and Center** the two titles on the **Forecast** sheet across all the active columns. Select the range **B5:G20** and apply **Comma Style**. Decrease the number of decimals showing to none.

15. The expected growth per month is expressed as a percentage. In cell **A25**, type **Expected Growth** Then, in cell **B25**, type **.0156** and format it as a percentage with two decimals.

16. Sales of products in February are expected to grow by 1.56% over January sales. Likewise, March sales are expected to grow 1.56% over February sales, and so forth through June. Create a formula in cell **C5** to compute the February forecast for the first product. The result, *145*, is the January usage plus the increase.

17. Copy the formula down for all products. With the range selected, copy the entire range across all months through June. The June total for *Tablecover* should be *92*.

18. Conduct a what-if analysis by proposing a growth percentage of 2.25% rather than 1.56%. On the Standard toolbar, click **Save**.

19. Right-click the **Forecast sheet tab**, and then click **Select All Sheets**. Click the **Print Preview** button to view the two worksheet pages (use [PageDown] to view the second sheet). On the Print Preview toolbar, click the **Print** button. Because you have selected all sheets, both sheets will print. Close the file and close Excel.

End **You have completed Project 2J**

Problem Solving

Project 2K — Sales Forecast

Objectives: *Enter Constant Values with AutoFill and the Fill Handle; Conduct a What-if Analysis; Insert, Delete, and Adjust Rows and Columns; Edit Formulas; and Copy Formulas.*

Using the data found in *e2K_Data*, create a workbook that computes a sales forecast for the next year assuming an increase in sales of 5 percent. List each month from January through December with a total forecast for each month and for the year. Include a footer with your first and last name. Select a company name of your choice, and create appropriate worksheet titles. Place the percentage in an assumption area below column A in your workbook. Save the workbook as *2K_Sales_Forecast_Firstname_Lastname*.

End **You have completed Project 2K** ——————————————

Project 2L — Gross Payroll

Objectives: *Enter Constant Values with AutoFill and the Fill Handle; Conduct a What-if Analysis; Insert, Delete, and Adjust Rows and Columns; Edit Formulas; and Copy Formulas.*

Create a weekly payroll report for The Perfect Party. The owners, Angie Nguyen and Gabriela Quinones, receive an annual salary of $40,000 each, paid weekly. The other employees, Tom Sundling, Corey Finstad, and Christina Stevens, each receive $20 per hour. Create a workbook that will enable the owners to enter the number of hours worked in one week for each of the hourly employees. Include formulas that will calculate the total gross pay for each employee, including the owners. The total gross payroll amount should also be displayed. Include a footer that contains your first and last name. Create appropriate worksheet titles. Save the workbook as *2L_Gross_Payroll_Firstname_Lastname*.

End **You have completed Project 2L** ——————————————

On the Internet

Excel Help on the Web

Microsoft is not the only source for additional information about Excel. Using Internet Explorer, type **Excel absolute cell reference** in the address bar, and press Enter.

MSN Search finds over 9,000 sites that refer to those search words. Review a few of those pages to see whether you can pick up some new information about using cell references in Excel. You might also want to try the same search in your favorite search engine to see whether you can find additional information on the Web.

Using Excel Help

In this exercise, you will use Microsoft Help to get help with absolute cell references.

1. If necessary, start Excel to open a new workbook.

2. At the right edge of the menu bar, click in the *Type a question for help* box, type **absolute reference** and then press the Enter key.

   The task pane opens, showing Search Results. Notice that you typed *absolute reference* as the question instead of *What is an absolute reference?* It is not actually necessary to ask the question *as* a question.

3. Click the link **Switch between relative**, **absolute**, **and mixed references**.

   A Microsoft Excel Help window displays with Help for the topic.

4. In the upper right corner of the Help window, click **Show All**.

   Detailed descriptions of the terms included on the help screen are displayed. Alternatively, you can click on the individual links associated with each term to display them as needed.

5. Review the information provided in the Help window.

6. Print the contents of the Help window with the expanded material.

7. Close the Help Window, and close the task pane.

3 chapterthree

Formatting a Worksheet

In this chapter, you will: complete these projects and practice these skills.

Project 3A **Format Numbers and Cells**	**Objectives** • Change Number Format • Change Alignment of Cell Contents • Apply Cell Formatting

Project 3B **Apply Workbook Formatting**	**Objective** • Apply Workbook Formatting

Project 3C **Print Gridlines and Insert Comments**	**Objectives** • Print Gridlines, Print Row and Column Headings, and Set Print Quality • View and Insert Comments in a Cell

Oceana Palm Grill

Oceana Palm Grill is a chain of 25 upscale, casual, full-service restaurants based in Austin, Texas. The company opened its first restaurant in 1975 and now operates 25 outlets in the Austin and Dallas areas. Plans call for 15 additional restaurants to be opened in North Carolina and Florida by 2008. These ambitious plans will require the company to bring in new investors, develop new menus and recruit new employees, all while adhering to the company's strict quality guidelines and maintaining its reputation for excellent service.

© Getty Images, Inc.

Formatting a Worksheet

In this chapter, you will learn how to change the format of numbers and decimals. You will change the alignment of text and numbers, indent text, rotate text, wrap text, and merge cells. You will change the appearance of cells by changing fonts and font size and by creating cell borders and shading. Additionally, you will format your worksheet for printing by creating headers and footers and changing the placement of your worksheet on the printed page.

Project 3A **Tableware**

In this project, you will use various methods to format numbers and the appearance of cells. Cell formatting includes adding color or patterns to a cell. You will also practice how to change the horizontal and vertical alignment of data in a cell.

In Activities 3.1 through 3.14, you will edit a workbook for Donna Rohan Kurian, Executive Chef for the Oceana Palm Grill, detailing tableware purchases for the Dallas location. Your workbook will look similar to Figure 3.1. You will save the workbook as *3A_Tableware_Firstname_ Lastname.*

Tableware Purchases, Dallas Location							
Item	Jan	Feb	Mar	Apr	May	Jun	Total
Linen table covers*	$1,050	$350	$200	$567	$450	$359	$2,976
Plates							
8 inch	170	65	85	75	123	60	$578
12 inch	77	125	243	189	150	150	$934
Coffee mugs	125	157	120	145	155	235	$937
Espresso cups	245	85	125	150	258	245	$1,108
Seafood Salad shells	90	432	130	155	260	255	$1,322
Silverware	1,245	865	350	160	262	265	$3,147
Baskets and Candles, Salt, Pepper, Butter	150	125	125	225	75	125	$825
Total	$2,102	$1,854	$1,178	$1,099	$1,283	$1,335	$8,851

*Order only in white or cream

3A Tableware-Firstname Lastname

Figure 3.1
Project 3A—Tableware

Objective 1
Change Number Format

Excel's power lies in its ability to perform calculations on numbers. Because there are many ways to write numbers—think of percentages, fractions, money—Excel has a variety of ways to help you enter numbers so that you get the results you want. Excel refers to the various ways to write numbers as **number formats**.

Activity 3.1 Using the Format Cells Dialog Box to Format Numbers

Formatting is the process of determining the appearance of cells and the overall layout of a worksheet. Formatting of cells is accomplished through the Format Cells dialog box. Additionally, the Formatting toolbar has some buttons that provide a one-click method of performing commonly used cell formatting without displaying the Format Cells dialog box.

Once applied, cell formats stay with the cell, even if you delete the contents of the cell. To delete the format from a cell, you must purposely clear the format using either the Clear Formats command or the Clear All command from the Edit menu.

The table in Figure 3.2 details the many ways Excel can format numbers for you.

Excel Number Formats

Number Format	Description
General	The General format is the default format for a number that you type in a cell. The General format displays a number exactly as you type it—with three exceptions:
	1. Extremely long numbers may be abbreviated to a shorthand version of numbers called scientific notation, and long decimal values may be rounded up. Even if this happens, Excel will still use the underlying value, not the displayed value, in any calculations.
	2. Trailing zeros will not display in the General format. For example, if you type the number *456.0* the cell will display 456 with no zero or decimal point.
	3. A decimal fraction entered without a number to the left of the decimal point will display with a zero. For example, if you type *.456* you will see 0.456 displayed in the cell.
Number	Number format is used for the general display of noncurrency numbers. The default format has two decimal places, and you may choose to check the option for using a comma as a thousand separator. Negative numbers can display in red, be preceded by a minus sign, be enclosed in parentheses, or display both in red and in parentheses.
Currency	Currency format is used for general monetary values, and you can select from a list of worldwide currency symbols—the U.S. dollar sign is the default symbol. When you click the Currency Style button on the Formatting toolbar, you apply a two-decimal-place Accounting format.
Accounting	Accounting format is similar to Currency format with two differences—the dollar sign (or other currency symbol) always displays at the left edge of the cell, rather than flush against the first number. Thus, both dollar signs and numbers are vertically aligned in the same column. Also, Accounting formats add a blank space equal to the width of a close parenthesis on the right side of positive values to ensure that decimal points align if a column has both positive and negative numbers.
Date	Date format provides many common ways to display dates. The default format in the Format Cells dialog box is month, day, and year, separated by a slash. The year displays as four digits by default, but may be changed in the Control Panel to a four-digit display.
Time	Time format provides many common ways to display time. The default format in the Format Cells dialog box is the hour and minute.
Percentage	Percentage format multiplies the cell value by 100 and displays the result with a percent sign. The default is two decimal places.
Fraction	Fraction format displays fractional amounts as actual fractions rather than as decimal values. The first three formats use single-digit, double-digit, and triple-digit numerators and denominators. For example, the single-digit format rounds up to the nearest value that can be represented as a single-digit fraction.
Scientific	Scientific format displays numbers in scientific (exponential) notation. This is useful for extremely large numbers.
Text	Text format treats a number as if it were text. The number is left-aligned like text.
Special	Special formats are used primarily with database functions. You can type postal codes, telephone numbers, and taxpayer ID numbers quickly without having to enter the punctuation.
Custom	Custom format is used to create your own number format. For example, perhaps your organization has a special format for invoice numbers.

Figure 3.2

1 Start Excel. On the **File** menu, click **Open**. In the **Open** dialog box, navigate to the student files that accompany this textbook, and open the file **e03A_Tableware**. Display the **View** menu, click **Header and Footer**, and then click the **Custom Footer** button. In the **Left section**, using your own name, type **3A Tableware-Firstname Lastname** and then click **OK** to close the dialog boxes.

2 From the **File** menu, click **Save As**. In the **Save As** dialog box, navigate to the location where you are storing your projects for this chapter, creating a new Chapter 3 folder if you want to do so. In the **File name** box, type **3A_Tableware_Firstname_Lastname** and then click **Save** or press Enter.

3 Click the **Format Cells Practice sheet tab**.

4 In cell **A1** type **52350** and press Enter. Click cell **A1** again to make it the active cell.

The default format for numbers is no commas, no decimal points, and aligned at the right boundary of the cell.

5 Display the **Format** menu, and then click **Cells**. If necessary, click the **Number tab**.

The Format Cells dialog box displays, as shown in Figure 3.3. Under Category, all of Excel's Number formats are listed. The first format, General, is highlighted. The **General format** is the default format for a number that you type in a cell. Unless you apply a different number format to a cell, Excel will use the General format. The General format displays a number exactly as you type it—with three exceptions, as noted in the table in Figure 3.2.

Format Cells dialog box ———

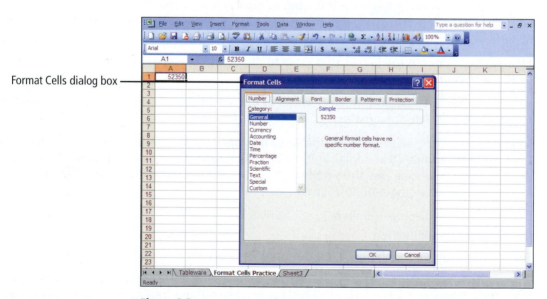

Figure 3.3

6 In the **Format Cells** dialog box, under **Category**, click **Number**, and then look at the right side of the dialog box under **Sample**.

Assuming the selected cell contains numbers, the Format Cells dialog box *Sample area* will always show you how the format will look with the numbers you have typed into the cell. The default number of decimal places for the Number format is two decimal places.

7 In the middle of the dialog box, click to select (place a check mark in) the **Use 1000 Separator (,)** check box, and then look again at the **Sample** area.

Excel demonstrates how your number will look if you apply this format.

8 In the **Decimal places** box, click once on the **up arrow** in the spin box to change the number of decimal places to **3**. Look at the **Sample** area to see the effect that three decimal places will have on your cell.

Note

A spin box enables you to move through a set of fixed values. A spin box is found in many dialog boxes throughout Windows-based applications. You can also type a valid value in the box if you prefer.

9 At the lower right corner of the dialog box, click the **Cancel** button to close the dialog box and reject any of the number formats that you examined.

Another Way ─── **Display the Format Cells Dialog Box**

There are three ways to display the Format Cells dialog box:

- From the menu bar, click Format, and then click Cells.

- Use the keyboard shortcut by holding down Ctrl and pressing 1 on the alphanumeric keyboard.

- Select a range of cells, right-click to display a shortcut menu, and then click Format Cells.

10 With **A1** as the active cell, press and hold down Ctrl and then press 1 at the top left of your keyboard.

The Format Cells dialog box displays. This is the keyboard shortcut for displaying the Format Cells dialog box. You cannot use the numeric keypad for this keyboard shortcut.

11 In the displayed **Format Cells** dialog box, under **Category**, click **Currency**, and then observe the **Sample** area. Click **Accounting** and observe the **Sample** area.

The Currency and Accounting formats always include the thousand comma separator where necessary. These two number formats are similar—there is only a slight difference in the way dollar signs are aligned and the way negative numbers are formatted. In the **Currency format**, the dollar sign is always flush against the first number. In the **Accounting format**, the dollar sign is always flush with the left cell boundary. See the examples shown in Figure 3.4.

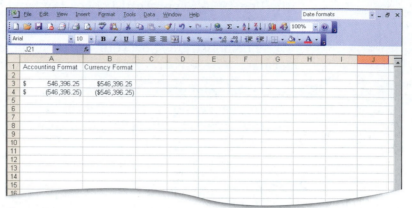

Figure 3.4

12 Under **Category**, click **Percentage**. At the bottom of the dialog box, read how percentage formats are handled and displayed. Then, at the lower right corner of the dialog box, click the **Cancel** button.

13 With cell **A1** as the active cell, press ⌈Delete⌋ to delete the contents of the cell.

More Knowledge

When you click the Comma Style button on the Formatting toolbar, Excel applies a two-decimal place Accounting format *without* currency symbols. When you click the Percent Style button on the Formatting toolbar, Excel applies a Percentage format *without* decimals.

Activity 3.2 Selecting and Applying the Currency Format

1 Click the **Tableware sheet tab**. Select the range **B3:H3**. Press and hold down ⌈Ctrl⌋ and select the range **B12:H12**. Recall that this is the technique to select nonadjacent ranges. With the two ranges selected, display the **Format** menu, and then click **Cells**.

2 If necessary, click the **Number tab**, and then, under **Category**, click **Currency**. Click the **Symbol arrow** to display the list of symbols, and from the displayed list, click **$**. In the **Decimal places** spin box, click the **down arrow** twice to set **0** decimal places. Click **OK**.

Recall that it is common practice to include the dollar sign ($) symbol in the first line of a worksheet and in the Total line of a worksheet. When you add totals to row 12, they will display with this format.

3 Select the range **B4:H11**, and then right-click to display the shortcut menu, as shown in Figure 3.5.

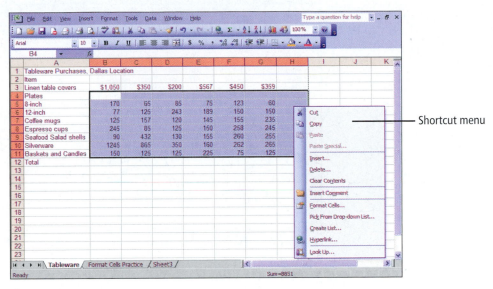

Shortcut menu

Figure 3.5

4 On the displayed shortcut menu, click **Format Cells**.

This is another way to display the Format Cells dialog box.

5 If necessary, click the **Number tab**. Under **Category**, click **Currency**. In the **Decimal places** box, click the **spin box arrows** as necessary to set **0** decimal places. Click the **Symbol arrow** and click **None**. Click **OK**. Click anywhere to cancel the selection.

The Currency format automatically includes the thousand comma separator where appropriate.

6 On the Standard toolbar, click the **Save** button ![save icon].

Objective 2
Change Alignment of Cell Contents

Alignment refers to the position of text or numbers within a cell. You have already used the alignment options on the toolbar, for example, Align Left, Center, and Align Right.

Options for more complex alignment, such as rotating cell contents, aligning the contents vertically and horizontally, and increasing or decreasing indentation, are available from the Format Cells dialog box.

Activity 3.3 Changing Horizontal Alignment Using the Format Cells Dialog Box

Within a cell, you can align data horizontally in a number of ways. *Horizontal alignment* is the positioning of data between the left and right boundaries of a cell. Recall that Excel's default horizontal alignment for numbers, dates, and times is right-aligned. Excel's default horizontal alignment for text is left-aligned. Other horizontal alignments include Center, General, Indent, Fill, Justify, and Center Across Selection. See Figure 3.6.

Examples of horizontal alignments

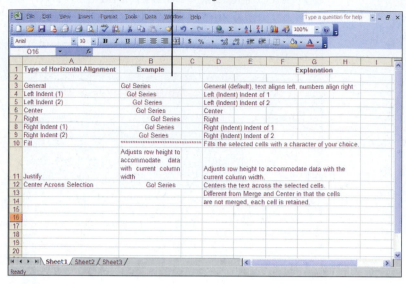

Figure 3.6

1 If necessary, **Open** 📂 your file **3A Tableware**. Click cell **A12**. On the Formatting toolbar, click the **Center** button 📊. The text is centered horizontally within the cell.

2 In cell **B2**, type **Jan** and then press ⏎. Click in cell **B2** again, position your pointer over the **fill handle**, and drag to the right to cell **G2** to fill in the series of month abbreviations *Jan* through *Jun*.

3 In cell **H2**, type **Total** and press ⏎.

4 Select the range **B2:G2**, position your pointer over the selected area, and then right-click to display the shortcut menu. Click **Format Cells**.

5 In the **Format Cells** dialog box, click the **Alignment tab**. Under **Text alignment**, click the **Horizontal arrow**, and then click **Center**, as shown in Figure 3.7.

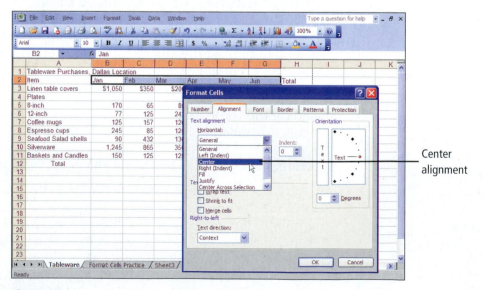

Center alignment

Figure 3.7

6 Click **OK**.

The text in each of the selected cells is centered horizontally between the left and right boundaries of the cell. You can accomplish horizontal centering either by clicking the Center button on the Formatting toolbar or, as you just did, from the Format Cells dialog box. This is another example of the convenience and speed of toolbar buttons.

7 In cell **H3**, click **AutoSum** and press Enter to sum the cost of linen table covers for the six-month period.

Notice that the Currency format with no decimal places is applied because earlier, you applied that format to the empty cell. Also, it is the format of the adjacent cells.

8 Click cell **H3** again, and then drag the **fill handle** downward to copy the formula through cell **H11**. Click cell **H4** and press Delete.

Because this row functions as a subheading for the two plate types, this cell needs no formula.

9 Click cell **B12**, click **AutoSum**, press Enter, and then copy the formula across through cell **H12**. Click anywhere to cancel the selection, and compare your screen with Figure 3.8.

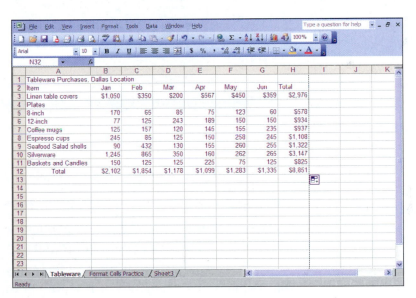

Figure 3.8

10 Click **Save**.

Activity 3.4 Indenting Cell Contents

Indenting increases the distance of the cell contents from either the left cell boundary (***left indent***) or the right cell boundary (***right indent***). Each time you increase the left indent by 1, the data in the cell begins one character width farther to the right. A character width in Excel is an approximate measurement equivalent to the width of an uppercase W. Zero is the default number of indents.

1 Click cell **A5**. From the **Format** menu, click **Cells**.

2 If necessary, click the **Alignment tab**. Under **Text alignment**, click the **Horizontal arrow**, and then click **Left (Indent)**. In the **Indent spin box**, click the **up arrow** to indent by **2**. See Figure 3.9. Click **OK**.

The cell contents are indented by two character widths. Recall that a character width is an approximate measurement equivalent to the width of an uppercase W, and thus it may appear that the indent is more than 2 characters because the characters above are much narrower than an uppercase W.

Apply left indent and increment by 2

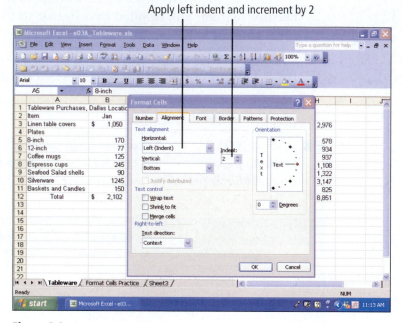

Figure 3.9

3 Click cell **A6**. On the Formatting toolbar, click the **Increase Indent** button once. Notice how the data indents to the right. Click the **Increase Indent** button again to align the data by two character widths—the same as the data in the cell above.

As you have just practiced, Right Indent can be applied from either the Format Cells dialog box or from the Formatting toolbar.

Activity 3.5 Filling a Cell

The **Fill** alignment repeats any character you type into a cell to fill the width of the cell or to fill a group of selected cells across two or more columns.

1 In cell **A13**, type ***** and then press [Enter]. Select the range **A13:H13**. With your mouse pointer positioned over the selection, right-click to display the shortcut menu, and then click **Format Cells**.

2 If necessary, click the **Alignment tab**. Under **Text alignment**, click the **Horizontal arrow**, and then click **Fill**. Click **OK**, and then click in a blank cell to cancel the selection. Compare your worksheet with Figure 3.10.

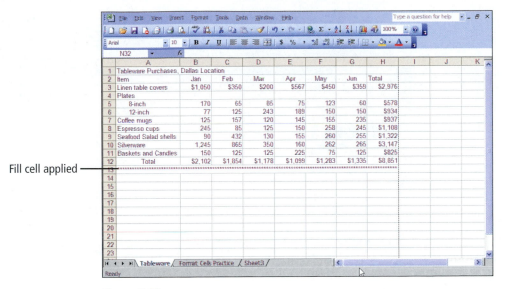

Fill cell applied ——

Figure 3.10

3 Select the range **A1:H1**. Press and hold down Ctrl and press 1 at the top left of your keyboard—recall that this is another way to display the **Format Cells** dialog box.

4 On the **Alignment tab** of the displayed **Format Cells** dialog box, click the **Horizontal arrow**, and then click **Center Across Selection**. Click **OK**.

The Center Across Selection alignment looks similar to the result you get when you use the Merge and Center button; however, the two features work differently. Merge and Center merges the selected cells and replaces them with a single cell. Thus, the first selected cell remains, but the other selected cells no longer exist. You cannot select them.

The Center Across Selection feature centers the text in one cell across all selected blank cells to the right. The cell contents remain in the first cell, and the remaining cells continue to exist as empty cells.

5 Click **Save** 🖫 to save the changes you have made to your workbook.

Activity 3.6 Aligning Cell Contents Vertically

Vertical alignment is the positioning of data between the top and bottom boundaries of a cell. Vertical alignment has four positions from which you can choose: top, bottom, center, and justify. The default vertical alignment for all data is bottom—aligned along the lower boundary of the cell.

1 Position your mouse pointer over the **row 1 heading**, and right-click to simultaneously select the row and display the shortcut menu. On the shortcut menu, click **Row Height**.

The Row Height dialog box displays, as shown in Figure 3.11.

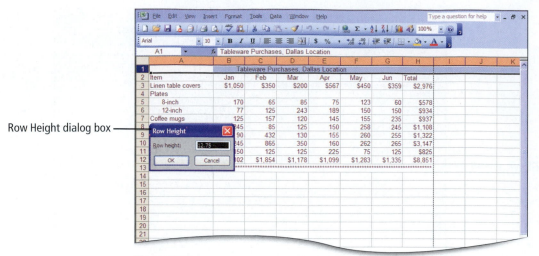

Row Height dialog box ——

Figure 3.11

---

2 With 12.75 highlighted, type **30** and then click **OK**.

Your new typing replaces the highlighted text, and the height of row 1 is changed to 30 pts. Recall that a pt. is ½₂ of an inch.

3 Select the range **A1:H1**, position your pointer over the selected area, and then right-click to display the shortcut menu. Click **Format Cells**.

4 In the **Format Cells** dialog box, click the **Alignment tab**. Under **Text alignment**, click the **Vertical arrow**, scroll this small box as necessary, and then click **Top**. Click **OK**.

The data is vertically aligned with the top boundary of the cell, as shown in Figure 3.12.

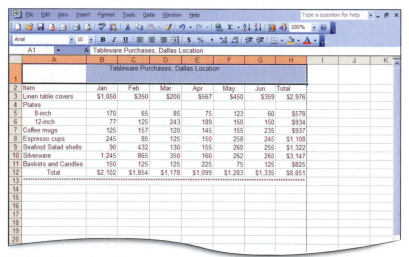

Figure 3.12

5 With the range **A1:H1** still selected, press and hold down Ctrl and press 1 at the upper left corner of your keyboard. In the **Alignment tab** of the **Format Cells** dialog box, click the **Vertical arrow**, and then click **Center**. Click **OK**, and then click anywhere to cancel the selection.

The data in the cells is vertically centered. Compare your screen with Figure 3.13.

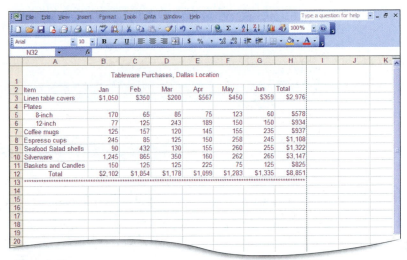

Figure 3.13

Activity 3.7 Rotating Text

The Orientation section of the Alignment tab in the Format Cells dialog box lets you change the angle of cell contents to read vertically from top to bottom (***stacked***), or at an angle of your choice—from 90 degrees counterclockwise to 90 degrees clockwise—for a total of 180 degrees. See Figure 3.14.

Examples of cell rotation

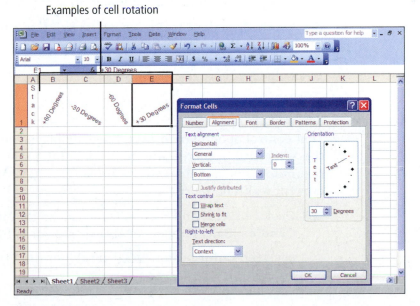

Figure 3.14

1 Select the range **B2:G2**, and then use any method to display the **Format Cells** dialog box. (Hint: When you have a group of cells selected, right-clicking is probably the quickest way to display the **Format Cells** dialog box. Remember that your mouse pointer must be over the selection when you right-click.)

2 If necessary, click the **Alignment tab**. Under **Orientation**, point to the **small red diamond** to the right of the word *Text*. Hold down the left mouse button, and drag the diamond upward until the **Degrees** spin box indicates *30*. Alternatively, click the up spin box arrow until *30* displays, or type **30** directly into the spin box. See Figure 3.15.

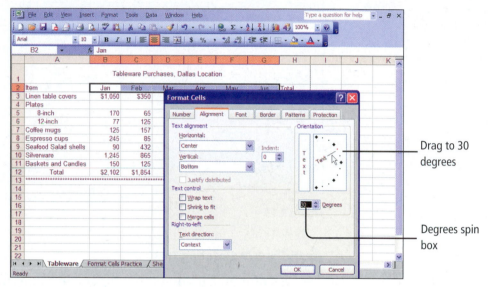

Drag to 30 degrees

Degrees spin box

Figure 3.15

3 Click **OK**.

The text in the selected cells is rotated 30 degrees, and the row height is automatically adjusted to accommodate the rotated text.

4 On the Standard toolbar, click **Save** 🔲 to save the changes you have made to your workbook.

Activity 3.8 Wrapping Text in a Cell

Recall that when you type text that is too long for the active cell, Excel lets the text spill over into adjacent cells—if they are empty. Using the Text control option **Wrap text**, Excel displays your text entirely within the active cell by increasing the *height* of the row and then wrapping the text onto additional lines in the same cell. Thus, Wrap text maintains the current width of the cell.

1 Click cell **A11**, and then edit the cell so that it indicates **Baskets and Candles, Salt, Pepper, Butter** as shown in Figure 3.16, and then click the **Enter** button ✅ on the Formula Bar.

Click Enter on Formula Bar   Edit cell

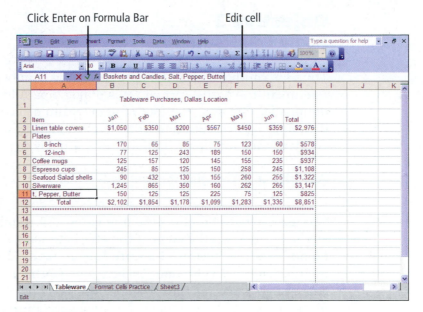

Figure 3.16

2 With **A11** as the active cell, use any method to display the **Format Cells** dialog box.

3 If necessary, click the **Alignment tab**. Under **Text control**, click to place a check mark in the **Wrap text** check box, as shown in Figure 3.17.

Wrap text check box

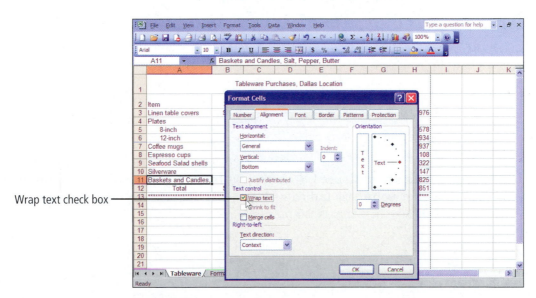

Figure 3.17

4 Click **OK**. On the Standard toolbar, click **Save** to save the changes you have made to your workbook.

Objective 3
Apply Cell Formatting

Thus far you have used the options on the Number tab and the Alignment tab of the Format Cells dialog box. Additional tabs provide options for changing the font of data within cells and also for adding borders and pattern effects to cells. In the following activities, you will change fonts and apply borders and patterns to cells in your worksheet.

Activity 3.9 Changing the Font and Font Size

A *font* is a set of characters with the same design and shape. There are two basic types of fonts—serif and sans serif. **Serif fonts** have extensions, or lines, on the ends of the characters and are good for large amounts of text because they are easy to read. Examples of serif fonts include Times New Roman, Copperplate Gothic Light, and Garamond. **Sans serif fonts** do not have lines on the ends of characters. Sans serif fonts are good for worksheets because worksheets normally contain more numbers than text. The default font for an Excel worksheet is Arial—a commonly used sans serif font. Other sans serif fonts include Impact and Comic Sans MS. See Figure 3.18.

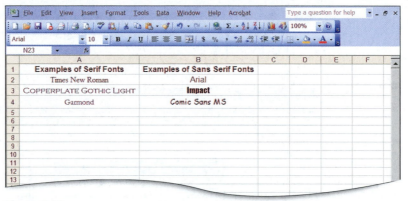

Figure 3.18

Fonts are measured in points, with one point equal to $\frac{1}{72}$ of an inch. A higher point size indicates a larger font size. See Figure 3.19. The default font size in Excel is 10 points.

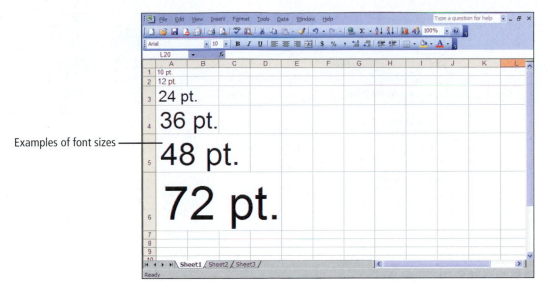

Examples of font sizes ——

Figure 3.19

You can apply a new font to cells in a worksheet from either of two places:

- The Font list on the Formatting toolbar
- The Font tab on the Format Cells dialog box

Font styles are used to emphasize text using bold, italic, and underline. You can apply font styles in three ways:

- On the Formatting toolbar, click the Bold, Italic, or Underline buttons.
- Select the font style from the Font tab of the Format Cells dialog box.
- Use the keyboard shortcuts Ctrl + B (Bold), Ctrl + I (Italic), or Ctrl + U (Underline).

1 If necessary, **Open** 📂 your file **3A_Tableware**.

2 Click cell **A1**, which contains the centered text *Tableware Purchases, Dallas Location*. On the Formatting toolbar, click the **Font button arrow** Arial ▾, as shown in Figure 3.20.

The Font list displays the fonts available on your system. Each font name displays in its actual design so that you have an immediate indication of the way the font will appear on your screen and on your printed page.

Font button arrow —

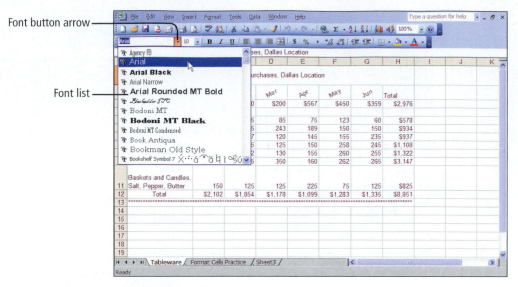

Figure 3.20

Note

Many fonts are TrueType, indicated by the two overlapping *Ts* to the left of the font name in the font list. Text formatted in a TrueType font prints exactly as it appears on your screen, provided that the font is installed on the system from which you are printing.

3 In the **Font** list, scroll down to find, and then click, **Century Schoolbook**. If Century Schoolbook is not available on the Font list, select Times New Roman.

The text *Tableware Purchases, Dallas Location* is formatted in the Century Schoolbook font. Century Schoolbook is a serif font—it has small line extensions on the ends of the letters.

4 With cell **A1** still selected, move to the Formatting toolbar and click the **Font Size arrow** 10 , as shown in Figure 3.21, and from the displayed list, click **18**.

Font Size arrow —

List of font sizes —

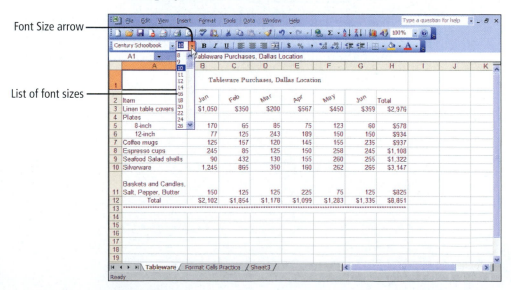

Figure 3.21

5 With cell **A1** selected, move to the Formatting toolbar and click the **Bold** button **B**.

The Bold style is applied to your text.

6 With cell **A1** still selected, display the **Format** menu, and then click **Cells** to display the **Format Cells** dialog box. Click the **Font tab**. Under **Font**, notice that *Century Schoolbook* is selected and that a preview of the font is also displayed under **Preview**.

7 Under **Font style**, click **Italic**, and notice that the Preview changes to reflect your selection. Click **OK**.

8 With cell **A1** still selected, move to the Formatting toolbar, and then click the **Underline** button **U**. The **Underline** button places a single underline under the contents of a cell.

The Bold, Italic, and Underline buttons on the Formatting toolbar are ***toggle buttons***, which means that you can click once to turn the formatting on and click again to turn it off.

9 With cell **A1** selected, move to the Formatting toolbar and click the **Underline** button **U** again.

The Underline font style is removed from the text, but the Bold and Italic styles remain.

10 Click cell **A2**. On the Formatting toolbar, click the **Bold** button **B** and click the **Center** button **≡**. Click the **Font Size arrow** ⌊10 ▾⌋, and from the displayed list, click **12**.

11 Click cell **H2**. On the Formatting toolbar, click the **Bold** button **B** and click the **Align Right** button **≡**. Click in an empty cell, and then compare your worksheet with Figure 3.22.

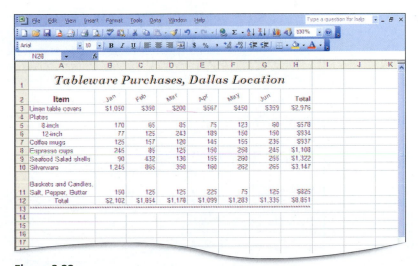

Figure 3.22

12 Click cell **A3**, press ⌈F2⌉ to turn on Edit mode, and with the insertion point positioned following *s* type ***** and then press ⌈Enter⌉.

13 Select cell **A14**. Type ***Order only in white or cream** and press ⌈Enter⌉.

Because the adjacent cell is empty, the text spills into cell B14. To avoid having to adjust the column width, you can *shrink* the size of a font in a cell.

14 Click to select cell **A14**, display the **Format Cells** dialog box, and then click the **Alignment tab**. Under **Text control**, select the **Shrink to fit** check box, as shown in Figure 3.23, and then click **OK**.

Shrink to fit check box ————

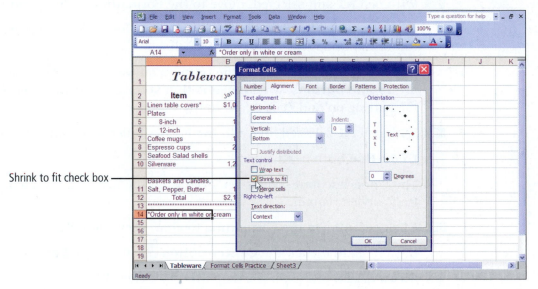

Figure 3.23

15 Save 🖫 your workbook and compare your screen with Figure 3.24.

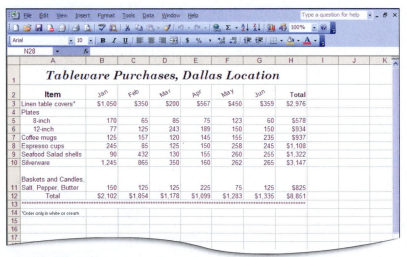

Figure 3.24

Activity 3.10 Merging Cells

Recall that an Excel worksheet is a **grid**—a network of uniformly spaced vertical and horizontal lines. Occasionally, it is desirable to have non-uniform cells. In those instances you can merge cells together.

After you merge a group of cells to form one large cell, the new, larger cell uses the address of the cell that was in the upper left corner of the selected group.

1 Select the range **I3:I11**. Use the shortcut menu to display the **Format Cells** dialog box. If necessary, click the **Alignment tab**. Under **Text control**, click to place a check mark in the **Merge cells** check box. Click **OK**. See Figure 3.25.

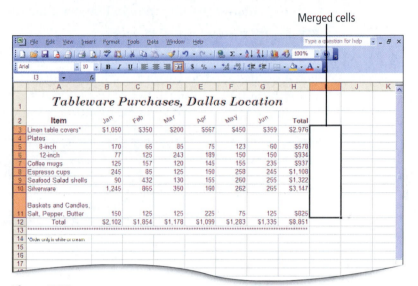

Merged cells

Figure 3.25

2 Click anywhere outside the selected cell. Click cell **I12** and look at the Name Box to the left of the Formula Bar. Notice that *I12* displays. Click in the **large merged cell above cell I12** and notice that *I3* displays in the name box.

When a group of cells are merged, the first cell in the selection becomes the cell address of the new, larger cell. The other cells cease to exist.

3 With cell **I3** still selected, type **First Half** and press Enter. Select cell **I3** again, display the **Format Cells** dialog box, and click the **Alignment tab**. Click the **Vertical arrow**, and then click **Center**. Click **OK**.

The text is vertically centered within the cell.

4 To separate the merged cells, select cell **I3**. Display the **Format Cells** dialog box, and then display the **Alignment tab**. Under **Text control**, clear (click to remove the check mark) the **Merge cells** check box. Click **OK**.

The cells are separated, and the text displays in cell I3.

5 Click cell **I3** and press Delete to delete the cell contents.

6 On the Standard toolbar, click **Save** 🖫 to save the changes you have made to your workbook.

Activity 3.11 Applying Cell Borders

Apply cell borders to visually differentiate one part of a worksheet from another and to draw the reader's eye to specific data. Use cell borders to add the type of underline and double underline that is often found in an accounting-style worksheet. You can customize borders by adjusting color and width. You can apply cell borders in two ways:

• On the Formatting toolbar, click the Borders button.

• Select the border from the Border tab of the Format Cells dialog box.

1 Select the range **A1:H1**. Display the **Format Cells** dialog box, and then click the **Border tab**.

Here you can specify where you want the border and select the style and color of the line that will be used for the border.

2 Under **Presets**, click **Outline**.

Under Border, your selection is previewed. The Outline preset places a border around the outer edges of the selected group of cells. Additionally, under Line, in the Style list, the default line style—a single line—is selected and blinking, as shown in Figure 3.26.

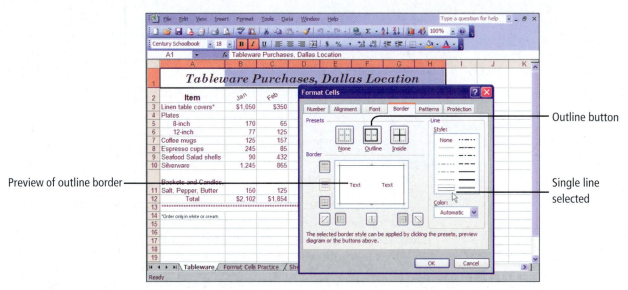

Figure 3.26

3 Under **Line**, in the **Style** list, click the **fifth line style in the second column**—a medium-thick solid line. Under **Presets**, click the **Outline** button again to apply the new line style to the outline of the selected cells.

Your selected line style is surrounded by dots, indicating that it is the selected line style, and a line blinks beneath it. After you select a new line style, you have to reapply the border to the selected areas. You can do this by clicking the Outline button, or by clicking the Border buttons that surround the border preview area.

4 Click **OK**. Click in an empty cell so you can see the border that has been applied.

On some computer screens, the applied border is not as readily visible as on others.

5 To visualize how your bordered cells will look, on the Formatting toolbar click the **Print Preview** button 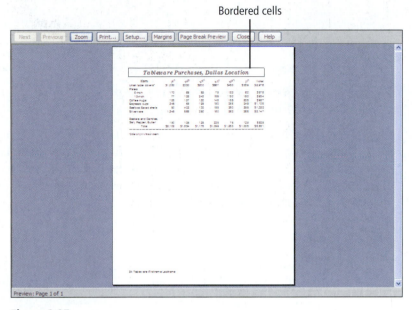. Compare your screen with Figure 3.27.

Bordered cells

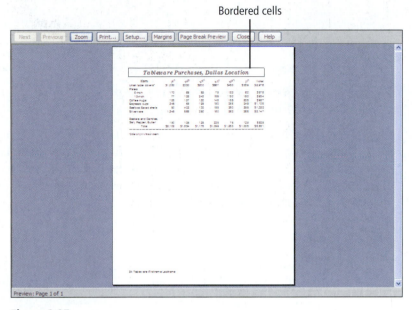

Figure 3.27

6 On the Print Preview toolbar, click the **Close** button.

7 Select the range **A11:H11** and display the **Format Cells** dialog box. If necessary, click the **Border tab**.

8 Under **Border**, move your mouse pointer into the white area. Point to the lower edge of the white preview area, and click the left mouse button once.

A line displays, and the **Bottom border** button appears "pressed." See Figure 3.28.

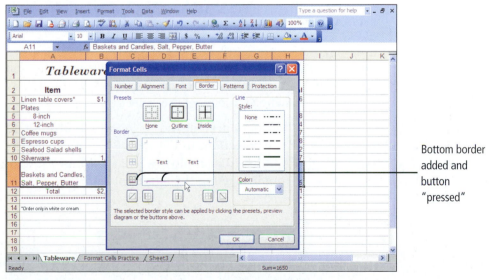

Bottom border added and button "pressed"

Figure 3.28

Note

To apply color to cell borders, click the **Color arrow** on the **Border tab** of the **Format Cells** dialog box.

9 Click **OK** to close the dialog box.

10 Select the range **A2:H12**. On the Formatting toolbar, click the **Borders arrow** 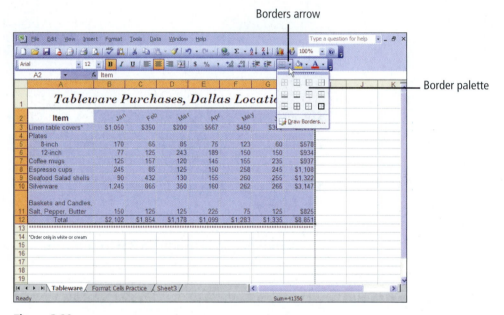 to display the Border palette, as shown in Figure 3.29.

The content of and ScreenTip for the Border button reflect its most recent use and thus can vary. Clicking the button will apply the border indicated on the button. Clicking the Border arrow, however, will always display the Border palette, from which you can choose any of the border styles.

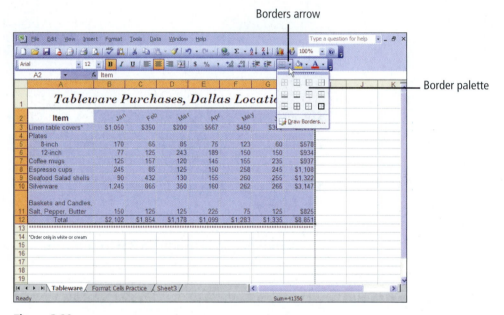

Figure 3.29

11 On the displayed Border palette, in the last row, click the second button, **All Borders**, as shown in Figure 3.30, and then click anywhere to cancel the selection.

Borders are applied to the top, bottom, left, and right of each *cell* in the selection. In Figure 3.31, notice that in row 2, the borders are applied diagonally. Row 2 contains rotated text, and the borders are applied using the same rotation.

Note — Applying Borders

The border applied in this step overrides the outline border applied to the lower edge of cells A1:H1.

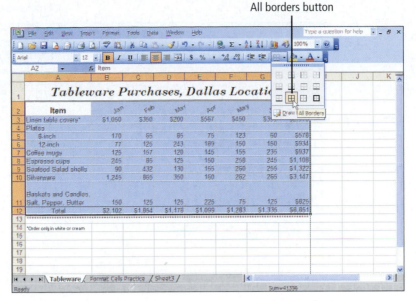

All borders button

Figure 3.30

12 Click **Save** 🖫 . Compare your screen with Figure 3.31.

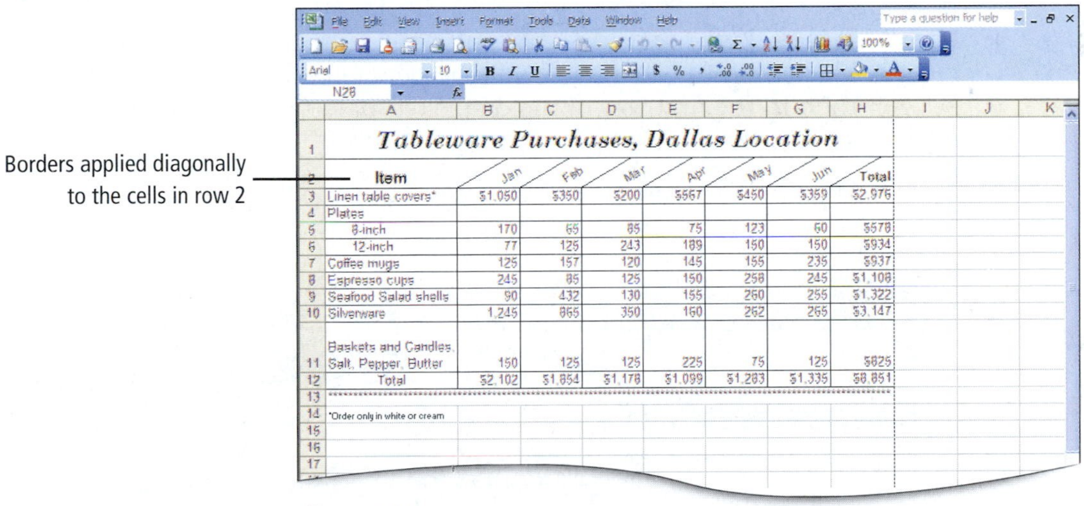

Borders applied diagonally to the cells in row 2

Figure 3.31

Activity 3.12 Applying Cell Shading

Applying shading to cells is another way to visually differentiate one part of a worksheet from another and to draw the reader's eye to specific data or to a group of cells. You can select colors and patterns for shading. You can apply shading to cells in two ways:

- Click the Fill Color button on the Formatting toolbar.

- Select the shading from the Patterns tab of the Format Cells dialog box.

1 Select the range **A1:H1**. On the Formatting toolbar, click the **Fill Color arrow** 🎨▾ to display the color palette, as shown in Figure 3.32.

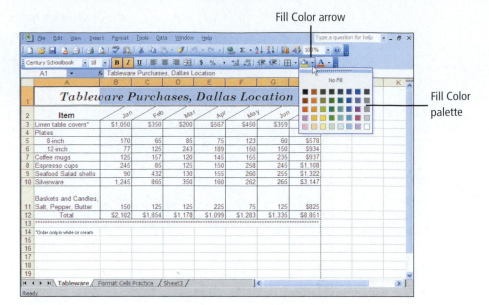

Fill Color arrow

Fill Color palette

Figure 3.32

2 On the displayed color palette, in the last row, click the sixth color— **Pale Blue**.

3 Select the range **A12:H12**. Display the **Format Cells** dialog box, and then click the **Patterns tab**.

4 In the lower portion of the dialog box, click the **Pattern arrow**, and then in the first row of the displayed palette, click the fifth pattern— **12.5% Gray**—as shown in Figure 3.33.

You can see a preview of the pattern in the Sample area after the pattern is selected.

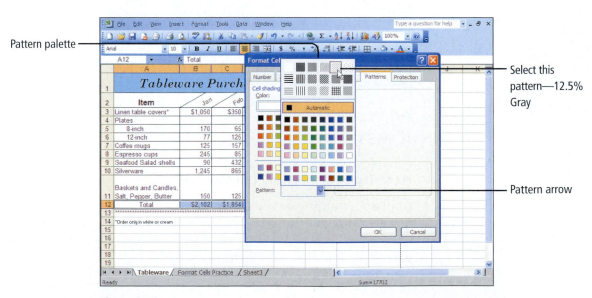

Pattern palette

Select this pattern—12.5% Gray

Pattern arrow

Figure 3.33

5 Click **OK**, and then click anywhere to cancel the selection. On the Standard toolbar, click **Save** ![save icon] to save the changes you have made to your workbook.

Activity 3.13 Using Format Painter

Format Painter copies all formatting from one selection of cells to another selection of cells. This differs from copy and paste because the cell contents are not copied. Instead, only the formatting of the cell is copied. Any type of formatting applied to the selected cells—number format, alignment, font, font style, borders, or patterns—is copied.

1 Click cell **A3** to make it the active cell. On the Formatting toolbar, click the **Font button arrow** Arial , scroll the displayed list as necessary, and change the font to **Comic Sans MS**. Then, on the Formatting toolbar, click the **Italic** button *I*, and then click the **Center** button to apply Italic style and Center alignment to the cell.

2 With cell **A3** still selected, move to the Standard toolbar and click the **Format Painter** button. Move the pointer into the grid area, and notice that the Format Painter button is highlighted. Also, cell A3 displays a moving border, and the mouse pointer displays with a small paintbrush attached to it, as shown in Figure 3.34.

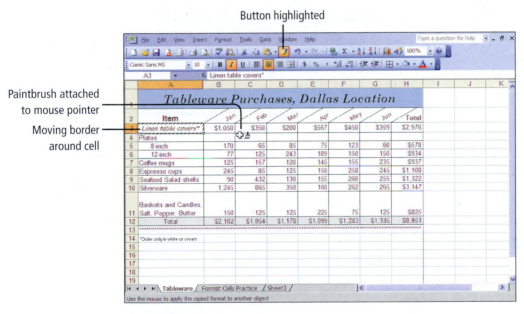

Figure 3.34

3 Select the range **A4:A11**.

As you release the left mouse button, notice that the range of cells has acquired the same formatting—font style of Comic Sans MS, Italic, and Centering—as cell A3. The paintbrush is no longer attached to the mouse pointer, and the Format Painter button is no longer highlighted. This is a convenient way to copy *formats* to other cells without having to reapply each format individually.

4 Select cell **A3**. On the Formatting toolbar, change the font to **Century Schoolbook**, be sure the **Font Size** 10 is **10**, and change the alignment to **Align Left**.

5 On the Standard toolbar, *double-click* the **Format Painter** button.

Double-clicking the Format Painter button causes it to remain active until you click the button again to turn it off.

6 Click cell **A10**.

The format from cell A3—Century Schoolbook, 10 pt, left aligned—is copied to cell A10.

7 Move your mouse pointer anywhere into the grid area of your worksheet and verify that the paintbrush is still attached to the pointer. This indicates that Format Painter is still active.

If you do not see the paintbrush, it is likely that your hand moved slightly when you attempted your double-click of the Format Painter button, and it was interpreted as a single click. Double-click the Format Painter button again.

8 Click cell **A4**.

The format from cell A3 is copied to cell A4.

9 Drag to select the range **A7:A11**.

The format from cell A3 is copied to the selected range.

10 Click the **Format Painter** button once to turn it off.

The button is no longer highlighted, and the paintbrush is no longer attached to the mouse pointer.

11 Select cell **A11,** display the **Format Cells** dialog box, click the **Alignment tab**, and select the **Wrap text** check box. Click **OK**.

12 On the Standard toolbar, click **Save** to save the changes you have made to your workbook. Compare your screen with Figure 3.35.

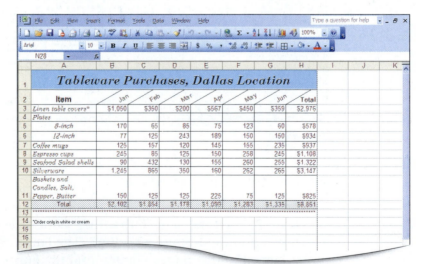

Figure 3.35

Note

You can apply formatting to individual characters in a text entry (but not a numeric entry) by first selecting only the characters and then applying any of the cell formats.

Activity 3.14 Clearing Cell Formats

Once applied, cell formats stay with the cell, even if you delete the contents of the cell. To delete the *format* from a cell, you must purposely clear the format using the Clear Formats or Clear All commands from the Edit menu.

1 If necessary, **Open** 📁 your file **3A_Tableware**.

2 Click to make cell **A5** the active cell. On the menu bar, click **Edit**, point to **Clear**, and then click **Formats**.

All the formatting for the cell—the Comic Sans font, Italic, and Centering—are removed from the cell, and the default font (Arial) and alignment for text (left) are applied to the cell.

3 Click to make cell **A6** the active cell. Press Delete to delete the contents of the cell. Type **13-inch** and then press Enter.

Notice that deleting the contents of the cell does not delete the formatting.

4 Click cell **A6** again. To delete the cell contents and the cell formats at the same time, display the **Edit** menu, point to **Clear**, and then click **All**.

This command deletes the cell contents and removes all cell formatting—all at the same time.

5 Type **12-inch** and then press Enter.

6 To reapply the original formatting, click cell **A4**, and then click the **Format Painter** button 🖌. With the Format Painter paintbrush attached to the mouse pointer, drag to select the range **A5:A6**. With the range **A5:A6** still selected, click the **Increase Indent** button 🔲 two times.

7 Select the range **A14:H14**. Display the **Format Cells** dialog box, click the **Alignment tab**, and then click the **Horizontal arrow**. Click **Center Across Selection**, and then click **OK**.

8 On the Standard toolbar, click **Save** 💾 to save the changes you have made to this workbook since your last Save operation.

9 View your worksheet in **Print Preview**, and then on the Print Preview toolbar, click **Print**, in the **Print** dialog box click **OK**. On the menu bar, click **File**, and then click **Close** to close the workbook.

End **You have completed Project 3A** ──────────────────────────

Project 3B **Suppliers**

In this project, you will change the appearance of your printed workbook by changing the page orientation, the scale of the worksheet, and the paper size. You will also set margins and center the worksheet on the printed page, and insert a picture within a header or footer.

Jin Bae, Food and Beverage Manager   Dallas Location
                                                      10/20/2003

Supplier Accounts Summary

Company Name	Cost Center	Invoice Amount	No. of Items	Last Invoice Date	Last Check Number	Total
Texas Refreshments	Beverage	$ 477	1	2/24	684	$ 477
Laura Provisions	Restaurant	$ 1,566	1	4/3	758	$ 1,566
All Steel Utensils	Kitchen	$ 325	1	5/12	832	$ 325
POS Service Company	Management	$ 798	7	6/20	906	$ 5,586
Austin Forms	Management	$ 1,765	1	7/29	980	$ 1,765
Universal Office Supply	Management	$ 379	1	9/6	954	$ 379
Acme Provisions	Restaurant	$ 1,190	2	10/15	128	$ 2,380
Benjamin Beverage Service	Beverage	$ 475	6	11/23	202	$ 2,850
Atlas Meats	Restaurant	$ 822	1	1/1	276	$ 822
National Restaurant Supply	Restaurant	$ 732	1	2/9	350	$ 732
Texas Floral Supply	Management	$ 509	1	3/20	424	$ 509
Doyle Range	Kitchen	$ 589	4	4/28	498	$ 2,356
Massey Refrigeration	Kitchen	$ 921	4	6/6	572	$ 3,684
Victory Ventilation Service	Kitchen	$ 367	4	7/15	646	$ 1,468

3B Suppliers-Firstname Lastname

Figure 3.36
Project 3B—Suppliers

In Activities 3.15 through 3.18, you will edit a workbook for Jin Bae, Food and Beverage Manager for the Oceana Palm Grill, listing recent payments to suppliers. You will save the file as *3B_Suppliers_Firstname_Lastname.* Your completed worksheet will look similar to Figure 3.36.

Objective 4
Apply Workbook Formatting

In the remainder of the chapter, you will practice methods to format the printed worksheet using the *Page Setup* command. Settings that you adjust in the Page Setup dialog box affect only the active worksheet, not the entire workbook. To adjust settings for the entire workbook, use the Select All Sheets command before displaying the Page Setup dialog box. To select two or more adjacent sheets, use the Shift plus click technique to select sheets before displaying the Page Setup dialog box. Use the Ctrl plus click technique to select nonadjacent sheets.

Activity 3.15 Selecting Page Orientation, Scaling, and Paper Size

The default page orientation in Excel is *portrait* orientation. In portrait orientation, the paper is taller than it is wide. You can also select a *landscape* orientation in which the paper is wider than it is tall. The default paper size in Excel is 8½-inches by 11 inches—standard business letter-size paper.

1 Start Excel. On the **File** menu, click **Open**. In the **Open** dialog box, navigate to the student files that accompany this textbook, and then open the file **e03B_Suppliers**. Display the **View** menu, click **Header and Footer**, and then click the **Custom Footer** button. In the **Left section**, type **3B Suppliers-Firstname Lastname** and then click **OK** to close the dialog boxes.

2 From the **File** menu, click **Save As**. In the **Save As** dialog box, navigate to the location where you are storing your projects for this chapter. In the **File name** box, type **3B_Suppliers_Firstname_Lastname** and then click **Save** or press Enter.

3 On the Standard toolbar, click the **Print Preview** button. In the **Print Preview** window, notice at the lower left corner *Preview: Page 1 of 2*, as shown in Figure 3.37.

Next button —

Page 1 of 2 indicated —

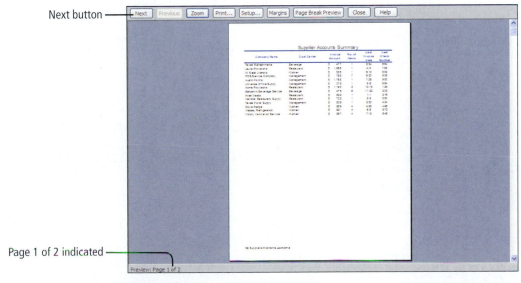

Figure 3.37

4 On the Print Preview toolbar, click the **Next** button.

Page 2 of the worksheet displays in the Print Preview window. Because all the columns on this worksheet cannot print on one page as the page is currently set up, the Print Preview displays the worksheet as two pages.

5 On the Print Preview toolbar, click the **Previous** button to redisplay Page 1 of the worksheet.

The preview is shown in portrait orientation—the paper is taller than it is wide.

6 On the Print Preview toolbar, click the **Close** button to close Print Preview.

The boundary between columns F and G displays as a dotted line. As you saw in the Print Preview, columns to the right of the dotted line will print on the second page as the page is currently set up.

7 From the **File** menu, click **Page Setup**. In the displayed **Page Setup** dialog box, click the **Page tab**. Under **Scaling**, click the **Fit to** option button with the default of *1 page(s) wide by 1 tall*.

8 In the upper right portion of the dialog box, click **Print Preview**.

Excel has *scaled* (shrunk) the data to fit on one page in the portrait orientation, as shown in Figure 3.38. Scaling is a good choice when the data is slightly too wide to display on one page, or if you need to keep the worksheet in a portrait orientation.

Data scaled to fit on one page

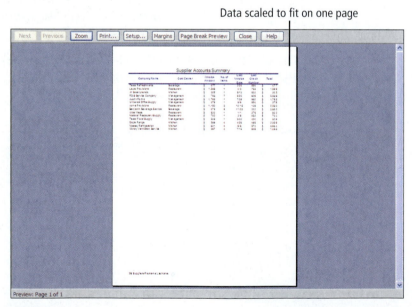

Figure 3.38

9 On the Print Preview toolbar, click **Setup** to return to the **Page Setup** dialog box.

Under Scaling, your print has been scaled to 88% (or a number close to 88%). The two options under *Scaling* on the Page tab of the Page Setup dialog box enable you to override the default size of your print-out by specifying a scaling factor of 10% to 400%, or by automatically fitting the data to a specified number of pages—as you did here. Use caution with this feature, because Excel will scale the print both horizontally and vertically, so some distortion is possible. Always use Print Preview to view your results before printing.

10 Under **Scaling**, click the **Adjust to** option button, and then, in the **Adjust to** spin box, click the **up arrow** until **100** displays. This will return the data to a full-size printout. Click **OK**, and then, on the Print Preview toolbar, click the **Close** button to close Print Preview.

11 From the **File** menu, click **Page Setup**. On the **Page tab**, under **Orientation**, click the **Landscape** option button. In the lower portion of the dialog box, click the **Paper size arrow**.

It is likely that the default paper size, Letter, is already selected, but here you can view the different sizes available.

12 Scroll through the list, and then click **Letter**.

As you make changes to the setup of your worksheet, you will want to look at it in Print Preview; thus, a Print Preview button is conveniently placed at the upper right of this dialog box.

13 Click the **Print Preview** button in the dialog box to view your worksheet in landscape orientation as it would print on letter-size paper.

In this orientation, all the columns will print on one sheet. If necessary, you can return to the Page Setup dialog box from this screen by clicking the *Setup* button on the toolbar of the Print Preview window.

14 On the Print Preview window's toolbar, click **Close**. On the Standard toolbar, click **Save** .

Activity 3.16 Setting Margins and Centering the Worksheet

The default margins in Excel are 1 inch for the top and bottom margins and ¾ (.75) inch for the left and right margins.

1 From the **File** menu, click **Page Setup**, and in the displayed **Page Setup** dialog box, click the **Margins tab**.

As shown in the small preview picture on the dialog box, Excel will begin the print starting at the top and left margins—within the settings that you select. See Figure 3.39.

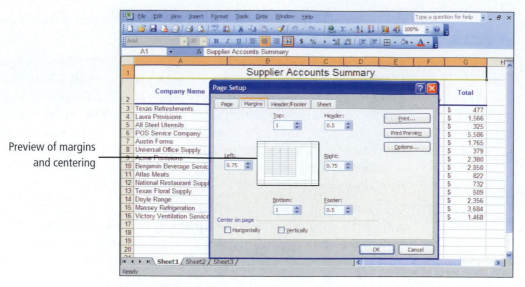

Preview of margins and centering

Figure 3.39

2 Click to position the insertion point within the **Right** box.

On the small picture in the middle of the dialog box, a black line displays to give you a visual indication that you are working with the right margin of the worksheet.

3 Click in the **Top** box.

The black line moves to indicate that you are working with the top margin.

4 In the **Top** box, click the **up arrow** in the spin box so that the top margin is **1.75** inches.

5 At the bottom of the dialog box, under **Center on page**, click to select the **Horizontally** check box.

The preview changes to give a visual indication of the horizontal centering you have chosen. If you center your printout horizontally on the page, you need not be concerned with left and right margins. If you center your printout vertically on the page, you need not be concerned with top and bottom margins.

6 In the **Page Setup** dialog box, click the **Print Preview** button to view the changes you have made to your workbook. Then, on the Print Preview toolbar, click the **Close** button.

7 On the Standard toolbar, click **Save** 🔳 to save the changes you have made to your workbook.

More Knowledge

From the Print Preview toolbar's Margins button, you can change margins visually by dragging the margin boundaries with the mouse.

Activity 3.17 Creating Headers and Footers with Inserted Pictures

Headers and *footers* refer to text and graphics that appear at the top (headers) or bottom (footers) of a worksheet in a workbook. For example, a header might contain the company or department name and a company logo. A footer might contain the page number and the time and date the worksheet was printed. You are already familiar with creating a custom footer containing your name and the project name.

Headers and footers can display character formatting such as bold and italic. You can also align the characters, apply borders and shading, and insert pictures. Excel's default setting is to display no header and no footer.

You can create headers and footers in Excel in two ways:

- Use one of Excel's predefined headers and footers.

- Create your own custom header or footer.

In this activity, you will use both methods to place a header and footer in your worksheet.

1 From the **View** menu, click **Header and Footer**. Alternatively, on the menu bar, click File, Page Setup, and then click the Header/Footer tab.

The Header/Footer tab of the Page Setup dialog box displays. Notice that under Header, *(none)* displays, and under Footer, the custom footer that you already created for this project displays. See Figure 3.40.

No header applied ——

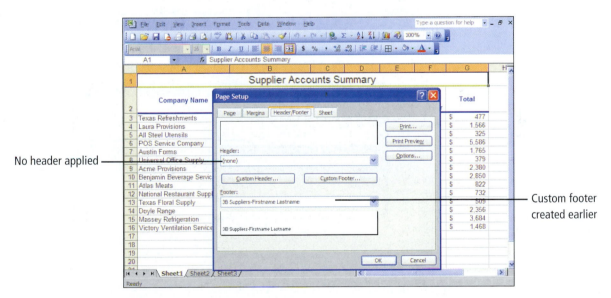

—— Custom footer created earlier

Figure 3.40

2 Click the **Header arrow** to view a list of predefined headers. Scroll down the list, and notice that Excel has included several variations of the file name as one of the predefined headings.

Excel always displays the file name as a possible header or footer as well as other variations of possible headers that include the file name.

3 In the displayed list, click **(none)**. Click the **Custom Header** button. The **Header** dialog box displays. Click in the **Left section**, and then type **Jin Bae, Food and Beverage Manager**

Text in the Left section is aligned at the left, and as you type, the text wraps to a second line.

4 Click in the **Center section**, and then type **Dallas Location** Text in the **Center section** is centered. Press Enter. On the **Header** dialog box toolbar, click the **Date** button 🔲 to insert today's date. Compare your screen with Figure 3.41.

Although a code displays, the current date will display and print in your worksheet. Excel has codes that begin with an ampersand and are enclosed in brackets to represent things you might want to insert into a header or footer—such as the current time, current date, and page number. You do not have to know the codes; they are automatically inserted using one of the buttons on the dialog box's toolbar.

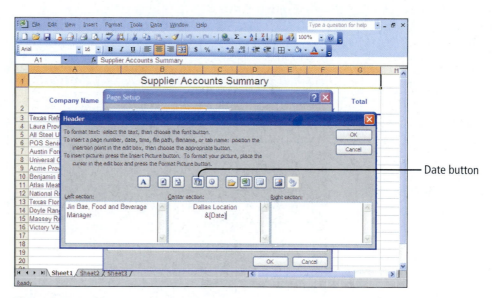

Figure 3.41

5 Take a moment to review the table in Figure 3.42 that describes the buttons on the Header (and Footer) dialog box toolbar.

Header and Footer Toolbar Buttons

Button	Action
A	Opens the Font dialog box in which you can change the font, font style, font size, underline, or effects.
#	Inserts the page number.
	Inserts the total number of pages in a worksheet.
	Inserts the current date.
	Inserts the current time.
	Inserts the directory path and file name.
	Inserts the name of the Excel file.
	Inserts the name on the sheet tab.
	Displays the Insert Picture dialog box, from which you can insert a picture.
	Displays the Format Picture dialog box, from which you can format an inserted picture.

Figure 3.42

Note

To print header or footer text on more than one line, press Enter at the end of the line.

6 Click in the **Right section**, and then on the **Header** dialog box toolbar, click the **Insert Picture** button [icon], as shown in Figure 3.43.

Insert Picture button

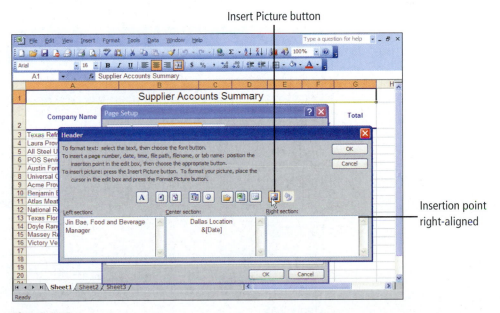

Insertion point right-aligned

Figure 3.43

7 In the displayed **Insert Picture** dialog box, click the **Look in arrow**, and then navigate to the student files that accompany this textbook. Click to select the file **03B_Chef**, and then, in the lower right corner, click the **Insert** button.

&[Picture] displays, and the Format Picture button becomes active, as shown in Figure 3.44.

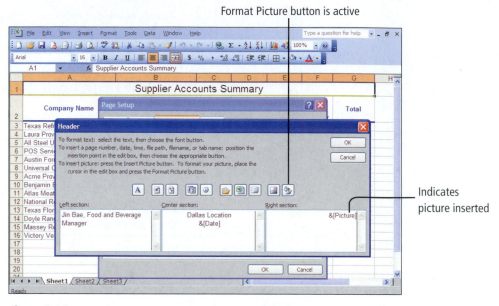

Figure 3.44

8 Click the **Format Picture** button on the toolbar, located to the right of the Insert Picture button.

9 In the displayed **Format Picture** dialog box, under **Size and rotate**, in the **Height** spin box, click the **down arrow** until **0.5** displays in both the **Height** and **Width** spin box, as shown in Figure 3.45.

This will reduce the size of the chef picture to fit within the header.

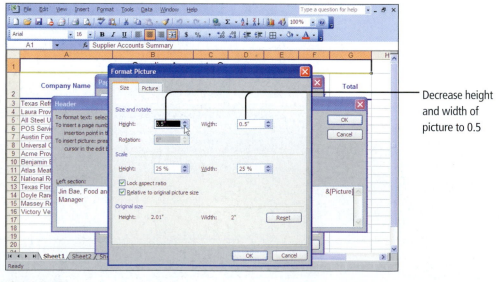

Figure 3.45

10 In the lower right corner of the dialog box, click **OK**. In the upper right corner of the **Header** dialog box, click **OK**.

Do not be concerned if, in the Page Setup dialog box, it appears that your header elements are layered on top of one another.

11 In the **Page Setup** dialog box, click the **Print Preview** button. Compare your screen with Figure 3.46.

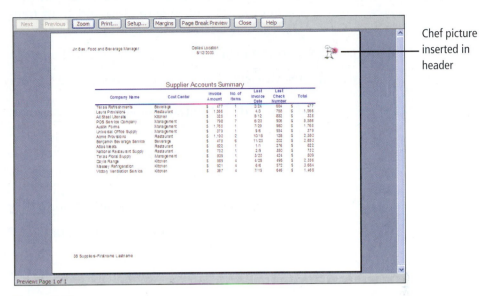

Chef picture inserted in header

Figure 3.46

12 On the Print Preview toolbar, click the **Setup** button to return to the **Header/Footer tab** of the **Page Setup** dialog box, and then click the **Custom Header** button.

13 In the **Left section**, select the entire text if it is not already selected, and then click the **Font** button [A] to display the **Font** dialog box. Under **Font**, scroll as necessary, and click **Comic San MS**. Change the **Font style** to **Bold** and the **Size** to **9**, as shown in Figure 3.47, and then click **OK**.

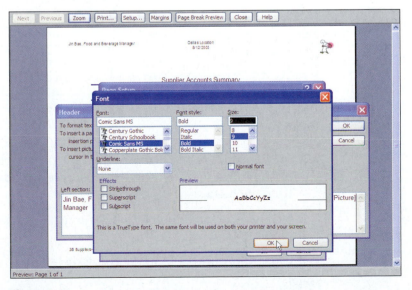

Figure 3.47

14 Click **OK** to close the **Header** dialog box. Click **OK** to close the **Page Setup** dialog box.

To edit (make changes to) headers or footers, display the dialog box and make changes directly within a section.

15 Examine the Print Preview on your screen.

Your worksheet data is centered horizontally on the page, and the header and footer use the left and right margins as set on the Margins tab of the Page Setup dialog box.

16 On the Print Preview toolbar, click the **Close** button.

17 **Save** 🖫 the changes you have made to your workbook.

Activity 3.18 Setting Header and Footer Margins

Use the Margins tab of the Page Setup dialog box to adjust the distance between the header and the top of the page or to adjust the distance between the footer and the bottom of the page. This setting should always be less than the setting for the corresponding top or bottom margin. Otherwise, the text from the header or footer will overlap into the worksheet data.

1 On the menu bar, click **File** and then click **Page Setup**. If necessary, click the **Margins tab**.

2 Using the spin box arrows, increase the **Header** margin to **0.75**. Then, increase the **Footer** margin to **0.75**. Compare your screen with Figure 3.48.

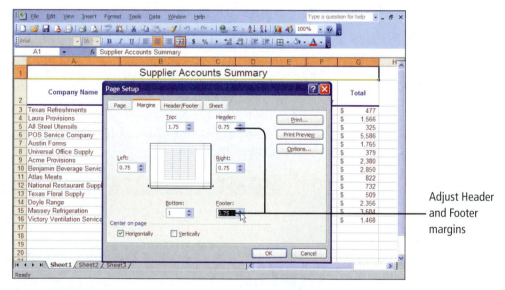

Adjust Header and Footer margins

Figure 3.48

3 In the upper right corner of the dialog box, click the **Print Preview** button, and then, on the **Print Preview** toolbar, click **Print**, and then click **OK**.

4 On the Standard toolbar, click **Save** 🖫 to save the changes you have made to your workbook.

5 Close the workbook, and close Excel.

End **You have completed Project 3B**

Project 3C Totals

In this project, you will practice how to print a worksheet with the gridlines, row headings, and column headings that you see on your screen. You will also insert a comment in a cell, and view and edit a comment in a cell.

In Activities 3.19 through 3.20, you will edit a workbook for Jin Bae, Food and Beverage Manager. You will save your file as *3C_Totals_Firstname_Lastname*. Your completed worksheet will look similar to Figure 3.49.

	A	B	C	D	E	F	G
1							
2	Company Name	January	February	March	April	May	June
3	Texas Refreshments	$ 426	$ 733	$ 837	$ 837	$ 200	$ 387
4	Laura Provisions	387	387	426	426	226	1,426
5	All Steel Utensils	1,426	1,286	344	344	386	200
6	POS Service Company	200	1,876	243	243	342	226
7	Acme Provisions	226	472	837	243	243	386
8	National Restaurant Supply	386	387	426	733	243	243
9	Atlas Meats	342	1,324	344	387	733	837
10	Texas Floral Supply	128	243	243	1,286	387	426
11	Massey Refrigeration	234	234	243	1,876	426	344
12	Totals	$ 3,755	$ 6,942	$ 3,943	$ 6,375	$ 3,186	$ 4,475

3C Totals-Firstname Lastname   9/22/2003

Figure 3.49
Project 3C—Totals

Objective 5
Print Gridlines, Print Row and Column Headings, and Set Print Quality

When you work in Excel, you see the row headings (numbers 1, 2, 3, and so on), the column headings (letters A, B, C, and so on) and the gridlines (the vertical and horizontal lines that define cells). By default, row headings, column headings, and gridlines do not print, but if you want to print them, you can do so by displaying the Page Setup dialog box and adjusting the settings.

Activity 3.19 Printing Gridlines, Printing Row and Column Headings, and Setting Print Quality

1 Start Excel. On the **File** menu, click **Open**. In the **Open** dialog box, navigate to the student files that accompany this textbook, and then open the file **e03C_Totals**. Display the **View** menu, click **Header and Footer**, and then click the **Custom Footer** button. In the **Left section**, type 3C Totals-Firstname Lastname and then click **OK** to close the dialog boxes.

2 From the **File** menu, click **Save As**. In the **Save As** dialog box, navigate to the location where you are storing your projects for this chapter. In the **File name** box, type 3C_Totals_Firstname_Lastname and then click **Save** or press Enter.

3 From the **File** menu, click **Page Setup**. In the **Page Setup** dialog box, click the **Sheet tab**.

4 Under **Print**, select the **Gridlines** check box and the **Row and column headings** check box. In the upper right corner of the dialog box, click the **Print Preview** button. Compare your screen with Figure 3.50.

Notice that gridlines, column headings, and row headings are displayed and will print.

Gridlines, column headings, and row headings display

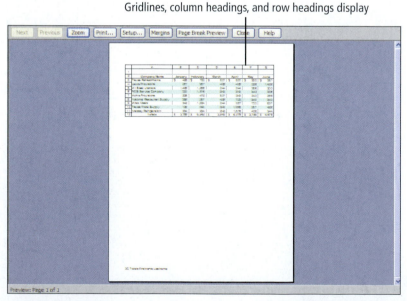

Figure 3.50

5 On the Print Preview toolbar, click the **Setup** button to return to the **Page Setup** dialog box.

6 Under **Print**, select the **Black and white** check box, as shown in Figure 3.51.

If background colors and patterns have been applied to your work-sheet, as they are in this worksheet, but you are using a black-and-white printer (most laser printers are black and white), selecting this option signals Excel to use only black and white when printing. The result is that the printer will *not* use shades of gray for the areas that are in color.

Select black and white ———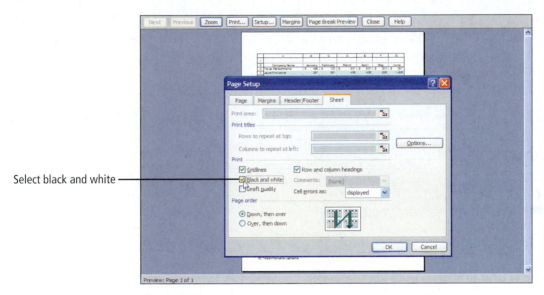

Figure 3.51

7 Click **OK** to close the dialog box, and then, on the Print Preview tool-bar, click **Close** to close the Print Preview screen.

8 On the menu bar, click **View**, and then click **Header and Footer**. Click the **Custom Footer** button. In the **Center section**, click the **Date** button ⊞. In the **Footer** dialog box, click the **OK** button, and then, in the **Page Setup** dialog box, click **OK** again.

9 On the Standard toolbar, click the **Print Preview** button ⊠. Notice that the date is displayed (and will print) at the bottom center of your worksheet.

10 **Close** the Print Preview, and then, on the Standard toolbar, click **Save** 🖫 to save the changes you have made to your workbook.

Objective 6
View and Insert Comments in a Cell

Comments provide reminders, document work, or provide clarifying information about data within a cell. You can attach one comment to a cell. When you move the mouse pointer over the cell, the comment and the name of the computer user who created the comment display.

Activity 3.20 Viewing and Inserting Comments in a Cell

1 Look at cell **A6** and notice the small red triangle in upper right corner of the cell.

The red triangle indicates that a comment is applied to the cell.

2 Move your mouse pointer over cell **A6**, and notice the comment that displays, as shown in Figure 3.52.

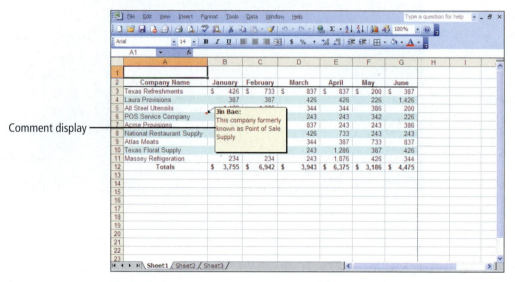

Comment display

Figure 3.52

3 Right-click cell **A9** to simultaneously select it and display the shortcut menu.

4 From the displayed shortcut menu, click **Insert Comment**.

The name that displays is the name of the person or organization to whom your computer is registered, derived from your computer system's information.

5 Replace the name with your name, position your insertion point after the colon, and press Enter. Turn off bold if necessary, and then type **Atlas Meats supplies only beef products.** Compare your screen with Figure 3.53.

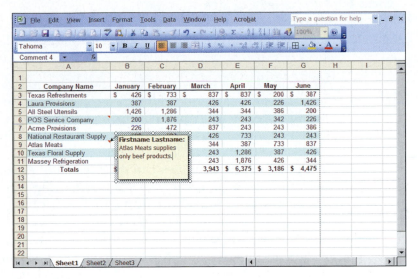

Figure 3.53

6 Click in any empty cell, and then move your mouse pointer over cell **A9** to view your comment.

Alert!

Hiding and Unhiding Comments

If your comment does not close when you click an empty cell, the Show/Hide Comments feature may be turned on. To turn this off and hide the comments, right-click on the cell containing the comment and from the shortcut menu click Hide Comments.

7 On the Standard toolbar, click the **Save** button. Print your worksheet, and then close the file and close Excel. Your worksheet will print with the column heading letters, the row heading letters, and the gridlines.

Note

Comments do not automatically print. To print comments, access the **Sheet tab** of the **Page Setup** dialog box, and select the appropriate check box.

End **You have completed Project 3C**

Summary

You can change the look of your worksheet in two primary ways. First, you can format the individual cells or groups of cells on your worksheet by changing cell alignment, applying cell borders, and shading cells. Second, you can format the worksheet itself by changing margins, centering the data vertically and horizontally on the page, and adding headers and footers. Graphics can be inserted in a header or footer to display, for example, a company logo. Cell formatting can be accomplished by using buttons on the Formatting toolbar, or by using the Format Cells dialog box. The dialog box offers more options and control, while the toolbar buttons are quicker to use. You can copy the format from one cell or group of cells to another by using the Format Painter. Worksheet formatting is accomplished using the Page Setup dialog box. Here you have control over the page orientation, margin settings, placement of the worksheet on the page, as well as the header and footer area.

Comments can be viewed and inserted in a cell to assist you in documenting your worksheets. Comments can also be printed. If desired, the gridlines and the row and column headings of a worksheet can be printed.

In This Chapter You Practiced How To

- Change Number Format
- Change Alignment of Cell Contents
- Apply Cell Formatting
- Apply Workbook Formatting
- Print Gridlines, Print Row and Column Headings, and Set Print Quality
- View and Insert Comments in a Cell

Concepts Assessments

Matching   Match each term in the second column with its correct definition in the first column by writing the letter of the term on the blank line in front of the correct definition.

_____ **1.** The various ways to display numbers in Excel.

_____ **2.** The process of determining the overall appearance of a worksheet.

_____ **3.** The default format for a number that you type in a cell.

_____ **4.** The position of text or numbers in a cell.

_____ **5.** The positioning of data between the left and right boundaries of a cell.

_____ **6.** The positioning of data between the top and bottom boundaries of a cell.

_____ **7.** An arrangement of cell contents that reads vertically from the top of the cell to the bottom of the cell.

_____ **8.** Fonts that have extensions or lines on the ends of the characters and that are good for large amounts of text because they are easy to read.

_____ **9.** A feature to emphasize text using bold, italic, and underline.

_____ **10.** A feature that copies all formatting from one selection of cells to another selection of cells.

_____ **11.** A page orientation in which the paper is wider than it is tall.

_____ **12.** The default page orientation in Excel, in which the paper is taller than it is wide.

_____ **13.** A text control option that displays text entirely within the active cell by increasing the height of the row and then wrapping the text onto additional lines in the same cell—thus maintaining the current width of the cell.

_____ **14.** A feature that repeats your cell entry to occupy the entire width of the cell.

_____ **15.** A set of characters with the same design and shape.

A Alignment

B Fill

C Font

D Font styles

E Format Painter

F Formatting

G General format

H Horizontal alignment

I Landscape

J Number formats

K Portrait

L Serif fonts

M Stacked

N Vertical alignment

O Wrap text

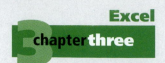

Concepts Assessments (continued)

Fill in the Blank Write the correct answer in the space provided.

1. In addition to formatting individual cells, Excel also enables you to format the overall layout of the _____.

2. Once applied, cell formats stay with the _____, even if you delete the contents of the cell.

3. Unless you apply a different number format to a cell, Excel will use the _____ format.

4. The General number format displays a number exactly as you type it—with _____ exceptions.

5. The default number of decimal places for the Number format is _____.

6. Excel's default horizontal alignment for text is _____ aligned.

7. The default vertical alignment for all data in a cell is _____.

8. Because worksheets usually contain more numbers than text, a _____ type of font is a good choice.

9. The default font for an Excel worksheet is _____.

10. After merging a group of cells to form one large cell, the new, larger cell uses the address of the cell that was in the _____ corner of the selected group.

Project 3D — Costs

Objectives: *Change Number Format, Change Alignment of Cell Contents, Apply Cell Formatting, and Apply Workbook Formatting.*

In the following Skill Assessment, you will edit a workbook for Felicia Mabry, President of the Oceana Palm Grill, which details the operating costs at the various restaurant locations. Your completed workbook will look similar to the one shown in Figure 3.54. You will save the workbook as *3D_Costs_Firstname_Lastname.*

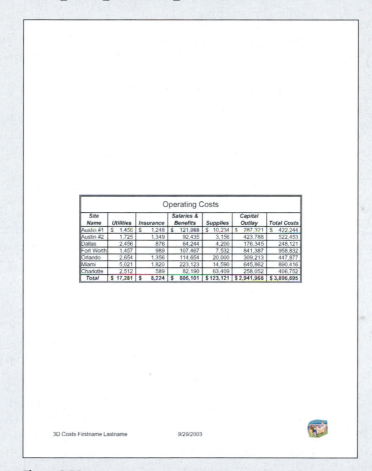

Operating Costs						
Site Name	Utilities	Insurance	Salaries & Benefits	Supplies	Capital Outlay	Total Costs
Austin #1	$ 1,456	$ 1,245	$ 121,988	$ 10,234	$ 287,321	$ 422,244
Austin #2	1,725	1,349	92,435	3,156	423,788	522,453
Dallas	2,456	876	64,244	4,200	176,345	248,121
Fort Worth	1,457	989	107,467	7,532	841,387	958,832
Orlando	2,654	1,356	114,654	20,000	309,213	447,877
Miami	5,021	1,820	223,123	14,590	645,862	890,416
Charlotte	2,512	589	82,190	63,409	258,052	406,752
Total	$ 17,281	$ 8,224	$ 806,101	$ 123,121	$ 2,941,968	$ 3,896,695

3D Costs-Firstname Lastname   9/29/2003

Figure 3.54

1. Start Excel. From the **File** menu, click **Open**. In the **Open** dialog box, navigate to the student files that accompany this textbook, and open the file **e03D_Costs**. Display the **View** menu, click **Header and Footer**, and then click the **Custom Footer** button. In the **Left section**, type **3D Costs-Firstname Lastname** and then close the dialog boxes.

2. From the **File** menu, click **Save As**. In the **Save As** dialog box, navigate to the location where you are storing your projects for this chapter. In the **File name** box, type **3D_Costs_Firstname_Lastname** and then click **Save** or press Enter.

(Project 3D–Costs continues on the next page)

(Project 3D–Costs continued)

3. Select the range **A2:G2**. From the **Format** menu, click **Cells**, and then click the **Alignment tab**. Under **Text control**, select the **Wrap text** check box so that the headings that do not fit within the cell margins display on two lines.

4. Under **Text alignment**, click the **Horizontal arrow**, and then click **Center** to center the text between the left and right boundaries of each cell. Click **OK**. Notice that the text in cells **A2**, **D2**, **F2**, and **G2** has wrapped to two lines. The rows were made taller to accommodate the wrapped text.

5. With the range **A2:G2** still selected, move to the Formatting toolbar, and then click **Bold** and **Italic**. Select **column C**, and then from the column heading area, drag its right edge to the right slightly to accommodate the entire word *Insurance*.

6. Click cell **A1**. On the Formatting toolbar, click the **Font Size arrow**, and then click **14** to enlarge the worksheet title. From the **Format** menu, point to **Row**, and then click **Height**. Change the height of the row to **31.5** and then click **OK**.

7. Select the range **A1:G1**. Press and hold down Ctrl, and then press 1 to display the **Format Cells** dialog box. Click the **Alignment tab**. Under **Text alignment**, click the **Horizontal arrow**, and then click **Center Across Selection**. Click the **Vertical arrow**, click **Center**, and then click **OK**.

8. Click cell **G3**, and then on the Standard toolbar, click **AutoSum** and press Enter. This totals the operating costs for the Austin #1 location. Copy the formula down through cell **G9** to total the costs for each location. Click cell **B10**, click **AutoSum** and press Enter. Copy the formula across through cell **G10** to total the costs in each category and the total for all locations.

9. Select the range **B3:G3**. Point to the selection, right-click, and from the displayed shortcut menu, click **Format Cells**. Click the **Number tab**, and then under **Category**, click **Accounting**. Change the number of **Decimal places** to zero (0), and verify that under **Symbol**, a $ displays. Click **OK**.

10. With the range **B3:G3** still selected, move to the Standard toolbar, and then click **Format Painter**. Point to cell **B10**, and then press and hold down the left mouse button and drag the **Format Painter** pointer across cells **B10:G10**. Release the left mouse button to apply the Accounting format to the selection. Select the columns that are now too narrow, display the **Format** menu, point to **Column**, and then click **AutoFit Selection**.

(Project 3D–Costs continues on the next page)

(Project 3D–Costs continued)

11. Select the range **B4:G9**. Press Ctrl + 1 to display the **Format Cells** dialog box. On the **Number tab**, under **Category**, click **Number**. Change the number of **Decimal places** to 0, and then select the **Use 1000 Separator (,)** check box.

12. Under **Negative numbers**, click the third option—**(1,234)**. Recall that the Accounting format automatically displays negative numbers with parentheses. In the event that you have negative numbers, to align the digits correctly, you must choose the option that includes the parentheses. Click **OK**.

13. Select the range **A10:G10**. On the Formatting toolbar, click **Bold**. Click cell **A10**. On the Formatting toolbar, click **Increase Indent**, and then on the Formatting toolbar, click **Italic**.

14. Select the range **A2:G10**. On the Formatting toolbar, click the **Borders arrow** to display the **Border palette**. In the last row, click the second button, **All Borders**.

15. Select the range **A1:G10**. From the **Format** menu, click **Cells**, and then click the **Border tab**. Under **Line**, in the **Style** list, click the **last style in the second column**—the double line. Under **Presets**, click **Outline**, and then click **OK**.

16. On the Standard toolbar, click **Print Preview** to view the borders you have applied. **Close** Print Preview.

17. From the **File** menu, click **Page Setup**, and then click the **Margins tab**. Under **Center on page**, select the **Horizontally** and **Vertically** check boxes. Click the **Header/Footer tab**, and then click **Custom Footer**. Click in the **Center section**, and then click the **Date** button. Press Tab once to move the insertion point to the **Right section**, and then, on the **Footer** dialog box toolbar, click the **Insert Picture** button.

18. In the displayed **Insert Picture** dialog box, click the **Look in arrow**, and navigate to the student files for this textbook. Select **e03D_Dining** and then click the **Insert** button.

19. On the **Footer** dialog box toolbar, click the **Format Picture** button. In the displayed **Format Picture** dialog box, decrease the height and width of the picture to **0.5** either by using the spin box arrows or by typing directly in the box. Click **OK**.

20. Click **OK** to close the **Footer** dialog box, and then, in the **Page Setup** dialog box, click **Print Preview**. On the **Print Preview** dialog box, click **Print**. In the **Print** dialog box, click **OK**.

21. On the Standard toolbar, click **Save**, close your file, and close Excel.

End You have completed Project 3D

Project 3E — POS

Objectives: *Change Alignment of Cell Contents, Apply Cell Formatting, and Apply Workbook Formatting.*

In the following Skill Assessment, you will edit a workbook for Laura Mabry Hernandez, Director of Point of Sale (POS) Systems for the Oceana Palm Grill, that lists the point of sale equipment at the restaurant locations. Your completed workbook will look similar to the one shown in Figure 3.55. You will save the workbook as *3E_POS_Firstname_Lastname*.

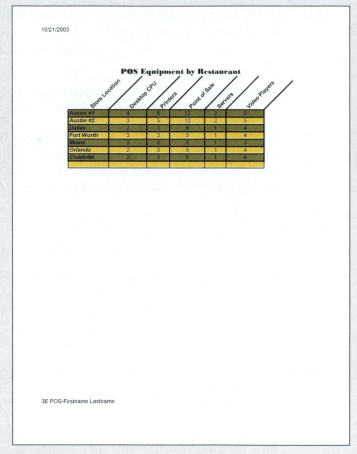

Figure 3.55

(**Project 3E–POS** continues on the next page)

(Project 3E–POS continued)

1. Start Excel. From the **File** menu, click **Open**. In the **Open** dialog box, navigate to the student files that accompany this textbook, and open the file **e03E_POS**. Display the **View** menu, click **Header and Footer**, and then click the **Custom Footer** button. In the **Left section**, type **3E POS-Firstname Lastname** and then close the dialog boxes.

2. From the **File** menu, click **Save As**. In the **Save As** dialog box, navigate to the location where you are storing your projects for this chapter. In the **File name** box, type **3E_POS_Firstname_Lastname** and then click **Save** or press ⏎.

3. Select the range **A2:F10**. From the **Edit** menu, point to **Clear**, and then click **Formats** to clear all formatting from the selected range. Click anywhere to cancel the selection, and notice that the shading format is removed from the selected cells.

4. Click cell **A1**. On the Formatting toolbar, click the **Font arrow**, and then click **Britannic Bold**. If this font is not available on your system, choose another serif font. Recall that a serif font contains extensions (lines) on the ends of the characters. Click the **Font Size arrow**, and then click **14**.

5. Select the range **A2:F2**. On the Formatting toolbar, click **Bold**. Point to the selection, and then click the right mouse button to display the shortcut menu. Click **Format Cells**. Click the **Alignment tab**. Under **Orientation**, point to the **red diamond**, press and hold down the left mouse button, and then drag upward so that **45** displays in the **Degrees** box. Alternatively, you can type **45** in the degrees box or click the spin box arrows. Under **Text alignment**, click the **Horizontal arrow**, and then click **Center**. Click **OK**.

6. Select the range **A1:G1**. Display the **Format Cells** dialog box. On the **Alignment tab**, click the **Horizontal arrow**, and then click **Center Across Selection**. Recall that when you use this method, all the cells remain intact—none is merged into the first cell in the selection, as is the case with the Merge and Center button. Click **OK**.

7. Select the range **A3:A9**. On the Formatting toolbar, click **Italic**, and then click **Bold**.

8. Select the range **A3:F9**. On the Formatting toolbar, click the **Borders arrow** to display the **Borders palette**. In the last row, click the second button, **All Borders**. From the **Format** menu, click **Cells**, click the **Border tab**, and then under **Line**, in the **Style** list, click the **fifth line style** in the second column. In the **Presets** area click the **Outline** and the **Inside** buttons to apply the new line style to the borders. Click **OK**.

(Project 3E–POS continues on the next page)

(Project 3E–POS continued)

9. Select the range **A2:F2**. When you select this range, a portion of the word *Players* may not appear to be included in the selection. Because the text is formatted at a 45-degree angle, it may not display within the selection. From the **Format** menu, click **Cells**. Under **Border**, in the white preview area, click to apply a **Right** border and a **Center** border—the button with the vertical line displayed in the center. Notice that in the white preview area, the left and top edges of the sample cells do not contain a border. Click **OK**.

10. Select the range **B3:F9** (all of the cells with numbers). On the Formatting toolbar, click the **Center** button. On the Standard toolbar, click **Save**. Then, on the Standard toolbar, click the **Print Preview** button to see the changes you have made. On the Print Preview toolbar, click **Close** to return to the worksheet.

11. From the **File** menu, click **Page Setup**, and then click the **Margins tab**. Change the **Top** margin to **1.5**, and then change the **Footer** margin to **1**. Under **Center on page**, select the **Horizontally** check box.

12. Click the **Header/Footer tab**, and then click **Custom Header**. With the insertion point positioned in the **Left section**, click the **Date** button. Click **OK**.

13. In the displayed **Page Setup** dialog box, click the **Print Preview** button to view your worksheet. On the Print Preview toolbar, click **Print**, and then click **OK**. Save the changes you have made to your worksheet since the last Save operation, and then close the file and close Excel.

 You have completed Project 3E ———————————————

Project 3F — Time Sheets

Objectives: *Change Number Format, Change Alignment of Cell Contents, Apply Cell Formatting, Apply Workbook Formatting, and View and Insert Comments in a Cell.*

In the following Skill Assessment, you will edit a workbook for Seth Weddel, Controller for the Oceana Palm Grill, that lists the time sheets and weekly salaries for the Austin #1 location. Your completed workbook will look similar to the one shown in Figure 3.56. You will save the workbook as *3F_Time_Sheets_Firstname_Lastname*.

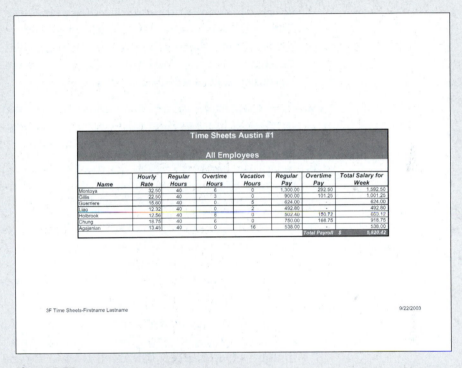

Figure 3.56

1. Start Excel. From the **File** menu, click **Open**. In the **Open** dialog box, navigate to the student files that accompany this textbook, and open the file **e03F_Time_Sheets**. Display the **View** menu, click **Header and Footer**, and then click the **Custom Footer** button. In the **Left section**, type **3F Time Sheets-Firstname Lastname** and then close the dialog boxes.

2. From the **File** menu, click **Save As**. In the **Save As** dialog box, navigate to the location where you are storing your projects for this chapter. In the **File name** box, type **3F_Time_Sheets_Firstname_Lastname** and then click **Save** or press Enter.

(Project 3F–Time Sheets continues on the next page)

(Project 3F–Time Sheets continued)

3. Select the range **A1:H3**. Press and hold down Ctrl and press 1 to display the **Format Cells** dialog box. Click the **Alignment tab**, and then click the **Horizontal arrow**. Click **Center Across Selection**. Click the **Patterns tab**. Under **Cell shading**, in the second row of the palette, click the last color—**Dark Gray**. Click the **Font tab**, and then under **Font style**, click **Bold**, and under **Size**, click **16**. Click the **Color arrow**, and in the fifth row of the palette, click the last color—**White**. Click **OK**.

4. Select the range **A6:H6**. Right-click the selection to display the shortcut menu, and then click **Format Cells**. Click the **Alignment tab**, and then, under **Text control**, select the **Wrap text** check box. Under **Text alignment**, click the **Horizontal arrow**, and then click **Center**. Click the **Font tab**. Change the **Size** to **12** and change the **Font style** to **Bold Italic**. Click **OK**.

5. Select the range **B7:B13**. Display the **Format** menu, click **Cells**, and then click the **Number tab**. Under **Category**, click **Number**. Verify that **2 Decimal places** display. Click **OK**.

6. Select the range **F7:H13**. On the Formatting toolbar, click the **Comma Style** button. Click cell **H14**, and then, on the Formatting toolbar, click the **Currency Style** button.

7. Click cell **H7**, and on the Standard toolbar, click the **AutoSum** button. Because you need only add the regular pay to the overtime pay to compute the total weekly salary, drag to select **F7:G7** so that the formula indicates =SUM(F7:G7) and then press Enter. Copy the formula down through cell **H13**.

8. In cell **H14**, click **AutoSum** to total the column—your result should be $5,820.42. Select the range **C7:E13**, and then, on the Formatting toolbar, click **Center**. Click cell **G14** and type **Total Payroll**

9. Select the range **G14:H14**. Press and hold down Ctrl and press 1 to display the **Format Cells** dialog box. Click the **Patterns tab**. Under **Cell shading**, in the second row of the palette, click the last color—**Dark gray**. Click the **Font tab**, and then click the **Color arrow**. In the fifth row of the palette, click the last color—**White**. Under **Font style**, click **Bold Italic**. Click **OK**.

10. Select the range **A6:H13**. On the Formatting toolbar, click the **Borders arrow** and then, in the third row, click the second button— **All Borders**. On the Standard toolbar, click **Save**. Recall that it is good practice to save your work periodically.

(Project 3F–Time Sheets continues on the next page)

(Project 3F–Time Sheets continued)

11. Select the range **A1:H14**. On the Formatting toolbar, click the **Borders arrow**. In the last row, click the last button—**Thick Box Border**. Click cell **D6**, right-click, and from the displayed shortcut menu, click **Insert Comment**. In the comment box, type **Overtime paid at 1.5 times hourly rate** and then change the inserted name to your name. Click in any empty cell to close the comment box. If necessary, right-click cell D6 and click Hide Comments from the shortcut menu.

12. On the menu bar, click **File**, and then click **Page Setup**. Click the **Margins tab**, and then under **Center on page**, select the **Horizontally** and **Vertically** check boxes. Change the **Footer margin** to **1**.

13. Click the **Header/Footer tab**, and then click **Custom Footer**. Press twice to position the insertion point in the **Right section**. On the **Footer** dialog box toolbar, click the **Date** button, and then click **OK**.

14. Click the **Page tab**. Under **Orientation**, click **Landscape**. Under **Scaling**, adjust the worksheet to **90%** of its normal size. Click **OK**.

15. On the Standard toolbar, click the **Save** button, and then click the **Print Preview** button. On the **Print Preview** toolbar, click **Print** and then click **OK**. Close your file, and then close Excel.

End **You have completed Project 3F**

Project 3G—Category Sales

Objectives: *Change Number Format, Change Alignment of Cell Contents, Apply Cell Formatting, and Apply Workbook Formatting.*

In the following Performance Assessment, you will edit a workbook for Donna Rohan Kurian, Executive Chef for the Oceana Palm Grill, that lists category sales for a recent Saturday. Your completed workbook will look similar to the one shown in Figure 3.57. You will save the workbook as *3G_Category_Sales_Firstname_Lastname.*

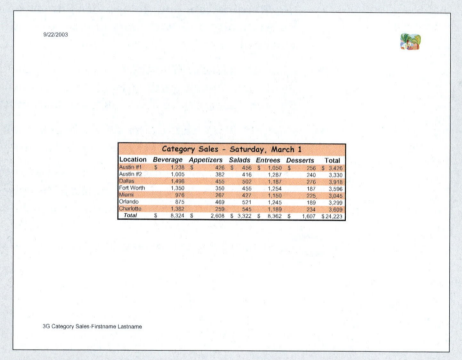

Figure 3.57

1. Start Excel. From the **File** menu, click **Open**. In the **Open** dialog box, navigate to the student files that accompany this textbook, and open the file **e03G_Category_Sales**. Display the **View** menu, click **Header and Footer**, and then click the **Custom Footer** button. In the **Left section**, type **3G Category Sales-Firstname Lastname** and then close the dialog boxes.

2. From the **File** menu, click **Save As**. In the **Save As** dialog box, navigate to the location where you are storing your projects for this chapter. In the **File name** box, type **3G_Category_Sales_Firstname_Lastname** and then click **Save** or press Enter.

(Project 3G–Category Sales continues on the next page)

(Project 3G–Category Sales continued)

3. Select the range **A1:G1**. Display the **Format Cells** dialog box, and click the **Font tab**. Change the **Font** to **Comic Sans MS**, change the **Font style** to **Bold**, and change the **Font Size** to **14 pt**. Click the **Alignment tab**, and apply the **Center Across Selection** horizontal alignment. Click **OK** to close the **Format Cells** dialog box.

4. In cell **B10**, use the **AutoSum** button to create a total for the Beverage category. Use the **fill handle** to copy the formula across through cell **F10**.

5. In cell **G3**, use the **AutoSum** button to create a total for the Austin #1 location. Use the **fill handle** to copy the formula through cell **G9**. Click cell **G10**, and total the column.

6. Select the range **B4:G9**, apply the **Comma Style**, and then click **Decrease Decimal** two times so that there are no decimal places. Select the range **B3:G3**, hold down Ctrl, and select **B10:G10**. Then, with the two nonadjacent ranges selected, apply **Currency Style**, and click **Decrease Decimal** two times. The total sales for all categories in cell **G10** should be $24,223.

7. Select the range **A2:G2**, change the **Font Size** to **12**, and then apply **Bold** to the selection. Select **columns A:G** and **AutoFit** the columns.

8. Apply **Italic** to the names of each of the categories. Click in cell **A10** and apply **Bold** and **Italic**, and then **Increase Indent** one time.

9. Select the range **A1:G1**. Display the **Format Cells** dialog box, click the **Patterns tab**, and under **Color**, in the fifth row of the palette, click the second color box—**Tan**. Click **OK**.

10. Select the range **A3:G3**. On the Formatting toolbar, click the **Fill Color arrow** (to the right of the **Borders** button) to display the color palette. In the last row, click the second color—**Tan**—to apply tan shading across the row. Notice that you can apply shading to cells either from the **Format Cells** dialog box or from the **Fill Color** button.

11. Repeat this shading for the data in rows **5**, **7**, and **9**. (Hint: After formatting the color for a row, you can select the next row's data and then press the Repeat key, F4. Do not use the Format Painter because this would apply the Currency style to rows where it is not appropriate.)

12. Select the range **A1:G10**. Apply a **Thick Box** border to the selection. Display the **Page Setup** dialog box, change the worksheet orientation to **Landscape**, and then center the worksheet on the page **horizontally** and **vertically**. Create a **Custom Header** that includes the **date** in the **Left section** and the picture **e03G_Waiter** in the **Right section**. Format the picture to a height and width of **0.5 inches**.

13. Save your worksheet, and then view it in **Print Preview**. Print the worksheet, close your file, and then close Excel.

End You have completed Project 3G

Project 3H—Restaurant Sales

Objectives: *Change Number Format, Change Alignment of Cell Contents, Apply Cell Formatting, Apply Workbook Formatting, and View and Insert Comments in a Cell.*

In the following Performance Assessment, you will edit a workbook for Felicia Mabry, President of the Oceana Palm Grill, that details restaurant sales for the first half of the year. Your completed workbook will look similar to the one shown in Figure 3.58. You will save the workbook as *3H_Restaurant_Sales_Firstname_Lastname*.

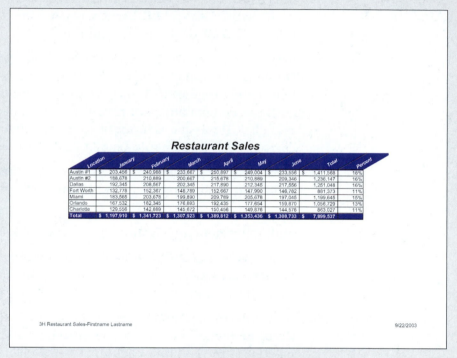

Figure 3.58

1. Start Excel. From the **File** menu, click **Open**. In the **Open** dialog box, navigate to the student files that accompany this textbook, and open the file **e03H_Restaurant_Sales**. Display the **View** menu, click **Header and Footer**, and then click the **Custom Footer** button. In the **Left section**, type **3H Restaurant Sales-Firstname Lastname** and then close the dialog boxes.

2. From the **File** menu, click **Save As**. In the **Save As** dialog box, navigate to the location where you are storing your projects for this chapter. In the **File name** box, type **3H_Restaurant_Sales_Firstname_Lastname** and then click **Save** or press Enter.

(Project 3H–Restaurant Sales continues on the next page)

(Project 3H–Restaurant Sales continued)

3. In cell **A1**, change the **Font Size** to **22**, and apply **Bold** and **Italic**. Select the range **A1:I1**. Display the **Format Cells** dialog box, and from the **Alignment tab**, apply the **Center Across Selection** horizontal alignment.

4. In cell **B2**, type **January** and then use the **fill handle** to complete the series across through June.

5. Select the range **A2:I2**. Using the Formatting toolbar buttons, apply **Bold** and **Italic**, and then **Center** the text. From the **Alignment tab** of the **Format Cells** dialog box, change the orientation to **30 Degrees**, and change the **Vertical alignment** to **Center**.

6. In cell **H3**, use the **AutoSum** button to create a formula that calculates the January through June total for the Austin #1 location. Use **AutoFill** to copy the formula for the remaining locations. In cell **H2**, type **Total**

7. In cell **A10**, type **Total** In cell **B10**, use the **AutoSum** button to create a formula that calculates the January total. Use **AutoFill** to copy the formula for each month and the Total column.

8. Select the range **B3:H3**. Using the Formatting toolbar button, apply the **Currency Style**. Use the **Decrease Decimal** button to decrease the number of decimals to zero (0). Click **Format Painter**, and copy the formatting to the Total row—cells **B10:H10**.

9. Select the range **B4:H9**. Using the Formatting toolbar button, apply the **Comma Style**. Use the **Decrease Decimal** button to decrease the number of decimals to zero (0). **AutoFit** any columns if necessary.

10. Click cell **I2** and type **Percent** Click in cell **I3**. Create a formula that calculates the percent that each location's total is of the total income. (To create this formula, divide the total for Austin #1 location, cell **H3**, by the total in cell **H10**. Be sure to make the cell reference to cell **H10** absolute—**$H$10**.) Copy the formula down through cell **I9**. Select the range **I3:I9**, and using the Formatting toolbar button, apply the **Percent Style**. Click **Save**.

11. Select the range **A2:I2**. Use the **Fill Color** button to apply the **Blue** fill color to the range—the sixth color in the second row of the color palette. To provide better contrast of the text on the blue background, display the **Format Cells** dialog box, and from the **Font tab**, change the **Font Color** to **White**—the last color in the fifth row. Select the range **A10:I10**, and apply the same **Fill Color** and **Font Color** as you did in **row 3**. (Hint: The Fill Color button is now the same color—Blue—and you can click the arrow on the Font Color button and click White from the displayed palette.) Apply **Bold**. Widen columns if necessary.

(Project 3H–Restaurant Sales continues on the next page)

(Project 3H–Restaurant Sales continued)

12. Select the range **A3:I10**. Using the Formatting toolbar button, apply the **All Borders** border style to the selection.

13. Select the range **A2:I2**. Display the **Format Cells** dialog box, and click the **Border tab**. Apply a single line border style to the bottom and to the center of the selection.

14. Display the **Page Setup** dialog box. Change the worksheet orientation to **Landscape** and then, under **Scaling**, scale the worksheet to **90%**. Center the worksheet on the page **horizontally** and **vertically**. Create a **custom footer** that includes the **date** in the **Right section**.

15. In cell **I3**, add the following comment, using your own name: **Same percentage as last year**

16. Save your worksheet, and then view it in **Print Preview**. Print the worksheet, close your file, and then close Excel.

 You have completed Project 3H ———————————————

Project 3I—Employee Sales

Objectives: *Change Number Format, Change Alignment of Cell Contents, Apply Cell Formatting, and Apply Workbook Formatting.*

In the following Performance Assessment, you will edit a workbook for Seth Weddel, Controller for the Oceana Palm Grill, that details restaurant sales by employee. Your completed workbook will look similar to the one shown in Figure 3.59. You will save the workbook as *3I_Employee_Sales_Firstname_Lastname.*

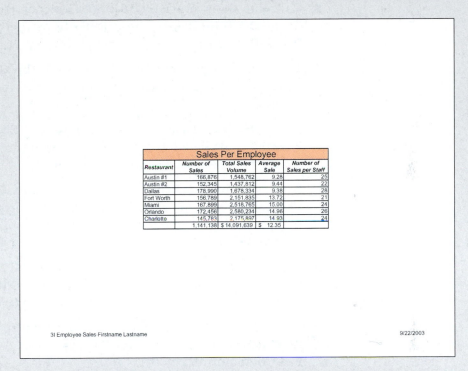

	Sales Per Employee			
Restaurant	Number of Sales	Total Sales Volume	Average Sale	Number of Sales per Staff
Austin #1	166,876	1,548,762	9.28	25
Austin #2	152,345	1,437,812	9.44	22
Dallas	178,990	1,678,334	9.38	28
Fort Worth	156,789	2,151,835	13.72	21
Miami	167,899	2,518,765	15.00	24
Orlando	172,456	2,580,234	14.96	26
Charlotte	145,783	2,175,897	14.93	24
	1,141,138	$ 14,091,639	$ 12.35	

3I Employee Sales-Firstname Lastname   9/22/2003

Figure 3.59

1. Start Excel. From the **File** menu, click **Open**. In the **Open** dialog box, navigate to the student files that accompany this textbook, and open the file **e03I_Employee_Sales**. Display the **View** menu, click **Header and Footer**, and then click the **Custom Footer** button. In the **Left section**, type **3I Employee Sales-Firstname Lastname** and then close the dialog boxes.

2. From the **File** menu, click **Save As**. In the **Save As** dialog box, navigate to the location where you are storing your projects for this chapter. In the **File name** box, type **3I_Employee_Sales_Firstname_Lastname** and then click **Save** or press Enter.

(**Project 3I**–Employee Sales continues on the next page)

(Project 3I–Employee Sales continued)

3. Select the range **A2:E2**, and then display the **Format Cells** dialog box. Use the appropriate tabs in the dialog box to activate **Wrap text**, and center the text in the cells both **horizontally** and **vertically**. Apply **Bold** and **Italic**. Drag to adjust the width of each column so that the column titles make sense, display on no more than two lines, and look attractive. See Figure 3.59.

4. Create totals in **row 10** for the **Number of Sales** and the **Total Sales Volume**.

5. To create the Average Sale formula for each location, click in cell **D3**, divide the Total Sales Volume (cell **C3**) by the Number of Sales (cell **B3**). Fill the formula down through row 10.

6. To format the title, change the font to **Berlin Sans FB** or some other sans sarif font, **16 pt**, and then **center** the title over the worksheet columns.

7. Select the nonadjacent ranges **B3:B10** and **E3:E9**. Display the **Format Cells** dialog box. Apply the **Number** format with the **1000 separator** and **zero (0)** decimal places.

8. Select the range **C3:C9**, and use the **Format Cells** dialog box (not the toolbar button) to apply the **Currency** format with **zero (0)** decimal places and **no dollar sign**. Select the range **D3:D9** and apply the **Currency** format with **2 decimal places** and **no dollar sign**.

9. Select cell **C10**, click the **Currency Style** button, and then click **Decrease Decimal** twice. If necessary, **AutoFit** to display results. Select cell **D10**, and click the **Currency Style** button.

10. Select the range **A1:E10**, click the **Borders button arrow**, and apply **All Borders**. To the range **A1:E1**, apply **Tan** cell shading from the **Fill Color** button palette.

11. Use the **Page Setup** dialog box to change the worksheet orientation to **Landscape**. Center the worksheet on the page **horizontally** and **vertically**. Create a **custom footer** that includes the **date** in the **Right section**.

12. Save your worksheet, and then view it in **Print Preview**. Print the worksheet, close your file, and then close Excel.

End **You have completed Project 3I**

Project 3J — Seafood Sales

Objectives: *Change Number Format, Change Alignment of Cell Contents, Apply Cell Formatting, and Apply Workbook Formatting.*

In the following Mastery assessment, you will edit a workbook for Donna Rohan Kurian, Executive Chef for the Oceana Palm Grill, that details the sales of seafood specials during a one-week period in July at the two Austin restaurants. Your completed workbook will look similar to the one shown in Figure 3.60. You will save the workbook as *3J_Seafood_Sales_Firstname_Lastname*.

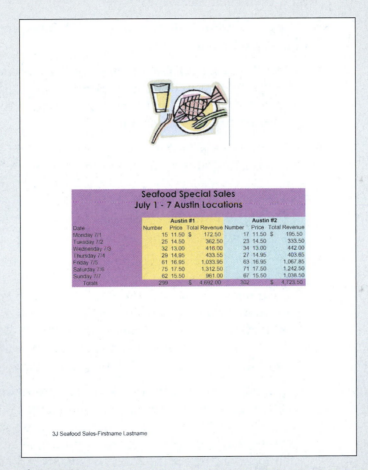

Figure 3.60

(**Project 3J**–Seafood Sales continues on the next page)

Mastery Assessments (continued)

(Project 3J–Seafood Sales continued)

1. Start Excel. On the **File** menu, click **Open**. In the **Open** dialog box, navigate to the student files that accompany this textbook, and open the file **e03J_Seafood_Sales**. Display the **View** menu, click **Header and Footer**, and then click the **Custom Footer** button. In the **Left section** type **3J Seafood Sales-Firstname Lastname** and then click **OK** to close the dialog boxes.

2. From the **File** menu, click **Save As**. In the **Save As** dialog box, navigate to the location where you are storing your projects for this chapter. In the **File name** box, type **3J_Seafood_Sales_Firstname_Lastname** and then click **Save** or press Enter.

3. Select **columns A:G**, and from the **Format** menu, point to **Column** and **AutoFit Selection**.

4. Select the range **A1:G2** and display the **Format Cells** dialog box. Change the font to **Century Gothic**, change the font style to **Bold**, change the font size to **16**, and then change the horizontal alignment to **Center Across Selection**.

5. Select the range **B4:D4**, change the font style to **Bold**, and change the horizontal alignment to **Center Across Selection**. Repeat for the range **E4:G4**. Select the range **B4:D12** and from the **Fill Color arrow**, apply **Light Yellow** shading. Select the range **E4:G12** and apply **Light Turquoise** shading. To the ranges **A1:G3** and **A4:A12**, apply **Lavender** shading.

6. In cell **D6**, create a formula to calculate the total revenue for the seafood specials sold at the Austin #1 location for Monday, July 1. Copy the formula down through cell **D12**. In cells **D7:D12**, use the **Format Cells** dialog box to format the numbers as **Currency** with **two decimal places** and **no symbol**. To cell **D6**, use the **Format Cells** dialog box to apply the **Currency** style with the **$** symbol. Repeat the calculation and the formatting for the Austin #2 location.

7. In cell **A13**, type **Totals** and **Increase Indent** twice. In cells **D13** and **G13**, compute total revenue for each location. If necessary, apply currency formatting with two decimal places to the two cells. In cells **B13** and **E13**, compute the total number of seafood specials sold for each location. Select the range **B13:G13**, and apply **Lavender** shading. Save your worksheet.

8. Create a custom header, and in the center section, insert the picture **e03J_Seafood**. Format the picture as **2 inches high** and **2 inches wide**. Change the **header margin** to **1.5**, and center the worksheet both **horizontally** and **vertically** on the page.

9. Save your workbook, view it in **Print Preview**, and then print it. Close the file, and then close Excel.

End You have completed Project 3J

Project 3K — Chef Expenses

Objectives: *Change Number Format, Change Alignment of Cell Contents, Apply Cell Formatting, Apply Workbook Formatting, and View and Insert Comments in a Cell.*

In the following Mastery assessment, you will edit a workbook that details chef expenses for all locations of the Oceana Palm Grill. Your completed workbook will look similar to the one shown in Figure 3.61. You will save the workbook as *3K_Chef_Expenses_Firstname_Lastname*.

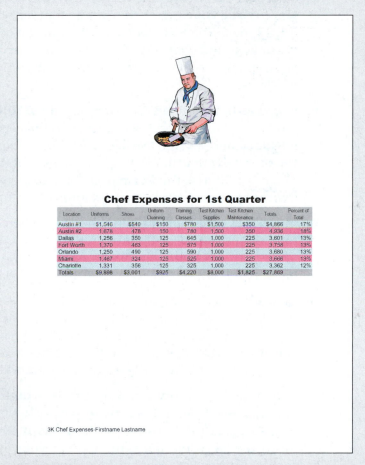

Figure 3.61

(Project 3K–Chef Expenses continues on the next page)

(Project 3K–Chef Expenses continued)

1. Start Excel. On the **File** menu, click **Open**. In the **Open** dialog box, navigate to the student files that accompany this textbook, and open the file **e03K_Chef_Expenses**. Display the **View** menu, click **Header and Footer**, and then click the **Custom Footer** button. In the **Left section** type 3K Chef Expenses-Firstname Lastname and then click **OK** to close the dialog boxes. Save the file in your storage location for this chapter as **3K_Chef_Expenses_Firstname_Lastname**

2. Select cell **A1**. Center the contents across cells **A1:I1**, change the font to **Arial Black**, and change the font size to **18**. Select the range **A2:G2**, wrap the text, center the text in the cells **horizontally** and **vertically**, and change the font to **Arial Narrow**. If necessary, adjust any columns so that the text displays attractively on no more than two lines.

3. In cell **A10**, type **Totals** and then in cells **B10:G10**, compute the totals in each category. Select the nonadjacent ranges **B3:G3** and **B10:G10** and use the **Format Cells** dialog box to apply the **Currency Style** with no decimal places and the $ symbol. To the range **B4:G9**, use the **Format Cells** dialog box to apply the **Currency Style** with no symbol and no decimal places.

4. In cell **H2**, type **Totals** and in cell **I2,** type **Percent of Total** In cell **H3**, total the expenses for the Austin #1 location, and then copy the formula to the remaining locations. Click cell **G4**, click the **Format Painter** button, and then format the range **H4:H9**.

5. In cell **H10**, compute the grand total for all expenses at all locations. In cell **I3**, construct a formula to compute the percentage that this location represents of the total expenses. Be sure to make your reference to cell **H10** absolute. Copy the formula down for each location, and apply the **Percent Style**. Save your workbook.

6. Shade the data in **rows 3**, **5**, **7**, and **9** in **Light Turquoise**. Shade the data in **rows 4**, **6**, and **8** in **Rose**. Select the nonadjacent ranges **A2:I2** and **A10:I10**, and apply **25 percent Gray** shading. In cell **D2**, insert the following comment, and use your own name: **New cleaning service, Kitchen Pro Cleaners, being tested this quarter.**

7. Center the page **horizontally** and **vertically**, and set the header margin to **1 inch**. Create a custom header, and in the center section, insert the picture **03K_Chef_at_Work**. Format the size of the picture to **2.5 inches high** and **1.5 inches wide**.

8. Save your workbook. View the workbook in **Print Preview**, print it, close the workbook, and close Excel.

End You have completed Project 3K

Project 3L — Budget

Objectives: *Change Number Format, Change Alignment of Cell Contents, Apply Cell Formatting, and Apply Workbook Formatting.*

Using the data found in e03L_Budget, use the techniques you have learned in this chapter to attractively format the data in the workbook. Compute totals where appropriate. Use each of the following at least once: apply currency format, indent cell contents, rotate text, change font and font size, apply cell borders, apply cell shading, insert a picture in a header or footer (use e03L_Table), and center the worksheet horizontally and vertically. Insert your name in the footer, print the worksheet, and save the workbook as *3L_Budget_Firstname_Lastname.*

 End **You have completed Project 3L** ————————————

Project 3M — Schedule

Objectives: *Change Number Format, Change Alignment of Cell Contents, Apply Cell Formatting, and Apply Workbook Formatting.*

Select three of the restaurant locations for the Oceana Palm Grill, and create a weekly schedule for the hours when various chefs will be supervising the kitchen. At each location, a supervising chef is in the kitchen every day between 8 a.m. and 12 midnight. Chefs work an eight-hour shift in the kitchen—either 8 a.m.–4 p.m. or 4 p.m.–midnight. Use the techniques you have practiced in this chapter to format the worksheet attractively. Use each of the following at least once: indent cell contents, rotate text, change font and font size, apply cell borders, apply cell shading, insert a picture in a header or footer (use e03M_Chef), and center the worksheet horizontally and vertically. Insert your name in the footer, print the worksheet, and save the workbook as *3M_Schedule_Firstname_Lastname.*

 End **You have completed Project 3M** ————————————

On the Internet

Locate Corporate Financial Information

Go to the Web site **http://www.thecheesecakefactory.com/financial.html** and look at the various types of financial information that is generated for a restaurant. Then, use a search engine to locate financial information about a restaurant chain about which you think you might like to learn more or in which you might possibly invest in some stock.

GO! with Help

Print Comments in a Worksheet

In this exercise, you will use Microsoft Help to get help with printing comments.

1. If necessary, start Excel to open a new workbook.

2. At the right edge of the menu bar, click in the **Type a question for help** box, type **print comments** and then press the Enter key.

   The task pane opens, showing Search Results. Notice that you typed *print comments* as the question instead of *How do I print comments?* It is not actually necessary to ask the question *as* a question.

3. Click the link **Print comments**.

   A Microsoft Excel Help window displays with Help for the topic.

4. In the upper right corner of the Help window, click **Show All**.

5. Review the information provided in the Help window. Notice that there are two ways to format comments on your printed worksheet.

6. Print the contents of the Help window with the expanded material.

7. Close the Help Window, and then close the task pane.

4 chapterfour

Ranges and Functions

In this chapter, you will: complete these projects and practice these skills.

Project 4A **Creating and Using Named Ranges**	**Objectives** • Create Range Names • Use Range Names in a Formula

Project 4B **Using Statistical Functions**	**Objective** • Create Statistical Functions

Project 4C **Using Date and Financial Functions**	**Objective** • Create Date & Time and Financial Functions

Project 4D **Using Logical Functions and Controlling the Print Area**	**Objectives** • Create Logical Functions • Set and Clear a Print Area

Owens Family Builders

Owens Family Builders was founded in 1968 as Owens and Sons Builders; in 1980 the name was changed to reflect the extended family that had joined the business. Today the company has more than 300 employees, including 50 members of the Owens family.

Focusing on home building, the company is known for quality construction, innovative design, and customer service. Owens Family Builders has built more than 3,000 homes in the Orlando area and has also built many schools, shopping centers, and government buildings.

© Getty Images, Inc.

Ranges and Functions

In this chapter you will create range names and use them in a formula. You will also create statistical, date and time, financial, and logical functions. Finally, you will set and clear a print area.

Project 4A **Construction Costs**

In this project, you will work with groups of cells, referred to as ranges. You will name, modify, and delete ranges and use row and column labels to name ranges.

In Activities 4.1 through 4.5, you will edit a workbook created by Warren Owen, president of the Owens Custom Home division of Owens Family Builders, which details the construction costs for the past year by quarter. The two worksheets of your completed workbook will look similar to Figure 4.1. You will save the workbook as *4A_Construction_ Costs_Firstname_Lastname.*

Owens Family Builders
Construction Costs by Quarter
Custom Home Division

	1st Qtr		2nd Qtr		3rd Qtr		4th Qtr
Land Acquisition	$	1,155,547	$	1,153,544	$	953,541	$	827,647
Surveying		14,867		18,463		9,683		5,385
Grading		136,548		152,529		127,527		145,527
Utilities		14,987		28,982		32,981		10,932
Roads		574,802		327,801		319,800		474,082
Concrete Supplies		129,510		127,014		128,532		125,432
Lumber Supplies		264,184		143,183		175,181		167,182
Electrical Supplies		112,806		94,803		72,836		62,854
Plumbing Supplies		92,187		134,928		61,987		53,187
Roof Tiles		64,436		42,956		58,867		52,329
Appliances		56,893		65,839		31,736		56,983
Decorating		9,432		12,345		14,874		21,984
Front Landscaping		16,389		19,384		48,567		37,482
Total by Quarter	$	2,642,588	$	2,321,771	$	2,036,112	$	2,041,006

4A_Construction_Costs_Firstname_Lastname

Owens Family Builders
Annual Construction Costs
Custom Home Division

Land Costs	$	6,485,175
Building Costs		2,164,394
Interior Costs		270,086
Front Landscaping		121,822
Total	$	9,041,477

4A_Construction_Costs_Firstname_Lastname

Figure 4.1
Project 4A—Construction Costs

Objective 1
Create Range Names

Recall that a range is a group of two or more cells that can be adjacent (touching one another) or nonadjacent (not touching one another). When you select a range of cells, all the cells in the range can, as a group, be formatted, moved, copied, or deleted. If the cells are adjacent, the range is referred to by the first and last cell in the range, for example, B3:B7. If the cells are nonadjacent, commas are used between each cell reference, for example B3, B7, B10. Another way to refer to a range of cells is by **range name**. A range name usually defines the purpose of the selected cells and provides a distinctive, easy-to-remember name.

Activity 4.1 Naming a Range

By assigning a name to a range of cells, you can use the name in a formula to refer to the group of cells. This makes it easier for you and others to understand the meaning of formulas in a worksheet. It also simplifies navigation in large worksheets because you can use the Go To command to move to a named range.

1 **Start** Excel. Click the **Open** button , navigate to the student files that accompany this textbook, and then open the file **e04A_Construction_Costs**.

2 From the **File** menu, click **Save As**. In the **Save As** dialog box, navigate to the location where you are storing your projects for this chapter, creating a new folder for Chapter 4 if you want to do so. In the **File name** box, type **4A_Construction_Costs_Firstname_Lastname** and then click **Save** or press Enter.

3 Select the range **A1:E1**, and then click the **Merge and Center** button . Select the range **A2:E2**, and then press F4, the repeat key, to repeat the merge and center action. Repeat for the range **A3:E3**.

4 Click cell **B5**, type **1st Qtr** and then press Enter. Click cell **B5** again, and then drag the fill handle to the right through **E5** to create a series of four quarters. With the range **B5:E5** selected, on the Formatting toolbar, click the **Bold** button **B** and the **Align Right** button .

5 Click cell **A18**, type **Total by Quarter** and then, in cell **B18**, use **AutoSum** Σ to create a total of the 1st Qtr costs. Copy the formula across through cell **E18**, and leave the range selected.

6 With the range **B18:E18** selected, hold down Ctrl and select the range **B6:E6**.

The two nonadjacent ranges are selected, as shown in Figure 4.2.

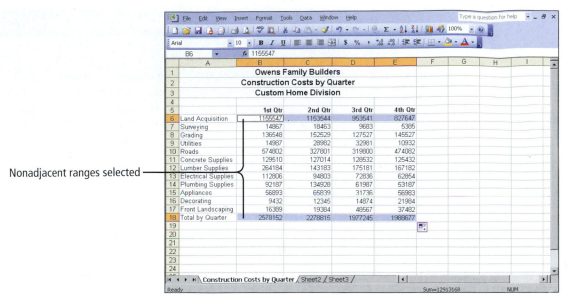

Nonadjacent ranges selected

Figure 4.2

7 On the Formatting toolbar, click the **Currency Style** button $, and then click the **Decrease Decimal** button two times. Select the range **B7:E17**. On the Formatting toolbar, click the **Comma Style** button , and then click the **Decrease Decimal** button two times.

8 Select the range **B6:E10**. To the right of the Formula Bar, click in the **Name Box**. The cell reference *B6* moves to the left edge of the box and is highlighted in blue. Type **Land_Costs** as shown in Figure 4.3, and then press Enter.

The name *Land_Costs* is assigned to the group of values in the range. These values represent the costs involved in getting land ready for construction. Excel has some rules for naming ranges, which are described in the table in Figure 4.4. Take a moment to study this information.

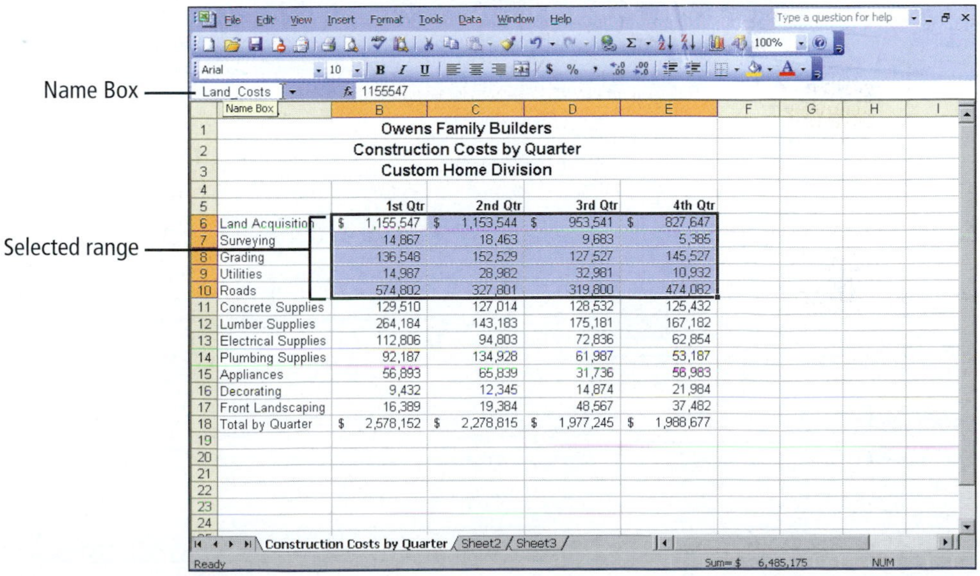

Name Box

Selected range

Figure 4.3

Rules for Naming a Range of Cells in Excel

Characteristic	Rule
Characters	The first character of the name must be a letter or an underscore (_). Although you can use a maximum of 255 characters, short, meaningful names are the most useful. Numbers can be part of a name, but symbols other than the underscore (_) or period (.) cannot.
Words	Names can be more than one word, but there cannot be spaces between the words. Use an underscore or a period as a separator in range names that have multiple words, for example, Land_Costs.
Cell references	Names cannot be the same as cell references, for example, A1.
Case	Names can contain uppercase and lowercase letters. Excel does not distinguish between uppercase and lowercase characters in range names. For example, if you have created the name *Land* and then create another name called *LAND* in the same workbook, the second name will replace the first one.

Figure 4.4

9 Select the range **B11:E13**. From the **Insert** menu, point to **Name**, and then click **Define**.

This is another method to name a range. The Define Name dialog box displays, as shown in Figure 4.5. Notice that in the large box under *Names in workbook*, the first range that you named, *Land_Costs*, is listed. At the bottom of the dialog box, the selected range, *B11:E13*, is indicated by absolute cell references—dollar signs. In the *Names in workbook* box, Excel suggests *Concrete_Supplies* as the name for this range, which is the text in the first cell to the left of the selected range.

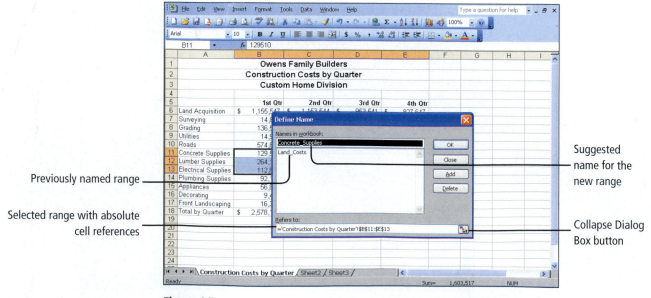

Previously named range

Selected range with absolute cell references

Suggested name for the new range

Collapse Dialog Box button

Figure 4.5

Note — Properties of Named Ranges

A range name is always absolute. If you insert rows, the range adjusts to the new cell address to represent the cells that were originally defined by the range name. Also, if you move the cells, the range name goes with them to the new location.

10 At the bottom of the dialog box, locate the **Refers to** box, as shown in Figure 4.5. Then, at the right edge of the **Refers to** box, point to and click the **Collapse Dialog Box** button.

The dialog box collapses (shrinks) so that only the *Refers to* box is visible, and the selected range is surrounded by a moving border, as shown in Figure 4.6. A Collapse dialog button temporarily shrinks a dialog box so that you have a larger view of the data in your worksheet while still being able to complete commands within the dialog box.

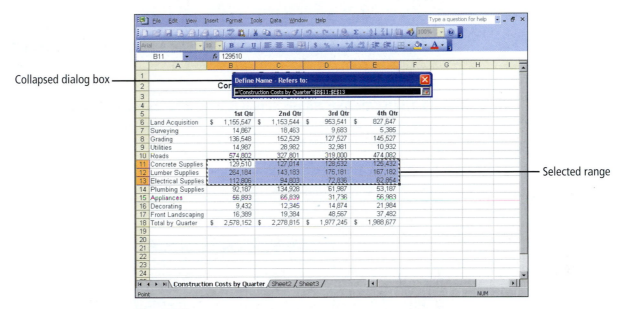

Collapsed dialog box

Selected range

Figure 4.6

11 If necessary, drag the collapsed dialog box by its title bar to the upper right of your screen so that it is not blocking the selection. Then, change the range selection by dragging to select the range **B11:E14**.

A moving border surrounds the new range, and the range, formatted with absolute cell references, displays in the *Refers to* box of the collapsed dialog box, as shown in Figure 4.7.

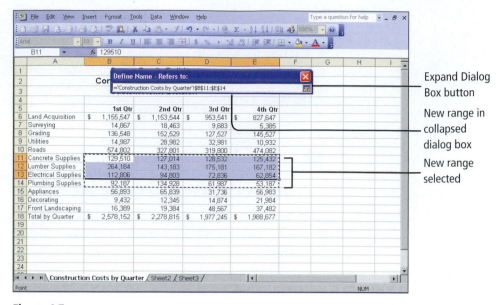

Figure 4.7

12 At the right edge of the collapsed dialog box, click the **Expand Dialog Box** button, as shown in Figure 4.7, to restore the dialog box to its original size.

13 In the **Define Name** dialog box, under **Names in workbook**, click in the box and delete the text *Concrete_Supplies*. Type **Supply_Costs** as shown in Figure 4.8.

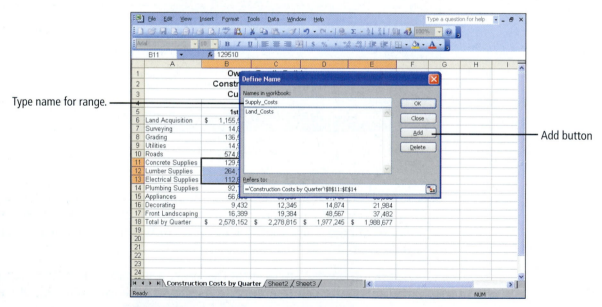

Figure 4.8

14 Click the **Add** button. The range name *Land_Costs* displays above the range name *Supply_Costs*. Click **OK** to close the dialog box and return to the worksheet. Click anywhere to cancel the selection.

15 Click the **Name Box arrow**.

The two range names that you have created display, in alphabetical order, as shown in Figure 4.9.

Name Box arrow

List of named ranges

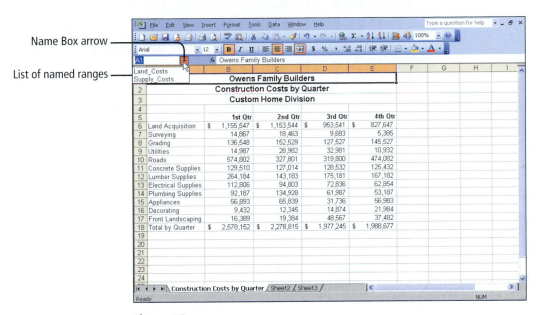

Figure 4.9

16 From the displayed list, click **Land_Costs** and notice that the range of values that make up land costs is highlighted, as shown in Figure 4.10.

Range name in Name Box

Selected range is highlighted.

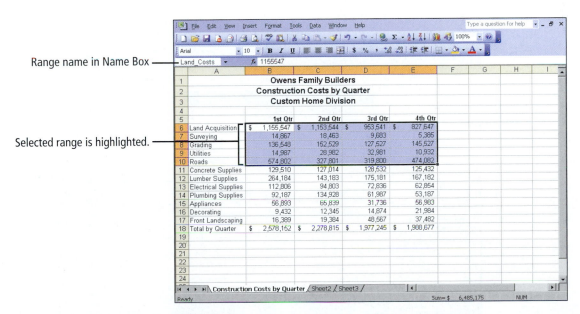

Figure 4.10

17 Click the **Name Box arrow** again, and on the displayed list, click **Supply_Costs**.

The range of values that make up Supply Costs is highlighted.

18 Select the range **B15:E16**. Click in the **Name Box**, type **Interior_Costs** and then press [Enter] to create the range name.

19 Click the heading for **row 15** to select the entire row. From the **Insert** menu, click **Rows**. A new **row 15** is inserted, and the remaining rows move down one row.

20 Click the **Name Box arrow**, and then click **Interior_Costs**. Notice that Excel highlights the correct range of cells, adjusting for the newly inserted row.

21 On the Standard toolbar, click the **Save** button 💾.

Activity 4.2 Modifying a Range

In this activity you will modify the range named *Supply_Costs* to include new data, and then name the new range *Building_Costs*.

1 Click cell **A15**, type **Roof Tiles** and then press [Tab]. In cell **B15**, type **64436** and press [Tab]. In cell **C15**, type **42956** and press [Tab]. In cell **D15**, type **58867** and press [Tab]. In cell **E15**, type **52329** and press [Enter].

The cells in the newly inserted row adopt the format (thousand comma separator) of the cells in the row above.

2 Hold down [Ctrl] and press [F3], which is the keyboard shortcut for displaying the **Define Name** dialog box.

3 In the **Names in workbook** list, click **Supply_Costs**. At the bottom of the dialog box, click in the **Refers to** box and edit the reference, changing **E14** to **E15** as shown in Figure 4.11.

This action will include the *Roof Tiles* values in the named range.

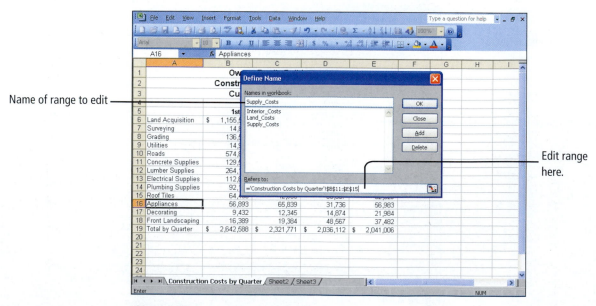

Name of range to edit ⎯

Edit range here.

Figure 4.11

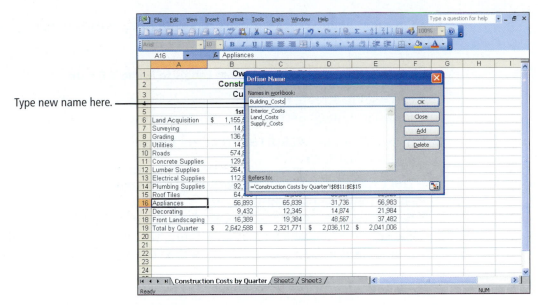

Type new name here. ————

Figure 4.12

---

4 Click the **Names in workbook** box, delete *Supply_Costs*, and then type **Building_Costs** as shown in Figure 4.12.

5 Click **OK** to close the dialog box. On the Standard toolbar, click **Save** 🖫 to save the changes you have made to your workbook.

Activity 4.3 Deleting a Range Name

If you create a range name and decide that you no longer need it, you can easily delete the range name and its accompanying range reference. Deleting a range name does not modify the cell contents or formatting of the cells.

1 Click the **Name Box arrow**. Four named ranges display on the list. Click **Supply_Costs** and notice the range that is highlighted.

This was the range of cells and range name that you created before adding the data regarding Roof Tiles.

2 Click the **Name Box arrow** again, click **Building_Costs**, and notice that the updated range, including **Roof Tiles**, is highlighted.

3 To delete the range name *Supply_Costs*, which is no longer needed, display the **Insert** menu, point to **Name**, and then click **Define**.

4 In the displayed **Define Name** dialog box, under **Names in workbook**, click **Supply_Costs**, and then, on the right side of the dialog box, click the **Delete** button. Click **OK** to close the dialog box.

Deleting a range name does not delete any cells or any values. It only deletes the name that you have applied to a group of cells.

5 Click the **Name Box arrow**, and notice that only three ranges display and that they are arranged alphabetically.

6 On the Standard toolbar, click **Save** 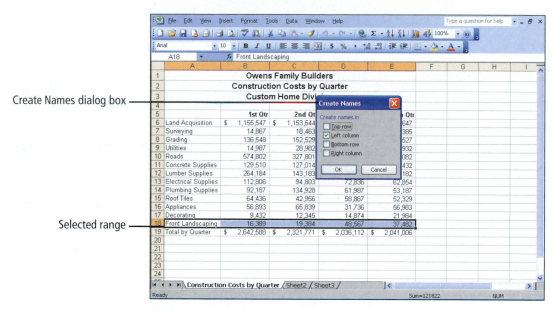 to save the changes you have made to your workbook.

Activity 4.4 Using Row and Column Labels to Name a Range

You can use the Create command to use existing row or column labels as the name for a range of cells. This will save you the step of typing a name.

1 Select the range **A18:E18**. From the **Insert** menu, point to **Name**, and then click **Create**.

The Create Names dialog box displays, as shown in Figure 4.13. A check mark displays in the *Left column* check box, which indicates that Excel will use the contents of the cell in the leftmost column of the selection as the range name. Using this dialog box, instead of the Define Names dialog box, saves you the step of typing a name.

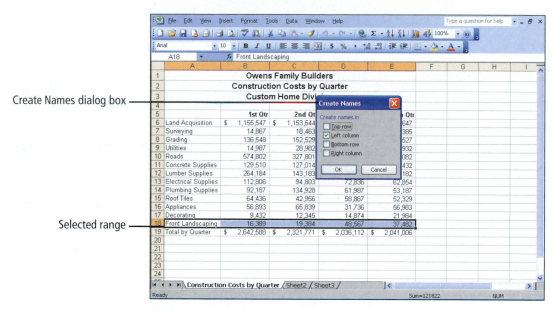

Figure 4.13

2 In the **Create Names** dialog box, click **OK**, and then click anywhere to cancel the selection.

3 Click the **Name Box arrow**, and then click the name **Front_Landscaping**. Notice that in the new range name, Excel inserted the underscore necessary to fill a blank space in the range name. Also notice that the actual range consists of only the numeric values, as shown in Figure 4.14.

This method is convenient for naming a range of cells without having to actually type a name—Excel uses the text of the first cell to the left of the selected range as the range name and then formats the name properly.

Range name formatted properly by Excel

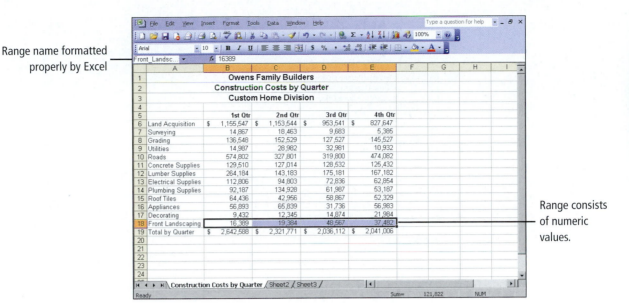

Range consists of numeric values.

Figure 4.14

4 On the Standard toolbar, click **Save** 🔲 to save the changes you have made to your workbook.

Objective 2
Use Range Names in a Formula

After you establish a name for a range of cells, you can use the name in a formula. The name can also be made available to other worksheets in the same workbook or in worksheets in other workbooks, which is easier to recall than having to remember and type the worksheet name and cell reference. In Activity 4.5, you will use range names in formulas.

Activity 4.5 Creating Formulas Using Range Names

1 If necessary, **Open** 📂 your file **4A_Construction_Costs_ Firstname_Lastname**.

2 Click the **Sheet2** tab. Rename the sheet tab either by pointing to and then double-clicking the Sheet2 tab or by pointing to and right-clicking the Sheet2 tab, and then clicking Rename. Type **Annual Costs** as the name for Sheet 2.

3 In cell **B5**, type **=sum(Land_Costs)** as shown in Figure 4.15, and then press Enter.

Recall that SUM is a *function* (a formula already built by Excel) that adds all the cells in a range. Thus, Excel sums all the cells in the range you defined as *Land_Costs* on the first worksheet in the workbook and then places the result in cell B5 of this worksheet. Your result should be 6485175.

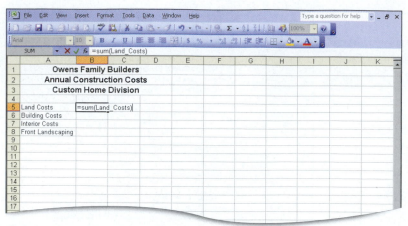

Figure 4.15

4 In cell **B6**, type **=sum(Building_Costs)** and press Enter.

You may type *sum* using lowercase letters; Excel will convert it to uppercase letters when you press Enter.

5 In cell **B7**, type **=sum(Interior_Costs)** and press Enter.

6 In cell **B8**, type **=sum(Front_Landscaping)** and press Enter.

7 In cell **A9**, type **Total** and then, in cell **B9**, use the **AutoSum** function button Σ ▾ to compute the total annual costs.

Your result should be 9041477.

8 Format the range **B6:B8** using the **Comma Style** button ▾ , and then click the **Decrease Decimal** button ▾ twice so that you have zero decimal places.

9 Click cell **B5**, hold down Ctrl, and then click cell **B9** to select the two nonadjacent cells. Format cells **B5** and **B9** using the **Currency Style** button $, and then click the **Decrease Decimal** button ▾ twice so that you have zero decimal places. Compare your worksheet with Figure 4.16.

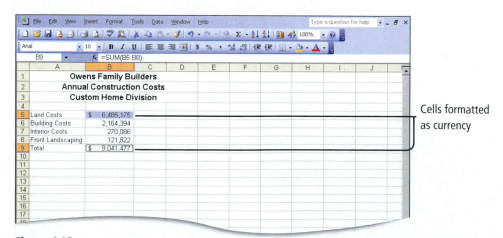

Cells formatted as currency

Figure 4.16

10 Click anywhere to deselect the cells. Right-click the **Annual Costs** sheet tab, and then click **Select All Sheets**.

Recall that by selecting all sheets, workbook formatting such as footers and page centering is applied to all sheets in the workbook.

Another Way ── **To Change Page Setup for Multiple Worksheets**

If you select two or more sheet tabs by holding down Ctrl, and then make changes in the Page Setup dialog box, the changes affect only the selected sheets—not all the sheets in the workbook.

---

11 From the **File** menu, click **Page Setup**. Click the **Margins tab**, and then, under **Center on page**, select the **Horizontally** check box. Click the **Header/Footer tab**, and then click **Custom Footer**. With the insertion point positioned in the **Left section**, on the dialog box toolbar click the **File name** button.

&[File] displays, as shown in Figure 4.17. This code will place the file name in the footer.

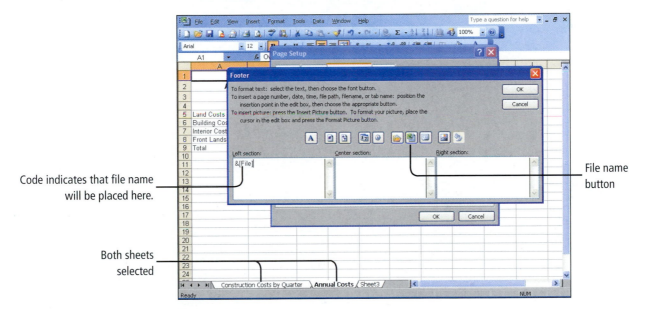

Code indicates that file name will be placed here.

File name button

Both sheets selected

Figure 4.17

12 Click **OK** twice to close the dialog boxes. On the Standard toolbar, click the **Print Preview** button [icon]. Because you have selected all sheets, both sheets can be viewed in Print Preview. Press `PageDown` to view the second worksheet, and then press `Page Up` to return to the print preview of the first worksheet. On the Print Preview toolbar, click the **Close** button.

13 **Save** [icon] your file. From the **File** menu, click **Print**. Because the sheets are still grouped, both worksheets will print, and it is not necessary to click the *Entire Workbook* option button. Click **OK**.

14 Right-click the **Annual Costs** sheet tab, and then click **Ungroup Sheets**. Hold down `Ctrl` and press `'` to display the formulas. Display the **Page Setup** dialog box, click the **Page tab**, and under **Scaling**, click the **Fit to** option button. On the Standard toolbar, click the **Print** button [icon] to print the formulas.

Recall that `'` is located below `Esc` on most keyboards. It is used with `Ctrl` to toggle between the worksheet numbers and the formulas.

15 Hold down `Ctrl` and press `'` again to redisplay the worksheet. Close the workbook, saving changes if prompted to do so.

End **You have completed Project 4A** ————————————————

Project 4B **Projected Revenues**

In this project, you will use Excel functions—prebuilt formulas—to compute various statistics such as median, average, minimum, and maximum.

In Activities 4.6 through 4.10, you will edit a workbook created by John Zeidler, Chief Financial Officer for Owens Family Builders, which projects the various sources of revenue for the company over the next three years. Your completed worksheet will look similar to Figure 4.18. You will save your workbook as *4B_Projected_Revenues_Firstname_Lastname*.

Owens Family Builders
Statement of Projected Revenues Over Next Three Years

		YEAR 1		YEAR 2		YEAR 3
Revenue Income by Source						
Custom Homes	$	1,809,347	$	1,191,525	$	1,205,816
Office Buildings		3,200,567		3,789,000		3,978,654
Shopping Centers		2,509,879		3,567,890		2,908,397
Public Schools		4,567,890		5,400,678		4,900,567
Municipal Facilities		2,345,675		1,987,554		2,346,787
Roadways		5,467,890		6,789,003		7,567,909
Bridges		2,456,785		2,345,785		3,457,892
Design Fees		69,915		71,548		89,915
Construction Management Fees		2,543,256		2,456,734		2,765,889
Total Revenue by Source	$	24,971,204	$	27,599,717	$	29,221,826
Investment Earnings						
Investment Earnings	$	450,687	$	500,876	$	550,678
Total Investment Earnings						
Rental Income						
Office Rental Income	$	147,000	$	152,321	$	168,521
Total Rental Income						
Transfers from Other Funds						
Sale of Easements		213,557		251,246		198,354
Projected Insurance Excess Reserves		234,990		235,467		260,987
Total Transfers from Other Funds	$	448,547	$	486,713	$	459,341
Total Projected Revenue From All Sources	$	51,437,189	$	56,826,057	$	60,081,533

Summary Data

		YEAR 1		YEAR 2		YEAR 3
Median Revenue	$	2,509,879	$	2,456,734	$	2,908,397
Minimum Revenue	$	69,915	$	71,548	$	89,915
Maximum Revenue	$	5,467,890	$	6,789,003	$	7,567,909
Average Annual Income Over the Three-Year Period	$	56,114,926				
Number of Different Revenue Sources		9				

4B_Projected_Revenues_Firstname_Lastname

Figure 4.18
Project 4B—Projected Revenues

Objective 3
Create Statistical Functions

Recall that a cell can contain either a constant value (text, numbers, dates, and times) or a formula. Recall also that a function is a formula that has already been built for you by Excel. For example, Excel's SUM function adds a series of cell values. This function is used so frequently that it has a button on the Standard toolbar. You can sum a column of numbers by writing a formula to add the specific cells, or you can use the SUM function. Compare the following two formulas:

=A1+A2+A3+A4+A5+A6+A7+A8+A9+A10
=SUM(A1:A10)

Both formulas instruct Excel to add together the values in cells A1 through A10, and both give the same result. It is much easier, however, to type the shortened version. And that is what a function is—a short, predefined formula.

Activity 4.6 Using the Insert Function Command to Create the MEDIAN Function

Excel has defined many complex formulas that are regularly used in business. You have access to these functions (predefined formulas) from the Insert Function dialog box. You can display the Insert Function dialog box from the Insert menu or by clicking the Insert Function button—*fx*—to the left of the Formula Bar.

All functions begin with an equal sign (=), which indicates the beginning of a formula. The equal sign is followed by the ***function name***, for example, *SUM*, which indicates the type of calculation that will be performed. The function name is followed by a set of ***arguments***—the information that Excel needs to make the calculation—set off in parentheses. The proper format of typing the equal sign, the function name, and the arguments is referred to as the ***function syntax***.

1 **Start** Excel. Click the **Open** button [icon], navigate to the student files that accompany this textbook, and open the file **e04B_Projected_Revenues**.

2 From the **File** menu, click **Save As**. In the **Save As** dialog box, navigate to the location where you are storing your projects for this chapter. In the **File name** box, type **4B_Projected_Revenues_Firstname_Lastname** and then click **Save** or press Enter.

3 Take a moment to familiarize yourself with the data in this worksheet, which lists the various sources of income projected over the next three years. Then, scroll down as necessary and click cell **B30**.

In this cell, you will use an Excel function to determine the *median* revenue in Year 1. Within a set of values, the median is the value below and above which there are an equal number of values. It is the value that falls in the middle of a ranked set of values.

4 From the **Insert** menu, click **Function**.

The Insert Function dialog box displays.

5 Under **Search for a function**, click the **Or select a category arrow** to display Excel's list of function categories as shown in Figure 4.19.

There are nine categories of functions, and within each, Excel has numerous predefined formulas. Three additional categories include *Most Recently Used*, which catalogs the functions you have used most recently so that they are easily located to use again; *All*, which lists all of Excel's predefined formulas in alphabetic order; and *User Defined*, which enables you to make up your own formulas and assign them a short function name.

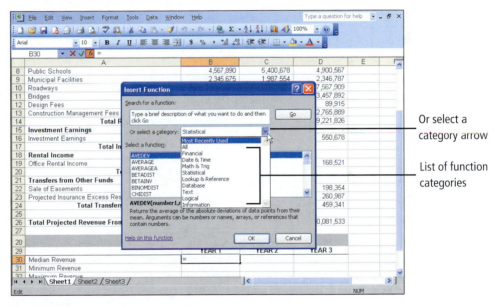

Figure 4.19

6 From the displayed list, click **Statistical**, and then, under **Select a function**, scroll down the alphabetic list and click **MEDIAN**.

Notice that at the bottom of the Insert Function dialog box, the function syntax and a brief description of the function display, as shown in Figure 4.20. This information is helpful in explaining what the formula will calculate.

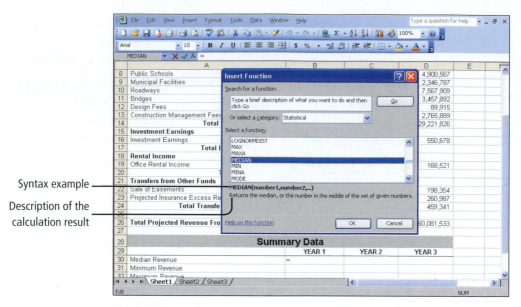

Syntax example ———

Description of the calculation result ———

Figure 4.20

7 Click **OK**.

The Function Arguments dialog box for the MEDIAN function displays, as shown in Figure 4.21.

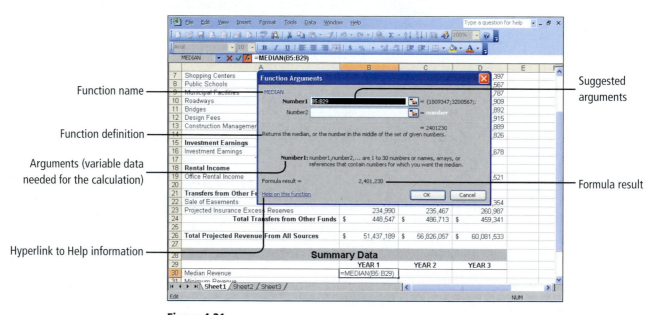

Function name ———

Function definition ———

Arguments (variable data needed for the calculation) ———

Hyperlink to Help information ———

——— Suggested arguments

——— Formula result

Figure 4.21

8 Take a moment to study Figure 4.21 to see each part of the **Function Arguments** dialog box.

9 Look at cell **B30** and notice that Excel will attempt to define a group of cells for the arguments—the information needed to perform the calculation. See Figure 4.21.

In this instance, this is not the group of cells among which you want to find the median.

10 In the **Function Arguments** dialog box, at the right edge of the **Number 1** box, click the **Collapse Dialog Box** button. Point to the blue title bar, and then drag the collapsed dialog box to the upper right corner of the screen, as shown in Figure 4.22.

The dialog box collapses (shrinks), leaving only the Number 1 box, and is moved off the worksheet area.

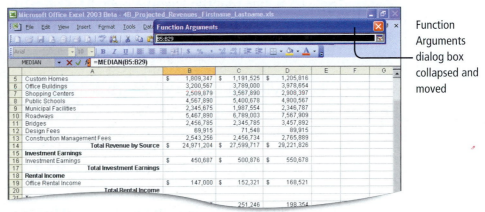

Function Arguments dialog box collapsed and moved

Figure 4.22

11 With the dialog box in the upper right corner of your screen, scroll the worksheet so that **rows 5 through 15** are visible, and then select the range **B5:B13**.

A moving border surrounds the cells, and the range displays as the argument—information needed for the calculation—in the Number1 box and in the Formula Bar. See Figure 4.23. The newly selected range also displays in the destination cell B30.

Formula displays in the Formula Bar.

Moving border surrounds selection.

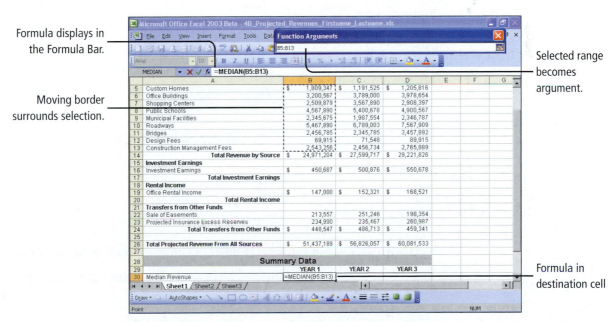

Selected range becomes argument.

Formula in destination cell

Figure 4.23

12 At the right edge of the collapsed dialog box, click the **Expand Dialog Box** button to redisplay the full dialog box.

Notice that the result of the formula—2,509,879—displays in the lower portion of the dialog box.

13 Click **OK**.

The result displays in cell B30. Look up at the Formula Bar and notice that the formula =MEDIAN(B5:B13) displays as the underlying formula. Excel looked at all the numbers in the group, ranked them in order of smallest to largest, and then determined which value fell in the middle of the group. This is how the mathematical median is calculated. When ranked in order from smallest to largest, half the values are below 2,509,879 and half the values are above 2,509,879.

14 With cell **B30** as the active cell, position your mouse pointer over the fill handle, and then drag to the right to copy the MEDIAN function to cells **C30** and **D30**. Compare your screen with Figure 4.24 and identify the function name and arguments in the formula displayed on the Formula Bar.

Excel copies the formula relative to the new locations. The median revenue income is 2,456,734 for Year 2 and 2,908,397 for Year 3.

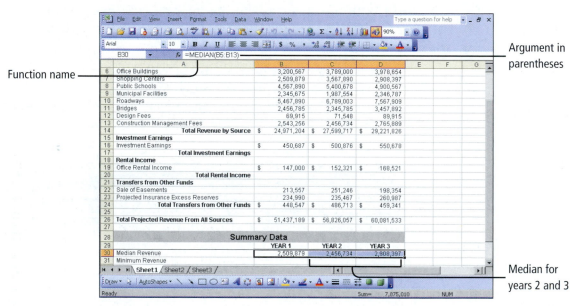

Figure 4.24

15 On the Standard toolbar, click the **Save** button.

Activity 4.7 Using the Insert Function Command to Create the MIN Function

1 Click cell **B31**. On the left edge of the **Formula Bar**, click the **Insert Function** button f_x.

Recall that you can display the Insert Function dialog box either from the Insert menu or by clicking the Insert Function button on the Formula Bar.

2 Check that the **Statistical** category displays in the **Or select a category** box, and then, under **Select a function**, scroll down the alphabetic list and click **MIN**.

The MIN function—minimum—looks at a set of values and determines which value is the smallest. In determining the smallest value among a set of values, Excel does not consider any cells that contain text or logical values such as TRUE or FALSE.

3 Click **OK**.

The Function Arguments dialog box displays.

4 To get a clearer view of your worksheet, move your pointer into the **Function Arguments** dialog box, and then, at the right edge of the **Number1** box, click the **Collapse Dialog Box** button.

The dialog box collapses (shrinks), leaving only the Number1 box.

5 Scroll the worksheet so that **rows 5 through 15** are visible, and then select the range **B5:B13**.

A moving border surrounds the cells, and the range displays as the argument in the Number1 box and also in the Formula Bar, as shown in Figure 4.25.

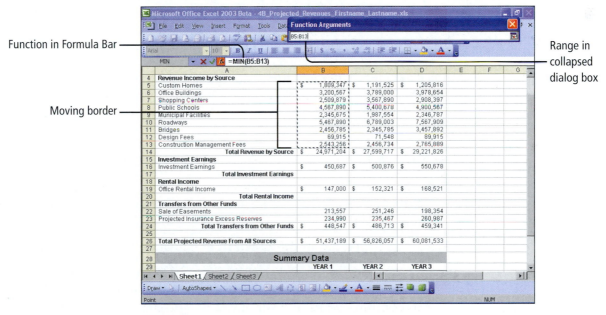

Figure 4.25

6 At the right edge of the collapsed dialog box, click the **Expand Dialog Box** button to redisplay the full dialog box.

Notice that the result of the formula—69,915—displays in the lower portion of the dialog box.

7 Click **OK**.

The minimum (smallest) value within the selected range—69,915—displays in cell B31. In a short list such as this one, you could probably find the smallest value by looking through the list, but you can see that in a long list of values, Excel can quickly determine the smallest value.

8 With cell **B31** as the active cell, use the fill handle to copy the formula to cells **C31** and **D31**.

You can see that in each year, income from Design Fees is the smallest source of income.

9 On the Standard toolbar, click **Save** 🖫 to save the changes you have made to your workbook.

Another Way — **To Enter Functions Without Using the Insert Function Dialog Box**

Two other methods can be used.

You can get access to some of the most common functions by clicking the arrow on the AutoSum button found on the Standard toolbar. First, click in the cell where you want the results of the function to be displayed, click the AutoSum button arrow, and then choose the function from the displayed list. Verify that the default cell range is correct, or drag to adjust the range, and then press [Enter] to see the results. If the function you want is not displayed on the AutoSum button list, click the More Functions command at the end of the list to open the Insert Function dialog box.

Alternatively, if you know the function name and the syntax for the arguments, you can type the formula for the function directly in the destination cell. For example, to calculate the minimum, type =MIN(B5:B13), where B5:B13 is the range of cells you want evaluated.

Activity 4.8 Using the Insert Function Command to Create the MAX Function

1 Click cell **B32**. Using either the Insert menu or the Insert Function button to the left of the Formula Bar, display the **Insert Function** dialog box.

2 Be sure you are in the **Statistical** category. Scroll down the alphabetic list, click **MAX**, and then click **OK**.

The Function Arguments dialog box displays. The MAX function—maximum—looks at a set of values and determines which value is the largest. In determining the largest value among a set of values, Excel does not consider any cells that contain text or logical values such as TRUE or FALSE.

3 In the **Number1** box of the **Function Arguments** dialog box, notice that the box is highlighted, indicating that if you begin to type, your new keystrokes will replace any existing text. Type **b5:b13** as shown in Figure 4.26, and then click **OK**.

The result in cell B32 is 5,467,890. As you have practiced, you can insert arguments into the boxes of the Function Arguments dialog box by dragging to select a range of cells or by typing the cell reference for a range of cells.

Formula displays
in Formula Bar.

Cell range
entered

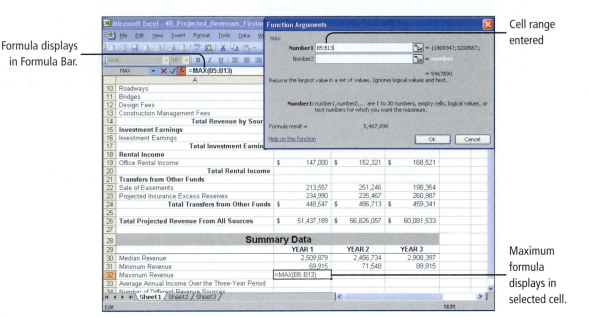

Maximum
formula
displays in
selected cell.

Figure 4.26

4 With cell **B32** as the active cell, copy the formula to cells **C32** and
D32. Compare your screen with Figure 4.27.

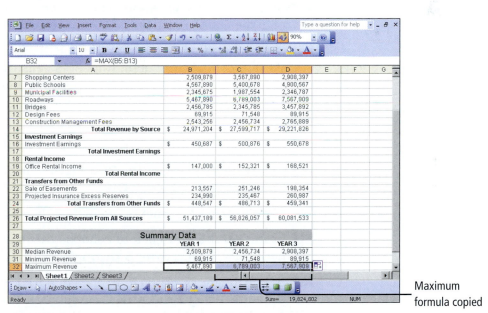

Maximum
formula copied

Figure 4.27

5 On the Standard toolbar, click **Save** 🖫 to save the changes you have
made to your workbook.

Activity 4.9 Using the Insert Function Command
to Create the AVERAGE Function

In this activity, you will compute the average annual revenue from all sources over the three-year period. To compute this average value, you must add the total projected revenue for each of the three years, and then divide the total by 3. Of course, Excel has a function for computing an arithmetic average—all you have to do is define which cells to use in the calculation.

1 Click cell **B33**, and then display the **Insert Function** dialog box.

2 Be sure you are in the **Statistical** category, and then click the **AVERAGE** function.

3 Click **OK** to display the **Function Arguments** dialog box. If necessary, scroll so that **row 26** is visible.

4 Select the range **B26:D26**, and then click **OK**.

The result, 56,114,926, displays in cell B33. The projected revenue from all sources will average $56,114,926 in each year of the three-year period.

5 On the Standard toolbar, click **Save** 🖫 to save the changes you have made to your workbook.

Activity 4.10 Using the Insert Function Command
to Create the COUNT Function

Within a range of selected cells, the COUNT function counts the number of cells that contain numbers. It ignores cells that contain text, logical values (such as TRUE or FALSE), or that are blank. In a short worksheet, it is easy to visually count the number of cells in a range, but in a large worksheet, this feature is very useful.

1 Click cell **B34** and display the **Insert Function** dialog box.

2 Check that you are in the **Statistical** category, click the **COUNT** function, and then click **OK**.

The Function Arguments dialog box displays.

3 In the **Value1** box, click to collapse the dialog box, and then scroll as necessary to view **rows 5 through 15**.

4 Select the range **B5:B13**. In the collapsed dialog box, click the **Expand Dialog Box** button to redisplay the full **Function Arguments** dialog box.

Notice that the result, 9, displays in the Function Arguments dialog box, as shown in Figure 4.28.

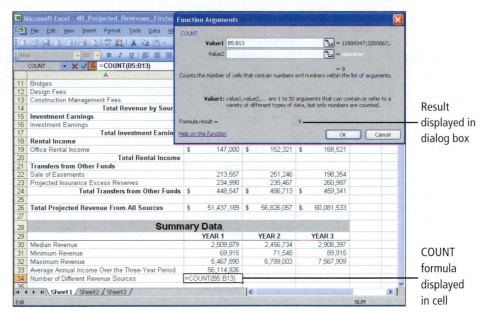

Figure 4.28

5 Click **OK** to display the result of the formula in the cell.

On a short worksheet like this, it would be easy to count the various revenue sources, but you can see that on a large worksheet, this formula would be quite useful.

6 Select the range **B30:D32**, hold down [Ctrl], and then click cell **B33**.

On the Formatting toolbar, click the **Currency Style** button [$], and then click the **Decrease Decimal** button [.00→.0] twice. Click in a blank cell to cancel the selection, and then compare your worksheet with Figure 4.29.

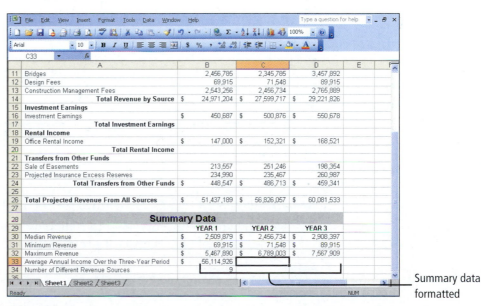

Figure 4.29

7 From the **File** menu, click **Page Setup**. Click the **Page tab**, and then, under **Orientation**, click the **Landscape** option button. Click the **Margins tab**, and then, under **Center on page**, select the **Horizontally** check box. Click the **Header/Footer tab**, and then click **Custom Footer**. With the insertion point positioned in the **Left section**, click the **File name** button [icon]. Click **OK** twice.

8 **Save** [icon] your file, and then click the **Print Preview** button [icon].

On the Print Preview toolbar, click the **Print** button [icon], and then click **OK**.

9 Hold down [Ctrl] and press [`] to display the formulas. Click the **Print Preview** button [icon].

The formulas expand the worksheet across two pages.

10 On the Print Preview toolbar, click **Setup**. In the **Page Setup** dialog box, click the **Page tab**. Under **Orientation**, be sure **Landscape** is selected. Under **Scaling**, click the **Fit to** option button, and then click **OK**.

The scaling option shrinks the font as necessary so that the formulas will display on one page, as shown in Figure 4.30.

Formulas display on one page. ————

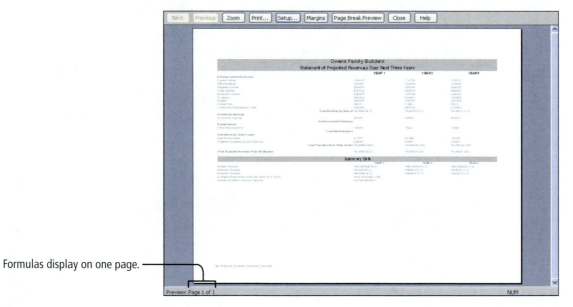

Figure 4.30

11 On the Print Preview toolbar, click **Print**, and then click **OK**.

12 Hold down [Ctrl] and press [`] to redisplay the worksheet. Close the workbook, saving changes if prompted to do so.

End **You have completed Project 4B** ————————————

Project 4C New Benefits

In Project 4C you will use functions within the Date & Time, Financial, and Logical categories. Using these functions, you will compute monthly loan payments and annuity values.

In Activities 4.11 through 4.13, you will edit a workbook created by Juan Sanchez, Director of Employee Benefits for Owens Family Builders, which details the cost of a new plan to provide pick-up trucks for each of the 24 construction managers and also to provide an annuity benefit for the construction managers and construction crew members. An *annuity* is an investment that pays the beneficiary an amount of money in a lump sum or as a series of equal annual payments. The two worksheets of your workbook will look similar to Figure 4.31. You will name the workbook *4C_New_Benefits_Firstname_Lastname.*

Proposed Annuity Benefit
Construction Managers and Crew Members

	Number of Eligible Employees	Total Initial Purchase Cost	Annual Payment Cost	Total Cost for the Life of the Annuity
Managers	24	$ 360,000	$ 48,000	$1,080,000
Crew Members	75	$1,125,000	$150,000	$3,375,000
Total	99	$1,485,000	$198,000	$4,455,000
Average Return Rate	10%			
Contributing Years	15			
Annual Contribution	2000			
Initial Contribution per Employee	15000			
Computed on:	12/18/2003 13:12			

Annuity Value Per Employee at the End of 15 Years	$132,558.18

4C_New_Benefits_Firstname_Lastname

Figure 4.31a
Project 4C—New Benefits
Proposed Annuity Benefit worksheet

Pick-up Truck Financing Proposal
9/24/2004

Item	24 Pick-up Trucks
Purchase Price	600000
Down Payment	60000
Loan Amount	540000
Rate	0.06
Term of Loan	3
Monthly Payment	($16,427.85)

4C_New_Benefits_Firstname_Lastname

Figure 4.31b Pick-up Truck Financing Proposal worksheet

Objective 4
Create Date & Time and Financial Functions

Excel assigns a serial value to a date and then uses that value to calculate the number of days between two dates. For example, in the period July 16, 2004, to July 31, 2004 (a typical payroll period), Excel looks at the serial numbers of the two dates and subtracts the smaller one from the larger one. Excel also has numerous functions for complex business calculations.

Activity 4.11 Applying the DATE and NOW Functions

The DATE function places, in the selected cell, a serial value that represents a particular day, month, and year. Excel has assigned the number 1 to the date January 1, 1900, and continues numbering the days consecutively. For example, January 1, 2008, has the serial value 39,448 because there are 39,448 days between the base date of January 1, 1900, and January 1, 2008.

1 **Start** Excel. Click the **Open** button, navigate to the student files that accompany this textbook, and open the file **e04C_New_Benefits**.

2 From the **File** menu, click **Save As**. In the **Save As** dialog box, navigate to the location where you are storing your projects for this chapter. In the **File name** box, type 4C_New_Benefits_Firstname_Lastname and then click **Save** or press Enter.

3 Be sure that **Truck Financing** is the active sheet, and then click cell **A2**.

4 From the **Insert** menu, click **Function**. Click the **Or select a category arrow**, and from the displayed list, click **Date & Time**. Under **Select a function**, click **DATE**, and then click **OK**.

The Function Arguments dialog box displays with three different boxes for arguments—*Year*, *Month*, and *Day*.

5 Using the date September 24, 2004, type each argument—year first—as a number, as shown in Figure 4.32.

The formula =DATE(2004,9,24) displays in the cell and in the Formula Bar. Notice the number—38254—displayed in the dialog box as the serial value for this date.

Formula displayed

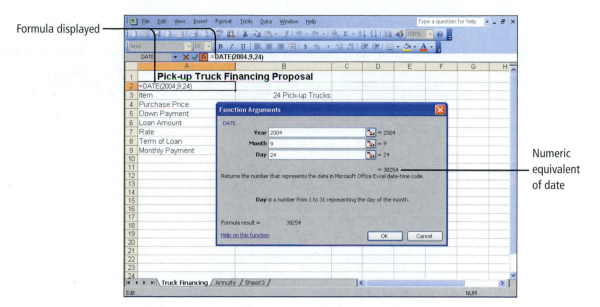

Numeric equivalent of date

Figure 4.32

6 Click **OK** to close the dialog box.

The date—9/24/2004—displays in cell A2.

> **Note** — Does Your Date Display Leading Zeros?
>
> Your date may display with leading zeros—09/24/2004. This is controlled by the date configuration set for your operating system and does not change the purpose or results of the date functions.

7 With cell **A2** as the active cell, display the **Format Cells** dialog box, and then click the **Number tab**. Under **Category**, click **General**, and then click **OK**.

The serial value of the date, 38254, displays. Recall that all cells have the General format by default; however, the DATE function applies the Date format to the cell. To view the sequential serial number that represents a particular date, you must reformat the cell to the General format.

8 On the Standard toolbar, click the **Undo** button [↶▾] to restore the cell format to Date and display the date.

9 Click the **Annuity** sheet tab, and then click cell **B11**. On the Formula Bar, click the **Insert Function** button f_x. In the displayed **Insert Function** dialog box, with **Date & Time** as the category, scroll as necessary, and then click the **NOW** function. Click **OK**.

The Function Arguments dialog box displays, as shown in Figure 4.33. The NOW function places, in the selected cell, a serial value that represents today's date and the current time. This is a volatile function, that is, a function that is subject to change, because each time you open a workbook that contains the NOW function, the day, month, year, and time can be updated by gathering the date and time from your computer's internal calendar and clock.

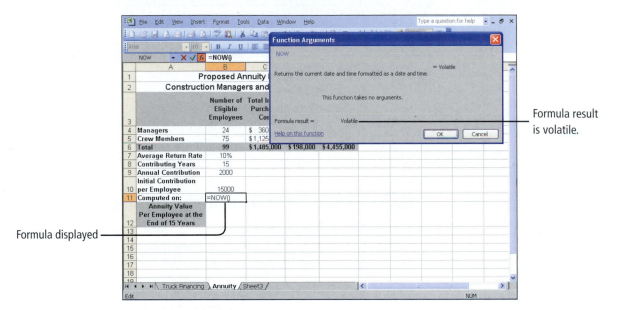

Formula displayed

Formula result is volatile.

Figure 4.33

Note — Working with the NOW Function

If you open a workbook containing the NOW function, you will be prompted to save your changes even if you do not perform any editing in the cells. This is because the NOW function will attempt to update the cell where it is used to the current date and time.

10 In the **Function Arguments** dialog box, notice that the NOW function has no arguments. The function captures the current date and time from your computer system's internal calendar and clock. Click **OK**.

The current date and time display in cell B11.

11 With cell **B11** as the active cell, display the **Format Cells** dialog box, and then, on the **Number tab**, click **General**. In the **Sample** area, notice that the serial value for the date and time is displayed. See Figure 4.34.

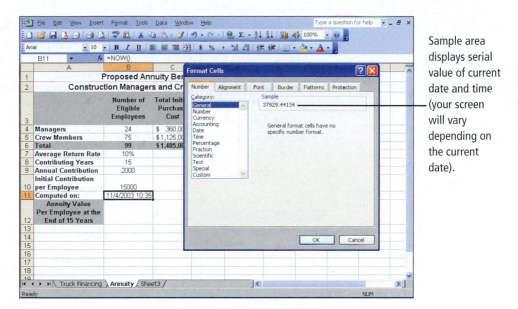

Sample area displays serial value of current date and time (your screen will vary depending on the current date).

Figure 4.34

12 In the lower right corner of the **Format Cells** dialog box, click **Cancel** so that the format of the cell is not changed from the Date format.

13 On the menu bar, click the **Save** button ▣.

Activity 4.12 Applying the Financial Function FV

The **FV** function calculates **future value**. Future value is the value of an investment at the end of a specified period of time, based on periodic, constant payments and a constant interest rate.

For example, Owens Family Builders wants to purchase an annuity for employees who have 10 or more years of service with the company. After an additional 15 years of service, this investment would provide each employee with a sum of money that would be paid as a lump sum or as a series of equal annual payments.

1 If necessary, click the **Annuity** sheet tab, and then click cell **B12**.

2 From the **Insert** menu, click **Function**. In the displayed **Insert Function** dialog box, click the **Or select a category arrow**, and then click **Financial**. Under **Select a function**, click **FV**.

Using this function, you will calculate the value of a $15,000 annuity at the end of 15 years, assuming that the company contributes $2,000 to each employee's annuity at the beginning of each year and that there is an average rate of return of 10 percent per year for each of the 15 remaining years.

3 At the bottom of the dialog box, locate the information in bold, which is the structure of the FV formula, and the descriptive information, as shown in Figure 4.35.

The FV function uses the structure *(rate, number of periods, payment, present value, type)*. You need not, of course, be concerned with the exact structure of the calculation because Excel has done that work for you by predefining the formula as a function. You need only supply the arguments (needed information) with which Excel should make the calculations.

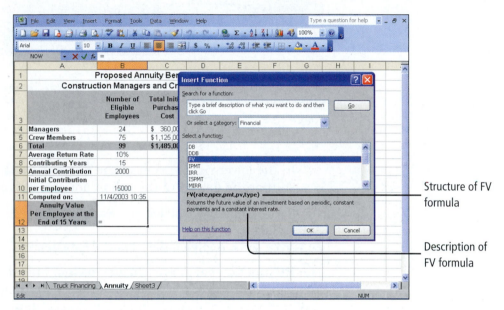

Structure of FV formula

Description of FV formula

Figure 4.35

4 In the lower right corner, click **OK** to display the **Function Arguments** dialog box. If necessary, drag the dialog box to the right side of your screen. With the insertion point positioned in the **Rate** box, click cell **B7**, which contains the percentage rate of return per year.

B7 displays in the Rate box, cell B7 is surrounded by a moving border, and a definition and example of Rate is provided.

5 Press ⟨Tab⟩ to move the insertion point to the **Nper** box, and then click cell **B8**.

B8 displays in the Nper box, and cell B8 is surrounded by a moving border. **Nper** is the total number of payment periods—15—in the annuity investment.

6 Press ⟨Tab⟩ to move the insertion point to the **Pmt** box, type - (minus sign), and then click cell **B9**.

-B9 displays in the Pmt box, and cell B9 is surrounded by a moving border. **Pmt** represents the payment that will be made in each annual period. Because this amount will be paid out, it should be entered as a negative number.

7 Press (Tab) to move the insertion point to the **Pv** box, type **-** (minus sign), and then click cell **B10**.

-B10 displays in the Pv box, and cell B10 is surrounded by a moving border. **Pv** represents the present value—what the annuity is worth now—which is $15,000, the employee's initial contribution. This is also an amount that will be paid out. Thus, the value should be entered as a negative number.

8 Press (Tab) to move the insertion point to the **Type** box, and type **1**

Type represents the timing of the payment—whether it will be paid at the beginning of each period (indicated by a 1) or at the end of the period (indicated by a 0). Compare your Function Arguments dialog box with Figure 4.36.

Function formula displayed in Formula Bar

Arguments entered for FV function

Formula partially displayed in destination cell

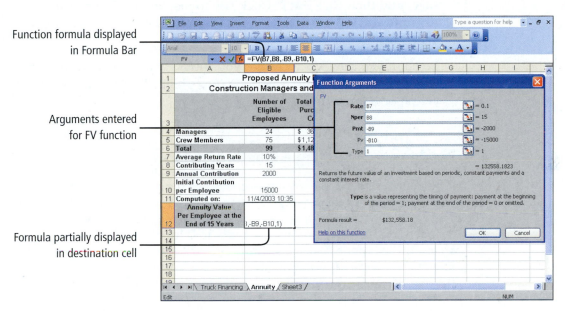

Figure 4.36

9 Notice that cell **B12** is the active cell and that the function formula is partially displayed in the cell. Move to the lower right corner of the **Function Arguments** dialog box, and then click **OK**.

The result, $132,558.18, displays in cell B12. At the end of 15 years, the annuity investment for each employee will be worth $132,558.18. Using Excel's FV function, you can see how quickly an investment of this type can add up.

10 On the Standard toolbar, click the **Save** button to save the changes you have made to your workbook.

Activity 4.13 Applying the Financial Function PMT

The **PMT** function calculates the payment for a loan based on constant payments and a constant interest rate. The structure for the function is *PMT(rate, number of periods, present value, future value, type)*.

For example, Juan Sanchez wants to calculate the monthly payments the company will have to make to finance the purchase of 24 new pick-up trucks. The total cost of the trucks, less the down payment, is $540,000. Juan wants to finance this amount over three years at an annual interest rate of 6 percent.

1 Click the **Truck Financing** sheet tab, and then click cell **B9**.

2 From the **Insert** menu, click **Function** to display the **Insert Function** dialog box. Within the **Financial** category, scroll as necessary, and then click **PMT**. Click **OK** to display the **Function Arguments** dialog box for the PMT function. If necessary, drag the dialog box to the right of your screen.

To complete the PMT formula, you must first determine the total number of loan payment periods (months), which is 12 months × 3 years, or 36 months.

Note — Calculating a Monthly Payment

When borrowing money, the interest rate and term—length of the loan—is quoted in years. The payments on a loan, however, are usually made monthly. Therefore, the term, stated in years, and annual interest rate have to be changed to a monthly equivalent in order to calculate the monthly payment amount. This is done by dividing the interest rate by 12 to derive a monthly interest rate and multiplying the term by 12 to convert the number of years to the number of months (payment periods) for the term of the loan.

3 With your insertion point positioned in the **Rate** box, type **b7/12**

This will instruct Excel to divide the annual interest rate of 6 percent—0.06 in decimal notation—located in cell B7 by 12 (months), which will result in a monthly interest rate.

4 Press Tab to move the insertion point to the **Nper** box.

5 At the bottom of the dialog box, notice that *Nper* represents the number of payments for the loan (number of periods).

6 Click cell **B8**, and then type ***12** so that Excel converts the number of years in the loan to the total number of months.

Recall that this function is calculating a monthly payment. Thus, all values in the function must be expressed in months.

7 Press `Tab` to move your insertion point to the **Pv** box.

Pv represents the present value—the total value that a series of future payments is worth now.

8 Click cell **B6** to instruct Excel to use the value 540000 in cell **B6**. Compare your dialog box with Figure 4.37. Notice that the different parts of the PMT argument are separated by commas (,).

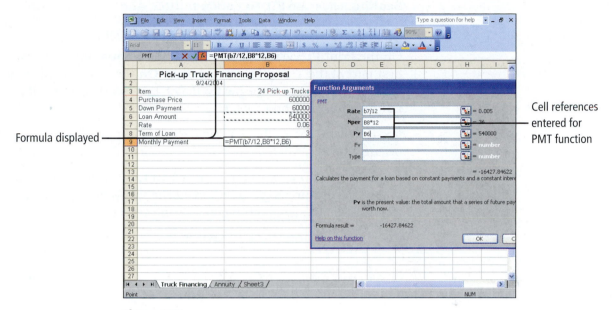

Formula displayed

Cell references entered for PMT function

Figure 4.37

9 Click **OK**.

The monthly payment amount, ($16,427.85), displays in cell B9. The amount is displayed in red and in parentheses to show that it is a negative number, a number that will be paid out.

10 On the **Truck Financing sheet tab**, right-click, and then click **Select All Sheets**. From the **File** menu, click **Page Setup**. Click the **Margins tab**, and then under **Center on page**, select the **Horizontally** check box.

11 Click the **Header/Footer tab**, and then click **Custom Footer**. With the insertion point positioned in the **Left section**, click the **File Name** button. Click **OK** twice.

12 On the Standard toolbar, click the **Save** button, and then click the **Print Preview** button. Because you have grouped the sheets, both worksheets can be viewed in Print Preview. On the Print Preview toolbar, click **Print**, and then click **OK**.

13 With the sheets still grouped, hold down Ctrl and press `'` to display the formulas. Click the **Print Preview** button again. On the Print Preview toolbar, click **Next** three times to see the four formula pages.

Both worksheets display but are spread across four pages.

14 On the Print Preview toolbar, click **Setup**. In the **Page Setup** dialog box, click the **Page tab**. Under **Orientation**, click **Landscape**, under **Scaling**, click the **Fit to** option button, and then click **OK**.

The Annuity Benefit sheet displays on one page.

15 On the Print Preview toolbar, click the **Previous** button twice to see the first part of the Truck Financing page. On the Print Preview toolbar, click **Setup**. In the **Page Setup** dialog box, on the **Page tab**, click **Landscape**, and then click **OK**.

For this worksheet, the scaling option is not needed—the landscape orientation is sufficient to display the formulas on one page.

16 On the Print Preview toolbar, click **Print**, and then click **OK**. Hold down Ctrl and press `'` to redisplay the worksheet numbers. Close the workbook, saving changes if prompted to do so.

The formulas print for both worksheets.

End You have completed Project 4C ————————————

Project 4D **Office Payroll**

In Project 4D, you will use Excel's Logical functions, which apply a conditional test to determine whether a condition is true or false. You will also print a portion of a worksheet.

In Activities 4.14 through 4.15, you will edit a workbook created by Jennifer Owen, Payroll Manager, that lists the number of hours worked and the hourly pay rate of the administrative staff at Owens Family Builders. Your completed worksheet will look similar to Figure 4.38. You will name the workbook *4D_Admin_Payroll_Firstname_Lastname.*

Administrative Office Payroll - Week of July 23					
Employee	Hours	Hourly Pay Rate	Regular Pay	Overtime Pay	Total Weekly Salary
Fong, B.	52	$35.50	$1,420.00	$639.00	$2,059.00
Owen-Hughes, M.	38	$22.50	$855.00	$0.00	$855.00
Freeman, M.	61	$22.50	$900.00	$708.75	$1,608.75
Daly, M.	58	$17.50	$700.00	$472.50	$1,172.50
Ensler, V.	36	$21.75	$783.00	$0.00	$783.00
Sobel, D.	47	$40.00	$1,600.00	$420.00	$2,020.00
Rhode, A.	42	$15.50	$620.00	$46.50	$666.50
Total Weekly Payroll					$9,164.75

4D_Admin_Payroll_Firstname_Lastname

Figure 4.38
Project 4D—Office Payroll

Objective 5
Create Logical Functions

Most of the functions that fall in the category of Logical functions use a **conditional test** to determine whether a specified condition is true or false. A conditional test is performed by using an equation to compare two values (or two functions or two formulas).

A conditional test must have at least one **logical operator**—a mathematical symbol that tests the relationship between the two elements of the conditional test. Take a moment to become familiar with the logical operator symbols in the table shown in Figure 4.39.

Logical Operators

Logical Operator Symbol	Definition
=	Equal to
>	Greater than
<	Less than
>=	Greater than or equal to
<=	Less than or equal to
<>	Not equal to

Figure 4.39

Activity 4.14 Applying the IF Function

The IF Logical function helps you make a decision about assigning a value to a cell dependent on a **logical test**. A logical test is any value or expression that can be evaluated as true or false. For example, $C8=100$ is an expression that can be evaluated as true or false. If the value in cell C8 is equal to 100, the expression is true. If the value in cell C8 is not 100, the expression is false.

1 **Start** Excel. Click the **Open** button 📂, navigate to the student files that accompany this textbook, and open the file **e04D_Admin_Payroll**. From the **File** menu, click **Save As**. In the **Save As** dialog box, navigate to the location where you are storing your projects for this chapter. In the **File name** box, type **4D_Admin_Payroll_Firstname_Lastname** and then click **Save** or press Enter.

2 From the **View** menu, click **Header and Footer**. Click the **Custom Footer** button. With the insertion point positioned in the **Left section**, click the **File Name** button 📄. Click **OK** twice. Then, take a moment to familiarize yourself with the data in the workbook.

In this worksheet, you will use the IF function to determine whether or not an employee has earned any overtime pay. All hours over 40 worked in a week are paid as overtime, and the overtime hourly pay rate is one and a half times the regular hourly pay rate.

3 Click cell **D3**. On the Formula Bar, click the **Insert Function** button
[fx]. In the displayed **Insert Function** dialog box, click the **Logical**
category, and then, under **Select a function**, click **IF**. Click **OK**. If
necessary, drag the dialog box to the right side of your screen.

The IF function determines whether a condition is met and returns one
value if the condition is true and another value if the condition is false.

4 With the insertion point positioned in the **Logical_test** box, type **b3>40**

This directs Excel to look at the value in cell B3, the hours worked
during the week, and then determine whether the value is greater
than 40. This will determine whether or not the employee has
worked any overtime hours during the week.

5 Press [Tab] to move the insertion point to the **Value_if_true** box, and
then type **c3*40**

This directs Excel to multiply the value in cell C3 (the hourly pay
rate) times 40 if the condition in the argument above is TRUE
(greater than 40). Recall that the first 40 hours worked in any week
are paid at the regular hourly rate.

6 Press [Tab] to move the insertion point to the **Value_if_false** box, and
then type **b3*c3**

This directs Excel to multiply the value in cell B3 (the number of hours
worked) times the value in cell C3 (the regular hourly pay rate for 40 or
fewer hours worked). Compare your dialog box with Figure 4.40.

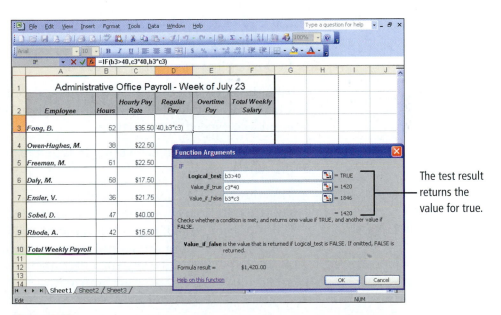

Figure 4.40

7 Click **OK**.

The result, $1,420.00, displays in cell D3. In this cell, the true value was returned because cell B3 is greater than 40.

8 Using the fill handle, copy the formula down through cell **D9**, and then compare your worksheet with Figure 4.41.

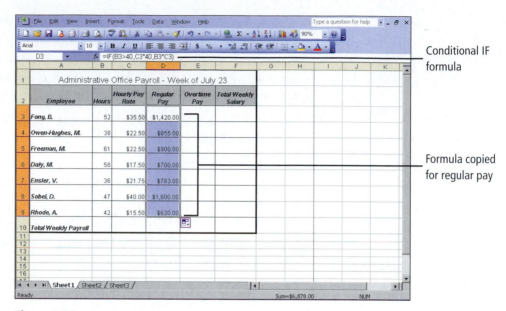

Figure 4.41

9 Click cell **E3**, and then display the **Insert Function** dialog box. Click the **IF** function, and then click **OK**.

10 In the **Logical_test** box, type **b3>40**

This directs Excel to look at the value in cell B3 and determine whether it is greater than 40, which will indicate whether or not the employee earned any overtime.

11 Press [Tab] to move to the **Value_if_true** box, and then type **(b3-40)*(1.5*c3)**

This directs Excel, provided that the logical test result is true, to subtract 40 from the value in cell B3, and then multiply the result times one and a half times the value in cell C3. More specifically, Excel calculates the number of hours worked over 40, and then multiplies that number by the overtime hourly rate—which is one and a half times the regular hourly rate.

More Knowledge — How Excel Performs Calculations

Order of Operations

When performing calculations, Excel follows a set of mathematical rules referred to as **order of operations**. Moving from left to right, it performs operations from the highest level to the lowest. First it applies negation (-), then percentage (%), then exponentiation (^), followed by division (/) or multiplication (*), and finally addition (+) or subtraction (-). You can override this order by the use of parentheses because any operations inside of parentheses are performed first. For example, substituting the values for cells B3—52—and C3—$35.50—in the formula in Step 11 results in (52-40)*(1.5*35.50). Performing the operations inside the parentheses first simplifies the equation to 12*53.25, or $639. If the parentheses are removed from this formula, the result would be different, and not the desired result. Parentheses play an important part in assuring that you get the correct results in your formulas.

12 Press Tab to move to the **Value_if_false** box, and type **0.00**

If the logical test is FALSE, the employee does not earn any overtime pay, and the result in this column should display as zero dollars.

13 Click **OK**.

The result, $639.00, displays in cell E3, which is the value 12 (number of hours over 40 worked) times the overtime hourly rate (1.5 × 35.50 = 53.25).

14 Using the fill handle, copy the formula down through cell **E9**, and then compare your worksheet with Figure 4.42.

By examining your worksheet, you can see that the employees who worked fewer than 40 hours per week (Owens-Hughes and Ensler) received no overtime pay.

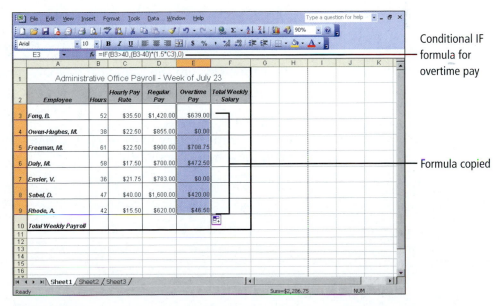

Figure 4.42

15 Click cell **F3**. On the Standard toolbar, click the **AutoSum** button $\boxed{\Sigma \cdot}$.

AutoSum proposes to add the values in cells B3:E3. To calculate the Total Weekly Salary, you need only add the Regular Pay to the Overtime Pay.

16 With the moving border displayed around the range **B3:E3**, select the range **D3:E3**, and then press Enter. Click cell **F3** again, and then copy the formula down through cell **F9**. In cell **F10**, use the **AutoSum** button $\boxed{\Sigma \cdot}$ to compute the total weekly Administrative Office Payroll cost. Compare your screen with Figure 4.43.

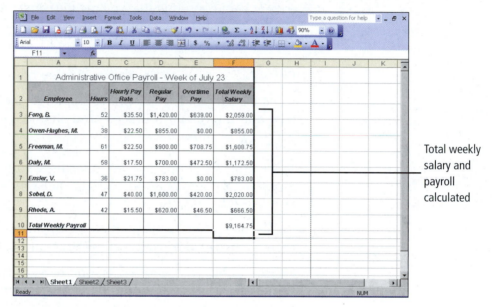

Total weekly salary and payroll calculated

Figure 4.43

17 From the **File** menu, click **Page Setup**, and then click the **Margins tab**. Under **Center on page**, select the **Horizontally** check box, and then click **OK**. On the Standard toolbar, click the **Save** button, and then click the **Print Preview** button to view your worksheet as it will print.

18 On the Print Preview toolbar, click **Close**, and leave the workbook open for the next activity.

Objective 6
Set and Clear a Print Area

Sometimes you do not need to print an entire worksheet; rather, you need to print only a portion of a worksheet. If you need to print a worksheet portion only once, select the cells, and then, in the Print dialog box, click the Selection option button.

If, on the other hand, you are likely to print the same portion of a worksheet over and over again, you can save time by naming the area *Print_Area*. For example, Jennifer Owen frequently prints a list of the Administrative Office employees and the number of hours they have worked in a given week—without the accompanying salary information. After you have set a print area, you also need to know how to clear it when necessary.

Activity 4.15 Setting and Clearing the Print Area

1 If necessary, **Open** 📂 your file **4D_Admin_Payroll**.

2 Select the range **A2:B9**. From the **File** menu, point to **Print Area**, and then click **Set Print Area**.

The selected area is surrounded by a dashed border.

Another Way ── **To Set the Print Area**

On the menu bar, click File, click Page Setup, click the Sheet tab, and then type the range into the Print area box.

3 Click in any blank cell, and notice that a smaller dashed border continues to surround the area. As shown in Figure 4.44, click the **Name Box arrow**, and then click **Print_Area**.

The Print Area is selected and once again surrounded by a thin, dashed border.

Name Box arrow —

Print area highlighted —

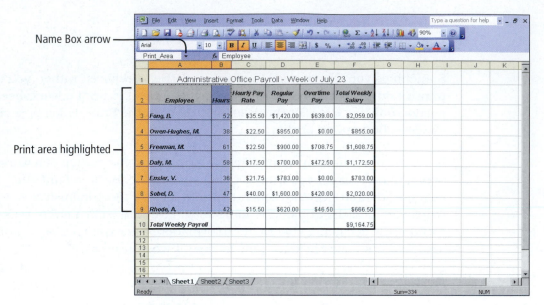

Figure 4.44

4 On the menu bar, click the **Print Preview** button. Notice that only the print area displays and will print. On the Print Preview toolbar, click the **Print** button, and then click **OK**.

5 To clear the Print Area, display the **File** menu, point to **Print Area**, and then click **Clear Print Area**. The print area is cleared.

6 On the Standard toolbar, click the **Save** button. Hold down Ctrl and press ` to display the formulas. Click the **Print Preview** button.

The formulas display across two pages.

7 On the Print Preview toolbar, click **Setup**. In the **Page Setup** dialog box, on the **Page tab**, click the **Landscape** and **Fit to** option buttons, and then click **OK**. On the Print Preview toolbar, click **Print**, and click **OK**.

8 Hold down Ctrl and press ` to redisplay the worksheet. Close the workbook, saving changes if prompted to do so. Close Excel.

End **You have completed Project 4D**

Summary

In this chapter, you created range names and used the names in a formula. By assigning a name to a range of cells, you can use the name in a formula. This makes it easier for you and other users of your worksheet to understand the meaning of the formula. Using a range name, you can also navigate to a specific section of a worksheet.

Naming ranges involves a few rules. The first character must be a letter, and you cannot use spaces. After you name ranges, you can modify or delete them. Modifying or deleting a range does not change the contents of the cells in the range.

In this chapter, you also worked with more of Excel's functions. A function is a predefined formula, and Excel provides many such formulas for use in complex calculations. When using the Date & Time functions, recall that Excel assigns a serial value to a date for the purpose of calculating the number of days between two dates. Using Statistical functions, you practiced calculating some of the most common statistical measures—average, median, minimum, maximum, and count.

Using Financial functions, you practiced calculating common financial transactions such as a future value and loan payments. Using Logical functions, you practiced performing conditional tests to determine whether a specified condition was true or false.

In This Chapter You Practiced How To

- Create Range Names
- Use Range Names in a Formula
- Create Statistical Functions
- Create Date & Time and Financial Functions
- Create Logical Functions
- Set and Clear a Print Area

Matching   Match each term in the second column with its correct definition in the first column by writing the letter of the term on the blank line in front of the correct definition.

_O_   **1.** Within an Excel function, a value that represents the timing of the payment—whether it will be paid at the beginning of each period (indicated by a 1) or at the end of the period (indicated by a 0).

_B_   **2.** The information that Excel uses to make the calculation within a function.

_H_   **3.** A mathematical symbol that tests the relationship between the two elements of a conditional test, for example, greater than (>), less than (<), or equal (=).

_N_   **4.** A specific name given to a range of cells, which can then be used to refer to the range in a function or formula.

_D_   **5.** A test performed by using an equation to compare two values (or two functions or two formulas).

_G_   **6.** An Excel function that calculates future value—the value of an investment at the end of a specified period of time—based on periodic, constant payments and a constant interest rate.

_I_   **7.** Within a set of values, the value below and above which there are an equal number of values—the value that falls in the middle of a ranked set of values.

_A_   **8.** A sum of money payable in a lump sum or as a series of equal annual payments.

_L_   **9.** Within an Excel function, the value that represents what an annuity is worth now.

_J_   **10.** Within an Excel function, the total number of payment periods in an annuity investment.

_C_   **11.** A button within a dialog box that temporarily shrinks the dialog box so that you have a larger view of the data in your worksheet.

_K_   **12.** Within an Excel function, the payment that will be made in each annual period.

_E_   **13.** A formula that has already been built for you by Excel.

_M_   **14.** A group of cells referred to by the first and last cell in the group, for example, B3:G7.

_F_   **15.** The proper format of typing the equal sign, the function name, and the arguments when constructing a function.

A Annuity

B Arguments

C Collapse Dialog Box button

D Conditional test

E Function

F Function syntax

G FV   future value

H Logical operator

I Median

J Nper   total # of payment

K Pmt   payment each annual period

L Pv   present value

M Range

N Range name

O Type

Fill in the Blank   Write the correct answer in the space provided.

1. By assigning a ___*range name*___ to a range of cells, it is easier for you and others to understand the meaning of formulas in a worksheet.

2. Assigning a name to a range of cells makes navigating a worksheet easier because you can use the ___*Go to*___ command to move to a named range.

3. The first character of a range name must be a(n) ___*letter*___ or a(n) ___*underscore*___.

4. Range names can be more than one word; however, there can be no ___*spaces*___ between the words.

5. Deleting a range name does not modify or delete the cell ___*contents*___ or ___*formatting*___ of the cells.

6. To view and get access to all of Excel's functions, display the ___*collapse*___ dialog box.

7. A function, like a formula, always begins with a(n) ___*equal sign*___.

8. Excel has ___*9*___ different categories of functions, plus three additional categories: Most Recently Used, All, and User Defined.

9. Within a range of selected cells, the ___*count*___ function returns the number of cells that contain numbers.

10. Excel has assigned the serial value of 1 to the date ___*Jan 1/1900*___.

11. The ___*date*___ function places, in the selected cell, a serial value that represents a particular day, month, and year.

(Fill in the Blank–continues on the next page)

(Fill in the Blank–continued)

12. If you open a workbook containing the _____*now*_____ function, when closing the workbook you will be prompted to save changes even if you did not perform any editing in the cells because the function attempts to update the cell in which it is used to contain the current date and time.

13. The symbol > is the logical operator that indicates _*greater than*_.

14. The symbol < is the logical operator that indicates _*less than*_.

15. The symbols >= form the logical operator that indicates

*greater or equal to*

Project 4E — Home Price

Objectives: *Create Range Names, Use Range Names in a Formula, and Create Statistical Functions.*

In the following Skill Assessment, you will calculate statistics regarding the prices of various new home plans that are built by the Owens Custom Homes division of Owens Family Builders. Your completed worksheet will look similar to Figure 4.45. You will save your workbook as *4E_Home_Price_Firstname_Lastname.*

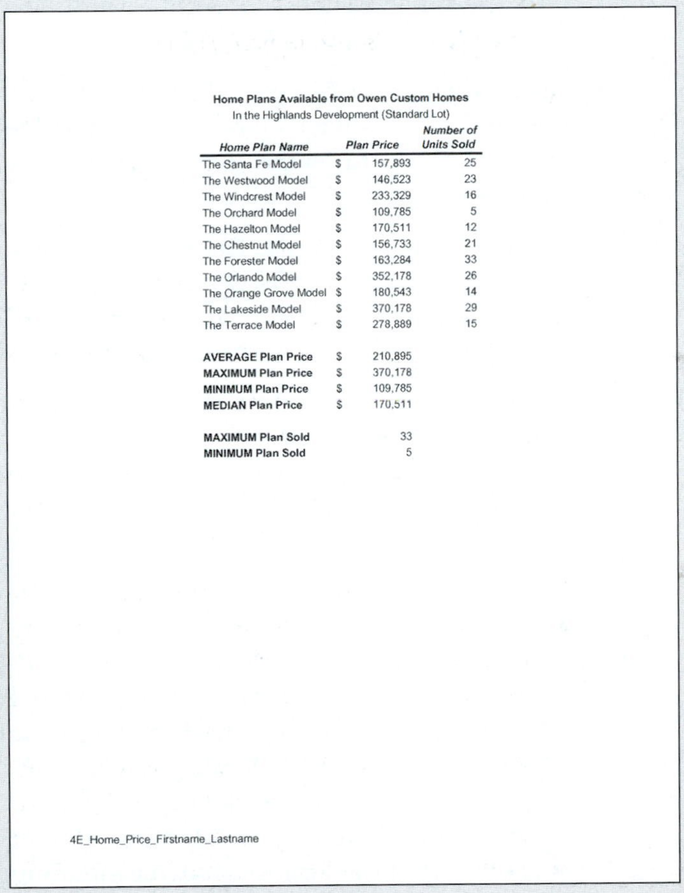

Home Plans Available from Owen Custom Homes
In the Highlands Development (Standard Lot)

Home Plan Name	Plan Price	Number of Units Sold
The Santa Fe Model	$ 157,893	25
The Westwood Model	$ 146,523	23
The Windcrest Model	$ 233,329	16
The Orchard Model	$ 109,785	5
The Hazelton Model	$ 170,511	12
The Chestnut Model	$ 156,733	21
The Forester Model	$ 163,284	33
The Orlando Model	$ 352,178	26
The Orange Grove Model	$ 180,543	14
The Lakeside Model	$ 370,178	29
The Terrace Model	$ 278,889	15
AVERAGE Plan Price	$ 210,895	
MAXIMUM Plan Price	$ 370,178	
MINIMUM Plan Price	$ 109,785	
MEDIAN Plan Price	$ 170,511	
MAXIMUM Plan Sold		33
MINIMUM Plan Sold		5

4E_Home_Price_Firstname_Lastname

Figure 4.45

1. **Start** Excel. On the Standard toolbar, click the **Open** button, navigate to the student files that accompany this textbook, and open the file **e04E_Home_Price**.

2. From the **File** menu, click **Save As**. In the **Save As** dialog box, navigate to the location where you are storing your projects for this chapter. In the **File name** box, type **4E_Home_Price_Firstname_Lastname** and then click **Save** or press Enter.

(Project 4E–Home Price continues on the next page)

(Project 4E–Home Price continued)

3. Select the range **B3:B14**. You will use the column label in cell **B3** to create a range name for the price data. From the **Insert** menu, point to **Name**, and then click **Create**. In the **Create Names** dialog box, if necessary, click to place a check mark in the **Top row** check box. This will instruct Excel to use the label in the first row of the selection— **row 3**—as the name for the range you are creating. Click **OK**.

4. Select the range **C4:C14**. To create this range name, from the **Insert** menu, point to **Name**, and then click **Define**. In the **Names in workbook** box, type **Units** and then verify that in the **Refers to** box, the range =Sheet1!$C$4:$C$14 displays. Click **OK** to define the range name.

5. Click an empty cell to cancel the selection. Click the **Name Box arrow**, and from the displayed list, click **Plan_Price**. The range B4:B14 is selected. Click the **Name Box arrow** again, click **Units**, and be sure that the range C4:C14 is selected.

6. Click cell **B16**. From the **Insert** menu, click **Function**. Click the **Or select a category arrow**, and then from the displayed list, click **Statistical**. Under **Select a function**, click **AVERAGE**, and then click **OK** to display the **Function Arguments** dialog box.

   In the **Number1** box, type **Plan_Price** to indicate the range that Excel should average. Recall that you defined Plan_Price as the range B4:B14 and that it is acceptable to use a range name in a function or formula. Click **OK**. The result, $210,895, displays. Thus, the average price for a new home in this development is $210,895.

7. Click cell **B17**. To the left of the Formula Bar, click the **Insert Function** button. Under **Select a function**, scroll as necessary, and then click **MAX**. Click **OK**. In the displayed **Function Arguments** dialog box, in the **Number1** box, type **Plan_Price** to denote the range B4:B14 and to have Excel find the largest amount in that range. Click **OK**. The result, $370,178, displays, indicating that this is the most expensive plan in the development. Look at the list of numbers in the column labeled *Plan Price*. It is easy to determine visually, in this short list, that the largest (maximum) amount is $370,178, but in a longer worksheet, you can see that the MAX function is quite useful.

8. Click cell **B18**. Display the **Insert Function** dialog box, and then, in the **Statistical** category, scroll as necessary and click **MIN**. Click **OK** to display the **Function Arguments** dialog box. In the **Number1** box, type **Plan_Price** to denote the range B4:B14. Click **OK**. The result, $109,785, displays, indicating that this is the lowest-priced home plan in the development.

(Project 4E–Home Price continues on the next page)

(Project 4E–Home Price continued)

9. Click cell **B19**. Display the **Insert Function** dialog box, and then, in the **Statistical** category, scroll as necessary and click **MEDIAN**. Click **OK**, and then, in the **Number1** box, type **Plan_Price** Click **OK**. The result, $170,511, displays, indicating that half the plans are more expensive than $170,511, and half are less expensive.

10. Click cell **B17** and look at the Formula Bar. You can see that the pattern for inserting a function is the equal sign, the function abbreviation, and then the cells to be calculated enclosed in parentheses. In this case, the range of cells has been named. Click cell **B21** and type **=MAX(Units)** and notice that a blue border surrounds the range that you named *Units*. Press . The result, 33, displays, indicating that the most popular model has sold 33 units.

11. Click cell **B22**. Using either the **Insert Function** dialog box, or by typing, insert the formula to find the minimum number of units—the least popular plan. Your result should be 5.

12. From the **File** menu, click **Page Setup**, and then click the **Margins tab**. Under **Center on page**, select the **Horizontally** check box. Click the **Header/Footer tab**, and then click **Custom Footer**. In the **Left section**, click the **File Name** button, and then click **OK** twice.

13. On the Standard toolbar, click the **Save** button, and then click the **Print Preview** button to view how your worksheet will print. On the Print Preview toolbar, click **Print**, and then click **OK**.

14. Hold down Ctrl and press ` to display the formulas. Click the **Print Preview** button. On the Print Preview toolbar, click **Setup**. In the **Page Setup** dialog box, click the **Page tab**. Under **Scaling**, click the **Fit to** option button, and then click **OK**. On the Print Preview toolbar, click **Print**, and then click **OK**.

15. Hold down Ctrl and press ` to display the worksheet. Close the workbook, saving changes if prompted to do so.

End You have completed Project 4E ────────────────────────

Project 4F—Auto Purchase

Objective: *Create Financial Functions.*

In the following Skill Assessment, you will compute the payment for eight automobiles that Owens Family Builders is purchasing for the members of its sales staff. The purchase will be financed over a period of two years. Your completed worksheet will look similar to Figure 4.46. You will save your workbook as *4F_Auto_Purchase_Firstname_Lastname.*

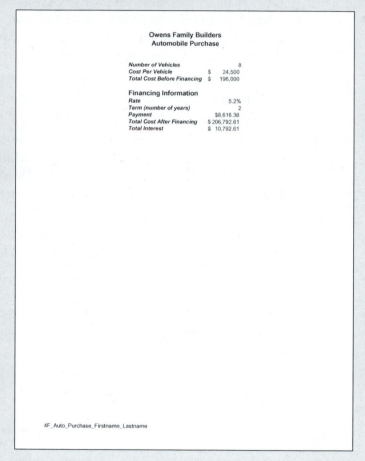

Owens Family Builders
Automobile Purchase

Number of Vehicles		8
Cost Per Vehicle	$	24,500
Total Cost Before Financing	$	196,000

Financing Information

Rate	5.2%
Term (number of years)	2
Payment	$8,616.36
Total Cost After Financing	$ 206,792.61
Total Interest	$ 10,792.61

4F_Auto_Purchase_Firstname_Lastname

Figure 4.46

1. **Start** Excel. On the Standard toolbar, click the **Open** button, navigate to the student files that accompany this textbook, and open the file **e04F_Auto_Purchase**.

2. From the **File** menu, click **Save As**. In the **Save As** dialog box, navigate to the location where you are storing your projects for this chapter. In the **File name** box, type **4F_Auto_Purchase_Firstname_Lastname** and then click **Save** or press Enter.

(Project 4F–Auto Purchase continues on the next page)

(Project 4F–Auto Purchase continued)

3. Click cell **B7**. In this cell, you will compute the total purchase price for all eight vehicles. This calculation is the number of vehicles purchased multiplied by the cost per vehicle. Type or use the point-and-click method to enter the formula **=B5*B6** and then press Enter. The result, $196,000, displays. Notice that the cell adopted the format of the cell above it.

4. Click cell **B12**. The total purchase will be financed over two years at an interest rate of 5.2 percent. From the **Insert** menu, click **Function**. In the **Insert Function** dialog box, click the **Or select a category arrow**. From the displayed list, click **Financial**. Under **Select a function**, scroll as necessary, and then click **PMT**. Notice that this function calculates the payment for a loan based on constant payments and a constant interest rate.

5. Click **OK**. With your insertion point positioned in the **Rate** box, click cell **B10** to insert it in the **Rate** box, and then type **/12** This instructs Excel to divide the annual interest rate of 5.2 percent located in cell **B10** by 12 (months), which will result in a monthly interest rate. Press Tab to move the insertion point to the **Nper** box.

6. Nper is the total number of payments over the life of the loan. Click cell **B11** (number of years) to insert it into the **Nper** box, and then type ***12** to convert the number of years in the loan to the number of months. Recall that this function is calculating a monthly payment. Thus, all values in the function must be expressed in months. Press Tab to move the insertion point to the **Pv** box.

7. Pv represents the present value. Click cell **B7** to instruct Excel to use the *Total Cost Before Financing* as the present value. Click **OK** to compute the payment. The result, ($8,616.36), displays in red and in parentheses.

8. The payment displays as a negative number because it represents money paid out. In the Formula Bar, click to position the insertion point after the equal sign (=). Type - and then press Enter so that the result displays as a positive number.

9. To compute the total cost of the purchase and financing, you will construct a formula that multiplies the monthly payment by the total number of monthly payments. Click cell **B13**, type **=24*** and then click cell **B12**. Press Enter. The result, $206,792.61, displays.

10. To compute the total amount of interest that will paid over the life of the loan, you will construct a formula that subtracts the cost before financing from the total cost after financing. Click cell **B14**. Use either the point-and-click method or type to construct the formula as follows: **=B13-B7** The total amount of interest that will be paid is $10,792.61.

(Project 4F–Auto Purchase continues on the next page)

(Project 4F–Auto Purchase continued)

11. From the **File** menu, click **Page Setup**, and then click the **Margins tab**. Under **Center on page**, select the **Horizontally** check box. Click the **Header/Footer tab**, and then click **Custom Footer**. In the **Left section**, click the **File Name** button, and then click **OK** twice.

12. On the Standard toolbar, click the **Save** button, and then click the **Print Preview** button to view how your worksheet will print. On the Print Preview toolbar, click **Print**, and then click **OK**.

13. Hold down Ctrl and press ` to display the formulas. Click the **Print Preview** button. Verify that the formulas display on one page, and then, on the Print Preview toolbar, click **Print**. Click **OK**. Hold down Ctrl and press ` to redisplay the worksheet. Close the workbook, saving changes if prompted to do so.

End **You have completed Project 4F**

Project 4G — Bonus

Objectives: *Create Statistical Functions, Create Logical Functions, and Set and Clear a Print Area.*

In the following Skill Assessment, you will compute the average sale amount for the first quarter for sales associates in the Custom Home Division of Owens Family Builders. Using logical functions, you will also determine which associates qualify for a bonus. Your completed worksheet will look similar to Figure 4.47. You will save your workbook as *4G_Bonus_Firstname_Lastname.*

1. **Start** Excel. On the Standard toolbar, click the **Open** button, navigate to the student files that accompany this textbook, and then open the file **e04G_Bonus**.

2. From the **File** menu, click **Save As**. In the **Save As** dialog box, navigate to the location where you are storing your projects for this chapter. In the **File name** box, type **4G_Bonus_Firstname_Lastname** and then click **Save** or press Enter.

3. Click cell **E5**. In this cell, you will compute the average monthly sales amount for the sales associate in the first quarter. From the **Insert** menu, click **Function**. Click the **Or select a category arrow**, and from the displayed list, click **Statistical**. Under **Select a function**, click **AVERAGE**, and then click **OK**. The **Function Arguments** dialog box displays.

4. If necessary, drag the dialog box to the right so that you have a clear view of the data in the worksheet. In the **Number1** box, Excel has proposed the range B5:D5, which is the correct range that you want to average—the sales amounts for January, February, and March. Click **OK**. The result, $460,218.00, displays.

(Project 4G–Bonus continues on the next page)

(Project 4G–Bonus continued)

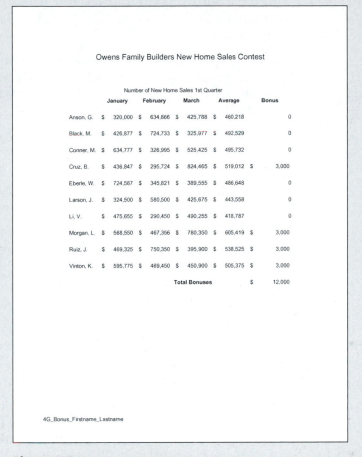

Owens Family Builders New Home Sales Contest

Number of New Home Sales 1st Quarter

	January	February	March	Average	Bonus
Anson, G.	$ 320,000	$ 634,866	$ 425,788	$ 460,218	0
Black, M.	$ 426,877	$ 724,733	$ 325,977	$ 492,529	0
Conner, M.	$ 634,777	$ 326,995	$ 525,425	$ 495,732	0
Cruz, B.	$ 436,847	$ 295,724	$ 824,465	$ 519,012	$ 3,000
Eberle, W.	$ 724,567	$ 345,821	$ 389,555	$ 486,648	0
Larson, J.	$ 324,500	$ 580,500	$ 425,675	$ 443,558	0
Li, V.	$ 475,655	$ 290,450	$ 490,255	$ 418,787	0
Morgan, L.	$ 568,550	$ 467,356	$ 780,350	$ 605,419	$ 3,000
Ruiz, J.	$ 469,325	$ 750,350	$ 395,900	$ 538,525	$ 3,000
Vinton, K.	$ 595,775	$ 469,450	$ 450,900	$ 505,375	$ 3,000
			Total Bonuses	$	12,000

4G_Bonus_Firstname_Lastname

Figure 4.47

5. Point to the fill handle so that the small black cross displays. Drag down to copy the formula through cell **E14**. With the range **E5:E14** selected, on the Formatting toolbar, click **Decrease Decimal** two times.

6. Sales associates who averaged $500,000 or more per month in sales over the three-month quarter qualify for a bonus of $3,000. You will use the Logical IF function to determine which associates will receive a bonus. Click cell **F5**. At the left edge of the Formula Bar, click the **Insert Function** button. Click the **Logical** category, click the **IF** function, and then click **OK**. The **Function Arguments** dialog box displays.

7. If necessary, drag the dialog box to the right of your screen so that you have a clear view of the data. With the insertion point in the **Logical_test** box, click cell **E5**, and then type **>=500000** This instructs Excel to determine if the value in cell **E5** is greater than or equal to 500000. Press ⌨Tab.

(Project 4G–Bonus continues on the next page)

(Project 4G–Bonus continued)

8. With the insertion point in the **Value_if_true** box, type **3000** This instructs Excel to insert 3000 in the cell if the value in cell **E5** is greater than or equal to 500000. Press Tab.

9. With the insertion point in the **Value_if_false** box, type **0.00** This instructs Excel to insert 0.00 in the cell if the value in cell E5 is not greater than or equal to 500000. Click **OK**. The result for sales associate Anson is zero.

10. Point to the fill handle, and then drag down through cell **F14**. You can see that four sales associates averaged over $500,000 per month and will receive a bonus. Select the range **F12:F14**, hold down Ctrl, and then click cell **F8**. With the four cells selected, click the **Currency Style** button, and then click the **Decrease Decimal** button twice.

11. Click cell **F15**, and then, on the Standard toolbar, click the **AutoSum** button. Verify that the range **F5:F14** is selected, and then press Enter to calculate the total bonuses paid to the sales associates. If necessary, format cell F15 using the Currency Style button, and then click Decrease Decimal two times.

12. From the **File** menu, click **Page Setup**, and then click the **Margins tab**. Under **Center on page**, select the **Horizontally** check box. Click the **Header/Footer tab**, and then click **Custom Footer**. In the **Left section**, click the **File Name** button, and then click **OK** twice.

13. To print only the sales figures, without the bonuses, select the range **A3:E14**. Then, from the **File** menu, point to **Print Area**, and click **Set Print Area**. On the menu bar, click the **Print Preview** button and verify that only the selected area displays. On the Print Preview toolbar, click **Print**, and then click **OK**.

14. From the **File** menu, point to **Print Area**, and then click **Clear Print Area**. Click any cell to cancel the selection.

15. On the Standard toolbar, click the **Save** button, and then click the **Print Preview** button to view how your worksheet will print. On the Print Preview toolbar, click **Print**, and then click **OK** to print the full worksheet.

16. Hold down Ctrl and press ` to display the formulas. Click the **Print Preview** button. On the Print Preview toolbar, click **Setup**. In the **Page Setup** dialog box, click the **Page tab**. Under **Orientation**, click **Landscape**, under **Scaling**, click the **Fit to** option button, and then click **OK**. On the Print Preview toolbar, click **Print**, and then click **OK**.

17. Hold down Ctrl and press ` to display the worksheet. Close the workbook, saving changes if prompted to do so.

End **You have completed Project 4G**

Project 4H — Survey

Objectives: *Create Range Names, Use Range Names in a Formula, Create Statistical Functions, and Set and Clear a Print Area.*

In the following Performance Assessment, you will calculate statistics regarding a survey conducted by the marketing department at Owens Family Builders. The survey polled residents in five adjacent neighborhoods about a proposal to construct a shopping area and adjoining park that would serve the residents of these neighborhoods. Your completed worksheet will look similar to Figure 4.48. You will save your workbook as *4H_Survey_Firstname_Lastname*.

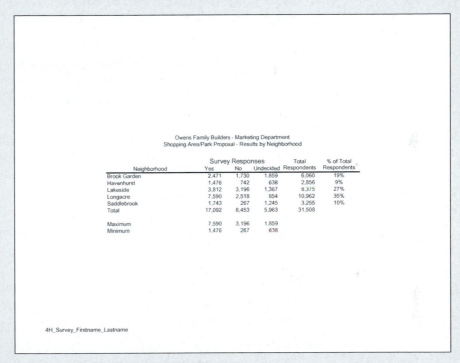

Owens Family Builders - Marketing Department
Shopping Area/Park Proposal - Results by Neighborhood

Neighborhood	Survey Responses			Total Respondents	% of Total Respondents
	Yes	No	Undecided		
Brook Garden	2,471	1,730	1,859	6,060	19%
Havenhurst	1,476	742	638	2,856	9%
Lakeside	3,812	3,196	1,367	8,375	27%
Longacre	7,590	2,518	854	10,962	35%
Saddlebrook	1,743	267	1,245	3,255	10%
Total	17,092	8,453	5,963	31,508	
Maximum	7,590	3,196	1,859		
Minimum	1,476	267	638		

4H_Survey_Firstname_Lastname

Figure 4.48

1. **Start** Excel. On the Standard toolbar, click the **Open** button, navigate to the student files that accompany this textbook, and then open the file **e04H_Survey**.

2. From the **File** menu, click **Save As**. In the **Save As** dialog box, navigate to the location where you are storing your projects for this chapter. In the **File name** box, type **4H_Survey_Firstname_Lastname** and then click **Save** or press Enter.

3. In cell **E6**, use the **AutoSum** button to calculate the Total Respondents from the Brook Garden neighborhood. Then, copy the formula down through cell **E10** to calculate the number of respondents from each of the remaining neighborhoods.

(Project 4H–Survey continues on the next page)

(Project 4H–Survey continued)

4. In cell **B11**, calculate the number of Yes respondents, and then copy the formula across through cell **E11**. Select the range **B6:E11** and apply **Comma Style** formatting with zero decimal places.

5. In cell **F6**, create a formula that calculates the percentage that the Brook Garden neighborhood represents out of the total respondents. To create this formula, divide the total respondents for the Brook Garden neighborhood by the total respondents in cell **E11**. (Hint: Make the reference to E11 absolute so that you can copy the formula down through the remaining neighborhoods. Recall that you can use the [F4] function key to make a cell reference absolute.) Copy the formula down through cell **F10**. With the range selected, apply **Percent Style** formatting with zero decimal places, and **Center** the percentages.

6. Select the range **B5:D10**. From the **Insert** menu, point to **Name**, and then click **Create**. In the **Create Names** dialog box, be sure the **Top row** check box is selected. Click **OK**. The label in the first row at the top of each column becomes the range name for each respective column.

7. Click the **Name Box arrow**, and verify that all three ranges were created using the column names. From the displayed list, click **Yes**, and verify that the range includes **B6:B10**. Repeat for the ranges named *No* and *Undecided*.

8. Click cell **B13**. Type **=MAX(Yes)** to instruct Excel to display the largest number within the *Yes* range of cells. Press [Enter]. In cells **C13** and **D13**, construct a similar formula to instruct Excel to display the largest number within the *No* range of cells and within the *Undecided* range of cells. In cells **B14:D14**, construct similar formulas using the **MIN** function. Format the range **B13:D14** using **Comma Style** and zero decimal places.

9. Change the **Page Orientation** to **Landscape**, and center the worksheet **Horizontally** and **Vertically** on the page. Create a custom footer and insert the file name in the **Left section**.

10. To print only the survey response information, select the range **A4:D11**. Then, from the **File** menu, point to **Print Area**, and click **Set Print Area**. On the menu bar, click the **Print Preview** button, and verify that only the selected area displays. On the Print Preview toolbar, click the **Print** button, and then click **OK**.

11. From the **File** menu, point to **Print Area**, and then click **Clear Print Area**. Click in any cell to cancel the selection.

12. On the Standard toolbar, click the **Save** button, and then click the **Print Preview** button to view how your worksheet will print. On the Print Preview toolbar, click **Print**, and then click **OK**.

(Project 4H–Survey continues on the next page)

(Project 4H–Survey continued)

13. Hold down Ctrl and press ' to display the formulas. Click the **Print Preview** button. On the Print Preview toolbar, click **Setup**. In the **Page Setup** dialog box, on the **Page tab**, click the **Landscape** and **Fit to** option buttons, and then click **OK**. On the Print Preview toolbar, click **Print**, and then click **OK**.

14. Hold down Ctrl and press ' to display the worksheet. Close the workbook, saving changes if prompted to do so.

End You have completed Project 4H ─────────────────────

Project 4I—Annuity

Objective: *Create Date & Time and Financial Functions.*

In the following Performance Assessment, you will calculate the value of a $5,000 annuity at the end of 10 years, assuming that the company contributes $1,200 to the annuity at the beginning of each year and that the average rate of return is 8 percent per year for each of the 10 remaining years. Your completed worksheet will look similar to Figure 4.49. You will save your workbook as *4I_Annuity_Firstname_Lastname*.

1. **Start** Excel. On the Standard toolbar, click the **Open** button, navigate to the student files that accompany this textbook, and then open the file **e04I_Annuity**.

2. From the **File** menu, click **Save As**. In the **Save As** dialog box, navigate to the location where you are storing your projects for this chapter. In the **File name** box, type **4I_Annuity_Firstname_Lastname** and then click **Save** or press Enter.

3. Click cell **B18**. Display the **Insert Function** dialog box, select the **Financial** category, and then click the **FV** (future value) function. Click **OK**. If necessary, drag the **Function Arguments** dialog box to the right of your screen so that you have a clear view of the worksheet.

4. With the insertion point positioned in the **Rate** box, click the cell that contains the Average Return Rate of 8%. In the **Nper** box, click the cell that contains the number of Contributing Years. In the **Pmt** box, click the cell that contains the Annual Contribution amount. In the **Pv** box, click the cell that contains the Initial Contribution per Employee. In the **Type** box, type **1** to indicate that the payment into the annuity will be made at the beginning of each year. Click **OK** to calculate the future value of the annuity for each employee.

(Project 4I–Annuity continues on the next page)

(Project 4I–Annuity continued)

Owens Family Builders
Employee Annuity Plan by Department

	Total Eligible Employees	Total Initial Purchase Cost	Annual Payment Cost	Total Cost Life of the Annuity
Executives	6	$ 30,000	$ 7,200	$ 102,000
Managers	18	$ 90,000	$ 21,600	$ 306,000
Clerical	32	$ 160,000	$ 38,400	$ 544,000
Marketing	7	$ 35,000	$ 8,400	$ 119,000
Design	12	$ 60,000	$ 14,400	$ 204,000
Construction Mangement	12	$ 60,000	$ 14,400	$ 204,000
Security	15	$ 75,000	$ 18,000	$ 255,000
Total		$ 510,000	$ 122,400	$ 1,734,000

Computed On:	12/27/2003 7:43
Average Return Rate	8%
Contributing Years	10
Annual Contribution	$1,200
Initial Contribution per Employee	$5,000
Future Value of Annuity per Employee	$29,569.21

4I_Annuity_Firstname_Lastname

Figure 4.49

5. The result, ($29,569.21), displays as a negative number. To display a positive number, edit the formula so that a minus sign (-) is inserted between the equal sign (=) and the function name (FV).

6. In cell **C4**, create a formula that multiplies the number of Executives by the Initial Contribution per Employee, and make the reference to the Initial Contribution absolute. By doing so, you can copy the formula to other cells. Copy the formula down through cell **C10**. In cell **C11**, total the column.

7. In cell **D4**, create a formula that multiplies the number of Executives by the Annual Contribution, and make the reference to the Annual Contribution absolute. Copy the formula down through cell **D10**. In cell **D11**, total the column.

8. In cell **E4**, type **=(d4*b15)+c4** For each employee group, this formula instructs Excel to multiply the annual payment (cell **D4**) by the number of years (cell **B15**), and then add that figure to the initial payment (cell **C4**). Copy the formula down through cell **E10**. In cell **E11**, total the column.

(Project 4I–Annuity continues on the next page)

(Project 4I–Annuity continued)

9. Click cell **B13**, and then insert the **NOW** function from the **Date & Time** category. Recall that this function has no arguments; rather, it obtains the current date and time from your system's internal calendar and clock.

10. Display the **Page Setup** dialog box, and center the worksheet **Horizontally** on the page. Create a custom footer, and insert the file name in the **Left section**.

11. On the Standard toolbar, click the **Save** button, and then click the **Print Preview** button to view how your worksheet will print. On the Print Preview toolbar, click **Print**, and then click **OK**.

12. Hold down Ctrl and press `'` to display the formulas. Click the **Print Preview** button. On the Print Preview toolbar, click **Setup**. In the **Page Setup** dialog box, on the **Page tab**, click the **Landscape** and **Fit to** option buttons, and then click **OK**. On the Print Preview toolbar, click **Print**, and then click **OK**.

13. Hold down Ctrl and press `'` to display the worksheet. Close the workbook, saving changes if prompted to do so.

End **You have completed Project 4I**

Project 4J — Prices

Objectives: *Create Range Names, Use Range Names in a Formula, and Create Statistical Functions.*

In the following Performance Assessment, you will calculate statistics regarding home prices in selected U.S. cities for Laura Owen Shafku, President of Owens Family Builders, who is interested in comparing the prices of homes in the Orlando area with those in other cities. Your completed worksheet will look similar to Figure 4.50. You will save your workbook as *4J_Prices_Firstname_Lastname*.

1. **Start** Excel. On the Standard toolbar, click the **Open** button, navigate to the student files that accompany this textbook, and then open the file **e04J_Prices**.

2. From the **File** menu, click **Save As**. In the **Save As** dialog box, navigate to the location where you are storing your projects for this chapter. In the **File name** box, type **4J_Prices_Firstname_Lastname** and then click **Save** or press Enter.

3. Select the range **B3:D41**. You will use the column labels in **row 3** to create range names for each year's data. From the **Insert** menu, point to **Name**, and then click **Create**. In the **Create Names** dialog box, be sure the **Top row** check box is selected. This will instruct Excel to use the labels in the top row of the selection as the range names. Click **OK**.

(Project 4J–Prices continues on the next page)

(Project 4J–Prices continued)

Average Home Prices In US Cities	In Thousands			Average Price Over 3-Year Period
City	Year 2000	Year 2001	Year 2002	
Albany/Schenectady/Troy, NY	111.1	121.6	130.5	121.1
Atlantic City, NJ	121.5	125.7	143.6	130.3
Austin/San Marcos, TX	142.8	152.0	156.5	150.4
Birmingham, AL	125.5	133.6	137.4	132.2
Boston, MA	314.2	356.6	405.0	358.6
Chattanooga, TN/GA	101.1	107.3	112.3	106.9
Cincinnati, OH/KY/IN	126.7	130.2	134.1	130.3
Dallas, TX	122.5	131.1	135.2	129.6
Daytona Beach, FL	85.3	93.7	108.3	95.8
Ft. Myers/Cape Coral, FL	97.6	121.1	133.6	117.4
Gainesville, FL	113.1	118.0	130.0	120.4
Greenville/Spartanburg, SC	118.1	124.5	125.3	122.6
Honolulu, HI	295.0	299.9	335.0	310.0
Indianapolis, IN	112.3	116.9	116.8	115.3
Lansing/East Lansing, MI	111.2	119.5	126.4	119.0
Madison, WI	153.6	162.5	177.0	164.4
Milwaukee, WI	140.7	149.4	173.8	154.6
New Orleans, LA	112.0	117.4	123.5	117.6
Monmouth/Ocean, NJ	179.0	208.6	251.7	213.1
Pensacola, FL	101.1	105.0	112.2	106.1
Philadelphia, PA/NJ	125.2	134.8	146.1	135.4
Pittsburgh, PA	93.6	97.8	101.5	97.6
Portland, OR	170.1	172.3	180.4	174.3
Raleigh/Durham, NC	158.4	168.2	172.2	166.3
Richmond/Petersburg, VA	129.8	133.3	142.3	135.1
Sacramento, CA	145.2	173.2	209.5	176.0
Salt Lake City/Ogden, UT	141.5	147.6	148.8	146.0
Sarasota, FL	132.0	168.1	176.2	158.8
Seattle, WA	230.1	245.4	254.0	243.2
Spokane, WA	104.2	108.0	108.7	107.0
Springfield, MA	120.4	127.4	139.8	129.2
Tacoma, WA	151.1	159.5	170.4	160.3
Tallahassee, FL	122.5	129.7	136.9	129.7
Tampa/St. Petersburg/Clearwater, FL	110.8	123.6	133.5	122.6
Topeka, KS	80.6	88.7	89.0	86.1
Tucson, AZ	120.5	128.8	146.4	131.9
Washington, DC/MD/VA	182.6	213.9	250.2	215.6
Worcester, MA	131.8	152.6	187.7	157.4
Average	137.8	149.1	162.2	149.7
Maximum	314.2	356.6	405.0	358.6
Minimum	80.6	88.7	89.0	86.1
Median	123.9	130.7	141.1	131.1
Average 2002 Price In Florida Cities	133.0			

4J_Prices_Firstname_Lastname

Figure 4.50

4. Click the **Name Box arrow,** and verify that the three ranges have been named.

5. Click cell **A12**, hold down (Ctrl), and then click cell **D12**. Continue holding down (Ctrl), and then click cell **A13**, and then cell **D13**. Continue holding down (Ctrl), and then, in a similar manner, click each remaining city in the state of Florida (**FL**), and then its **Year 2002** data. (There are seven cities in Florida.) With this nonadjacent range of cells selected, display the **Insert** menu, point to **Name**, and then click **Define**. Under **Names in workbook**, type FL_2002 The existing text is deleted. Click the **Add** button. The new range name is added to the list of named ranges. Click **OK** to close the dialog box, and then click anywhere to cancel the selection.

6. Click cell **E4**. For each city in the list, you will calculate the average home price over the three-year period. On the Standard toolbar, click the **AutoSum button arrow**, and then, from the displayed list, click

(Project 4J–Prices continues on the next page)

(Project 4J–Prices continued)

Average. Recall that you can select some of the more common functions using the AutoSum button. In cell **E4**, be sure Excel has proposed the correct range of cells to average—**B4:D4**—and then press Enter. Copy the formula down through cell **E41**.

7. Click cell **B43**. Type **=AVERAGE(Year_2000)** and notice that Excel borders the cells that comprise the range *Year_2000*. Press Enter. Format cell **B43** with one decimal place.

8. Click cell **C43**, display the **Insert Function** dialog box, display the **Statistical** category, click the **AVERAGE** function, and then click **OK**. In the **Number1** box, type **Year_2001** and then click **OK**. Format the cell with one decimal place. Look at the Formula Bar, and notice that the formula is the same format as the formula you typed in cell **B43**. You can either type functions or use the **Insert Function** dialog box to create them.

9. Using either the typing method or the dialog box method, calculate the Average statistic for Year 2002 in cell **D43** and the Average statistic for the 3-Year Period column in cell **E43**. (Hint: There is no defined range for the numbers in the 3-Year column. If you want, define and name the range. Otherwise, you will have to define the range in the dialog box by either dragging or typing; or you can type the function name into the cell, and then drag to select the range.) If necessary, format the cell with one decimal place.

10. For each of the four columns, compute the Maximum, Minimum, and Median statistics. Format the cells with one decimal place.

11. In cell **A48**, type **Average 2002 Price In Florida Cities** and then click cell **B48**. Type **=AVERAGE(FL_2002)** and notice that Excel borders the nonadjacent range that you defined. Press Enter. Format the cell with one decimal place.

12. Display the **Page Setup** menu, and center the worksheet **Horizontally** and **Vertically** on the page. Create a custom footer, and insert the file name in the **Left section**.

13. On the Standard toolbar, click the **Save** button, and then click the **Print Preview** button to view how your worksheet will print. On the Print Preview toolbar, click **Print**, and then click **OK**.

14. Hold down Ctrl and press ` to display the formulas. Click the **Print Preview** button. On the Print Preview toolbar, click **Setup**. In the **Page Setup** dialog box, on the **Page tab**, click the **Landscape** and **Fit to** option buttons, and then click **OK**. On the Print Preview toolbar, click **Print**, and then click **OK**.

15. Hold down Ctrl and press ` to redisplay the worksheet. Close the workbook, saving changes if prompted to do so.

End **You have completed Project 4J**

Project 4K — Rates

Objectives: *Create Range Names, Use Range Names in a Formula, Create Statistical Functions, and Create Logical Functions.*

In the following Mastery Assessment, you will calculate water rates that will be applied to users in the new planned-development community recently completed by Owens Family Builders. This new, large community includes residential, commercial, and industrial buildings. Your completed worksheet will look similar to Figure 4.51. You will save your workbook as *4K_Rates_Firstname_Lastname.*

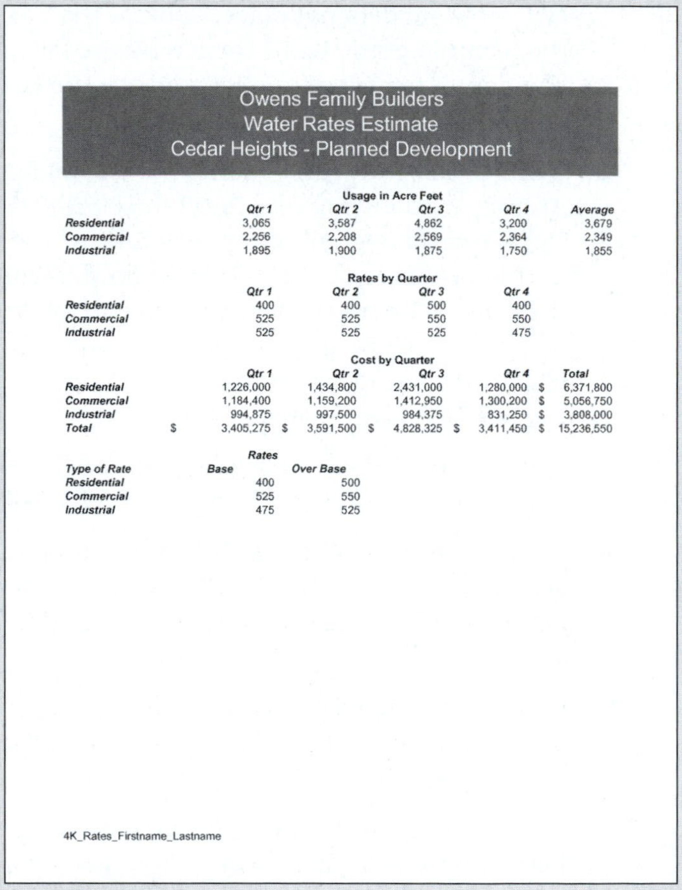

Owens Family Builders
Water Rates Estimate
Cedar Heights - Planned Development

Usage in Acre Feet

	Qtr 1	Qtr 2	Qtr 3	Qtr 4	Average
Residential	3,065	3,587	4,862	3,200	3,679
Commercial	2,256	2,208	2,569	2,364	2,349
Industrial	1,895	1,900	1,875	1,750	1,855

Rates by Quarter

	Qtr 1	Qtr 2	Qtr 3	Qtr 4
Residential	400	400	500	400
Commercial	525	525	550	550
Industrial	525	525	525	475

Cost by Quarter

	Qtr 1	Qtr 2	Qtr 3	Qtr 4	Total
Residential	1,226,000	1,434,800	2,431,000	1,280,000	$ 6,371,800
Commercial	1,184,400	1,159,200	1,412,950	1,300,200	$ 5,056,750
Industrial	994,875	997,500	984,375	831,250	$ 3,808,000
Total	$ 3,405,275	$ 3,591,500	$ 4,828,325	$ 3,411,450	$ 15,236,550

Rates

Type of Rate	Base	Over Base
Residential	400	500
Commercial	525	550
Industrial	475	525

4K_Rates_Firstname_Lastname

Figure 4.51

1. **Start** Excel. On the Standard toolbar, click the **Open** button, navigate to the student files that accompany this textbook, and then open the file **e04K_Rates**.

2. From the **File** menu, click **Save As**. In the **Save As** dialog box, navigate to the location where you are storing your projects for this chapter. In the **File name** box, type **4K_Rates_Firstname_Lastname** and then click **Save** or press [Enter].

(Project 4K–Rates continues on the next page)

(Project 4K–Rates continued)

3. Click cell **B27**. From the **Insert** menu, point to **Name**, and then click **Define**. Under **Names in workbook**, delete *Residential*, type **Res_Base** and then click the **Add** button. Click **OK**.

4. Click cell **B28**, and then click the **Name Box**. Type **Comm_Base** and then press Enter. Click the **Name Box arrow** to view the two range names that you have created.

5. Using either the **Define Names** dialog box or the **Name Box**, name the following cells as indicated:

   B29   Ind_Base

   C27   Res_Over

   C28   Comm_Over

   C29   Ind_Over

6. Click the **Name Box arrow** and verify that you have six named ranges. In cell **F8**, use the **AVERAGE** function to calculate the average quarterly water usage for Residential users, and then copy the formula down for the Commercial and Industrial users.

7. Water rates are determined on a quarterly basis. Up to a certain level, the Base rate is used. If more water is used, the Over Base rate applies. Click cell **B14**, and insert the **IF** Logical function. Insert the arguments based on the following: If the Qtr 1 usage is less than or equal to the 4-quarter average usage, the rate is equal to the Res_Base rate. Otherwise, the rate is equal to the Res_Over rate. (Hint: For purposes of copying the formula across the quarters, cell **F8**, which contains the quarterly average, must be an absolute cell reference in the logical test portion of the argument. In the Value_if_true and Value_if_false portion of your function arguments, click the appropriate cells—the range names that you created will be inserted.) Copy the formula through cell **E14**.

8. Use the same type of IF function to determine the Commercial rates in cells **B15:E15** and the Industrial rates in cells **B16:E16**.

9. Click cell **B20**. Calculate the cost for residential customers in Qtr 1 by multiplying the Residential Qtr 1 rate (cell **B14**) times the Residential Qtr 1 usage (cell **B8**). Copy the formula over through the fourth quarter. Use the same technique to calculate the quarterly costs for the Commercial users in cells **B21:E21** and the Industrial customers in cells **B22:E22**. In cells **F20:F22**, use AutoSum to total the four quarters for each type of user. Format the range **F20:F23** using the **Currency Style** button and zero decimal places. Total the Cost by Quarter and total columns, beginning with cell **B23**, and apply the same format.

(Project 4K–Rates continues on the next page)

(Project 4K–Rates continued)

10. Display the **Page Setup** dialog box, and center the worksheet **Horizontally** on the page. Create a custom footer that contains the file name on the left.

11. Set a **Print Area** showing only the Cost by Quarter. **Print** the area, and then **Clear** the Print Area.

12. On the Standard toolbar, click the **Save** button, and then click the **Print Preview** button to view how your worksheet will print. On the Print Preview toolbar, click **Print**, and then click **OK**.

13. Display the formulas and AutoFit columns B:F so that the formulas are fully displayed on the worksheet. Click the **Print Preview** button, and then click **Setup**. In the **Page Setup** dialog box, click the **Landscape** and **Fit to** option buttons. On the Print Preview toolbar, click **Print**, and then click **OK**.

14. Hold down Ctrl and press ` to display the worksheet. Readjust the column widths, if necessary, to display all the figures. Close the workbook, saving changes if prompted to do so.

End **You have completed Project 4K**

Project 4L — Paving

Objectives: *Create Date & Time, Financial, and Logical Functions.*

In the following Mastery Assessment, you will calculate the payment and create an amortization schedule for three pieces of paving equipment being purchased by Owens Family Builders. Your completed worksheet will look similar to Figure 4.52. You will save your workbook as *4L_Paving_Firstname_Lastname*.

1. **Start** Excel. On the Standard toolbar, click the **Open** button, navigate to the student files that accompany this textbook, and then open the file **e04L_Paving**.

2. From the **File** menu, click **Save As**. In the **Save As** dialog box, navigate to the location where you are storing your projects for this chapter. In the **File name** box, type **4L_Paving_Firstname_Lastname** and then click **Save** or press Enter.

3. Click cell **B11**. The total purchase will be financed over three years at an interest rate of 4.2 percent. From the **Financial** category, insert the **PMT** function, and then click **OK** to display the **Function Arguments** dialog box.

(Project 4L–Paving continues on the next page)

(Project 4L–Paving continued)

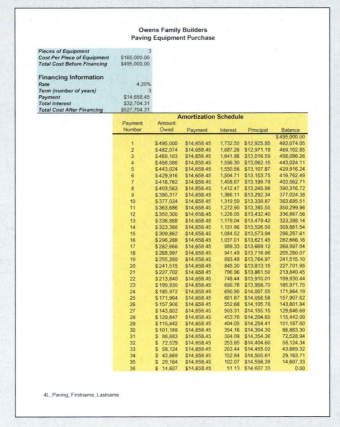

Owens Family Builders
Paving Equipment Purchase

Pieces of Equipment	3
Cost Per Piece of Equipment	$165,000.00
Total Cost Before Financing	$495,000.00
Financing Information	
Rate	4.20%
Term (number of years)	3
Payment	$14,658.45
Total Interest	$32,704.31
Total Cost After Financing	$527,704.31

Amortization Schedule

Payment Number	Amount Owed	Payment	Interest	Principal	Balance
					$495,000.00
1	$495,000	$14,658.45	1,732.50	$12,925.95	482,074.05
2	$482,074	$14,658.45	1,687.26	$12,971.19	469,102.85
3	$469,103	$14,658.45	1,641.86	$13,016.59	456,086.26
4	$456,086	$14,658.45	1,596.30	$13,062.15	443,024.11
5	$443,024	$14,658.45	1,550.58	$13,107.87	429,916.24
6	$429,916	$14,658.45	1,504.71	$13,153.75	416,762.49
7	$416,762	$14,658.45	1,458.67	$13,199.78	403,562.71
8	$403,563	$14,658.45	1,412.47	$13,245.98	390,316.72
9	$390,317	$14,658.45	1,366.11	$13,292.34	377,024.38
10	$377,024	$14,658.45	1,319.59	$13,338.87	363,685.51
11	$363,686	$14,658.45	1,272.90	$13,385.55	350,299.96
12	$350,300	$14,658.45	1,226.05	$13,432.40	336,867.56
13	$336,868	$14,658.45	1,179.04	$13,479.42	323,388.14
14	$323,388	$14,658.45	1,131.86	$13,526.59	309,861.54
15	$309,862	$14,658.45	1,084.52	$13,573.94	296,287.61
16	$296,288	$14,658.45	1,037.01	$13,621.45	282,666.16
17	$282,666	$14,658.45	989.33	$13,669.12	268,997.04
18	$268,997	$14,658.45	941.49	$13,716.96	255,280.07
19	$255,280	$14,658.45	893.48	$13,764.97	241,515.10
20	$241,515	$14,658.45	845.30	$13,813.15	227,701.95
21	$227,702	$14,658.45	796.96	$13,861.50	213,840.45
22	$213,840	$14,658.45	748.44	$13,910.01	199,930.44
23	$199,930	$14,658.45	699.76	$13,958.70	185,971.75
24	$185,972	$14,658.45	650.90	$14,007.55	171,964.19
25	$171,964	$14,658.45	601.87	$14,056.58	157,907.62
26	$157,908	$14,658.45	552.68	$14,105.78	143,801.84
27	$143,802	$14,658.45	503.31	$14,155.15	129,646.69
28	$129,647	$14,658.45	453.76	$14,204.69	115,442.00
29	$115,442	$14,658.45	404.05	$14,254.41	101,187.60
30	$101,188	$14,658.45	354.16	$14,304.30	86,883.30
31	$ 86,883	$14,658.45	304.09	$14,354.36	72,528.94
32	$ 72,529	$14,658.45	253.85	$14,404.60	58,124.34
33	$ 58,124	$14,658.45	203.44	$14,455.02	43,669.32
34	$ 43,669	$14,658.45	152.84	$14,505.61	29,163.71
35	$ 29,164	$14,658.45	102.07	$14,556.38	14,607.33
36	$ 14,607	$14,658.45	51.13	$14,607.33	0.00

4L_Paving_Firstname_Lastname

Figure 4.52

4. If necessary, move the dialog box to the right of the screen. With your insertion point positioned in the **Rate** box, click cell **B9** to insert it in the **Rate** box, and then type **/12** This instructs Excel to divide the annual interest rate of 4.2 percent located in cell **B9** by 12 (months), which will result in a monthly interest rate. Press Tab to move the insertion point to the **Nper** box.

5. Click cell **B10** (number of years) to insert it in the **Nper** box, and then type ***12** to convert the number of years in the loan to the number of months. Press Tab to move the insertion point to the **Pv** box.

6. Click cell **B6** to instruct Excel to use the Total Cost Before Financing as the present value. Click **OK** to compute the payment. Widen the column as necessary. The result, ($14,658.45), displays in red.

7. In the Formula Bar, click to position the insertion point after the equal sign (=). Type - and then press Enter so that the result displays as a positive number.

8. To compute the total cost of the purchase and financing, you will construct a formula that multiplies the monthly payment by the total number of monthly payments. Click cell **B13**, type **=36*** and then click cell **B11**. Press Enter. The result, $527,704.31, displays.

(Project 4L–Paving continues on the next page)

(Project 4L–Paving continued)

9. In cell **B12**, compute the total amount of interest that will be paid over the life of the loan. Your result should be $32,704.31.

10. Click cell **B17**, type **1** and then press Enter. In cell **B18**, type **2** and then press Enter. Select both cells, and then point to the fill handle in cell **B18**. Drag down until the ScreenTip displays **36** (to the end of the yellow shading).

11. Click cell **G16**. Type **=b6** and then press F4 so that the entry is absolute. Press Enter. Click cell **G16** again, and click the **Increase Decimal** button twice. This is the opening balance for the loan.

12. Click cell **C17**. The amount owed is the balance from the previous period. Type **=g16** and then press Enter.

13. Click cell **D17**. Type **=b11** and then press F4 so that the entry is absolute. Press Enter. This is the payment amount as computed using the PMT function.

14. Click cell **E17**. The interest for the period is equal to the monthly interest rate multiplied by the balance owed. Type **=** and then click cell **C17**. Type ***** and then click cell **B9**. Press the F4 function key to make cell B9's entry absolute. Type **/12** so that the yearly rate is converted to a monthly rate. Press Enter. Your result should be 1,732.50.

15. Click cell **F17**. The amount applied to the loan principal is equal to the payment amount minus the interest amount. Type **=d17-e17** and then press Enter.

16. Click cell **G17**. The new balance is equal to the previous balance minus the principal amount. Type **=g16-f17** and then press Enter.

17. Select the range **C17:G17**, and then point to the fill handle in cell **G17**. Drag down to fill the formulas through the 36 payments. The Balance column should display zero for payment 36.

18. Display the **Page Setup** dialog box. Center the worksheet horizontally on the page. Create a custom footer with the file name in the **Left section**.

19. On the Standard toolbar, click the **Save** button, and then click the **Print Preview** button to view how your worksheet will print. On the Print Preview toolbar, click **Print**, and then click **OK**.

20. Display the formulas. Click the **Print Preview** button, and then click **Setup**. In the **Page Setup** dialog box, click the **Landscape** and **Fit to** option buttons, and then click **OK**. On the Print Preview toolbar, click **Print**, and then click **OK**.

21. Hold down Ctrl and press ` to redisplay the worksheet. Close the workbook, saving changes if prompted to do so.

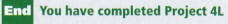

End You have completed Project 4L

Project 4M — Investments

Objectives: *Create Date & Time, Financial, and Logical Functions.*

John Zeidler, the Chief Financial Officer for Owens Family Builders, is considering two investment alternatives for the employee pension fund. In this project, you will complete a worksheet that will compare the two investments and determine which one will result in a better return. You will save the workbook as *4M_Investments_Firstname_Lastname.*

1. **Start** Excel. Locate and open the file **e04M_Investments**. Save the file using the name **4M_Investments_Firstname_Lastname**

2. In cell **B3**, enter the **NOW** function formula.

3. The Bond Fund requires an initial investment of $100,000 and annual payments of $1,000 for each employee over the next 10 years—the term of the investment. Based on past returns, Mr. Zeidler is estimating that the rate will be 7.5 percent on average. Enter the figures in the appropriate cells in the worksheet, and then, in cell **B9**, use the **FV** function to calculate the total value of the investment at the end of the term.

4. The Balanced Fund requires an initial investment of $250,000 and annual payments of $250,000 for the 10-year term of the investment. The estimated annual rate on this investment is 8 percent. Enter the figures in the appropriate cells in the worksheet, and then, in cell **C9**, use the **FV** function to calculate the ending value.

5. Format all the numbers in the worksheet appropriately.

6. In cell **B12**, use the IF function to display the name of the investment and the best investment return.

7. Center the worksheet horizontally on the page, and add a custom footer that displays the file name in the left section.

8. Save, and then print the worksheet. Display and print the formulas on one page.

 End **You have completed Project 4M** ————————————————

Project 4N — Hours Worked

Objectives: *Create Statistical Functions, Create Date & Time and Financial Functions, and Create Logical Functions.*

Benefits for employees are granted after a certain length of employment. In this project, you will complete a worksheet for Juan Sanchez, Director of Employee Benefits, that calculates when benefits are due based on hire date. You will save the workbook as *4N_Benefits Earned_Firstname_Lastname.*

1. **Start** Excel. Locate and open the file **e04N_Benefits_Earned**. Save the file using the name **4N_Benefits_Earned_Firstname_Lastname**

2. First, the hire date for each employee needs to be converted to a numeric equivalent. In **column C**, display the hire date for each employee as the numeric equivalent date.

3. Click cell **D4**, and enter **6/30/05** as the current date. Change this date to its numeric equivalent. Fill this number down through cell **D10**.

4. In cell **E4**, write a formula to determine the number of days the employee has been with the company. Fill this number through cell **E10**.

5. In cell **F4**, use the logical IF function to determine if the employee is eligible for health insurance. Evaluate whether the difference between the current date and the hire date—displayed in cell **E4**—is greater than or equal to the number in cell **C16**. Enter **Yes** in the true box and **No** in the false box. Copy this statement down **column F** to the other employees in the list.

6. In cell **G4**, write a similar statement to determine if the employee has met the requirement for life insurance shown in cell **C17**. In cell **H4**, write a statement to evaluate if the employee is eligible for Dental Insurance as shown in cell **C18**. Finally, in cell **I4** write a statement to evaluate if the employee is eligible for the Retirement program as shown in cell **C19**.

7. Fill all three formulas to the rest of the employees.

8. Open the **Page Setup** dialog box. Change the page orientation to landscape. Center the worksheet horizontally on the page, and add a custom footer that displays the file name in the left section.

9. Save, and then print the worksheet. Display and print the formulas on one page.

End **You have completed Project 4N**

On the Internet

Researching the Cost of Financing a Home or Car

Several sites on the Internet can help you determine the cost of financing a home, car, boat, or other large purchase. Open your browser, and then use your favorite search engine, such as Google.com, to search for information about financing a house or a car. For keywords, enter **car loan** or **home loan** Pick one of the sites that result from the search. Many of these sites have a quick calculation to provide you with a payment estimate based on the amount borrowed and length of the loan. Click on the Loan Calculator button, and enter appropriate figures for the type of loan you are researching. After you see the results, check the figures provided by setting up a payment function in Excel. Open a new workbook, and enter each component used for the loan and the figures used in the Web site loan calculation. Use the PMT function to calculate the payment. Compare your results with the one provided by the Internet Web site.

GO! with Help

Special Column Formats

In this chapter, you practiced how to create IF functions. Use Excel Help to learn how to use text in an IF function.

1. From your student files, **Open** the worksheet **e04O_Help**.

2. In the **Type a question for help** box, type **How do I create an IF function?** and then press Enter. In the **Search Results** task pane, click **Create conditional formulas by using the If Function**. Read the topic to review the IF function. Under the Examples section of the Help window, notice that in the first example, text is included in the argument and that the text is enclosed in quotation marks. **Close** the Help window.

3. In cell **F5**, create an IF statement that uses text for the value_if_true and the value_if_false as follows: If the total of undecided respondents per district is greater than 30 percent of the total number of respondents per district, "Send Additional Information to Voters". Otherwise, "Additional Mailing Not Necessary". (Hint: In the **Logical test** box, type **D5>E5*.3** You do not need to type the quotation marks when you type the text in the **Value_if_true** and **Value_if_false** boxes because Excel will insert the quotation marks for you.) Copy the formula from cell **F5** through cell **F9**.

5 chapter five

Creating Charts and Diagrams

In this chapter, you will: complete this project and practice these skills.

Project 5A Charting Attendance by Location

Objectives

- Create a Column Chart
- Modify a Column Chart
- Print a Chart
- Create and Modify a Line Chart
- Create and Modify a 3-D Pie Chart
- Create a Diagram
- Organize and Format Worksheets

Greater Atlanta Job Fair

The Greater Atlanta Job Fair is a nonprofit organization supported by the Atlanta Chamber of Commerce and Atlanta City Colleges. The organization holds several targeted job fairs in the Atlanta area each year. Candidate registration is free and open to area residents and students enrolled in certificate or degree programs at any of the City Colleges. Employers pay a nominal fee to participate in the fairs. When candidates register for a fair, their resumes are scanned into an interactive, searchable database that is provided to the employers.

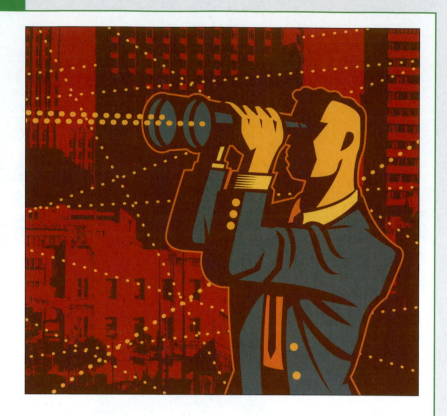

Creating Charts and Diagrams

A *chart* is a graphic representation of data in a worksheet. In many instances, data presented as a chart is easier to understand than a table of numbers. The most commonly used chart types are *column charts*, which are used to make comparisons among related numbers, *pie charts*, which show the contributions of each piece to the whole, and *line charts*, which show a trend over time. A chart can be placed on a separate sheet, called a *chart sheet*, or it can be *embedded* (placed within) the same worksheet as the data. You can also create diagrams using Excel. A *diagram* is a graphical illustration of a concept or relationship. When you have multiple worksheets in a workbook, it is helpful to name the sheets. You can also add color coding to the sheet tabs, add, delete, or hide sheets, or reposition sheets in the workbook.

5A

Project 5A **Attendance**

Graphical representation of numbers helps a reader understand implications and trends in a visual manner that is easier to interpret than by reading the numbers alone. The Excel Chart Wizard helps you create a wide variety of charts that can be displayed either with the worksheet data or on a separate sheet. The Diagram Gallery provides six options for creating a diagram. In this chapter, you will create and modify each of these main chart types. You will also create a diagram and practice organizing worksheets.

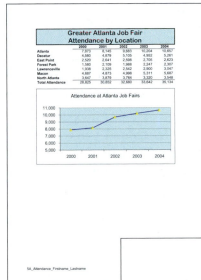

In Activities 5.1 through 5.28, you will create and modify column, pie, and line charts for the Greater Atlanta Job Fair that display attendance patterns at the fairs over a five-year period. You will examine the purpose of each chart type and practice selecting the data to display, using the Chart Wizard, and modifying and formatting various chart components. You will create a chart on a separate sheet and one that is embedded within the worksheet. You will also create a diagram to show the continuous process of holding job fairs. Finally, you will practice some techniques for organizing and formatting multiple worksheets. Your completed worksheets will look similar to Figure 5.1. You will save your workbook as *5A_Attendance_Firstname_Lastname.*

Embedded line chart

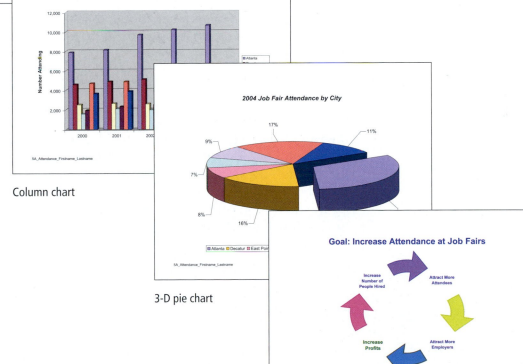

Column chart

3-D pie chart

Cycle diagram

Figure 5.1
Project 5A—Attendance

Objective 1
Create a Column Chart

Charts are used to make a set of numbers easier to understand. The type of chart used is determined by the data in your worksheet and the kind of relationship that you want your data to show. The Excel Chart Wizard makes it easy to create a variety of chart types. One of the most frequently used charts is the column chart, which compares groups of related numbers. A column chart presents the data in vertical columns. Groups of related numbers can also be represented in a bar chart, which uses horizontal bars instead of vertical columns.

Activity 5.1 Creating a 3-D Column Chart

To create a chart, first select the data you want to *plot*—represent graphically—and then access the **Chart Wizard**. The Chart Wizard is a feature that guides you, step by step, through the process of creating a chart.

1 **Start** Excel. On the Standard toolbar, click the **Open** button. Navigate to the location where the student files for this textbook are stored. Locate and open the Excel file **e05A_Attendance**.

2 From the **File** menu, click **Save As**. In the **Save As** dialog box, navigate to the location in which you are storing your files, creating a new folder for this chapter if you want to do so.

3 In the **File name** box, type **5A_Attendance_Firstname_Lastname** and then click **Save**.

The data displayed shows the number of applicants who have attended job fairs held over the past five years at various locations in the greater Atlanta area.

4 Examine the data displayed in this worksheet. Locate the data that is identified in Figure 5.2.

When you create a chart, first decide whether you are going to plot the values representing totals or the values representing details. (You cannot plot both in the same chart.) In this example, you will select the details—the number of attendees at each location each year. To help the reader understand the chart, you will also select the *labels* for the data—the column and row headings that describe the values. In this spreadsheet, the labels will consist of the location names and the years.

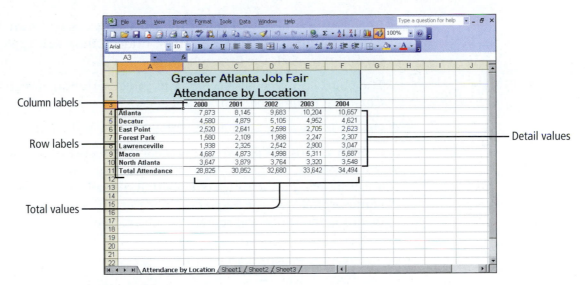

Figure 5.2

Column labels

Row labels

Total values

Detail values

5 Select the range **A3:F10**, and then, on the Standard toolbar, click the **Chart Wizard** button. Alternatively, from the Insert menu, click Chart.

The Chart Wizard opens to the first step in the wizard with the Standard Types tab selected. The selected data is highlighted on the worksheet. In the first step of the wizard, you select the type of chart you want to use. On the left side of the Chart Wizard dialog box, you can select from among fourteen *standard chart types*—predefined chart designs. On the right side, you can choose the *chart sub-type*— variations of the selected standard chart type. The default chart is the clustered column chart. A description of the selected chart displays at the lower right of the dialog box. See Figure 5.3.

You can also use this dialog box to create a *custom chart*, which offers more advanced chart options and allows you to add your own features.

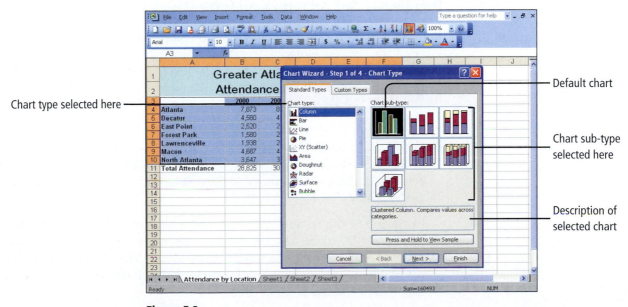

Chart type selected here

Default chart

Chart sub-type selected here

Description of selected chart

Figure 5.3

6 Be sure the **Standard Types tab** is selected. Under **Chart type**, be sure **Column** is selected, and then, under **Chart sub-type**, in the second row, click the first sub-type.

The chart sub-type is selected, and the description changes to *Clustered column with 3-D visual effect.*

7 On the lower right side of the dialog box, click the **Next** button.

In Step 2 of the Chart Wizard you can see a preview of the data as it will display in the chart. Notice that the Data range box displays the sheet name and the range of cells that are selected as an absolute value—recall that the $ symbol indicates an absolute reference, meaning the range will remain constant. See Figure 5.4.

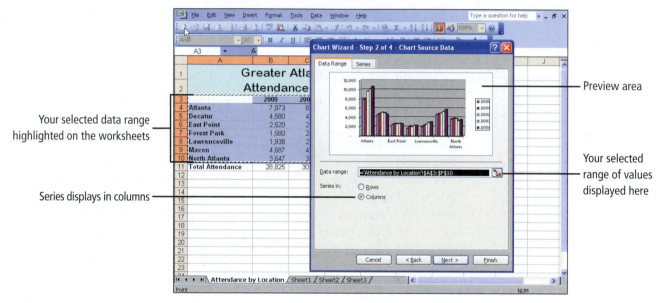

Your selected data range highlighted on the worksheets

Series displays in columns

Preview area

Your selected range of values displayed here

Figure 5.4

Note — Not All Data Labels Display

You may notice that not all of the location labels display along the lower edge of the preview window. This is because of the limited space in the dialog box. The labels will display when you view the finished chart, at which time you can adjust the label format as needed.

8 Verify that the **Data range** box displays *='Attendance by Location'!$A$3:$F$10,* and then click the **Next** button to accept the settings in Step 2 and move to Step 3 in the Chart Wizard. Click the **Titles tab**.

In Step 3 of the wizard, you can add a title to the chart or to the **Category (X) axis**—the horizontal axis, or to the **Value (Z) axis**—the vertical axis along the left side of the chart. This shows the range of numbers needed to display the **data points**, the numeric values of the selected worksheet figures.

More Knowledge — Value (Y) Axis

Typically, the value axis in a chart is known as the y-axis. In this example, the value axis has been changed by the Chart Wizard to the z-axis because a 3-D chart sub-type was selected. If a two-dimensional chart were used, such as the default clustered column chart, the label for the vertical axis in the wizard would be Value (Y) axis.

9 In the **Chart title** box, click to position the insertion point, and then type **Attendance by Location**

After a moment, the title displays in the chart Preview area, and the chart area is resized. See Figure 5.5. Adjustments to the chart can be made after the chart is complete—the Preview area only gives you an idea of how the chart will display.

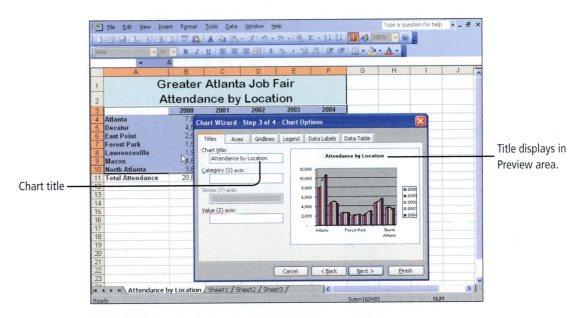

Figure 5.5

10 Click **Next**.

Step 4 of the Chart Wizard displays. Here you must decide the location of the chart. You can place the chart on a separate chart sheet in the workbook in which the chart fills the entire page or accept the default to display the chart as an object within the worksheet, which is an embedded chart. If you place the chart on a separate sheet, it's a good idea to rename the sheet to indicate the chart's location.

11 Click the **As new sheet** option button. In the **As new sheet** box, type **Attendance Chart**

The chart will be placed on a separate sheet named *Attendance Chart*. See Figure 5.6.

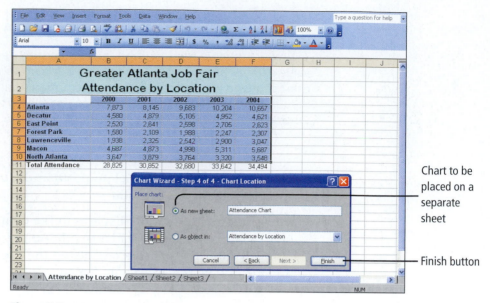

Figure 5.6

12 Click the **Finish** button.

The Chart Wizard dialog box closes, and the chart displays on a separate sheet. See Figure 5.7.

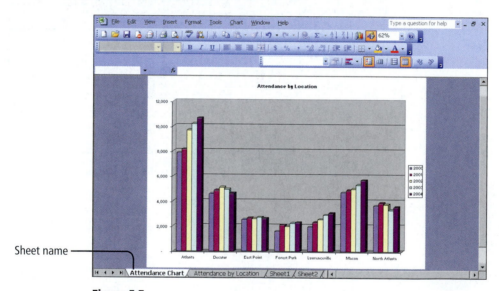

Figure 5.7

13 On the Standard toolbar, click the **Save** button ▣.

Activity 5.2 Identifying Chart Elements

Before you can modify a chart, you need to be able to locate and identify different parts of the chart. **Chart objects** are the elements that make up a chart. As you move the mouse pointer around the chart, ScreenTips display to identify the name of different chart objects.

1 Point to the title at the top of the chart. A ScreenTip displays the name of the chart object—**Chart Title**—as shown in Figure 5.8. Move your mouse pointer around the chart and display the ScreenTip for each of the chart objects labeled in Figure 5.8. When the ScreenTip displays, click the chart object to select it.

Clicking a chart object is one way to select it. When a chart object is selected, *sizing handles* display at each corner of the chart object. Sizing handles, also known as *selection handles*, are the small boxes that surround a chart object to indicate that the object is selected and can be modified.

Figure 5.8

Note — Is It a Sizing Handle or a Selection Handle?

Sizing handles and selection handles look the same, and the terms are often used interchangeably. If a two-headed resize arrow—⬍ ⬌ ⬉—displays when you point to boxes surrounding an object, it is a sizing handle; otherwise, it is a selection handle. Some objects in a chart cannot be resized, such as the category axis or the value axis, but they can be selected and then reformatted.

---

2 A Chart menu and a Chart toolbar display when a chart is active. The Chart toolbar may be anchored under the Standard and Formatting toolbars or floating on your screen. Locate the Chart toolbar and point to each button to identify the button and display the ScreenTip name. The table in Figure 5.9 explains the purpose of each button. Take a moment to examine this information.

The Chart Toolbar

Button	Button Name	Description
	Chart Objects	Displays a list of chart objects. Clicking an object in the list selects the object.
	Format Selected Object	Opens the Format Selected Object dialog box. The ScreenTip displays the name of the selected object.
	Chart Type	Changes the chart type.
	Legend	Toggles the legend on and off.
	Data Table	Toggles the data table on and off.
	By Row	Displays the data series in rows.
	By Column	Displays the data series in columns.
	Angle Clockwise	Angles the selected text downward at a 45-degree angle.
	Angle Counterclockwise	Angles the selected text upward at a 45-degree angle.

Figure 5.9

Alert!

If the Chart Toolbar Does Not Display

The Chart toolbar should be displayed on your screen. If it is not, right-click any toolbar and from the displayed list, click Chart. The Chart toolbar may float on your screen or be anchored. To anchor the Chart toolbar, point to the title bar and drag it up under the second toolbar at the top of the screen. Release the mouse button.

3 The table in Figure 5.10 lists the objects that are typically found in a chart. Take a moment to study this information.

Excel Chart Objects

Object	Description
Chart area	The entire chart and all its elements.
Plot area	The area bounded by the category axis (x-axis) and the value axis (y-axis) that includes the data series.
Gridlines	Lines in the plot area that aid the eye in determining the plotted values.
Axis	A line that borders one side of the plot area, providing a frame of reference for measurement or comparison in a chart. For most charts, categories are plotted along the category axis, which is usually horizontal (the x-axis), and data values are plotted along the value axis, which is usually vertical (the y-axis).
Category axis	The horizontal axis (also called the x-axis) containing the data categories being plotted.
Value axis	The vertical axis (also called the y-axis) containing the numerical scale upon which the plotted data is based.
Data point	A single value from a worksheet cell.
Data marker	The graphic element that represents a single data point (a value that originates from a worksheet cell). Data markers with the same pattern represent one data series.
Data series	A group of related data points that are plotted in a chart. Each series in a chart has a unique color or pattern and is represented in the chart legend. You can plot one or more data series in a chart (except in a pie chart, which can contain only one data series).
Data label	A label that provides additional information about a data marker (a graphic element that represents a single data point or value that originates from a worksheet cell). Data labels can be applied to a single data marker, an entire data series, or all data markers in a chart. Depending on the chart type, data labels can show values, names of data series or categories, percentages, or a combination of these.
Legend	A small box that identifies the patterns or colors that are assigned to the data series or categories in a chart.
Tick marks	Small lines of measurement, similar to divisions on a ruler, that intersect an axis.
Tick mark labels	Identifying information for a tick mark generated from the cells on the worksheet used to create the chart.
Walls and floor	The areas surrounding a 3-D chart that give dimension and boundaries to the chart. Two walls and one floor are displayed within the plot area.

Figure 5.10

4 On the Chart toolbar, click the **Chart Objects arrow**, and then click on each item listed to locate the item on the chart.

The Chart Objects button is another way to select chart objects. While you are learning, this method is sometimes preferable.

5 Click the tallest column displayed for the **Atlanta** category.

All the columns representing the Series "2004" are selected—selection handles display at the corners of each column in the series—and a ScreenTip displays the value for the column you are pointing to. A **data series** is a group of related data—in this case, the attendees to all the job fairs that were held in 2004. Also notice that the Formula Bar displays the address for the selected data series. See Figure 5.11.

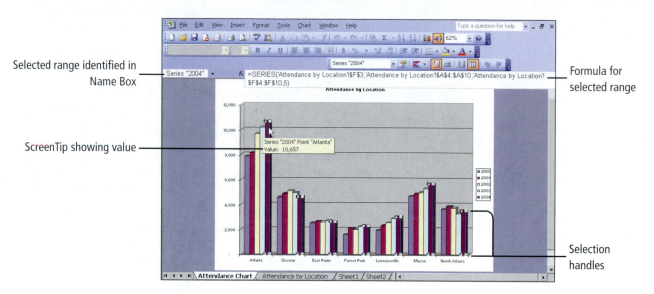

Selected range identified in Name Box

ScreenTip showing value

Formula for selected range

Selection handles

Figure 5.11

6 Locate the **Forest Park** category, and then click the shortest column displayed above the **Forest Park** category.

The selected series changes to those columns that represent the attendees at the job fairs in 2000. The Formula Bar and Name Box change and a new ScreenTip displays.

Objective 2
Modify a Column Chart

As you create a chart, you make choices about the data to include, the chart type, chart titles, and location. After the chart is created, you can change the chart type, change the way the data displays, add or change titles, select different colors, and modify the background, scale, or chart location.

Activity 5.3 Changing the Way the Data Displays

In the column chart you created, the attendance numbers are displayed along the value axis—the vertical axis—and the locations for each job fair are displayed along the category axis—the horizontal axis. The cells you select for a chart include the row and column labels from your worksheet. In a column or line chart, Excel selects whichever has *fewer* items—either the rows or the columns—and uses those labels to plot the data series, in this case, the years. After plotting the data series, Excel uses the remaining labels—in this example, the locations identified in the row headings—to create the labels on the category axis. A *legend*—the key that defines the colors used in the chart—identifies the data series, in this example, the years. A different color is used for each year in the data series. The chart, as currently displayed, compares the change in attendance year to year grouped by category location. You can change the chart to display the years on the category axis and the locations as the data series identified in the legend.

1 In the **Atlanta** category, click the second column, which is maroon in color.

All the columns with the same color are selected. The ScreenTip displays *Series "2001" Point "Atlanta" Value 8,145*.

2 Point to each of the other maroon columns that are selected and read the ScreenTip that displays.

The ScreenTip for each column identifies it as *Series "2001"*.

3 On the Chart toolbar, click the **By Row** button ▦.

The chart changes to display the locations as the data series. The locations are the row headings in the worksheet and are now identified in the legend. The years display as the category labels, as shown in Figure 5.12.

Note — Using the By Row and By Column Buttons

It is not necessary to select the columns or data series before clicking the By Row button or By Column button. In this instance, it is coincidental that columns are selected.

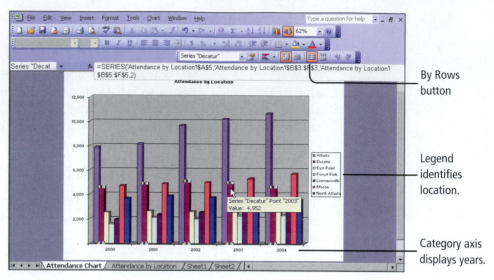

By Rows button

Legend identifies location.

Category axis displays years.

Figure 5.12

4 If necessary, click one of the maroon columns. Point to each maroon column and read the ScreenTip.

The ScreenTips for the maroon columns now identify this as the Decatur series.

5 Click outside the chart to cancel the selection of the columns. On the Standard toolbar, click the **Save** button.

More Knowledge — Changing the Range of Data in a Chart

After you have created a chart, you can adjust the range of data that is displayed in the chart. To do this, from the menu click Chart, Source Data. Edit the source address displayed in the Data Range box, or drag the data in the worksheet to adjust the range as needed.

Activity 5.4 Adding, Formatting, and Aligning Axis Titles

You can add new titles to a chart or modify existing titles. You can also change the format of the value and category axis labels.

1 From the menu bar, click **Chart**. From the displayed list, click **Chart Options**.

The Chart Options dialog box opens. Here you can change many different chart elements. The six tabs across the top of the dialog box—*Titles, Axes, Gridlines, Legend, Data Labels, Data Table*—identify the types of chart elements that can be modified.

2 If necessary, click the **Titles tab**.

3 Click in the **Value (Z) axis** box and type **Number Attending**

After a moment, the new title displays on the left side of the chart in the Preview area. See Figure 5.13.

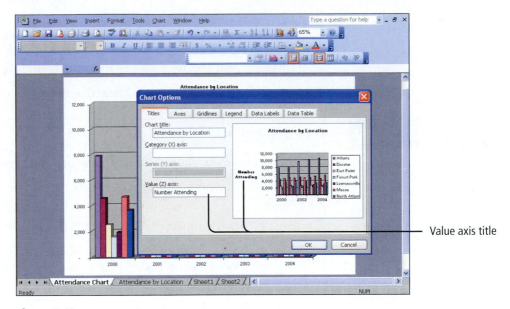

Figure 5.13

4 Click **OK**.

The dialog box closes, and the title is added to the left side of the chart. The axis title displays horizontally, but it would look better if aligned vertically.

5 Right-click the **Value Axis Title** you just added, and then, from the displayed shortcut menu, click **Format Axis Title**.

The Format Axis Title dialog box displays. Here you can change the format of the axis title, including the font, font size, style, or color, or the alignment of the text.

6 Click the **Font tab**, and then, in the list under the **Size** box, scroll as necessary and click **14**.

7 Click the **Alignment tab**. Under **Orientation**, drag the red diamond up to the top until the **Degrees** box displays **90**. See Figure 5.14.

The title alignment will change to 90 degrees.

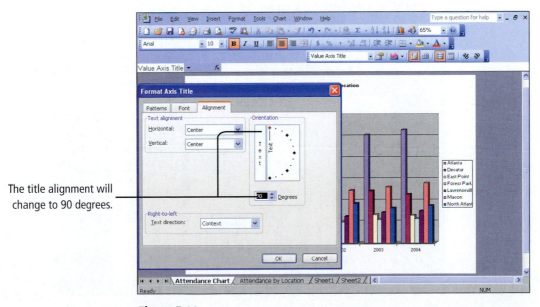

Figure 5.14

8 Click **OK**.

The dialog box closes. The orientation of the Value Axis Title is vertical, and the font size is increased to 14 pt.

9 On the Standard toolbar, click the **Save** button .

Another Way — **To Select Chart Objects**

You can use any of several methods to select and modify a chart object:

• Right-click the object and select the format option from the shortcut menu.

• Double-click the object, which opens the related format dialog box.

• On the Chart toolbar, click the Chart Objects arrow, from the displayed list click the chart object to select it, and then click the Format Object button.

Activity 5.5 Formatting Axis Labels

The labels along the value and category axes are the axis labels. These labels can be formatted in the same way as any other text.

1 On the left side of the chart, point to any number on the value axis. When the **Value Axis** ScreenTip displays, double-click to select the value axis and open the **Format Axis** dialog box.

In the Format Axis dialog box, you can change the patterns, scale, font, number format, and alignment of the axis labels.

2 Click the **Font tab**. Under **Size**, scroll as necessary, and then click **12**.

3 Click **OK**.

The dialog box closes. The value axis labels change to 12 pt.

4 On the Chart toolbar, click the **Chart Objects arrow** [_____] and, from the displayed list, click **Category Axis**.

The Category axis is selected, and selection handles display at each end of the category axis. See Figure 5.15.

Chart object box displays name of selected object.

Category axis selection handles

Figure 5.15

5 On the Formatting toolbar, click the **Font Size arrow** ⬚12⬚ and, from the displayed list, click **12**.

The Category axis labels change to 12 pt. You can use the Formatting toolbar to format text on a chart in the same was as you do in the worksheet. If you want to change only the font, it is quicker to use the Formatting toolbar than the Format Axis dialog box.

6 On the Standard toolbar, click the **Save** button 🖫.

Activity 5.6 Formatting the Chart Title

1 Right-click the **Chart Title**—*Attendance by Location*—and then click **Format Chart Title**.

The Format Chart Title dialog box opens and displays the same formatting options as the Format Axis Title dialog box.

2 Click the **Font tab**. Under **Font style**, click **Bold Italic**. In the **Size** list, scroll as necessary, and then click **20**.

The Preview area displays the changes.

3 Click the **Color arrow**, and then, in the second row, click the sixth color—**Blue**.

4 Click the **Underline arrow**, and then click **Single**.

Compare your dialog box with Figure 5.16.

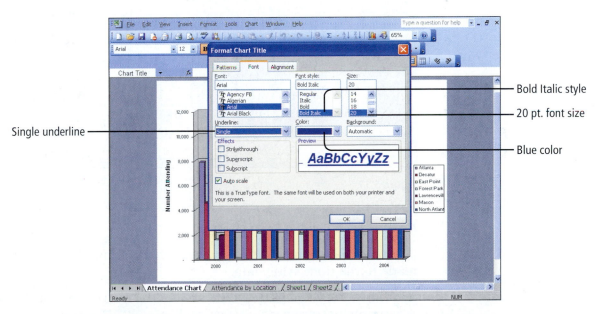

Figure 5.16

5 Click **OK**. Click in a white area of the chart to cancel the selection of the title and view your changes. On the Standard toolbar, click the **Save** button 🖫.

Activity 5.7 Editing the Chart Title

Because you have changed the data displayed in the chart in a manner that focuses on the attendance by year rather than the attendance by location, you should also change the chart title to reflect the data.

1 If necessary, click the **Chart Title**—*Attendance by Location*—to select it.

The title is selected, and a patterned box surrounds the title.

2 In the selected title, position the mouse pointer to the left of *Location*, and then click to place the insertion point.

To edit a title, click once to select the chart object, and then click a second time to position the insertion point in the title and change to editing mode.

3 Select *Location*, type **Years** and then click outside the title.

The title is changed to reflect the change in the data display. Compare your chart with Figure 5.17.

Chart title edited and formatted

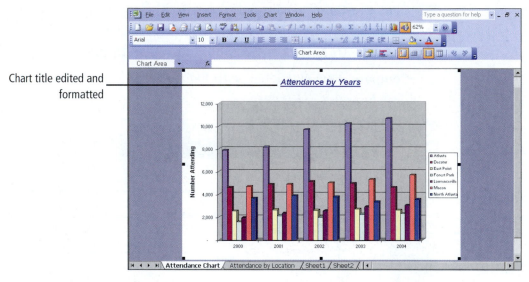

Figure 5.17

Activity 5.8 Editing Source Data

One of the characteristics of an Excel chart is that it reflects changes made to the underlying data.

1 Click anywhere in the white area of the chart. Then, in the **2004** column cluster, point to the second column—**Decatur**.

Notice that the Value for this column is 4,621.

2 Click the **Attendance by Location sheet tab** to move to the worksheet data.

3 Click cell **F5**, type **5261** and then press Enter.

The number of attendees at the 2004 Decatur Job Fair is updated.

4 Click the **Attendance Chart sheet tab**, and then point to the **Decatur** column for 2004.

The size of the column has expanded to reflect the change in data, and the new Value—5,261—displays in the ScreenTip. See Figure 5.18.

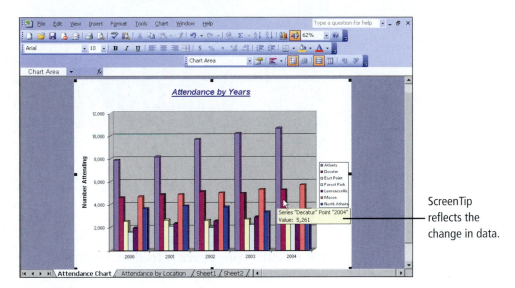

ScreenTip reflects the change in data.

Figure 5.18

5 On the Standard toolbar, click the **Save** button.

Objective 3
Print a Chart

Charts that are placed on their own sheet display in landscape orientation. If a chart is embedded with the worksheet, both the worksheet and chart print on the same page, and the orientation is controlled in the Page Setup dialog box.

Activity 5.9 Previewing and Printing a Chart

Before you print a chart, you should preview it.

1 With the *Attendance Chart* displayed, on the Standard toolbar click the **Print Preview** button.

2 From the Print Preview toolbar, click **Setup**, and then click the **Header/Footer tab**. Click the **Custom Footer** button. With the insertion point in the **Left section**, click the **File Name** button. Click **OK** twice.

The file name will print in the footer of the chart. Compare your screen with Figure 5.19.

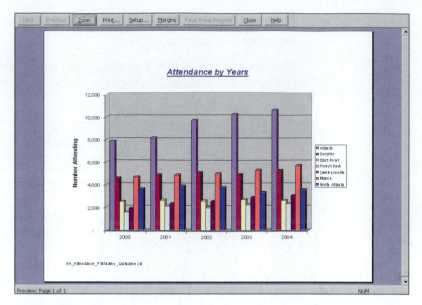

Figure 5.19

3 On the Print Preview toolbar, click the **Print** button . In the displayed **Print** dialog box, click **OK**.

The chart prints, and the Print Preview window closes.

4 On the Standard toolbar, click the **Save** button .

Objective 4
Create and Modify a Line Chart

Line charts are used to show trends over time. A line chart can consist of one line, such as the price of stock over time, or it can display more than one line to show a comparison of related numbers over time. For example, charts tracking stock or mutual fund performance often display the price of the mutual fund on one line and an industry standard for that particular type of fund on a different line.

Activity 5.10 Creating a Line Chart

In this activity, you will create a line chart showing the change in attendance at the Atlanta job fair over the five-year period covered by the worksheet.

1 With your **5A_Attendance_Firstname_Lastname** file open on your screen, click the **Attendance by Location sheet tab** to display the worksheet.

2 Select the range **A3:F4**, and then, on the Standard toolbar, click the **Chart Wizard** button .

The range is selected, and the Chart Wizard opens to Step 1 of the wizard. Cell A3 must be included in the selection, even though it is empty, because there must be the same number of cells in each row that is selected. The Chart Wizard will identify the first row as a category because of the empty first cell.

3 In the **Chart Wizard** dialog box, under **Chart type**, click **Line**.

The Chart sub-type area changes to display various styles of line charts, and the default line type—*Line with markers displayed at each data value*—is selected. See Figure 5.20.

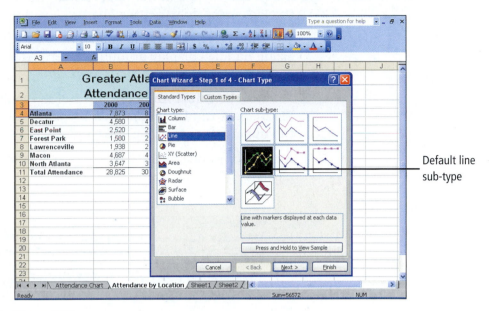

Default line sub-type

Figure 5.20

4 In the **Chart Wizard** dialog box, click the **Finish** button.

The dialog box closes, and the line chart displays on the worksheet. If you do not want to make any changes to the selected chart type and want it *embedded* in the worksheet—displayed on the same worksheet as the source data—you can skip Steps 2 through 4 of the wizard after you have selected the type of chart you want to create. See Figure 5.21.

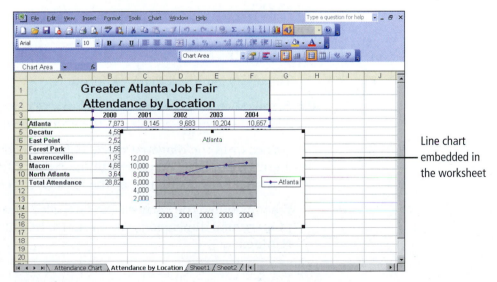

Line chart embedded in the worksheet

Figure 5.21

Activity 5.11 Moving and Resizing an Embedded Chart

When a chart is embedded in a worksheet it usually needs to be moved to a new location on the sheet, and often the size of the chart needs to be adjusted.

1 If necessary, click in the **Chart Area**—the white area surrounding the Plot Area—to select the chart.

Use the ScreenTip to help you identify the Chart Area. Recall that sizing handles display around the perimeter of the selected chart object—in this case the chart area.

2 Point to the **Chart Area**, and then drag the chart as shown in Figure 5.22 until the upper left corner of the chart is positioned at the upper left corner of cell **A13**.

A dotted outline displays to show the position of the chart as you move it.

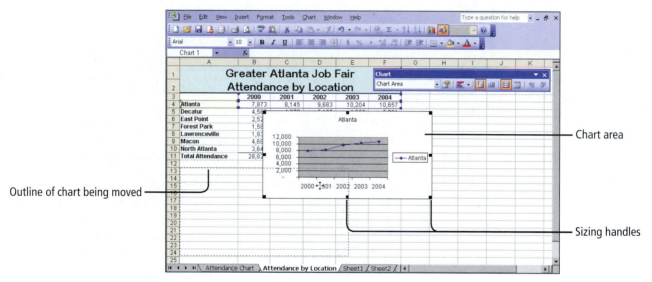

Figure 5.22

3 Release the mouse.

The chart is moved to a new location.

4 Scroll down as necessary to view **row 30**. Be sure the chart is selected. Move the pointer to the sizing handle in the lower right corner until the diagonal resize pointer ⬃ displays, as shown in Figure 5.23. Drag down and to the right until the lower right corner of the chart is positioned at the lower right corner of cell **F29**.

When you use the corner sizing handles to resize an object, the proportional dimensions—the relative height and width—are retained.

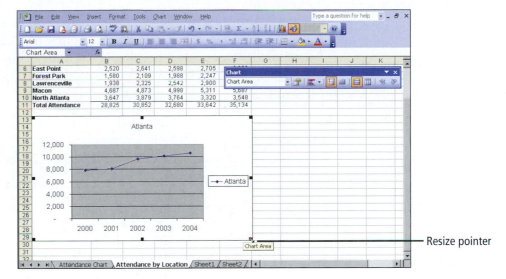

Resize pointer

Figure 5.23

5 On the Standard toolbar, click the **Save** button 🖫.

More Knowledge — Using Snap to Grid

You can hold down Alt while you are moving or resizing an object to have the object align with the edge of the cell gridlines.

Activity 5.12 Deleting Legends and Changing Chart Titles

When you use the Chart Wizard to select the chart type, the resulting chart may have some elements that you want to delete or change. In the line chart, the title is *Atlanta*, and there is a legend that also indicates *Atlanta*. Because there is only one line of data, a legend is unnecessary, and the chart title can be made more specific.

1 In the embedded chart, click the **Legend**—*Atlanta*—to select it. Press Delete.

The legend is removed from the chart, and the chart plot area expands.

2 Click the **Chart Title**—*Atlanta*. Click a second time to activate editing mode.

3 Select the title *Atlanta*, and then type **Attendance at Atlanta Job Fairs** to replace the selected text.

4 Click in the **Chart Area** to exit editing mode, and then click the new **Chart Title** to select it.

To format text in a chart, you can either select the text or select the chart object. In this instance, you are selecting the chart object so that you can change the font size.

5 On the Formatting toolbar, click the **Font Size arrow** [12 ▾], and then click **14**. Alternatively, right-click the Chart Title, click Format Chart Title, and use the displayed dialog box to change the font size.

The size of the title increases, and the plot area decreases slightly. Compare your chart with Figure 5.24.

Chart title changed and font size increased ——

Legend removed and plot area expanded horizontally

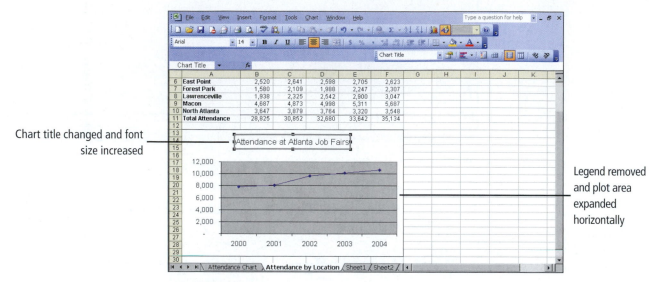

Figure 5.24

6 On the Standard toolbar, click the **Save** button [💾].

Activity 5.13 Changing the Value Scale

In some cases, you will want to change the value *scale* on a chart to increase or decrease the variation among the numbers displayed. The scale is the range of numbers in the data series; the scale controls the minimum, maximum, and incremental values on the value axis. In the line chart, the attendance figures for Atlanta are all higher than 7,000, but the scale begins at zero, and the line occupies only the upper area of the chart.

1 On the left side of the line chart, point to the **Value Axis**, and when the ScreenTip displays, right-click. From the displayed shortcut menu, click **Format Axis**.

The Format Axis dialog box displays.

2 In the **Format Axis** dialog box, click the **Scale tab**.

Here you can change the beginning and ending numbers displayed on the chart and also change the unit by which the major gridlines display.

3 In the **Minimum** box, select the displayed number and type **5000** In the **Major unit** box, select the displayed number and type **1000** Compare your screen with Figure 5.25.

The Value Axis will start at 5000 with major gridlines at intervals of 1000. This will emphasize the change in attendance over the five years by starting the chart at a higher number and decreasing the interval for gridlines from 2000 to 1000. Notice that when you enter a number in one of the boxes, the check mark is removed. This indicates that the new number overrides the default settings.

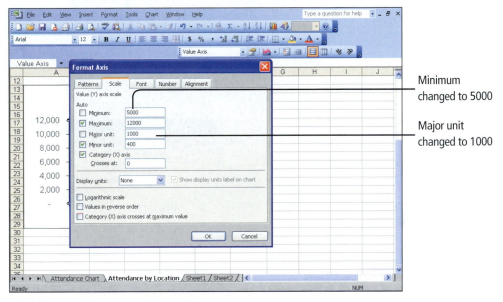

Minimum changed to 5000

Major unit changed to 1000

Figure 5.25

4 Click **OK**. On the Standard toolbar, click the **Save** button.

The dialog box closes, and the value axis on the chart changes to the new settings. See Figure 5.26.

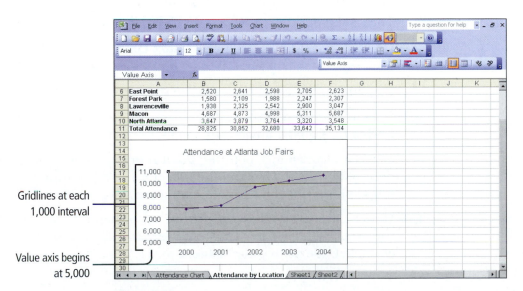

Gridlines at each 1,000 interval

Value axis begins at 5,000

Figure 5.26

Activity 5.14 Formatting the Plot Area and the Data Series

You can change the format of the Plot Area and the data series.

1 Right-click anywhere within the gray **Plot Area**, and then from the displayed shortcut menu, click **Format Plot Area**.

The Format Plot Area dialog box displays. Here you can change the border of the plot area or the background color.

2 Under **Area**, in the fifth row, click the fifth color—light turquoise.

The color displays in the Sample area. This is the same color shown in the title area on the worksheet. Compare your screen with Figure 5.27.

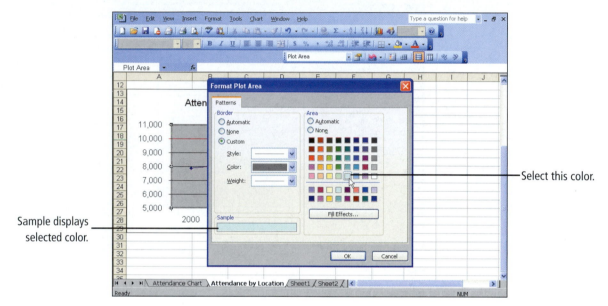

Sample displays selected color.

Select this color.

Figure 5.27

3 Click **OK**.

The background of the Plot Area changes to the selected color.

4 On the Chart toolbar, click the **Chart Objects arrow** [   ], and then from the displayed list, click **Series "Atlanta"**.

The line on the chart representing the data series *Atlanta* is selected.

5 Click the **Format Data Series** button [icon] to display the **Format Data Series** dialog box. If necessary, click the **Patterns tab**.

Here you can change both the *data markers*—the indicators for a data point value, which on the line chart is represented by a diamond shape—or the line connecting the data markers.

6 Under **Line**, click the **Weight arrow**, and then click the third line in the displayed list. Click the **Color arrow**, and then, in the second row, click the sixth color—**Blue**.

7 Under **Marker**, click the **Style arrow**, and then, from the displayed list, click the **triangle**—the third symbol in the list. Click the **Foreground arrow** and, in the fourth row, click the third color— **Yellow**. Click the **Background arrow**, and then click **Yellow**. Compare your dialog box with Figure 5.28.

The foreground is the border color surrounding the symbol, and the background is the fill color in the middle of the symbol.

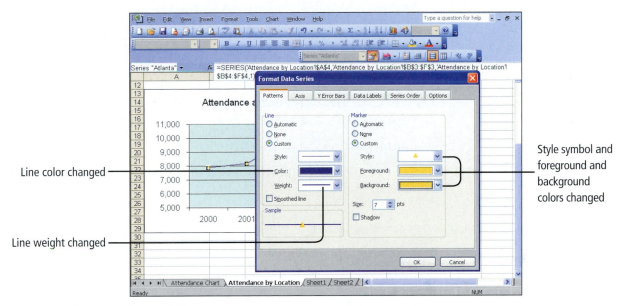

Line color changed

Line weight changed

Style symbol and foreground and background colors changed

Figure 5.28

8 Click **OK**. Click in any cell to cancel the selection of the chart.

The dialog box closes, and the data line and series markers change. See Figure 5.29.

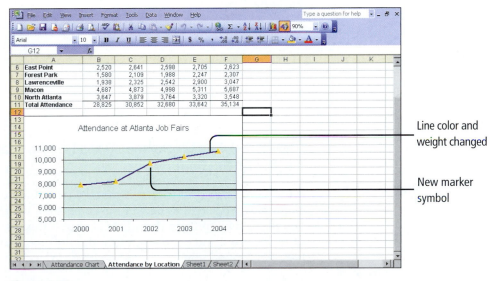

Line color and weight changed

New marker symbol

Figure 5.29

Activity 5.15 Printing a Worksheet with an Embedded Chart

1 Be sure the chart is not selected. On the Standard toolbar, click the **Print Preview** button.

The worksheet data and the chart display on a single page in the Print Preview window. You can see that the worksheet will look more professional if it is centered on the page.

2 On the Print Preview toolbar, click the **Setup** button. In the **Page Setup** dialog box, click the **Margins tab**.

The Page Setup dialog box displays the Margins tab.

3 In the lower part of the **Page Setup** dialog box, under **Center on page**, select the **Horizontally** check box.

4 Click the **Header/Footer tab**, and then click the **Custom Footer** button. With the insertion point in the **Left section**, click the **File Name** button. Click **OK** twice.

The file name will print in the footer. Compare your screen with Figure 5.30.

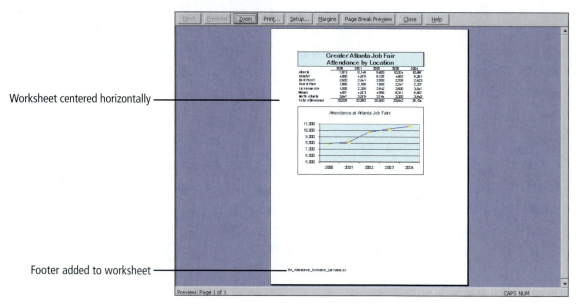

Worksheet centered horizontally

Footer added to worksheet

Figure 5.30

Note — The Worksheet Does Not Appear Exactly in the Center of the Page

If the right edge of the chart is touching the line between columns F and G, column G is included as part of the chart area, which causes the centering to appear to be slightly to the left of center. If this is a concern, you can use the right middle sizing handle to move the right edge of the chart off of the line between the columns.

5 On the **Print Preview** toolbar, click the **Print** button 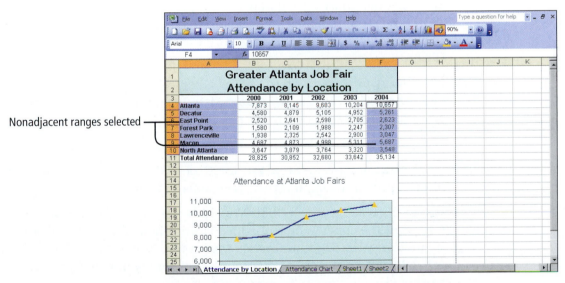, and then click **OK**.

6 On the Standard toolbar, click the **Save** button.

Objective 5
Create and Modify a 3-D Pie Chart

Pie charts show the relationship of parts to a whole. For example, a pie chart can show contributions to income by products or services. It might also be used to show expenses by category to help understand and control expenses. It can be particularly useful when there are competitive goals among divisions or regions in a company.

Activity 5.16 Selecting Nonadjacent Data and Creating a Pie Chart

In this activity, you will create a pie chart to show how attendance at each individual city contributed to the overall attendance of the Job Fair in 2004. In the two previous charts, adjacent areas of the worksheet were selected for graphing. Sometimes you will need to select nonadjacent areas, such as the titles in one column or row and the totals in another.

1 With your **5A_Attendance** file open on your screen, be sure the **Attendance by Location** worksheet is displayed.

2 Scroll up if necessary, and then select the range **A4:A10**. Hold down Ctrl, and then select the range **F4:F10**.

Two nonadjacent data ranges are selected—the labels in column A and the numeric values in column F. See Figure 5.31.

Nonadjacent ranges selected —

Figure 5.31

3 On the Standard toolbar, click the **Chart Wizard** button 📊.

The Chart Wizard opens with the default column chart selected.

4 In the **Chart Wizard** dialog box, under **Chart type**, click **Pie**.

Six pie chart sub-types display. The first one in the first row is selected as the default pie chart. See Figure 5.32.

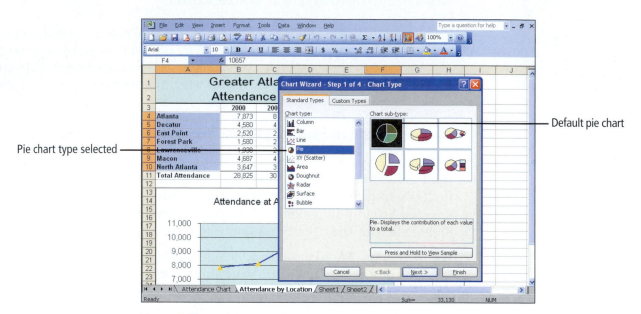

Pie chart type selected ⎯⎯⎯

Default pie chart

Figure 5.32

5 Click **Next**.

Step 2 of the Chart Wizard displays. In the worksheet, the selected data range is outlined by a moving border, and the pie sample displays in the Chart Wizard. No changes are needed in this step of the Chart Wizard.

6 Click **Next** to move to Step 3 of the Chart Wizard. Be sure the **Titles tab** is selected. Click in the **Chart title** box and type **2004 Job Fair Attendance by City**

After a moment, the chart title displays on the chart Preview area.

7 Click **Next** to move to Step 4 in the Chart Wizard. Click the **As new sheet** option button, and then type **2004 Attendance**

Recall that Step 4 of the Chart Wizard is used to determine whether you want the chart to be embedded within the worksheet or displayed on its own sheet. By entering a name in the *As new sheet* box, you are setting a name for the new worksheet that will be inserted in the workbook.

8 Click the **Finish** button to close the Chart Wizard. On the Standard toolbar, click the **Save** button 💾.

The pie chart displays on a separate sheet. Compare your screen with Figure 5.33.

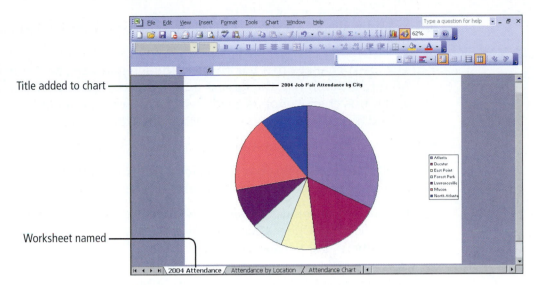

Title added to chart

Worksheet named

Figure 5.33

Activity 5.17 Changing Chart Type

After a chart is created, you can change the chart type from the Chart menu or by clicking the Chart Type button arrow on the Chart toolbar.

1 On the Chart toolbar, click the **Chart Type button arrow** [icon].

A palette of chart types displays. Although not every available chart type in Excel displays on the palette, it provides a quick way to change chart types. A ScreenTip displays the name of the chart types as you point to each one. See Figure 5.34.

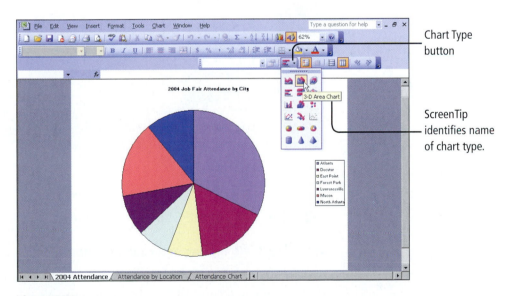

Chart Type button

ScreenTip identifies name of chart type.

Figure 5.34

2 From the displayed palette, in the second row, click the first chart type—**Bar Chart**.

The chart changes to a bar chart. Although you can see that the Atlanta location had the largest number of attendees in the year 2004, this chart is not as good a visual representation of how the attendance at each location contributed to the whole.

3 On the menu bar, click **Chart**, and then click **Chart Type**.

The Chart Type dialog box opens with the Bar chart type selected. Here you have access to the full range of the available charts in Excel.

4 Be sure the **Standard Types tab** is selected, and then under **Chart type** click **Pie**. Under **Chart sub-type**, in the first row click the second option—**Pie with a 3-D visual effect**. Notice the description in the lower right portion of the dialog box. Under the description, point to the **Press and Hold to View Sample** button, and hold down the left mouse button.

A sample of the new chart type displays. See Figure 5.35.

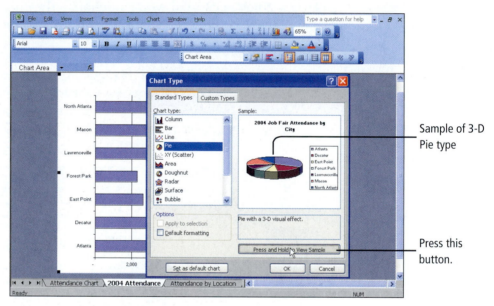

Figure 5.35

5 Click **OK**. On the Standard toolbar, click the **Save** button.

Activity 5.18 Moving and Changing the Legend

The default location for a legend is the right side of the chart, but you can move the legend to another position.

1 On the right side of the chart, point to the legend, and when the **Legend** ScreenTip displays, right-click. From the displayed shortcut menu, click **Format Legend**.

The Format Legend dialog box displays. Here you can change the font of the legend text, the patterns—borders and background color of the legend box—or the placement of the legend.

2 Point to the **Format Legend** title bar and drag the dialog box to the left so that the legend is visible. Click the **Font tab**. Under **Size**, scroll as necessary and click **12**.

The Preview area displays the new font size, but the legend is not changed yet. It changes only after you click OK.

3 Click the **Placement tab**, and under **Placement**, click **Bottom**.

There are five options—Bottom, Corner, Top, Right, Left—for placement of the legend. Alternatively, you can drag the legend to a new location.

4 In the lower right side of the **Format Legend** dialog box, click **OK**.

The font size is increased, and the legend is placed at the lower edge of the chart, as shown in Figure 5.36. Because the legend was removed from the right side of the chart, the chart plot area expanded to the right.

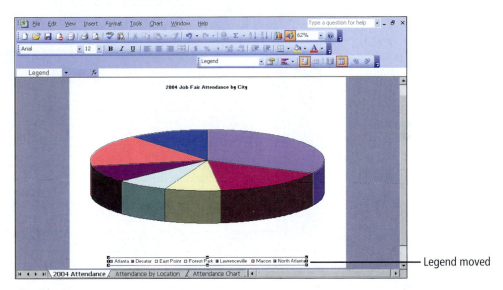

Legend moved

Figure 5.36

5 Click the **Chart Title** to select it. On the Formatting toolbar, click the **Font Size arrow** [12 ▼], scroll as necessary, and then click **18**. On the same toolbar, click the **Italic** button [*I*].

The font size is increased, and italic emphasis is added to the title.

6 On the Standard toolbar, click the **Save** button [🖫].

Activity 5.19 Adding and Formatting Data Labels

Data labels are labels that display the value, percentage, and/or category of each particular data point, which you recall is each single value in a worksheet that is plotted on the chart. The data point value is represented in the chart by a data marker such as a column, bar, line, or in this example, a pie piece.

1 From the **Chart** menu, click **Chart Options**.

The Chart Options dialog box displays.

2 In the **Chart Options** dialog box, click the **Data Labels tab**.

Data labels can contain one or more of the choices listed—Series name, Category name, Value, or Percentage. Labels can be used with any type of chart but are most often used with a pie chart.

3 Under **Label Contains**, select the **Value** and **Percentage** check boxes.

The preview window displays the chart with both labels. Sometimes it is difficult to determine whether the chart will look attractive and understandable until you look at the full-size chart. In the preview, the position of the value, followed by the percentage, looks like it could be confusing to a reader of your chart. See Figure 5.37.

Value and percentage data labels selected

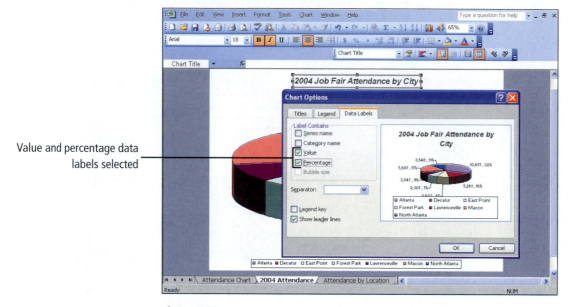

Figure 5.37

4 Click to clear the **Value** check box, and then click **OK**.

The data labels display next to each pie piece, indicating the percentage each pie slice represents of the entire pie. You can see that the data labels would be easier to read if they were larger and were moved away from the pie.

5 Point to any of the data labels and click.

Selection handles are displayed on each data label, indicating that all the labels are selected. Notice that the Formatting toolbar is active, which means it can be used to format the selected chart object.

6 On the Formatting toolbar, click the **Font Size arrow** 12 ▾ , and then, from the displayed list, click **14**.

The size of the labels increases, and the pie shrinks slightly.

7 On the chart, click the **11%** data label to select it. Point to the patterned outline around the label; when the pointer changes to a white arrow, drag up, away from the pie until the leader line displays, as shown in Figure 5.38.

A *leader line* is a line that connects the data label to its pie piece. You must drag the data label a minimum distance before the line will display.

Data label moved —

Leader line connects data label to pie piece.

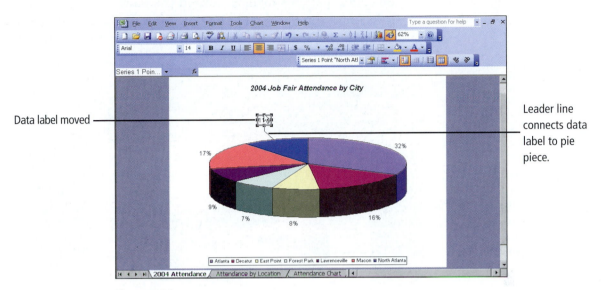

Figure 5.38

8 Click **17%** to select the data label, and then drag the label to the left, slightly away from the pie. Continue around the pie, dragging each data label away from the pie. Compare your screen with Figure 5.39.

The data labels are moved away from the pie, and leader lines display between each label and data marker.

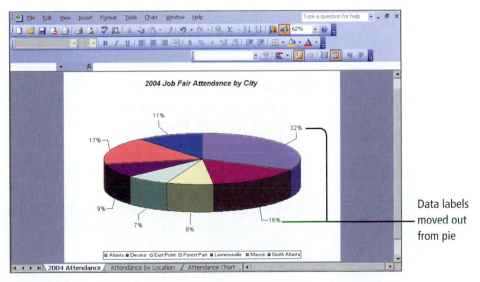

Data labels moved out from pie

Figure 5.39

9 On the Standard toolbar, click the **Save** button 🖫.

Activity 5.20 Formatting Chart Data Points

The colors used in column, bar, or pie charts can be changed, just as you changed the data markers for a line chart.

1 Point to the pie and click once to select it. Point to the pie piece labeled *9%*, which is the *Lawrenceville* data point, and click again to select only the **Lawrenceville** pie piece. See Figure 5.40.

Selection handles display around the Lawrenceville pie piece. To select a particular data point, click once to select the entire data series, in this instance the pie, and then click a second time on a specific data point to select it.

Pie piece selected ——

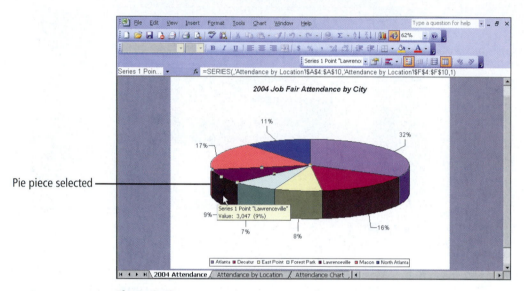

Figure 5.40

2 Right-click the selected pie piece, and from the displayed shortcut menu, click **Format Data Point**.

The Format Data Point dialog box opens. The color used for the selected pie piece displays in the Sample area and is pushed in—selected—under Area in the sixth row, fifth color. Notice that ScreenTips do not display to name the colors.

3 Point to the title bar of the dialog box and drag it to the upper right corner of your screen so that you can see the front half of the pie. Notice that the colors used in this chart are the colors in the sixth row under Area.

There are eight colors in each row, but only seven colors have been used in this chart.

4 In the **Format Data Point** dialog box, under **Area**, in row six, click the last color to change the color of the Lawrenceville data point to a lighter color.

The color displays in the Sample area.

5 In the lower right corner of the dialog box, click **OK**.

The color of the Lawrenceville pie piece changes, and the corresponding color in the legend also changes.

6 Point to the piece labeled *8%* for *East Point* and click to select that piece. Right-click the **East Point** piece, and from the displayed shortcut menu, click **Format Data Point**.

7 In the **Format Data Point** dialog box, under **Area**, in the fifth row, click the first color—**Rose**—and then click **OK**.

The color of the East Point pie piece changes, and the corresponding color in the legend also changes.

8 To the right of the *East Point* piece, double-click the piece labeled **16%—Decatur**. In the displayed dialog box, under **Area**, in the fourth row, click the second color—**Gold**—and then click **OK**.

The color of the *Decatur* piece changes, and the corresponding color in the legend also changes. Compare your screen with Figure 5.41.

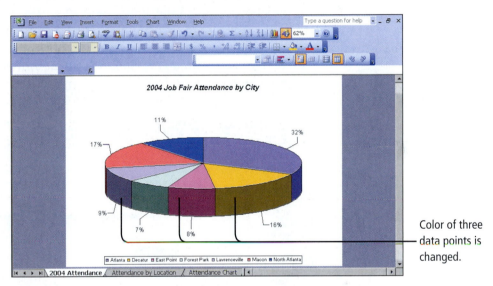

Color of three data points is changed.

Figure 5.41

9 On the Standard toolbar, click the **Save** button.

More Knowledge — Identifying Color Names

As you have experienced in this activity, not all the dialog boxes use ScreenTips to identify the names of colors. Fortunately, there is consistency of color placement among color palettes used in dialog boxes. To identify the name of a color, select some text, and then on the Formatting toolbar, click the Font Color arrow. Use the ScreenTips that display in this color palette to identify the names of the colors in other dialog boxes.

Activity 5.21 Adjusting the 3-D View Options

With a pie chart, you can change the orientation of the chart. For example, you can adjust the chart so that a different pie piece is moved toward the front of the chart for emphasis.

1 From the **Chart** menu, click **3-D View**.

The 3-D View dialog box opens. Using this dialog box you can rotate the chart and change the *elevation*—the angle at which a chart is tilted on the screen.

2 Under **Rotation**, click the **clockwise rotation** button—the one on the left—three times.

The rotation box changes to 30, and the graphic changes to show the effect. You can change the rotation by clicking either button to the right of the Rotation box. The button on the left rotates the pie clockwise—to the right—and the other button rotates the pie counterclockwise—to the left. You can also type a number in the rotation box if you have an idea of how much you want to rotate the pie. Each time you click one of the buttons, the rotation graphic and the rotation number change by 10 degrees. See Figure 5.42.

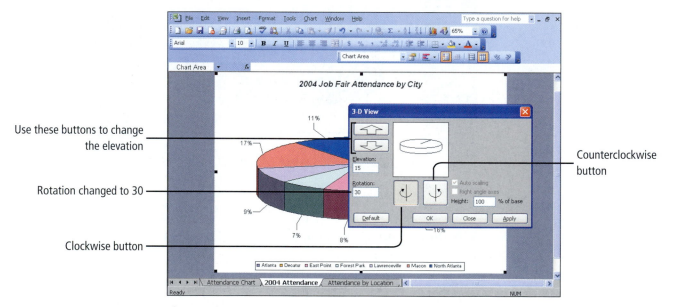

Figure 5.42

3 In the **Rotation** box, select **30**, type **60** and then, in the lower right corner of the dialog box, click **Apply**. Drag the dialog box out of the way as needed so that you can see the pie.

The Rotation box changes to 60, and the chart is rotated. See Figure 5.43. In some dialog boxes, you can use the Apply button to see the effect of a change before you decide to make the change. To accept the change, you must click OK. If you close the dialog box without clicking OK, the change is not made to the chart.

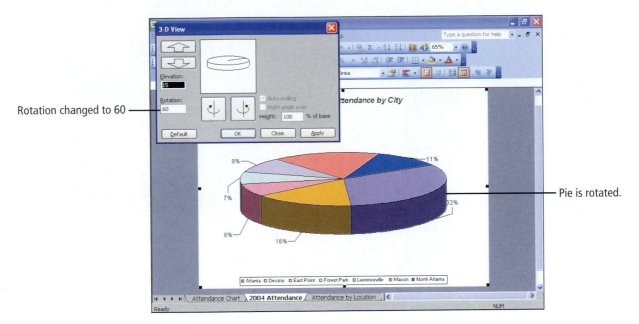

Rotation changed to 60

Pie is rotated.

Figure 5.43

4 In the **3-D View** dialog box, click **OK**. On the Standard toolbar, click the **Save** button ⊟.

The 60-degree rotation is accepted, and the dialog box closes. If the leader lines and data labels have moved, do not be concerned. You will adjust those in the next activity.

Activity 5.22 Exploding a Pie Chart

You can display all the pieces of a pie chart as separate pieces pulled away from the center of the pie; or you can selectively move a piece away from the pie. Pulling one or more pie pieces away from the pie is referred to as *exploding*.

1 Click the pie to select it, and then click the largest piece, labeled *32%*, which represents Atlanta.

Recall that to select a single data point, you first select the pie, and then select the specific data point—in this case, the Atlanta pie piece.

2 Point to the selected piece, and then drag it away from the pie as shown in Figure 5.44.

As you drag, an outline indicates the location of the pie piece.

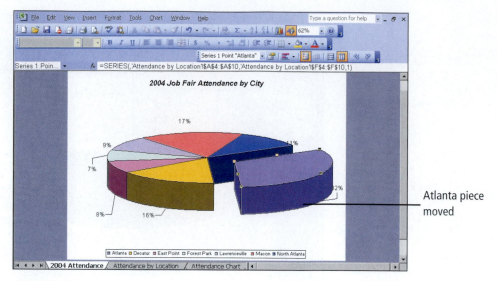

Atlanta piece moved

Figure 5.44

3 Using the technique you practiced in Activity 5.19, adjust any data labels that may have become disconnected or moved too far from their pie piece. Recall that you must first click any data label to select the group of labels, and then drag the individual label that needs to be adjusted. Be sure each data label has a leader line displayed.

4 From the **View** menu, click **Header/Footer**. Click **Custom Footer**. In the **Left section**, click the **File Name** button, and then click **OK** twice.

5 On the Standard toolbar, click the **Save** button, and then click the **Print Preview** button to view the chart as it will print. On the Print Preview toolbar, click the **Print** button, and then click **OK**. Leave the workbook open for the next activity.

Objective 6
Create a Diagram

In addition to creating charts, Excel has six predefined diagrams that can be used to illustrate a concept or relationship. Unlike charts, *diagrams* do not depend on any underlying data in a worksheet; rather, they are graphical tools that help depict ideas or associations. For example, a diagram such as an organizational chart shows the reporting relationship among managers, supervisors, and employees. In the following activities, you will use the diagram program to create a cycle diagram to illustrate how the number of people hired through the job fairs increases the number of attendees, which, in turn, increases the number of employers who elect to have booths at the fairs.

Activity 5.23 Creating a Continuous Cycle Diagram

A cycle diagram illustrates a continuous process, which is a course of action that loops through the same cycle on an ongoing basis. The end result positively affects the beginning of the cycle.

1 To the left of the horizontal scroll bar, locate the **tab scrolling** buttons. Click the **right-most arrow** to move Sheet1 through Sheet3 into view, and then click the **Sheet1 tab**.

An empty worksheet, Sheet1, displays on your screen.

2 Click cell **A1** and type **Goal: Increase Attendance at Job Fairs** and then press Enter.

3 Click cell **A1** to select it. On the Formatting toolbar, click the **Font Size arrow** 12, scroll as necessary, and then click **24**. Click the **Bold** button B. Click the **Font Color arrow** A and in the second row, click the sixth color—**Blue**. Select the range **A1:J1**, and then click the **Merge and Center** button.

The title for your diagram is formatted.

4 From the **Insert** menu, click **Diagram**.

The Diagram Gallery dialog box opens, displaying six diagram types. See Figure 5.45.

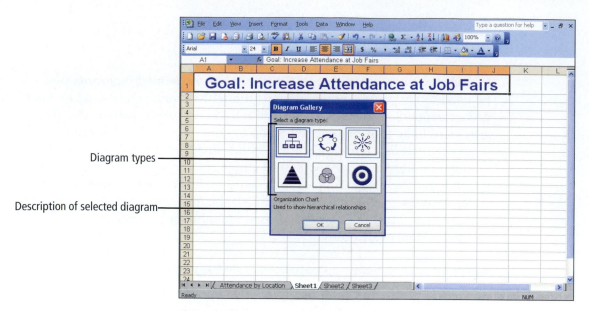

Diagram types

Description of selected diagram

Figure 5.45

5 Click on each diagram and read the description that explains the purpose of the diagram. Then, take a moment to examine the table in Figure 5.46.

Description of Diagrams

Diagram Name	What the Diagram Shows
Organization Chart	Hierarchical relationships
Cycle	A process with a continuous cycle
Radial	Relationships of a core element
Pyramid	Foundation-based relationships
Venn	Areas of overlap among elements
Target	Steps toward a goal

Figure 5.46

6 In the first row, click the second option—**Cycle Diagram**—and then click **OK**.

The cycle diagram graphic displays on the worksheet, and a text box on the right is selected ready for you to enter text. The Diagram toolbar floats on the screen. See Figure 5.47. The Diagram toolbar has commands that help you format and modify your diagram. You will use this toolbar in the next activity.

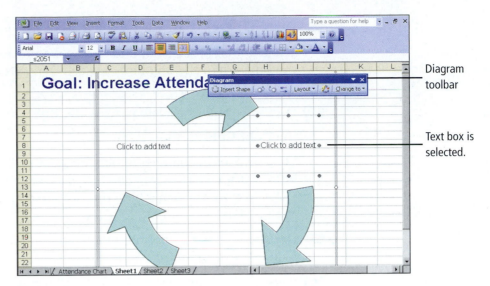

Diagram toolbar

Text box is selected.

Figure 5.47

7 Be sure the text box at the right of the diagram is selected, and then type **Attract More Attendees**

The text displays in the text box on the right side of the diagram. Notice that the text wraps to a second line.

8 Scroll as needed to display the text box at the bottom of the diagram. Click on the words **Click to add text** and type **Attract More Employers** On the left of the diagram, click on the words **Click to add text** and type **Increase Number of People Hired**

Text is added to the text boxes. The active text box is surrounded by a slashed border. Compare your diagram with Figure 5.48.

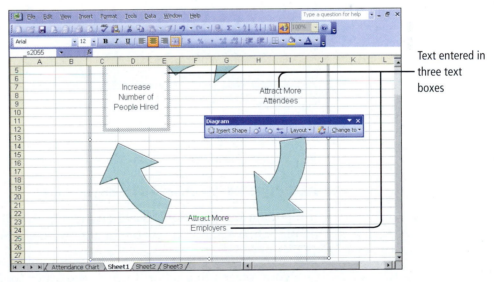

Text entered in three text boxes

Figure 5.48

9 On the left text box, click anywhere on the border.

The text box is selected, and circles display around the perimeter of the box. When the text box is selected in this manner, the text and text box can be formatted.

10 On the Formatting toolbar, click the **Bold** button ⬚B, and then click the **Font Color** button ⬚A⬚.

The text font is changed to blue and bold. Recall that the Font Color button displays the last color selected, so when you click the Font Color button, the same blue that was used for the title is applied to the text box.

11 Use the technique you just practiced to change the font to blue and bold for the remaining two text boxes.

12 Point to the left outside edge of the diagram to display the four-way move pointer ⬚, which displays with the white pointer arrow attached. Drag down and to the left to center the diagram under the title on the worksheet, as shown in Figure 5.49.

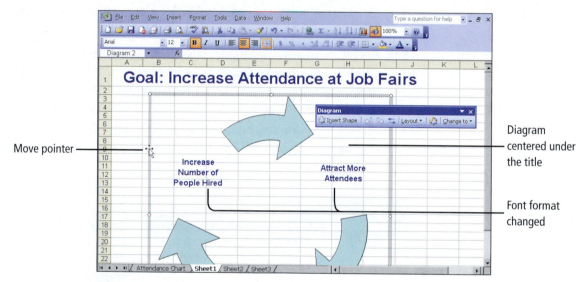

Move pointer

Diagram centered under the title

Font format changed

Figure 5.49

13 On the Standard toolbar, click the **Save** button ⬚.

Activity 5.24 Inserting and Moving a Shape

If the diagram does not have enough shapes to illustrate the concept or display the relationship, you can add more shapes.

1 Point to the title bar of the Diagram toolbar and drag it to the top of your screen to anchor it under the other toolbars.

2 On the Diagram toolbar, click the **Insert Shape** button ⟨Insert Shape⟩.

An arrow and text box are inserted in the upper left corner of the diagram.

3 Click the new text box and type **Increase Profits**

4 Click the patterned border surrounding the new text box. From the Formatting toolbar, change the font to **14** point, **Bold** with **Green** font color.

5 With the **Increase Profits** text box still selected, on the Diagram toolbar click the **Move Shape Backward** button ⟨◻⟩.

The selected text box moves backward one position. To move a shape, first select it, and then click the Move Shape Forward or Move Shape Backward button. Each time you click one of these two directional buttons, the selected text box moves one position forward or back. Compare your diagram with Figure 5.50.

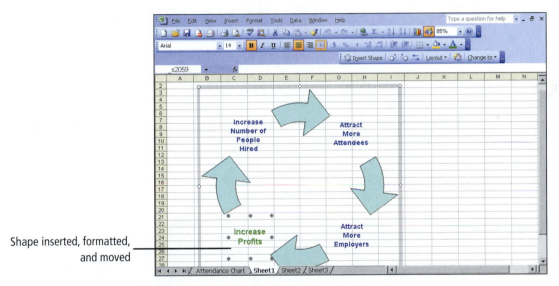

Shape inserted, formatted, and moved

Figure 5.50

6 On the Standard toolbar, click the **Save** button ⟨▣⟩.

Activity 5.25 Changing the Diagram Style

Excel offers a selection of preformatted styles that can be applied to a diagram.

1 On the Diagram toolbar, click the **Reverse Diagram** button ⟨⇄⟩.

The arrows reverse direction, and the boxes rotate counterclockwise one position. See Figure 5.51.

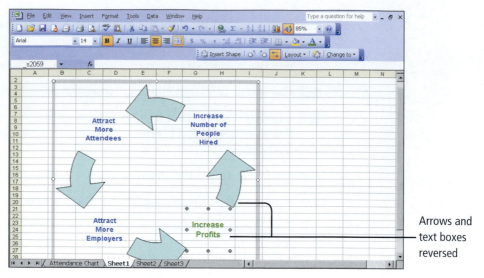

Arrows and text boxes reversed

Figure 5.51

2 On the Diagram toolbar, click the **Reverse Diagram** button again to return the diagram to its original configuration.

3 On the Diagram toolbar, click the **AutoFormat** button .

The Diagram Style Gallery dialog box opens. Ten different styles can be used for this diagram.

4 In the **Diagram Style Gallery** dialog box, under **Select a Diagram Style**, click on each style to see the style displayed in the preview window. After reviewing the style selections, click **Primary Colors**. See Figure 5.52.

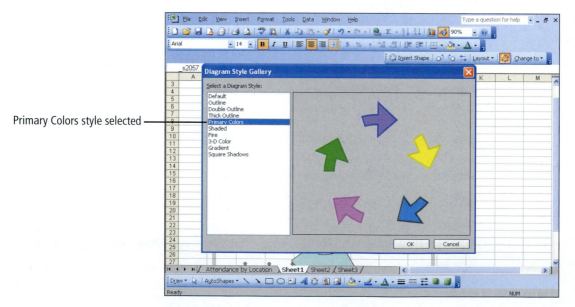

Primary Colors style selected

Figure 5.52

5 In the lower right corner of the dialog box, click **OK**.

The new style is applied to the diagram.

6 On the Standard toolbar, click the **Save** button 🖫.

7 From the **File** menu, click **Page Setup**. Click the **Page tab**, and then, under **Orientation**, click the **Landscape** option button. Click the **Margins tab**, and then, under **Center on page**, select the **Horizontally** check box. Click the **Header/Footer tab**, and then click **Custom Footer**. With the insertion point positioned in the **Left section**, click the **File Name** button 🔲. Click **OK** twice.

8 **Save** 🖫 your file, and then click the **Print Preview** button 🔍. On the Print Preview toolbar, click the **Print** button, and then click **OK**.

Objective 7
Organize and Format Worksheets

Worksheets can be deleted, inserted, and repositioned within a workbook. You have learned how to name a worksheet, but you can also add color to a sheet tab to help differentiate one from another. It is also possible to hide a worksheet within a workbook.

Activity 5.26 Inserting and Deleting Worksheets

1 Display the **Insert** menu, and then click **Worksheet**.

Sheet4 is inserted to the left of the Sheet1 tab, and Sheet4 becomes the active worksheet. Inserted worksheets are numbered consecutively.

Another Way ── **Use the Shortcut Menu to Insert Worksheets**

You can also right-click a sheet tab and from the displayed shortcut menu, click Insert. From the displayed Insert dialog box, click the Worksheet icon and click OK to add a new worksheet.

2 Right-click the **Sheet4 tab**, and from the displayed shortcut menu, click Delete. Alternatively, from the Edit menu, click Delete Sheet.

Sheet4 is deleted. Because there was no data on this sheet, Excel does not warn you that you are about to delete a worksheet, nor can you click the Undo button.

3 Click the **Sheet2 tab**. In cell **A1**, type **September 2004** and press Enter.

Now that you have added text to this worksheet, you will be able to see what happens when you delete a sheet than contains data.

4 Hold down `Ctrl` and click the **Sheet3 tab** to select both Sheets 2 and 3. Display the **Edit** menu, and then click **Delete Sheet**.

A dialog box displays, warning you that data may exist in one or more of the selected sheets. This gives you a chance to change your mind and helps prevent you from inadvertently deleting active worksheets. See Figure 5.53.

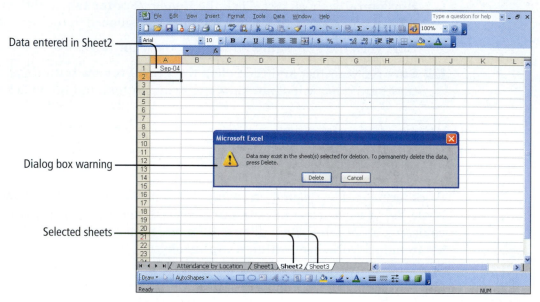

Data entered in Sheet2

Dialog box warning

Selected sheets

Figure 5.53

5 In the displayed dialog box, click **Delete**. Click the **Save** button 🖫.

Both sheets are deleted, and Sheet1 displays on the screen.

Activity 5.27 Formatting and Moving Worksheets

1 Double-click the **Sheet1 tab**, type **Attend Diagram** and then press `Enter`.

The name of the sheet is changed. Recall that you can double-click a sheet tab to change to the editing mode, or you can right-click the sheet tab and from the displayed shortcut menu click Rename, which also selects the sheet name and activates the editing mode.

2 Right-click the **Attend Diagram sheet tab** and, from the displayed shortcut menu, click **Tab Color**.

The Format Tab Color dialog box opens, as shown in Figure 5.54.

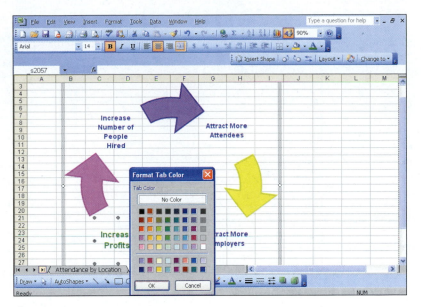

Figure 5.54

3 Under **Tab Color**, in the last row, click the second color—**Pink**—and then click **OK**.

The sheet tab displays a pink line under the sheet name.

4 If necessary, use the tab scrolling buttons to display the **Attendance by Location** sheet. Right-click the **Attendance by Location sheet tab**, and from the displayed list, click **Tab Color**. In the displayed **Format Tab Color** dialog box, in the fifth row, click the fifth color— **Light Turquoise**—to match the color used in this worksheet. Click **OK**.

5 Use the technique you just practiced to apply **Coral** to the **2004 Attendance sheet tab** and **Ocean Blue** to the **Attendance Chart sheet tab**. Both colors are in the sixth row of the color palette, the sixth and seventh colors, respectively.

Notice that the active sheet displays the sheet tab color as an underscore under the sheet name, and the inactive sheet tabs display the full color. If necessary, the color of the font changes to white to maintain a contrast with the color of the sheet tab. Refer to Figure 5.55.

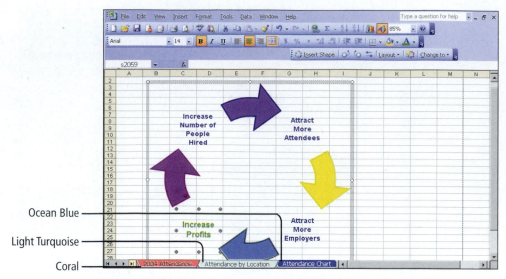

Ocean Blue

Light Turquoise

Coral

Figure 5.55

6 Click the **Attendance by Location tab** to make it the active sheet. On the **Attendance by Location tab**, click and hold down the left mouse button until a sheet icon displays. See Figure 5.56.

When you see the Sheet icon, you can drag to move the selected sheet to the left or right of the other sheet tabs.

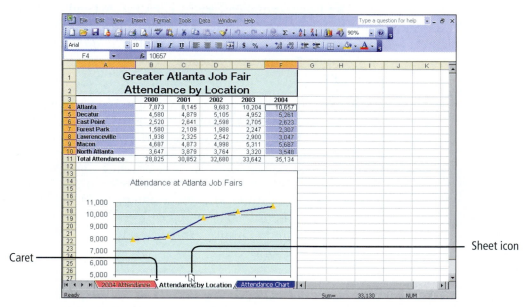

Caret

Sheet icon

Figure 5.56

7 Drag the **Attendance by Location sheet icon** to the left of the **2004 Attendance sheet tab**. Release the mouse.

As you move the sheet, notice the tiny triangle—called a *caret*—that indicates the location where the worksheet will be positioned.

8 On the Standard toolbar, click the **Save** button 📄.

Activity 5.28 Hiding and Unhiding Worksheets

You can hide a worksheet in a workbook. For example, you may have a workbook of diagrams and charts that you want to share, but you do not want to include the worksheet data to discourage someone from changing the data, or you may not want to include all the diagrams or charts that are in the workbook.

1 If necessary, use the tab scrolling buttons to bring the **Attend Diagram** into view. Click the **Attend Diagram tab** to make it the active worksheet.

2 Display the **Format** menu, point to **Sheet**, and then click **Hide**.

The active worksheet—Attend Diagram—is hidden, and the chart worksheet displays on your screen.

3 Display the **Format** menu, point to **Sheet**, and click **Unhide**.

The Unhide dialog box displays, as shown in Figure 5.57, and under Unhide Sheet, the Attend Diagram sheet is listed.

Unhide dialog box lists hidden worksheet(s)

Attend Diagram worksheet tab not displayed

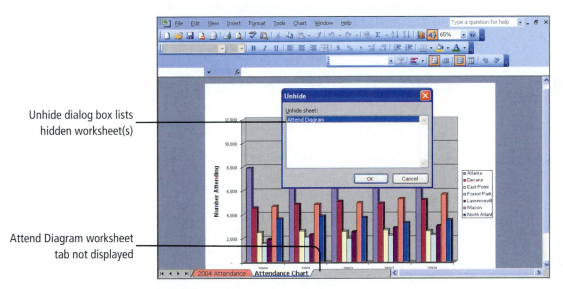

Figure 5.57

4 With the Attend Diagram sheet selected in the dialog box, click **OK** to return the sheet to view. Save your changes and close the workbook.

End **You have completed Project 5A**

Summary

The Excel charting feature provides a broad array of chart options for creating a graphical illustration of the numbers in a worksheet. In this chapter, the three main chart types were demonstrated: charts that show a relationship among data, charts that show trends over time, and charts that show the parts of a whole. You created and modified a column chart to show a comparison among related numbers, a line chart to display a trend over time, and a pie chart to show the contribution of parts to a whole. Within each chart type, you identified and modified various chart objects and created and formatted titles and labels.

Excel also offers six predefined diagram types. You created and modified a cycle diagram to practice working with some of the diagram features and options.

It is typical to have several worksheets in a workbook. To help you organize a workbook, you practiced inserting, deleting, moving, hiding, and unhiding worksheets. You also changed the tab color on the worksheets.

In This Chapter You Practiced How To

- Create a Column Chart
- Modify a Column Chart
- Print a Chart
- Create and Modify a Line Chart
- Create and Modify a 3-D Pie Chart
- Create a Diagram
- Organize and Format Worksheets

Concepts Assessments

Matching   Match each term in the second column with its correct definition in the first column by writing the letter of the term on the blank line in front of the correct definition.

_I_ **1.** A chart that is inserted into the same worksheet that contains the data used to create the chart.

_E_ **2.** A type of chart that shows comparisons among data.

_K_ **3.** A type of chart that uses lines to show a trend over time.

_L_ **4.** A type of chart that shows the proportion of parts to the whole.

_G_ **5.** A group of related data points.

_J_ **6.** In a multicolumn chart, a key that identifies the data series by colors.

_C_ **7.** A tool that walks you step by step through the process of creating a chart.

_H_ **8.** A tool that is used to graphically illustrate a concept or relationship.

_M_ **9.** The chart object that graphically represents the numbers in a worksheet.

_N_ **10.** The range of numbers in the data series that controls the minimum, maximum, and incremental values on the value axis.

_O_ **11.** Small boxes that surround an object or chart and that can be used to resize it.

_B_ **12.** Variations on a main chart type.

____ **13.** The default chart type that displays when you open the Chart Wizard.

_F_ **14.** A single value in a worksheet represented by a data marker in a chart.

_A_ **15.** A separate worksheet used to display an entire chart.

A Chart sheet

B Chart sub-type

C Chart Wizard

D Clustered column chart

E Column chart

F Data point

G Data series

H Diagram

I Embedded chart

J Legend

K Line chart

L Pie chart

M Plot area

N Scale

O Sizing handles

Fill in the Blank Write the correct answer in the space provided.

1. Elements that make up a chart are known as chart
chart objects.

2. The numbers along the left side of a chart display in the
_____Value_____ axis.

3. The graphic element, such as a column or pie slice, that represents a single data point is known as _____

_____.

4. Text or numbers that provide additional information about a data marker, including values, percentages, data series, or categories are

_____.

5. To create more advanced chart designs and incorporate your own features, you can click _____custom chart_____ types in the Chart Wizard.

6. The data along the bottom of a chart displays in the
_____category_____ axis.

7. The areas surrounding a 3-D chart that give dimension and boundaries to the chart are the _____.

8. If you pull a pie piece away from the center of the pie, it is referred to as _____exploding_____ the pie.

9. To reposition a sheet tab, _____ it to the left or right of the adjacent sheet tabs.

10. A diagram that is used to show hierarchical relationships is the

_____.

Project 5B — Industry

Objectives: *Print a Chart, and Organize and Format Worksheets.*

Janice Dawson, the employer coordinator for the Greater Atlanta Job Fair, is responsible for attracting new employers to the fairs. She wants to know the percentage each industry group represents of the total number of employers attending the fairs and has gathered the data together in a worksheet. In the following Skill Assessment, you will create and modify a pie chart that shows the distribution of employers across several industry categories. Your completed chart will look similar to the one shown in Figure 5.58. You will save your workbook as *5B_Industry_Firstname_Lastname.*

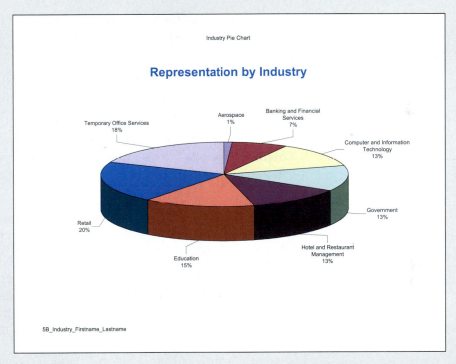

Figure 5.58

1. **Start** Excel. On the Standard toolbar, click the **Open** button. Navigate to the location where the student files for this textbook are stored. Locate and open **e05B_Industry**.

2. From the **File** menu, click **Save As**. In the **Save As** dialog box, use the **Save in arrow** to navigate to the location where you are storing your files for this chapter. In the **File name** box, type **5B_Industry_Firstname_Lastname** Click the **Save** button.

3. At the bottom of the worksheet, double-click the **Sheet1 tab**, type **2004 Industries** and then press Enter.

(Project 5B–Industry continues on the next page)

(Project 5B–Industry continued)

4. Right-click the **2004 Industries sheet tab**, and from the displayed shortcut menu, click **Tab Color**. In the displayed **Format Tab Color** dialog box, in the third row, click the first color—**Red**. Click **OK**.

5. Select the range **A3:B10**, and then, on the Standard toolbar, click the **Chart Wizard** button.

6. In Step 1 of the displayed **Chart Wizard** dialog box, under **Chart type**, click **Pie**, and then under **Chart sub-type**, in the first row click the second sub-type—**Pie with 3-D visual effect**. At the lower right of the dialog box, click **Next**.

7. In Step 2 of the **Chart Wizard**, verify that the **Data range** box displays ='2004 Industries'!$A$3:$B$10, and then click **Next**.

8. In Step 3 of the **Chart Wizard**, be sure the **Titles tab** is selected. Click the **Chart title** box, type **Representation by Industry** and then click **Next**.

9. In Step 4 of the **Chart Wizard**, delete the text in the **As new sheet** box, type **Industry Pie Chart** and then click **Finish**. On the Standard toolbar, click the **Save** button.

10. Right-click the **Legend** and from the displayed shortcut menu, click **Format Legend**. In the **Format Legend** dialog box, click the **Placement tab**, and then click **Bottom**. Click **OK**.

11. At the top of the chart, click the **Chart Title** to select it. From the Formatting toolbar, click the **Font Size arrow**, and click **22**. Click the **Font Color arrow**. From the displayed palette, in the sixth row, click the seventh color—**Ocean Blue**.

12. Display the **Chart** menu, and then click **Chart Options**. Click the **Data Labels tab**. Under **Label Contains**, select the **Category name** and **Percentage** check boxes. Be sure the **Show leader lines** check box is selected, and then click **OK**. The data labels are added, and the plot area of the pie shrinks.

13. Because you added the category names to the data labels, the legend is no longer needed. Right-click the **Legend**, and from the displayed shortcut menu, click **Clear** to remove the legend from the chart.

14. On the Chart toolbar, click the **Chart Objects arrow**. From the displayed list, click **Plot Area**. A patterned border displays around the plot area. Point to the sizing handle in the lower left corner of the plot area outline. When the pointer changes to a two-way resize arrow, drag down and to the left to increase the size of the plot area by approximately 1 to 2 inches. Point to the slashed border outline, and drag the enlarged plot area so that it is approximately centered under the title. Use Figure 5.58 as a reference.

(Project 5B–Industry continues on the next page)

(Project 5B–Industry continued)

15. Click any one of the data labels. Recall that if you click one data label, all the data labels are selected. On the Formatting toolbar, click the **Font Size arrow**, and then click **10**.

16. Click the data label **Temporary Office Services**, and drag it away from its pie piece so that a leader line displays. Recall that when a patterned border displays around an individual data label, the label can be moved. Continue around the pie and drag each label out from the pie until leader lines show between each label and its related pie slice.

17. Click the **2004 Industries sheet tab**, and hold down the mouse until the sheet icon displays. Drag the 2004 Industry sheet to the left of the **Industry Pie Chart sheet tab**. Click **Sheet2**, hold down Ctrl, and click **Sheet3** to select both sheets. Right-click on one of the selected sheet tabs, and from the displayed shortcut menu, click **Delete** to remove the two empty sheets from the workbook.

18. Right-click the **Industry Pie Chart sheet tab**, and from the displayed shortcut menu, click **Tab Color**. In the **Format Tab Color** dialog box, in the sixth row, click the seventh color—**Ocean Blue**—and then click **OK**. Recall that ScreenTips do not display the color names in this dialog box, but this is the same color that was used earlier to format the chart title.

19. From the **View** menu, click **Header and Footer**. Click the **Custom Header** button. Click in the **Center section**, and then click the **Sheet Tab** button; the code $[Tab] displays in the Center section. Click **OK**. Click the **Custom Footer** button. With the insertion point positioned in the **Left section**, click the **File Name** button. Click **OK** twice.

20. On the Standard toolbar, click the **Save** button, and then click the **Print Preview** button to see how the worksheet will look when it prints. Compare your worksheet with Figure 5.58. Click the **Print** button, and then click **OK**. Close the file, saving changes if prompted to do so.

End You have completed Project 5B ————————————————

Project 5C—Atlanta Results

Objectives: *Create and Modify a Line Chart, Print a Chart, and Organize and Format Worksheets.*

Ben Ham, the administrative manager for the Greater Atlanta Job Fair, tracks expenses and attendance for the fairs to determine the average cost per attendee. In the following Skill Assessment, you will create and format a line chart to show the trend in expenses at the Atlanta fair over the past five years. Your completed worksheet will look similar to the one shown in Figure 5.59. You will save your workbook as *5C_Atlanta_Results_Firstname_Lastname.*

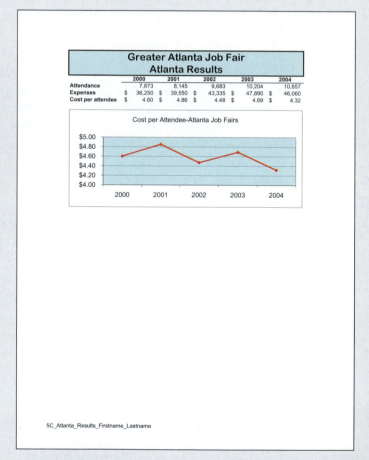

Figure 5.59

1. If necessary, **Start** Excel. On the Standard toolbar, click the **Open** button. Navigate to the location where the student files for this textbook are stored. Locate and open **e05C_Atlanta_Results**.

(Project 5C–Atlanta Results continues on the next page)

(Project 5C–Atlanta Results continued)

2. From the **File** menu, click **Save As**. In the **Save As** dialog box, use the **Save in arrow** to navigate to the location where you are storing your files for this chapter. In the **File name** box, type **5C_Atlanta_Results_Firstname_Lastname** Click the **Save** button.

3. In cell **A6**, type **Cost per attendee** and press Tab. Recall that a cell adopts the formatting of the cell above it. In cell **B6**, type **=b5/b4** and press Enter to calculate the cost per attendee for the 2000 fair. Click cell **B6** and use the fill handle to copy the formula to cells **C6:F6**. The cost per attendee is formatted as dollars, the same as the cells above.

4. Select the range **A3:F3**, hold down Ctrl, and select the range **A6:F6**. This selects the labels in **row 3** and the data to be charted in **row 6**. Recall that you must select the same number of cells in each row or column, even if one of the cells is empty. On the Standard toolbar, click the **Chart Wizard** button.

5. In Step 1 of the **Chart Wizard**, under **Chart type**, click **Line**. Under **Chart sub-type**, in the second row, click the first chart sub-type— *Line with markers displayed at each data value*. In the lower right corner of the Chart Wizard, click the **Next** button.

6. In Step 2 of the **Chart Wizard**, verify that the **Data range** box displays =*'Atlanta Results'!$A$3:$F$3,'Atlanta Results'!$A$6:$F$6*, and then click **Next**.

7. In Step 3 of the **Chart Wizard**, click the **Legend tab** and clear the **Show legend** check box. Recall that if there is only one line of data, a legend is not needed. Click **Next**.

8. In Step 4 of the **Chart Wizard**, be sure the **As object in** option is selected, and then click **Finish**. The chart displays on the worksheet.

9. Point to the **Chart Area** and drag the chart down and to the left. Position the upper left corner of the chart in the upper left corner of cell **A8**.

10. With the **Chart Area** selected, sizing handles display at the outside corners of the chart; point to the lower right corner. When a two-way resize arrow displays, drag as necessary to position the lower right corner of the chart aligned with the lower right corner of cell **F21**. The right edge of the chart aligns with the right edge of the data in the worksheet. On the Standard toolbar, click the **Save** button.

11. Click the **Chart Title** once to select it, and then click it a second time to place an insertion point in the title. Select the text, and then type **Cost per Attendee-Atlanta Job Fairs**

(Project 5C–Atlanta Results continues on the next page)

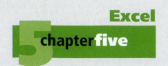
(Project 5C–Atlanta Results continued)

12. On the Chart toolbar, click the **Chart Objects arrow**, and from the displayed list click **Series "Cost per attendee"**. This selects the data series line on the plot area of the chart. On the **Chart** toolbar, click the **Format Data Series** button. Recall that the Format Selected Object button adopts the name of the selected object—in this instance, the data series.

13. In the **Format Data Series** dialog box, click the **Patterns tab** if necessary. Under **Line**, click the **Color arrow**, and then in third row, click the first color—**Red**. Click the **Weight arrow** and from the displayed list, click the third line. Under **Marker**, click the **Foreground arrow** and click **Red**; then click the **Background arrow** and click **Red**. Click **OK**. The data line and its marker change to red.

14. Right-click the **Plot Area**—the gray background—and from the displayed shortcut menu, click **Format Plot Area**. In the **Format Plot Area** dialog box, under **Area**, in the fifth row, click the fifth color—**Light Turquoise**, the same color that is used in the title of the worksheet. Click **OK**. Click in an empty cell to cancel the selection of the chart.

15. From the **File** menu, click **Page Setup**. Click the **Margins tab** and under **Center on page**, click **Horizontally**. Click the **Header/Footer tab**, and then click the **Custom Footer** button. With the insertion point positioned in the **Left section**, click the **File Name** button. Click **OK** twice.

16. Click to select the **Sheet1 tab**, hold down , and then click the **Sheet2 tab** and the **Sheet3** tab. With the three sheets selected, display the **Edit** menu, and then click **Delete Sheet**.

17. On the Standard toolbar, click the **Save** button, and then click the **Print Preview** button to see the worksheet as it will print. Compare your worksheet with Figure 5.59. Click the **Print** button, and then click **OK**. Close the file, saving changes if prompted to do so.

End **You have completed Project 5C**

Project 5D—Hires

Objectives: *Create a Line Chart, Change the Line Chart to a Column Chart, Modify a Column Chart, Print a Chart, and Organize and Format Worksheets.*

Janice Dawson, the employer coordinator for the Greater Atlanta Job Fair, tracks the number of people who get hired by an employer at each fair. In the following Skill Assessment, you will create and modify a chart to display the number of people hired at the fairs in the past five years. Your completed worksheet will look similar to the one shown in Figure 5.60. You will save your workbook as *5D_Hires__Firstname_Lastname.*

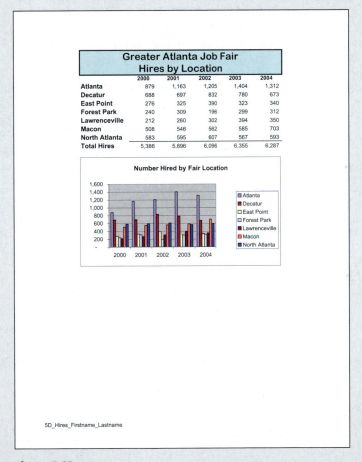

Figure 5.60

(Project 5D–Hires continues on the next page)

(Project 5D–Hires continued)

1. On the Standard toolbar, click the **Open** button. Navigate to the location where the student files for this textbook are stored. Locate and open **e05D_Hires**.

2. From the **File** menu, click **Save As**. In the **Save As** dialog box, use the **Save in arrow** to navigate to the location where you are storing your files for this chapter. In the **File name** box, type 5D_Hires_Firstname_ Lastname Click the **Save** button.

3. Select the range **A3:F10**. On the Standard toolbar, click the **Chart Wizard** button.

4. In Step 1 of the **Chart Wizard**, under **Chart type** click **Line**. Under **Chart sub-type**, in the second row, click the first option—**Line with markers displayed at each data value**. In the lower right corner of the Chart Wizard, click the **Next** button.

5. In Step 2 of the **Chart Wizard**, next to **Series in**, click the **Rows** option button. The preview changes to display the years on the category axis and the locations as the data series. Click **Next**.

6. In Step 3 of the **Chart Wizard**, click the **Titles tab**. Click the **Chart title** box and type Number Hired by Fair Location and then click **Next**.

7. In Step 4 of the **Chart Wizard**, be sure the **As object in** option is selected, and then click **Finish**. The chart displays on the worksheet.

8. Point to the **Chart Area** and drag the chart down and to the left. Position the upper left corner of the chart in the upper left corner of cell **A13**.

9. With the **Chart Area** selected, sizing handles display at the outside corners of the chart; point to the lower right corner. When a two-way resize arrow displays, drag as necessary until the lower right corner of the chart aligns with the lower right corner of cell **F28**. The right edge of the chart aligns with the right edge of the data in the worksheet. On the Standard toolbar, click the **Save** button.

10. On the Chart toolbar, click the **Chart Type button arrow**. From the displayed palette, in the third row, click the first chart—**Column Chart**. The chart type changes to columns grouped by year along the category axis.

(Project 5D–Hires continues on the next page)

(Project 5D–Hires continued)

11. On the Chart toolbar, click the **Chart Objects arrow**, and from the displayed list click **Value Axis**. On the Chart toolbar, click the **Format Axis** button. Recall that the Format Selected Object button takes on the name of the selected object—in this instance, Axis.

12. In the **Format Axis** dialog box, click the **Scale tab**. Under **Value (Y) axis scale**, select the value in the **Major unit** box and type **200** if necessary. Select the value in the **Minor unit** box and type **50** Click the **Font tab** and under **Size**, click **10**. In the lower right corner of the dialog box, click **OK**.

13. Double-click the **Legend**. In the displayed **Format Legend** dialog box, click the **Font tab**. Under **Size**, click **10**, and then click **OK**.

14. Click the **Chart Title**. On the Formatting toolbar, click the **Font Size arrow**, and then click **12**. Click the years on the **Category Axis**, on the Formatting toolbar click the **Font Size arrow**, and then click **10**. Click in an empty cell to cancel the selection of the chart.

15. Click cell **F9**, type **703** and then press Enter. The change is reflected in the chart for the Macon data series in 2004.

16. From the **File** menu, click **Page Setup**. Click the **Margins tab** and under **Center on page**, select **Horizontally**. Click the **Header/Footer tab**, and then click the **Custom Footer** button. With the insertion point positioned in the **Left section**, click the **File Name** button. Click **OK** twice.

17. Click to select the **Sheet1 tab**, hold down Ctrl, and then click the **Sheet2 tab** and the **Sheet3 tab**. With the three sheets selected, display the **Edit** menu, and then click **Delete Sheet**.

18. On the Standard toolbar, click the **Save** button, and then click the **Print Preview** button to see the worksheet as it will print. Compare your worksheet with Figure 5.60. Click the **Print** button, and then click **OK**. Close the file, saving changes if prompted to do so.

 End **You have completed Project 5D**

Project 5E—Atlanta Expenses

Objectives: *Organize and Format Worksheets, Create and Modify a 3-D Pie Chart, and Print a Chart.*

Ben Ham, the administrative director for the Greater Atlanta Job Fair, has created a worksheet showing the income and expenses for the 2004 Atlanta Job Fair. In the following Performance Assessment, you will create a pie chart that shows the percentage that each expense represents out of the total for this fair. Your completed worksheet will look similar to the one shown in Figure 5.61. You will save your workbook as *5E_Atlanta_Expenses_Firstname_Lastname.*

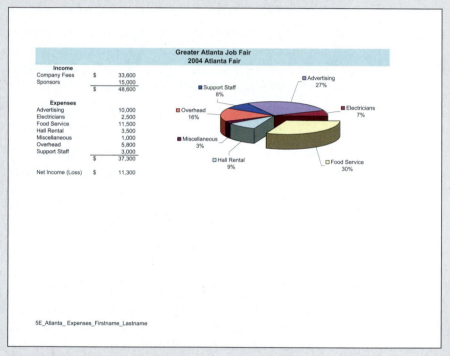

Figure 5.61

1. **Start** Excel. On the Standard toolbar, click the **Open** button. Navigate to the location where the student files for this textbook are stored. Locate and open **e05E_Atlanta_Expenses**.

2. From the **File** menu, click **Save As**. In the **Save As** dialog box, use the **Save in arrow** to navigate to the location where you are storing your files for this chapter. In the **File name** box, type 5E_Atlanta_Expenses_ Firstname_Lastname Click the **Save** button.

3. Select the range **A9:B15**. On the Standard toolbar, click the **Chart Wizard** button. In Step 1 of the **Chart Wizard**, under **Chart type**, click **Pie**. Under **Chart sub-type**, in the first row, click the second option—**Pie with 3-D visual effect**. Click the **Finish** button. Recall that you can click **Finish** after you have selected the chart type, and then make modifications using the various charting tools.

(Project 5E–Atlanta Expenses continues on the next page)

(Project 5E–Atlanta Expenses continued)

4. Drag the chart to the right of the worksheet data, placing the left edge of the chart in the middle of **column C** and the top edge of the chart at the top of **row 3**. Using the lower right sizing handle, drag to expand the chart until the lower right corner of the chart is at the lower right corner of cell **K18**.

5. From the **Chart** menu, click **Chart Options**. In the **Chart Options** dialog box, click the **Legend tab** and clear the **Show legend** check box. Click the **Data Labels tab**, and under **Label Contains**, select the **Category name** and **Percentage** check boxes. On the lower left of the dialog box, click as needed to select both the **Legend key** check box and the **Show leader lines** check box. Click **OK** to close the dialog box.

6. From the **Chart** menu, click **3-D View**. In the **3-D View** dialog box, click the **counterclockwise rotation arrow**—the one on the right—three times, until the rotation box displays *330*. Click **OK**. On the Standard toolbar, click the **Save** button.

7. On the Chart toolbar, click the **Chart Objects arrow**, and then click **Plot Area**. A patterned border displays around the pie. Point to the lower left sizing handle and drag down and to the left to expand the plot area to align with the middle of **column E**. Use the upper right sizing handle to expand the plot area to align with the right edge of **column I**.

8. On the Chart toolbar, click the **Chart Objects arrow**, and then click **Series 1 Data Labels**. On the Formatting toolbar, click the **Font Size arrow**, and then click **10**.

9. Click the data label **Support Staff**. A patterned border displays around the label to indicate that it is selected. Drag the **Support Staff** label away from the pie slightly to display the leader line. Continue around the pie and drag each label out from the pie to display the leader line.

10. Click the pie, and then click the **Food Service** data marker—the yellow pie piece. Drag the **Food Service** slice away from the pie about 1/2 inch. Use Figure 5.61 as a reference.

11. Click cell **A1**. On the Formatting toolbar, click the **Merge and Center** button to unmerge this heading. Select cells **A1:K1**, and then click the **Merge and Center** button again to center the title over the worksheet and the chart. Repeat these actions to merge and center cell **A2** over cells **A2:K2**.

12. At the bottom of the worksheet, right-click the sheet tab **2004 Atlanta Fair**. From the shortcut menu, click **Tab Color**. In the **Format Tab Color** dialog box, in the third row, click the sixth color—**Light Blue**—and then click **OK**.

(Project 5E–Atlanta Expenses continues on the next page)

(Project 5E–Atlanta Expenses continued)

13. Click **Sheet1**, hold down Shift and click **Sheet3**. You can select a contiguous group of sheets using the Shift key. From the **Edit** menu, click **Delete Sheet**. The three empty sheets are deleted, and the 2004 Atlanta Fair sheet displays on your screen.

14. From the **File** menu, click **Page Setup**. Click the **Page tab**, and under **Orientation**, click **Landscape**. Click the **Header/Footer tab**, and then click the **Custom Footer** button. With the insertion point positioned in the **Left section**, click the **File Name** button. Click **OK** twice.

15. Right-click the white **Chart Area**. From the shortcut menu, click **Format Chart Area**. In the **Format Chart Area** dialog box, click the **Patterns tab**. Under **Border**, click **None**, and then click **OK**. The border surrounding the chart is removed.

16. On the Standard toolbar, click the **Save** button, and then click the **Print Preview** button to see the worksheet as it will print. Compare your worksheet with Figure 5.61. Click the **Print** button, and then click **OK**. Close the file, saving changes if prompted to do so.

End You have completed Project 5E

Project 5F — Communities

Objective: *Create a Diagram.*

Michael Augustino, executive director, has asked the marketing department for a diagram that shows all the locations where job fairs are held in the greater Atlanta area. In the following Performance Assessment, you will create a radial diagram. Your completed diagram will look similar to the one shown in Figure 5.62. You will save your workbook as *5F_Communities_Firstname_Lastname*.

1. **Start** Excel. In a new worksheet, in cell **A1** type **Communities We Serve** and press Enter.

2. Select the range **A1:M1** and click the **Merge and Center** button. Change the **Font Size** to **24** pt., the **Font Color** to **Aqua**—the third row, fifth color of the **Font Color** palette—and then apply **Bold**.

3. On the Standard toolbar, click the **Save** button. In the **Save As** dialog box, navigate to the location where you are storing your files for this chapter. In the **File name** box, type **5F_Communities_Firstname_ Lastname** and then click the **Save** button.

4. From the **Insert** menu, click **Diagram**. In the **Diagram Gallery** dialog box, in the first row, click the third diagram—**Radial Diagram**—and then click **OK**.

(Project 5F–Communities continues on the next page)

(Project 5F–Communities continued)

Figure 5.62

5. Point to the patterned border around the diagram. When the four-way **move pointer** displays, drag the diagram so that the top edge of the diagram outline is on the lower edge of **row 2** and the center sizing handle is positioned under the **column G** heading. If the Diagram toolbar is not docked at the top of your screen, drag it to a location where it is not blocking your view of the diagram.

6. Click in the circle at the top of the diagram, and type **Atlanta** Click in the center circle, and type **Greater Atlanta Job Fairs** The text wraps to three lines in the circle. Click in the circle on the lower left, and type **Macon** and in the circle on the lower right, type **Decatur**

7. On the Diagram toolbar, click the **Insert Shape** button. In the new circle, type **East Point** Click the **Insert Shape** button again and, in the new circle, type **Forest Park** Add another circle and type **Lawrenceville** and then add the last circle and type **North Atlanta** Seven total circles are around the perimeter. You will adjust the spacing of *Lawrenceville* later.

8. Alphabetically going clockwise, the *Macon* circle is out of order. Click the **Macon** circle, and then on the Diagram toolbar, click the **Move Shape Backward** button one time.

9. On the Diagram toolbar, click the **AutoFormat** button. From the **Diagram Style Gallery**, under **Select a Diagram Style**, click **Double Outline**, and then click **OK**.

(Project 5F–Communities continues on the next page)

(Project 5F–Communities continued)

10. Drag the right-middle sizing handle to the right edge of **column K**. Drag the left-middle sizing handle to the left edge of **column C**. Scroll down as needed, and use the lower-middle sizing handle and drag the outline to the top of **row 35**.

11. Lawrenceville does not fit on one line at this size font. Click between the *e* and *v* in *Lawrenceville* and type a hyphen so that *ville* wraps to a second line. Refer to Figure 5.62.

12. Click outside of the diagram so that it is not selected. From the **File** menu, click **Page Setup**. Click the **Page tab** and under **Orientation**, click **Landscape**. Click the **Margins tab** and under **Center on page**, click both **Horizontally** and **Vertically**. Click the **Header/Footer tab**, and then click the **Custom Footer** button. With the insertion point positioned in the **Left section**, click the **File Name** button. Click **OK** twice.

13. On the Standard toolbar, click the **Save** button, and then click the **Print Preview** button to see the worksheet as it will print. Compare your worksheet with Figure 5.63. Click the **Print** button, and then click **OK**. Close the file, saving changes if prompted to do so.

End You have completed Project 5F

Project 5G — 2004 Results

Objectives: *Create a Column Chart, Modify a Column Chart, Print a Chart, and Organize and Format Worksheets.*

Janice Dawson, employer coordinator, has gathered the figures for attendance and hires at the 2004 Job Fair and wants a chart to show the relative relationship of hires to attendance. In the following Performance Assessment, you will create a column chart and then change it to a bar chart. A bar chart is used for comparisons in a manner similar to a column chart, but the data is displayed in horizontal bars rather than in vertical columns. Your completed worksheet will look similar to the one shown in Figure 5.63. You will save your workbook as *5G_2004_Results_Firstname_Lastname*.

1. On the Standard toolbar, click the **Open** button. Navigate to the location where the student files for this textbook are stored. Locate and open **e05G_2004_Results**.

2. From the **File** menu, open the **Save As** dialog box. Navigate to the location where you are storing your files for this chapter. In the **File name** box, using your own name, type **5G_2004_Results_Firstname_Lastname** and then click the **Save** button.

(Project 5G–2004 Results continues on the next page)

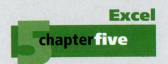
(Project 5G–2004 Results continued)

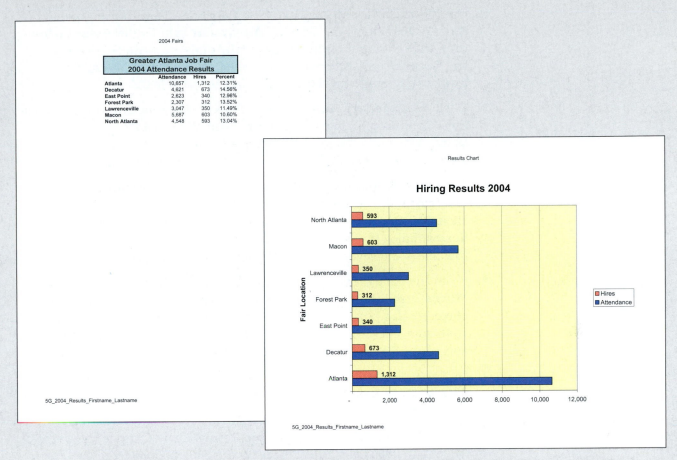

Figure 5.63

3. Select the range **A3:C10** and on the Standard toolbar, click the **Chart Wizard** button. With the **Column** Chart type selected, under **Chart sub-type**, in the first row click the second sub-type—**Stacked Column**—and then click **Next**.

4. In Step 2 of the **Chart Wizard**, click **Next**. In Step 3 of the **Chart Wizard**, click the **Titles tab**, and in the **Chart title** box, type Hiring Results 2004 In the **Category (X) axis** box, type Fair Location and then click **Next**.

5. In Step 4 of the **Chart Wizard**, be sure the **As object in** option button is selected, and then click **Finish**.

6. After a chart is created, you can change its location. Display the **Chart** menu and click **Location**. Click the **As new sheet** option button, and click **OK**.

7. Display the **Chart** menu, and click **Chart Type**. In the **Chart Type** dialog box, click **Bar**, and then under **Chart sub-type**, in the first row click the first sub-type—**Clustered Bar**. Click **OK**. The category axis displays along the left side of the chart and the value axis along the lower edge of the chart. On the Standard toolbar, click the **Save** button.

(Project 5G–2004 Results continues on the next page)

(Project 5G–2004 Results continued)

8. Double-click the category axis title **Fair Location**. In the **Format Axis Title** dialog box, click the **Alignment tab**. Under **Orientation**, drag the red diamond to the top of the diagram until **90** displays in the **Degrees** box. Alternatively, type **90** in the Degrees box. Click the **Font tab**, change the **Size** to **14**, and then click **OK**.

9. Click the **Category Axis** on the left side of the chart, and then, from the Formatting toolbar, change the **Font Size** to **12** pt. Click the **Value Axis** and change the **Font Size** to **12** pt. Change the **Font Size** for the **Chart Title** to **20** pt. and the **Legend** to **12** pt.

10. Double-click the **Plot Area**. In the **Format Plot Area** dialog box, under **Area**, in the sixth row, click the third color—**Ivory**—and then click **OK**. Double-click any of the blue bars to open the **Format Data Series** dialog box. Click the **Patterns tab**. Under **Area**, in the sixth row, click the seventh color—**Ocean Blue**—and then click **OK**.

11. From the Chart toolbar, click the **Chart Objects arrow**, click **Series "Hires"**, and then click the **Format Data Series** button. In the displayed dialog box, click the **Patterns tab**, and under **Area**, in the sixth row, click the sixth color—**Coral**. Click the **Data Labels tab**, and under **Label Contains**, select the **Value** check box. Click **OK**.

12. On the Chart toolbar, click the **Chart Objects arrow**, and then click **"Hires" Data Labels**. Using the Formatting toolbar, change the **Font Size** to **12** and click **Bold**.

13. Change the **Chart 1** sheet name to **Results Chart** Change the name of **Sheet1** to **2004 Fairs** Select **Sheet2** and **Sheet3** and from the **Edit** menu, click **Delete Sheet**. Drag the **2004 Fairs** sheet to the left of the **Results Chart** sheet.

14. With the **2004 Fairs sheet tab** selected, display the **Page Setup** dialog box. Click the **Margins tab** and select the **Horizontally** check box. Click the **Header/Footer tab**, and then click the **Custom Header** button. In the **Center section**, insert the **Tab name**. Click the **Custom Footer** button. With the insertion point positioned in the **Left section**, click the **File Name** button. Click **OK** twice.

15. Click the Results Chart sheet tab. Create a **Custom Footer**, and in the **Left section**, insert the **File Name**.

16. On the Standard toolbar, click the **Save** button. Select both worksheets (use the Select All Sheets command), and then click the **Print Preview** button to see the worksheets as they will print. Compare your worksheets with Figure 5.63. Click the **Print** button, and then click **OK**. Close the file, saving changes if prompted to do so.

End You have completed Project 5G

Project 5H—Profit

Objectives: *Create and Modify a Line Chart, Print a Chart, and Organize and Format Worksheets.*

Ben Ham, the administrative manager, has requested a chart showing the profit from each of the job fairs over the past five years. In the following Mastery Assessment, you will create and modify a line chart using multiple lines to show the trend in profit by fair. Your completed worksheets will look similar to Figure 5.64. You will save your workbook as *5H_Profit_Firstname_Lastname.*

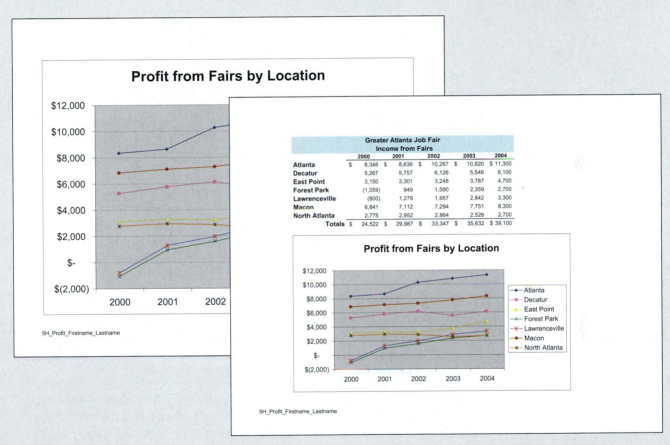

Figure 5.64

1. On the Standard toolbar, click the **Open** button. Navigate to the location where the student files for this textbook are stored. Locate and open **e05H_Profit**.

2. From the **File** menu, open the **Save As** dialog box. Navigate to the location where you are storing your files for this chapter. In the **File name** box, using your own information, type **5H_Profit_Firstname_Lastname** and then click the **Save** button.

3. Select the range **A3:F10**, and start the **Chart Wizard**. In Step 1 of the wizard, select a **Line chart** with markers displayed at each data value.

(Project 5H–Profit continues on the next page)

(Project 5H–Profit continued)

4. In Step 2, format the data range in **Rows**. In Step 3, insert **Profit from Fairs by Location** as the chart title. Display the chart as an object in the worksheet.

5. Position the upper left corner of the chart in cell **A13** and the lower right corner in cell **H33**. Save your work.

6. Change the **Font Size** of the **Chart Title** to **18** pt. If necessary, change the **Font Size** of the **Value Axis** to **12** pt., the **Category Axis** to **12** pt., and the **Legend** to **12** pt.

7. Click the **Value Axis** and open the **Format Axis** dialog box. Click the **Scale tab**, if necessary, select the **Category (X) axis** check box, and then, in the **Crosses at** box, type **-2000** Two of the figures in this chart had losses, so it is necessary to change the number for value (x) axis to cross the category (y) axis to a negative number. This also places the category titles under the plot area at the edge of the category axis.

8. Click the **North Atlanta** data line. On the Chart toolbar, click the **Format Data Series** button. Under **Line**, change the **Color** to **Orange**. Under **Marker**, click the **Style arrow**, and click the fifth option. Change the **Foreground** to **Green**. Click **OK**. Select the **Forest Park** data line and open the **Format Data Series** dialog box. Change the **Line** color to **Bright Green**, change the **Foreground Marker** color to **Blue**, and then click **OK**. Select the **Lawrenceville** data line and open the **Format Data Series** dialog box. Change the **Line** color to **Light Blue**, change the **Foreground Marker** color to **Red**, and then click **OK**.

9. With the chart selected, click the **Print Preview** button. On the Print Preview toolbar, click the **Setup** button. In the **Page Setup** dialog box, click the **Header/Footer tab**, and then click the **Custom Footer** button. With the insertion point positioned in the **Left section**, click the **File Name** button. Click **OK** twice. On the Print Preview toolbar, click the **Print** button, and then click **OK**.

10. Be sure the chart is not selected. Double-click the **Sheet1 tab**, type **Profit** and press [Enter]. Right-click the **Profit sheet tab** and click **Tab Color**. In the sixth row, click the second color—**Plum**. Select and delete **Sheet2** and **Sheet3**.

11. Be sure the chart is not selected, and then click the **Print Preview** button. The worksheet and chart will not print completely in portrait orientation. On the Print Preview toolbar, click the **Setup** button. Click the **Page tab**, and then click **Landscape**. Click the **Margins tab**, and then select the **Horizontally** check box. Click the **Header/Footer tab** and insert the **File Name** in the **Left section** of the footer. Click **OK** twice, and then click the **Print** button.

12. On the Standard toolbar, click the **Save** button and close the file.

 You have completed Project 5H

Project 5I — Expenses

Objectives: *Create a Column Chart, Modify a Column Chart, and Print a Chart.*

Executive Director Michael Augustino has requested a chart comparing direct expenses of the fairs. In the following Mastery Assessment, you will create a chart to compare the direct expenses for the fairs. Your completed worksheet will look similar to the one shown in Figure 5.65. You will save your workbook as *5I_Expenses_Firstname_Lastname.*

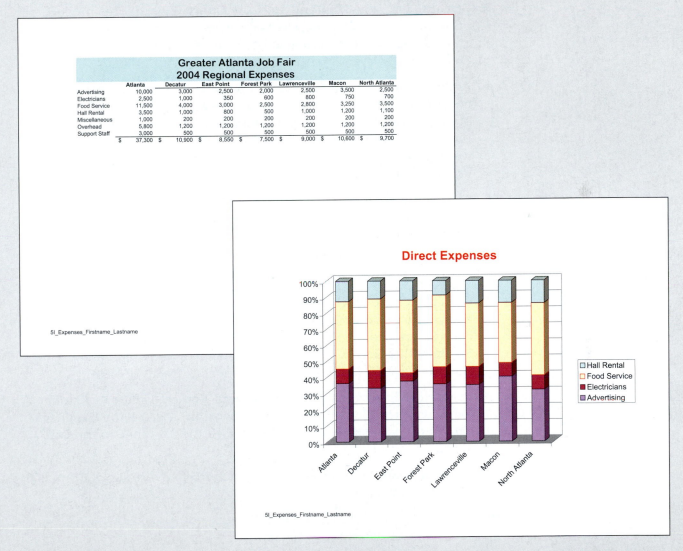

Greater Atlanta Job Fair
2004 Regional Expenses

	Atlanta	Decatur	East Point	Forest Park	Lawrenceville	Macon	North Atlanta
Advertising	10,000	3,000	2,500	2,000	2,500	3,500	2,500
Electricians	2,500	1,000	350	600	800	750	700
Food Service	11,500	4,000	3,000	2,500	2,800	3,250	3,500
Hall Rental	3,500	1,000	800	500	1,000	1,200	1,100
Miscellaneous	1,000	200	200	200	200	200	200
Overhead	5,800	1,200	1,200	1,200	1,200	1,200	1,200
Support Staff	3,000	500	500	500	500	500	500
$	37,300	$ 10,900	$ 8,550	$ 7,500	$ 9,000	$ 10,600	$ 9,700

5I_Expenses_Firstname_Lastname

Figure 5.65

(Project 5I–Expenses continues on the next page)

(Project 5I–Expenses continued)

1. On the Standard toolbar, click the **Open** button. Navigate to the location where the student files for this textbook are stored. Locate and open **e05I_Expenses**.

2. From the **File** menu, open the **Save As** dialog box. Navigate to the location where you are storing your files for this chapter. In the **File name** box, using your own name, type **5H_Expenses_Firstname_Lastname** and then click the **Save** button.

3. Select the range **A3:H7** and start the **Chart Wizard**. This range accounts for the direct expenses for each fair. Create a **Column** chart using the **100% stacked column with a 3-D visual effect** chart type.

4. Accept the defaults in Step 2. In Step 3, insert **Direct Expenses** as the chart title. In Step 4, click the **As new sheet** option button. A 100% stacked chart lets you compare the relative expense category by location. This type of chart can be used in place of a pie chart when you want to compare parts of the whole—in this instance, direct expenses—across several categories—fair locations.

5. Change the font size of the chart title to **22** and the font color to **Red**. Change the font size of the value axis, the category axis, and the legend to **14**. Save your changes.

6. Click the **Category Axis**. On the Chart toolbar, click the **Angle Counterclockwise** button so that all the location names display.

7. Click the **Chart Objects arrow**, and then click **Walls**. Click the **Format Walls** button. Under **Area**, click **None**, and then click **OK**. The wall color is removed. Right-click the ivory **Food Service** series and click **Format Data Series**. Click the **Patterns tab** if necessary, and under **Border**, click the **Color arrow**, and then click **Red**. Click **OK**.

8. From the **View** menu, click **Header and Footer**. Create a custom footer with the file name in the **Left section**. Display the **Expenses** worksheet, and add a custom footer with the file name in the **Left section**.

9. In the **Expenses** worksheet, change cell **D5** to **350** and cell **E5** to **600** Save your changes.

10. Print both sheets. Close the workbook.

End You have completed Project 5I ─────────────────

Project 5J — Organization Chart

Objective: *Create a Diagram.*

The Greater Atlanta Job Fair has added a new department responsible for expanding to new markets in the southeastern United States. Executive Director Michael Augustino has drafted an outline for a new organizational structure and has requested that it be entered in the computer so that it can be distributed. In this Problem Solving exercise, you will use the diagram feature in Excel to create an organizational chart. You will save your workbook as *5J_Organizational_Chart_Firstname_Lastname.*

1. Open a new workbook. Use the **Diagram Gallery** to select the **Organizational Chart** diagram.

2. In the top box, type **Michael Augustino Executive Director**. The text will wrap within the box.

3. In the three subordinate boxes, enter the following names and titles:

   Janice Dawson Employer Coordinator

   Ben Ham Administrative Manager

   Derek Michaels Development Manager

4. Click the box containing **Janice Dawson**, and then click the **Insert Shape** button. In the new subordinate box, type **Yolanda Strickland**

5. Add a subordinate box to Ben Ham, and type **Janna Sharma** in the new box. Add a second subordinate box to Ben Ham, and type **Joseph Sorokin**

6. Save the file with your other files for this chapter as **5J_Organizational_Chart_Firstname_Lastname**

7. Use the resizing handles to expand the organizational chart area. Select the text in each box, and change the font to **14** pt. or the largest size that will fit in that box.

8. Click the **AutoFormat** button, and select a style of your choice. Adjust the font size as needed to ensure that the names and titles are fully displayed.

9. Enter an appropriate title in the first cell of the worksheet. Increase the font size to **20** pt., and center it over the organizational chart. In the footer area, in the left section insert the **File name**. Change the page orientation to **Landscape**.

10. Save your changes, print the worksheet, and then close the file.

 End **You have completed Project 5J** ─────────────────────

Project 5K — Revenue

Objectives: *Create and Modify a 3-D Pie Chart, Print a Chart, and Organize and Manage Worksheets.*

The Greater Atlanta Job Fair needs a chart that will show the profit contribution of each of the fairs to the total revenue stream. In this Problem Solving exercise, you will create and modify a 3-D chart to display the amount and percentage each location has contributed to total revenues for 2004. You will save your workbook as *5K_Revenue_Firstname_Lastname.*

1. Locate and open the file **e5K_Revenue** Save it with your other files as **5K_Revenue_Firstname_Lastname**

2. Select the cells containing the location names, and using , select the cells containing the net income (loss) figures for each location. (Hint: Do not include the row labels.)

3. Use the Chart Wizard to create a 3-D pie chart. Include an appropriate chart title, and save the chart on a separate sheet. Name the chart sheet **Revenue Distribution** and add a tab color of your choice. Name Sheet1 **2004 Results** and add a tab color.

4. Add data labels that include value and percentage. Drag the data labels away from the pie so that the leader lines display. Place the legend at the bottom of the chart. Increase the font size of the chart title to **20** pt., the data labels to **12** pt., and the legend to **12** pt.

5. Display the **3-D View** dialog box, and rotate the chart so that the largest piece is in the lower left (front) section of the pie. Pull this pie piece away from the pie and change its color to **Teal**. Change the two pieces on either side to a lighter color for contrast.

6. Add the file name to the left section of the footer for both the worksheets. Set the data worksheet to print in landscape orientation. Save your changes, and close the file.

End **You have completed Project 5K**

On the Internet

Graph Styles and Theory

In this chapter, you examined three basic types of charts. Understanding which type of chart to use to display the data appropriately takes some practice. Graph theory is a branch of mathematics that studies the use of graphs—charts in Excel terms. Some interesting Web sites are available to help you better understand different chart options and the type of data that can be illustrated graphically.

1. Open your browser, and in the address box type: **http://www.corda. com/examples/graph_styles**

2. Examine the different graph styles explained and illustrated on this Web site.

3. In the left panel, click **Examples**. The Corda examples Web page displays.

4. Under the **PopChart+OptiMap 5**, click **Weather Example**. This page shows several graph types used to display current weather conditions for a specific location.

5. Replace the displayed postal code with your postal code, and press Enter . Graphs related to the weather in your area are displayed. If necessary, scroll the page to see all the graphs.

6. Explore this Web site to discover some of the other uses for charts. When you are finished, close your browser.

Display Data on Two Scales

Sometimes you will have two data series where the range of numbers varies widely, such as population of a geographic area and the number in that population who are customers; or data types that are mixed, such as quantity and price. To display this type of information in a chart, you need two scales (values axes)—one on the left and one on the right.

1. **Start** Excel. In the **Type a question for help** box, type **Display data on two scales** Scroll through the list of topics that displays in the **Search Results** task pane.

2. From this list of help topics, click **Add a second axis** and read the results.

3. From the **Search Results** task pane, click the topic **About combination charts**. Read this topic, and then, at the top of the Microsoft Office Excel Help pane, click the **Print** button. Close the **Help** task panes.

4. Start a new worksheet. In range **A2:A11**, enter the years from 1996 through 2005. Select range **A2:A11** and use the **Format Cells** dialog box to format this range as **Text**, not numbers. (Note: Cell **A1** should be empty.)

5. In cell **B1**, type **Population** In cell **C1**, type **Customers** In range **B2:B11**, enter random numbers ranging from 1 million to 5 million. In range **C2:C11**, enter random numbers ranging from 10,000 to 100,000. Format the numbers with commas and no decimals.

6. Select the range **A1:C11** and click the **Chart Wizard** button. Click the **Custom Types tab** and select one of the two combination charts that uses two axes. If necessary, use the Help information to guide you through this process.

7. Complete the rest of the steps in the Chart Wizard to see your results.

8. Close the file without saving the results, and close Excel.

Excel 2003

6 chaptersix

Working with Templates, Large Worksheets, and Other File Formats

In this chapter, you will: complete these projects and practice these skills.

Project 6A Using Excel Templates	**Objective** • Use Excel Templates
Project 6B Working with Large Worksheets and Sharing Worksheets	**Objectives** • Work with a Large Worksheet • Prepare a Worksheet to Share with Others
Project 6C Using AutoFormats, Styles, Drawing Tools and the Research Feature	**Objectives** • Enhance Worksheets with AutoFormats and Styles • Use Drawing Tools and Use the Research Feature
Project 6D Using Goal Seek	**Objective** • Use Goal Seek

Lake Michigan City College

Lake Michigan City College is located along the lakefront of Chicago—one of the country's most exciting cities. The college serves its large and diverse student body and makes positive contributions to the community through relevant curricula, partnerships with businesses and nonprofit organizations, and learning experiences that allow students to be full participants in the global community. The college offers three associate degrees in 20 academic areas, adult education programs, and continuing education offerings on campus, at satellite locations, and online.

© Getty Images, Inc.

Working with Templates, Large Worksheets, and Other File Formats

In this chapter, you will use an Excel template to report expenses, work with a large worksheet, save a worksheet as a Web page, and save worksheets in other file formats for easy transportation of data. You will practice creating and applying styles to a worksheet and use the AutoFormat feature to format a worksheet. You will add drawing objects to a worksheet and insert text using the Research feature. Finally, you will use the Goal Seek function to determine the interest rate necessary to reach a desired investment goal.

Project 6A **Expense Report**

Excel offers several predefined templates that can be used for common financial reports such as an expense report, time card, balance sheet, sales invoice, or purchase order.

Clarence Krasnow, Director of Resource Development, needs to submit his expense report for the month of September, which must include the advance he received to cover expenses related to a conference he attended in Denver. In Activity 6.1, you will open and complete an Excel template for reporting expenses. Your completed worksheet will look similar to Figure 6.1. You will save your workbook as *6A_Expense_Report_ Firstname_Lastname.*

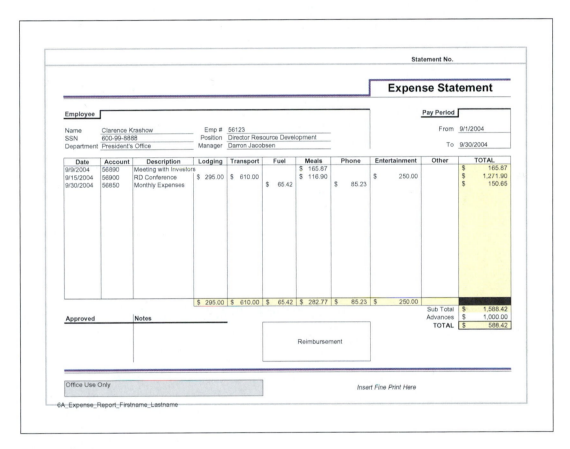

Figure 6.1
Project 6A—Expense Report

Objective 1
Use Excel Templates

A ***template*** is a workbook used as a pattern for creating other workbooks. Excel has several templates that you can use as the basis for creating common financial forms such as expense reports, time cards, and balance sheets. Templates are preformatted and have built-in formulas for performing calculations based on the data that you enter. The cells that contain the formulas are ***locked***, which prevents you from changing the formulas in the template.

Activity 6.1 Using an Excel Template

To open an Excel template, click the New command on the File menu. Alternatively, on the Getting Started task pane, click *Create a new workbook*, which will display the New Workbook task pane. From the New Workbook task pane, you can locate templates that are already on your computer or locate additional templates from the Web.

1 Start Excel. On the menu bar, click **File**, and then from the displayed list, click **New**.

The New Workbook task pane displays. From this task pane, you can locate templates from your computer or from the Web.

2 In the **New Workbook** task pane, under **Templates**, click **On my computer**. In the displayed **Templates** dialog box, click the **Spreadsheet Solutions tab**.

Several template options are available, as shown in Figure 6.2. The templates that display on your screen may not match the figure exactly.

Template options ——

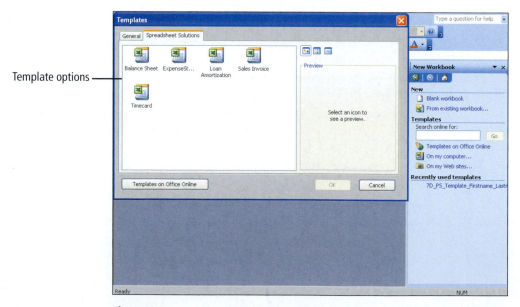

Figure 6.2

3 From the displayed templates, click **ExpenseStatement**, and then click **OK**.

The Expense Statement workbook opens at 85% zoom.

4 Change the zoom if necessary so that you can see the entire width of the worksheet on the screen, and then examine the form.

This template is used to report expenses. Notice that there is a bordered rectangle in the space next to *Name*. This is the active cell and the position at which you will begin entering data. Column labels are included in the body of the form—*Date*, *Description*, *Lodging*, and so forth. The ivory shaded areas contain formulas for calculating totals, and the cells there are locked so that you cannot enter anything in these areas or accidentally delete the formulas. See Figure 6.3.

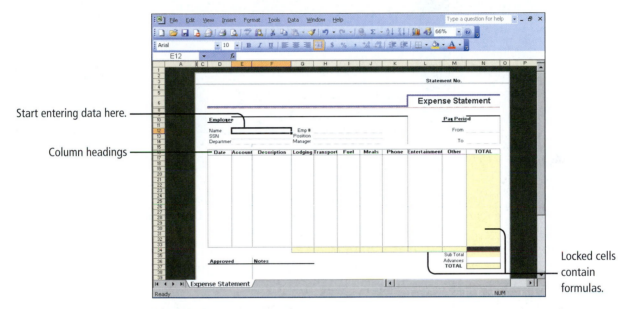

Start entering data here.

Column headings

Locked cells contain formulas.

Figure 6.3

5 Type **Clarence Krasnow** and press Tab.

The employee name is entered and the next *field*—a predefined area for a specific type of data—becomes the active cell. In this field, you will enter the employee number. In a form like this expense statement, categories of information are designated as fields, such as name, employee number, and social security number. Fields are useful because the information in a field can be gathered together in a database or used to create a report of all employees who have completed an expense report in a particular reporting period.

6 In the **Emp #** field, type **56123** and then press ⎡Tab⎤ to move to the **From**—beginning date—field. Notice the ScreenTip that displays with a message to tell you what information belongs in this field, as shown in Figure 6.4.

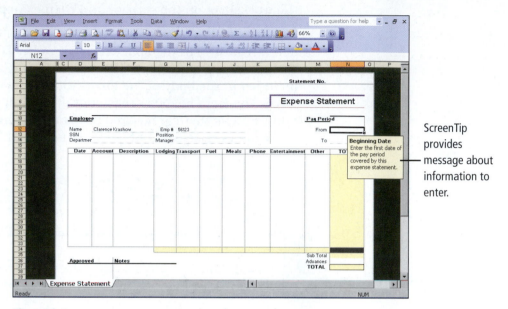

ScreenTip provides message about information to enter.

Figure 6.4

7 Type **9/1/04** and press ⎡Tab⎤ to move to the next field. In the **SSN** (Social Security Number) field, type **600-99-8888** and then press ⎡Tab⎤ to move to the **Position** field. Continue entering the data in the upper portion of the form as shown in the list that follows. If you make an error, hold down ⎡Shift⎤ and press ⎡Tab⎤ to move back one field at a time.

Position	**Director Resource Development**
Department	**President's Office**
Manager	**Darron Jacobsen**
To	**9/30/04**

The data for the upper portion of the form is complete.

8 If necessary, press ⎡Tab⎤ to move to the active cell under *Date*. Enter the information that follows. As you enter information for the expenses, not all categories or fields will be completed for each date. Press ⎡Tab⎤ as necessary to skip empty fields.

Date	Account	Description	Lodging	Transport	Fuel	Meals	Phone	Entertainment	Other
9/9/2004	56890	Meeting with Investors				165.87			
9/15/2004	56900	RD Conference	295.00	610.00		116.90		250.00	
9/30/2004	56850	Monthly Expenses			65.42		85.23		

Notice that as you enter monetary values, the ivory shaded areas at the right and end of the columns display the totals of the columns or rows. Compare your screen with Figure 6.5.

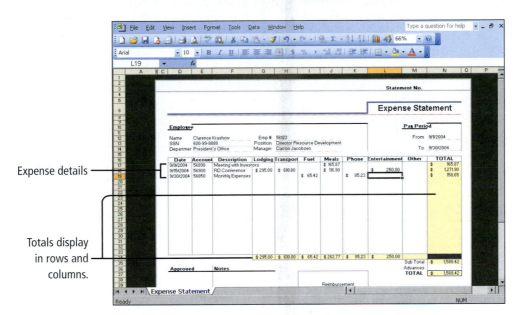

Expense details

Totals display in rows and columns.

Figure 6.5

9 From the **File** menu, click **Save As**. In the **Save As** dialog box, use the **Save in arrow** to navigate to the location where you are storing your files for this chapter, creating a new folder for Chapter 6 if you want to do so. In the **File name** box, delete the existing text and type **6A_Expense_Report_Firstname_Lastname** Click the **Save** button.

10 Try to click a cell in the ivory shaded areas on the Expense Statement report.

Notice that you cannot make any cell in the shaded areas the active cell. The cells are locked and may not be selected, thus protecting the formulas in these cells.

11 In the lower right side of the form, click in the white area to the right of *Advances*, read the displayed ScreenTip, type **1000** and then press Enter. Click in an empty white cell to close the ScreenTip that blocks the view of the total area.

The total amount is adjusted to reflect the advance that was given to this employee prior to the trip to the RD Conference. You can see that Krasnow needs to be reimbursed $588.42 for expenses.

12 From the **View** menu, click **Header and Footer**. Click the **Custom Footer** button. With the insertion point positioned in the **Left section**, click the **File name** button . Click **OK** twice.

13 On the Standard toolbar, click the **Save** button , and then click the **Print Preview** button to see the worksheet as it will print. Compare your worksheet with Figure 6.6. Click **Print**, and then click **OK**. Close the file, saving changes if prompted to do so.

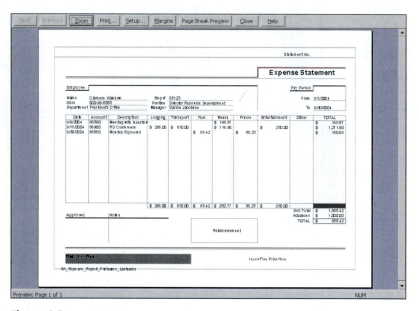

Figure 6.6

End **You have completed Project 6A** ───────────────────────

Project 6B **Class Schedule**

Worksheets are often wider and longer than a single screen can display. Techniques for navigating in a large worksheet are necessary to help locate and update information. When worksheets are shared with other people, it is sometimes necessary to save the files in different formats to accommodate the needs of others.

When you work with large worksheets, you can use various techniques to help you navigate the worksheet and quickly find the information you need. For example, you can sort specific rows, columns, or ranges of cells in a different order or look only at specific information. You can also view two worksheets at the same time. Samantha Pruett, coordinator of the computer courses for the Business division, needs to update some records and determine which classes still need instructors for the fall semester. In Activities 6.2 through 6.16, you will work with a large worksheet that lists the class schedule for the Business Office Systems and Computer Information Systems departments at Lake Michigan City College. Your completed worksheets will look similar to Figure 6.7. You will save your workbook as *6B_Class_Schedule_Firstname_Lastname.*

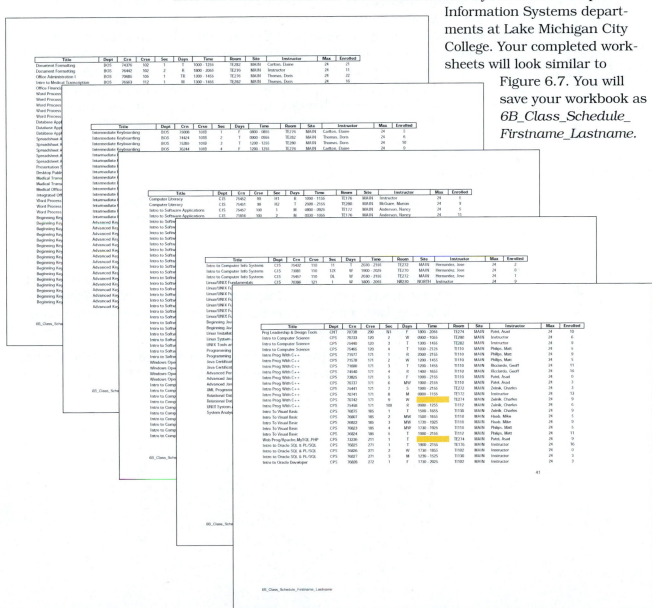

Figure 6.7
Project 6B—Class Schedule

Objective 2
Work with a Large Worksheet

You cannot view all the columns and rows of a large worksheet on your screen at one time. Therefore, Excel provides features that help you control what is displayed on the screen and navigate the worksheet to locate information quickly. For example, you can hide columns, sort information by rows and columns, and *filter* the data—limit the data displayed to match a stated condition. The **Freeze Panes** command is especially useful because it sets the column and row headings so that they remain on the screen while you scroll up and down the rows and across the columns. Finally, the Find and Replace command locates information anywhere in your worksheet.

Activity 6.2 Freezing and Unfreezing Panes

In a large worksheet, if you scroll down more than 30 rows or scroll across beyond column O (the exact row number and column letter varies, depending upon your screen resolution), you will no longer see row 1 or column A, where identifying information about the data is usually typed. Viewing cells that have no identifying row or column headings makes it practically impossible to work with data in any meaningful way. Fortunately, the Freeze Panes command allows you to select one or more rows or columns and freeze (lock) them into place. The locked rows and columns become separate *panes*. A pane is a portion of a worksheet window bounded by and separated from other portions by vertical or horizontal bars.

1 Start Excel. On the Standard toolbar, click the **Open** button 📂. Navigate to the location where the student files for this textbook are stored. Locate and open the file **e06B_Class_Schedule**.

2 From the **File** menu, click **Save As**. In the **Save As** dialog box, use the **Save in arrow** to navigate to the location where you are storing your files for this chapter. In the **File name** box, type **6B_Class_Schedule_Firstname_Lastname** Click the **Save** button. Scroll through the worksheet to examine the data.

The worksheet lists the computer courses that are available for the fall semester at Lake Michigan City College. See Figure 6.8.

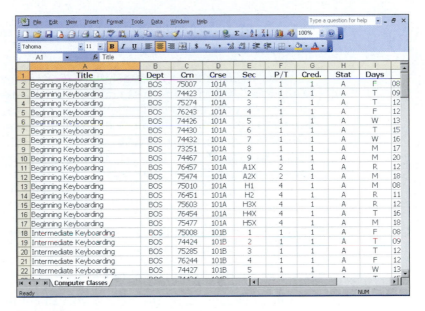

Figure 6.8

Note — Does Your Screen Look Different?

The amount of data that is displayed on your screen may be different than that shown in the figure. This is because of a difference in the resolution setting on your monitor. For newer monitors, the typical resolution setting is 1024 × 768 or higher. The figures in this book are shown at a resolution of 800 × 600, which displays fewer rows and columns at the same zoom setting.

3 Hold down Ctrl and press End to move to the last entry in the worksheet, cell **O170**. Notice that the column headings at the top and the course descriptions on the left are no longer in view, as shown in Figure 6.9.

You can see that working with data that has no identifying row and column headings makes it almost impossible to determine meaningful information from the displayed data.

Column headings do not display.

Course titles do not display.

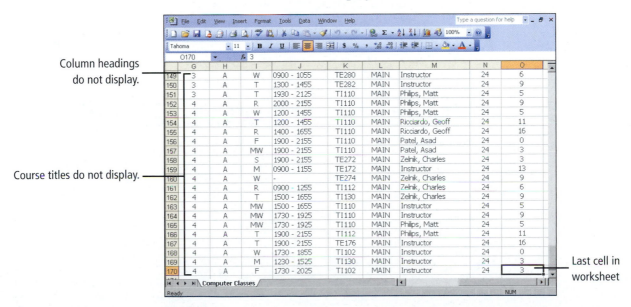

Last cell in worksheet

Figure 6.9

Columns are identified by capital letters. A reference to the cell in column O and row 5 is O5. Because a capital O looks a lot like a zero, use caution when referring to the O column in complex formulas. To identify the 26 columns to the right of column Z, the column headings are two letters that start with A, for example, AA, AB, AC, and so on. The next 26 columns start with B, for example, BA, BB, BC, and so on. The maximum number of columns in an Excel worksheet is 256.

4 Hold down [Ctrl] and press [Home] to move to cell **A1** at the upper left corner of the worksheet.

5 Click cell **B2**. From the **Window** menu, click **Freeze Panes**.

A line displays along the right border of column A and across the lower border of row 1. All the row(s) above the selected cell and all the column(s) to the left of the selected cell are frozen on the screen and will remain on the screen when you scroll through the worksheet.

6 Hold down [Ctrl] and press [End] to move to the last entry in the worksheet. Notice that the column headings display in **row 1** and the course titles display in **column A** on the left, as shown in Figure 6.10.

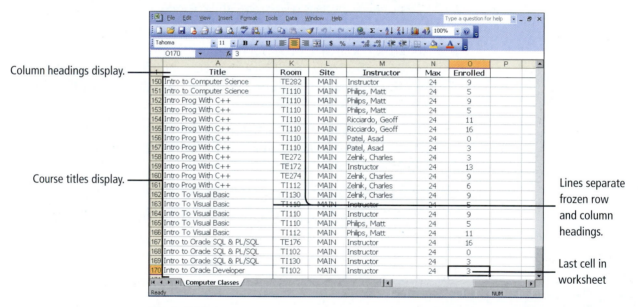

Column headings display.

Course titles display.

Lines separate frozen row and column headings.

Last cell in worksheet

Figure 6.10

7 Hold down (Ctrl) and press (Home) again to move back to cell **B2**, the location of the Freeze Panes command, which now functions as the home cell for the worksheet. At the bottom of the window, on the horizontal scroll bar, click the **right scroll arrow** three times.

Columns B, C, and D scroll off the screen to the left, but the identifying information in column A still displays.

8 In the lower right corner of the window, click the **down scroll arrow** five times.

Rows 2 through 6 scroll off the screen, but the identifying information in row 1 still displays.

9 Display the **Window** menu and notice that the Freeze Panes command has changed to *Unfreeze Panes*. Click **Window** again to close the menu without removing the Freeze Panes command.

The Freeze Panes command is a toggle switch that is used to activate or deactivate the command.

Activity 6.3 Finding and Replacing Information

The *Find* command can search for and locate specific data each time it occurs in your worksheet. Excel finds the data you specify and moves the active cell to its location. The *Replace* command finds specific data and then replaces it with data that you specify. You can instruct Excel to stop at each cell containing the data to be replaced, at which point you can decide whether or not to make the replacement. Alternatively, you can instruct Excel to replace all occurrences without waiting for your input. In a worksheet that is too big to reliably scan visually, the Find and Replace commands help you confirm that you have found all instances of specific data. In this activity, you will use the Find and Replace commands to change all occurrences of the course number for the Windows Operating System class from 117 to 107.

1 Press (Ctrl) + (Home) to return to the top of the worksheet. Be sure cell **B2** (the home cell in the unfrozen portion of the worksheet) is the active cell. From the **Edit** menu, click **Find**. Alternatively, press (Ctrl) + (F) as the keyboard shortcut.

The Find and Replace dialog box displays. Here you can locate specific information and search the worksheet by row or column to find matching text.

2 In the **Find what** box, type **117** and then click **Find Next**. The first occurrence of *117* is located, and cell **D119** becomes the active cell. If necessary, click the title bar of the **Find and Replace** dialog box and drag it out of the way so that you can see cell **D119**.

You can see that the Find command is useful if you are looking for a specific piece of data in a large worksheet.

3 In the **Find and Replace** dialog box, click the **Replace tab**.

The dialog box expands, and the *Replace with* box displays.

4 In the **Replace with** box, type **107** and then click **Replace**.

The first occurrence of *117* is replaced with *107*, and the next occurrence of *117* is located, as shown in Figure 6.11.

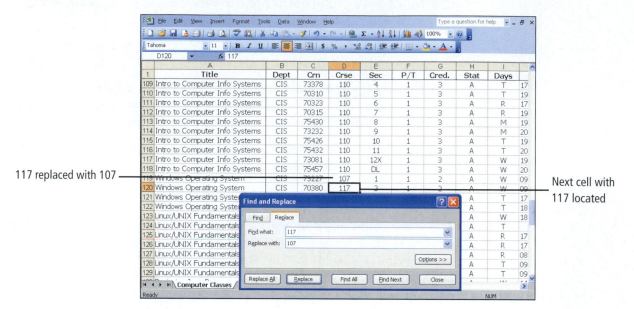

117 replaced with 107

Next cell with 117 located

Figure 6.11

5 In the **Find and Replace** dialog box, click **Replace All**.

A message box displays indicating that three instances of *117* have been found and replaced with *107*.

6 Click **OK** to acknowledge the message. In the **Find what** box, select **117**, and type **Applebee** In the **Replace with** box, select **107** and type **Applebee-Meyers** and then click **Find Next**.

The first occurrence of *Applebee* is located in cell M12. Before data can be replaced, you must first initiate the Find command.

7 Click **Replace All**.

A message box displays indicating that Excel has made eight replacements. Notice in cell M17 that the comma and first name of this instructor remain as part of the text in this cell. See Figure 6.12. Excel finds the data even if it is only part of a cell's contents.

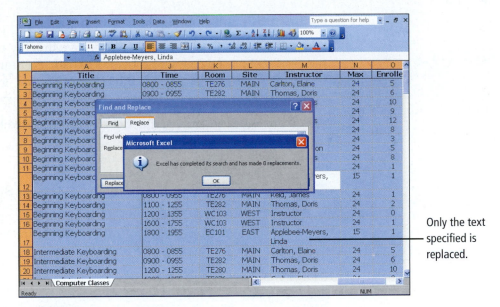

Only the text specified is replaced.

Figure 6.12

8 Click **OK** to acknowledge the message box, and then click **Close** in the **Find and Replace** dialog box.

The rows containing Applebee-Meyers expand, and the name wraps to a second line.

9 In the **column heading area**, drag the right border of **column M** to a width of **180 pixels**. Click the **Select All** box in the upper left corner of the worksheet (to the left of **column A** and above **row 1**). With the entire worksheet selected, display the **Format** menu, point to **Row**, and then click **AutoFit**.

The *Instructor* column expands to display the names without wrapping, and the rows readjust to the same height.

10 Press [Ctrl] + [Home] to cancel the selection of the worksheet and move to cell **B2**, the home cell in the unfrozen portion of the worksheet. On the Standard toolbar, click the **Save** button [icon].

More Knowledge — Find and Replace Options

The Options button in the Find and Replace dialog box enables you to control the Find operation by defining specific characteristics. For example, you can specify a format for data that is bold and italic, and Excel will locate only cells that have that formatting. Or, you can match the case—uppercase or lower-case letters—or match only the entire content of cells. You can also search an entire workbook so that all matching cells are located throughout the entire workbook rather than on only a single worksheet.

Because Excel finds and replaces part of the content of a cell, it is important to be cautious when using the Replace All button so that you do not replace data unintentionally. If the number of changes seems too high, you can always click the Undo button, and then review each replacement before agreeing to the change.

Activity 6.4 Using the Go To Command

You can use the Go To command to move quickly to a specific cell or range of cells in a large worksheet. The Go To command can also be used to move to cells that have special characteristics, for example, to cells that are blank or to cells that contain constants (as opposed to formulas).

1 From the **Edit** menu, click **Go To**. Alternatively, press [Ctrl] + [G] to use the keyboard shortcut.

The Go To dialog box displays.

2 At the bottom of the **Go To** dialog box, click **Special**.

The Go To Special dialog box displays. You can use this dialog box to move to cells that contain the various special options listed. See Figure 6.13.

Go To Special options

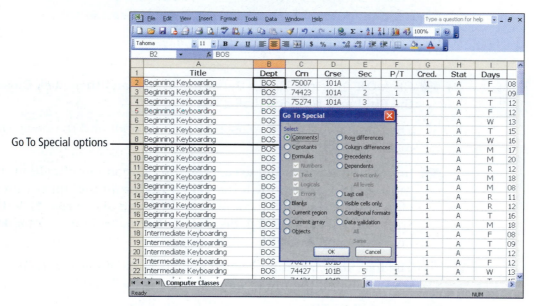

Figure 6.13

3 In the first column, click the **Blanks** option button, and then click **OK**.

The blank cells in the *active area* of the worksheet are located, and the first blank cell displays on the screen as the active cell. The active area is the area of the worksheet that contains data or has contained data—it does not include any empty cells that have not been used in this worksheet. Cell J124 is missing the time for a Linux/UNIX class held on Tuesday.

4 On the Formatting toolbar, click the **Fill Color (Yellow)** button .

The missing information needs to be researched before a time can be entered, and the yellow fill color will help locate this cell later, when you have determined the correct time for the class.

5 Scroll down the screen and locate the other two cells identified as blank—**J148** and **J160**.

When you initiated the Go To command for Blank cells, Excel located and selected all blank cells in the active area. Thus, the formatting you applied to the first blank cell, yellow fill, was applied to all the selected cells. See Figure 6.14.

Missing information highlighted

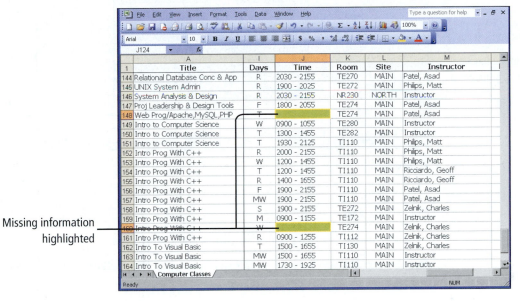

Figure 6.14

6 On the Standard toolbar, click the **Save** button.

Activity 6.5 Using the COUNTIF Function

The **COUNTIF** function counts the number of cells within a range that meet a certain condition. For example, in this worksheet, Samantha Pruett needs to determine how many classes have not been assigned to a specific faculty member. When a class is unassigned, the word *Instructor* displays in column M—the Instructor column.

1 Press Ctrl + End to move to the end of the active area in the worksheet, and then scroll as necessary to click in cell **M172**.

In this cell you are going to use the COUNTIF function to construct a formula that will count the number of times the word *Instructor* occurs in column M. The title of the column, *Instructor*, displays in cell M1. Thus, the range used in the formula will start with cell M2.

2 On the Formula Bar, click the **Insert Function** button to display the **Insert Function** dialog box. Click the **Or select a category arrow** and click **Statistical**. Under **Select a function**, scroll as necessary and click **COUNTIF**. Compare your screen with Figure 6.15.

The COUNTIF function has two arguments—the range of cells to be evaluated and the *criteria*—the conditions on which cells will be evaluated.

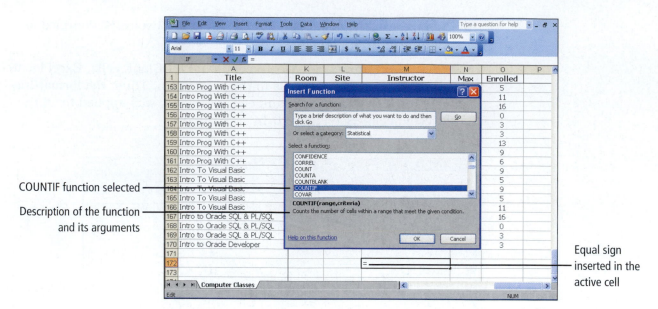

COUNTIF function selected

Description of the function and its arguments

Equal sign inserted in the active cell

Figure 6.15

3 Click **OK**.

The Function Arguments dialog box displays.

4 In the **Range** box, type **m2:m170** and in the **Criteria** box, type **Instructor**

Compare your screen with Figure 6.16.

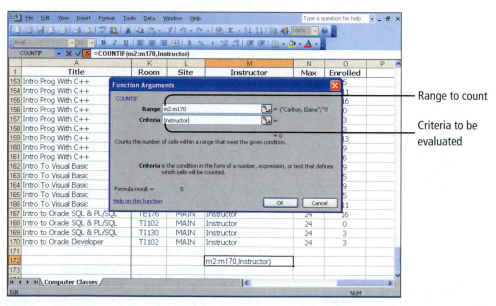

Range to count

Criteria to be evaluated

Figure 6.16

5 Click **OK**.

The result—*47*—displays in cell M172. This is the number of classes that, as yet, have no specific instructor assigned.

6 On the Standard toolbar, click the **Save** button.

Activity 6.6 Hiding and Unhiding Columns

In the next three activities, you will assign some classes to specific instructors. In a large worksheet, it is easier to work if you hide columns that are not necessary for the immediate task. You may also need to hide columns or rows to control the data that will print or to remove confidential information from view. For example, if you wanted to create a summary report, you could hide the columns between the row headings and the totals column, and the hidden columns would not display on the printed worksheet, resulting in a summary report.

1 Press Ctrl + Home. Scroll as necessary to view **columns F**, **G**, and **H** on your screen, and then select **columns F:H**.

2 From the **Format** menu, point to **Column**, and then, from the displayed list, click **Hide**.

Columns F, G, and H are hidden from view. Notice that the column labels skip from E to I, as shown in Figure 6.17. A dark line displays between columns E and I to indicate that columns from this location are hidden from view. After you click in another cell, however, this line will not be visible.

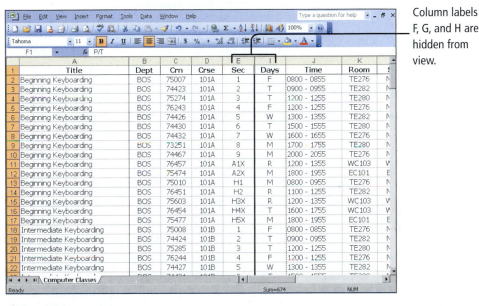

Column labels F, G, and H are hidden from view.

Figure 6.17

3 Select **columns E:I**.

To redisplay hidden columns, first select the columns on either side of the hidden columns, in this instance, columns E and I. Look for column or row headings that are missing letters or numbers in the sequence to determine whether a worksheet contains any hidden columns or rows.

4 From the **Format** menu, point to **Column**, and then click **Unhide**.

Columns F, G, and H redisplay.

5 Select **columns F**, **G**, and **H** again; right-click the selected columns and, from the shortcut menu, click **Hide**.

Columns F, G, and H are again hidden from view. You can also use the shortcut menu to hide or unhide selected columns or rows.

Activity 6.7 Arranging Workbooks and Splitting Worksheets

If you need to refer to information in one workbook while you have another workbook open, instead of jumping back and forth between the two workbooks, you can arrange the window to display sheets from more than one workbook. This is accomplished by using the Arrange command. Additionally, you can view separate parts of the same worksheet on your screen by using the Split command. This command helps you split the window into two or more panes.

1 With your **6B_Class_Schedule** workbook on the screen, on the Standard toolbar, click the **Open** button 📂. Navigate to the location where the student files for this textbook are stored. Locate and open the file **e06B_Requests**.

The *Requests* file opens, and the *Class Schedule* file is no longer visible on your screen. You will use the Requests file to find instructors to assign to unassigned classes based on requests that instructors have made. This worksheet shows a list of instructors who have sent in requests for classes they would like to teach. It is not necessary to save this file using a different name because you will not be making any changes to it.

2 Display the **Window** menu and, at the bottom of the list, click your **6B_Class_Schedule** file to make it the active worksheet.

You can use the Window menu to select which worksheet is currently displayed. Alternatively, click the Excel file name icon displayed in the taskbar at the bottom of your screen.

3 From the **Window** menu, click **Arrange**.

The Arrange Windows dialog box displays. See Figure 6.18. This dialog box is used to control how two or more worksheets from multiple workbooks are arranged on the screen.

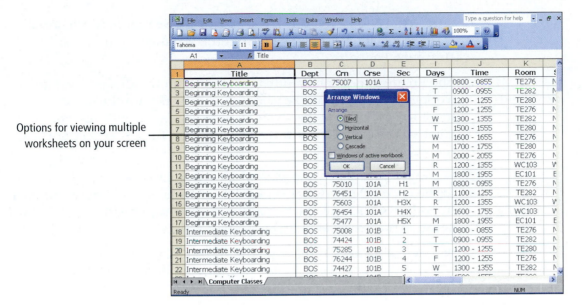

Options for viewing multiple worksheets on your screen

Figure 6.18

4 Click **Horizontal**, and then click **OK**.

The screen is split horizontally, and the *Requests* worksheet displays below the *Class Schedule* worksheet. The active window displays scroll bars, and its title bar displays in a darker shade of blue. See Figure 6.19.

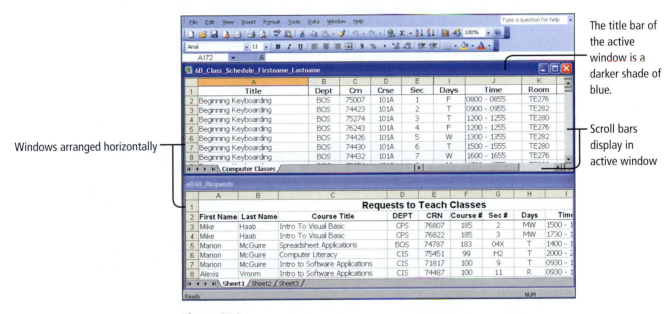

The title bar of the active window is a darker shade of blue.

Scroll bars display in active window

Windows arranged horizontally

Figure 6.19

5 If necessary, click the title bar of the **Class Schedule** worksheet to make it the active worksheet. From the **Window** menu, click **Unfreeze Panes**.

The Freeze Panes command is removed from the *Class Schedule* worksheet. When multiple worksheets are open on the screen, you must select the worksheet you want to activate before you choose a command. To activate a worksheet, click on the worksheet or click the worksheet's title bar.

6 With the **Class Schedule** worksheet active, press Ctrl + End to move to the end of the active area of the worksheet, scroll to view **column A**, and then click cell **A172**. On the vertical scroll bar, click the **down scroll arrow** twice so that you can see several empty rows.

You are going to split this window horizontally at row 172 so that you can view cell M172, which displays the number of classes that still need to have instructors assigned.

7 From the **Window** menu, click **Split**. Scroll to the right to display cell **M172**.

A gray horizontal bar displays at the top of row 172, as shown in Figure 6.20. Notice that there are two vertical scroll bars in the Class Schedule worksheet, one in each of the two worksheet parts displayed in this window.

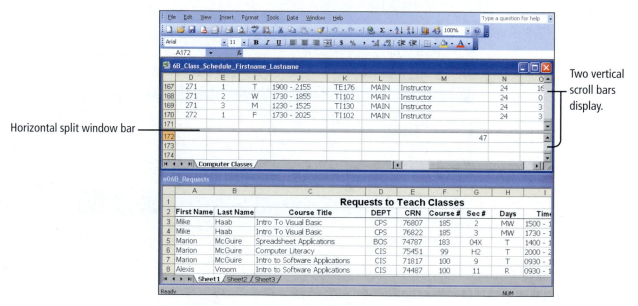

Figure 6.20

8 In the **Class Schedule** worksheet, scroll to the left. Above the split bar, click in any cell in **column C**. Press Ctrl + F to display the **Find and Replace** dialog box.

Column C lists the CRN—Course Registration Number—for each class. This is a unique number that identifies each class. You will use this information to locate the classes that need to be filled.

9 Look at the first request in the **Requests** worksheet, which is from Mr. Haab to teach Intro to Visual Basic. The CRN for this course is 76807. In the **Find what** box, type **76807** so that you can locate the course in the Class Schedule.

10 Click **Find Next**.

CRN 76807 is located in cell C163 of the Class Schedule worksheet.

11 Drag the **Find and Replace** dialog box out of the way—to the upper left of your screen. Verify that the information for this class in **row 163** of the **Class Schedule** worksheet matches the information listed in **row 3** of the **Requests** worksheet.

12 In the **Class Schedule** worksheet, scroll to the right, click in cell **M163**, type **Haab, Mike** to delete *Instructor*, and assign the class to Mr. Haab. Press Enter.

The class is assigned to Mr. Haab, and the total number of classes that still need to be assigned changes to 46. Compare your screen with Figure 6.21.

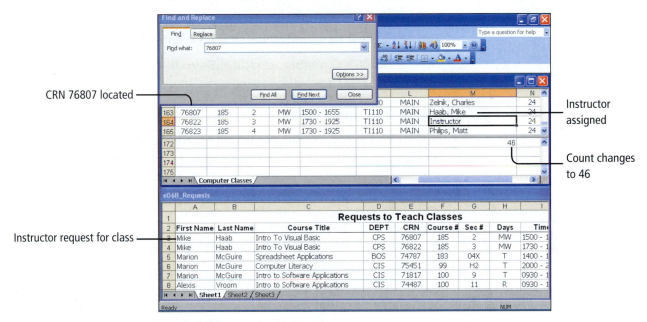

CRN 76807 located

Instructor assigned

Count changes to 46

Instructor request for class

Figure 6.21

13 In the **Requests** worksheet, look at **row 4** and notice that the next class that Mr. Haab requested to teach is also a Visual Basic class—CRN 76822.

This class is listed in the next row of the Class Schedule worksheet—row 164.

14 In the **Class Schedule** worksheet, verify that the course in **row 164** is the same class—CRN 76822. In cell **M164**, type **Haab, Mike** and when his name displays in the cell, press Enter to accept the AutoComplete suggestion.

The second class is assigned, and the total number of classes that needs to be assigned changes to 45.

15 In the **Find and Replace** dialog box, in the **Find what** box, type **74787** (the next requested CRN), and then click **Find Next**.

CRN 74787 in cell C66 is selected. This is the class that displays in row 5 of the Requests worksheet. Marion McGuire has requested to teach this class.

16 Click cell **M66**, type **McGuire, Marion** and then press Enter.

17 Continue to use the **Find and Replace** dialog box to locate the next three **CRNs** listed in the **Request** worksheet, and enter the appropriate instructor name for each class in **column M** of the **Class Schedule** worksheet.

After you have entered instructors for all six requests, there are 41 classes remaining that need to have instructors assigned.

18 Click **Close** in the **Find and Replace** dialog box. Click the **Requests** worksheet to make it active, and then click its **Close** button ❎.

19 From the **Window** menu, click **Remove Split**. On the **Class Schedule** title bar, click the **Maximize** button 🔲 to restore the size of the worksheet to its full size.

The worksheet expands again to fill the window.

20 On the Standard toolbar, click the **Save** button 💾 to save the changes to the **Class Schedule** worksheet.

Activity 6.8 Sorting a Worksheet

You can sort data in a worksheet based on the data in a row or a column. For example, in the Class Schedule worksheet, you could sort the data by the number of students enrolled (column N) from the lowest to the highest number. You could further sort in this manner within each department (column B). To sort a worksheet by a single column, you can use the Sort Ascending or Sort Descending buttons located on the Standard toolbar. To sort on more than one column, use the Sort dialog box.

1 Press Ctrl + Home to move to cell **A1**. Scroll down the worksheet and notice that the data is currently sorted first on **column B**—alphabetic by department. Within each department, the data is further sorted numerically on **column D—Crse**. Within each Crse group, the data is further sorted by **column E—Sec**.

The departments listed are BOS, CIS, CNT, and CPS. The course numbers are in *ascending* order—from the lowest number to the highest—within the department. Within each course number, the classes are sorted by section number—Sec. All the BOS courses are listed, and then all the CIS courses are listed, followed by CNT and CPS courses.

2 Scroll back to the top of the worksheet. From the **Data** menu, click **Sort**.

All the worksheet data in the active area is selected, and the Sort dialog box displays. From the Sort dialog box, you can sort on up to three columns of data.

3 Click the **Sort by arrow** and from the displayed list, click **Enrolled**. Be sure the **Ascending** option button is selected. Compare your **Sort** dialog box with the one shown in Figure 6.22.

This action will sort the data based on the numbers in column O—the enrollment number—with courses having the lowest enrollment listed first.

Worksheet will be sorted by number of students enrolled.

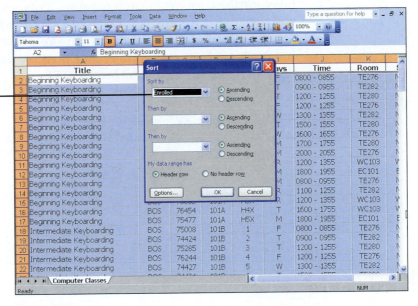

Figure 6.22

4 In the **Sort** dialog box, click **OK**. Scroll to the right so that you can see **column O**—Enrolled.

The data is sorted. The classes that have zero enrollments are listed first, as shown in Figure 6.23.

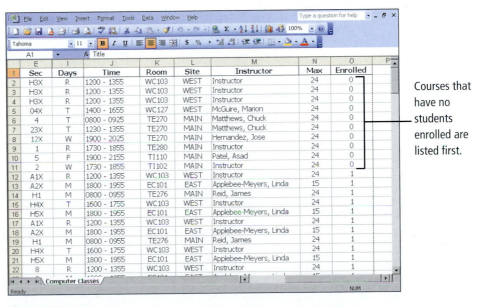

Courses that have no students enrolled are listed first.

Figure 6.23

5 From the **Data** menu, click **Sort**. Click the **Sort by arrow**, and then click **Days**. Click the first **Then by arrow** and then, from the displayed list, click **Time**. Click the second **Then by arrow** and then, from the displayed list, click **Room**. Be sure the **Ascending** option button is selected for all three sorts. Be sure the **Header row** option button is selected. See Figure 6.24.

The first row of the data is identified as a header row because it is a label for the content in each column. This sort will help determine whether there are any conflicts with room assignments. The data will first be sorted alphabetically by the *Days* field, which is known as the **major** sort, then by *Time*, and then by *Room*. The second and third sorts are known as **minor** sorts.

Data will be sorted on three columns.

Header row option selected

All sorts to be performed in Ascending order

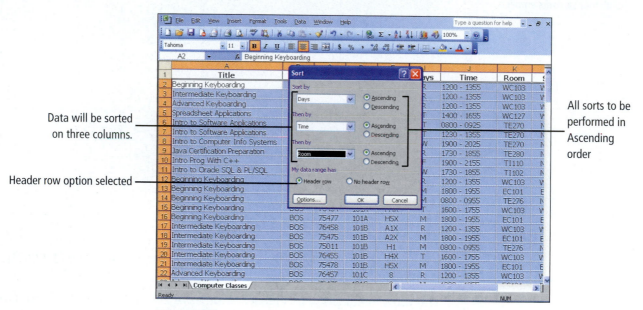

Figure 6.24

6 In the **Sort** dialog box, click **OK**. Compare your screen with Figure 6.25.

The data is sorted. Because the days are sorted alphabetically, F (for *Friday*) is listed first, and then the times for the Friday classes are sorted in ascending order. Within the Friday group, the classes are further sorted from the earliest to the latest. Within each time period, the data is further sorted by room.

Keyboarding classes on Friday —

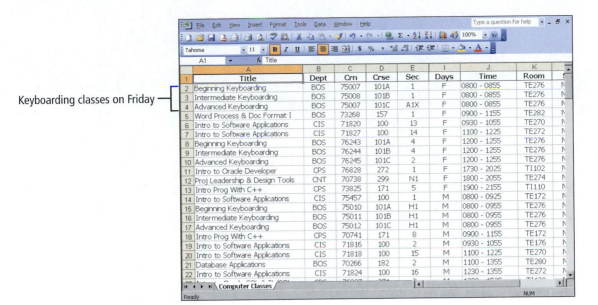

Figure 6.25

7 Examine the sorted data. Notice that the first three classes listed are on *Friday*, at *8:00*, in room *TE276*, with *Elaine Carlton* as the instructor.

These are all keyboarding classes, and the instructor teaches the three levels of keyboarding at the same time.

8 Scroll down until **rows 50** and **51** are in view. Notice that two *Visual Basic* classes are scheduled on *MW* at *17:30*—5:30—in room *TE110* with two different instructors listed.

This is a conflict of classroom assignment that will need to be resolved. Sorting data can help you identify such problems.

9 Press Ctrl + Home to make cell **A1** active again. From the **Data** menu, click **Sort**. Click the **Sort by arrow** and then, from the displayed list, click **Dept**. Click the first **Then by arrow** and click **Crse**. Click the second **Then by arrow**, click **Sec**, and then click **OK**.

The data is resorted. The sort is not identical to the original pattern, however, because Excel first sorts the course numbers that contain only numbers, and then sorts the course numbers that include letters, such as 101A, 101B, and 101C.

Activity 6.9 Using AutoFilter to Limit the Data Displayed

Another technique you can use when you are working with a large worksheet is to *filter*—limit the data displayed to match a specific condition.

1 If necessary, press Ctrl + Home to return to cell **A1**. From the **Data** menu, point to **Filter**, and then, from the displayed list, click **AutoFilter**.

Filter arrows are displayed next to each column heading, as shown in Figure 6.26.

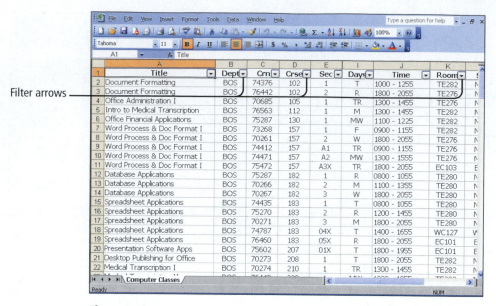

Filter arrows

Figure 6.26

2 In the **Instructor** column—**column M**—click the **Filter arrow**.

The list displays the names of the instructors assigned to classes. At the top of the list you can choose to display *All*, the *Top 10*, or a *Custom* list.

3 From the displayed list, click **Hernandez, Jose**.

Four classes are listed for Mr. Hernandez, as shown in Figure 6.27. Only the matching rows are displayed; all the other rows are hidden. The row numbers displayed on the left are the rows where this information is found. The color of the Filter arrow changes to indicate that a filter is applied.

4 In the **Instructor** column—**column M**—click the **Filter arrow**, scroll to the top of the list, and then click **All**.

All the rows display.

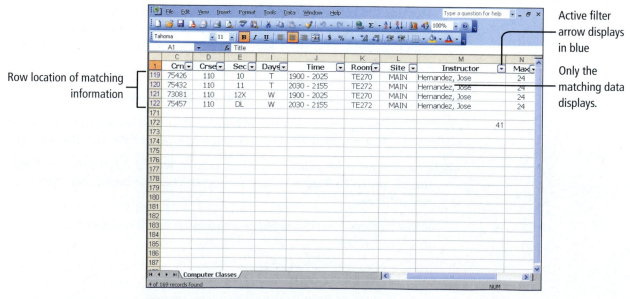

Row location of matching information

Active filter arrow displays in blue

Only the matching data displays.

Figure 6.27

5 In the **Dept** column—**column B**—click the **Filter arrow**, and then click **CPS**. In the **Crse** column—**column D**—click the **Filter arrow**, and then click **171**.

Only the CPS course 171 displays. In this manner, you can apply filters to multiple columns.

6 In **column B**, click the **Filter arrow**, and then click **All**. In **column D**, click the **Filter arrow**, and then click **All**. Alternatively, display the Data menu, point to Filter, and then click Show All.

All the records redisplay.

7 From the **Data** menu, point to **Filter**, and then click **AutoFilter**.

The filter arrows are removed. The AutoFilter command is a toggle command—click it once to turn it on, click it again to turn it off.

8 On the Standard toolbar, click the **Save** button.

Objective 3
Prepare a Worksheet to Share with Others

You can share a worksheet with others by printing and distributing paper copies, sending it electronically, or displaying it as a Web page. Other people with whom you share the worksheet may not have the Excel program or may need it in a different format. You can save an Excel file as a text file or as a **comma separated value (CSV)** file, which inserts a comma between the data in each cell in a row and eliminates the boxed cell structure entirely. This format can be read by other programs that work with data, including most database programs. You can also add a **hyperlink** to a worksheet, which, when clicked, takes you to another location in the worksheet, to another file, or to a Web page on the Internet or on your organization's intranet. In the following activities, you will prepare the Course Schedule worksheet to share with faculty and to post to the college Web site. To prepare this schedule, you will need to refer to another workbook that shows instructor contact information.

Activity 6.10 Previewing and Modifying Page Breaks

Before you print a large worksheet, preview it to see where the pages will break across the columns and rows. You can move the page breaks to a column or row that groups the data logically, and you can change the orientation between portrait and landscape if you want to display more rows on the page (portrait) or more columns on the page (landscape). You can also **scale** the data to force the worksheet into a selected number of pages.

1 With your **Class Schedule** worksheet displayed, press Ctrl + Home to return to cell **A1**. On the Standard toolbar, click the **Print Preview** button. On the Print Preview toolbar, click the **Next** button seven times to view the eight pages required to print this worksheet.

As you view each page, notice that pages 5 through 8 display the time, room, site, and instructor related to the first four pages of the printout. The printed worksheet would be easier to read if all the information related to a class were on the same page.

2 From the Print Preview toolbar, click **Page Break Preview**. If the **Welcome to Page Break Preview** dialog box displays, close it.

The Page Break Preview window displays. Blue dashed lines show where the page breaks are in the current setup for this worksheet. Compare your screen with Figure 6.28.

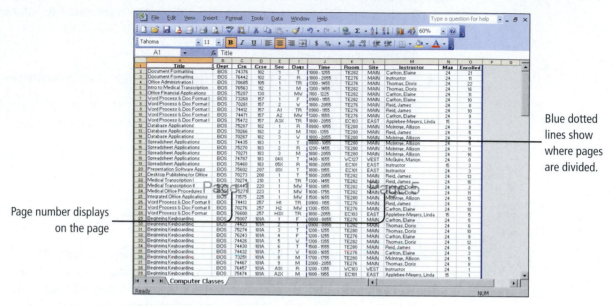

Page number displays on the page

Blue dotted lines show where pages are divided.

Figure 6.28

Note — A Dialog Box May Display

A Welcome to Page Break Preview dialog box may display with a message informing you that page breaks can be adjusted by clicking and dragging the breaks with your mouse. If this box displays, click OK to close it.

3 Scroll down to view the other pages and see where the page breaks are indicated. From the **View** menu, click **Normal** to redisplay the worksheet.

The Page Break view closes, and the Worksheet returns to the screen. When you are looking at the page breaks, the worksheet displays in a different view. When you close this view, the normal worksheet window returns—not the Print Preview window. Dashed lines display at the page break locations on the worksheet.

4 From the **File** menu, click **Page Setup**. On the **Page tab**, under **Orientation**, click **Landscape**. Under **Scaling**, click the **Fit to** option button. Be sure *1* displays in the **page(s) wide by** box, and then type **4** in the **tall** box.

The worksheet will print horizontally across the page with the time, room, site, and instructor information on the same row as the related class information.

5 Click the **Header/Footer tab**. Click **Custom Footer** and with the insertion point in the **Left section**, click the **File Name** button. Click **OK** twice.

6 On the Standard toolbar, click the **Print Preview** button.

The Print Preview window displays. Notice in the lower left corner that the worksheet has been reduced to four pages. Each complete row of data will fit on one page.

7 On the Print Preview toolbar, click **Page Break Preview**. If necessary, click **OK** to close the **Welcome to Page Break Preview** dialog box. Scroll down to display the page break between **Page 2** and **Page 3**.

The page break needs to be adjusted so that a break occurs between the BOS courses and the CIS courses so that separate printouts can be sent to the BOS and CIS department heads.

8 Point to the horizontal page break line between **Page 2** and **Page 3**.

When the vertical resize pointer displays, drag the line up between **row 76** and **row 77**. Compare your screen with Figure 6.29.

Page break line moved —

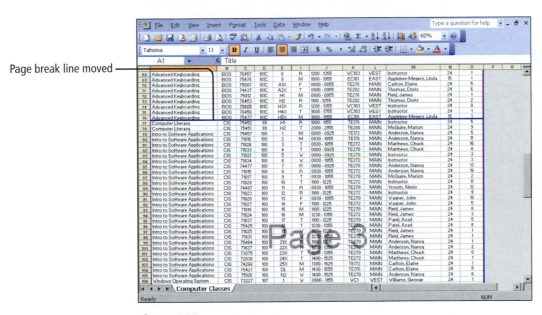

Figure 6.29

9 Scroll down to see the page break line between **Page 4** and **Page 5**. Drag the line up to break the page between **row 146** and **row 147**, which is the end of the CIS section.

10 On the Standard toolbar, click the **Print Preview** button. Click **Next** four times to scroll through the five pages that will print.

The BOS, CIS, and CNT/CPS courses will print on separate pages.

11 On the Print Preview toolbar, click **Normal View**. On the Standard toolbar, click the **Save** button.

Activity 6.11 Repeating Column or Row Headings

When a large worksheet is printed on several pages, you will usually want to repeat the column headings and, if necessary, the row headings on each page.

1 On the Standard toolbar, click the **Print Preview** button. On the Print Preview toolbar, click **Next** several times to view the pages.

Notice that the column headings display only on Page 1 and on none of the remaining pages. Repeating the column headings on each page will make it easier to understand and read the information on the printed pages.

2 On the Print Preview toolbar, click **Close**. From the **File** menu, click **Page Setup**. In the **Page Setup** dialog box, click the **Sheet tab**.

Here you can select rows to repeat at the top of each page or columns to repeat at the left of each page. To have access to this printing command, you must display the Page Setup dialog box from the Page Setup command on the File menu. It is not available from the Setup button on the Print Preview toolbar.

3 Under **Print titles**, click in the **Rows to repeat at top** box, and then, in the worksheet, click cell **A1**.

A moving border surrounds row 1, and the mouse pointer displays as a black select row arrow. The absolute reference $1:$1 displays in the Rows to repeat at top box. See Figure 6.30.

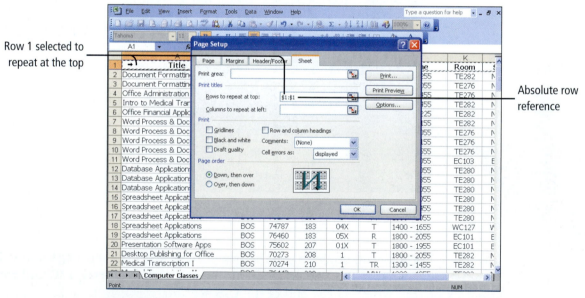

Row 1 selected to repeat at the top

Absolute row reference

Figure 6.30

More Knowledge — Using Expand and Collapse Boxes

On the Sheet tab of the Page Setup dialog box, the *Rows to repeat at top* box and the *Columns to repeat at left* box have the expand and collapse characteristic that you used previously in the function dialog boxes. Boxes that have this feature display a collapse arrow at the right side of the box that is used to collapse the larger dialog box so that you can see more of the worksheet. The destination box you are working with remains on the screen, and the arrow at the right end of the box changes to an expand arrow. This makes it easier to drag the reference area you want included in the box. After you select the reference area, click the expand arrow at the end of the collapsed box to redisplay the full dialog box and continue with the next action.

4 Click **OK**.

The Page Setup dialog box closes.

5 Press Ctrl + G to display the **Go To** box. In the **Go To** box, under **Reference**, type **k172** and press Enter.

You can use the Go To box to move to a specific cell on the worksheet. A label needs to be added to identify the number that displays in cell M172.

6 In cell **K172**, type **Unassigned classes:** and press Enter.

7 On the Standard toolbar, click the **Save** button 🖫, and then click the **Print Preview** button 🔍. On the Print Preview toolbar, click **Next**.

The second page displays, and the column headings from row 1 display at the top, as shown in Figure 6.31.

Column headings display on page 2.

Figure 6.31

8 Click **Next** to view the remaining pages of the worksheet, and notice the column headings on each page and the label at the end of the worksheet to identify the number of unassigned classes. Verify that the page breaks are still located between each department and make any adjustments that may be necessary. On the Print Preview toolbar, click **Print**, and then click **OK**. Save your changes.

The five pages of the worksheet print.

Activity 6.12 Inserting a Hyperlink in a Worksheet

Recall that a hyperlink is colored and underlined text that you click to go to a file, a location in a file, a Web page on the World Wide Web, or a Web page on your organization's intranet. Hyperlinks can be attached to text or to graphics. In this activity, you will add a hyperlink that will open a file that contains the instructors' names, phone numbers, office locations, and email addresses.

1 Press Ctrl + Home to move to cell **A1**. Scroll to the right and click cell

M1. On the Standard toolbar, click the **Insert Hyperlink** button. Alternatively, display the Insert menu and click Hyperlink.

The Insert Hyperlink dialog box displays.

2 On the **Link to** bar, if necessary, click **Existing File or Web Page**. Click the **Look in arrow** and navigate to the location where the student files for this textbook are stored. Click the **e06B_Faculty** file to select it.

The selected file contains the faculty phone numbers, office locations, and email addresses.

3 In the upper right corner of the **Insert Hyperlink** dialog box, click the **ScreenTip** button.

The Set Hyperlink ScreenTip dialog box displays.

4 In the **ScreenTip text** box, type **Click here for contact information**

When you point to the hyperlink on the worksheet, this is the text of the ScreenTip that will display. Compare your dialog box with the one shown in Figure 6.32.

ScreenTip text

File location

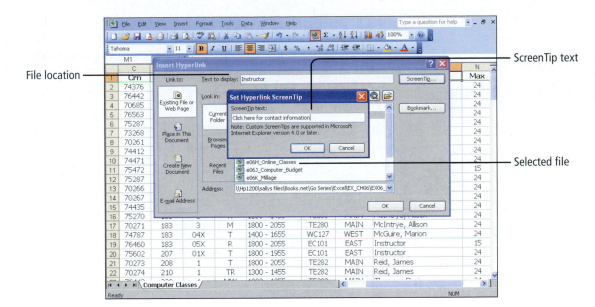

Selected file

Figure 6.32

5 Click **OK** in the **Set Hyperlink ScreenTip** dialog box, and then click **OK** in the **Insert Hyperlink** dialog box.

The Instructor column heading is blue and underlined, indicating a hyperlink.

6 Point to the **Instructor hyperlink** and read the ScreenTip that displays.

When you point to the hyperlink, the Link Select mouse pointer displays ⬛ and the ScreenTip text you entered displays, as shown in Figure 6.33.

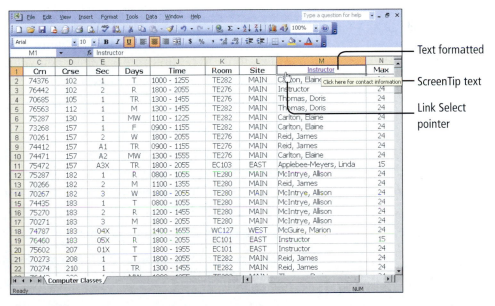

Text formatted

ScreenTip text

Link Select pointer

Figure 6.33

7 Click the **Instructor hyperlink**.

The Faculty file opens and displays the contact information for each faculty member, as shown in Figure 6.34. Additionally, the Web toolbar displays.

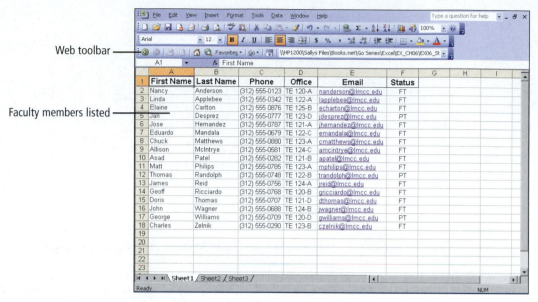

Web toolbar

Faculty members listed

Figure 6.34

8 On the Web toolbar, click the **Back** button .

The Class Schedule returns to the screen. The Instructor link changes color to indicate that it has been selected at least once.

9 On the Standard toolbar, click the **Save** button .

Activity 6.13 Modifying a Hyperlink

If the file to which the hyperlink refers is moved or renamed or a Web page to which a hyperlink refers gets a new address, the hyperlink needs to be modified to reflect the change.

1 On the Web toolbar, click the **Forward** button .

The Faculty worksheet displays.

2 From the **File** menu, click **Save As**. In the **Save As** dialog box, use the **Look in arrow** to navigate to the location where you are saving your files. In the **File name** box, type **6B_Faculty_Firstname_Lastname** and then click **Save**.

The file is saved in a new location with a new name.

3 To the right of the **Type a question for help** box, click the small **Close Window** button to close the Faculty file.

The Class Schedule file displays on your screen.

4 Right-click cell **M1**—the Instructor hyperlink—and from the displayed list, click **Edit Hyperlink**.

The Edit Hyperlink dialog box displays. The layout of this dialog box is the same as the Insert Hyperlink dialog box.

5 Click the **Look in arrow** and navigate to the location where you are saving the files for this chapter. Locate and select your file **6B_Faculty_Firstname_Lastname**.

6 Click **OK**. In cell **M1**, click the hyperlinked text—**Instructor**.

Your *6B_Faculty_Firstname_Lastname* file displays on your screen. The hyperlink has been changed to the new file and new file location.

7 Click the small **Close Window** button ☒ to close the Faculty file.

The Class Schedule worksheet redisplays on your screen.

Activity 6.14 Viewing and Saving a Worksheet as a Web Page

Before you save a worksheet as a Web page, it is a good idea to view it as a Web page to see how it will display.

1 Display the **File** menu, and then click **Web Page Preview**.

Your browser program (Internet Explorer or other browser program) opens, and the worksheet displays in the browser, as shown in Figure 6.35. (Depending on your browser setup and screen resolution, your screen may vary somewhat from the figure.)

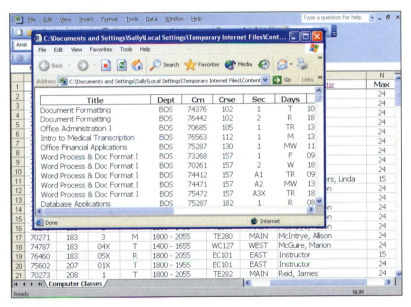

Figure 6.35

2 On the browser title bar, click the **Close** button ☒.

3 From the **File** menu, click **Save as Web Page**. The **Save As** dialog box opens. At the lower edge of the dialog box, be sure the **Save as type** box displays **Web Page**.

4 If necessary, click the **Save in arrow** and navigate to the location where you are saving your files for this chapter. You will not see your other files, because only files with the type *Web Page* will be visible.

5 In the lower portion of the dialog box, click the **Change Title** button.

The Set Page Title dialog box displays. The text that you type here will become the title of the Web page when it is displayed.

6 In the **Set Page Title** dialog box, in the **Page title** box, type **Business Division Computer Courses (Firstname Lastname)** using your own name as part of the page title. Compare your screen with Figure 6.36.

Location where file will be saved

Page title

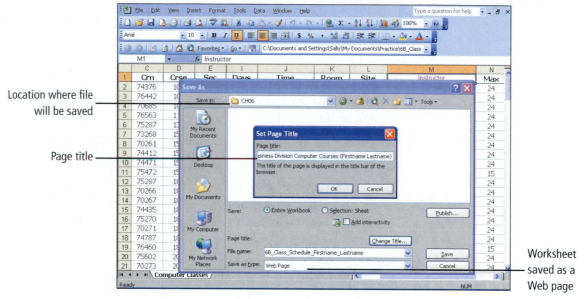

Worksheet saved as a Web page

Figure 6.36

7 In the **Set Page Title** dialog box, click **OK**. In the **Save As** dialog box, click **Save**.

The Save As dialog box closes.

8 On the right side of the blue Excel title bar, click the **Minimize** button ▬ to minimize the Excel program to a button on your taskbar. Start your browser program (Internet Explorer or other browser program). From the menu bar, click **File**, and then click **Open**. In the **Open** dialog box, click the **Browse** button.

A dialog box displays, similar to the Open dialog box in Excel. Depending on the style of the displayed dialog box, you can click the Browse button or use the Look in arrow to navigate to the file folder location, and then select the file you want to open.

9 Click the **Browse** button or the **Look in arrow**, and then navigate to the location where you have saved the files for this chapter. Click the HTML file **6B_Class_Schedule_Firstname_Lastname**, and then click **Open**.

The name of the file you selected displays in the Open dialog box.

10 In the **Open** dialog box, click **OK**.

The Class Schedule file opens in your browser. The browser title bar displays the text you typed in the Set Page Title dialog box—Business Division Computer Courses. The file name may display .htm at the end, which is the extension that is given to files that are saved as Web pages. Compare your screen with Figure 6.37.

Page title —

File address —

Extension of .htm indicates Web page

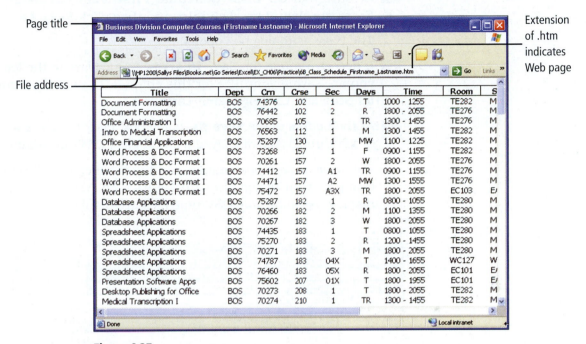

Title	Dept	Crn	Crse	Sec	Days	Time	Room	S
Document Formatting	BOS	74376	102	1	T	1000 - 1255	TE282	M
Document Formatting	BOS	76442	102	2	R	1800 - 2055	TE276	M
Office Administration I	BOS	70685	105	1	TR	1300 - 1455	TE276	M
Intro to Medical Transcription	BOS	76563	112	1	M	1300 - 1455	TE282	M
Office Financial Applications	BOS	75287	130	1	MW	1100 - 1225	TE282	M
Word Process & Doc Format I	BOS	73268	157	1	F	0900 - 1155	TE282	M
Word Process & Doc Format I	BOS	70261	157	2	W	1800 - 2055	TE276	M
Word Process & Doc Format I	BOS	74412	157	A1	TR	0900 - 1155	TE276	M
Word Process & Doc Format I	BOS	74471	157	A2	MW	1300 - 1555	TE276	M
Word Process & Doc Format I	BOS	75472	157	A3X	TR	1800 - 2055	EC103	E/
Database Applications	BOS	75287	182	1	R	0800 - 1055	TE280	M
Database Applications	BOS	70266	182	2	M	1100 - 1355	TE280	M
Database Applications	BOS	70267	182	3	W	1800 - 2055	TE280	M
Spreadsheet Applications	BOS	74435	183	1	T	0800 - 1055	TE280	M
Spreadsheet Applications	BOS	75270	183	2	R	1200 - 1455	TE280	M
Spreadsheet Applications	BOS	70271	183	3	M	1800 - 2055	TE280	M
Spreadsheet Applications	BOS	74787	183	04X	T	1400 - 1655	WC127	W
Spreadsheet Applications	BOS	76460	183	05X	R	1800 - 2055	EC101	E/
Presentation Software Apps	BOS	75602	207	01X	T	1800 - 1955	EC101	E/
Desktop Publishing for Office	BOS	70273	208	1	T	1800 - 2055	TE282	M
Medical Transcription I	BOS	70274	210	1	TR	1300 - 1455	TE282	M

Figure 6.37

11 From the **File** menu, click **Page Setup**. In the **Page Setup** dialog box, change the Orientation to **Landscape**, and then click **OK**.

12 From the **File** menu, click **Print**. In the **Print** dialog box, change the page range from **All** to **1**, and then click **Print**.

The first page of the Class Schedule Web page prints. Depending on your printer, several of the columns on the right do not print. Do not be concerned about this; Web pages are meant to be viewed, not printed.

13 On the browser title bar, click the **Close** button ☒. On your taskbar, click the **6B_Class_Schedule** icon that displays to restore the Excel program and redisplay the worksheet.

The browser closes, and the Class Schedule worksheet displays on your screen.

Activity 6.15 Saving a Worksheet as a Comma Separated Values File

You can save an Excel worksheet as a comma separated value (CSV) file, which saves the contents of the cells by placing commas between them and an end-of-paragraph mark at the end of each row. This type of file can be readily exchanged with various database programs, in which it is referred to as a *comma delimited file*.

1 Be sure your **6B_Class_Schedule_Firstname_Lastname** file is open. From the menu bar, click **File**, and then click **Save As**.

The Save As dialog box opens.

2 If necessary, use the **Save in arrow** to navigate to the location where you are saving your files for this chapter. In the **File name** box type **6B_Schedule_CSV_Firstname_Lastname**

3 At the bottom of the **Save As** dialog box, click the **Save as type arrow**. Scroll through the displayed list and click **CSV (Comma delimited)**.

The Save as type box enables you to save files in different formats. Compare your dialog box with Figure 6.38. Your other files no longer display, because only CSV type files are displayed.

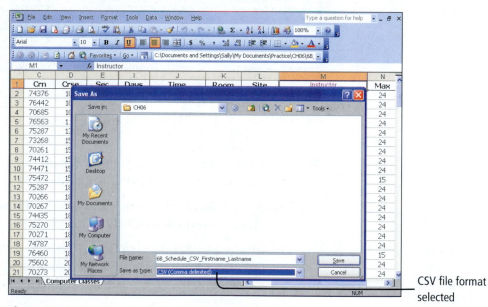

CSV file format selected

Figure 6.38

4 Click **Save**.

A dialog box displays to inform you that some features of the file may not be compatible with the CSV format. Features such as merged cells and formatting are lost. You can save the file and leave out incompatible features by clicking *Yes*, preserve the file in an Excel format by clicking *No*, or see what might be lost by clicking *Help*. See Figure 6.39.

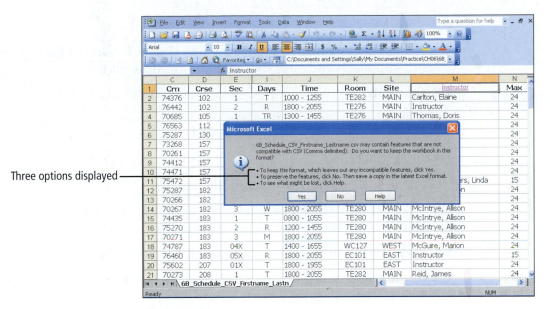

Three options displayed

Figure 6.39

Alert! A Different Warning

You may see a different warning message about the selected format not supporting a workbook that has multiple sheets. Click OK to save the active worksheet and acknowledge the warning.

5 Click **Yes** to keep the CSV format.

The file is saved in the new format. The new file name displays in the title bar. If file extensions—the three letters that identify the type of files—are displayed on your computer, you will also see *.csv* after the file name.

6 Close your **6B_Schedule_CSV** file. Click **Yes** to save changes, and then click **Yes** to acknowledge the warning message.

Activity 6.16 Saving an Excel File as a Text File

1 On the Standard toolbar, click the **Open** button. Navigate to the location where you are saving your files and open your Excel file (not the Web page file) **6B_Faculty_Firstname_Lastname**. (The file type shown at the bottom of the dialog box controls which types of files display here.)

2 From the **File** menu, click **Save As**. In the **Save As** dialog box, if necessary, use the **Save in arrow** to navigate to the location where you are saving your files for this chapter. In the **File name** box, type **6B_Faculty_TXT_Firstname_Lastname**

3 At the bottom of the **Save As** dialog box, click the **Save as type arrow**. Scroll through the displayed list and click **Text (Tab delimited)**.

A *tab delimited* text file is similar to a comma separated values file except that a tab character, rather than a comma, is used to separate the cell contents in the rows. Database programs can also read this type of data format easily.

4 Click **Save**.

A message box displays, advising you that the selected file type does not support workbooks that contain multiple sheets.

5 Click **OK**.

A second warning box displays, advising you that the file may contain features that are not compatible with the Text file format.

6 Click **Yes** to keep the format.

The new file name displays on the title bar.

7 Close the file. Click **Yes** to save the changes, click **OK**, and then click **Yes** to acknowledge the warning messages.

8 **Start** Microsoft Word. On the Standard toolbar, click the **Open** button.

9 In the **Open** dialog box, use the **Look in arrow** to navigate to the location where you are storing your files for this chapter.

10 At the bottom of the **Open** dialog box, click the **Files of type arrow** and, from the displayed list, click **Text Files**.

The *6B_Faculty_TXT_Firstname_Lastname* file displays on the list.

11 Click the **6B_Faculty_TXT_Firstname_Lastname** file to select it, and then click **Open**.

The file opens with tab characters inserted between each cell's data. Each row is treated as a paragraph. See Figure 6.40.

Tabs display between the data. ⎯⎯⎯

Paragraph marks indicate the end of a row of data.

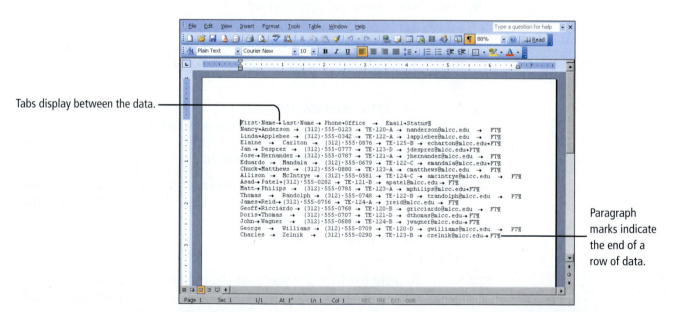

Figure 6.40

12 From the **View** menu, display the Header and Footer toolbar, and then click the **Switch Between Header and Footer** button ⊞. With the insertion point on the left side of the footer, on the Header and Footer toolbar, click the **Insert AutoText** button, and then click **Filename**.

13 Close the Header and Footer toolbar. On the Standard toolbar, click the **Print** button to print the one-page text file.

14 Close your **6B_Faculty_TXT** file, saving the changes when prompted to do so. If necessary, click **Yes** to acknowledge the warning message.

15 On the Word Standard toolbar, click the **Open** button ⊞. At the lower edge of the displayed **Open** dialog box, click the **Files of type arrow** and, from the displayed list, click **All Word Documents**. In the dialog box's title bar, click the **Close** button ⊠. Close Word.

16 In the Excel program, click **View**, point to **Toolbars**, and then click **Web** to close the Web toolbar. Then, from the **File** menu, click **Open**, and at the bottom of the dialog box, click the **Files of type arrow** and click **Microsoft Office Excel Files**. Close Excel.

More Knowledge — Using a Tab Delimited Text File

After a file has been saved as a text file, it can be converted from tab delimited text to a Word table. Word has a *Convert Text to Table* command that can easily convert a tabbed file into a table. A table displays in a row and column format, like an Excel spreadsheet.

End **You have completed Project 6B** ——————————————

Project 6C **Programming Classes**

Excel has several more tools for improving the visual appeal of your worksheet. You can format a worksheet by using the AutoFormat command or by creating your own styles. You can add graphic elements to a worksheet such as circles, rectangles, arrows, and text boxes. The Research tool can help you locate information that is related to your worksheet content.

In Activities 6.17 through 6.20, you will use AutoFormat, styles, drawing tools, and research tools to format a worksheet for the Computer Science and Computer Systems Information departments. Your completed worksheets will look similar to Figure 6.41. You will save your workbook as *6C_Programming_Classes_Firstname_Lastname.*

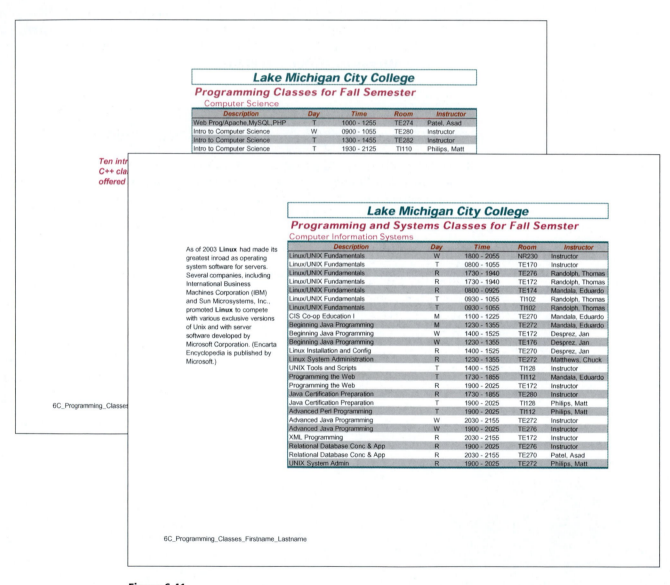

Figure 6.41
Project 6C—Programming Classes

Objective 4
Enhance Worksheets with AutoFormats and Styles

In addition to formatting cells from the Formatting toolbar and the Format Cells dialog box, you can also use the *AutoFormat* command. The AutoFormat feature provides a selection of predefined formats that can be applied to cells on a worksheet. Another alternative is to create your own *styles*, which are formats that you design and save and which can then be applied to cells in multiple worksheets or other workbooks.

Activity 6.17 Applying an AutoFormat

1 Start Excel. On the Standard toolbar, click the **Open** button. Navigate to the location where the student files for this textbook are stored. Locate and open the file **e06C_Programming_Classes**.

2 From the **File** menu, click **Save As**. In the **Save As** dialog box, use the **Save in arrow** to navigate to the location where you are storing your files for this chapter. In the **File name** box, type **6C_Programming_Classes_Firstname_Lastname** and then click the **Save** button.

This worksheet lists the programming courses that are available for the fall semester through the Computer Science department. Notice that the workbook contains two worksheets, one named CPS and the other, CIS.

3 On the **CPS** sheet, make cell **A1** the active cell. Display the **Insert** menu, and then click **Rows**. In the new cell **A1**, type **Lake Michigan City College** and press [Enter].

4 Click the **CIS tab**. With the insertion point in cell **A1**, display the **Insert** menu, and then click **Rows**. In the new cell **A1**, type **Lake Michigan City College** and press [Enter].

5 Click the **CPS tab**. Select the range **A4:E27**. From the **Format** menu, click **AutoFormat**.

The AutoFormat dialog box opens and displays predefined formats.

6 Scroll down the list, locate and then click the **List 1** AutoFormat.

This format applies gray to alternate lines, which helps lead the eye across a row of information. See Figure 6.42.

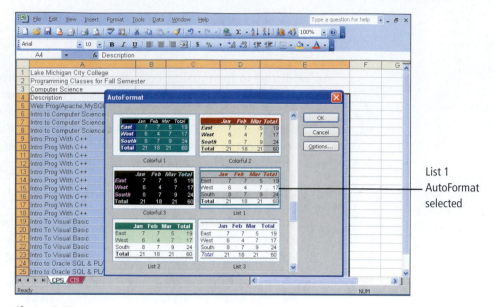

Figure 6.42

7 Click **OK**, and then click in any empty cell to view the results.

The format is applied to the selected cells.

8 Select columns **B**, **C**, and **D** and then, on the Formatting toolbar, click the **Center** button . With the three columns selected, widen **columns B**, **C**, and **D** to **12 (89 pixels)**. Click in any empty cell and compare your screen with Figure 6.43.

Columns widened and data centered

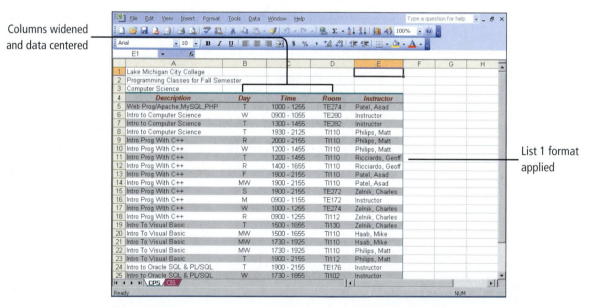

Figure 6.43

9 Click the **CIS tab**. Select cells **A4:E29**. From the **Format** menu, click **AutoFormat**. In the **AutoFormat** dialog box, click **List 1**, and then click **OK**. Center ⊟ columns **B**, **C**, and **D**, and then widen **columns B**, **C**, and **D** to **12 (89 pixels)**.

10 On the Standard toolbar, click the **Save** button 🖫.

Activity 6.18 Creating Styles

1 Click the **CPS tab** and click cell **A1**. From the **Format** menu, click **Style**.

The Style dialog box opens and displays the name and formats of the current style—*Normal*—that is applied to this cell. The **Normal** style is the default style that is applied to new worksheets. It includes Arial 10 pt. font and the other formats listed in the dialog box, as shown in Figure 6.44.

Style name box ——

Normal style formats

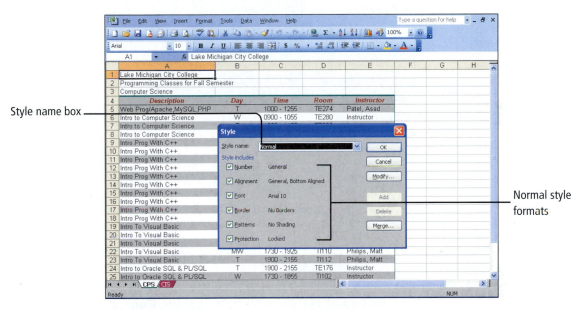

Figure 6.44

2 In the **Style name** box, type **LMCC** and then click the **Modify** button.

The Format Cells dialog box opens. Here you can define the format for your LMCC style.

3 Click the **Font tab**. Under **Font**, click **Tahoma**, under **Font style**, click **Bold Italic**, and under **Size**, click **18**. Click the **Color arrow** and then, in the second row, click the fifth color—**Teal**.

4 Click the **Border tab**. In the lower right corner of the dialog box, click the **Color arrow** and in the second row, click the fifth color—**Teal**. Under **Presets**, click **Outline**.

An outline displays in the Border area.

5 Click **OK**.

The Format Cells dialog box closes. The Style dialog box shows the selections you have made. Compare your dialog box with the one in Figure 6.45.

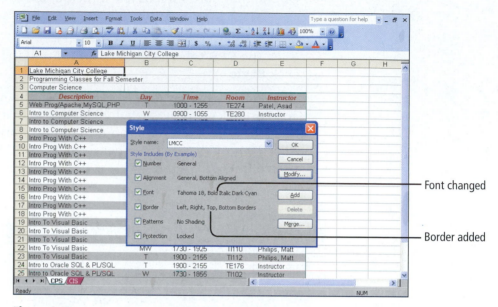

Figure 6.45

6 Click the **Add** button.

After you define the style, you must click Add to retain the selections you have made.

7 Click **OK**.

The Style is applied to cell A1.

8 Click cell **A2**. On the Formatting toolbar, change the **Font** to **Arial Rounded MT Bold** and change the **Font Size** to **16**. Click the **Font Color arrow** and then, in the fourth row, click the seventh color—**Plum**.

Now that you have set the formats you want, you can open the Style dialog and name this style. This is another way to create a style.

9 From the **Format** menu, click **Style**. In the **Style** dialog box, in the **Style name** box, type **Title** Notice that, after you assign a name, the font formats you have chosen are displayed under **Style Includes**, as shown in Figure 6.46.

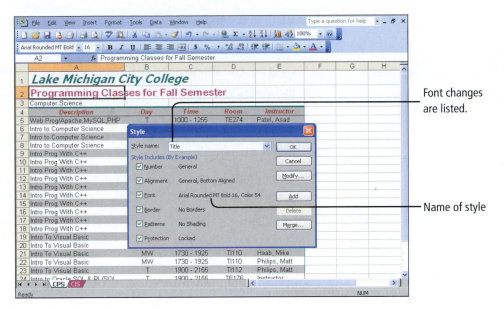

Font changes are listed.

Name of style

Figure 6.46

🔟 Click **Add**, and then click **OK**.

The style is applied to the selected cell, and the dialog box closes.

1️⃣1️⃣ Click cell **A3**. Use one of the two methods you just practiced to create a style for this cell named **Department** Use **12** pt. **Arial Rounded MT Bold** font, **Plum** font color, and **Center** alignment. Compare your results with Figure 6.47.

Your three created styles applied to the three title lines

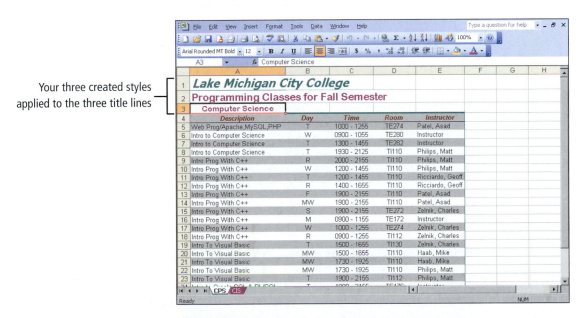

Figure 6.47

1️⃣2️⃣ On the Standard toolbar, click the **Save** button 🖫.

Activity 6.19 Applying Styles to Other Worksheets

1 Click the **CIS tab**, and then click cell **A1**.

2 Display the **Format** menu, and then click **Style**.

The Style dialog box opens with the Normal style listed in the Style name box.

3 Click the **Style name arrow**, from the displayed list click **LMCC**, and then click **OK**.

The LMCC style is applied to cell A1. The styles you created in Activity 6.18 are available to use with other worksheets in this workbook.

4 Click cell **A2**. Display the **Format** menu and click **Style**. In the **Style** dialog box, click the **Style name arrow**, click **Title**, and then click **OK**.

5 Click cell **A3** and from the **Style** dialog box, apply the **Department** style. Widen **column A** to **35.00 (250 pixels)**. Save your work and click in any empty cell.

The three styles you created for the CPS worksheet have been applied to the CIS worksheet. Compare your screen with Figure 6.48.

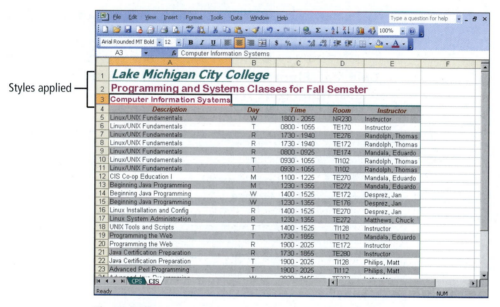

Figure 6.48

More Knowledge — Using Styles in Other Workbooks

Styles you create in one workbook are not automatically available for use in other workbooks. However, if you create styles in one workbook, you can merge the styles with other workbooks. Open the workbook that contains the styles, and then open the workbook where you want to use the styles. In the workbook where you want to add the styles, open the Styles dialog box and click the Merge button. A Merge Styles dialog box displays and lists the open workbook containing the styles. Select the workbook containing the styles, and then click OK. The styles are available for you to use in the new workbook.

Activity 6.20 Modifying Styles

After you create a style, you can alter it and the changes will be reflected in any cell that uses that style. In the following activity, you will change the Title style to bold italic. The border used in the LMCC style needs to be adjusted so that it covers the full length of the cells where the Lake Michigan Community College title displays.

1 Be sure the **CIS** worksheet is displayed. Click cell **A2**. From the **Format** menu, display the **Style** dialog box.

The Style dialog box opens with the Title style selected.

2 In the **Style** dialog box, click the **Modify** button.

The Format Cells dialog box displays.

3 Click the **Font tab**, under **Font style** click **Bold Italic**, and then click **OK**.

In the Style dialog box, the font for the Title style is changed to include Bold Italic. See Figure 6.49. Notice that the font in cell A2 has not yet been changed to Bold Italic.

Change in style not displayed in text

Font style changed in dialog box

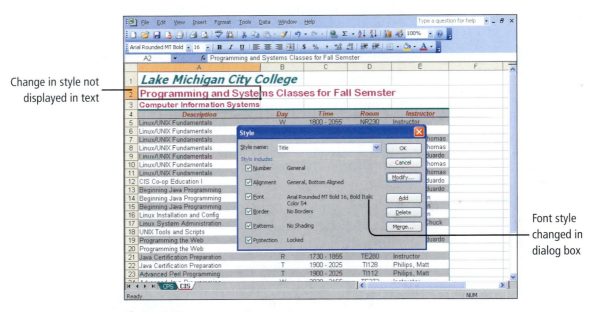

Figure 6.49

4 Click **OK**.

The Style dialog box closes, and the font in cell A2 changes to Bold Italic. The change in style is applied only after the Style dialog box is closed.

5 Select cells **A1:E1** and then, on the Formatting toolbar, click the **Merge and Center** button ⊞. Click in any empty cell and notice that the Teal border no longer displays around the cell.

Because you cannot initiate the Merge and Center cells command from the Format Cells dialog box, you must make that formatting change before displaying the Style dialog box for the purpose of changing the style.

6 Click the **CPS tab**. Notice that the font for the Title in cell **A2** has changed to Bold Italic.

In most cases, changes to a style are updated to any cell in the workbook that uses that style.

7 Select **A1:E1** and then, on the Formatting toolbar, click the **Merge and Center** button ![merge and center icon]. Display the **Format** menu and click **Style**.

The Style dialog box opens with the LMCC style listed in the Style name box. The Alignment needs to be changed to Center.

8 In the **Style** dialog box, click the **Modify** button. In the **Format Cells** dialog box, click the **Alignment tab**, under **Text alignment**, click the **Horizontal arrow**, and then click **Center**.

The text will be centered over the merged cell range, and the border displays over the merged cell area.

9 Click **OK** twice to close both dialog boxes.

10 Click the **CIS tab**. Click in any empty cell and notice that the border does not display around cell **A1**, even though a change was made to the LMCC format.

11 Click cell **A1**. Display the **Style** dialog box. Notice that the **Alignment** specifies **Horizontal Center, Bottom Aligned**.

12 Click **OK**. Click in any empty cell. On the Standard toolbar, click the **Save** button ![save icon].

The style is reapplied. You need to reapply the style to the merged cell so that the border displays around the entire merged area. Compare your screen with Figure 6.50.

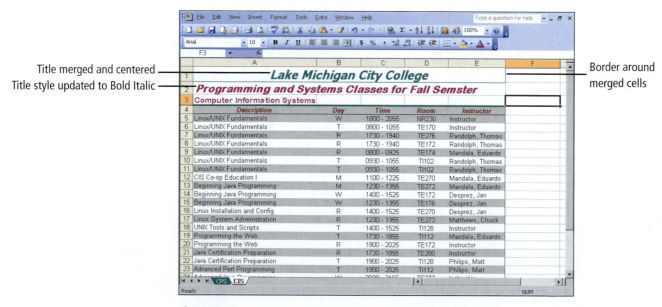

Title merged and centered
Title style updated to Bold Italic

Border around merged cells

Figure 6.50

Objective 5
Use Drawing Tools and Use the Reaserch Feature

Drawing objects are shapes such as lines, arrows, rectangles, and circles that can be added to a worksheet and are especially useful to provide a place to document information or to draw attention to a particular cell or area of a worksheet. Additionally, the **Research** feature can be used to look up relevant information that can be placed within a drawing object. A button on the Standard toolbar opens the Research task pane, which provides an assortment of research tools such as a dictionary, thesaurus, encyclopedia, or other reference tools using the MSN Learning and Research Web site.

Activity 6.21 Using Drawing Tools

Drawing tools are objects such as lines, arrows, rectangles, and circles that can be added to a worksheet. The most common use in Excel is to add a *text box* for explanatory information related to the worksheet. A text box is a container into which you can type or insert text. Because a text box is a drawing object, it is not constrained by the dimension of a cell. You can resize, move, and format drawing objects.

1 Click the **CPS tab**, and then click anywhere in **column A**. From the **Insert** menu, click **Columns**.

An empty column is inserted to the left, and the remaining columns move to the right.

2 Widen **column A** to **30.00 (215 pixels)**. If the Drawing toolbar is not already displayed at the bottom of your screen, right-click on one of the toolbars and, from the displayed list, click Drawing. Alternatively, on the Standard toolbar, click the Drawing button.

The Drawing toolbar opens. On most systems, the Drawing toolbar docks at the lower edge of the window. See Figure 6.51.

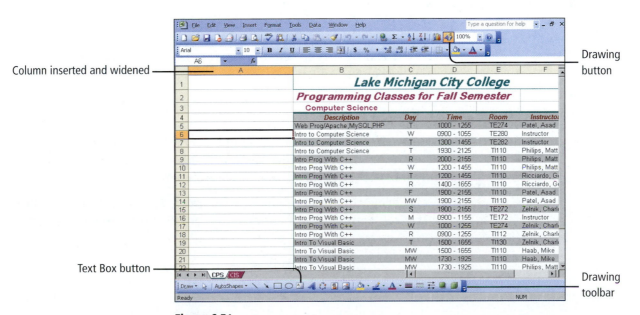

Column inserted and widened

Drawing button

Text Box button

Drawing toolbar

Figure 6.51

3 On the Drawing toolbar, click the **Text Box** button 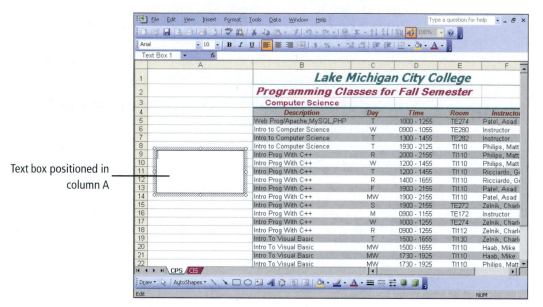 and move the mouse pointer into the screen to the left side of cell **A9**.

The mouse pointer changes to a crosshair.

4 Look at Figure 6.52 to visualize how your box will be drawn, and then position the cross portion of the pointer at the upper boundary of cell **A9**, not quite at the left boundary. Drag down and to the right to the upper boundary of **row 14** and almost to the right boundary of **column A**.

As you draw, the mouse pointer changes shape slightly. When you release the mouse button, the text box displays with a slashed border and the insertion point inside the box, as shown in Figure 6.52. If you are not satisfied with your result, click the slashed border to display a pattern of dots, press Delete, click the Text Box button, and begin again.

Text box positioned in column A

Figure 6.52

5 Inside the text box, type **Ten introductory C++ classes will be offered in the fall.**

6 Click the edge of the text box to display a pattern of dots.

To modify the text in a text box, you can either drag to select the text or display the pattern of dots. Displaying the pattern of dots acts to select all the text and the text box itself (although the text is not visibly selected) for the purpose of changing its format.

7 On the Formatting toolbar, change the **Font Size** to **12** pt., add **Bold** and **Italic** for emphasis, and then change the **Font Color** to **Plum**.

8 On the Drawing toolbar, click the **Line Color button arrow** 🖌️▾. At the top of the displayed palette, click **No Line**. Click in any empty cell.

The font is formatted to match the spreadsheet format, and the line around the text box is removed. Compare your screen with Figure 6.53.

Text box font formatted ————

Perimeter line removed from text box

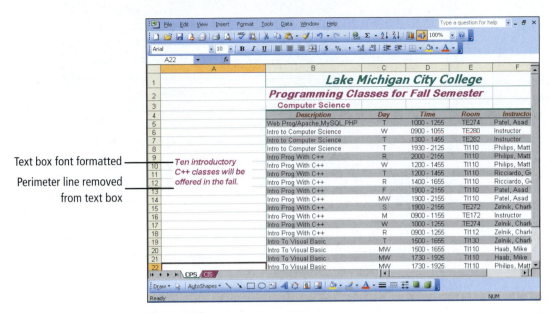

Figure 6.53

9 Look at Figure 6.54 to visualize how your arrow will be drawn. On the Drawing toolbar, click the **Arrow** button ➘. Move the mouse pointer into the text box, to the right of the word *fall*, and then drag from the text box to the left edge of cell **B14**. If you are not satisfied with your result, press Delete, click the Arrow button, and begin again.

An arrow is drawn on the screen pointing to the C++ class offerings for this fall. Two small circles at either end indicate that the arrow object is selected. See Figure 6.54 to verify the placement of your arrow.

10 With the arrow still selected, on the Drawing toolbar, click the **Arrow Style** button ⇄. From the displayed list, point to the arrows to see the ScreenTips, and then locate and click **Arrow Style 9**. Click in any empty cell to cancel the selection and view the arrow's changed shape.

11 Click the arrow to select it, click the **Line Color button arrow** 🖌️▾, and in the fourth row, click the seventh color—**Plum**. Compare your screen with Figure 6.54.

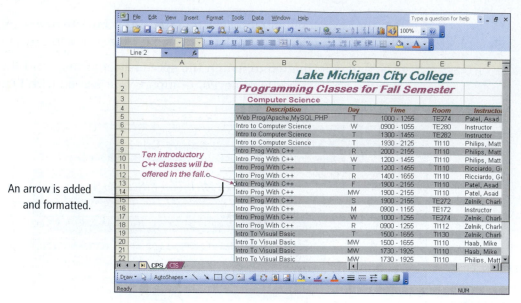

An arrow is added and formatted.

Figure 6.54

12 On the Standard toolbar, click the **Save** button.

Activity 6.22 Locating and Inserting Supporting Information

The Research tool can help you locate information related to topics or words in your worksheet.

1 Click the **CIS tab**, and then click anywhere in **column A**. From the **Insert** menu, click **Columns**. Widen the new **column A** to **30.00 (215 pixels)**.

An empty column is inserted and widened to the left of the data.

2 On the Drawing toolbar, click the **Text Box** button. Using the technique you practiced, in **column A**, draw a text box extending from cell **A4** to cell **A10**. If your computer is not connected to the Internet, read the Alert box following Step 4 and complete the instructions. Otherwise, continue with Step 3.

3 On the Standard toolbar, click the **Research** button.

The Research task pane opens on the right of the window.

4 In the **Search for** box, type **Linux** and then click the **All Reference Books arrow**. From the displayed list, click **Encarta Encyclopedia: English (North America)**.

The Research feature searches the designated reference and locates information and articles related to Linux. See Figure 6.55.

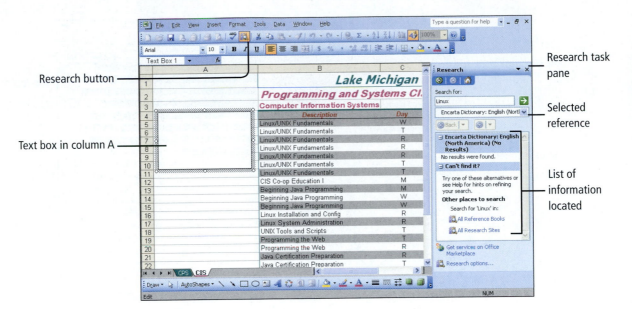

Research button

Text box in column A

Research task pane

Selected reference

List of information located

Figure 6.55

Alert!

If Your Computer Is Not Connected to the Internet

If your computer is not connected to the Internet, you will see a message box indicating that Excel cannot complete the operation. To continue with this activity, start Microsoft Word. On the Standard toolbar, click the Open button. In the folder that contains the files for this chapter, locate and open the Word File e06C_Linux. Use the techniques you have practiced in previous chapters to copy the text, and then close Word. On your Excel worksheet, click inside the text box and then, on the Formatting toolbar, click the Paste button. Continue the exercise at Step 9.

5 Scroll through the list. Locate the reference to *Open Source Software article* and click the **Article—Encarta Encyclopedia** hyperlink.

The task pane moves to the left side of the screen, and the MSN Learning and Research window opens to the Open Source Software article.

6 Scroll through the article and locate the paragraph beginning *As of 2003 Linux.* Starting at that point, drag to select the lines through the end of the parenthetical reference—ending *published by Microsoft.)* See Figure 6.56.

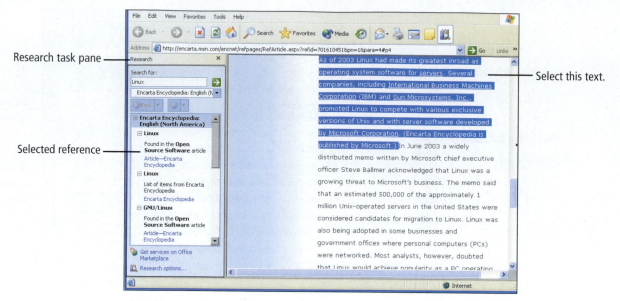

Research task pane ⟶

Selected reference ⟶

Select this text. ⟵

Figure 6.56

7 Press ⌃Ctrl + ⒞ to copy the selected text. Alternatively, from the Edit menu, click Copy. **Close** ❌ the MSN Learning & Research window.

8 In **column A**, click in the text box, and then press ⌃Ctrl + ⓋV to paste the copied text. Alternatively, on the Standard toolbar, click the Paste button 📋 ▾.

The reference to the Linux program displays in the text box.

9 On the lower edge of the text box, drag the middle sizing handle down until the entire reference is displayed. Compare your screen with Figure 6.57.

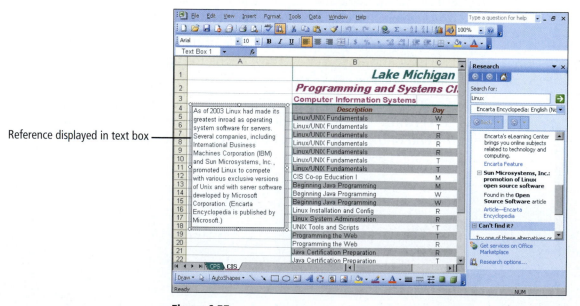

Reference displayed in text box ⟶

Figure 6.57

10 **Close** ☒ the **Research** task pane if it is still displayed. In the text box, in the first line, double-click the word **Linux**, and then click the **Bold** button **B**. Repeat this action to apply bold to the second occurrence of *Linux* in the article. On the Drawing toolbar, click the **Line Color button arrow** and at the top of the list, click **No Line** to remove the line from around the text box.

11 Select both worksheets. (Hint: Use the **Select All Sheets** command or the ⌨ Ctrl key.) From the **File** menu, display the **Page Setup** dialog box. On the **Page tab**, click **Landscape**. On the **Margins tab**, under **Center on page**, select the **Horizontally** check box. On the **Header/Footer tab**, open the **Custom Footer** and, with the insertion point in the **Left section**, insert the **File Name**. Click **OK** twice.

12 On the Standard toolbar, click the **Save** button 🖫, and then click the **Print Preview** button 🔍. Scroll to view both worksheets, and then click **Print**. Click **OK** to print, and then close the workbook.

End **You have completed Project 6C** ——————————————————————

Project 6D Pension

Goal Seek is one of the Excel what-if analysis tools that can help you answer questions and plan for the future.

Pension Funding	
Investment	100,000
Annual Payment	100,000
Interest Rate	6.89%
Term	30
Future Value	$10,000,000.00

In Activity 6.23 you will use Goal Seek to determine the interest rate that is required to meet the investment goal for a pension fund investment. You will save your file as *6D_Pension_Firstname_Lastname.* Your completed worksheet will look similar to Figure 6.58.

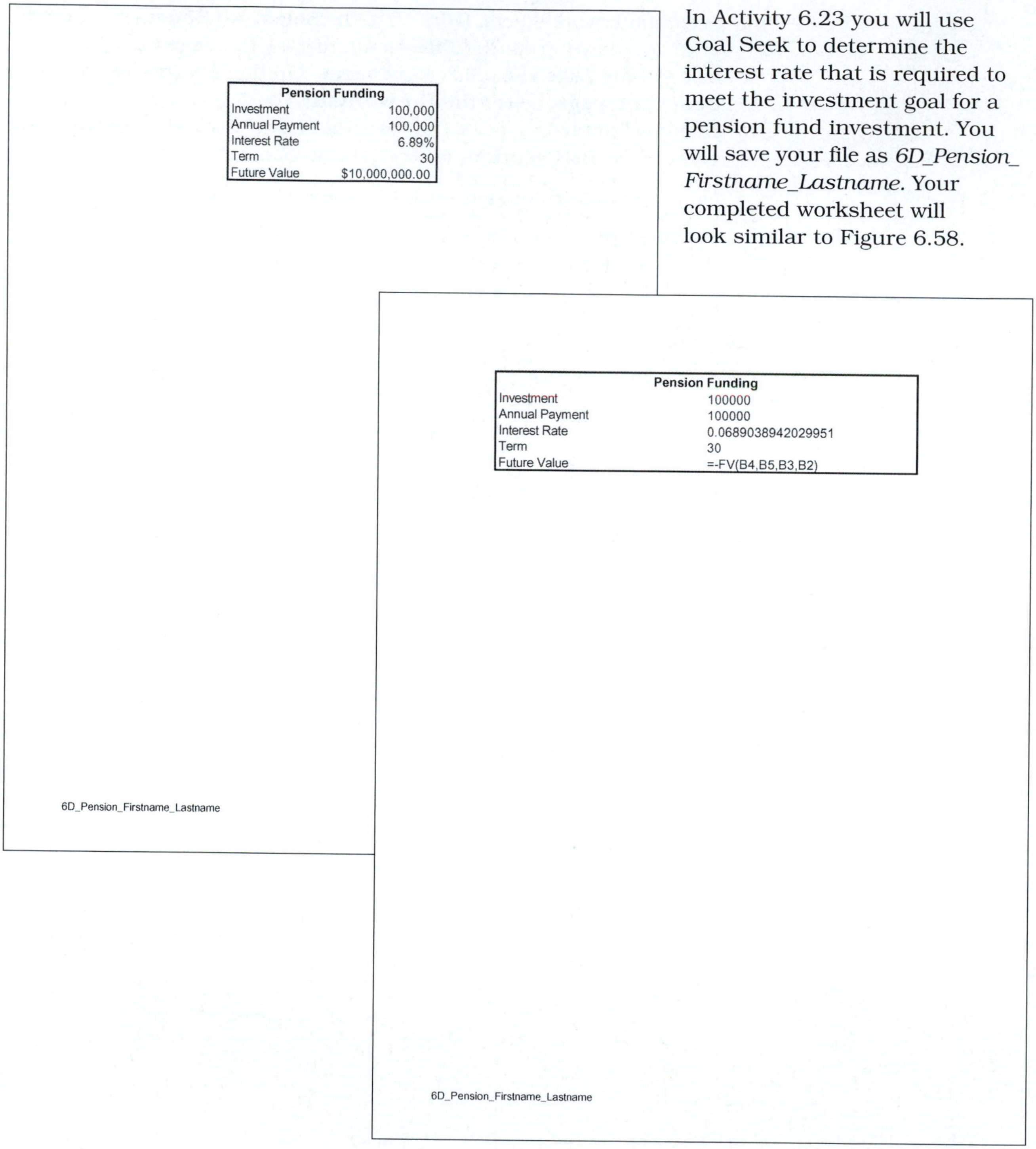

Pension Funding	
Investment	100000
Annual Payment	100000
Interest Rate	0.0689038942029951
Term	30
Future Value	=-FV(B4,B5,B3,B2)

6D_Pension_Firstname_Lastname

6D_Pension_Firstname_Lastname

Figure 6.58
Project 6D—Pension

Objective 6
Use Goal Seek

Goal Seek is a what-if analysis tool that can help you answer questions. Goal Seek is useful when you know the desired result of a formula but not the input value the formula needs to determine the result. For example, if you need to borrow money to buy a car but can only afford a payment of $200 a month, Goal Seek can help you answer the question, "How much can I borrow?" In the following activity, you will determine, for David Hanna, Vice President of Finance, the minimum interest rate required to meet the fund goal for a new investment for the employee pension fund. Mr. Hanna knows the amount of money that will be invested annually and the total amount that will be needed at the end of the term.

Activity 6.23 Using Goal Seek

1 Start Excel if necessary. On the Standard toolbar, click the **Open** button. Navigate to the location where the student files for this textbook are stored. Locate and open the file **e06D_Pension**.

2 Be sure only the Standard and Formatting toolbars are displayed. Close any other toolbars. From the **File** menu, click **Save As**. In the **Save As** dialog box, use the **Save in arrow** to navigate to the location where you are storing your files for this chapter. In the **File name** box, type **6D_Pension_Firstname_Lastname** Click the **Save** button.

This worksheet displays the figures for a pension fund investment.

3 In cell **B4**, type **6%** and press Enter.

This is an estimate of the interest rate to use in the Future Value formula.

4 Click cell **B6**. On the Formula Bar, click the **Insert Function** button. In the **Insert Function** dialog box, click the **Or select a category arrow**, and then click **Financial**.

The Financial functions display in the Select a function box.

5 In the **Select a function** box, click **FV**, and then click **OK**.

The Function Arguments dialog box displays. Recall that you used this function in an earlier chapter to determine the value of an annuity.

6 In the **Function Arguments** dialog box, click the **Rate** box, and then click cell **B4**—the estimated interest rate. Click the **Nper** box, and then click cell **B5**—the term of the investment. Click the **Pmt** box, and then click cell **B3**—the annual payments—and, finally, click the **Pv** box and click cell **B2**—the initial amount invested. Compare your screen with Figure 6.59.

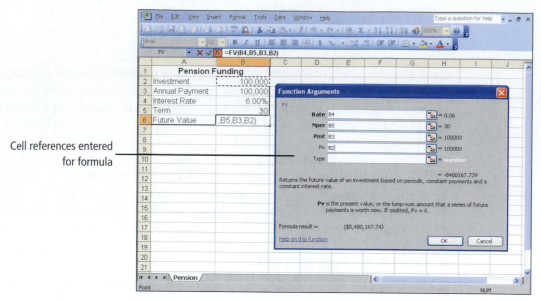

Figure 6.59

Cell references entered for formula

7 Click **OK**.

The Function Argument dialog box closes and the result— ($8,480,167.74)—displays in cell B6.

The result displays as a negative number because these are funds that are paid out.

8 Click cell **B6** if necessary and, in the Formula Bar, edit the formula to place a minus sign after the equal sign. Verify that the formula displays as *=-FV(B4,B5,B3,B2)* and press Enter.

The results displays as a positive number—$8,480,167.74.

9 Make **B6** the active cell and then, from the **Tools** menu, click **Goal Seek**.

The Goal Seek dialog box opens, and B6 displays in the *Set cell* box. This is the cell in which you want to set the value to a specific amount—$10,000,000.

10 In the **Goal Seek** dialog box, click the **To value** box and type **10,000,000**—ten million.

This is the amount that you want the pension to be worth after the 30-year term. When you enter a number in this box, it is not necessary to use commas.

11 Click the **By changing cell** box, and then click cell **B4**—the interest rate.

The interest rate is the variable you are trying to find. Notice that the reference in the *By changing cell* box is absolute. Compare your screen with Figure 6.60.

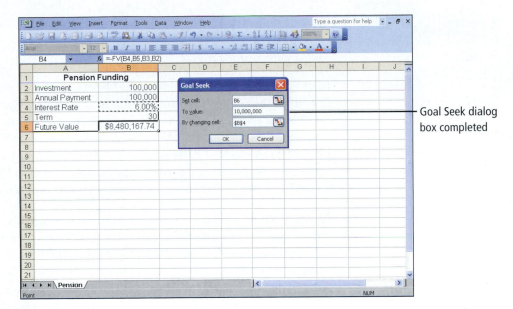

Goal Seek dialog box completed

Figure 6.60

12 Click **OK**.

The Goal Seek Status dialog box opens, stating that it found a solution. The Future Value in cell B6 displays $10,000,000.00, and the interest rate in cell B4 displays as 6.89%. This answers the question: "At what interest rate must I invest $100,000 to have the total value of the pension fund equal $10,000,000 after 30 years?"

13 In the **Goal Seek Status** dialog box, click **OK**.

The new numbers display in the worksheet.

14 From the **File** menu, display the **Page Setup** dialog box. On the **Margins tab**, under **Center on page**, select the **Horizontally** check box. On the **Header/Footer tab**, create a **Custom Footer** and place the **File Name** in the **Left section**. Click **OK** twice.

15 Save your file, and then print it. Press Ctrl + ` to display the formula. Print the formula page, and then press Ctrl + ` to return the page to the worksheet figures. After printing the file, close the file, saving changes if prompted to do so.

End You have completed Project 6D

Summary

Excel offers several template worksheets that you can use for common financial tasks such as completing an expense report, time card, sales invoice, or purchase order. These preformatted forms are quick and easy to use because they use a fill-in-the-blank approach. The formulas are prewritten in locked cells so that the user does not need to know how to use Excel to produce a report that has the appropriate totals. In Project 6A, you were introduced to templates when you completed an expense report.

Project 6B focused on several techniques for working with large worksheets. These included using the Freeze Panes command to keep column and row headings in place while scrolling the rest of the window; using the Find and Replace dialog box to locate and change information; using the Go To function to locate blank cells; and using the COUNTIF function to determine the number of cells that matched a certain condition. You hid columns to control what was displayed on the worksheet, and you practiced splitting the screen so that you could see two nonadjacent parts of the worksheet at the same time and scroll each area separately. The Arrange Workbooks feature was used so that you could view two worksheets from different workbooks at the same time. Finally, you used the Sort command to control the order of the data and the AutoFilter command to restrict the data that was displayed to only those rows that matched specific criteria.

Additional tools were introduced for sharing a large worksheet with others. You practiced how to repeat the column and row headings on each page and control the break between pages so that the data printed in a logical and organized manner. A hyperlink was inserted to another workbook to provide quick reference to contact information. You viewed and saved a worksheet as a Web Page, as a comma separated value file, and as a text file.

In Project 6C, the AutoFormat feature was introduced, and you practiced creating, applying, and modifying styles. Drawing tools were introduced, and you added a text box and an arrow to insert related comments on the worksheet. The Research tool was used to locate related information, and then you added that text to a text box.

Finally, in Project 6D, you used Goal Seek to determine the interest rate required to meet a specific funding goal for a pension investment.

In This Chapter You Practiced How To

- Use Excel Templates

- Work with a Large Worksheet

- Prepare a Worksheet to Share with Others

- Enhance Worksheets with AutoFormats and Styles

- Use Drawing Tools and Use the Research Feature

- Use Goal Seek

Concepts Assessments

Matching Match each term in the second column with its correct definition in the first column by writing the letter of the term on the blank line in front of the correct definition.

_____ **1.** A function that enables you to determine the number of cells in a range that meet a specified condition.

_____ **2.** The drawing object that is used most frequently to type comments or related information.

_____ **3.** The file type that is used when you want to save an Excel file with tabs between each cell in a row.

_____ **4.** A command that gives you a choice of predesigned formats that can be applied to a group of cells.

_____ **5.** The default style that is applied to new workbooks.

_____ **6.** The name for the group of objects such as lines, arrows, rectangles, and circles that can be added to a worksheet.

_____ **7.** The what-if analysis tool that finds the input needed in one cell in order to determine the desired result in another cell.

_____ **8.** The file type that is used when you need to save an Excel file so that there is a comma between each cell and a paragraph return at the end of each row.

_____ **9.** A tool that can be used to help locate information related to the data in your worksheet.

_____ **10.** The command that is used when you need to view multiple worksheets on your screen at the same time.

_____ **11.** Predesigned and preformatted financial forms that have built-in formulas for calculating totals based on the data that is entered.

_____ **12.** Colored and underlined text or a graphic that you click to go to a file, a location in a file, a Web page on the World Wide Web, or a Web page on your organization's intranet.

_____ **13.** The command that is used to set the column and row headings so that they remain on the screen while you scroll to other parts of the worksheet.

_____ **14.** Categories of information organized in columns.

_____ **15.** The term used for a condition on which cells are evaluated, for the purpose of displaying only those rows that meet that condition.

A Arrange

B AutoFormat

C Comma separated value (CSV)

D COUNTIF

E Criteria

F Drawing objects

G Fields

H Freeze Panes

I Goal Seek

J Hyperlink

K Normal

L Research

M Templates

N Text Box

O Text (tab delimited)

Fill in the Blank Write the correct answer in the space provided.

1. In the Sort dialog box, if you want to sort the selected column in alphabetical order, click the _____ option button.

2. Some cells in a template are _____ to prevent the user from entering data in that cell or accidentally overwriting formulas.

3. When sorting data, the first sort is known as the _____ sort.

4. If the rows or the columns are locked so that they do not scroll, it is known as _____.

5. If you want to sort numerical data from the highest value to the lowest, choose _____.

6. When sorting on multiple columns, the second or third sort is known as a _____ sort.

7. When printing a large worksheet, you can change the rows or columns that print on each page by using the _____ view.

8. When printing a large worksheet, you can select rows or columns to repeat on each page using the _____ dialog box.

9. To be able to view and scroll two different areas on a worksheet at the same time, use the _____ _____ command.

10. To limit the data displayed to only those records that match a stated condition, use the _____ command.

Project 6E—Loan

Objectives: *Use Excel Templates, Work with a Large Worksheet, and Prepare a Worksheet to Share with Others.*

David Hanna, Vice President of Finance, is considering different financing options for the purchase of new equipment for the college. He has requested a spreadsheet calculating the loan payment and an amortization schedule as one of three financing options he is considering. In this project, you will use the Excel Loan Amortization template to calculate the payment and related amortization schedule. Your completed worksheet will look similar to the one shown in Figure 6.61. You will save your workbook as *6E_Loan_Firstname_Lastname*.

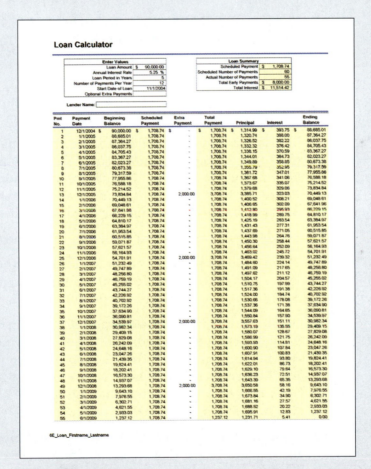

Figure 6.61

1. **Start** Excel. On the menu bar, click **File** and, from the displayed list, click **New**. In the **New Workbook** task pane, under **Templates**, click **On my computer**. In the displayed **Templates** dialog box, click the **Spreadsheet Solutions tab**. Click the **Loan Amortization** icon, and then click **OK**.

(Project 6E–Loan continues on the next page)

(Project 6E–Loan continued)

2. In the displayed **Loan Amortization** worksheet, in cell **D6** type **90,000** and then press Enter. Recall that templates are preformatted, and the value you entered displays in currency format with two decimals.

3. The active cell moves to cell **D7**—the Annual Interest Rate. Type **.0525** and press Enter. Recall that interest rates are usually entered in decimal format but display as percentages—5.25%.

4. The active cell moves to cell **D8**—the length or term of the loan in years. Type **5** and press Enter.

5. In the **Number of Payments Per Year** cell—**D9**—type **12** and then press Enter. In the **Start Date** cell—**D10**—type **11/1/2004** and then press Enter.

   The loan payment is calculated to be *$1,708.74*, and the interest paid for the term of the loan is *$12,524.31*. The amortization schedule is completed. A ScreenTip displays that describes how to use the Extra Payment option.

6. On the Standard toolbar, click the **Save** button. Save the file in your folder for this chapter with the name **6E_Loan_Firstname_Lastname**

7. Mr. Hanna thinks the college will be able to make additional payments of $2,000 at the end of each year of the loan—payment numbers 13, 25, 37, and 49. Click cell **E18**. From the **Window** menu, click **Freeze Panes**. Recall that freezing panes makes it easier to scroll the window and still see the identifying row or column titles.

8. Scroll down and click cell **E30**, type **2000** and press Enter.

   The additional payment at the beginning of the second year of the loan—payment 13—is recorded, and the worksheet recalculates. *$2000* displays in cell H9—*Total Early Payments*.

9. Scroll down, click cell **E42**, type **2000** and then press Enter. The worksheet is recalculated, and the early payment total displays $4,000.00. Continue in this manner and enter an extra payment of $2,000 in cells **E54** and **E66**. Notice that the *Actual Number of Payments* shows as 55, the *Total Early Payments* as *$8,000.00*, and the *Total Interest* is reduced to *$11,514.42*.

10. From the **Window** menu, click **Unfreeze Panes**. From the **View** menu, click **Header and Footer**. Add the file name to the **Custom Footer** as you have in the past. Click the **Save** button.

11. Display the **File** menu and click **Web Page Preview**.

(Project 6E–Loan continues on the next page)

(Project 6E–Loan continued)

12. In the browser window, display the **File** menu and click **Save As**. Use the **Save in arrow** to navigate to the folder where you are saving your files for this chapter. In the **File name** box, be sure *6E_Loan_Firstname_Lastname* displays. In the **Save as type** box, be sure **Web Page, complete (*.htm;*.html)** displays, and then click **Save**.

The file is saved as a Web page so that Mr. Hanna can view it using the college intranet.

13. Close the browser. From the **File** menu, display the **Page Setup** dialog box and, on the **Page tab**, under **Scaling**, click the **Fit to** option button. Be sure to fit to 1 page. In the **Page Setup** dialog box, click the **Print Preview** button and then, on the Print Preview toolbar, click the **Print** button and click **OK**.

14. Close the file, saving changes if prompted to do so.

End You have completed Project 6E ————————————————

Project 6F — Degrees

Objectives: *Prepare a Worksheet to Share with Others and Enhance Worksheets with AutoFormats and Styles.*

Henry Sabaj, Vice President of Academic Affairs, wants to review the programs offered by departments and their related degrees. In this exercise, you will work with a large spreadsheet and create and apply styles. Your completed file will look similar to the one shown in Figure 6.62. You will save your workbook as *6F_Degrees_Firstname_Lastname*.

1. On the Standard toolbar, click the **Open** button. Navigate to the location where the student files for this textbook are stored. Locate and open the file **e06F_Degrees**.

2. From the **File** menu, click **Save As**. In the **Save As** dialog box, use the **Save in arrow** to navigate to the location where you are storing your files for this chapter. In the **File name** box, type **6F_Degrees_Firstname_Lastname** Click the **Save** button.

3. Click cell **A2**. From the Formatting toolbar, click the **Font arrow**, and then click **Tahoma**. Click the **Font Size arrow**, and then click **16**. Click the **Bold** button and the **Center** button. Click the **Font Color arrow** and in the second row, click the fifth color—**Teal**.

(Project 6F–Degrees continues on the next page)

(Project 6F–Degrees continued)

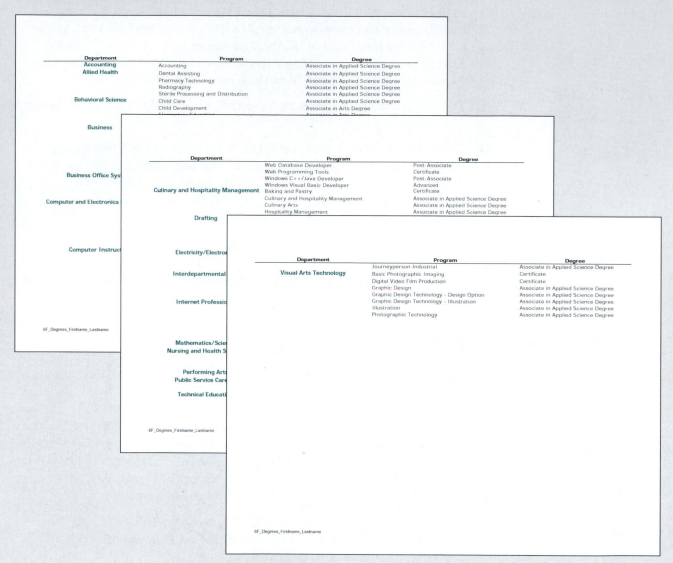

Figure 6.62

4. From the **Format** menu, click **Style**. In the **Style** dialog box, in the **Style name** box, type **Dept** Examine the changes to the **Style** dialog box to be sure it displays the choices you made in the previous step. (You may notice the font color displays Dark Cyan instead of Teal. The correct color has been selected, so do not be concerned about this naming difference.) Click **OK**.

5. Click cell **A3**, hold down Ctrl, and then click cells **A7** and **A11**. From the **Format** menu, click **Style**. Click the **Style name arrow**, click **Dept**, and then click **OK**.

The font size is likely too large for the longer department names and thus should be modified before it is applied to the rest of the worksheet.

(Project 6F–Degrees continues on the next page)

(Project 6F–Degrees continued)

6. Click cell **A11**, display the **Format** menu, and click **Style**. Be sure that *Dept* displays in the **Style name** box, and then click the **Modify** button. In the **Format Cells** dialog box, click the **Font tab**, and then change the **Size** to **14**. Click **OK** twice.

All the cells that have been formatted using the Dept style are changed to a smaller font.

7. Hold down Ctrl and continue down the **Department** column to select the cells that contain department names. Next, use the **Style** dialog box to apply the **Dept** style to the cells that display a department name.

8. From the **File** menu, click **Page Setup**. On the **Page tab**, click **Landscape**. Under **Scaling**, click the **Fit to** option button, and then change the **tall** box to **3**. Click the **Header/Footer tab** and add the file name to the custom footer as you have in the past. Click the **Sheet tab** and, under **Print titles**, click in the **Rows to repeat at top** box, and then click the **row 1 heading** to select **row 1** to repeat at the top of each printed page. Click the **Print Preview** button. Scroll through the pages to see how they will display when printed.

9. On the Print Preview toolbar, click **Print**. Click **OK** in the **Print** dialog box. On the Standard toolbar, click the **Save** button, and then close your file.

End **You have completed Project 6F** ———————————

Project 6G — Enrollment

Objectives: *Enhance Worksheets with AutoFormats and Styles, Use Drawing Tools and Use the Research Feature, and Use Goal Seek.*

Joyce Walker-MacKinney, President of Lake Michigan City College, has a goal to grow student enrollment to 20,000 in the next ten years. She wants to know what the target student population should be in each intervening year and the rate of growth that is needed to achieve this goal. In this exercise you will use Goal Seek to answer these questions. Your completed worksheet will look similar to the one shown in Figure 6.63. You will save your workbook as *6G_Enrollment_Firstname_Lastname*.

1. Open a new, blank worksheet. In cell **A1**, type **Lake Michigan City College** and in cell **A2**, type **Enrollment Projection**

2. On the Standard toolbar, click the **Save** button. In the **Save As** dialog box, navigate to the location where you are storing your files for this chapter. In the **File name** box, type **6G_Enrollment_Firstname_ Lastname** and then click **Save**.

(Project 6G–Enrollment continues on the next page)

(Project 6G–Enrollment continued)

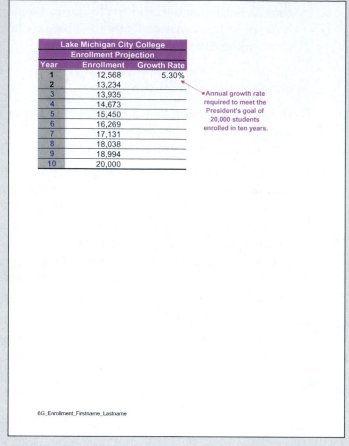

Lake Michigan City College
Enrollment Projection

Year	Enrollment	Growth Rate
1	12,568	5.30%
2	13,234	
3	13,935	
4	14,673	
5	15,450	
6	16,269	
7	17,131	
8	18,038	
9	18,994	
10	20,000	

Annual growth rate required to meet the President's goal of 20,000 students enrolled in ten years.

6G_Enrollment_Firstname_Lastname

Figure 6.63

3. In cell **A3**, type **Year** and in cell **B3**, type **Enrollment** and in cell **C3**, type **Growth Rate**

4. In cell **A4**, type **1** and in cell **A5**, type **2** Select the range **A4:A5**, point to the fill handle in the corner of **A5**, and drag down to create the series 1 through 10.

5. In cell **B4**, type **12568** and press [Enter]. This is the current student enrollment. Click cell **B4**, on the Formatting toolbar click the **Comma Style** button, and then click the **Decrease Decimal** button twice.

(Project 6G–Enrollment continues on the next page)

(Project 6G–Enrollment continued)

6. In cell **B5**, type **=b4*(1+c4)** and press Enter. This formula multiplies the previous year's enrollment—cell **B4**—by 1 plus the growth rate that will display in cell **C4**. The absolute cell reference is applied to cell **C4** so that you can copy the formula to years 3 through 10 and maintain cell **C4** in the formula. The growth rate will be calculated when you use Goal Seek. Click cell **B5** and, using the fill handle, copy the formula to cells **B6:B13**. Because there is no value yet in cell C4, all the numbers display as *12568*. With the cells selected, on the Formatting toolbar, click the **Comma Style** button, and then click the **Decrease Decimal** button twice.

   The results—*12,568*—display in cells B6:B13. The result for each year displays the same number until the growth rate factor is determined using Goal Seek.

7. Click cell **B13**. In this cell, you want to set the value equal to the desired enrollment of 20,000. With cell **B13** the active cell, display the **Tools** menu and click **Goal Seek**. In the **Goal Seek** dialog box, be sure that *B13* displays in the **Set cell** box. In the **To value** box, type **20,000** and then press Tab. In the **By changing cell** box, type **c4** which is the cell you have designated to display the growth rate. Click **OK**.

   Goal Seek calculates the growth rate to be 0.052975. The dialog box shows that Goal Seek found an answer that results in 20,000 students enrolled in year 10.

8. In the **Goal Seek Status** dialog box, click **OK**. Click cell **C4** and format it as a percentage with two decimals so that it displays as *5.30%*. Save your changes.

9. Select the range **A3:C13**. From the **Format** menu, display the **AutoFormat** dialog box. Click the **Classic 2** format and click **OK**. Select the range **A1:C13** and change the **Font Size** to **14** pt. Widen **column A** to **65 pixels** and **columns B** and **C** to **145 pixels**.

10. Click cell **A3**. On the Formatting toolbar, double-click the **Format Painter** button, and then click cell **A1** and cell **A2**. Click the **Format Painter** button to turn it off. Recall that the Format Painter can be used to apply formats from one cell to another. Only the first part of the text in these cells may display. This will be corrected in the next step.

11. Select **A1:C1** and, from the Formatting toolbar, click the **Merge and Center** button. Repeat this action to merge and center cells **A2:C2**.

(Project 6G–Enrollment continues on the next page)

(Project 6G–Enrollment continued)

12. If necessary, on the Standard toolbar, click the Drawing button to display the Drawing toolbar. On the Drawing toolbar, click the **Text Box** button. Look at Figure 6.63 to visualize the location of the text box. Starting in the middle of the upper boundary of cell **D6**, drag down and to the right, to the lower-right corner of cell **F10**. In the text box you just created, type **Annual growth rate required to meet the President's goal of 20,000 students enrolled in ten years.**

13. Click the edge of the text box to display a pattern of dots indicating that it is selected. On the Formatting toolbar, change the **Font Size** to **12**, change the **Font Color** to **Plum**, change the alignment to **Center**, and apply **Bold**. On the Drawing toolbar, click the **Line Color button arrow**, and then click **No Line**. Recall that this removes the line from the border of the text box. Adjust the size of the text box so that the text displays on five lines.

14. On the Drawing toolbar, click the **Arrow** button. Draw an arrow from the text box to cell **C4** as shown in Figure 6.63. With the arrow selected, on the Drawing toolbar, click the **Line Color button arrow**, and then click **Plum**. Click the **Arrow Style** button, and then click **Arrow Style 8**.

15. Display the **Header and Footer** dialog box and add the file name to the custom footer as you have previously. From the **Page Setup** dialog box, center the worksheet horizontally on the page. Save your changes, and then click the **Print Preview** button to see the worksheet as it will print. Compare your worksheet with Figure 6.63. Print the file, and then close it.

End **You have completed Project 6G** ——————————————————

Performance Assessments

Project 6H—Online Classes

Objectives: *Work with a Large Worksheet and Enhance Worksheets with AutoFormats and Styles.*

The Academic Affairs office is promoting its increased offering of online classes. A worksheet has been developed listing the classes, but it needs to be formatted to make it more visually appealing. In this project, you will use the AutoFormat feature and create styles to apply to the worksheet. You will also update a name change. Your completed worksheet will look similar to the one shown in Figure 6.64. You will save your workbook as *6H_Online_Classes_Firstname_Lastname*.

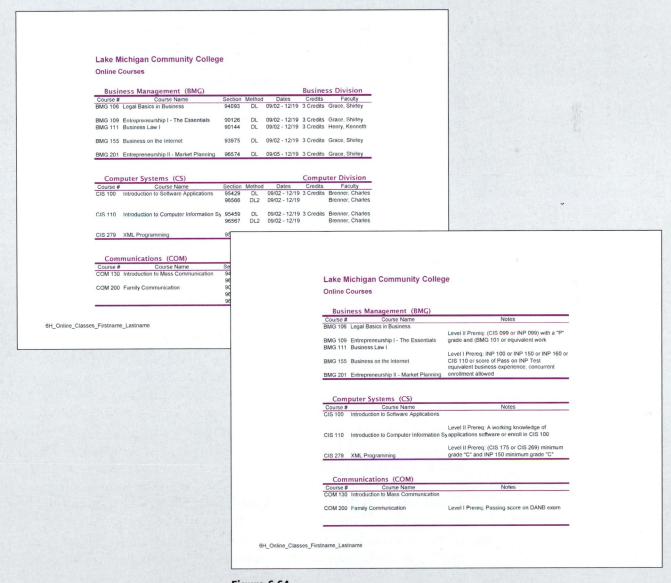

Figure 6.64

(Project 6H–Online Classes continues on the next page)

(Project 6H–Online Classes continued)

1. Start Excel. On the Standard toolbar, click the **Open** button. Navigate to the location where the student files for this textbook are stored. Locate and open the file **e06H_Online_Classes**. Save the file in your folder with the name **6H_Online_Classes_Firstname_Lastname**

2. Click cell **A4**. Change the **Font** to **Lucida Sans**, the **Font Size** to **12** pt., and the **Font Color** to **Violet**. From the **Format** menu, open the **Style** dialog box. In the **Style name** box, type **Program** click **Add**, and then click **OK**.

3. Click cell **F4**. Open the **Style** dialog box, click the **Style name arrow**, click **Program**, and then click **OK**. Apply the **Program** style to the Program and Division titles in **rows 13** and **22** (Hint: Hold down Ctrl to select all the cells, and then apply the style to the multiple selection.)

4. Select the range **A5:H10**. Display the **Format** menu and click **AutoFormat**. Click the **Accounting 2** AutoFormat and then, at the right side of the dialog box, click the **Options** button. At the bottom of the dialog box, under **Formats to apply**, clear the check boxes for **Number, Alignment** and **Width/Height** This area of the **AutoFormat** dialog box enables you to customize the selected AutoFormat. Click **OK**.

5. Apply the same AutoFormat to the range **A14:H19** and **A23:H28**. (Hint: You cannot apply AutoFormat to multiple selections.)

6. Select cells **A1:A2**—the title lines. Click the **Font Color** button to apply the **Violet** color. Select **row 2** and increase its height to **27 pt. (36 pixels)**. Click cell **A2** and display the **Format Cells** dialog box. On the **Alignment tab**, under **Text alignment**, click the **Vertical arrow**, and then click **Center**. Click **OK**.

7. Click cell **A1**. Press Ctrl + F to open the **Find** dialog box. In the **Find what** box, type **Goetze** Click the **Replace tab** and, in the **Replace with** box, type **Rhoades** Click **Find Next**, and then click **Replace**. Replace all occurrences of Goetze with the new name.

8. From the **File** menu, open the **Page Setup** dialog box. Add the **File Name** to the **Left section** of the footer area. Click the **Print Preview** button. Click the **Next** button to view each of the two pages. Notice that as currently set up, each row of information would be split on two pages. **Close** the Print Preview window.

9. Display the **Page Setup** dialog box. On the **Sheet tab**, click in the **Rows to repeat at top** box, and then select **rows 1:2** so that the title rows repeat at the top of each page. Click in the **Columns to repeat at left** box, and then select **columns A:B**. Click the **Margins tab**, and center the worksheet both **Horizontally** and **Vertically.**

10. Click the **Print Preview** button. Verify that the two title lines display at the top of each page and that the columns containing the Course # and Course Name display on each page.

11. Save, print, and then close the file.

 You have completed Project 6H ————————————

Project 6I — Timecard

Objectives: *Use Excel Templates, Work with a Large Worksheet, and Prepare a Worksheet to Share with Others.*

In this project, you will complete the Excel Timecard template to report the hours that Mary Adair, an hourly employee at the college, has worked for the past two weeks. You will also save the file as a CSV file so it can be uploaded to a database program. Your timecard template and CSV file will look similar to the ones shown in Figure 6.65. You will save your workbook as *6I_Timecard_Firstname_Lastname*.

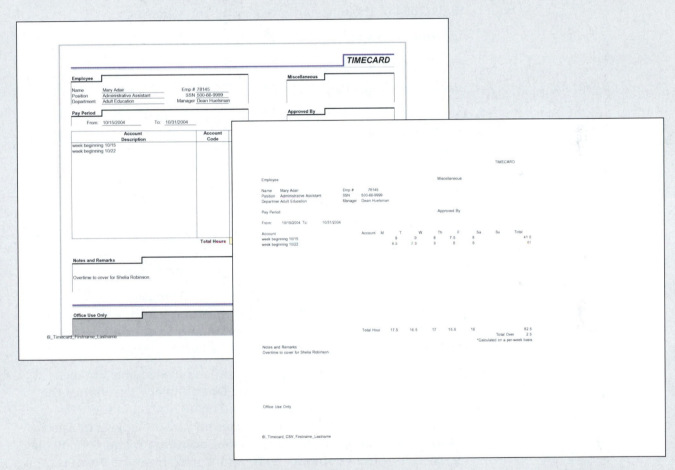

Figure 6.65

1. Start Excel. From the **File** menu, click **New**. In the **New Workbook** task pane, under **Templates**, click **On my computer**. In the **Templates** dialog box, click the **Spreadsheet Solutions tab**, click **Timecard**, and then click **OK**.

(**Project 6I–Timecard continues on the next page**)

(Project 6I–Timecard continued)

2. In the **Name** box, type **Mary Adair** In the **Emp #** box, type **78145** Enter the remainder of the employee information in the appropriate areas as follows:

Position	**Administrative Assistant**
SSN	**500-66-9999**
Department	**Adult Education**
Manager	**Dean Huelsman**

3. In the **From** field, type **10/15/2004** and, in the **To** field, type **10/31/2004** In the time card area, enter the following:

Account Description	M	T	W	Th	F
week beginning 10/15	**9**	**9**	**8**	**7.50**	**8**
week beginning 10/22	**8.5**	**7.5**	**9**	**8**	**8**

4. Display the **Page Setup** dialog box, click the **Header/Footer tab**, create a **Custom Footer**, and in the **Left section**, insert the **File Name**. Save the file in your folder for this chapter with the name **6I_Timecard_Firstname_Lastname**

5. In the *Notes and Remarks* area, type **Overtime to cover for Shelia Robinson**

6. On the Standard toolbar, click the **Save** button, and then click the **Print Preview** button to see the worksheet as it will print. Compare your worksheet with Figure 6.65. Click the **Print** button.

7. From the **File** menu, click **Save As**. In the **Save As** dialog box, change the **Save as type** box to **CSV (Comma Delimited)**. Change the **File name** to **6I_Timecard_CSV_Firstname_Lastname** Click **Save**, and then click **Yes** to acknowledge the information message.

8. Close the file, saving your changes and acknowledging any messages. Click the **Open** button. In the **Open** dialog box, change the **Files of type** box to display *All Files*. Locate and open the **6I_Timecard_CSV_Firstname_Lastname** file. It displays in Excel without the template formatting. Widen **columns E** and **G** to display all the cells. Select **columns A**, **B**, and **C** and, from the **Format** menu, point to **Column**, and then click **Hide**.

9. Click the **Print Preview** button. Open the **Page Setup** dialog box and add a custom footer with the file name as you have in the past. On the **Page tab**, click the **Fit to** option button and **Landscape** orientation. Print the file.

10. Save the changes and close the file, acknowledging the message boxes if they display. Click **Yes** to save the changes to the file.

End **You have completed Project 6I** ──────────────

Project 6J — Computer Budget

Objectives: *Prepare a Worksheet to Share with Others, Enhance Worksheets with AutoFormats and Styles, Use Drawing Tools and Use the Research Feature, and Use Goal Seek.*

The price of computers has continued to drop over the years, so either the college budget for this item can be reduced or more computers and software can be purchased for the same amount of money each year. In this project, you will use Goal Seek to prepare a projection for Margaret Young, the Information Technology Director, for the cost of replacing computers based on past price reductions. Your completed worksheet will look similar to the one shown in Figure 6.66. You will save your workbook as *6J_Computer_Budget_Firstname_Lastname*.

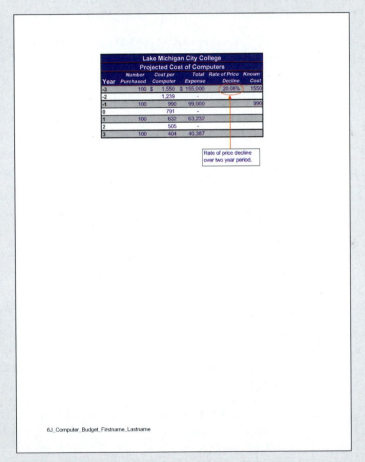

Figure 6.66

(Project 6J–Computer Budget continues on the next page)

(Project 6J–Computer Budget continued)

1. On the Standard toolbar, click the **Open** button. Navigate to the location where the student files for this textbook are stored. Locate and open the file **e06J_Computer_Budget**.

2. Open the **Save As** dialog box. Save the file in the folder with the other files for this chapter, using the name **6G_Computer_Budget_Firstname_Lastname** Display the **Header and Footer** dialog box and add the file name to the custom footer as you have previously done.

3. Rather than showing specific years, the year column displays negative numbers for previous years, zero for the current year, and positive numbers for future years. Click cell **D4** and enter a formula that calculates the total expense for the computers purchased three years ago. Copy the formula to cells **D5:D10**. Zeros will display in these cells until the cost per computer is calculated.

4. In cell **C5**, type **=c4*(1-e4)** and press Enter. Copy this formula to cells **C6:C10**. This is the formula to calculate the rate of decline in computer prices, where the value in *E4* (not yet calculated) will be a rate of decline in price.

5. Click cell **C6** and display the **Goal Seek** dialog box. In the **To value** box, type **990** which is the known cost of computers last year. In the **By changing cell** box, type **e4** and then press Enter. The result shows a rate of decline of approximately *0.2008* in cell **E4**. Click **OK**.

6. Format cell **E4** as a percentage with two decimals. Format cells **C5:D10** using the **Comma Style** with no decimals. Format cells **C4:D4** using the **Currency Style** and no decimals. Save your changes.

7. Select the range **A3:F10**. Display the **AutoFormat** dialog box and apply the **Classic 3** style. Select cells **A6:F6**, press Ctrl, and select cells **A8:F8** and **A10:F10**. On the Formatting toolbar, click the **Fill Color arrow**, and then click **Gray 25%**.

8. Click cell **A3**, and then double-click the **Format Painter** button. Click cells **A1** and **A2**. **Merge and Center** the title in cell **A1** over cells **A1:F1**. Do the same for the title in cell **A2**.

9. On the Drawing toolbar, click the **Text Box** button, and then draw a box from the lower left corner of cell **D12** to the lower right side of cell **F14**. In the text box, type **Rate of price decline over two year period** Click the edge of the box to display a pattern of dots, click the **Font Color arrow**, and then click **Dark Blue**. This matches the font color used in the AutoFormat style that has been applied. Adjust the size of the text box as needed to display the text on two lines in an open space under the formatted area in **column E**.

(Project 6J–Computer Budget continues on the next page)

(Project 6J–Computer Budget continued)

10. On the Drawing toolbar, click the **Oval** button. Position the crosshair pointer above and to the left of cell **E4**. Drag down and to the right to draw a white oval over the number in cell **E4**. With the white oval selected, on the Drawing toolbar, click the **Fill Color arrow** and, at the top of the color palette, click **No Fill**. Click the **Line Color arrow** and click **Red**.

11. On the Drawing toolbar, click the **Arrow** button and draw an arrow from the text box to the number in cell **E4**. Click the **Line Color** button and apply **Red** to the arrow.

12. Display the **Page Setup** dialog box and center the page **Horizontally**.

13. On the Standard toolbar, click the **Save** button, and then click the **Print Preview** button. Compare your worksheet with Figure 6.66. Print the worksheet, and then close the file.

 End **You have completed Project 6J** ————————————————————

Project 6K — Millage

Objectives: *Use Drawing Tools and Use the Research Feature and Use Goal Seek.*

Lake Michigan City College is partially funded by taxes assessed on property owners in the county. The current rate of 3.84 mills per $1,000 value in property will drop to 2.34 mills three years from now. Expenses are rising at an average of 7 percent a year. David Hanna, Vice-President of Finance, needs to determine how many mills to request in the next election cycle to continue the support of the college. In this project, you will determine how many mills (the fraction 1/1000 frequently used as a measurement of tax on property values) are needed to keep the college from going into a deficit. Your completed worksheet will look similar to the one shown in Figure 6.67. You will save your workbook as *6K_Millage_Firstname_Lastname.*

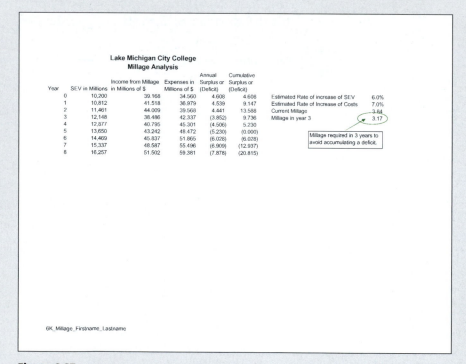

Figure 6.67

1. On the Standard toolbar, click the **Open** button. Navigate to the location where the student files for this textbook are stored. Locate and open the file **e06K_Millage**.

2. From the **File** menu, open the **Save As** dialog box. Navigate to the location where you are storing your files for this chapter. Save the file with the name **6K_Millage_Firstname_Lastname**

3. In cell **B5**, type **=b4*(1+i4)** to determine the rate of increase in property values. Copy the formula to cells **B6:B12**. Compare your worksheet with Figure 6.67 to verify the results for this range.

(Project 6K–Millage continues on the next page)

Mastery Assessments (continued)

(Project 6K–Millage continued)

4. In cell **C4**, type **=b4*i6/1000** This is the current value of taxable property in the county—cell **B4**—times the current mills—cell **I6**. The amount is divided by 1000 because millages are assessed on each thousand dollars of property value. Fill this formula to cells **C5** and **C6**. In cell **C7**, type **=b7*i7/1000** The millage drops in three years to 2.34 mills as listed in cell **I7**; therefore, the income from millage will drop to $28.427 million as calculated in this cell. Copy this formula to cells **C8:C12**. Compare your results with those shown in Figure 6.68.

5. In cell **D5**, type **=d4*(1+i5)** Expenses at the college are going up every year at a rate of 7 percent, as shown in cell **I5**. This formula calculates the estimated expenses based on this rate of increase. Fill this formula to cells **D6:D12**. Compare your results with those shown in Figure 6.68.

6. In cell **E4**, calculate the surplus or deficit by subtracting the expense from the income. Copy this formula to cells **E5:E12**. The college will have a shortfall (deficit) of $13.910 million in year 3. In 8 years, the deficit will be $21.339 million.

7. In cell **F4**, type **=e4** which is the surplus for year 0. In cell **F5**, write a formula to add the current year's surplus in cell **E5** to the previous year's surplus in **F4**. Fill this formula to cells **F6:F12**.

The cumulative amount changes to a deficit of (0.322) in year 3 when the millage drops from 3.84 to 2.84. The total cumulative deficit in year 8 is (90,975). Millage for the college is voted on in the general election every three years, which is due to take place two years from year zero. Hanna needs to know how many mills to request to ensure that the college does not go into deficit and to keep it in a positive cash flow for at least three years after the vote. Compare your results with those in Figure 6.68.

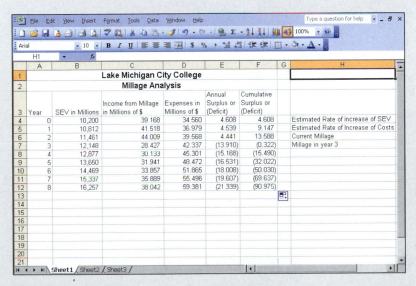

Figure 6.68

(Project 6K–Millage continues on the next page)

(Project 6K–Millage continued)

8. Click cell **F9**. You want the deficit at this point to be zero. Display the **Goal Seek** dialog box. Type **0** in the **To value** box. Click the **By changing cell** box and click cell **I7**. Click **OK**. The new millage needs to total 3.17.

9. Draw a text box from the middle of cell **H9** to the upper right boundary of cell **I11** and type **Millage required in 3 years to avoid accumulating a deficit**. Draw an **Arrow** from the text box to the number in **F9**. Draw an oval over **F9**. Change the **Fill Color** of the oval to **No Fill** and change the **Line Color** of the oval and the arrow to **Green**. Compare your screen with Figure 6.67.

10. Display the **Page Setup** dialog box. Change the orientation to **Landscape**. On the **Header/Footer tab**, add the file name as you have previously done. Save your changes. **Print** the file.

 End **You have completed Project 6K**

Project 6L — Organizations

Objectives: *Work with a Large Worksheet, Prepare a Worksheet to Share with Others, and Enhance Worksheets with AutoFormats and Styles.*

James Smith, Vice President of Student Affairs, has requested an updated listing of all the student organizations on campus. In the following Mastery Assessment, you will work with a large worksheet listing the student organizations. You will reorganize the information and apply styles. Your completed worksheet will look similar to the one shown in Figure 6.69. You will save your workbook as *6L_Organizations_Firstname_Lastname*.

1. On the Standard toolbar, click the **Open** button. Navigate to the location where the student files for this textbook are stored. Locate and open the file **e06L_Organizations**. Save the file with your other files for this chapter using the name **6L_Organizations_Firstname_Lastname**

2. Click cell **A3** and then, from the **Data** menu, click **Sort**. Sort in **Ascending** order by **Name of Organization**.

(Project 6L–Organizations continues on the next page)

(Project 6L–Organizations continued)

Lake Michigan City College Student Organizations

Name of Organization	Sponsor	Contact
A.C.E. ACTION COMMUNITY EDUCATION	Student Affairs Office	Fredia Lot, flot@lmcc.org
ARTISTS CLUB	Art Department	Robert Kelly rkelly@lmcc.org
BUSINESS PROFESSIONAL ASSOCIATION	Business Education Department	Doris Thomas
CHESS CLUB	Math Department	Rachel Orkey rorkey@lmcc.org
CRIMINAL JUSTICE CLUB	Policy Academy	Judy McDaniels
DANCE CLUB	Theater Department	Nancy Andrews nandrews@lmcc.org
DENTAL ASSISTANTS CLUB	Health and Human Services Dept	
DRAMA CLUB	Theater Department	Alisha Weber
EUCLIDEANS	Math Department	Robert Donalson rdon@lmcc.org
FRENCH CLUB	Foreign Lanugage Dept	Kim Sneely ksneely@lmcc.org
FRENCH CLUB (BEGINNERS)	Foreign Lanugage D	
GEOLOGY CLUB	Geography Departm	
GERMAN LANGUAGE AND CULTURE CLUB (GLACC)	Foreign Language D	
HUNGARIAN-AMERICAN FILM CLUB	Theater Department	
I.S.A. (INTERNATIONAL STUDENT ASSOCIATION)	Student Affairs Offic	
INTERNET PROFESSIONAL CLUB	Internet Professiona	
LMCC DIGITIZERS (digital photography club)	Art Department	
LMCC PRIDE	Student Affairs Offic	
MAGIC THE GATHERING GAMING CLUB	Computer Departme	
PHI THETA KAPPA	Student Affairs Offic	
RADIOGRAPHY	Health and Human	
SOCIETY FOR CREATIVE ANACHRONISM	Student Affairs Offic	
SPANISH CLUB	Foreign Language D	
STUDENT ADVOCACY CLUB	Student Affairs Offic	
STUDENT GOVERNMENT ASSOCIATION	Student Affairs Offic	
STUDENT NURSING CLUB	Health and Human	

6L_Organizations_Firstname_Lastname

Lake Michigan City College Student Organizations

Name of Organization	Contact Number	Meeting Day	Meeting Place
A.C.E. ACTION COMMUNITY EDUCATION	555-3565	Tue 3:00 - 4:30 pm	LA 236
ARTISTS CLUB	555-2408	Tue 5:00 - 9:00 pm	LA 371
BUSINESS PROFESSIONAL ASSOCIATION	555-5111		
CHESS CLUB	555-3500	Tue 1230 - 230 pm, Thur 5:00-7:00 pm	Food Court
CRIMINAL JUSTICE CLUB	555-0880	Tue 11:45 am - 1:00 pm	Mini Theatre, SCB
DANCE CLUB	555-3378	Wed 8:30 - 9:30 pm, Sat 10:00 am - Noon	Dance Studio, MLB
DENTAL ASSISTANTS CLUB	555-0672		
DRAMA CLUB			
EUCLIDEANS	555-0321	Mon 7:00 - 9:00 PM	BEB 120
FRENCH CLUB		Fri 1:30 - 3:00 pm (French 2)	Campus Book Store
FRENCH CLUB (BEGINNERS)		Fri 3:00 - 4:30 pm (French 1)	Campus Book Store
GEOLOGY CLUB	555-3582		
GERMAN LANGUAGE AND CULTURE CLUB (GLACC)	555-8567	Wed 3:30 - 4:30 pm	Mini theatre, SCB
HUNGARIAN-AMERICAN FILM CLUB	555-9870	Sun 6:00 - 9:00 pm	LA 175
I.S.A. (INTERNATIONAL STUDENT ASSOCIATION)	555-5128		
INTERNET PROFESSIONAL CLUB	555-3089		
LMCC DIGITIZERS (Digital photography club)			
LMCC PRIDE		Fri 5:30 - 7:00 pm	LA 175
MAGIC THE GATHERING GAMING CLUB			
PHI THETA KAPPA	555-3691		
RADIOGRAPHY	555-5119		
SOCIETY FOR CREATIVE ANACHRONISM	555-5215		
SPANISH CLUB	555-8567	Thu twice a month, 3:30-4:30 pm	LA 374
STUDENT ADVOCACY CLUB	555-3500		
STUDENT GOVERNMENT ASSOCIATION			
STUDENT NURSING CLUB	555-5015		

6L_Organizations_Firstname_Lastname

Figure 6.69

3. With cell **A3** as the active cell, from the **Data** menu display the **AutoFilter arrows** on the column labels in **row 3**. In **column B**, click the **Sponsor filter arrow**, and then click **Foreign Language Dept**. Change the **Contact** and **Contact Number** for the *German Language and Culture Club* to **Rochelle Gray** the same as shown for the *Spanish Club*. (Hint: You will need to scroll over to view **column A** to determine the row for the German Language Club. Use copy and paste.) Display all the rows again. (Hint: From the **Data** menu, point to **Filter** and click **Show All**.)

4. Use the **AutoFilter** to display only those records that are missing a **Contact Number**. (Hint: Click **Blanks** from the bottom of the list.) You should see seven clubs that list no Contact Number.

(Project 6L–Organizations continues on the next page)

(Project 6L–Organizations continued)

5. Display all the rows again and turn off the **AutoFilter** feature. Click cell **A3**. Change the alignment to **Center**, change the **Font Color** to **Blue**, change the **Font** to **Comic Sans MS**, **14** pt. **Italic** and **Bold**. Open the **Style** dialog box and name this style **Heading** Click **Add**, and then click **OK**. Select the remaining headings in **row 3** and apply the style you created. Adjust the width of **column D** to accommodate the new heading style.

6. Click cell **A4**. Create a new style that includes **Comic Sans MS 12** pt. Name the style **Organization** and then apply it to the all the other organization names in **column A**.

7. The worksheet is too wide to print on one page and still be legible. Remove the **Merge and Center** from **row 1** so that you can select **column A** to repeat. (Hint: Click cell **A1** and click the **Merge and Center** button.) Display the **Sheet tab** of the **Page Setup** dialog box, set **row 3** to **repeat at the top** of the page, and then set **column A** to **repeat at the left** of every page. Change the scaling to **75% of normal size**.

8. Display the **Header/Footer tab** and add the file name to the **Left section** of the footer area. Save the file, view the **Print Preview**, and then print.

End **You have completed Project 6L**

Project 6M — Early Payoff

Objectives: *Use Excel Templates and Use Goal Seek.*

Goal Seek is a powerful tool that can help you answer questions concerning your own finances. Use the Loan Amortization template to set up a loan for a 30-year mortgage at a 6 percent interest rate. Pick a loan amount that would make sense for your circumstances. After the loan payment is calculated and the amortization schedule is complete, use Goal Seek to determine an Optional Extra Payment—cell D11—that would result in paying off the loan five years early. (Hint: You need to set cell H8 equal to 300.) Add a footer to the worksheet and save the file as *6M_Early_Payoff_ Firstname_Lastname*.

 End **You have completed Project 6M** ────────────

Project 6N — Registration

Objectives: *Prepare a Worksheet to Share with Others, Enhance Worksheets with AutoFormats and Styles, Use Drawing Tools and Use the Research Feature.*

Lake Michigan City College recently implemented an online registration process. James Smith, Vice-President of Student Affairs, wants a graphic flow chart created to show the registration process using this new method. In this project, you will use the drawing tools to create a flow chart that illustrates the steps involved in registration. You will save your workbook as *6N_Registration_Firstname_Lastname*.

1. Open a blank worksheet. Add a footer in the usual location and save the file as **6N_Registration_Firstname_Lastname**

2. Add the Lake Michigan City College title to the top of the worksheet. Add a title in **row 2** that identifies the purpose of the worksheet.

3. Remove the gridlines from the worksheet. Use drawing tools to illustrate the registration process. Explore the shapes that are included in the **AutoShapes** button. Use the registration process that is followed at your school as your example. Draw arrows between each box and label appropriately.

4. Use the buttons on the Drawing toolbar to change the fill color, line color, and text color of the drawing objects.

5. Preview the worksheet and be sure it is evenly spaced and will print on one page. Print the file.

6. Save your changes and close the file.

 End **You have completed Project 6N** ────────────

Exploring Microsoft Office Online Templates

In this chapter, you worked with the templates that are installed as part of the Excel 2003 program. Other templates are available from the Microsoft Web site.

1. Start Excel. Click **File**, **New**. In the **New Workbook** task pane, click the **Templates on Office Online** link.

2. In the **Microsoft Office Online Web** site, examine some of the templates that are listed in the **Quick links** pane.

3. Explore other parts of the Web site and open the templates that are of interest to you. Try downloading a template and using it.

4. When you are finished, close your browser.

GO! with Help

Merging Styles with Another Workbook

In this chapter you created, applied, and modified styles. You also used styles in multiple worksheets. Importing styles to another workbook was discussed in a More Knowledge box in Activity 6.19. Styles create a uniformity of appearance and help to create an organizational identity. In addition to merging styles from another workbook, you can also save styles to use in any new workbook. This is particularly useful if you want to create a style to be used in all departments in an organization. If the styles are saved, they can be easily moved to multiple computers for use by staff members in all areas of the organization.

1. Start Excel. In the **Type a question for help** box, type **Styles**

2. From the list of related help topics, click **Save styles to use in new workbooks**.

3. Read the instructions for this topic. Print the instructions if you want.

4. Open one of the files from this chapter that used styles, such as Project 6C.

5. Follow the procedure in the Help topic to save the styles from the Project as an .xlt file.

6. Open a new workbook and click the **File**, **New** command to see the available templates.

7. Select the template file you saved that contains the sample styles, and then use the styles in the new workbook.

8. Close the file without saving the results and close Excel.

Excel 2003 Task Guide

Each book in the *GO! Series* is designed to be kept beside your computer as a handy reference, even after you have completed all the activities. Any time you need to recall a sequence of steps or a shortcut needed to achieve a result, look up the general category in the alphabetized listing that follows and then find your task. To review how to perform a task, turn to the page number listed in the second column to locate the step-by-step activity or other detailed description. Additional entries without page numbers describe tasks that are closely related to those presented in the chapters.

Excel Task	Page	Mouse	Menu Bar	Shortcut Menu	Shortcut Keys
Absolute reference, create	137	Edit cell reference to precede the column letter and/or row number with $, such as $B$6			While typing formula, select cell, press F4 In Formula Bar, click cell reference, press F4 (repeat to cycle through options)
Align, cell contents	177		Format | Cells | Alignment tab	Format Cells | Alignment tab	Ctrl + 1 | Alignment tab
Align, center across selection	180		Format | Cells | Alignment tab, Horizontal: Center Across Selection	Format Cells | Alignment tab	Ctrl + 1 | Alignment tab
Align, fill cell(s) with character(s)	179		Format | Cells | Alignment tab, Horizontal: Fill	Format Cells | Alignment tab	Ctrl + 1 | Alignment tab
Align, indent cell contents	177	increase or decrease on Formatting toolbar	Format | Cells | Alignment tab, Indent	Format Cells | Alignment tab	Ctrl + 1 | Alignment tab
Align, left-align cell contents	104	on Formatting toolbar	Format | Cells | Alignment tab, Horizontal: Left (Indent)	Format Cells | Alignment tab	Ctrl + 1 | Alignment tab
Align, merge and center cells	105, 180	on Formatting toolbar	Format | Cells | Alignment tab, Horizontal: Center, under Text Control select Merge cells	Format Cells | Alignment tab	Ctrl + 1 | Alignment tab
Align, merge cells	191	on Formatting toolbar (also centers)	Format | Cells | Alignment tab, Merge cells	Format Cells | Alignment tab	Ctrl + 1 | Alignment tab
Align, right-align cell contents	104	on Formatting toolbar	Format | Cells | Alignment tab, Horizontal: Right (Indent)	Format Cells | Alignment tab	Ctrl + 1 | Alignment tab
Align, rotate cell contents	183	In Format Cells dialog box, Alignment tab, Orientation, drag red diamond	Format | Cells | Alignment tab, Orientation or Degrees	Format Cells | Alignment tab	Ctrl + 1 | Alignment tab
Align, shrink to fit cell contents	186		Format | Cells | Alignment tab, Shrink to fit	Format Cells | Alignment tab	Ctrl + 1 Press | Alignment tab

Excel Task	Page	Mouse	Menu Bar	Shortcut Menu	Shortcut Keys
Align, vertically	181		Format | Cells | Alignment tab, Vertical	Format Cells | Alignment tab	Ctrl + 1 Press | Alignment tab
Align, wrap text in cell	184		Format | Cells | Alignment tab, Wrap text	Format Cells | Alignment tab	Ctrl + 1 Press Alt + Enter to move specific text to the next line in the cell
Arrange, view of workbooks	412		Window | Arrange		
Arrow style, change	445	Click line or arrow [icon] on Drawing toolbar			
Arrow, draw	445	[icon] on Drawing toolbar			
AutoComplete, use	42				Begin typing the first few letters; when a ScreenTip displays, press Enter
AutoFill Options, smart tag	94	Use AutoFill, click [icon] to select a fill option			
AutoFill, ascending	94	Select cell fill handle, drag [icon] down or right	Edit | Fill | Down Edit | Fill | Right		
AutoFill, descending	94	Select cell fill handle, drag [icon] up or left	Edit | Fill | Up Edit | Fill | Left		
AutoFill, duplicate data	96	Use AutoFill, click [icon], click Copy Cells			
AutoFilter, apply or remove	419		Data | Filter | AutoFilter		
AutoFit, fit column(s) to widest entry	120	Double-click vertical bar at right of column heading	Format | Column | AutoFit Selection		
AutoFormat, apply	437		Format | AutoFormat		
AutoSum, insert	55	[Σ icon] on Standard toolbar	Insert | Function | SUM		Alt + =
AutoSum, select range	125	Select range, [Σ icon] on Standard toolbar [Σ icon] on Standard toolbar, and then drag to select range	Insert | Function | SUM		Alt + =
Bold, apply to font	186	[B icon] on Formatting toolbar	Format | Cells | Font, Font style: Bold	Format Cells | Font tab	Ctrl + B

Excel Task	Page	Mouse	Menu Bar	Shortcut Menu	Shortcut Keys
Border, apply to cell(s)	192	on Formatting toolbar; click arrow for predefined border style	Format | Cells | Border tab; choose a preset style or choose line style, color, and position	Format Cells | Border tab	Ctrl + Shift + 7 (outline border) Ctrl + 1 | Border tab, then Alt + T (top) or Alt + B (bottom) or Alt + L (left) or Alt + R (right)
Cancel an entry	44, 47	on Formula Bar			Esc (entire entry) or Bksp (characters left of insertion point)
Chart, 3-D View options	352	Drag corner(s) where walls or floor intersect	Click blank area in chart, Chart | 3-D View	Right-click blank area in chart, 3-D View	
Chart, add axis title	328	Click in title text box, edit	Click blank area in chart, Chart | Chart Options | Titles tab	Right-click blank area in chart, Chart Options | Titles tab	
Chart, add data labels	347		Click blank area in chart, Chart | Chart Options | Data Labels tab	Right-click blank area in chart, Chart Options | Data Labels tab	
Chart, align axis title	328	Click axis title, on Chart toolbar, then click Alignment tab Double-click axis title, then click Alignment tab	Click axis title, Format | Selected Axis Title | Alignment tab	Right-click axis title, Format Axis Title | Alignment tab	Select axis title, Ctrl + 1
Chart, change data display (axis)	327	or on Chart toolbar	Click blank area in chart, Chart | Source Data | Data Range tab, Rows or Columns	Right-click blank area in chart, Source Data | Data Range tab, Rows or Columns	
Chart, change type	345	Click arrow on on Chart toolbar	Click blank area in chart, Chart | Chart Type	Right-click blank area in chart, Chart Type	
Chart, change value(s)	25	Edit value(s) in worksheet			
Chart, create	318		Insert | Chart		
Chart, create in existing worksheet	334	; in Chart Location step, under *Place chart,* click As object in	Insert | Chart; in Chart Location step, under *Place chart,* click As object in		
Chart, create in new worksheet	318, 343	; in Chart Location step, under *Place chart,* click As new sheet	Insert | Chart; in Chart Location step, under *Place chart,* click As new sheet		
Chart, edit chart title	332, 337	Click in title text box, edit	Click blank area in chart, Chart | Chart Options | Titles tab	Right-click blank area in chart, Chart Options | Titles tab	

Excel Task	Page	Mouse	Menu Bar	Shortcut Menu	Shortcut Keys
Chart, edit source data	332	Click worksheet cell, edit Drag data point on chart			
Chart, edit source data range	327		Click blank area in chart, Chart | Source Data | Data Range tab	Right-click blank area in chart, Source Data | Data Range tab	
Chart, explode pie slice	353	Click pie chart, click a slice, drag slice away from center of pie			
Chart, format axis label	330	Click axis, on Chart toolbar Chart Area ▼ arrow on Chart toolbar, click Category Axis or Value Axis Double-click axis	Click axis, Format | Selected Axis	Right-click axis label, Format Axis	Select axis label, Ctrl + 1
Chart, format axis title	328	Click axis title, on Chart toolbar, then click Font tab Double-click axis title, then click Font tab	Click axis title, Format | Selected Axis Title | Font tab	Right-click axis title, Format Axis Title | Font tab	Select axis title, Ctrl + 1
Chart, format chart title	331	Click chart title, on Chart toolbar, then click Font tab Double-click chart title, then click Font tab	Click chart title, Format | Selected Chart Title | Font tab	Right-click chart title, Format Chart Title | Font tab	Select chart title, Ctrl + 1
Chart, format data labels	347	Double-click a data label, click Font tab Click a data label, on Chart toolbar, click Font tab	Select data label, Format | Selected Data Labels | Font tab	Right-click data label, Format Data Labels | Font tab	Select data label, Ctrl + 1
Chart, format data point	350	Click data point twice; double-click data point	Click data point twice, Format | Selected Data Point	Click data point twice; right-click data point, Format Data Point	Select data point, Ctrl + 1
Chart, format data series	340	Double-click a data marker, click Patterns tab	Click data series, Format | Selected Data Series | Patterns tab	Right-click data series, Format Data Series | Patterns tab	Select data series, Ctrl + 1
Chart, format legend	346	Click legend, on Chart toolbar, then click Font tab Double-click legend, then click Font tab	Click legend, Format | Selected Legend | Font tab	Right-click legend, Format Legend | Font tab	Select legend, Ctrl + 1
Chart, format plot area	340	Double-click plot area Click plot area, on Chart toolbar	Click plot area, Format | Selected Plot Area	Right-click plot area, Format Plot Area	Select plot area, Ctrl + 1
Chart, legend placement	346	Drag legend text box	Click blank area in chart, Chart | Chart Options | Legend tab	Right-click blank area in chart, Chart Options | Legend tab	

Excel Task	Page	Mouse	Menu Bar	Shortcut Menu	Shortcut Keys
Chart, move	336	Click blank area in chart, drag chart area			
Chart, move data label	347	Click data label, drag			
Chart, print chart only	333	Click blank area in chart, ⎙ on Standard toolbar	Click blank area in chart, File | Print		Click blank area in chart, Ctrl + P
Chart, print on same page with worksheet	342	Click a cell (to deselect chart), ⎙ on Standard toolbar	Click a cell (to deselect chart), File | Print		Click a cell (to deselect chart), Ctrl + P
Chart, print preview of chart only	333	Click blank area in chart, 🔍 on Standard toolbar	File | Print Preview File | Print, Preview		
Chart, print preview on same page with worksheet	342	Click a cell (to deselect chart), 🔍 on Standard toolbar	Click a cell (to deselect chart), File | Print Preview		
Chart, remove legend	337	🔳 on Chart toolbar	Click blank area in chart, Chart | Chart Options | Legend tab, clear Show legend	Right-click blank area in chart, Chart Options | Legend tab, clear Show legend	Select legend, Delete
Chart, scale value axis	338	Double-click value axis (or value), click Scale tab Click value axis, 🔳 on Chart toolbar, then click Scale tab	Click axis, Format | Selected Axis | Scale tab	Right-click axis, Format Axis | Scale tab	Select axis, Ctrl + 1
Chart, select and modify chart object	328	Chart Area ▾ arrow on Chart toolbar, click object name, then click 🔳 on Chart toolbar Double-click object		Right-click object, Format <object>	
Chart, size	336	Click blank area in chart, drag a selection handle			
Chart, snap to grid	336	Alt + drag chart area			
Clear, cell contents	50		Edit | Clear | Contents	Clear Contents	Del
Clear, cell contents and formatting	199		Edit | Clear | All		
Clear, cell formats	199		Edit | Clear | Formats		
Clipboard, clear	106	✖ Clear All in Clipboard task pane			

Excel Task	Page	Mouse	Menu Bar	Shortcut Menu	Shortcut Keys
Clipboard, collect and paste	110	Display Clipboard task pane, [icon] or [icon] multiple objects; in new location(s), click objects on Clipboard to paste or [icon] Paste All	Collect objects on Clipboard using Edit | Copy or Edit | Cut or Insert | Picture | Clip Art, and then paste in new location (must use Clipboard task pane)	Display Clipboard; right-click objects, Copy or Cut; right-click objects in Clipboard, Paste	With Clipboard displayed, Ctrl + C or Ctrl + X, and then paste (must use Clipboard task pane)
Clipboard, display task pane	106	[icon] in any task pane, and then click Clipboard	Edit | Office Clipboard		Ctrl + F1, choose Clipboard
Close, task pane	4, 36	[X] in task pane	View | Task Pane		Ctrl + F1
Close, workbook	11, 61	[X] on menu bar	File | Close		Ctrl + F4 or Ctrl + W
Collect and paste, multiple selections	110	Display Clipboard task pane, [icon] or [icon] multiple objects; in new location(s), click objects on Clipboard to paste or [icon] Paste All	Collect objects on Clipboard using Edit | Copy or Edit | Cut or Insert | Picture | Clip Art, and then paste in new location (must use Clipboard task pane)	Display Clipboard; right-click objects, Copy or Cut; right-click objects in Clipboard, Paste	With Clipboard displayed, Ctrl + C or Ctrl + X, and then paste (must use Clipboard task pane)
Color, fill	195	[icon] on Formatting toolbar	Format | Cells | Patterns tab, Color	Format Cells | Patterns tab	Ctrl + 1 | Patterns tab
Column width, change	98	Drag vertical bar at right of column heading left or right	Format | Column | Width	Right-click vertical bar to right of column heading, and then click Column Width	
Column, delete	101		Edit | Delete | Entire column	Right-click column heading; click Delete	Ctrl + −
Column, insert	101		Insert | Columns	Right-click column heading; click Insert	Ctrl + Shift + +
Columns, hide/ unhide	411		Format | Hide or Unhide	Right-click column heading, Hide or Unhide	
Columns, select multiple	98	Point to column heading until pointer changes to [↓], drag over column headings			
Comment, insert in cell	214	[icon] on Reviewing toolbar	Insert | Comment	Insert Comment	
Comment, view	214	Point to cell containing red triangle	View | Comments		
Copy and paste, multiple ranges from another workbook	112	Display Clipboard, [icon]; in source workbook. In destination workbook, paste (click) each Clipboard item	Display Clipboard; in source workbook, Edit | Copy workbook ranges. In destination workbook, paste (click) each Clipboard item	Display Clipboard; in source workbook, right-click selected range, click Copy. In destination workbook, paste (click) each Clipboard item	Ctrl + C
Copy, cell contents	106	[icon] on Standard toolbar	Edit | Copy	Copy	Ctrl + C

Excel Task	Page	Mouse	Menu Bar	Shortcut Menu	Shortcut Keys
Copy, formula with absolute cell references	137	For cell references that should not change, create absolute references in formula; copy (and paste)			
Copy, formula with relative cell references	135	Point to fill handle of formula cell; drag ⊞ to copy formula to adjacent cell(s)	Select formula cell, Edit | Copy; click another cell, Edit | Paste	Right-click formula cell, click Copy; click another cell, right-click, and then click Paste	Ctrl + C and then, in another cell, Ctrl + V
Copy, worksheet	111	Click sheet tab, hold down Ctrl, drag to location	Click sheet tab, Edit | Move or Copy Sheet	Right-click sheet tab, Move or Copy	
Countif function, use	409	*fx*, click Statistical category, click COUNTIF function	Insert | Function, click Statistical category, click COUNTIF function		Shift + F3
Create, new folder	32	📁 in Open or Save As dialog box			
Create, new workbook	36	Start Excel (opens blank workbook) 📄 on Standard toolbar Click Create a new workbook in Getting Started task pane Click Blank workbook in in New Workbook task pane	File | New		Ctrl + N
Cut, cell contents	116	✂ on Standard toolbar	Edit | Cut	Cut	Ctrl + X
Date, enter in cell	45	Type date in allowed format, such as m/d/yy, and then click another cell			Type date in allowed format, such as m/d/yy, and then press Enter or Tab
Decimal places, decrease (for selected styles)	123	.00→.0 on Formatting toolbar	Format | Cells | Number tab	Format Cells | Number tab	Ctrl + 1 | Number tab
Decimal places, increase (for selected styles)	123	←.0.00 on Formatting toolbar	Format | Cells | Number tab	Format Cells | Number tab	Ctrl + 1 | Number tab
Delete, row or column	101		Edit | Delete | Entire row or Entire column	Right-click row heading or column heading; click Delete	Ctrl + −
Deselect, row or column	14	Click any cell			
Diagram, change style	359	🖉 on Diagram toolbar			
Diagram, create	355		Insert | Diagram, select diagram type		

Excel Task	Page	Mouse	Menu Bar	Shortcut Menu	Shortcut Keys
Diagram, insert shape	358	Insert Shape on Diagram toolbar		Right-click a shape, Insert Shape	
Diagram, move shape	358	or on Diagram toolbar			
Display, underlying formulas	142				Ctrl + ` (below Esc); repeat to return display to normal
Draw, arrow	445	on Drawing toolbar			
Draw, text box	445	on Drawing toolbar			
Edit, data in cell	47, 134	Double-click cell, type changes, in Formula bar			F2, type and use ←, →, Bksp, Del as needed, and then Enter
Edit, data in Formula Bar	131	Click in Formula Bar, and then type Double-click cell reference in Formula Bar, click a cell, and then press Enter			In Formula Bar, type and use ←, →, Bksp, Del as needed, and then Enter
Edit, overtype mode	47				Ins
Exit Excel	32	X	File | Exit		Alt + F4
File name, view on taskbar	36	Point to taskbar button, view ScreenTip			
Filter, data	419		Data | Filter | AutoFilter		
Find, text	405		Edit | Find		Ctrl + F
Font, apply style	186	**B** *I* on Formatting toolbar	Format | Cells | Font, Font style	Format Cells | Font tab	Ctrl + B or Ctrl + I
Font, apply underline	186	U on Formatting toolbar	Format | Cells | Font, Underline	Format Cells | Font tab	Ctrl + U
Font, change (face)	186	Arial ▼ on Formatting toolbar	Format | Cells | Font, Font	Format Cells | Font tab	
Font, change size	186	10 ▼ on Formatting toolbar	Format | Cells | Font, Size	Format Cells | Font tab	
Format numbers	172		Format | Cells | Number tab, choose Category	Format Cells | Number tab	Ctrl + 1 | Number tab

Excel Task	Page	Mouse	Menu Bar	Shortcut Menu	Shortcut Keys
Format numbers, comma style	124, 172	**,** on Formatting toolbar	Format | Cells | Number tab, Category: Currency, Symbol: None	Format Cells | Number tab	Ctrl + 1 | Number tab
Format numbers, currency style	120, 176	**$** on Formatting toolbar (precisely, accounting style)	Format | Cells | Number tab, Category: Currency	Format Cells | Number tab	Ctrl + Shift + 4 Ctrl + 1 | Number tab
Format numbers, percent style	122	**%** on Formatting toolbar	Format | Cells | Number tab, Category: Percentage	Format Cells | Number tab	Ctrl + Shift + 5 Ctrl + 1 | Number tab
Format Painter	197	on Standard toolbar (double-click to apply repeatedly)			
Format, apply AutoFormat	437		Format | AutoFormat		
Formula Bar, edit within	131	Click in Formula Bar, and then type Double-click cell reference in Formula Bar, click a cell, press Enter			In Formula Bar, type and use ←, →, Bksp, Del as needed, and then Enter
Formula, create using range name	253	Type = followed by formula, replacing range reference with range name			
Formula, display underlying	142				Ctrl + ` (below Esc); repeat to return display to normal
Formula, enter in cell	51	Type = followed by formula			
Formula, enter using point-and-click method	53	Type = and then click cells and type operators to enter formula			
Freeze/unfreeze, panes	402		Window | Freeze/Unfreeze Panes		
Function, average	266	_fx_, click Statistical category, click AVERAGE function	Insert | Function, click Statistical category, click AVERAGE function		Shift + F3
Function, count	266	_fx_, click Statistical category, click COUNT function	Insert | Function, click Statistical category, click COUNT function		Shift + F3
Function, countif	409	_fx_, click Statistical category, click COUNTIF function	Insert | Function, click Statistical category, click COUNTIF function		Shift + F3

Excel Task	Page	Mouse	Menu Bar	Shortcut Menu	Shortcut Keys
Function, date	270	f_x, click Date & Time category, click DATE function	Insert | Function, click Date & Time category, click DATE function		Shift + F3
Function, future value	273	f_x, click Financial category, click FV function	Insert | Function, click Financial category, click FV function		Shift + F3
Function, if	280	f_x, click Logical category, click IF function	Insert | Function, click Logical category, click IF function		Shift + F3
Function, insert	258–284, 409	f_x, click category, click function	Insert | Function, click category, click function		Shift + F3
Function, maximum	264	f_x, click Statistical category, click MAX function	Insert | Function, click Statistical category, click MAX function		Shift + F3
Function, median	258	f_x, click Statistical category, click MEDIAN function	Insert | Function, click Statistical category, click MEDIAN function		Shift + F3
Function, minimum	262	f_x, click Statistical category, click MIN function	Insert | Function, click Statistical category, click MIN function		Shift + F3
Function, now	270	f_x, click Date & Time category, click NOW function	Insert | Function, click Date & Time category, click NOW function		Shift + F3
Function, payment	276	f_x, click Financial category, click PMT function	Insert | Function, click Financial category, click PMT function		Shift + F3
Go to, specified cell	408		Edit | Go To		F5 Ctrl + G
Goal seek	453		Tools | Goal Seek		
Header/footer, create	29, 92, 205		View | Header and Footer, Custom Header or Custom Footer File | Page Setup | Header/Footer tab, Custom Header or Custom Footer		
Header/footer, insert picture	205	in Header dialog box or Footer dialog box	View | Header and Footer, Custom Header or Custom Footer		
Help, close window	61	in Help window			

Excel Task	Page	Mouse	Menu Bar	Shortcut Menu	Shortcut Keys
Help, display in Excel	61	[icon] on Standard toolbar. Click the *Type a question for help* box; type text and press Enter	Help | Microsoft Excel Help		F1
Help, print help topic	61	[icon] in Help window		Print	Ctrl + P in Help window
Hide/unhide, columns	411		Format | Hide or Unhide	Right-click column letter; Hide or Unhide	
Hyperlink, insert	426	[icon] on Standard toolbar	Insert | Hyperlink	Right-click selection, Hyperlink	Ctrl + K
Hyperlink, modify	428	[icon] on Standard toolbar	Insert | Hyperlink	Right-click hyperlink, Edit Hyperlink	Ctrl + K
Insert, hyperlink	426	[icon] on Standard toolbar	Insert | Hyperlink	Right-click selection, Hyperlink	Ctrl + K
Insert, row or column	101		Insert | Rows or Columns	Right-click row or column heading; click Insert	Ctrl + Shift + +
Italic, apply to font	186	[icon] on Formatting toolbar	Format | Cells | Font, Font style: Italic	Format Cells | Font tab	Ctrl + I
Line color, change	445	[icon] on Drawing toolbar			
Look up, supporting information	448	[icon] on Standard toolbar	Tools | Research	Look Up	Alt + click
Menus, display full	8	Double-click menu name in menu bar Wait a few seconds after displaying menu Click double arrows at bottom of menu	Tools | Customize | Options tab, Always show full menus		
Move active cell, down one cell	22	Click cell			Enter ↓
Move active cell, down one full screen	22				PgDn
Move active cell, left one cell	22	Click cell			Shift + Tab ←
Move active cell, left one full screen	22				Alt + Page Up
Move active cell, left/right/up/down one cell	22	Click cell			← or → or ↑ or ↓

Excel Task	Page	Mouse	Menu Bar	Shortcut Menu	Shortcut Keys
Move active cell, right one cell	22	Click cell			Tab →
Move active cell, right one full screen	22				Alt + PgDn
Move active cell, to cell A1	22				Ctrl + Home
Move active cell, to column A of current row	22				Home
Move active cell, up one cell	22	Click cell			Shift + Enter ↑
Move active cell, up one full screen	22				PgUp
Move active cell, use Name box	22	Click Name box (left of Formula Bar); type cell reference, Enter			
Move to last cell of active area	22				Ctrl + End
Move, cell contents	116, 118	✂ on Standard toolbar, and then, in new location, 📋▾ Select range, drag to new location, drop (release mouse button)	Edit | Cut, and then, in new location, Edit | Paste	Cut, and then, in new location, right-click and then click Paste	Ctrl + X, and then, in new location, Ctrl + V
Move, to another worksheet	24	Click sheet tab			
Name, range	244	Select cells, type name in Name box on Formula Bar, press Enter	Select cells, Insert | Name | Define		Ctrl + F3
Normal View, return to	421		View | Normal		
Number, enter in cell	44	Type number in cell, click another cell			Type number in cell, press Enter or Tab
Open, workbook	11	📂 on Standard toolbar More or workbook name in Getting Started task pane	File | Open File | workbook name at bottom of File menu		Ctrl + O
Page setup, center worksheet on page	201		File | Page Setup | Margins tab, Horizontally and/or Vertically		

Excel Task	Page	Mouse	Menu Bar	Shortcut Menu	Shortcut Keys
Page setup, header or footer	205		View | Header and Footer, Custom Header or Custom Footer File | Page Setup | Header/Footer tab, Custom Header or Custom Footer		
Page setup, header or footer margins	210		File | Page Setup | Margins tab, Header or Footer		
Page setup, margins	201		File | Page Setup | Margins tab; Top, Bottom, Left, Right		
Page setup, page settings (orientation, scaling, paper size)	143, 201		File | Page Setup | Page tab		
Page setup, sheet settings (print area, rows/ columns to repeat, gridlines, row/column headings, page order)	212		File | Page Setup | Sheet tab		
Panes, freeze/ unfreeze	402		Window | Freeze/Unfreeze Panes		
Paste (after Cut or Copy)	106	on Standard toolbar Click item in Office Clipboard	Edit | Paste	Paste	Ctrl + V
Paste options	106	after pasting			
Pattern, apply to cell(s)	195		Format | Cells | Patterns tab, Pattern	Format Cells | Patterns tab	Ctrl + 1 | Patterns tab
Preview, as Web page	429		File | Web Page Preview		
Preview, page breaks	421	on Standard toolbar, Page Break Preview	View | Page Break Preview File | Print Preview, click Page Break Preview		
Print, entire workbook	118	Click first sheet tab, Shift + click last sheet tab, then	File | Print, Entire workbook		Ctrl + P | Entire workbook
Print, Preview	31, 60	on Standard toolbar	File | Print Preview File | Print, click Preview button in the dialog box		

Excel Task	Page	Mouse	Menu Bar	Shortcut Menu	Shortcut Keys
Print, preview multiple sheets	253	Select sheet tabs, [icon] on Standard toolbar	Select sheet tabs, File | Print Preview Select sheet tabs, File | Print, Preview		
Print, worksheet(s)	31	[icon] on Standard toolbar	File | Print, Active sheet(s)		Ctrl + P
Print area, clear	285		Select range, File | Print Area | Clear Print Area		
Print area, set	285		Select range, File | Print Area | Set Print Area File | Page Setup | Sheet tab		
Range, create name using row or column label	252		Select cells, Insert | Name | Create		
Range, define name	244	Select cells, type name in Name Box on Formula Bar, press Enter	Select cells, Insert | Name | Define		Ctrl + F3
Range, delete name	251		Insert | Name | Define, Delete		Ctrl + F3, Delete
Range, modify reference	250		Insert | Name | Define, Refers to		Ctrl + F3
Range, select named range	244	Click Name Box arrow, click range name	Edit | Go To, click range name		Ctrl + G
Redo	50	[icon] on Standard toolbar	Edit | Redo		Ctrl + Y
Repeat row/column headings	424		File | Page Setup | Sheet tab		
Replace, text	405		Edit | Replace Edit | Find | Replace tab		Ctrl + H
Research	448	[icon] on Standard toolbar	Tools | Research	Look Up	Alt + click
Row height, change	98	Drag horizontal line between row headings up or down	Format | Row | Height	Right-click horizontal line between row headings, and then click Row Height	
Row, delete	101		Edit | Delete | Entire row	Right click row heading; click Delete	Ctrl + −
Row, insert	101		Insert | Rows	Right-click row heading; click Insert	Ctrl + Shift + +
Save, as comma separated values	432		File | Save As, click Save as type, select CSV (Comma delimited)		

Excel Task	Page	Mouse	Menu Bar	Shortcut Menu	Shortcut Keys
Save, as text file	433		File | Save As, click Save as type, select Text (Tab delimited)		
Save, as Web page	429		File | Save as Web Page		
Save, new workbook	38	💾	File | Save As		Ctrl + S or F12
Save, workbook	38	💾	File | Save		Ctrl + S
Save, workbook (new name, location, or type)	32		File | Save As		F12
Scroll, multiple columns to right/left	20	Click between scroll box and scroll arrow on horizontal scroll bar			
Scroll, multiple rows down/up	20	Click between scroll box and scroll arrow on vertical scroll bar			
Scroll, one column to right/left	20	Click right/left scroll arrow on horizontal scroll bar			
Scroll, one row down/up	20	Click down/up scroll arrow on vertical scroll bar			
Select, all cells	14	Click Select All button (where row and column headings intersect)			Ctrl + A
Select, multiple columns	98	Point to column heading until the pointer changes to ↓, drag over column headings			
Select, multiple rows	98	Point to row heading until the pointer changes to →, drag over row headings			
Select, nonadjacent cells	14				Click first cell, Ctrl + click remaining cells
Select, nonadjacent ranges	343	Select first range, Ctrl + select remaining ranges			
Select, range (adjacent cells)	14	Click first cell, drag to last cell			Click first cell, Shift + click last cell
Select, row or column	14	Click row or column heading in worksheet frame			Shift + Spacebar (row); Ctrl + Spacebar (column)
Sort, ascending	416	⬇ on Standard toolbar	Data | Sort, Ascending		
Sort, descending	416	⬇ on Standard toolbar	Data | Sort, Descending		

Excel Task	Page	Mouse	Menu Bar	Shortcut Menu	Shortcut Keys
Spelling check	59	[icon] on Standard toolbar	Tools | Spelling		F7
Split, worksheet (or remove split)	412		Window | Split or Remove Split		
Start Excel	4	[start] on Windows taskbar, and then locate and click Microsoft Office Excel 2003	Start | All Programs | Microsoft Office | Microsoft Office Excel 2003		
Style, apply	416		Format | Style, select a name		
Style, create	416		Format | Style, type a name, Modify		Alt + ' (apostrophe)
Style, modify	443		Format | Style, select a name, Modify		
Styles, use in another workbook	442		Format | Style, Merge		
Template, use to create workbook	396		File | New | On my computer (in task pane) | Spreadsheet Solutions tab		
Text box, draw	445	[icon] on Drawing toolbar			
Text, enter in cell	39	Type in cell, click another cell			Type in cell, press Enter or Tab
Text, find	405		Edit | Find		Ctrl + F
Text, replace	405		Edit | Replace; Edit | Find | Replace tab		Ctrl + H
Toolbar buttons, identify	8	Point to button, view ScreenTip			
Toolbars, show on one or two rows	8	[icon] on Standard or Formatting toolbar, Show Buttons on One Row / Two Rows	Tools | Customize | Options tab, Show Standard and Formatting toolbars on two rows; View | Toolbars | Customize | Options tab, Show Standard and Formatting toolbars on two rows	Right-click any toolbar, and then click Customize; on Options tab, select or clear Show Standard and Formatting toolbars on two rows	
Trace Error, smart tag	131	Click cell containing green triangle; point to smart tag, read error in ScreenTip, and then click and select an option			
Underline, apply to font	186	[icon] on Formatting toolbar	Format | Cells | Font, Underline	Format Cells | Font tab	Ctrl + U
Undo	50	[icon] on Standard toolbar	Edit | Undo		Ctrl + Z

Excel Task	Page	Mouse	Menu Bar	Shortcut Menu	Shortcut Keys
View, return to normal	421		View | Normal		
Web page, preview	429		File | Web Page Preview		
Web page, save as	429		File | Save as Web Page		
Workbook, arrange multiple	412		Window | Arrange		
Workbook, close	11, 61	☒ on menu bar	File | Close		$Ctrl$ + $F4$ or $Ctrl$ + W
Workbook, create new	36	Start Excel (opens blank workbook) ⬜ on Standard toolbar Click Create a new workbook in Getting Started task pane Click Blank workbook in New Workbook task pane	File | New		$Ctrl$ + N
Workbook, maximize	412	⬜ in workbook title bar			
Workbook, open	11	⬜ on Standard toolbar More or workbook name in Getting Started task pane	File | Open File | workbook name at bottom of File menu		$Ctrl$ + O
Worksheet, copy	111	Click sheet tab, hold down $Ctrl$, drag to location	Click sheet tab, Edit | Move or Copy Sheet	Right-click sheet tab, Move or Copy	
Worksheet, delete	361		Edit | Delete Sheet	Right-click sheet tab, Delete	
Worksheet, format sheet tab	362		Format | Sheet | Tab Color	Right-click sheet tab, Tab Color	
Worksheet, hide	365		Format | Sheet | Hide		
Worksheet, insert	361		Insert | Worksheet	Right-click sheet tab, Insert	
Worksheet, move	362	Drag sheet tab to new location in sheet tab row	Edit | Move or Copy sheet	Right-click sheet tab, Move or Copy	
Worksheet, rename	26	Double-click sheet tab, type new name		Right-click sheet tab, click Rename, type new name	
Worksheet, select all (group)	27	Click first sheet, hold down $Shift$ and click last sheet		Right-click sheet tab, click Select All Sheets	
Worksheet, select multiple (group)	361	Click first worksheet tab, $Ctrl$ + click other tab(s)			
Worksheet, split or remove split	412		Window | Split or Remove Split		

Excel Task	Page	Mouse	Menu Bar	Shortcut Menu	Shortcut Keys
Worksheet, ungroup multiple worksheets	27	Click an inactive sheet tab		Right-click a grouped work-sheet tab, click Ungroup Sheets	
Worksheet, unhide	365		Format | Sheet | Unhide		
Zoom	57	`100%` ▾ on Standard toolbar	View | Zoom		

Glossary

Absolute cell reference A cell address in which both the column letter and the row number of the cell are preceded with dollar signs. An absolute cell reference in a formula, such as $A$1, always refers to a cell in a specific location. When an absolute cell reference is used in a formula and the formula is copied to another cell, the cell references in the new cell are not adjusted to fit the new location of the formula; they remain as they are in the source cell.

Accounting format A format for numbers in which the currency symbol displays flush with the left boundary of the cell, a format which conforms to formats necessary for creating profit and loss statements and balance sheets.

Active area The area of the worksheet that contains data or has contained data—it does not include any empty cells that have not been used in the worksheet.

Active cell The cell in which the next keystroke or command will take place. A black border surrounds the cell when it is active.

Alignment The position of data within a cell.

Annuity A sum of money payable in a lump sum or as a series of equal annual payments.

Arguments The information that Excel uses to perform the calculation within a function.

Ascending When sorting data, a sort in alphabetical order (A–Z) or numerical order from lowest to highest.

Asterisk The term used to refer to the * symbol.

AutoComplete An Excel feature that speeds your typing and lessens the likelihood of errors. If the first few characters you type in a cell match an existing entry in the column, Excel fills in the remaining characters for you.

AutoFill Extending values into adjacent cells based on the values of selected cells.

AutoFill Options button An Excel feature that provides instant access to commands and actions that are relevant to an AutoFill operation.

AutoFormat A formatting command that provides a selection of predefined formats that can be applied to cells on a worksheet.

AutoSum A function (predefined formula) that adds a series of cell values by selecting a range.

Caret When moving a worksheet, the tiny triangle that displays to indicate the new location where the worksheet will be positioned.

Category (x) axis The horizontal axis along the bottom of a chart that displays labels.

Cell The intersection of a column and a row.

Cell address The intersecting column letter and row number of a cell.

Cell content Anything typed into a cell.

Cell reference The intersecting column letter and row number of a cell. Also referred to as a cell address.

Chart A graphic representation of numbers in a worksheet used to display comparisons, change over time, contributions to the whole, or some other relationship.

Chart objects The elements that make up a chart.

Chart sheet A separate worksheet in which a chart fills the entire page in landscape orientation.

Chart sub-type Variations on a standard chart type.

Chart Wizard An Excel tool that walks you through four steps in creating a chart.

Collect and paste The process of copying a group of items to the Office Clipboard and then pasting them into various locations in a worksheet.

Column A vertical group of cells in a worksheet.

Column chart A graph with vertical columns that is used to make comparisons among related numbers.

Column heading The heading that appears above the topmost cell in a column and that is identified by a unique letter.

Comma delimited file Also known as comma separated value (CSV) file, a type of file format in which each field is separated by a comma. This type of file may be readily exchanged with database programs.

Comma separated value (CSV) A file format in which each cell is separated by a comma and an end-of-paragraph mark at the end of each row. Excel files can be saved in this format for transferring information to other programs.

Comma style A cell style in which Excel sets the formatting of a cell to display numeric values with two decimal places and with commas in the thousand, million, and billion (and higher) places.

Comment A note attached to a cell and which is separate from other cell content.

Conditional test A test performed by using an equation to compare two values (or two functions or two formulas).

Constant value Numbers, text, dates, or times of day that are typed into a cell.

Context-sensitive Information or commands related to the current task.

COUNTIF The Excel function that sums the number of occurrences in a given range that match a condition or value. This function has two arguments, the range and the condition.

Criteria A condition on which a cell is evaluated for the purpose of matching the specified value.

Currency style A cell style in which Excel sets the formatting of a cell to display numeric values with two decimal places, with commas in the thousand, million, and billion (and higher) places, and with a leading dollar sign. Also referred to as currency format.

Custom chart Advanced charts that can include your own features.

Cut A command in which selected data is removed from the worksheet and placed on the Office Clipboard.

Data Labels A label that provides additional information about a data marker.

Data marker An indicator with the same pattern such as a column, bar, pie slice, or symbol that represents a data series or data point.

Data point A single value in a worksheet represented by a data marker in a chart.

Data series A group of related data points.

Deselect To cancel the selection of one or more cells.

Diagram A tool used to graphically illustrate a concept or relationship.

Displayed value The value that appears in a formatted cell.

Double-click The act of clicking the left mouse button twice without moving the position of the mouse pointer.

Drag-and-drop Repositioning cell data by dragging to a new location with the mouse.

Drawing objects Shapes such as lines, arrows, rectangles, and circles that can be drawn on a worksheet for the purpose of adding information or to illustrate an idea.

Drawing tools Buttons that are used to draw objects such as lines, arrows, rectangles, circles, and text boxes.

Edit The process of updating and making changes in a worksheet.

Elevation The angle at which a chart is titled on the screen.

Embedded chart A chart that is inserted into the same worksheet that contains the data used to create the chart.

Explode A feature used for 3-D pie charts in which one or more pie pieces is pulled away from the center of the chart.

Field A predefined area for a specific type of data such as name, employee number, or social security number.

Fill handle The small black square in the lower right corner of a selected cell.

Filter A process that limits the data displayed to only those records that match a stated condition.

Find A command that is used to search and locate specific data each time it occurs.

Font A set of characters with the same design and shape.

Font size The size of characters in a font, measured in points.

Font style Bold, italic, or underline emphasis added to characters.

Footer An area that prints on all worksheets at the bottom of each page. Displays only in Print Preview or on the printed page of a worksheet.

Format painter A command that enables you to copy the formatting of one cell to one or more other cells.

Formatting Characteristics that determine how data typed into the cell will look.

Formula An equation that you type into a cell and that acts as an instruction to Excel to perform mathematical operations (such as adding and subtracting) on data within a worksheet.

Freeze Panes The Excel command that enables you to select one or more rows or columns and freeze (lock) them into place. This is frequently used to keep column and row headings visible while scrolling a large worksheet.

Function A predefined formula that performs calculations by using specific values, called arguments, in a particular order or structure. For example, Excel's SUM function, which is so frequently used that a button for it appears on the Standard toolbar, adds a series of cell values by selecting a range of cells.

Function name The word is used to label a function, which indicates the type of calculation that will be performed, for example, SUM or AVERAGE.

Function syntax The proper format of typing the equal sign, the function name, and the arguments when constructing a function.

Future value (FV) An Excel function that calculates future value—the value of an investment at the end of a specified period of time—based on periodic, constant payments and a constant interest rate.

General format The default number format in Excel, which formats numbers exactly as you type them, with no commas or decimal points.

Goal Seek A what-if analysis tool that can help you answer questions. It is used to find the input needed in one cell in order to arrive at the desired result in another cell.

Grave accent The ` symbol on the keyboard.

Grid A pattern of horizontal and vertical lines.

Header An area that prints on all worksheets at the top of each. Displays only in Print Preview or on the printed page of a worksheet.

Horizontal alignment The alignment of data within a cell relative to the left and right cell boundaries.

Hyperlink A hypertext link that, when clicked, takes you to another location in the worksheet, to another file, or to a Web page on the Internet or on your organization's intranet.

Indent Adding space between the cell data and its left or right cell boundaries.

Insert mode The default mode in which characters move to the right to make space for new characters.

Insertion point A blinking vertical bar that indicates the point at which anything you type will be inserted.

Labels Column and row headings used in a chart to describe the values in the chart.

Landscape orientation A page orientation in which the paper is wider than it is tall.

Leader line In a chart, a line that connects a data label with its data marker.

Left-align A cell format in which data is aligned with the left boundary of the cell.

Legend A key that identifies a data series by color.

Line chart A graph with lines that show a change or trend in each element over time.

Locked A condition applied to cells that prevents the user from accidentally overwriting them. This is frequently used to preserve built-in formulas or data that should not be changed.

Logical operator A mathematical symbol that tests the relationship between the two elements of a conditional test, for example, greater than (>), less than (<), or equal (=).

Logical test Any value or expression that can be evaluated as true or false.

Major sort The term used for the first sort in a multiple-field sort. In Excel, the value that is placed in the Sort by box.

Median Within a set of values, the value below and above which there are an equal number of values; the value that falls in the middle of a ranked set of values.

Menu A list of Excel commands organized by category.

Merge and Center The process of combining cells in a row or column into one cell and then centering the cell contents within the new cell.

Minor sort The second or third sort in a multiple-field sort. In Excel, the values that are placed in the then by boxes.

Navigate The act of moving from one point to another in a worksheet or between worksheets in the same workbook.

Normal The default style that is applied to new worksheets. In Excel, the Normal style includes Arial 10-point font.

Nper Within an Excel function, the total number of payment periods in a loan over a specific span of time.

Number formats The various ways that Excel displays numbers.

Operator A symbol that represents a mathematical operation in a formula.

Option buttons The round buttons to the left of each option in a dialog box.

Order of operations The mathematical rules for performing multiple calculations within a formula.

Overtype mode The mode in which typed characters replace existing characters.

Pane A portion of a worksheet window bounded by and separated from other portions by vertical or horizontal bars.

Paste The process of moving items from the Office Clipboard to a location within a worksheet.

Pie chart A graph in the shape of a pie that is used to show the contribution of each part to the whole.

Plot To represent numbers graphically on a chart.

Plot area The area on the chart bounded by the category axis (x-axis) and the value axis (y-axis) that includes the data series.

PMT function An Excel function that calculates the payment for a loan based on constant payments and a constant interest rate. The structure for the function is *PMT(rate, number of periods, present value, future value, type)*.

Pmt Within an Excel function, such as the FV (Future Value) function, the payment that will be made in each annual period.

Points The unit of measure for font size. One point is equal to ½ of an inch.

Portrait orientation The page orientation in which the paper is taller than it is wide.

Pv Within an Excel function, the value that represents the amount an annuity is worth now, also referred to as the present value.

Quarters A three-month period within a fiscal year.

Range A group of adjacent cells.

Range name A specific name given to a range of cells that can then be used to refer to the range in a function or formula.

Relative cell reference In a formula, the address of a cell based on the relative position of the cell that contains the formula and the cell referred to.

Replace A command that finds specific data, and then replaces it with data that you specify.

Research A feature that can be used to look up information in an encyclopedia, dictionary, thesaurus, or other reference tool using the MSN Learning and Research Web site.

Right-align A cell format in which the data aligns with the right boundary of the cell.

Right-click Clicking the right mouse button once.

Row A horizontal group of cells in a worksheet.

Row heading The heading that appears to the left of the leftmost cell in a row and that is identified by a unique number.

Sample area A preview area of cell formats within the Format Cells dialog box.

Sans serif font Fonts that do not have small lines at the bottom of the characters.

Scale The range of numbers in the data series that controls the minimum, maximum, and incremental values on the value axis of a chart.

Scale to fit An Excel feature that enables you to control the number of pages that are required to print a worksheet. The font, rows, and columns are resized to force the worksheet into a selected number of pages.

Scaling The ability of Excel to increase or decrease the size of printed characters so that the worksheet will fit within a specific number of pages.

ScreenTip A box that displays when you position the mouse pointer over a button or screen element, and which describes the name and/or function of the button or screen element.

Scroll The action of moving the worksheet window either vertically (from top to bottom) or horizontally (from left to right) to bring different areas of the worksheet into view on your screen.

Selecting The process of highlighting, by dragging with your mouse, one or more cells so that the highlighted area can be edited, formatted, copied, or moved. Excel treats the selected area as a single unit; thus, you can make the same change or combination of changes to more than one cell at a time.

Selection handles Small black boxes surrounding an object to indicate the object is selected and can be modified or moved. Also referred to as sizing handles.

Serif font Font that has small lines at the bottom of the characters which serve to guide the reader's eye.

Sheet tab A label located at the lower border of the worksheet window. It identifies each worksheet in a workbook and is used to navigate between worksheets.

Shortcut menu A menu that offers a quick way to activate the most commonly used commands for a selected area.

Sizing handles Small black boxes surrounding an object or a chart that are used to resize the object. Also called selection handles.

Smart tag A button that displays when Excel recognizes a specific type of data.

Standard chart type Fourteen predefined chart designs that are available in the Excel Chart Wizard.

Styles Formats designed by the user that can be applied to cells in multiple worksheets or other workbooks.

Tab delimited file A text file in which a tab character is used to separate the cell contents in rows. Excel files can be saved in this format for transferring information to various database or other types of programs.

Task pane A window within a Microsoft Office application that displays commonly used commands. Its location and small size give easy access to use of these commands while you are still working in your workbook.

Template A workbook used as a pattern for creating other workbooks. Templates are preformatted and have built-in formulas for calculating totals based on the data that is entered.

Text box A drawing object container into which you can type or insert text that is not constrained by the dimension of a cell.

Toggle button A button that when clicked once is turned on and when clicked again is turned off.

Trace error A message displayed by Excel when anomalies in formulas are recognized.

Truncate To cut off or shorten.

Type Within an Excel function, a value that represents the timing of the payment, whether it will be paid at the beginning of each period (indicated by a 1) or at the end of the period (indicated by a 0).

Underlying formula The formula entered in a cell and visible only on the Formula Bar.

Value Numbers, text, dates, or times of day that are typed into a cell. Also referred to as a constant value.

Value (y) axis The vertical line on the left side of the chart that displays the numeric scale for numbers in the selected data.

Vertical alignment The alignment of data in a cell relative to its top and bottom boundaries.

What-if analysis A process of changing the values in cells to see how those changes affect the outcome of formulas on the worksheet, for example, varying the interest rate used in an amortization table to determine the amount of the payments at different rates.

Workbook An Excel file that contains one or more worksheets.

Worksheet A page formatted as a pattern of uniformly spaced horizontal and vertical lines.

Wrap text An Excel feature in which the content of a cell is split onto two or more lines when the width of the cell is not sufficient to display all the content on one line.

Index

Symbols

+ (addition), order of operations, 283

* (asterisk), multiplication operator, 55, 283

/ (division), order of operations, 283

= (equal sign)
    formula operator, 258
    logical operator, 280

^ (exponentiation), order of operations, 283

` (grave accent), displaying formulas, 142

- (negation/subtraction), order of operations, 283

( ) (parentheses), order of operations, 283

% (percentage), order of operations, 283

3-D charts
    column charts, 320–322
    pie charts, 343–344, 352–354
    value axis, 321
    view options, 352–353

3-D View dialog box, 352–353

A

absolute cell references, copying formulas, 137–140

Accounting format, 176

active area, 23, 408

active cells, 6–7, 15–16, 40–41
    clearing formats, 199
    Clipboard, 113
    moving location of
      keyboard shortcuts, 23
      using Enter key, 42
    in templates, 397

active sheet, tab color, 363

addition (+), order of operations, 283

adjacent cells in ranges, 244

Adjust to spin box, 203

Align Left button (Formatting toolbar), 104

Align Right button (Formatting toolbar), 105, 189, 244

aligning cell contents, 177–180
    fill, 180–181
    Format Cells dialog box, 177–180
    horizontal, 104–106
    left, 40, 105
    right, 44, 104–105
    vertical, 181–183

alphabetical sort. *See* sorting data

Alt key, 337

analysis tool, 453–455

Angle Clockwise button (Chart toolbar), 324

Angle Counterclockwise button (Chart toolbar), 324

arguments, 258. *See also* Function Arguments dialog box
    estimating values using Goal Seek, 453–455
    specifying cells, 274–277

specifying ranges, 253–254, 260–264

typing arguments, 270, 281–282

Arrange command (Window menu), 412

Arrange Windows dialog box, 412–413

arranging worksheets on screen, 412–413

Arrow button (Drawing toolbar), 447

Arrow Style button (Drawing toolbar), 447

arrows
    drawing objects, 445, 447–448
    two-headed resize arrows, 323

ascending order, sorting, 416

asterisk (*), multiplication operator, 54–55

Auto Fill Options button, 95–97

AutoComplete, 42–43, 92

AutoFill
    constant values generated, 92
    duplicating data, 96
    series created, 94–96

AutoFilter, 419–421

AutoFit command. *See* Row command (Format menu)

AutoFit Selection command (Format menu), 99, 130, 136

AutoFormat button (Diagram toolbar), 360

AutoFormat dialog box, 437–439

AutoSum function, 55–56, 125–130, 179, 244, 254, 264, 284

AVERAGE function, 266

axes, charts
    axis labels, 330–331
    axis titles, 320, 328–329
    axis types, 320–321, 325, 327
    changing
      data displayed in charts, 327
      value scales, 338–339

B

bar charts, 318

blank cells, finding, 408–409

Bold button (Formatting toolbar), 187, 189, 244, 358

borders, applying to cells, 192–194

buttons, 29. *See also* toolbars
    toggling, 189

By Column button (Chart toolbar), 324, 327

By Row button (Chart toolbar), 324, 327–328

C

calculations, 53
    order of operations, 283. *See also* formulas

Cancel button, 47–48

category axis, 320, 323, 325, 327

cells. *See also* relative cell reference
    active, 40–41, 397. *See also* active cells
    address or reference, 15–16, 52
    aligning, 104–105, 177–185
    applying styles, 440, 444
    borders, 192–194
    clearing, 50
    copying and moving, 106–118
    copying formulas containing absolute, 137–140
    counting cells meeting a condition, 409–410
    cutting and pasting, 106–109
    editing data in, 47–49
    fill handles, 94–96
    filling, 180–181
    finding blank, 408–409
    formatting, 172–176, 186–199
      Comma Style button, 124–125
      Currency Style button, 120–121
      Percent Style button, 122–123
    going to specified cells, 408–409
    gridlines, 212
    indent content, 179–180
    locking in data, 40–42, 396–399
    merging, 105–106, 191
    printing selected, 285
    range, 16. *See also* ranges
    selecting, 14
    shading, 195
    specifying as function arguments, 274–277
    truncated values, 94
    typing formula in, 51–52
    view and insert comments, 214
    worksheets, 4

Cells command (Format menu), 174, 179

Center button (Formatting toolbar), 104, 178, 189, 197, 438

centering
    cell contents, 177–185
    columns, 438
    embedded charts, 342
    text in merged cells, 444
    worksheets, 203–204

Change button, 60

chart area, 323–325

Chart menu commands, 323
    3-D View, 352
    Chart Options, 328, 347
    Chart Type, 346
    Source Data, 328

chart objects
    formatting, 330
    list of chart objects, 324
    ScreenTip display, 323
    selecting, 323, 326, 330
    selection handles, 323
    sizing handles, 323, 336–337

Chart Objects button arrow (Chart toolbar), 323–326, 330, 340

Microsoft menu characteristics, 10
Select All Sheets, 92, 115, 120, 143, 201
starting, keyboard shortcuts, 9
Tools menu
Customizing, 9
Goal Seek, 454
Options, 8, 42
Options, Formulas, 142
Ungroup Sheets, 93
View menu
Custom Footer button, 201
Header and Footer, 40, 92, 120, 174, 205, 212–213
Normal, 422
Zoom, 57
Window menu
Arrange, 412
Freeze Panes, 404
Remove Split, 416
Split, 412, 414
Unfreeze Panes, 405, 414
comments
printing, 215
viewing and inserting, 214
comparing values. *See* logical functions
conditional tests, 280. *See also* logical functions
constant value
cell content, 39
generated with AutoFill, 92
context-sensitive tags or buttons, 95
Control Panel, Regional and Language Options, 46
Copy button, 107, 112
Copy command (Edit menu), 450
copying
cell contents, 106–109
entire worksheets, 111–112
formulas, 135–140
using collect and paste, 110–111, 114
using Format Painter, 197–198
COUNT function, 266–267
COUNTIF function, 409–410
counting cells meeting a condition, 409–410
Create command. *See* Name command (Insert menu)
Create Names dialog box, 252
Create New Folder button, 33
CSV (comma separated value) files, 421, 432–433
Currency format, selecting and applying, 176–177
Currency Style button (Formatting toolbar), 120–121, 173, 245, 254
custom charts, creating, 319
Custom Footer button, 28, 40, 92, 120, 174, 201, 212–213
Custom Header button, 209
Customizing command (Tools menu), 9
customizing toolbars, 10
Cut button, 116
cutting/moving cell contents, 116–117
Cycle (diagram type), 317, 356–358

D

data. *See also* information
displaying graphically. *See* charts
editing, 47–51
entering, 39–46
in templates, 397
filtering, 402, 419–421
finding and replacing, 402, 405–407, 414–416
formatting. *See* formatting, cells
labels in charts, 320, 325, 347–349
locking in cells, 40–42, 396–399
markers in charts, 325, 340–341
sorting, 416
Data menu commands
Filter
AutoFilter, 419, 421
Show All, 421
Sort, 416, 418
data points, 320
charts, 325, 350–351. *See also* data, labels in charts
Data Range box, Chart Wizard, 320, 328
data series, charts, 325
changing data displayed, 327
formatting, 340–341
selecting, 326
Data Table button (Chart toolbar), 324
DATE function, 270–271. *See also* NOW function
dates
DATE function, 270–271
default format, 46
entering, 46
leading zeros displayed in, 271
NOW function, 272
serial values of, 271–272
typing into worksheets, 45–46
days
DATE function, 270–271
NOW function, 272
serial values of dates, 271–272
decimal places, increasing and decreasing, 123
Decimal places spin box, 176
Decrease Decimal button (Formatting toolbar), 124, 245, 254
defaults
alignment, 40
format for dates, 46
Define command. *See* Name command (Insert menu)
Define Name dialog box, 246, 250–251
Degrees spin box, 184
Delete command (Edit menu), 101
Delete Sheet command (Edit menu), 361
deleting
legends, 337
range names, 251–252
rows and columns, 101–103
worksheets, 361–362

delimited files
comma separated value (CSV) files, 421, 432–433
tab delimited (text) files, 433–434
deselecting columns, 18
diagonal sizing box, 12–13
Diagram command (Insert menu), 355
Diagram Gallery, 317
Diagram Gallery dialog box, 355–356
Diagram Style Gallery dialog box, 360
Diagram toolbar, 356–357
AutoFormat button, 360
Insert Shape button, 359
Move Shape Backward button, 359
Move Shape Forward button, 359
Reverse Diagram button, 359–360
diagrams, 316–317, 355. *See also* charts
adding footers, 361
changing style, 360–361
creating, 356–358
cycle diagrams, 356–358
formatting, 358
inserting shapes, 358–359
moving shapes, 359
reversing direction, 359–360
types of diagrams, 355–356
dialog boxes
3-D View, 352–353
Arrange Windows, 412–413
AutoFormat, 437, 439
Chart Options, 328–329, 347
Chart Type, 346
Chart Wizard, 319, 335, 344
collapsing, 247, 261, 263, 425
Create Names, 252
Define Name, 246, 250–251
deleting worksheets, 362
Diagram Gallery, 355–356
Diagram Style Gallery, 360
Edit Hyperlink, 429
expanding, 248, 263, 425
Find and Replace, 405–407, 415–416
Font, 29, 207, 209
Footer, 28–30, 93, 120, 213
Format Axis, 330, 338
Format Axis Title, 329
Format Cells, 437
Alignment tab, 178–185, 190–191, 444
Border tab, 192–194, 439
Font tab, 187, 189, 439
Number tab, 174–177, 271–272
Patterns tab, 195
Format Chart Title, 331
Format Data Point, 350–351
Format Data Series, 340
Format Legend, 346
Format Picture, 207–208
Format Plot Area, 340
Format Selected Object, 324
Format Tab Color, 362